THE BOOK OF
COMMON PRAYER
2018

THE BOOK OF
COMMON PRAYER
2018

THE CHRISTIAN EPISCOPAL CHURCH
OF CANADA

XULON PRESS

Xulon Press
2301 Lucien Way #415
Maitland, FL 32751
407.339.4217
www.xulonpress.com

Unless otherwise indicated, Scripture quotations taken from the King James Version (KJV)–*public domain*.

Printed in the United States of America.

ISBN-13: 9781545634844

A NOTE CONCERNING COPYRIGHT

To the honour and glory of
ALMIGHTY GOD,
and in Thanksgiving to Him for
the Life and Reign of
Her Majesty ELIZABETH the Second,
by the grace of God of
the United Kingdom of Great Britain
and Northern Ireland,
CANADA,
and all other her Realms and Territories
QUEEN,
Head of the Commonwealth,
Defender of the Faith,
this First Edition of
the Book of Common Prayer of
the Christian Episcopal Church of Canada
is lovingly and loyally
dedicated.

FOREWORD

FROM the Right Reverend the Lord Bishop of the See and Diocese of Richmond and Custodian of the Book of Common Prayer of the Christian Episcopal Church of Canada, to All the Faithful of the One Holy Catholic and Apostolic Church throughout the World, and more especially to those who are true adherents of the orthodox Anglican tradition: Grace be unto you, and peace, from God our Father, and the Lord Jesus Christ.

THIS Year of Our Lord 2018 marks the centenary of the publication of the first revision of the Book of Common Prayer made specifically for the use of the Anglican Church here in Canada. In 1918, the Church of England in the Dominion of Canada published the first Canadian Book of Common Prayer. This venerable Prayer Book was ratified by the General Synod of the Church of England in Canada in 1922, and it remained in use until the General Synod of the Anglican Church of Canada published a second revision of the Prayer Book in 1959, which revision was given its final authorisation in 1962.

When the first and founding members of the Christian Episcopal Church of Canada first found themselves fully separated from the Anglican Church of Canada for reasons of conscience and conviction, the only Liturgy that they had known and which was available to them was the 1962 Book of Common Prayer of the Anglican Church of Canada, and it was natural for them to desire to continue to use that Prayer Book as their Public Liturgy. However, this was not allowed them; and the hierarchy of the Anglican Church of Canada were determined to deny permission for use of the Prayer Book to any person or body of persons not fully under their ecclesiastical authority. This placed the Christian Episcopal Church of Canada in an awkward and uncomfortable position: that of working to maintain the traditional Faith, Doctrine, Order, Worship, and Discipline of their Church whilst being prevented from using its Prayer Book in which was set forth all those things for which they were contending.

Nevertheless, the Lord will often use awkward and uncomfortable situations in order to further His will, and to provide and bring about blessings for His people. In answer to this dilemma, the First Lord Primate and Metropolitan of the Christian Episcopal Church of Canada and First Lord Bishop of Richmond, the Most Reverend A. Donald Davies, gave permission for a revision of the Book of Common Prayer to be made and used within his jurisdiction. This permission was given, and the work of overseeing that revision was entrusted by Archbishop Davies to his successor the Right Reverend Robert D. Redmile. Bishop Redmile was appointed to supervise the revision, and was then entrusted with the responsibility of being the custodian of that revision on behalf of the Bishops and National Synod of the Canadian Church. And at such time as it shall please the Lord to call the soul of the present Lord Bishop of Richmond unto Himself, the custodianship of the revised Book of Common Prayer will then pass to his lawful successor.

It was determined from the very beginning that this revised Book of Common Prayer would be a restoration of the liturgical and doctrinal integrity of the Book of Common Prayer of the Church of England of 1662; and that it would incorporate into this revision all that which was good in the Canadian Book of Common Prayer of 1918; those things which were useful and admirable in the First English Book of Common Prayer of 1549; and such things as were edifying and meaningful in the Scottish Books of Common Prayer of 1637, 1764, and 1912, as well as in the proposed Book of Common Prayer of the Church of England of 1928, the Books of Common Prayer of the

Episcopal Church in the United States of America of 1892 and 1928, and the traditional liturgies of the Church in the Province of South Africa, the Church in the Province of the West Indies, and the Church of India, Burma, and Ceylon.

And what might give a certain distinction of liturgical character to this present revision is that it also incorporates certain prayers and devotions taken from the magnificent Liturgy of the Catholic Apostolic Church, as well as some from the Latin Rite of the Church in communion with the Holy See which had been authorised and promulgated by Pope Paul the Sixth after the Second Vatican Council and which had become incorporated into the liturgies of many Anglican parish, collegiate, and cathedral churches in Canada and other parts of the Anglican Communion.

The work which has been entrusted by God to the Christian Episcopal Church of Canada is to be faithful and obedient to Him, and true to His Word and the Faith of His Church. The Book of Common Prayer is, for all orthodox Anglican Christians, the way and means of doing this very thing. In it, the Scripture is apportioned and laid out for regular daily and seasonal reading; the Scripture is arranged and utilised for liturgical and devotional use; and the Scripture is presented as the source and foundation of the Doctrine, Order, Worship, and Discipline of the holy Catholic and Apostolic Church of God, and especially of that portion of the Church to which we belong.

In this way, it is hoped that the words of Saint Paul the Apostle will be fulfilled for all those faithful who may use this present version of the Book of Common Prayer, "I thank my God always on your behalf, for the grace of God which is given you by Jesus Christ; that in everything ye are enriched by Him, in all utterance, and in all knowledge; even as the testimony of Christ was confirmed in you: so that ye come behind in no gift; waiting for the coming of our Lord Jesus Christ: Who shall also confirm you unto the end, that ye may be blameless in the day of our Lord Jesus Christ" (I Corinthians 1. 4-8.); which echoes the words of the Psalmist, "For the Lord God is a Sun and Shield: the Lord will give grace and glory: no good thing will He withhold from them that walk uprightly." (Psalm 84. 11.)

May this Book of Common Prayer, revised with the permission and at the behest of the First Lord Primate and Metropolitan of the Christian Episcopal Church of Canada, approved and duly ratified by the successive National Synods canonically required, and published and issued by the authority of the Lord Primate and Bishops of the Christian Episcopal Church of Canada, be a source of strength, hope, spiritual comfort, and guidance to all who use it, and a mighty help to prepare, at the very least, this portion of the Catholic Church to be as the faithful Bride awaiting the return of the Bridegroom, and her entrance into the joy of the Presence of her only and long-expected Husband: her Lord and Saviour Jesus Christ.

✠ Robert David: Richmond.

Richmond, British Columbia.
Whitsuntide, 2018.

THE BOOK OF
COMMON PRAYER

AND

ADMINISTRATION OF

THE SACRAMENTS

AND OTHER RITES AND CEREMONIES OF

THE CHURCH

ACCORDING TO THE USE OF

THE CATHOLIC AND APOSTOLIC ANGLICAN CHURCH IN CANADA

ESTABLISHED AND KNOWN AS

THE CHRISTIAN EPISCOPAL CHURCH OF CANADA

2018

THE CONTENTS OF THIS BOOK

AN ACT
OF THE
NATIONAL SYNOD
OF
THE CHRISTIAN EPISCOPAL
CHURCH OF CANADA
INSTITUTING AND ESTABLISHING
THE BOOK OF COMMON PRAYER
2008

WHEREAS the Christian Episcopal Church of Canada is a national Catholic and Apostolic Church of the Anglican tradition, and a true and legitimate descendant and heir of the Church of England and of the Church of England in the Dominion of Canada;

AND WHEREAS the Christian Episcopal Church of Canada is an integral portion and living branch of the One Holy Catholic and Apostolic Church of Jesus Christ, with all the rights, privileges, powers, and authority belonging thereunto;

AND WHEREAS the Christian Episcopal Church of Canada, having separated itself from the fellowship of those with whom they had once enjoyed full communion in order to remain faithful to the orthodox Catholic and Apostolic Christian Faith and Religion from which their erring brethren had fallen away, has found it necessary to establish its own Public Liturgy, Constitution, and Canon Law to serve the needs of its own members;

AND WHEREAS the National Synod of the Christian Episcopal Church of Canada, acting in full accordance with the Constitution and Canons of the Christian Episcopal Church of Canada, accepted and adopted a draught proposed Book of Common Prayer duly submitted by His Excellency the Lord Bishop of Richmond on behalf of the Prayer Book Revision Committee to the National Synod for its consideration on the Thirteenth Day of October in the Year of Our Lord 2007, with the provision that any corrections that may need to be made to the text to ensure grammatical, literal and theological accuracy be made prior to its ratification by the next meeting of the National Synod;

AND WHEREAS the Constitution of the Christian Episcopal Church of Canada provides that any Canon respecting the Public Liturgy shall require to be passed by a majority of two-thirds of both Houses of the National Synod sitting separately at two consecutive sessions thereof held in two different years before coming into effect, and therefore the acceptance and adoption of the draughft proposed Book of Common Prayer requires to be ratified by a subsequent meeting of the National Synod convened for that purpose;

AND WHEREAS this present meeting of the National Synod has been convened and duly constituted with the express purpose of ratifying the acceptance and adoption of the said draught proposed Book of Common Prayer, with all necessary corrections made to the text thereof, and thereby instituting and establishing the said draught proposed Book of Common Prayer as the official Public Liturgy of the Christian Episcopal Church of Canada;

THEREFORE be it enacted by His Grace The Most Reverend Theodore Chris Casimes, acting on behalf and with the authorisation of His Grace The Most Reverend Archibald Donald Davies, Lord Primate and Metropolitan of Canada, by and with the advice and consent of His Excellency The Right Reverend Robert David Redmile, Lord Bishop of Richmond, and the Delegates from the Clergy and the Laity of the Christian Episcopal Church of Canada, now assembled in National Synod, the following: That the acceptance and adoption of the draught proposed Book of Common Prayer duly submitted to the National Synod on the Thirteenth Day of October in the Year of Our Lord 2007 be now ratified; and that the said draught proposed Book of Common Prayer, with all necessary corrections made to the text thereof, be hereby instituted and established as the sole official Book of Common Prayer of the Christian Episcopal Church of Canada to be used in all acts of worship in the Christian Episcopal Church of Canada whether public or private; and that every Bishop, Priest, Deacon, and licenced Lay-Minister of the Christian Episcopal Church of Canada shall use the said Book and none other at all times of their ministrations whether public or private.

PROVIDED ALWAYS that the Book of Common Prayer of the Church of England of 1662 and the Book of Common Prayer of the Church of England in the Dominion of Canada of 1918 and the Book of Common Prayer of the Anglican Church of Canada of 1962 shall be respected as historical documents of the Christian Episcopal Church of Canada; and that any of the said Books may be used from time to time where it may be considered expedient at the discretion of the Ordinary for pastoral reasons with his written permission without prejudice to the intention and tenor of this Act.

GIVEN under Our Hands at the City of Richmond, in the Province of British Columbia of the Dominion of Canada, this Nineteenth Day of January in the Year of Our Lord 2008.

> ✠ THEODORE CHRIS CASIMES,
>   Acting Primate of Canada.
>
> ✠ ARCHIBALD DONALD DAVIES,
>   Lord Primate and Metropolitan of Canada.
>
> ✠ ROBERT DAVID REDMILE,
>   Lord Bishop of Richmond.
>
> ✠ TIMOTHY JOSEPH KLEREKOPER,
>   Bishop Co-adjutor of Seattle.

THE PREFACE TO
THE BOOK OF COMMON PRAYER
1662

IT hath been the wisdom of the Church of England, ever since the first compiling of her Public Liturgy, to keep the mean between the two extremes, of too much stiffness in refusing, and in too much easiness in admitting any variation from it. For, as on the one side common experience sheweth, that where a change hath been made of things advisedly established (no evident necessity so requiring) sundry inconveniences have thereupon ensued; and those many times more and greater than the evils, that were intended to be remedied by such change: So on the other side, the particular Forms of Divine worship and the Rites and Ceremonies appointed to be used therein, being things in their own nature indifferent, and alterable, and so acknowledged; it is but reasonable, that upon weighty and important considerations, according to the various exigency of times and occasions, such changes and alterations should be made therein, as to those that are in place of Authority should from time to time seem either necessary or expedient. Accordingly we find, that in the Reigns of several Princes of blessed memory since the Reformation, the Church, upon just and weighty considerations her thereunto moving, hath yielded to make such alterations in some particulars, as in their respective times were thought convenient: Yet so, as that the main Body and Essentials of it (as well in the chiefest materials, as in the frame and order thereof) have still continued the same unto this day, and do yet stand firm and unshaken, notwithstanding all the vain attempts and impetuous assaults made against it, by such men as are given to change, and have always discovered a greater regard to their own private fancies and interests, than to that duty they owe to the public.

By what undue means, and for what mischievous purposes the use of the Liturgy (though enjoined by the Laws of the Land, and those Laws never yet repealed) came, during the late unhappy confusions, to be discontinued, is too well known to the world, and we are not willing here to remember. But when, upon His Majesty's happy Restoration, it seemed probable, that, amongst other things, the use of the Liturgy also would return of course (the same having never been legally abolished) unless some timely means were used to prevent it; those men who under the late usurped powers had made it a great part of their business to render the people disaffected thereunto, saw themselves in point of reputation and interest concerned (unless they would freely acknowledge themselves to have erred, which such men are very hardly brought to do) with their utmost endeavours to hinder the restitution thereof. In order whereunto divers Pamphlets were published against the Book of Common Prayer, the old Objections mustered up, with the addition of some new ones, more than formerly had been made, to make the number swell. In fine, great importunities were used to His Sacred Majesty, that the said Book might be revised, and such Alterations therein, and Additions thereunto made, as should be thought requisite for the ease of tender Consciences: whereunto His Majesty, out of his pious inclination to give satisfaction (so far as could be reasonably expected) to all his subjects of what persuasion soever, did graciously condescend.

In which review we have endeavoured to observe the like moderation, as we find to have been used in the like case in former times. And therefore of the sundry Alterations proposed unto us, we have rejected all such as were either of dangerous consequence (as secretly striking at some established Doctrine, or laudable Practice of the Church of England, or indeed of the whole Catholic Church of Christ) or else of no consequence at all, but utterly frivolous and vain. But such

Alterations as were tendered to us (by what persons, under what pretences, or to what purpose soever so tendered) as seemed to us in any degree requisite or expedient, we have willingly, and of our own accord assented unto: not enforced so to do by any strength of Argument, convincing us of the necessity of making the said Alterations: For we are fully persuaded in our judgements (and we here profess it to the world) that the Book, as it stood before established by Law, doth not contain in it anything contrary to the Word of God, or to sound Doctrine, or which a godly man may not with a good Conscience use and submit unto, or which is not fairly defensible against any that shall oppose the same; if it shall be allowed such just and favourable construction as in common Equity ought to be allowed to all human Writings, especially such as are set forth by Authority, and even to the very best translations of the Holy Scripture itself.

Our general aim therefore in this undertaking was, not to gratify this or that party in any their unreasonable demands; but to do that, which to our best understandings we conceived might most tend to the preservation of Peace and Unity in the Church; the procuring of Reverence, and exciting of Piety and Devotion in the Public Worship of God; and the cutting off occasion from them that seek occasion of cavil or quarrel against the Liturgy of the Church. And as to the several variations from the former Book, whether by Alteration, Addition, or otherwise, it shall suffice to give this general account, That most of the Alterations were made, either first, for the better direction of them that are to officiate in any part of Divine Service; which is chiefly done in the Calendars and Rubrics: Or secondly, for the more proper expressing of some words or phrases of ancient usage in terms more suitable to the language of the present times, and the clearer explanation of some other words and phrases, that were either of doubtful signification, or otherwise liable to misconstruction: Or thirdly, for a more perfect rendering of such portions of Holy Scripture, as are inserted into the Liturgy; which, in the Epistles and Gospels especially, and in sundry other places, are now ordered to be read according to the last Translation: and that it was thought convenient, that some Prayers and Thanksgivings, fitted to special occasions, should be added in their due places; particularly for those at Sea, together with an office for the Baptism of such as are of Riper Years: which although not so necessary when the former Book was compiled, yet by the growth of Anabaptism, through the licentiousness of the late times crept in amongst us, is now become necessary, and may be always useful for the baptising of Natives in our Plantations, and others converted to the Faith. If any man, who shall desire a more particular account of the several Alterations in any part of the Liturgy, shall take the pains to compare the present Book with the former; we doubt not but the reason of the change may easily appear.

And having thus endeavoured to discharge our duties in this weighty affair, as in the sight of God, and to approve our sincerity therein (so far as lay in us) to the consciences of all men; although we know it impossible (in such variety of apprehensions, humours and interests, as are in the world) to please all; nor can expect that men of factious, peevish, and perverse spirits should be satisfied with anything that can be done in this kind by any other than themselves: Yet we have good hope, that what is here presented, and hath been by the Convocations of both Provinces with great diligence examined and approved, will be also well accepted and approved by all sober, peaceable, and truly conscientious Sons of the Church of England.

THE PREFACE TO THE CANADIAN BOOK OF COMMON PRAYER 1918

THE Book of Common Prayer is a priceless possession of our Church. By its intrinsic merits, as a book designed for the reverent and seemly worship of Almighty God, as well as by its historic associations, it has endeared itself to generation after generation of devout Christians throughout the world. None would desire or advocate any change therein which would impair or lessen this deep-seated affection.

But through the lapse of some three hundred years many changes have taken place in the life of the Church and in its outlook upon the world. The present life and larger outlook of the Church are seeking more adequate expression than the Book of Common Prayer has hitherto afforded, and seem to require judicious adaptation and enrichment of the Book in order that it may more fully meet the needs of the Church in this age and in this Dominion.

Therefore the General Synod of the Church of England in Canada determined to make such adaptations and enrichments in the body of the Book as would serve this purpose. But to avoid the risk of changes that might impair the character of the Book, the General Synod clearly ordained the limits within which such adaptation and enrichment might be made, forbidding any change in text or rubric which would involve or imply a change of doctrine or principle of the Church of England as set forth in the Book of Common Prayer, or any other change not in accordance with the 27th Resolution of the Lambeth Conference of 1908.

The chief results of the present Revision will be found to be: the adaptation of rubrics to customs generally accepted at the present time; the provision of directions for the combined use of the different Services; the adaptation and enrichment of the Occasional Offices; the supplying of Forms for Additional Services in use throughout the Church though not provided for in the Book of Common Prayer heretofore; the addition of many new Prayers for Special Occasions; the revision of the Calendar, the Lectionary, and the Psalter.

This present book, the fruit of much prayer and toil, is set forth in the firm belief that, by the alterations and additions herein made, it will both provide greater variety in Public Worship and better meet the needs of the Church in this land: and in good hope that, thus adapted and enriched, it may prove more generally serviceable to both Clergy and people in the worship of God throughout this Dominion.

The Preface to
the Present Revision of
the Book of Common Prayer
2018

The Book of Common Prayer, which was authorised and given to the Church of England by King Charles the Second in 1662 at the time of the Restoration of the Monarchy, became the vehicle by which the Gospel of Jesus Christ and the Worship of His Church were carried throughout the English-speaking world. That revised and restored Book of Common Prayer became the compendium of the Faith, Doctrine, Order, and Discipline held and maintained by the Church of England: that same Church which was first brought to the British Isles in Apostolic times and again to England by Saint Augustine, and which was later established by Law and has since continued without break as the national Church of the English and English-speaking peoples unto our own time.

And even when within that ancient and established Anglican Church there were those who were disloyal to her Faith, opposed to her Doctrine, and who despised her Establishment, there were ever yet faithful men and women who upheld the Faith and Order of the One undivided Church as set forth in their Book of Common Prayer; and who, with God's help, maintained the integrity and continuity of their portion of the Catholic and Apostolic Church. Thus the Book of Common Prayer has become for many generations of faithful Anglican Christians their beloved and priceless treasure, and the principal means whereby they can remain loyal to and steadfast in their defence of the Faith and Church which they received from their forefathers, and to worship God as their ancestors did.

It was in this same spirit that the Christian Episcopal Church of Canada was established by Canadian Anglican Christians who could not in good conscience accept the innovations and alterations being made to the Doctrine, Order, and Discipline of the Anglican Church of Canada by successive general, provincial, and diocesan synods following the Tenth Lambeth Conference of 1968. Rather than abandon the Anglican tradition embodied in their Book of Common Prayer, they chose instead to remain loyal to the Faith and Order of the undivided Church, and the witness thereunto of the restored and established Church of England; and to separate themselves from the corrupted body, in order to preserve, maintain, and transmit unimpaired to succeeding generations the true Anglican expression of the Catholic Religion.

However, in the more than three and a half centuries since the Book of Common Prayer of the Church of England was last revised, the world has changed greatly; and the venerable Liturgy of the Church of England, has, in many instances, not been fully adequate to meet the needs of Christians living outside the British Isles, nor of those living under constitutional and social circumstances quite different from those of Great Britain and its Dependencies. It was this fact which led to the first official revision of the Book of Common Prayer for the Church of England in the Dominion of Canada in 1918.

Moreover, the rediscovery and reclamation of some of the forgotten ancient devotional and liturgical heritage of the Church of England, and the inspired movement within the Anglican Communion for reconciliation with other historic particular and national Catholic Churches from which the Church of England became separated at the time of the Reformation, have necessitated some thoughtful and careful revision to the Public Liturgy of the Church. This is especially true in light of the great liturgical renewal brought about by the Second Vatican Council which substantially altered many of the accepted practices of the western Church. And since the Anglican Churches have always considered themselves to be integral portions of the One Church, it was a matter of course that the Anglican Use of the Divine Liturgy and Common Prayer would require some sort of careful revision in order to accommodate these alterations, and to bring the Anglican usages into line with the usages lawfully permitted and now prevailing within the Catholic Church in the west.

It is for this reason, therefore, that the Christian Episcopal Church of Canada, now building upon the first revision of the Book of Common Prayer made by the Church of England in Canada of 1918, and considering its subsequent revision by the Anglican Church of Canada in 1962, has determined to further the work of previous generations of Canadian Anglicans by setting forth a new revision of the Book of Common Prayer drawn up specifically for use within the Christian Episcopal Church of Canada and Churches in full communion with her.

This present revision of our Canadian Book of Common Prayer is intended to be faithful to the Book of Common Prayer of the Church of England of 1662 and that of the Church of England in the Dominion of Canada of 1918, while incorporating certain prayers, devotions, and usages which have become common in the Church since the last Canadian revision of 1962, as well as certain prayers, and forms of prayer, found in other revisions of the Book of Common Prayer used throughout the wider Anglican Communion. It is also intended that this present revision should reflect the intention of the Christian Episcopal Church of Canada to be a faithful witness to and preserver of the fullness of the orthodox Faith and Order of the One undivided Catholic and Apostolic Church which was given to us by Our Lord Jesus Christ Himself through His holy Apostles, and which has been handed down faithfully from generation to generation by orthodox Christians at all times and in all places.

And so it is to this end that this present revision of the Canadian Book of Common Prayer, which was begun with the acceptance of a draught proposal of a revised Prayer Book in 2008, and which after a decade of correction, redaction, and refinement, is now completed and offered to the faithful of the Christian Episcopal Church of Canada as an acceptable vehicle for the proper worship of Almighty God and the effective and effectual preservation and transmission of the orthodox Christian Faith and the authentic Anglican tradition within the setting of the wider fellowship of the One Holy Catholic and Apostolic Church of God.

CONCERNING
THE SERVICE OF THE CHURCH
1549

THERE was never any thing by the wit of man so well devised, or so sure established, which in continuance of time hath not been corrupted: As, among other things, it may plainly appear by the Common Prayers in the Church, commonly called Divine Service. The first original and ground whereof if a man would search out by the ancient Fathers, he shall find, that the same was not ordained but of a good purpose, and for a great advancement of godliness. For they so ordered the matter, that all the whole Bible (or the greatest part thereof) should be read over every year; intending thereby, that the Clergy, and especially such as were Ministers in the congregation, should (by often reading, and meditation in God's word) be stirred up to godliness themselves and be more able to exhort others by wholesome doctrine, and to confute them that were adversaries to the truth; and further, that the people (by daily hearing of Holy Scripture read in the Church) might continually profit more and more in the knowledge of God, and be the more inflamed with the love of His true Religion.

But these many years passed, this godly and decent order of the ancient Fathers hath been so altered, broken, and neglected, by planting in uncertain Stories, and Legends, with multitude of Responds, Verses, vain Repetitions, Commemorations, and Synodals; that commonly when any Book of the Bible was begun, after three of four Chapters were read out, all the rest were unread. And in this sort the Book of Isaiah was begun in Advent, and the Book of Genesis in Septuagesima; but they were only begun, and never read through: after like sort were other Books of Holy Scripture used. And moreover, whereas Saint Paul would have such language spoken to the people in the Church, as they might understand, and have profit by hearing the same; the Service in this Church of England these many years hath been read in Latin to the people, which they understand not; so that they have heard with their ears only, and their heart, spirit and mind, have not been edified thereby. And furthermore, notwithstanding that the ancient Fathers have divided the Psalms into seven portions, whereof everyone was called a Nocturn: now of late time a few of them have been daily said, and the rest utterly omitted. Moreover, the number and hardness of the Rules called the Pie, and the manifold changings of the Service, was the cause, that to turn the book only was so hard and intricate a matter, that many times there was more business to find out what should be read, than to read it when it was found out.

These inconveniences therefore considered, here is set forth such an Order, whereby the same shall be redressed. And for a readiness in this matter, here is drawn out a Calendar for that purpose, which is plain and easy to be understood; wherein (so much as may be) the reading of Holy Scripture is so set forth, that all things shall be done in order, without breaking one piece from another. For this cause be cut off Anthems, Responds, Invitatories, and such like things as did break the continual course of the reading of the Scripture.

Yet, because there is no remedy, but that of necessity there must be some Rules; therefore certain Rules are here set forth; which, as they are few in number, so they are plain and easy to be understood. So that here you have an Order for Prayer, and for the reading of the Holy Scripture, much agreeable to the mind and purpose of the old Fathers, and a great deal more profitable and commodious, than that which of late was used. It is more profitable, because here are left out many things, whereof some are untrue, some vain and superstitious; and nothing is ordained to be read, but the very pure Word of God, the Holy Scriptures, or that which is agreeable to the same; and that in such a Language and Order as is most easy and plain for the understanding both of the Readers and Hearers. It is also more commodious, both for the shortness thereof, and for the plainness of the Order, and for that the Rules be few and easy.

And whereas heretofore there hath been great diversity in saying and singing in Churches within this Realm; some following Salisbury Use, some Hereford Use, and some the Use of Bangor, some of York, some of Lincoln; now from henceforth all the whole Realm shall have but one Use.

And forasmuch as nothing can be so plainly set forth, but doubts may arise in the use and practice of the same; to appease all such diversity (if any arise) and for the resolution of all doubts, concerning the manner how to understand, do, and execute, the things contained in this Book; the parties that so doubt, or diversely take anything, shall alway resort to the Bishop of the Diocese, who by his discretion shall take order for the quieting and appeasing of the same; so that the same order be not contrary to anything contained in this Book. And if the Bishop of the Diocese be in doubt, then he may send for the resolution thereof to the Archbishop.

THOUGH it be appointed, that all things shall be read and sung in the Church in the English Tongue, to the end that the Congregation may be thereby edified; yet it is not meant, but that when men say Morning and Evening Prayer privately, they may say the same in any language that they themselves do understand.

And all Priests and Deacons are to say daily the Morning and Evening Prayer either privately or openly, not being let by sickness, or some other urgent cause.

And the Curate that ministereth in every Parish-Church or Chapel, being at home, and not being otherwise reasonably hindered, shall say the same in the Parish-Church or Chapel where he ministereth, and shall cause a Bell to be tolled thereunto a convenient time before he begin, that the people may come to hear God's Word, and to pray with him.

OF CEREMONIES
WHY SOME BE ABOLISHED AND SOME RETAINED
1549

OF such Ceremonies as be used in the Church, and have had their beginning by the institution of man, some at the first were of godly intent and purpose devised, and yet at length turned to vanity and superstition: some entered into the Church by undiscreet devotion, and such a zeal as was without knowledge; and for because they were winked at in the beginning, they grew daily to more and more abuses, which not only for their unprofitableness, but also because they have much blinded the people, and obscured the glory of God, are worthy to be cut away, and clean rejected: other there be, which although they have been devised by man, yet it is thought good to reserve them still, as well for a decent order in the Church, (for the which they were first devised) as because they pertain to edification, whereunto all things done in the Church (as the Apostle teacheth) ought to be referred.

And although the keeping or omitting of a Ceremony, in itself considered, is but a small thing; yet the wilful and contemptuous transgression and breaking of a common order and discipline is no small offence before God, Let all things be done among you, saith Saint Paul, in a seemly and due order: the appointment of the which order pertaineth not to private men; therefore no man ought to take in hand, nor presume to appoint or alter any publick or common Order in Christ's Church, except he be lawfully called and authorised thereunto.

And whereas in this our time, the minds of men are so diverse, that some think it a great matter of conscience to depart from a piece of the least of their Ceremonies, they be so addicted to their old customs; and again on the other side, some be so new-fangled, that they would innovate all things, and so despise the old, that nothing can like them, but that is new: it was thought expedient, not so much to have respect how to please and satisfy either of these parties, as how to please God, and profit them both. And yet lest any man should be offended, whom good reason might satisfy, here be certain causes rendered, why some of the accustomed Ceremonies be put away, and some retained and kept still.

Some are put away, because the great excess and multitude of them hath so increased in these latter days, that the burden of them was intolerable; whereof Saint Augustine in his time complained, that they were grown to such a number, that the estate of Christian people was in worse case concerning that matter, than were the Jews. And he counselled that such yoke and burden should be taken away, as time would serve quietly to do it. But what would Saint Augustine have said, if he had seen the Ceremonies of late days used among us; whereunto the multitude used in his time was not to be compared? This our excessive multitude of Ceremonies was so great, and many of them so dark, that they did more confound and darken, than declare and set forth Christ's benefits unto us. And besides this, Christ's Gospel is not a Ceremonial Law, (as much of Moses' Law was,) but it is a Religion to serve God, not in bondage of the figure or shadow, but in the freedom of the Spirit; being content only with those Ceremonies which do serve to a decent Order and godly Discipline, and such as be apt to stir up the dull mind of man to the remembrance of his duty to God, by some notable and special signification, whereby he might be edified. Furthermore, the most weighty cause of the abolishment of certain Ceremonies was, That they were so far abused, partly by the superstitious blindness of the rude and unlearned, and partly by the unsatiable avarice of such as sought more their own lucre, than the glory of God, that the abuses could not well be taken away, the thing remaining still.

But now as concerning those persons, which peradventure will be offended, for that some of the old Ceremonies are retained still: If they consider that without some Ceremonies it is not possible to keep any Order, or quiet Discipline in the Church, they shall easily perceive just cause to reform their judgements. And if they think much, that any of the old do remain, and would rather have all devised anew: then such men granting some Ceremonies convenient to be had, surely where the old may be well used, there they cannot reasonably reprove the old only for their age, without bewraying of their own folly. For in such a case they ought rather to have reverence unto them for their antiquity, if they will declare themselves to be more studious of unity and concord, than of innovations and new-fangleness, which (as much as may be with the true setting forth of Christ's Religion) is always to be eschewed. Furthermore, such shall have no just cause with the Ceremonies reserved to be offended. For as those be taken away which were most abused, and did burden men's consciences without any cause; so the other that remain, are retained for a discipline and order, which (upon just causes) may be altered and changed, and therefore are not to be esteemed equal with God's Law. And moreover, they be neither dark nor dumb Ceremonies, but are so set forth, that every man may understand what they do mean, and to what use they do serve. So that it is not like that they in time to come should be abused as other have been. And in these our doings we condemn no other Nations, nor prescribe anything but to our own people only: For we think it convenient that every Country should use such Ceremonies as they shall think best to the setting forth of God's honour and glory, and to the reducing of the people to a most perfect and godly living, without error or superstition; and that they should put away other things, which from time to time they perceive to be most abused, as in men's ordinances it often chanceth diversely in divers countries.

THE KALENDAR
AND OTHER TABLES

THE KALENDAR

THE Holy-days which are appointed to be observed, commonly called Red Letter Days, are indicated in small capitals. The other Holy-days and Commemorations, commonly called Black Letter Days, are indicated in lower case. Each Red Letter Day is provided with its own Propers. The Black Letter Days may be observed by using the Common Propers provided therefor, or other suitable Propers may be used with the permission of the Ordinary.

In this Kalendar are commemorated the principal events in the lives of our Lord Jesus Christ and of His Mother the Blessed Virgin Mary, and the anniversaries of the deaths or principal events in the lives of the Saints who are venerated throughout the universal Church, as well as the Saints of the Churches of England, Wales, Scotland, and Ireland, and of other particular or national Churches with which those Churches have long had ties of kinship and affinity. Local commemorations approved by authority, but not included in this Kalendar, may also be observed if such observance is of ancient custom or long-standing use, and hath received permission from the Ordinary to be observed.

The names of persons of note who have departed this life in the communion of the Church of England or Churches of the wider Anglican Communion since the reign of Queen Elizabeth the First are not included in this Kalendar, with the exception of the two principal Anglican Martyrs. Nevertheless, here let it be noted that the names of such persons which may have been included in other Kalendars of this Church have been so included only to serve as examples for the instruction and edification of the faithful, without thereby enrolling or commending them as recognised Saints of the Church.

JANUARY HATH XXXI DAYS.

1. THE CIRCUMCISION OF OUR LORD.
2. Lucian of Beauvais, Bishop, Martyr, 290.
6. THE EPIPHANY OF OUR LORD.
7. Lucian of Antioch, Priest, Martyr, 312.
8. Cedd, Missionary in Northumbria, Bishop, 664.
9. Bertwald, Archbishop of Canterbury, Confessor, 731.
10. William, Archbishop of Canterbury, Martyr, 1645.
11. Ælred, Abbot of Rievaulx, 1167.
12. Benedict Biscop, Abbot, 689.
13. Hilary, Bishop of Poictiers, Doctor, 368.
14. Kentigern, Missionary in Scotland, Bishop, 603.
17. Anthony of Egypt, Abbot, 356.
18. Prisca, Virgin, Martyr, 270.
19. Wulfstan, Bishop of Worcester, Confessor, 1095.
20. Sebastian and Fabian, Martyrs, 250.
21. Agnes, Roman Virgin, Martyr, 304.
22. Vincent, Spanish Deacon, Martyr, 304.
24. Saint Timothy, Bishop of Ephesus, Martyr.
25. THE CONVERSION OF SAINT PAUL THE APOSTLE.
26. Polycarp, Bishop of Smyrna, Martyr, 155.
27. John Chrysostom, Patriarch of Constantinople, Doctor, 407.
28. Thomas Aquinas, Doctor, 1274.
29. Gildas, Abbot, Confessor, 570.
30. Charles, King of England and Scotland, Martyr, 1649.

FEBRUARY HATH XXVIII DAYS (AND IN EVERY LEAP YEAR 29 DAYS.)

1. Bridget, Virgin, Abbess of Kildare, 525.
2. THE PURIFICATION OF OUR LADY.
3. Blaise, Bishop of Sebaste, Martyr, 316.
4. Anskar, Missionary in Scandinavia, Bishop, 864.
5. Gilbert, Abbot of Sempringham, Confessor, 1189.
6. Saint Titus, Bishop of Crete, Confessor.
7. Apollonia, Virgin, Deaconess, Martyr, 249.
8. Agatha, Virgin, Martyr, 251.
9. Cyril, Patriarch of Alexandria, Doctor, 444.
10. Scholastica, Virgin, Sister to Benedict, Abbess, 543.
11. Caedmon, English Poet, Confessor, 680.
13. Ælflæda, Virgin, Abbess of Whitby, 714.
14. Valentine, Priest, Martyr, 270.
18. Colman, Bishop of Lindisfarne, Confessor, 676.
19. The Triumph of the True Faith, 842.
23. Milburga, Virgin, Abbess of Wenlock, 715.
24. SAINT MATTHIAS THE APOSTLE AND MARTYR.
26. Æthelbert, King of England, Confessor, 616.
28. Oswald, Archbishop of York, Confessor, 992.

MARCH HATH XXXI DAYS.

1. David, Archbishop of Menevia, Patron of Wales, 544.
2. Chad, Missionary in Mercia, Bishop, 673.
5. Piran, Missionary and Abbot, Patron of Cornwall, 480.
6. The Forty-two Martyrs of Amorium, 845.
7. Perpetua and Felicity, and their Companions, 673.
8. Felix, Missionary to the East Anglians, Bishop, 647.
9. Gregory, Bishop of Nyssa, Confessor, 395.
11. Oswin, King of Northumbria, Martyr, 651.
12. Gregory the Great, Pope of Rome, Doctor, 604.
17. Patrick, Missionary to the Irish, Patron of Ireland, 465.
18. Edward, King of the West Saxons, Martyr, 979.
19. SAINT JOSEPH OF NAZARETH, SPOUSE OF OUR LADY.
20. Cuthbert, Missionary in Northumbria, Bishop, 687.
21. Benedict of Nursia, Abbot of Monte Casino, 543.
25. THE ANNUNCIATION OF OUR LADY.
27. John of Damascus, Doctor, 749.
28. Stephen, Abbot of Citeaux, 1134.
30. Osburga, Virgin, Abbess of Coventry, 1018.

APRIL HATH XXX DAYS.

1. Gilbert, Bishop of Caithness, Confessor, 1245.
3. Richard, Bishop of Chichester, Confessor, 1253.
4. Ambrose, Bishop of Milan, Doctor, 397.
5. Isidore, Archbishop of Seville, Doctor, 636.
10. Hedda, Abbot of Peterborough, Martyr, 870.
11. Guthlac, Hermit, Confessor, 714.
16. Magnus, Earl of Orkney, Martyr, 1116.
17. Stephen Harding, Abbot, 1134.
19. Ælphege, Archbishop of Canterbury, Martyr, 1012.
21. Anselm, Archbishop of Canterbury, Doctor, 1109.
22. William, Bishop of Rochester, Confessor, 1201.
23. George, Martyr, Patron of England, 303.
24. Mellitus, Archbishop of Canterbury, Confessor, 624.
25. SAINT MARK THE EVANGELIST AND MARTYR.
26. Rusticus, Archbishop of Lyons, 501.
29. Robert of Molesme, Abbot of Citeaux, 1110.
30. Catherine of Siena, Virgin, 1380.

MAY HATH XXXI DAYS.

1. SAINT PHILIP AND SAINT JAMES, APOSTLES AND MARTYRS
2. Athanasius, Patriarch of Alexandria, Doctor, 373.
3. The Invention of the Holy Cross, 326.
4. Monnica, Widow, Mother to Augustine, 387.
7. John of Beverley, Archbishop of York, Confessor, 721.
8. Ida of Metz, Matron, 652.
9. Gregory, Patriarch of Constantinople, Doctor, 389.
11. Cyril and Methodius, Missionaries to the Slavs, Bishops, 885.
12. Pancras, Roman Martyr, 304.
13. Erconwald, Bishop of London, Confessor, 693.
16. Brendan, Abbot of Clonfert, 575.
19. Dunstan, Archbishop of Canterbury, Confessor, 988.
20. The Council of Nicæa, 325.
21. Godric, Hermit, 1170.
23. David, King of Scotland, Confessor, 1153.
24. Vincent of Lerins, Confessor, 445.
25. Aldhelm, Bishop of Sherborne, Confessor, 709.
26. Augustine of Canterbury, Missionary to the English, 605.
27. Bede, Priest of Jarrow, Confessor, Doctor, 735.
29. Oda, Archbishop of Canterbury, Confessor, 985.
30. Hubert, Bishop of Maastricht, Confessor, 727.
31. SAINT JOSEPH OF ARIMATHÆA.

JUNE HATH XXX DAYS.

1. Justin, Martyr, 165.
2. Erasmus, Bishop of Formiae, Martyr, 300.
4. Edfrith, Bishop of Lindisfarne, Confessor, 721.
5. Boniface, Missionary to the Germans, Martyr, 755.
6. SAINT MARY AND SAINT MARTHA OF BETHANY.
7. Robert, Abbot of Newminster, 1159.
8. William, Archbishop of York, Confessor, 1154.
9. Columba, Abbot of Iona, 597.
10. Margaret, Queen of Scotland, Widow, 1093.
11. SAINT BARNABAS THE APOSTLE AND MARTYR.
13. Anthony of Padua, Doctor, 1231.
14. Basil the Great, Bishop of Caesarea, Doctor, 379.
15. Vitus and Modestus, Martyrs, 303.
17. Ephraim of Syria, Deacon, Doctor, 373.
18. Henry, Missionary to the Finns, Martyr, 1150.
22. Alban, First Martyr in Britain, 303.
24. THE NATIVITY OF SAINT JOHN THE BAPTIST.
25. David, Missionary to the Swedes, Bishop, 1080.
28. Irenæus, Bishop of Lyons, Martyr, 202.
29. SAINT PETER THE APOSTLE AND MARTYR.
30. Saint Silas, Bishop of Corinth, Martyr.

JULY HATH XXXI DAYS.

2. The Visitation of Our Lady to Saint Elizabeth.
7. Willibald, Bishop of Eichstatt, 787.
8. Edgar, King of England, Confessor, 975.
9. Stephen, Archbishop of Canterbury, 1228.
12. Saint Veronica.
13. Mildred, Virgin, Abbess of Minster, 700.
14. ALL HOLY APOSTLES OF OUR LORD.
15. Swithun, Bishop of Winchester, Confessor, 862.
16. Bonaventure, Bishop of Albano, Doctor, 1274.
18. Arnold, Bishop of Metz, 640.
20. Margaret, Virgin, Martyr of Antioch, 278.
22. SAINT MARY MAGDALENE.
25. SAINT JAMES THE APOSTLE AND MARTYR.
26. Saint Anne, Mother to Our Lady.
27. Christopher, Martyr, 295.
28. Samson, Missionary to the Bretons, Bishop, 565.
29. Olaf, King of Norway, Martyr, 1030.
31. Germanus, Bishop of Auxerre, Confessor, 448.

AUGUST HATH XXXI DAYS.

1. Saint Peter in Chains, called Lammas-Day.
2. Plegmund, Archbishop of Canterbury, 914.
4. Dominic, Confessor, 1221.
5. Oswald, King of Northumbria, Martyr, 642.
6. THE TRANSFIGURATION OF OUR LORD.
10. Laurence, Archdeacon of Rome, Martyr, 258.
12. Clare of Assisi, Virgin, Abbess, 1253.
13. Hippolytus, Priest at Rome, Martyr, 235.
15. THE FALLING ASLEEP OF OUR LADY.
16. Saint Joachim, Father to Our Lady.
18. Helen, Empress of Rome, Widow, 330.
20. Bernard of Clairvaux, Abbot, Doctor, 1153.
22. Sigfrid, Abbot of Wearmouth, 688.
24. SAINT BARTHOLOMEW THE APOSTLE AND MARTYR.
25. Louis, King of France, 1270.
26. Bregwine, Archbishop of Canterbury, 764.
28. Augustine, Bishop of Hippo, Doctor, 430.
29. THE BEHEADING OF SAINT JOHN THE BAPTIST.
31. Aidan, Bishop of Lindisfarne, Confessor, 651.

SEPTEMBER HATH XXX DAYS.

1. Giles of Provence, Abbot, 720.
6. Begge, Matron, Abbess of Andenne, 693.
7. Evurtius, Bishop of Orleans, Confessor, 340.
8. THE NATIVITY OF OUR LADY.
12. Laurence, Archbishop of Canterbury, Confessor, 619.
13. Cyprian, Bishop of Carthage, Doctor, Martyr, 258.
14. THE EXALTATION OF THE HOLY CROSS, 335.
16. Ninian, Missionary to the Picts, Bishop, 430.
17. Lambert, Bishop of Maastricht, Martyr, 709.
19. Theodore of Tarsus, Archbishop of Canterbury, 690.
20. Honorius, Archbishop of Canterbury, Confessor, 653.
21. SAINT MATTHEW THE EVANGELIST, APOSTLE AND MARTYR.
23. Linus, Pope of Rome, Martyr, 80.
25. Ceolfrith, Abbot of Wearmouth and Jarrow, 716.
26. Cosmas and Damian, Martyrs, 287.
28. Wenceslas, Duke of Bohemia, Martyr, 929.
29. SAINT MICHAEL AND ALL ANGELS.
30. Jerome, Priest at Bethlehem, Doctor, 420.

OCTOBER HATH XXXI DAYS.

1. Remigius, Bishop of Rheims, Confessor, 593.
2. The Holy Guardian Angels.
4. Francis of Assisi, Confessor, 1226.
6. Faith of Aquitaine, Virgin, Martyr, 290.
8. Bridget of Sweden, Abbess, 1373.
9. Denys, Bishop of Paris, Martyr, 272.
10. Paulinus, Archbishop of York, Confessor, 644.
12. Wilfrid, Archbishop of York, Confessor, 709.
13. Edward, King of England, Confessor, 1066.
14. Callistus, Pope of Rome, Martyr, 222.
16. Nothelm, Archbishop of Canterbury, 739.
17. Ætheldreda, Queen, Abbess of Ely, 679.
18. SAINT LUKE THE EVANGELIST.
19. Frideswide, Virgin, Abbess of Oxford, 735.
23. Æthelwold, Bishop of Winchester, 984.
25. Crispin and Crispinian, Martyrs, 288.
26. Ælfred, King of the West Saxons, Confessor, 899.
28. SAINT SIMON AND SAINT JUDE, APOSTLES AND MARTYRS.

NOVEMBER HATH XXX DAYS.

1. ALL SAINTS.
2. All Souls.
6. Leonard, Abbot, Confessor, 559.
7. Willibrord, Missionary to the Frisians, Bishop, 739.
8. The Four Crowned Martyrs, 304.
9. Leo the Great, Pope of Rome, Doctor, 461.
10. Justus, Archbishop of Canterbury, Confessor, 627.
11. Martin, Bishop of Tours, Confessor, 397.
13. Britius, Bishop of Tours, 444.
15. Machutus, Bishop in Britanny, 564.
16. Edmund, Archbishop of Canterbury, Confessor, 1240.
17. Hugh, Bishop of Lincoln, Confessor, 1200.
18. Hilda, Virgin, Abbess of Whitby, 680.
19. Elizabeth of Hungary, Queen, Widow, 1231.
20. Edmund, King of East Anglia, Martyr, 870.
22. Cecilia, Virgin, Martyr, 230.
23. Clement, Pope of Rome, Martyr, 100.
25. Catherine of Alexandria, Virgin, Martyr, 307.
30. SAINT ANDREW THE APOSTLE AND MARTYR.

DECEMBER HATH XXXI DAYS.

1. Botolph, Abbot, 680.
2. Viviana, Roman Virgin, Martyr, 363.
3. Osmund, Bishop of Salisbury, Confessor, 1099.
4. All Servants of God before the First Advent.
5. Birinus, Missionary to the West Saxons, Bishop, 650.
6. Nicholas, Bishop of Myra, Confessor, 342.
8. THE CONCEPTION OF OUR LADY.
11. Damasus, Pope of Rome, 384.
12. Edburga, Virgin, Abbess of Minster, 751.
13. Lucy, Virgin, Martyr, 304.
16. *O Sapientia.*
17. Ignatius, Bishop of Antioch, Martyr at Rome, 110.
19. David, King of Israel and Judah, Prophet.
21. SAINT THOMAS THE APOSTLE AND MARTYR.
25. THE NATIVITY OF OUR LORD.
26. SAINT STEPHEN THE MARTYR.
27. SAINT JOHN THE APOSTLE AND EVANGELIST.
28. THE HOLY INNOCENTS.
29. Thomas, Archbishop of Canterbury, Martyr, 1170.
30. Ecgwine, Bishop of Worcester, Confessor, 717.
31. Sylvester, Pope of Rome, Confessor, 335.

TABLES AND RULES
FOR THE
MOVEABLE AND IMMOVEABLE FEASTS
TOGETHER WITH THE
DAYS OF FASTING AND ABSTINENCE
THROUGH THE WHOLE YEAR

RULES TO KNOW WHEN THE MOVEABLE FEASTS AND HOLY-DAYS BEGIN.

EASTER-DAY (on which all the rest depend) is always the first SUNDAY after the Full Moon which happeneth upon, or next after, the Twenty-first day of *March*: and if the Full Moon shall happen upon a SUNDAY, EASTER-DAY is the SUNDAY after.

ADVENT SUNDAY is always the SUNDAY nearest to the Feast of SAINT ANDREW whether before or after.

SEPTUAGESIMA SUNDAY is Nine Weeks before EASTER.
SEXAGESIMA SUNDAY is Eight Weeks before EASTER.
QUINQUAGESIMA SUNDAY is Seven Weeks before EASTER.
ASH WEDNESDAY is Forty Days before EASTER.
QUADRAGESIMA SUNDAY is Six Weeks before EASTER.
ROGATION SUNDAY is Five Weeks after EASTER.
ASCENSION-DAY is Forty Days after EASTER.
WHITSUNDAY is Seven Weeks after EASTER.
TRINITY SUNDAY is Eight Weeks after EASTER.
CORPUS CHRISTI is the THURSDAY after TRINITY SUNDAY.

The OCTAVES of the Christian Year are reckoned as being the Holy-day itself and the six or seven days following next after. The OCTAVES appointed to observed are as followeth:

CHRISTMASTIDE, which is CHRISTMAS-DAY and seven days after.
EPIPHANYTIDE, which is EPIPHANY-DAY and seven days after.
EASTERTIDE, which is EASTER-DAY and seven days after.
ASCENSIONTIDE, which is ASCENSION-DAY and seven days after.
WHITSUNTIDE, which is WHITSUNDAY and six days after.
ASSUMPTIONTIDE, which is ASSUMPTION-DAY and seven days after.
MICHAELMASTIDE, which is MICHAELMAS-DAY and seven days after.
HALLOWMASTIDE, which is ALL SAINTS' DAY and seven days after.

The SEASONS of the Christian Year are: The four weeks of ADVENT; the twelve days of CHRISTMASTIDE; the weeks of GREAT EPIPHANYTIDE; the forty days of LENT; the two weeks of PASSIONTIDE; the forty days of EASTERTIDE; the three days of ROGATIONTIDE; and all the weeks from TRINITY SUNDAY until the SUNDAY NEXT BEFORE ADVENT which is called TRINITYTIDE.

A Table to Find Easter-Day
From the Present Time until the Year 2199 Inclusive.

Golden Number .	Days of the Month.		Sunday Letters.	
	Mar	21	C	This Table containeth so much of the Calendar as is necessary for the determining of Easter; to find which, look for the Golden Number of the year in the first Column of the Table, against which standeth the day of the Pascal Full Moon; then look in the third Column for the Sunday Letter, next after the day of the Full Moon, and the day of the Month standing against that Sunday Letter is Easter Day. If the Full Moon happeneth upon a Sunday, then (according to the first rule) the next Sunday after is Easter-Day.
XIV.	”	22	D	
III.	”	23	E	
	”	24	F	
XI.	”	25	G	
	”	26	A	
XIX.	”	27	B	
VIII.	”	28	C	
	”	29	D	
XVI.	”	30	E	To find the Golden Number, or Prime, add one to the Year of our Lord, and then divide by 19; the remainder, if any, is the Golden Number; but if nothing remaineth, then 19 is the Golden Number.
V.	”	31	F	
	April	1	G	
XIII.	”	2	A	
II.	”	3	B	
	”	4	C	To find the Dominical or Sunday Letter, according to the Calendar, until the Year 2099 inclusive, add to the Year of our Lord its Fourth Part, omitting Fractions; and also the Number 6: Divide the sum by 7; and if there be no remainder, then A is the Sunday Letter: But if any number remaineth, then the Letter standing against that number in the small annexed Table is the Sunday Letter.
X.	”	5	D	
	”	6	E	
XVIII.	”	7	F	
VII.	”	8	G	
	”	9	A	
XV.	”	10	B	
IV.	”	11	C	
	”	12	D	
XII.	”	13	E	
I.	”	14	F	
	”	15	G	
IX.	”	16	A	For the next Century, that is, from the year 2100 till the year 2199 inclusive, add to the current year its fourth part, and also the number 5, and then divide by 7, and proceed as in the last Rule.
XVII.	”	17	B	
VI.	”	18	C	
	”	19	D	
	”	20	E	
	”	21	F	Note, that in all Bissextile or Leap-Years, the Letter found as above will be the Sunday Letter, from the intercalated day exclusive to the end of the year.
	”	22	G	
	”	23	A	
	”	24	B	
	”	25	C	

Small annexed table:

0	A
1	G
2	F
3	E
4	D
5	C
6	B

A Table for Finding Sundays

JANUARY: 1A 2b 3c 4d 5e 6f 7g 8A 9b 10c 11d 12e 13f 14g 15A 16b 17c 18d 19e 20f 21g 22A 23b 24c 25d 26e 27f 28g 29A 30b 31c

FEBRUARY: 1d 2e 3f 4g 5A 6b 7c 8d 9e 10f 11g 12A 13b 14c 15d 16e 17f 18g 19A 20b 21c 22d 23e 24f 25g 26A 27b 28c 29 -

MARCH: 1d 2e 3f 4g 5A 6b 7c 8d 9e 10f 11g 12A 13b 14c 15d 16e 17f 18g 19A 20b 21c 22d-14 23e-3 24f 25g-11 26A 27b-19 28c-8 29d 30e-16 31f-5

APRIL: 1g 2A-13 3b-2 4c 5d-10 6e 7f-18 8g-7 9A 10b-15 11c-4 12d 13e-12 14f-1 15g 16A-9 17b-17 18c-6 19d 20e 21f 22g 23A 24b 25c 26d 27e 28f 29g 30A

NOTE: *The Numbers here added to the several Days between the Twenty-first Day of March and the Eighteenth Day of April, both inclusive, denote Days upon which those Full Moons do fall, which happen upon or next after the Twenty-first Day of March, in those Years, of which they are respectively the Golden numbers: And the Sunday Letter next following nay such Full Moon pointeth out Easter-Day for that Year. All which holdeth until the Year of our Lord 2199 inclusive.*

MAY: 1b 2c 3d 4e 5f 6g 7A 8b 9c 10d 11e 12f 13g 14A 15b 16c 17d 18e 19f 20g 21A 22b 23c 24d 25e 26f 27g 28A 29b 30c 31d

JUNE: 1e 2f 3g 4A 5b 6c 7d 8e 9f 10g 11A 12b 13c 14d 15e 16f 17g 18A 19b 20c 21d 22e 23f 24g 25A 26b 27c 28d 29e 30f

JULY: 1g 2A 3b 4c 5d 6e 7f 8g 9A 10b 11c 12d 13e 14f 15g 16A 17a 18b 19c 20d 21e 22f 23g 24A 25b 26c 27d 28f 29g 30A 31b

AUGUST: 1c 2d 3e 4f 5g 6A 7b 8c 9d 10e 11f 12g 13A 14b 15c 16d 17e 18f 19g 20A 21b 22c 23d 24e 25f 26g 27A 28b 29c 30d 31e

SEPTEMBER: 1f 2g 3A 4b 5c 6d 7e 8f 9g 10A 11b 12c 13d 14e 15f 16g 17A 18b 19c 20d 21e 22f 23g 24A 25b 26c 27d 28e 29f 30g

OCTOBER: 1A 2b 3c 4d 5e 6f 7g 8A 9b 10c 11d 12e 13f 14g 15A 16b 17c 18d 19e 20f 21g 22A 23b 24c 25d 26e 27f 28g 29A 30b 31c

NOVEMBER: 1d 2e 3f 4g 5A 6b 7c 8d 9e 10f 11g 12A 13b 14c 15d 16e 17f 18g 19A 20b 21c 22d 23e 24f 25g 26A 27b 28c 29d 30e

DECEMBER: 1f 2g 3A 4b 5c 6d 7e 8f 9g 10A 11b 12c 13d 14e 15f 16g 17A 18b 19c 20d 21e 22f 23g 24A 25b 26c 27d 28e 29f 30g 31A

A Table of Moveable Feasts

2000. Golden Number: VI. The Epact: 24. Sunday Letter: BA. Sundays after Epiphany: Six. Septuagesima Sunday: 20 February. The First Day of Lent: March 8. Easter Day: 23 April. Rogation Sunday: 28 May. Ascension Day: 1 June. Whitsunday: 11 June. Sundays after Trinity: 23. Advent Sunday: 3 December.

2001. Golden Number: VII. The Epact: 5. Sunday Letter: G. Sundays after Epiphany: Five. Septuagesima Sunday: 11 February. The First Day of Lent: 28 February. Easter Day: 15 April. Rogation Sunday: 20 May. Ascension Day: 24 May. Whitsunday: 3 June. Sundays after Trinity: 24. Advent Sunday: 2 December.

2002. Golden Number: VIII. The Epact: 16. Sunday Letter: F. Sundays after Epiphany: Two. Septuagesima Sunday: 27 January. The First Day of Lent: 13 February. Easter Day: 31 March. Rogation Sunday: 5 May. Ascension Day: 9 May. Whitsunday: 19 May. Sundays after Trinity: 26. Advent Sunday: 1 December.

2003. Golden Number: IX. The Epact: 27. Sunday Letter: E. Sundays after Epiphany: Five. Septuagesima Sunday: 16 February. The First Day of Lent: 5 March. Easter Day: 20 April. Rogation Sunday: 25 May. Ascension Day: 29 May. Whitsunday: 8 June. Sundays after Trinity: 23. Advent Sunday: 30 November.

2004. Golden Number: X. The Epact: 8. Sunday Letter: DC. Sundays after Epiphany: Four. Septuagesima Sunday: 8 February. The First Day of Lent: 25 February. Easter Day: 11 April. Rogation Sunday: 16 May. Ascension Day: 20 May. Whitsunday: 30 May. Sundays after Trinity: 24. Advent Sunday: 28 November.

2005. Golden Number: XI. The Epact: 19. Sunday Letter: B. Sundays after Epiphany: Two. Septuagesima Sunday: 23 January. The First Day of Lent: 9 February. Easter Day: 27 March. Rogation Sunday: 1 May. Ascension Day: 5 May. Whitsunday: 15 May. Sundays after Trinity: 26. Advent Sunday: 27 November.

2006. Golden Number: XII. The Epact: 30. Sunday Letter: A. Sundays after Epiphany: Five. Septuagesima Sunday: 12 February. The First Day of Lent: 1 March. Easter Day: 16 April. Rogation Sunday: 21 May. Ascension Day: 25 May. Whitsunday: 4 June. Sundays after Trinity: 24. Advent Sunday: 3 December.

2007. Golden Number: XIII. The Epact: 11. Sunday Letter: G. Sundays after Epiphany: Four. Septuagesima Sunday: 4 February. The First Day of Lent: 21 February. Easter Day: 8 April. Rogation Sunday: 13 May. Ascension Day: 17 May. Whitsunday: 27 May. Sundays after Trinity: 25. Advent Sunday: 2 December.

TABLES

A TABLE OF MOVEABLE FEASTS

2008. Golden Number: XIV. The Epact: 22. Sunday Letter: FE. Sundays after Epiphany: One. Septuagesima Sunday: 20 January. The First Day of Lent: 6 February. Easter Day: 23 March. Rogation Sunday: 27 April. Ascension Day: 1 May. Whitsunday: 11 May. Sundays after Trinity: 27. Advent Sunday: 30 November.

2009. Golden Number: XV. The Epact: 3. Sunday Letter: D. Sundays after Epiphany: Four. Septuagesima Sunday: 8 February. The First Day of Lent: 25 February. Easter Day: 12 April. Rogation Sunday: 17 May. Ascension Day: 21 May. Whitsunday: 31 May. Sundays after Trinity: 24. Advent Sunday: 29 November.

2010. Golden Number: XVI. The Epact: 14. Sunday Letter: C. Sundays after Epiphany: Three. Septuagesima Sunday: 31 January. The First Day of Lent: 17 February. Easter Day: 4 April. Rogation Sunday: 9 May. Ascension Day: 13 May. Whitsunday: 23 May. Sundays after Trinity: 25. Advent Sunday: 28 November.

2011. Golden Number: XVII. The Epact: 25. Sunday Letter: B. Sundays after Epiphany: Six. Septuagesima Sunday: 20 February. The First Day of Lent: 9 March. Easter Day: 24 April. Rogation Sunday: 29 May. Ascension Day: 2 June. Whitsunday: 12 June. Sundays after Trinity: 22. Advent Sunday: 27 November.

2012. Golden Number: XVIII. The Epact: 6. Sunday Letter: AG. Sundays after Epiphany : Four. Septuagesima Sunday: 5 February. The First Day of Lent: 22 February. Easter Day: 8 April. Rogation Sunday: 13 May. Ascension Day: 17 May. Whitsunday: 27 May. Sundays after Trinity: 25. Advent Sunday: 2 December.

2013. Golden Number: XIX. The Epact: 17. Sunday Letter: F. Sundays after Epiphany: Two. Septuagesima Sunday: 27 January. The First Day of Lent: 13 February. Easter Day: 31 March. Rogation Sunday: 5 May. Ascension Day: 9 May. Whitsunday: 19 May. Sundays after Trinity: 26. Advent Sunday: 1 December.

2014. Golden Number: I. The Epact: 29. Sunday Letter: E. Sundays after Epiphany: Five. Septuagesima Sunday: 16 February. The First Day of Lent: 5 March. Easter Day: 20 April. Rogation Sunday: 25 May. Ascension Day: 29 May. Whitsunday: 8 June. Sundays after Trinity: 23. Advent Sunday: 30 November.

2015. Golden Number: II. The Epact: 10. Sunday Letter: D. Sundays after Epiphany: Three. Septuagesima Sunday: 1 February. The First Day of Lent: 18 February. Easter Day: 5 April. Rogation Sunday: 10 May. Ascension Day: 14 May. Whitsunday: 24 May. Sundays after Trinity: 25. Advent Sunday: 29 November.

2016. Golden Number: III. The Epact: 21. Sunday Letter: CB. Sundays after Epiphany: Two. Septuagesima Sunday: 24 January. The First Day of Lent: 10 February. Easter Day: 27 March. Rogation Sunday: 1 May. Ascension Day: 5 May. Whitsunday: 15 May. Sundays after Trinity: 26. Advent Sunday: 27 November.

TABLES

A TABLE OF MOVEABLE FEASTS

2017. Golden Number: IV. The Epact: 2. Sunday Letter: A. Sundays after Epiphany: Five. Septuagesima Sunday: 12 February. The First Day of Lent: 1 March. Easter Day: 16 April. Rogation Sunday: 21 May. Ascension Day: 25 May. Whitsunday: 4 June. Sundays after Trinity: 24. Advent Sunday: 3 December.

2018. Golden Number: V. The Epact: 13. Sunday Letter: G. Sundays after Epiphany: Three. Septuagesima Sunday: 28 January. The First Day of Lent: 14 February. Easter Day: 1 April. Rogation Sunday: 6 May. Ascension Day: 10 May. Whitsunday: 20 May. Sundays after Trinity: 26. Advent Sunday: 2 December.

2019. Golden Number: VI. The Epact: 24. Sunday Letter: F. Sundays after Epiphany: Five. Septuagesima Sunday: 17 February. The First Day of Lent: 6 March. Easter Day: 21 April. Rogation Sunday: 26 May. Ascension Day: 30 May. Whitsunday: 9 June. Sundays after Trinity: 23. Advent Sunday: 1 December.

2020. Golden Number: VII. The Epact: 5. Sunday Letter: ED. Sundays after Epiphany: Four. Septuagesima Sunday: 9 February. The First Day of Lent: 26 February. Easter Day: 12 April. Rogation Sunday: 17 May. Ascension Day: 21 May. Whitsunday: 31 May. Sundays after Trinity: 24. Advent Sunday: 29 November.

2021. Golden Number: VIII. The Epact: 16. Sunday Letter: C. Sundays after Epiphany: Three. Septuagesima Sunday: 31 January. The First Day of Lent: 17 February. Easter Day: 4 April. Rogation Sunday: 9 May. Ascension Day: 13 May. Whitsunday: 23 May. Sundays after Trinity: 25. Advent Sunday: 28 November.

2022. Golden Number: IX. The Epact: 27. Sunday Letter: B. Sundays after Epiphany: Five. Septuagesima Sunday: 13 February. The First Day of Lent: 2 March. Easter Day: 17 April. Rogation Sunday: 22 May. Ascension Day: 26 May. Whitsunday: 5 June. Sundays after Trinity: 23. Advent Sunday: 27 November.

2023. Golden Number: X. The Epact: 8. Sunday Letter: A. Sundays after Epiphany: Four. Septuagesima Sunday: 5 February. The First Day of Lent: 22 February. Easter Day: 9 April. Rogation Sunday: 14 May. Ascension Day: 18 May. Whitsunday: 28 May. Sundays after Trinity: 25. Advent Sunday: 3 December.

2024. Golden Number: XI. The Epact: 19. Sunday Letter: GF. Sundays after Epiphany: Three. Septuagesima Sunday: 28 January. The First Day of Lent: 14 February. Easter Day: 31 March. Rogation Sunday: 5 May. Ascension Day: 9 May. Whitsunday: 19 May. Sundays after Trinity: 26. Advent Sunday: 1 December.

2025. Golden Number: XII. The Epact: 30. Sunday Letter: E. Sundays after Epiphany: Five. Septuagesima Sunday: 16 February. The First Day of Lent: 5 March. Easter Day: 20 April. Rogation Sunday: 25 May. Ascension Day: 29 May. Whitsunday: 8 June. Sundays after Trinity: 23. Advent Sunday: 30 November.

TABLES

A TABLE OF MOVEABLE FEASTS

2026. Golden Number: XIII. The Epact: 11. Sunday Letter: D. Sundays after Epiphany: Three. Septuagesima Sunday: 1 February. The First Day of Lent: 18 February. Easter Day: 5 April. Rogation Sunday: 10 May. Ascension Day: 14 May. Whitsunday: 24 May. Sundays after Trinity: 25. Advent Sunday: 29 November.

2027. Golden Number: XIV. The Epact: 22. Sunday Letter: C. Sundays after Epiphany: Two. Septuagesima Sunday: 24 January. The First Day of Lent: 10 February. Easter Day: 28 March. Rogation Sunday: 2 May. Ascension Day: 6 May. Whitsunday: 16 May. Sundays after Trinity: 26. Advent Sunday: 28 November.

2028. Golden Number: XV. The Epact: 3. Sunday Letter: BA. Sundays after Epiphany: Five. Septuagesima Sunday: 13 February. The First Day of Lent: 1 March. Easter Day: 16 April 16. Rogation Sunday: 21 May. Ascension Day: 25 May. Whitsunday: 4 June. Sundays after Trinity: 24. Advent Sunday: 3 December.

2029. Golden Number: XVI. The Epact: 14. Sunday Letter: G. Sundays after Epiphany: Three. Septuagesima Sunday: 28 January. The First Day of Lent: 14 February. Easter Day: 1 April. Rogation Sunday: 6 May. Ascension Day: 10 May. Whitsunday: 20 May. Sundays after Trinity: 26. Advent Sunday: 2 December.

2030. Golden Number: XVII. The Epact: 25. Sunday Letter: F. Sundays after Epiphany: Five. Septuagesima Sunday: 17 February. The First Day of Lent: 6 March. Easter Day: 21 April. Rogation Sunday: 26 May. Ascension Day: 30 May. Whitsunday: 9 June. Sundays after Trinity: 23. Advent Sunday: 1 December.

2031. Golden Number: XVIII. The Epact: 6. Sunday Letter: E. Sundays after Epiphany: Four. Septuagesima Sunday: 9 February. The First Day of Lent: 26 February. Easter Day: 13 April. Rogation Sunday: 18 May. Ascension Day: 22 May. Whitsunday: 1 June. Sundays after Trinity: 24. Advent Sunday: 30 November.

2032. Golden Number: XIX. The Epact: 17. Sunday Letter: DC. Sundays after Epiphany: Two. Septuagesima Sunday: 25 January. The First Day of Lent: 11 February. Easter Day: 28 March. Rogation Sunday: 2 May. Ascension Day: 6 May. Whitsunday: 16 May. Sundays after Trinity: 26. Advent Sunday: 28 November.

2033. Golden Number: I. The Epact: 29. Sunday Letter: B. Sundays after Epiphany: Five. Septuagesima Sunday: 13 February. The First Day of Lent: 2 March. Easter Day: 17 April. Rogation Sunday: 22 May. Ascension Day: 26 May. Whitsunday: 5 June. Sundays after Trinity: 23. Advent Sunday: 27 November.

2034. Golden Number: II. The Epact: 10. Sunday Letter: A. Sundays after Epiphany: Four. Septuagesima Sunday: 5 February. The First Day of Lent: 22 February. Easter Day: 9 April. Rogation Sunday: 14 May. Ascension Day: 18 May. Whitsunday: 28 May. Sundays after Trinity: 25. Advent Sunday: 3 December.

TABLES

A TABLE OF MOVEABLE FEASTS

2035. Golden Number: III. The Epact: 21. Sunday Letter: G. Sundays after Epiphany: Two. Septuagesima Sunday: 21 January. The First Day of Lent: 7 February. Easter Day: 25 March. Rogation Sunday: 29 April. Ascension Day: 3 May. Whitsunday: 13 May. Sundays after Trinity: 27. Advent Sunday: 2 December.

2036. Golden Number: IV. The Epact: 2. Sunday Letter: FE. Sundays after Epiphany: Four. Septuagesima Sunday: 10 February. The First Day of Lent: 27 February. Easter Day: 13 April. Rogation Sunday: 18 May. Ascension Day: 22 May. Whitsunday: 1 June. Sundays after Trinity: 24. Advent Sunday: 30 November.

2037. Golden Number: V. The Epact: 13. Sunday Letter: D. Sundays after Epiphany: Three. Septuagesima Sunday: 1 February. The First Day of Lent: 18 February. Easter Day: 5 April. Rogation Sunday: 10 May. Ascension Day: 14 May. Whitsunday: 24 May. Sundays after Trinity: 25. Advent Sunday: 29 November.

2038. Golden Number: VI. The Epact: 24. Sunday Letter: C. Sundays after Epiphany: Six. Septuagesima Sunday: 21 February. The First Day of Lent: 10 March. Easter Day: 25 April. Rogation Sunday: 30 May. Ascension Day: 3 June. Whitsunday: 13 June. Sundays after Trinity: 22. Advent Sunday: 28 November.

2039. Golden Number: VII. The Epact: 5. Sunday Letter: B. Sundays after Epiphany: Four. Septuagesima Sunday: 6 February. The First Day of Lent: 23 February. Easter Day: 10 April. Rogation Sunday: 15 May. Ascension Day: 19 May. Whitsunday: 29 May. Sundays after Trinity: 24. Advent Sunday: 27 November.

2040. Golden Number: VIII. The Epact: 16. Sunday Letter: AG. Sundays after Epiphany: Three. Septuagesima Sunday: 29 January. The First Day of Lent: 15 February. Easter Day: 1 April. Rogation Sunday: 6 May. Ascension Day: 10 May. Whitsunday: 20 May. Sundays after Trinity: 26. Advent Sunday: 2 December.

2041. Golden Number: IX. The Epact: 27. Sunday Letter: F. Sundays after Epiphany: Five. Septuagesima Sunday: 17 February. The First Day of Lent: 6 March. Easter Day: 21 April. Rogation Sunday: 26 May. Ascension Day: 30 May. Whitsunday: 9 June. Sundays after Trinity: 23. Advent Sunday: 1 December.

2042. Golden Number: X. The Epact: 8. Sunday Letter: E. Sundays after Epiphany: Three. Septuagesima Sunday: 2 February. The First Day of Lent: 19 February. Easter Day: 5 April. Rogation Sunday: 11 May. Ascension Day: 15 May. Whitsunday: 25 May. Sundays after Trinity: 25. Advent Sunday: 30 November.

2043. Golden Number: XI. The Epact: 19. Sunday Letter: D. Sundays after Epiphany: Two. Septuagesima Sunday: 25 January. The First Day of Lent: 11 February. Easter Day: 29 March. Rogation Sunday: 3 May. Ascension Day: 7 May. Whitsunday: 17 May. Sundays after Trinity: 26. Advent Sunday: 29 November.

A TABLE OF MOVEABLE FEASTS

2044. Golden Number: XII. The Epact: 30. Sunday Letter: CB. Sundays after Epiphany: Five.
Septuagesima Sunday: 14 February. The First Day of Lent: 2 March. Easter Day: 17 April.
Rogation Sunday: 22 May. Ascension Day: 26 May. Whitsunday: 5 June. Sundays after Trinity: 23.
Advent Sunday: 27 November.

2045. Golden Number: XIII. The Epact: 11. Sunday Letter: A. Sundays after Epiphany: Four.
Septuagesima Sunday: 5 February. The First Day of Lent: 22 February. Easter Day: 9 April.
Rogation Sunday: 14 May. Ascension Day: 18 May. Whitsunday: 28 May. Sundays after Trinity:
25. Advent Sunday: 3 December.

2046. Golden Number: XIV. The Epact: 22. Sunday Letter: G. Sundays after Epiphany: Two.
Septuagesima Sunday: 21 January. The First Day of Lent: 7 February. Easter Day: 25 March.
Rogation Sunday: 29 April. Ascension Day: 3 May. Whitsunday: 13 May. Sundays after Trinity: 27.
Advent Sunday: 2 December.

2047. Golden Number: XV. The Epact: 3. Sunday Letter: F. Sundays after Epiphany: Four.
Septuagesima Sunday: 10 February. The First Day of Lent: 27 February. Easter Day: 14 April.
Rogation Sunday: 19 May. Ascension Day: 23 May. Whitsunday: 2 June. Sundays after Trinity: 24.
Advent Sunday: 1 December.

2048. Golden Number: XVI. The Epact: 14. Sunday Letter: ED. Sundays after Epiphany: Three.
Septuagesima Sunday: 2 February. The First Day of Lent: 19 February. Easter Day: 5 April. Rogation
Sunday: 10 May. Ascension Day: 14 May. Whitsunday: 24 May. Sundays after Trinity: 25. Advent
Sunday: 29 November.

2049. Golden Number: XVII. The Epact: 25. Sunday Letter: C. Sundays after Epiphany: Five.
Septuagesima Sunday: 14 February. The First Day of Lent: 3 March. Easter Day: 1 April. Rogation
Sunday: 23 May. Ascension Day: 27 May. Whitsunday: 6 June. Sundays after Trinity: 23. Advent
Sunday: 28 November.

2050. Golden Number: XVIII. The Epact: 6. Sunday Letter: B. Sundays after Epiphany: Four.
Septuagesima Sunday: 6 February. The First Day of Lent: 23 February. Easter Day: 10 April.
Rogation Sunday: 15 May. Ascension Day: 19 May. Whitsunday: 29 May. Sundays after Trinity:
24. Advent Sunday: 27 November.

A Table of all the Feasts

THAT ARE TO BE OBSERVED
IN THIS PORTION OF THE CHURCH
THROUGHOUT THE YEAR

All the SUNDAYS in the Year.

SAINT ANDREW'S DAY.
THE CONCEPTION OF OUR LADY.
SAINT THOMAS'S DAY.
THE NATIVITY OF OUR LORD.
SAINT STEPHEN'S DAY.
SAINT JOHN'S DAY.
HOLY INNOCENTS' DAY.
THE CIRCUMCISION OF OUR LORD.
THE EPIPHANY OF OUR LORD.
THE CONVERSION OF SAINT PAUL.
THE PURIFICATION OF OUR LADY.
SAINT MATTHIAS' DAY.
SAINT JOSEPH'S DAY.
THE ANNUNCIATION OF OUR LADY.
SAINT MARK'S DAY.
SAINT PHILIP'S AND SAINT JAMES'S DAY.
THE ASCENSION OF OUR LORD.
SAINT MARY'S AND SAINT MARTHA'S DAY.
SAINT BARNABAS'S DAY.
CORPUS CHRISTI DAY.
SAINT JOHN THE BAPTIST'S DAY.
SAINT PETER'S DAY.
HOLY APOSTLES' DAY.
SAINT MARY MAGDALENE'S DAY.
SAINT JAMES'S DAY.
THE TRANSFIGURATION OF OUR LORD.
THE FALLING ASLEEP OF OUR LADY.
SAINT BARTHOLOMEW'S DAY.
THE BEHEADING OF SAINT JOHN THE BAPTIST.
HOLY CROSS DAY.
SAINT MATTHEW'S DAY.
SAINT MICHAEL'S AND ALL ANGEL'S DAY.
SAINT LUKE'S DAY.
SAINT SIMON'S AND SAINT JUDE'S DAY.
ALL SAINTS' DAY.

MONDAY and TUESDAY of EASTER-WEEK.
MONDAY and TUESDAY of WHITSUN-WEEK.

THE HOLY-DAYS OF OBLIGATION
TO BE KEPT BY THE FAITHFUL

ALL the SUNDAYS of the Year, and the following Holy-days: THE CONCEPTION OF OUR LADY, CHRISTMAS-DAY, EPIPHANY-DAY, CANDLEMAS-DAY, ASH WEDNESDAY, LADY-DAY, MAUNDY THURSDAY, GOOD FRIDAY, HOLY SATURDAY, ASCENSION-DAY, CORPUS CHRISTI, THE ASSUMPTION OF OUR LADY, THE NATIVITY OF OUR LADY, MICHAELMAS-DAY, and ALL SAINTS' DAY, are Holy-days of Obligation upon which the Christian faithful of this Church are obliged to attend the DIVINE LITURGY.

THE DAYS OF NATIONAL THANKSGIVING

ACCESSION-DAY

THE Sixth Day of February, being the Day upon which Her Most Gracious Majesty Queen *ELIZABETH* the Second began her happy Reign.

VICTORIA-DAY

THE Twenty-fourth Day of May, being the Birthday of Her Late Majesty Queen Victoria; and the Day upon which the Birthday of Her Most Gracious Majesty Queen *ELIZABETH* the Second is observed in the Dominion of Canada.

DOMINION-DAY

THE First Day of July, being the Day upon which the Provinces of British North America were confederated into one Nation, thereby establishing the Dominion of Canada.

THANKSGIVING-DAY

THE Second Monday in October, being the Day upon which the people of the Dominion of Canada render humble thanks to ALMIGHTY GOD for all the Blessings which they have received at His hand.

A DAY OF SOLEMN REMEMBRANCE

REMEMBRANCE-DAY

THE Eleventh Day of November, being the Day upon which the people of the Dominion of Canada remember all those who gave of their lives, and those who made the Supreme Sacrifice, in the service of ALMIGHTY GOD, their Sovereign, their Country, and the British Commonwealth and Empire.

THE VIGILS, FASTS, AND DAYS OF ABSTINENCE
APPOINTED TO BE OBSERVED
THROUGHOUT THE YEAR

THE VIGILS

THE following Eves are appointed to be observed as Vigils: THE EVE OF THE IMMACULATE CONCEPTION OF OUR LADY, CHRISTMAS-EVE, CANDLEMAS-EVE, SHROVE TUESDAY, THE EVE OF THE ANNUNCIATION OF OUR LADY, EASTER-EVE, ASCENSION-EVE, WHITSUN-EVE, THE EVE OF THE ASSUMPTION OF OUR LADY, THE EVE OF THE NATIVITY OF OUR LADY, MICHAELMAS-EVE, and ALL HALLOWS' EVE.

THE FAST-DAYS

THE following Days are appointed to be observed as Days of Fasting: ASH WEDNESDAY and GOOD FRIDAY.

THE DAYS OF ABSTINENCE

THE following Days are appointed to be observed as Days of Abstinence: The Forty Days of LENT; the three EMBER-DAYS at the Four Seasons, being the WEDNESDAY, FRIDAY, and SATURDAY, after : The Third SUNDAY in ADVENT, the First SUNDAY in LENT, the Feast of PENTECOST, and HOLY CROSS DAY; the three ROGATION-DAYS, being the MONDAY, TUESDAY, and WEDNESDAY, before the FEAST OF THE ASCENSION OF OUR LORD which is called HOLY THURSDAY; and all the FRIDAYS of the Year, except CHRISTMAS-DAY and the Friday after CHRISTMAS-DAY, the Feast of the EPIPHANY, the Friday after EASTER-DAY, and the Friday after HOLY THURSDAY.

THE DAYS AND SEASONS
WHEN MARRIAGES ARE FORBIDDEN TO BE SOLEMNISED

I.   Any SUNDAY of the Year; and (except the Ordinary permit):
II. From ADVENT SUNDAY until Eight Days after the EPIPHANY;
III. From SEPTUAGESIMA SUNDAY until Eight Days after EASTER.

THE ORDER HOW
THE PSALTER
IS APPOINTED TO BE READ

THE Psalter is to be read through once a month as it is there appointed, unless the Psalms are read according to one of the Tables following. On the thirty-first day of the month, the Psalms for the thirtieth are to be used. Upon any weekday for which no Proper Psalms are appointed, one Psalm may be omitted, provided that one Psalm, or one numbered portion of a Psalm, be always retained. This is principally intended for use on those days on which the shortened Service is permitted or when the Office is said by the Minister alone.

Psalms for special occasions for which provision is not already made are appointed by the Ordinary.

The *Gloria Patri* is to be said or sung after each Psalm, or numbered portion of a Psalm; or, at the discretion of the Minister, after the whole selection of Psalms. The *Gloria Patri* shall be omitted during Passiontide.

In the pointing of the Psalms (and of all the Canticles used in Divine Service) the sign / indicates the place in each verse where the chant changes. In reading, a pause is made at this sign.

Note that the word *hell* where used in the Psalter meaneth the *place of the dead*.

NOTE: The Psalter as it is used herein followeth the Division of the Hebrews, and the Translation of the Great Bible, set forth and authorised for use in the time of King *Henry* the Eighth, and again in the time of Queen *Elizabeth*. Howbeit, whereinsoever the Psalter of the Great Bible hath been deemed to be unclear in its proper meaning according to the general understanding of this present day, certain verses of the Psalms, or portions thereof, as they are translated in the Authorised Version of the Bible, set forth in the time of King *James* the First, have been used instead. And whereinsoever it is deemed expedient at certain times, with the permission of the Ordinary, the Psalms as they are set forth in the Authorised Version of the Bible may be used in the place of the Psalter of the Great Bible.

THE USE OF
THE PSALTER AT
THE HOLY EUCHARIST

A PSALM or a portion of a Psalm shall be said or sung as the Introit as the Priest proceedeth up to the Lord's Table. Except in Holy Week, the *Gloria Patri* shall follow the Psalm; and one of the verses thereof may be repeated for an Antiphon. This may also be done for the Psalms appointed to be used at the Asperges.

A Psalm or a portion thereof shall be used as the Gradual between the Epistle and the Gospel readings. Except during Advent and Lent, and other times of penitence, three *Alleluias* shall be added to the Psalm or portion thereof used for the Gradual: two *Alleluias* at the beginning of the Gradual, to be followed by one *Alleluia* at the end of the Gradual. However, where it is customary, six *Alleluias* may be used: three *Alleluias* at the beginning of the Gradual, and three *Alleluias* at the end of the Gradual. This custom is appropriate to be followed during Christmastide, Eastertide, Whitsuntide, and on Corpus Christi Day, Feasts of Our Lady, and the Feasts of Saint Michael and All Angels and All Saints.

The Introit and Gradual may be said or sung by the Priest and the people together, or by the Choir, or else recited by the Priest himself alone.

THE PSALMS OF DAVID
IN THEIR ORDER TO BE SAID OR SUNG AT
DIVINE SERVICE
DAILY THROUGHOUT THE YEAR

Day 1 – Morning Prayer: 1, 2, 3, 4, 5;
Day 1 – Evening Prayer: 6, 7, 8;

Day 2 – Morning Prayer: 9, 10, 11;
Day 2 – Evening Prayer: 12, 13, 14;

Day 3 – Morning Prayer: 15, 16, 17;
Day 3 – Evening Prayer: 18;

Day 4 – Morning Prayer: 19, 20, 21;
Day 4 – Evening Prayer: 22, 23;

Day 5 – Morning Prayer: 24, 25, 26;
Day 5 – Evening Prayer: 27, 28, 29;

Day 6 – Morning Prayer: 30, 31;
Day 6 – Evening Prayer: 32, 33, 34;

Day 7 – Morning Prayer: 35, 36;
Day 7 – Evening Prayer: 37;

Day 8 – Morning Prayer: 38, 39, 40;
Day 8 – Evening Prayer: 41, 42, 43;

Day 9 – Morning Prayer: 44, 45, 46;
Day 9 – Evening Prayer: 47, 48, 49;

Day 10 – Morning Prayer: 50, 51, 52;
Day 10 – Evening Prayer: 53, 54, 55;

Day 11 – Morning Prayer: 56, 57, 58;
Day 11 – Evening Prayer: 59, 60, 61;

Day 12 – Morning Prayer: 62, 63, 64;
Day 12 – Evening Prayer: 65, 66, 67;

Day 13 – Morning Prayer: 68;
Day 13 – Evening Prayer: 69, 70;

Day 14 – Morning Prayer: 71, 72;
Day 14 – Evening Prayer: 73, 74;

Day 15 – Morning Prayer: 75, 76, 77;
Day 15 – Evening Prayer: 78;

TABLES

Day 16 – Morning Prayer: 79, 80, 81;
Day 16 – Evening Prayer: 82, 83, 84, 85;

Day 17 – Morning Prayer: 86, 87, 88;
Day 17 – Evening Prayer: 89;

Day 18 – Morning Prayer: 90, 91, 92;
Day 18 – Evening Prayer: 93, 94;

Day 19 – Morning Prayer: 95, 96, 97;
Day 19 – Evening Prayer: 98, 99, 100, 101;

Day 20 – Morning Prayer: 102, 103;
Day 20 – Evening Prayer: 104;

Day 21 – Morning Prayer: 105;
Day 21 – Evening Prayer: 106;

Day 22 – Morning Prayer: 107;
Day 22 – Evening Prayer: 108, 109;

Day 23 – Morning Prayer: 110, 111, 112, 113;
Day 23 – Evening Prayer: 114, 115;

Day 24 – Morning Prayer: 116, 117, 118;
Day 24 – Evening Prayer: 119. 1-32;

Day 25 – Morning Prayer: 119. 33-72;
Day 25 – Evening Prayer: 119. 73-104;

Day 26 – Morning Prayer: 119. 105-144;
Day 26 – Evening Prayer: 119. 145-176;

Day 27 – Morning Prayer: 120, 121, 122, 123, 124, 125;
Day 27 – Evening Prayer: 126, 127, 128, 129, 130, 131;

Day 28 – Morning Prayer: 132, 133, 134, 135;
Day 28 – Evening Prayer: 146, 137, 138;

Day 29 – Morning Prayer: 139, 140, 141;
Day 29 – Evening Prayer: 142, 143;

Day 30 – Morning Prayer: 144, 145, 146;
Day 30 – Evening Prayer: 147, 148, 149, 150.

Day 31 – Morning Prayer: 144, 145, 146;
Day 31 – Evening Prayer: 147, 148, 149, 150.

A Table of Proper Psalms
for Sundays and Holy-Days

Sunday or Holy-Day	Mattins	Evensong
First Sunday in Advent	1, 7	46, 48
Second Sunday in Advent	9, 11	50, 67
Third Sunday in Advent	73	75, 76, 82
Fourth Sunday in Advent	94	96, 97, 98
Christmas-Eve	—	89
Christmas-Day	19, 85	132
First Sunday after Christmas	2, 8	45, 110, 113
New Year's Eve	—	90, 133, 134
Circumcision	119 (1-32)	91, 121
Second Sunday after Christmas	103	104
Eve of Epiphany	—	19, 87
Epiphany	72	96, 97, 117
First Sunday after Epiphany	46, 47, 67	18
Second Sunday after Epiphany	27, 36	68
Third Sunday after Epiphany	42, 43	33, 34
Fourth Sunday after Epiphany	60, 63	74
Fifth Sunday after Epiphany	99, 112	106
Sixth Sunday after Epiphany	80, 81	78
Septuagesima	104	147, 148
Sexagesima	139	25, 26
Quinquagesima	15, 20, 23	30, 31
Ash Wednesday	6, 32, 38	102, 130, 143
First Sunday in Lent	51	6, 32, 143
Second Sunday in Lent	119 (1-32)	119 (33-72)
Third Sunday in Lent	119 (73-104)	119 (105-144)
Mothering Sunday	119 (145-176)	39, 40
Passion Sunday	22	51
Palm Sunday	61, 62	86, 130
Monday in Holy Week	13, 25	26, 27, 28
Tuesday in Holy Week	31	88
Wednesday in Holy Week	41, 42, 43	54, 55
Maundy Thursday	56, 64	23, 109
Good Friday	22	40, 69
Holy Saturday	23, 30, 142	115, 116, 117
Easter-Day	2, 16, 111	113, 114, 118
Low Sunday	3, 57	103
Good Shepherd Sunday	120, 121, 122, 123	65, 66
Third Sunday after Easter	124, 125, 126, 127	81, 84

TABLES

SUNDAY OR HOLY-DAY	MATTINS	EVENSONG
Fourth Sunday after Easter	128, 129, 130, 131	145, 146
Rogation Sunday	132, 133, 134	107
Eve of Ascension	–	15, 97, 99
Ascension-Day	8, 21	24, 47, 110
Sunday after Ascension-Day	93, 96	148, 149, 150
Whitsun-Eve	–	48, 145
Whitsunday	68	104
Trinity Sunday	29, 33	93, 99, 115
First Sunday after Trinity	1, 3, 5	4, 7, 8
Second Sunday after Trinity	10, 12, 13	15, 16, 17
Third Sunday after Trinity	18	19, 20, 21
Fourth Sunday after Trinity	24, 25	22, 23
Fifth Sunday after Trinity	26, 28	27, 29, 30
Sixth Sunday after Trinity	31, 32	33, 36
Seventh Sunday after Trinity	34	37
Eighth Sunday after Trinity	39, 40	41, 42, 43
Ninth Sunday after Trinity	46, 47, 48	44, 45
Tenth Sunday after Trinity	50, 53	51, 54
Eleventh Sunday after Trinity	56, 57	61, 62, 63
Twelfth Sunday after Trinity	65, 66	68
Thirteenth Sunday after Trinity	71	67, 72
Fourteenth Sunday after Trinity	75, 76	73, 77
Fifteenth Sunday after Trinity	84, 85	89
Sixteenth Sunday after Trinity	86, 87	90, 91
Seventeenth Sunday after Trinity	92, 93	100, 101, 102
Eighteenth Sunday after Trinity	103	107
Nineteenth Sunday after Trinity	111, 112, 113	120, 121, 122, 123
Twentieth Sunday after Trinity	114, 115	124, 125, 126, 127
Twenty-first Sunday after Trinity	116, 117	128, 129, 130, 131
Twenty-second Sunday after Trinity	118	132, 133, 134
Twenty-third Sunday after Trinity	110, 135	137, 138, 139
Twenty-fourth Sunday after Trinity	136	140, 141, 142
Twenty-fifth Sunday after Trinity	49	79, 83
Twenty-sixth Sunday after Trinity	84, 144	105
Sunday next before Advent	145, 146	147, 148, 149, 150

THE TABLE OF LESSONS

GENERAL RUBRICS.

1. When the First Sunday in Advent shall occur in a year with an even number, the Lessons appointed for Year I shall be read, and when it shall occur in a year with an odd number, the Lessons appointed for Year II shall be read, for the whole of that ecclesiastical year.

2. Whensoever a Lesson shall begin with a pronoun, the Minister shall substitute the appropriate proper noun.

3. In this Table, all verses are stated inclusively.

4. Those verses which are printed within brackets are permissive additions to the appointed passages.

5. The letter a after the number of a verse signifieth the first part of that verse, and the letter b the second part thereof.

		Morning Prayer		Evening Prayer	
		First Lesson	Second Lesson	First Lesson	Second Lesson
First Sunday in	Year I	Isa. 1. 1-20	Matt. 24. 1-28	Isa. 2. 10-end	1 Thess. 5
Advent	Year II	1. 1-20	Rev. 2. 1-17	2. 10-end	John 3. 1-21
M.		Isa. 3. 1-15	Mark 1. 1-20	Isa. 4. 2-end	Rev. 6
Tu.		6	1. 21-end	8. 16-9. 7	7
W.		9. 8-10. 4	2. 1-22	10. 5-23	8
Th.		10. 24-end	2. 23-3. 12	13. 1-14. 2	9
F.		14. 3-27	3. 13-end	17	10
S.		18	4. 1-20	19. 1-17	11
Second Sunday in	Year I	Isa. 5. 1-16	Matt. 24. 29-end	Isa. 5. 18-end	2 Tim. 3. 14-4. 8
Advent	Year II	11. 1-10	Rev. 2. 18-3. 6	11. 10-12 end	Luke 1. 1-25
M.		Isa. 19. 18-end	Mark 4. 21-end	Isa. 21. 1-12	Rev. 12
Tu.		22. 1-14	5. 1-20	24	13
W.		28. 1-8	5. 21-end	29. 1-14	14
Th.		29. 15-end	6. 1-13	30. 19-end	15
F.		31	6. 14-29	38. 1-20	16
S.		40. 12-end	6. 30-end	41	17
Third Sunday in	Year I	Isa. 25. 1-9	Matt. 25. 1-30	Isa. 26. 1-13	1 Tim. 1. 12-2. 8
Advent	Year II	28. 9-22	Rev. 3. 7-end	32. 1-18	Matt. 3
M.		Isa. 42. 1-17	Mark 7. 1-23	Isa. 42. 18-43. 13	Rev. 18
Tu.		43. 14-44. 5	7. 24-8. 10	44. 6-23	19
W. Ember Day		44. 24-45. 13	8. 11-9. 1	45. 14-end	20
Th.		46	9. 2-32	47	21. 1-14
F. Ember Day		48	9. 33-end	49. 1-13	21. 15-22. 5
S. Ember Day		49. 14-end	10. 1-31	50. 4-10	22. 6-end
Fourth Sunday in	Year I	Isa. 35	Matt. 25. 31-end	Isa. 40. 1-11	2 Pet. 3. 1-14
Advent	Year II	30. 8-21	Rev. 14. 13-15. 4	40. 1-11	Luke 1. 26-45
M.		Isa. 51. 1-16	Mark 10. 32-end	Isa. 51. 17-52. 12	Jude 1-16
Tu.		52. 13-53 end	11. 1-26	54	17-end
W.		56. 1-8	11. 27-12. 12	57. 15-end	2 Pet. 1
Th.		59	12. 13-34	60. 1-7	2
F.		60. 8-end	12. 35-13. 13	61	3
S.		62	13. 14-end	-	-

TABLES

		Morning Prayer		Evening Prayer	
		First Lesson	Second Lesson	First Lesson	Second Lesson
Christmas-Eve		-	-	Zech. 2. 10-end	Heb. 2. 10-18
Christmas-Day		Isa. 9. 2-7	Matt. 1. 18-25	Isa. 7. 10-14	1 John 4. 7-end
St Stephen Martyr		Gen. 4. 1-10	Acts 6	2 Chron. 24. 15-22	Acts 7. 59-8. 8
St John Evangelist		Exod. 33. 9-end	John 13. 21-35	Isa. 6. 1-8	1 John 5. 1-12
The Innocents' Day		Baruch 4. 21-27	Rev. 6. 9-11	Jer. 31. 1-17	Matt. 18. 1-10
Sunday after Christmas Day	Years I & II	Isa. 41. 8-20	Col. 1. 1-20	Isa. 55	Luke 2. 22-40
29 December		Ruth 1. 1-18	John 1. 14-18	Ruth 1. 19-2. 13	Matt. 11. 2-6
30 December		2. 14-end	3. 16-21	3	16. 13-20
31 December		4. 1-17	6. 41-58	Mic. 4. 8-5. 4	Luke 22. 24-30
Octave-Day of Christmas		Gen. 17. 1-13	Rom. 2. 17-end	Deut. 30	Col. 2. 8-15
Second Sunday after Christmas	Years I & II	Isa. 41. 21-end	1 John 1. 1-2. 6	Isa. 55	Luke 2. 22-40
2 January		Isa. 63. 1-6	Matt. 1. 18-end	Isa. 63. 7-end	1 Thess. 1
3 January		64	2. 19-end	65. 1-16	2. 1-16
4 January		65. 17-end	3. 1-4. 11	66. 1-9	2. 17-3 end
5 January		66. 10-end	4. 12-5. 16	60. 1-7	Rom. 15. 8-21
Epiphany		Isa. 49. 1-13	Luke 3. 15-22	Isa. 60. 9-end	John 2. 1-11
M.	Weekdays	Amos 1	Matt. 5. 17-end	Amos 2	1 Thess. 4. 1-12
Tu.	between the	3	6. 1-18	4	4. 13-5. 11
W.	Epiphany and	5	6. 19-end	6	5. 12-end
Th.	the First Sunday	7	7	8	2 Thess. 1
F.	after Epiphany	9	8. 1-17	Mic. 1	2
S.		Mic. 2	8. 18-end	3	3
First Sunday after Epiphany	Year I Year II	Isa. 49. 13-23 42. 1-12	Matt. 17. 1-13 John 4. 1-26 (27-42)	Isa. 61 43. 1-13	Matt. 2 John 12. 20-36a
M.		Mic. 4. 1-5. 1	Matt. 9. 1-17	Mic. 5. 2-end	Gal. 1
Tu.		6	9. 18-34	7	2
W.		Hos. 1	9. 35-10. 23	Hos. 2. 1-13	3
Th.		2. 14-3 end	10. 24-end	4. 1-11	4. 1-5. 1
F.		5. 8-6. 6	11	8	5. 2-end
S.		9	12. 1-21	10	6
Second Sunday after Epiphany	Year I Year II	Isa. 43. 14-44. 5 Amos 3	Eph. 1 John 6. 22-40	Isa. 44. 6-23 Mic. 3. 5-end	Mark 1. 35-end John 4. 43-5. 9
M.		Hos. 11	Matt. 12. 22-end	Hos. 12	1 Cor. 1. 1-25
Tu.		13. 1-14	13. 1-23	14	1. 26-2 end
W.		Zeph. 1	13. 24-43	Zeph. 2	3
Th.		3	13. 44-end	Nahum 1	4. 1-17
F.		Nahum 2	14	3	4. 18-5 end
S.		Hab. 1	15. 1-28	Hab. 2	6

TABLES

		Morning Prayer		Evening Prayer	
		First Lesson	Second Lesson	First Lesson	Second Lesson
Third Sunday after Epiphany	Year I	Isa. 45. 9-end	Eph. 2	Isa. 46. 3-end	Mark 7. 24-end
	Year II	Amos 5. 6-24	John 6. 41-end	Mic. 4. 1-7	John 9
M.		Hab. 3. 2-end	1 Cor. 7	Mal. 1	1 Cor. 8
Tu.		Mal. 2. 1-16	9	2. 17-3. 12	10. 1-11. 1
W.		3. 13-4 end	11. 2-end	Obadiah	12. 1-27
Th.		Joel 1	12. 27-13 end	Joel 2. 1-14	14. 1-19
F.		2. 15-end	14. 20-end	3	15. 1-34
S.		Jonah 1 & 2	15. 35-end	Jonah 3 & 4	16
Fourth Sunday after Epiphany	Year I	Isa. 48. 12-end	Eph. 3	Isa. 54. 1-14	Luke 13. 1-17
	Year II	Amos 7	John 7. 53-8. 11	Mic. 5. 2-7	John 10. 1-18
M.		Jer. 1. 11-end	2 Cor. 1. 1-2. 11	Jer. 2. 1-13	2 Cor. 2 12-3 end
Tu.		4. 1-18	4	5. 1-19	5
W.		5. 20-end	5. 20-7. 1	6. 1-21	7. 2-end
Th.		7. 1-28	8	8	9
F.		9. 1-24	10	10	11
S.		14	12. 1-13	15	12. 14-13 end
Fifth Sunday after Epiphany	Year I	Isa. 59. 12-20	Eph. 5. 15-6. 9	Isa. 60	Mark 2. 1-12
	Year II	Amos 8. 4-end	John 7. 14-36	Mic. 6. 1-8	John 5. 19-29 (30-40)
M.		Jer. 17. 1-18	Acts 15. 1-29	Jer. 17. 19-end	Acts 15. 30-16. 5
Tu.		18. 1-17	16. 6-end	20	17. 1-15
W.		23. 9-32	17. 16-end	30. 1-22	18. 1-23
Th.		31. 1-20	18. 24-19. 7	31. 23-end	19. 8-20
F.		33. 1-13	19. 21-end	33. 14-end	20. 1-16
S.		35. 1-11	20. 17-end	35. 12-end	21. 1-16
Sixth Sunday after Epiphany	Year I	Isa. 63. 7-16	Eph. 6. 10-end	Isa. 64	Luke 7. 1-10
	Year II	Amos 9. 5-end	John 7. 37-52	Mic. 7. 1-9	John 8. 12-30
M.		Tobit 4. 5-19	Acts 21. 17-36	Tobit 13	Acts 21. 37-22. 22
Tu.		Baruch 1. 15-2. 10	22. 23-23. 11	Baruch 2. 11-end	23. 12-end
W.		3. 1-8	24. 1-23	3. 9-end	24. 24-25. 12
Th.		4. 21-30	25. 13-end	4. 36-5 end	26
F.		2 Macc. 4. 7-17	27. 1-26	2 Macc. 6. 12-end	27. 27-end
S.		7. 1-19	28. 1-15	7. 20-41	28. 16-end
Septuagesima	Year I	Gen. 1. 1-2. 3	John 1. 1-18	Gen. 2. 4-end	Rev. 4
	Year II	1. 1-2. 3	Rev. 21. 1-7	2. 4-end	Mark 10. 1-16
M.		Gen. 3	Matt. 15. 29-16. 12	Gen. 4. 1-16	Rom. 1
Tu.		6	16. 13-end	7	2
W.		8. 1-14	17. 1-23	8. 15-9. 17	3
Th.		11. 1-9, 27- 12. 10	17. 24-18. 14	13	4
F.		14	18. 15-end	15	5
S.		16	19. 1-15	17. 1-22	6

TABLES

		Morning Prayer		Evening Prayer	
		First Lesson	Second Lesson	First Lesson	Second Lesson
Sexagesima	Year I	Gen. 3	1 Cor. 10. 1-24	Gen. 4. 1-15	1 John 3. 1-15
	Year II	27. 1-40	6. 12-end	37	Luke 10. 25-37
M.		Gen. 18	Matt. 19. 16-20. 16	Gen. 19. 1-3, 12-29	Rom. 7
Tu.		21	20. 17-end	22. 1-19	8. 1-17
W.		23	21. 1-22	24. 1-28	8. 18-end
Th.		24. 29-end	21. 23-end	25. 7-11, 19-end	9
F.		26. 1-5, 12-end	22. 1-33	27. 1-40	10
S.	Year I	27. 41-28 end	22. 34-23. 12	29. 1-20	11
	Year II	27. 41-28. 9			
Quinquagesima	Year I	Gen. 12. 1-9	1 Cor. 12. 4-end	Gen. 6. 5-end	Luke 17. 20-end
	Year II	28. 10-end	12. 4-end	41. 1-40	1 John 4. 7-end
M.		Gen. 31. 1-21	Matt. 23. 13-end	Gen. 31. 22-32. 2	Rom. 12
Shrove Tuesday		32. 3-30	24. 1-28	33	13
Ash Wednesday		Isa. 57. 15-end	Mark 2. 13-22	Isa. 58	Heb. 3. 12-4. 13
Th.		Gen. 35. 1-20	Matt. 24. 29-end	Gen. 37	Rom. 14
F.		39	25. 1-30	40	15
S.		41. 1-40	25. 31-end	41. 41-end	16
First Sunday in Lent	Year I	Gen. 13	Matt. 9. 1-17	Gen. 8	Mark 14. 1-26
	Year II	29. 1-20	Heb. 4. 14-5. 10	42	Luke 22. 1-30
M.	Year I	Gen. 42	Matt. 26. 1-30	Gen. 43	Phil. 1
	Year II	43. 1-14	26. 1-30	43. 15-end	1
Tu.		44	26. 31-56	45. 1-15	2
W. Ember Day		45. 16-46. 7	26. 57-end	46. 26-47. 12	3
Th.		47. 13-end	27. 1-26	48	4
F. Ember Day		49. 1-32	27. 27-56	49. 33-50 end	Col. 1. 1-20
S. Ember Day		Exod. 1. 1-14, 22-2. 10	27. 57-28 end	Exod. 2. 11-22	1. 21-2. 7
Second Sunday in Lent	Year I	Gen. 18. 1-15	Luke 15. 11-end	Gen. 9. 1-17 (11. 1-9)	Mark 14. 27-52
	Year II	32. 1-30	Heb. 10. 19-end	43. 1-15 (16-26) 27-end	Luke 22. 31-53
M.		Exod. 2. 23-3 end	John 1. 1-28	Exod. 4. 1-23	Col. 2. 8-3. 11
Tu.		4. 27-6. 1	1. 29-end	6. 2-13 & 7. 1-7	3. 12-4. 1
W.		7. 8-end	2	8. 1-19	4. 2-end
Th.		8. 20-9. 12	3. 1-21	9. 13-end	Philemon
F.		10. 1-20	3. 22-end	10. 21-11 end	Eph. 1
S.		12. 1-20	4. 1-26	12. 21-36	2
Third Sunday in Lent	Year I	Gen. 18. 16-end	Luke 18. 1-14	Gen. 24. 1-28	Mark 14. 53-end
	Year II	33. 1-17	Heb. 12. 18-end	44. 1-45. 8	Luke 22. 54-end
M.		Exod. 12. 37-end	John 4. 27-end	Exod. 13. 1-16	Eph. 3
Tu.		13. 17-14. 14	5. 1-23	14. 15-end	4. 1-16
W.		15. 1-26	5. 24-end	15. 27-16 35	4. 17-30
Th.		17	6. 1-21	18	4. 31-5. 21
F.		19	6. 22-40	20. 1-21	5. 22-6. 9
S.		22. 20-23. 17	6. 41-end	23. 18-end	6. 10-end

		Morning Prayer		Evening Prayer	
		First Lesson	Second Lesson	First Lesson	Second Lesson
Mothering Sunday	Year I	Exod. 1. 8-14, 22-2. 10	Luke 18. 35-19. 10	Gen. 24. 29-end	Mark 15. 1-21
	Year II	Gen. 35. 1-15	Heb. 13. 1-21	45. 16-46. 7	Luke 23. 1-25
M.		Exod. 24	John 7. 1-24	Exod. 25. 1-22	1 Tim. 1. 1-17
Tu.		28. 1-4, 29-41	7. 25-end	29. 38-30. 16	1. 18-2 end
W.		32	8. 1-30	33	3
Th.		34	8. 31-end	35. 20-36. 7	4
F.		40. 17-end	9	Lev. 6. 8-end	5
S.		Lev. 19. 1-18, 30-end	10. 1-21	25. 1-24	6
Passion Sunday	Year I	Exod. 2. 23-3. 20	Mark 10. 32-45	Exod. 6. 2-13	Mark 15. 22-39
	Year II	2. 23-3. 20	10. 32-45	4. 27-6. 1	Luke 23. 26-49
M.		Num. 6	John 10. 22-end	Num. 9. 15-end &10. 29-end	Titus 1. 1-2. 8
Tu.		11. 10-33	11. 1-44	12	2. 9-3 end
W.		13. 1-3,17- end	11. 45-end	14. 1-25	2 Tim. 1
Th.		16. 1-35	12. 1-19	16. 36-17 end	2
F.		20	12. 20-end	22. 1-35	3
S.		22. 36-23. 26	13	23. 27-24 end	4
Palm Sunday	Years I & II	Exod. 11	Matt. 26	Isa. 52. 13-53 end	Luke 19. 29-end
M.		Hos. 13. 1-14	John 14. 1-14	Hos. 14	John 14. 15-end
Tu.		Isa. 42. 1-9	15. 1-16	Wisd. 2. 1, 12-end	15. 17-end
W.		Num. 21. 4-9	16. 1-15	Lev. 16. 2-24	16. 16-end
Maundy Thursday		Lam. 1. 1-14	17	Lam. 3. 1-33	13. 1-35
Good Friday		Gen. 22. 1-18	18. 1-32	Isa. 50. 4-10	19. 38-end
Holy Saturday		Zech. 9. 9-12	1 Pet. 2. 11-end	Job 19. 21-27	2. 13-22
Easter Day	Years I & II	Exod. 12. 1-14	Rev. 1. 4-18	Exod. 14. 5-end	John 20. 11-23
Easter Monday		Exod. 15. 1-18	Luke 24. 1-12	Isa. 12	Rev. 7. 9-end
Easter Tuesday		Isa. 25. 1-9	1 Pet. 1. 1-12	26. 1-19	Matt. 28. 1-10
W.		61	1. 13-end	Song of Songs 2. 8-end	John 21. 1-14
Th.		Job 14. 1-15	1 Thess. 4. 13-end	Dan. 12	Mark 5. 21-end
F.		Zeph. 3. 14-end	Acts 17. 16-31	2 Kings 4. 8-37	Luke 7. 11-17
Low Saturday		Jer. 31. 1-14	26. 1-23	Mic. 7. 7-end	John 11. 17-44
Low Sunday	Year I	Isa. 51. 1-16	Luke 24. 13-35	Exod. 15. 1-18	John 20. 24-end
	Year II	Ezek. 37. 1-14	24. 13-35	1 Kings 17. 8-end	20. 24-end
M.		Deut. 1. 3-18	Acts 1. 1-14	Deut. 1. 19-end	Acts 1. 15-end
Tu.		2. 1-25	2. 1-21	2. 26-3. 5	2. 22-end
W.		3. 18-end	3. 1-4. 4	4. 1-24	4. 5-31
Th.		4. 41-end	4. 32-5. 11	5. 1-21	5. 12-end
F.		5. 22-end	6. 1-7, 16	6	7. 17-34
S.		7. 1-11	7. 35-8. 4	7. 12-end	8. 4-25

TABLES

		Morning Prayer		Evening Prayer	
		First Lesson	Second Lesson	First Lesson	Second Lesson
Good Shepherd	Year I	Exod. 16. 2-15	1 Cor. 15. 1-26	Exod. 24	John 21. 1-14
Sunday	Year II	Num. 13. 1, 2, 17- end	Mark 5. 21-end	Deut. 4. 25-40	Rev. 20
M.		Deut. 8	Acts 8. 26-end	Deut. 9. 1-10	Acts 9. 1-31
Tu.		9. 11-end	9. 32-end	10	10. 1-23
W.		11. 1-12	10. 24-end	11. 13-end	11. 1-18
Th.		12. 1-14	11. 19-end	15. 1-18	12. 1-24
F.		16. 1-20	12. 25-13. 12	17. 8-end	13. 13-43
S.		18. 9-end	13. 44-14. 7	19	14. 8-end
Third Sunday after	Year I	Exod. 32. 1-14	1 Cor. 15. 35-end	Exod. 33. 7-end	John 21. 15-end
Easter	Year II	Num. 22. 1-21	Luke 7. 11-17	Deut. 5. 1-21	Rev. 21. 9-end
M.		Deut. 21. 22-22. 8	Acts 15. 1-21	Deut. 24. 5-end	Acts 15. 22-35
Tu.		26	15. 36-16. 5	28. 58-end	16. 6-end
W.		29. 10-end	17. 1-15	30	17. 16-end
Th.		31. 1-13	18. 1-23	31. 14-29	18. 24-19. 7
F.		31. 30-32. 14	19. 8-20	32. 15-47	19. 21-end
S.		33	20. 1-16	32. 48-end & 34	20. 17-end
Fourth Sunday after	Year I	Exod. 34. 1-10	1 Pet. 3. 8-end	Exod. 35. 30-36. 7	Luke 16. 19-end
Easter	Year II	Num. 22. 36-23. 12	John 11. 1-44	Deut. 10. 12-11. 1	Rev. 22
M.		Joshua 1	Acts 21. 1-16	Joshua 2	Acts 21. 17-36
Tu.		3	21. 37-22. 22	4. 1-5. 1	22. 23-23. 11
W.		5. 13-6. 20	23. 12-end	7	24. 1-23
Th.		9. 3-end	24. 24-25. 12	10. 1-15	25. 13-end
F.		21. 43-22. 8	26	22. 9-end	27
S.		23	28. 1-15	24. 1-28	28. 16-end
Rogation Sunday	Year I	Deut. 34	Acts 13. 26-43	Deut. 6	Luke 10. 38-11. 13
	Year II	Num. 24. 1-19	Rom. 6. 1-14	28. 1-13	Mark 4. 1-20
M. Rogation Day		Deut. 7. 6-13	Matt. 6. 5-18	Deut. 8	Matt. 6. 19-end
Tu. Rogation Day		11. 8-21	Luke 5. 1-11	1 Kings 8. 22-43	Jas. 5. 1-18
W. Rogation Day		Joel 2. 21-27	John 6. 22-40	Song of Three Childr. 29-37	Matt. 28. 16-end
Ascension Day		2 Kings 2. 1-15	17	Dan. 7. 9, 10, 13, 14	Heb. 1
F.		Judges 2. 6-end	Heb. 2	Judges 3. 12-end	3
S.		4	4. 1-13	5	4. 14-5. 10
Sunday after	Year I	Isa. 65. 17-end	Luke 24. 36-end	Jer. 31. 1-13	Eph. 5. 1-14
Ascension-Day	Year II	52. 1-12	Eph. 4. 1-16	Isa. 62	Rev. 5
M.		Judges 6. 1-35	Heb. 5. 11-6 end	Judges 6. 36-7. 23	Heb. 7
Tu.		7. 24-8. 28	8	8. 32-9. 24	9. 1-14
W.		9. 26-end	9. 15-end	10. 17-11. 28	10. 1-18
Th.		11. 29-12. 7	10. 19-end	13	11
F.		14	12. 1-13	15. 1-16. 3	12. 14-end
Whitsun-Eve		16. 4-end	13	Deut. 16. 9-12	Acts 18. 24-19. 7

TABLES

		Morning Prayer		Evening Prayer	
		First Lesson	Second Lesson	First Lesson	Second Lesson
Whitsunday	Year I	Joel 2. 28-end	Rom. 8. 1-17	Isa. 11. 1-9	Rom. 8. 18-end
	Year II				
Whit-Monday		Ezek. 11. 14-20	Acts 2. 12-36	Wisd. 1. 1-7	Acts 2. 37-end
Whit-Tuesday		Ezek. 37. 1-14	1 Cor. 12. 1-13	Wisd. 7. 15-8. 1	1 Cor. 12. 27-13 end
W. Ember Day		1 Kings 19. 1-18	2	9	3
Th.		2 Sam. 23. 1-5	Eph. 6. 10-20	Exod. 35. 30-36. 1	Gal. 5. 13-end
F. Ember Day		Num. 11. 16, 17, 24-29	2 Cor. 5. 14-6. 10	Jer. 31. 31-34	2 Cor. 3
S. Ember Day		Num. 27. 15-end	Matt. 9. 35-10. 20	Isa. 61	2 Tim. 1. 3-14
Trinity Sunday	Year I	Isa. 6. 1-8	Mark 1. 1-13	Isa. 40. 12-end	1 Pet. 1. 1-12
	Year II				
M.		Job 1	Jas. 1	Job 2	Mark 1. 14-31
Tu.		3	2. 1-13	4	1. 32-end
W.		5	2. 14-end	6	2. 1-22
Corpus Christi		7	3	8	2. 23-3. 12
F.		9	4	10	3. 13-end
S.		11	5	12	4. 1-34
First Sunday after	Year I	Joshua 1. 1-9	Mark 1. 21-34	1 Sam. 9. 1-10. 1	Acts 1. 1-14
Trinity	Year II	1 Kings 3. 5-14	Acts 9. 1-22 (23-31)	2 Kings 17. 1-23	John 13. 1-20
M.		Job 13	1 Pet. 1. 1-21	Job 14	Mark 4. 35-5. 20
Tu.		15. 1-16	1. 22-2. 10	16. 1-17. 2	5. 21-end
W.		17. 3-end	2. 11-3. 7	18	6. 1-29
Th.		19	3. 8-4. 6	21	6. 30-end
F.		22	4. 7-end	23	7. 1-23
S.		24	5	25 & 26	7. 24-8. 10
Second Sunday after	Year I	Joshua 2	Mark 2. 23-3. 19	1 Sam. 16. 1-13	Acts 2. 1-21
Trinity	Year II	1 Kings 8. 22-30 (9. 1-3)	Acts 13. 1-13 (14-26)	2 Kings 18. 17-22, 28-19. 7	John 13. 21-end
M.		Job 27	2 Pet. 1	Job 28	Mark 8. 11-9. 1
Tu.		29. 1-30. 1	2	31. 13-end	9. 2-29
W.		32	3	33	9. 30-end
Th.		38. 1-21	Jude	38. 22-end	10. 1-31
F.		39	1 John 1. 1-2. 6	40	10. 32-end
S.		41	2. 7-end	42	11. 1-26
Third Sunday after	Year I	Joshua 3	Mark 3. 20-end	1 Sam. 17. 1-11, 32-51	Acts 2. 22-42 (43-end)
Trinity	Year II	1 Kings 10. 1-13	Acts 16. 6-34	2 Kings 19. 8-35	John 14. 1-14
M.		Prov. 1. 1-19	1 John 3. 1-12	Prov. 1. 20-end	Mark 11. 27-12. 12
Tu.		2	3. 13-4. 6	3. 1-26	12. 13-34
W.		3. 27-4. 19	4. 7-end	4. 20-5. 14	12. 35-13. 13
Th.		6. 1-19	5	8	13. 14-end
F.		9	2 John	10. 1-22	14. 1-26
S.		11. 1-25	3 John	12. 10-end	14. 27-52

TABLES

		Morning Prayer		Evening Prayer	
		First Lesson	Second Lesson	First Lesson	Second Lesson
Fourth Sunday after Trinity	Year I	Joshua 5. 13-6. 20	Mark 4. 21-end	1 Sam. 18. 1-16	Acts 3. 1-16 (17-end)
	Year II	1 Kings 12. 1-20	Acts 17. 16-end	2 Kings 22	John 14. 15-end
M.		Prov. 14. 9-27	Rom. 1	Prov. 15. 18-end	Mark 14. 53-end
Tu.		16. 31-17. 17	2. 1-16	18. 10-end	15. 1-41
W.		20. 1-22	2. 17-end	22. 1-16	15. 42-16 end
Th.		24. 23-end	3	25	Luke 1. 1-23
F.		26. 12-end	4	27. 1-22	1. 24-56
S.		30. 1-16	5	31. 10-end	1. 57-end
Fifth Sunday after Trinity	Year I	Joshua 24. 1-5, 13-25	Mark 6. 7-32	1 Sam. 28. 3-end	Acts 4. 1-22 (23-31)
	Year II	1 Kings 18. 17-39	Acts 19. 21-end	Jer. 36. 1-26	John 15. 1-16
M.		1 Sam. 1	Rom. 6	1 Sam. 2. 1-21	Luke 2. 1-21
Tu.		2. 22-end	7	3	2. 22-end
W.		4	8. 1-17	7	3. 1-22
Th.		8	8. 18-end	9. 1-25	4. 1-30
F.		9. 26-10. 16	9	10. 17-end	4. 31-end
S.		11	10	12	5. 1-16
Sixth Sunday after Trinity	Year I	Judges 5	Mark 6. 53-7. 23	2 Sam. 1	Acts 6
	Year II	1 Kings 19. 1-18	Acts 20. 17-end	Jer. 38. 1-13	John 15. 17-end
M.		1 Sam. 13	Rom. 11. 1-24	1 Sam. 14. 1-23	Luke 5. 17-end
Tu.		14. 24-48	11. 25-end	15	6. 1-19
W.		16	12	17. 1-30	6. 20-38
Th.		17. 31-54	13	17. 55-18. 16	6. 39-7. 10
F.		19	14	20. 1-17	7. 11-35
S.		20. 18-end	15. 1-13	21. 1-22. 5	7. 36-end
Seventh Sunday after Trinity	Year I	Judges 7. 1-23	Mark 9. 14-29	2 Sam. 7. 1-17 (18-end)	Acts 8. 4-17
	Year II	1 Kings 21. 1-23 (24-end)	Acts 21. 15-36	Jer. 52. 1-11	John 16. 1-15
M.		1 Sam. 22. 6-end	Rom. 15. 14-end	1 Sam. 23	Luke 8. 1-21
Tu.		24	16	25. 2-42	8. 22-end
W.		26	1 Cor. 1. 1-25	28. 3-end	9. 1-17
Th.		31	1. 26-2 end	2 Sam. 1	9. 18-50
F.		2 Sam. 2. 1-3. 1	3	3. 17-end	9. 51-end
S.		5. 1-12	4. 1-17	6	10. 1-24
Eighth Sunday after Trinity	Year I	Judges 16. 4-end	Mark 9. 30-end	2 Sam. 11	Acts 8. 26-39
	Year II	1 Kings 22. 1-38	Acts 25. 1-12 (13-end)	Ezek. 33. 21-end	John 16. 16-22
M.		2 Sam. 7	1 Cor. 4. 18-5 end	2 Sam. 8	Luke 10. 25-end
Tu.		9	6	10	11. 1-28
W.		13. 38-14. 24	7	14. 25-15. 12	11. 29-end
Th.		15. 13-end	8	16	12. 1-34
F.		17. 1-23	9	17. 24-18. 18	12. 35-53
S.		18. 19-end	10. 1-11. 1	19. 1-23	12. 54-13. 9

TABLES

		Morning Prayer		Evening Prayer	
		First Lesson	Second Lesson	First Lesson	Second Lesson
Ninth Sunday after Trinity	Year I	1 Sam. 1. 1-20 (21-end)	Mark 10. 17-31	2 Sam. 12. 1-23	Acts 11. 1-18
	Year II	2 Kings 4. 8-37	Acts 27	Ezek. 36. 22-28, 34-36	John 16. 23-end
M.		2 Sam. 19. 24-end	1 Cor. 11. 2-end	2 Sam. 23. 1-17	Luke 13. 10-end
Tu.		24	12. 1-27	1 Kings 1. 5-31	14. 1-24
W.		1 Kings 1. 32-end	12. 27-13 end	1 Chron. 22. 2-end	14. 25-15. 10
Th.		1 Chron. 28. 1-29. 9	14. 1-19	29. 10-end	15. 11-end
F.		1 Kings 3	14. 20-end	1 Kings 4. 21-end	16
S.		5	15. 1-34	6. 1-14	17. 1-19
Tenth Sunday after Trinity	Year I	1 Sam. 3. 1-4. 1 a	Mark 12. 18-end	2 Sam. 18	Acts 15. 1-31
	Year II	2 Kings 5. 1-19 (20-end)	Acts 28. 11-end	Ezek. 37. 15-end	John 17
M.		1 Kings 8. 1-21	1 Cor. 15. 35-end	1 Kings 8. 22-53	Luke 17. 20-end
Tu.		8. 54-9. 9	16	10	18. 1-30
W.		11. 1-13, 26-end	2 Cor. 1. 1-22	12. 1-24	18. 31-19. 10
Th.		12. 25-13. 10	1. 23-2 end	13. 11-end	19. 11-28
F.		14. 1-20	3	2 Chron. 12	19. 29-end
S.		2 Chron. 13	4	14	20. 1-26
Eleventh Sunday after Trinity	Year I	Hos. 6. 1-6	Rom. 1. 1-25 (26-end)	Jer. 5. 1-19	Matt. 4. 23-5. 20
	Year II	Jer. 18. 1-17	Luke 4. 1-15	Zech. 2	Gal. 1
M.		2 Chron. 15	2 Cor. 5	2 Chron. 16	Luke 20. 27-21. 4
Tu.		1 Kings 16. 15-end	5. 20-7. 1	1 Kings 17	21. 5-end
W.		18. 1-16	7. 2-end	18. 17-end	22. 1-38
Th.		19	8	21	22. 39-53
F.		22. 1-40	9	2 Chron. 20. 1-30	22. 54-end
S.		2 Kings 1	10	2 Kings 2. 1-22	23. 1-25
Twelfth Sunday after Trinity	Year I	Hos. 11. 1-9a	Rom. 5. 1-11	Jer. 7. 1-16	Matt. 5. 21-end
	Year II	Jer. 26. 1-16	Luke 4. 16-30	Zech. 8. 1-17	Gal. 6. 1-10
M.		2 Kings 4. 1-37	2 Cor. 11	2 Kings 5	Luke. 23. 26-49
Tu.		6. 1-23	12. 1-13	6. 24-7. 2	23. 50-24. 12
W.		7. 3-end	12. 14-13 end	8. 1-15	24. 13-end
Th.		9	Gal. 1	11. 1-20	John 1. 1-28
F.		11. 21-12 end	2	13	1. 29-end
S.		14	3	2 Chron. 26	2
Thirteenth Sunday after Trinity	Year I	Hos. 14	Rom. 12	Jer. 17. 5-14	Matt. 6. 1-18
	Year II	Jer. 30. 1-3, 10-22	Luke 6. 20-38	Ezra 1. 1-8	1 Cor. 1. 1-25
M.		2 Kings 15. 17-end	Gal. 4. 1-5. 1	2 Kings 16	John 3. 1-21
Tu.		Isa. 7. 1-17	5. 2-end	Isa. 8. 1-18	3. 22-end
W.		2 Kings 17. 1-23	6	2 Kings 17. 24-end	4. 1-26
Th.		18. 1-8	Eph. 1. 1-14	2 Chron. 30	4. 27-end
F.		18. 13-end	1. 15-end	2 Kings 19	5. 1-23
S.		20	2. 1-10	2 Chron. 33	5. 24-end

TABLES

		Morning Prayer		Evening Prayer	
		First Lesson	Second Lesson	First Lesson	Second Lesson
Fourteenth Sunday after Trinity	Year I	Joel 2. 1-14	Rom. 14. 1-15. 3	Dan. 3	Matt. 6. 19-end
	Year II	Jer. 31. 27-34	Luke 6. 39-end	Ezra 3	1 Cor. 1. 26-2.9 (10-end)
M.		2 Kings 22	Eph. 2. 11-end	2 Kings 23. 1-20	John 6. 1-21
Tu.		23. 21-35	3	23. 36-24. 17	6. 22-40
W.		24. 18-25. 7	4. 1-16	25. 8-end	6. 41-end
Th.		Jer. 19	4. 17-30	Jer. 21. 1-10	7. 1-24
F.		22. 20-23. 8	4. 31-5. 21	24	7. 25-end
S.		25. 1-14	5. 22-end	27. 2-end	8. 1-30
Fifteenth Sunday after Trinity	Year I	Joel 2. 15-27	1 Pet. 1. 13-end	Dan. 5	Matt. 7. 1-14
	Year II	Ezek. 11. 14-20	Luke 7. 36-8. 3	Neh. 1	1 Cor. 3
M.		Jer. 28	Eph. 6. 1-9	Jer. 29. 1-20	John 8. 31-end
Tu.		32. 1-15	6. 10-end	32. 16-35	9
W.		32. 36-end	Phil. 1. 1-11	33. 1-13	10. 1-21
Th.		33. 14-end	1. 12-end	34. 8-end	10. 22-end
F.		37	2. 1-11	38. 1-13	11. 1-44
S.		38. 14-end	2. 12-end	39	11. 45-end
Sixteenth Sunday after Trinity	Year I	Job 1	1 Pet. 2. 1-17	Dan. 6. 1-23	Matt. 7. 15-end
	Year II	Ezek. 18. 1-4, 19-end	Luke 9. 46-end	Neh. 2	1 Cor. 13
M.		Jer. 40	Phil. 3	Jer. 41	John 12. 1-19
Tu.		42	4	43	12. 20-end
W.		44. 1-14	Col. 1. 1-20	44. 15-end	13
Th.		Ezek. 1. 1-14	1. 21-2. 7	Ezek. 1. 15-end	14
F.		2	2. 8-19	3. 1-14	15
S.		3. 15-end	2. 20-3. 11	8	16
Seventeenth Sunday after Trinity	Year I	Job 2	1 Pet. 4	Prov. 1. 20-end	Matt. 11. 2-19
	Year II	Ezek. 33. 1-11	Luke 10. 1-24	Ruth 1	Phil. 1. 12-end
M.		Ezek. 9	Col. 3. 12-4. 1	Ezek. 11. 1-13	John 17
Tu.		12. 1-16	4. 2-end	12. 17-end	18. 1-27
W.		13. 1-16	Philemon	14	18. 28-end
Th.		17	1 Thess. 1	20. 1-26	19. 1-30
F.		20. 27-44	2. 1-16	22. 23-end	19. 31-end
S.		24. 15-end	2. 17-3 end	28. 1-19	20
Eighteenth Sunday after Trinity	Year I	Job 4. 1 & 5. 6-end	1 Pet. 5. 1-11	Prov. 8. 1-17	Matt. 11. 20-end
	Year II	Ezek. 34. 1-16	Luke 11. 37-end	Ruth 2. 1-20a (4. 13-17)	Phil. 2. 1-18
M.		Ezek. 33. 12-20	1 Thess. 4. 1-12	Ezek. 33. 21-end	John 21
Tu.		34. 17-end	4. 13-5. 11	36. 22-end	Heb. 1
W.		37. 1-14	5. 12-end	37. 15-end	2
Th.		Ezra 1	2 Thess. 1	Ezra 3	3
F.		4	2	Hag. 1. 1-2. 9	4. 1-13
S.		Zech. 1. 1-17	3	Zech. 1. 18-2 end	4. 14-5. 10

TABLES

		Morning Prayer		Evening Prayer	
		First Lesson	Second Lesson	First Lesson	Second Lesson
Nineteenth Sunday after Trinity	Year I	Job 19. 1-27a	Col. 1. 21-2. 7	Prov. 8. 1, 22-end	Matt. 12. 22-45
	Year II	Prov. 14. 31-15. 17	Luke 12. 1-21	Jonah 1 & 2	Phil. 3. 1-16
M.		Zech. 3	1 Tim. 1. 1-17	Zech. 4	Heb. 5. 11-6 end
Tu.		6. 9-end	1. 18-2 end	7	7
W.		8	3	11	8
Th.		13	4	Hag. 2. 10-end	9. 1-14
F.		Ezra 5	5	Ezra 6	9. 15-end
S.		7	6	8. 15-end	10. 1-18
Twentieth Sunday after Trinity	Year I	Job 38 (42. 1-6)	Col. 3. 12-4. 6	Job 28	Matt. 13. 44-end
	Year II	Prov. 31. 10-end	Luke 12. 22-34	Jonah 3 & 4	Phil. 4
M.		Ezra 9	Titus 1. 1-2. 8	Ezra 10. 1-19	Heb. 10. 19-end
Tu.		Neh. 1	2. 9-3 end	Neh. 2	11. 1-16
W.		4	2 Tim. 1	5	11. 17-end
Th.		6. 1-7. 4	2	8	12. 1-13
F.		9. 1-23	3	9. 24-end	12. 14-end
S.		13	4	Dan. 1	13
Twenty-first Sunday after Trinity	Year I	Wisd. 2	Philemon	Ecclus. 4. 11-28	Matt. 14. 13-33
	Year II	9	Luke 12. 35-end	1 Macc. 2. 1-22	2 Cor. 1. 1-22
M.		Dan. 2. 1-24	Jas. 1. 1-11	Dan. 2. 25-end	Jas. 1. 12-end
Tu.		4. 1-18	2. 1-13	4. 19-end	2. 14-end
W.		7. 9-end	3	9	4
Th.		10	5	12	1 Pet. 1. 1-12
F.		Esther 1	1 Pet. 1. 13-end	Esther 2	2. 1-10
S.		3	2. 11-3. 7	4	3. 8-end
Twenty-second Sunday after Trinity	Year I	Wisd. 4. 7-17	Jas. 1. 1-13 (14-end)	Ecclus. 4. 29-6. 1	Matt. 16. 13-end
	Year II	11. 21-12. 2	Luke 13. 18-end	1 Macc. 2. 49-69	2 Cor. 4
M.		Esther 5	1 Pet. 4. 1-11	Esther 6 & 7	1 Pet. 4. 12-end
Tu.		Eccles. 1	5	Eccles. 2. 1-23	1 John 1. 1-2. 6
W.		3	1 John 2. 7-17	4	2. 18-end
Th.		5	3. 1-18	6. 1-7. 14	3. 19-4. 6
F.		7. 15-end	4. 7-end	8	5
S.		9	2 John	10	3 John
Twenty-third Sunday after Trinity	Year I	Wisd. 6. 1-21	Jas. 2. 1-13 (14-end)	Ecclus. 11. 7-28	Matt. 18. 1-20
	Year II	Ecclus. 18. 1-13	Luke 14. 15-end	1 Macc. 3. 42-end	2 Cor. 5
M.		1 Macc. 1. 1-19	Acts 1	1 Macc. 1. 20-40	Acts 2. 1-21
Tu.		1. 41-end	2. 22-end	2. 1-28	3. 1-4. 4
W.		2. 29-48	4. 5-31	2. 49-end	4. 32-5. 11
Th.		3. 1-26	5. 12-end	3. 27-41	6. 1-7. 16
F.		4. 1-25	7. 17-34	4. 26-35	7. 35-8. 4
S.		4. 36-end	8. 4-25	6. 1-17	8. 26-end

		Morning Prayer		Evening Prayer	
		First Lesson	Second Lesson	First Lesson	Second Lesson
Twenty-fourth	Year I	Wisd. 7. 15-8. 1	Jas. 3	Ecclus. 15. 11-end	Matt. 21. 12-32
Sunday after Trinity	Year II	Ecclus. 27. 30-28. 9	Luke 15. 1-10	1 Macc. 14. 4-15	2 Cor. 9
M.		1 Macc. 6. 18-47	Acts 9. 1-31	1 Macc. 6. 48-end	Acts 9. 32-end
Tu.		7. 1-20	10. 1-23	7. 21-end	10. 24-end
W.		9. 1-22	11. 1-18	13. 41-end	11. 19-end
Th.		Ecclus. 1. 1-10	12. 1-24	Ecclus. 1. 11-end	12. 25-13. 12
F.		2	13. 13-43	6. 14-31	13. 44-14. 7
S.		7. 27-end	14. 8-end	10. 6-8, 12-24	15. 1-21
Twenty-fifth Sunday	Year I	2 Esdras 16. 53-67	Jas. 4	Baruch 3. 1-14	Matt. 21. 33-end
after Trinity	Year II	Ecclus. 3. 17-29	Luke 17. 1-10	Ecclus. 38. 24-end	1 Tim. 6. 1-16
					(17-end)
M.		Ecclus. 14. 20-15. 10	Acts 15. 22-35	Ecclus. 16. 1-14	Acts 15. 36-16. 5
Tu.		16. 17-end	16. 6-end	17. 1-24	17. 1-15
W.		18. 15-end	17. 16-end	19. 13-end	18. 1-23
Th.		20. 1-20	18. 24-19. 7	20. 21-end	19. 8-20
F.		21. 1-17	19. 21-end	22. 6-22	20. 1-16
S.		22. 27-23. 15	20. 17-end	24. 1-22	21. 1-16
Twenty-sixth Sunday	Year I	Prayer of Manasses	Jas. 5. (1-6) 7-end	Baruch 4. 36-5 end	Matt. 23. 1-22
after Trinity	Year II	Ecclus. 42. 15-end	Luke 20. 1-19	Ecclus. 43. 13-26	2 Tim. 1. 1-14
					(15-2. 7)
M.		Ecclus. 24. 23-end	Acts 21. 17-36	Ecclus. 31. 1-11	Acts 21. 37-22. 22
Tu.		34. 9-end	22. 23-23. 11	35	23. 12-end
W.		37. 1-15	24. 1-23	38. 1-14	24. 24-25. 12
Th.		39. 1-11	25. 13-end	39. 13-end	26
F.		43. 1-12	27. 1-26	50. 1-24	27. 27-end
S.		51. 1-12	28. 1-15	51. 13-end	28. 16-end
Sunday next before	Years I	Eccles. 11 & 12	Heb. 11. 1-16	Mal. 3. 13-4 end	Heb. 11. 17-12. 2
Advent	& II				
M.		Wisd. 1	Matt. 5. 1-16	Wisd. 2	Rev. 1
Tu.		3. 1-9	5. 17-end	4. 7-end	2. 1-17
W.		5. 1-16	6. 1-18	6. 1-21	2. 18-3. 6
Th.		7. 15-8. 4	6. 19-end	8. 5-18	3. 7-end
F.		8. 21-9 end	7. 1-14	10. 15-11. 10	4
S.		11. 21-12. 2	7. 15-end	12. 12-21	5

NOTE: *The Lessons for the First Sunday after Christmas will be read only when the 29th, 30th, or 31st of December is a Sunday.*

NOTE: *The Lessons for the Second Sunday after Christmas will be read only when 2nd, 3rd, 4th, or 5th of January is a Sunday, and in the last case the Lessons for Morning Prayer only.*

LESSONS PROPER FOR HOLY-DAYS

NOT INCLUDED IN THE FOREGOING TABLE

		FIRST EVENSONG		MATTINS		SECOND EVENSONG	
		FIRST LESSON	SECOND LESSON	FIRST LESSON	SECOND LESSON	FIRST LESSON	SECOND LESSON
St Andrew	30 Nov.	Ecclesiasticus 14. 20-end	1 Corinthians 4. 9-16	Zechariah 8. 20-end	John 1. 35-42	Ezekiel 47. 1-12	John 12. 20-32
St Thomas	21 Dec.	2 Samuel 15. 17-21	John 11. 1-16	Job 42. 1-6	John 14. 1-7	Ecclesiasticus 2	1 Peter 1. 3-9
Conversion of St Paul	25 Jan.	Isaiah 56. 1-8	Acts 26. 1-23	Jeremiah 1. 4-10	Galatians 1. 11-end	Ecclesiasticus 39. 1-10	Philippians 3. 1-14
Purification of St Mary the Virgin	2 Feb.	Exodus 13. 11-16	Galatians 4. 1-7	1 Samuel 1. 21- end	Hebrews 10. 1-10	Haggai 2. 1-9	Romans 12. 1-5
St Matthias	24 Feb.	Isaiah 22. 15-22	Matthew 11. 25-30	1 Samuel 2. 27-35	Matthew 7. 15-27	1 Samuel 16. 1-13	1 Corinthians 4. 1-8
Annunciation of our Lady	25 Mar.	Genesis 3.1-15	Romans 5. 12-end	Isaiah 52. 7-12	Hebrews 2. 5- end	1 Samuel 2. 1-10	Matthew 1. 18-23
St Mark	25 April	Ezekiel 1. 1-14	Acts 12. 25-13. 13	Ecclesiasticus 51. 13-end	Acts 15. 35-end	Isaiah 62. 6-end	2 Timothy 4. 1-11
St Philip and St James	1 May	Isaiah 30. 15-21	John 1. 43-end	Proverbs 4. 10-18	John 6. 1-14	Job 23. 1-12	John 17. 1-8
St Barnabas	11 June	Job 29. 11-16	Acts 4. 32-end	Jeremiah 9. 23,24	Acts 9. 19b-31	Tobit 4. 5-11	Acts 14. 8-end
Nativity of St John Baptist	24 June	Malachi 3. 1-6	Matthew 3	Judges 13. 1-7	Luke 1. 5-25	Malachi 4	Matthew 11. 2-19
St Peter	29 June	Ezekiel 2. 1-7	Acts 9. 32-end	Ezekiel 3. 4-11	Acts 11. 1-18	Ezekiel 34. 11-16	John 21. 15-22
St Mary Magdalene	22 July	1 Samuel 16. 14-end	Luke 8. 1-3	Isaiah 25. 1-9	John 20. 1-10	Zephaniah 3. 14-end	Mark 15. 40-end
St James	25 July	Jeremiah 26. 1-15	Mark 1. 14-20	2 Kings 1. 1-15	Luke 9. 46-56	Jeremiah 45	Mark 14. 32-42
Transfiguration of our Lord	6 Aug.	Exodus 24. 12-end	Luke 9. 28-45	Exodus 34. 29- end	2 Corinthians 3	Ecclesiasticus 46. 1-16	1 John 3. 1-8
The Falling Asleep of our Lady	15 Aug.	Ecclesiasticus 24. 23-31	Luke 11. 27-28	Proverbs 8. 22-35	John 19. 25-27	Judith 13. 22-25	Revelation 12. 1-6
St Bartholomew	24 Aug.	Genesis 28. 10-17	John 1. 43-end	Deuteronomy 18. 15-19	Matthew 10. 1-15	Isaiah 49. 1-13	Matthew 10. 16-22
St Matthew	21 Sept.	1 Kings 19. 15-end	1 Timothy 6. 6-19	Proverbs 3. 1-17	Matthew 19. 16-end	1 Chronicles 29. 9-18	Matthew 6. 19-end
St Michael and All Angels	29 Sept.	Daniel 12. 1-4	Revelation 8. 1-6	2 Kings 6. 8-17	Acts 12. 1-11	Daniel 10. 4-end	Revelation 5
St Luke	18 Oct	Isaiah 55	Luke 1. 1-4	Isaiah 61. 1-6	2 Timothy 3. 10-end	Ecclesiasticus 38. 1-14	Colossians 4. 7-end
St Simon and St Jude	28 Oct.	Isaiah 28. 9-16	Ephesians 2. 11-end	Jeremiah 3. 12-18	Luke 6. 12-19	Wisdom 5. 1-16	John 14. 15-24
All Saints	1 Nov.	2 Esdras 2. 42-end	Hebrews 11. 32-12.2	Wisdom 3. 1-9	Revelation 19. 6-10	Ecclesiasticus 44. 1-15	1 Corinthians 1. 1-8

PSALMS AND LESSONS
PROPER FOR SERVICES ON SPECIAL OCCASIONS

ACCESSION-DAY OR VICTORIA-DAY
Psalm: 20, 21. 1-7, or 101, 121.
First Lesson: *Joshua* 1. 1-9, or *Proverbs* 8. 1-16.
Second Lesson: *Romans* 13. 1-10, or *Revelation* 21. 22-22. 3.

DOMINION-DAY
AND OTHER OCCASIONS OF NATIONAL THANKSGIVING
Psalm: 46, 67, 72, or 145, 148.
First Lesson: *Deuteronomy* 6. 1-15, or *Deuteronomy* 8,
or *Deuteronomy* 28. 1-14, or *Joshua* 24. 14-25.
Second Lesson: *Matthew* 25. 14-30, or *Romans* 13. 1-10,
or *I Timothy* 2. 1-8.

FOR YOUNG PEOPLE
Psalms: 23, or 24, or 121, 122.
First Lesson: *Job* 28. 12-end, or *Proverbs* 4.
Second Lesson: *Matthew* 25. 1-13, or *II Timothy* 1. 1-14.

FOR MISSIONS
Psalm: 47, or 67, or 96, 97, or 132.
First Lesson: *Isaiah* 49. 13-23, or *Isaiah* 60. 1-14.
Second Lesson: *John* 10. 1-16, or *Ephesians* 3.

REMEMBRANCE-DAY
Psalm: 46, 144.
First Lesson: *Micah* 4. 1-5, or *Ecclesiasticus* 51. 1-12.
Second Lesson: *Romans* 8. 31-end, or *I Corinthians* 15. 50-end.

THE COMMEMORATION OF THE FAITHFUL DEPARTED
Psalm: 90, or 121, or 130.
First Lesson: *Isaiah* 38. 10-20, or *Isaiah* 43. 1-7, or *Job* 19. 21-27a.
Second Lesson: *John* 5. 24-29, or *I Corinthians* 15. 50-end, or *Revelation* 1. 9-18.

THE CONSECRATION OF A CHURCH OR DEDICATION FESTIVAL
Psalm: 84, or 122, or 132.
First Lesson: *I Kings* 8. 22-30, or *I Chronicles* 29. 6-19, or *Zechariah* 8. 9-end.
Second Lesson: *Hebrews* 10. 19-25.

THE DIVINE OFFICE

THE ORDER FOR

MORNING PRAYER

DAILY THROUGHOUT THE YEAR.

The daily Office of Morning Prayer, commonly called Mattins, shall be said or sung in the accustomed place of the Church, Chapel, or Chancel; except it shall be otherwise determined by the Ordinary of the Place. And at the beginning of Morning Prayer, the Minister shall stand in the place of the Church, Chapel, or Chancel appointed for the saying or singing of the Divine Office; and, turning himself to the people, he shall call them to worship, reading in a loud voice some one or more of these Sentences of the holy Scriptures following, the first according to the Season, and then those of Worship and Penitence that follow thereafter, as he shall determine in his discretion.

THE CALL TO WORSHIP AND PREPARATION.

Advent. Repent ye; for the kingdom of heaven is at hand. *Saint Matthew* 3. 2.

Christmastide. Behold, I bring you good tidings of great joy which shall be to all people. For unto you is born this day in the city of David a Saviour, which is Christ the Lord.
Saint Luke 2. 10-11.

Epiphanytide. The earth shall be filled with the knowledge of the glory of the Lord, as the waters cover the sea. *Habakkuk* 2. 14.

Lent. The sacrifices of God are a broken spirit: a broken and contrite heart, O God, Thou wilt not despise. *Psalm* 51. 17.

Rend your heart, and not your garments, and turn unto the Lord your God; for He is gracious and merciful, slow to anger, and of great kindness, and repenteth Him of the evil. *Joel* 2. 13.

Passiontide. God commendeth His love toward us, in that, while we were yet sinners, Christ died for us. *Romans* 5. 8.

Palm Sunday. Hosanna to the Son of David: Blessed is He that cometh in the Name of the Lord; Hosanna in the highest. *Saint Matthew* 21. 9.

Good Friday. All we like sheep have gone astray; we have turned everyone to his own way; and the Lord hath laid on Him the iniquity of us all. *Isaiah* 53. 6.

Easter-Even. For Christ also hath once suffered for sins, the just for the unjust, that He might bring us to God. I *Saint Peter* 3. 18.

Eastertide. The Lord is risen indeed. *Saint Luke* 24. 34.

Thanks be to God, which giveth us the victory through our Lord Jesus Christ.
I *Corinthians* 15. 57.

Rogationtide. The Lord is nigh unto all them that call upon Him, to all that call upon Him in truth. *Psalm* 145. 18.

Ascensiontide. Seeing then that we have a great high Priest that is passed into the heavens, Jesus the Son of God, let us come boldly unto the throne of grace, that we may obtain mercy, and find grace to help in time of need. *Hebrews* 4. 14,16.

Whitsuntide. It shall come to pass in the last days, saith God, I will pour out of my Spirit upon all flesh. *Acts* 2. 17.

Trinity Sunday. God is love; and he that abideth in love abideth in God, and God in him. I *Saint John* 4. 16.

Saints' Days. Wherefore seeing we also are compassed about with so great a cloud of witnesses, let us lay aside every weight, and the sin which doth so easily beset us, and let us run with patience the race that is set before us, looking unto Jesus the Author and Finisher of our faith. *Hebrews* 12. 1-2.

National Occasions. Blessed is the nation whose God is the Lord, and the people whom He hath chosen for His own inheritance. *Psalm* 33. 12.

Of Morning Prayer. O hearken Thou unto the voice of my calling, my King and my God; for unto Thee will I make my prayer. My voice shalt Thou hear betimes, O Lord; early in the morning will I direct my prayer unto Thee, and will look up. *Psalm* 5. 2-3.

Of Worship. The Lord is in His holy temple: let all the earth keep silence before Him. *Habakkuk* 2. 20.

O worship the Lord in the beauty of holiness, let the whole earth stand in awe of Him. *Psalm* 96. 9.

Thus saith the high and lofty One that inhabiteth eternity, Whose Name is Holy: I dwell in the high and holy place, with him also that is of a contrite and humble spirit. *Isaiah* 57. 15.

I was glad when they said unto me, Let us go into the house of the Lord. *Psalm* 122. 1.

The hour cometh, and now is, when the true worshippers shall worship the Father in spirit and in truth; for the Father seeketh such to worship Him. *Saint John* 4. 23.

Of Penitence. I will arise and go to my Father, and will say unto Him, Father, I have sinned against heaven, and before Thee, and am no more worthy to be called Thy son. *Saint Luke* 15. 18-19.

If we say that we have no sin, we deceive ourselves, and the truth is not in us: but if we confess our sins, He is faithful and just to forgive us our sins, and to cleanse us from all unrighteousness. I *Saint John* 1. 8-9.

I acknowledge my transgressions, and my sin is ever before me. *Psalm* 51. 3.

Hide Thy face from my sins, and blot out all mine iniquities. *Psalm* 51. 9.

The sacrifices of God are a broken spirit; a broken and a contrite heart, O God, Thou wilt not despise. *Psalm* 51. 17.

Enter not into judgement with Thy servant, O Lord; for in Thy sight shall no man living be justified. *Psalm* 143. 2.

O Lord, correct me, but with judgement: not in Thine anger, lest Thou bring me to nothing. *Jeremiah* 10. 24.

When the wicked man turneth away from his wickedness that he hath committed, and doeth that which is lawful and right, he shall save his soul alive. *Ezekiel* 18. 27.

To the Lord our God belong mercies and forgivenesses, though we have rebelled against Him: neither have we obeyed the voice of the Lord our God, to walk in His laws which He set before us. *Daniel* 9. 9-10.

Seek ye the Lord while He may be found, call ye upon Him while He is near: let the wicked forsake his way and the unrighteous man his thoughts; and let him return unto the Lord, and He will have mercy upon him; and to our God, for He will abundantly pardon. *Isaiah* 55. 6-7.

The Minister, still facing the people, shall say the Exhortation as followeth. However, from time to time, at the discretion of the Minister (it not being a Sunday in Christmastide, Eastertide, or Whitsuntide) the second Exhortation may be read instead.

DEARLY beloved brethren, the Scripture moveth us in sundry places to acknowledge and confess our manifold sins and wickedness; and that we should not dissemble nor cloak them before the face of Almighty God our heavenly Father; but confess them with an humble, lowly, penitent, and obedient heart; to the end that we may obtain forgiveness of the same, by His infinite goodness and mercy. And although we ought, at all times, humbly to acknowledge our sins before God; yet ought we chiefly so to do, when we assemble and meet together to render thanks for the great benefits that we have received at His hands, to set forth His most worthy praise, to hear His most holy Word, and to ask those things which are requisite and necessary, as well for the body as the soul. Wherefore I pray and beseech you, as many as are here present, to accompany me with a pure heart, and humble voice, unto the throne of the heavenly grace, saying after me:

Or this.

DEARLY beloved brethren, at this morning hour, we are come together into the presence of Almighty God our heavenly Father; and, as beginneth this day which He hath made, to make unto Him confession of all our sins, and to ask His pardon; to hear His holy Word; to offer, through our Lord Jesus Christ, our glad service of worship, praise, and thanksgiving; to pray, as well for others as for ourselves, that we may know more truly the greatness of God's love for us, and shew forth in our lives the fruits of His grace; and to ask on behalf of all men all such things as their well-being and eternal salvation may require. Wherefore, my brethren, let us now confess our sins unto Almighty God, and with pure hearts, and humble voices, come before the throne of the heavenly grace, saying after me:

A general Confession to be said of the whole Congregation after the Minister,
all meekly and devoutly kneeling upon their knees.

ALMIGHTY and most merciful Father, We have erred, and strayed from Thy ways like lost sheep, We have followed too much the devices and desires of our own hearts, We have offended against Thy holy laws, We have left undone those things which we ought to have done, And we have done those things which we ought not to have done, And there is no health in us: But thou, O Lord, have mercy upon us, miserable offenders; Spare Thou them, O God, which confess their faults, Restore

Thou them that are penitent, According to Thy promises declared unto mankind in Christ Jesu our Lord: And grant, O most merciful Father, for His sake, That we may hereafter live a godly, righteous, and sober life, To the glory of Thy holy Name. Amen.

Then shall this Prayer for Absolution be said by the Minister alone, still kneeling.
ALMIGHTY God, Father of our Lord Jesus Christ, Who desirest not the death of a sinner, but rather that he may turn from his wickedness and live; and pardonest and absolvest all them that truly repent, and unfeignedly believe Thy holy Gospel: We beseech Thee to grant us true repentance, and Thy Holy Spirit; that those things may please Thee which we do at this present, and that the rest of our life hereafter may be pure and holy; so that at the last we may come to Thine eternal joy; through Jesus Christ our Lord.
The people shall answer here, and at the end of all common prayers,
Amen.

If the Bishop or a Priest be present, he shall stand up;
and turning himself to the people, he shall pronounce this Absolution following.
MAY the Almighty and most merciful Lord God grant unto you pardon, ✠ absolution, and remission of all your sins; give you time for amendment of life, and the grace and comfort of His Holy Spirit; deliver you from all evil; preserve and strengthen you in all goodness; and bring you finally to everlasting life; through Jesus Christ our Lord. *Amen.*

Then shall the Minister, together with the people, say or sing the Lord's Prayer.
OUR Father, which art in heaven, hallowed be Thy Name. Thy kingdom come. Thy will be done in earth, as it is in heaven. Give us this day our daily bread. And forgive us our trespasses, As we forgive them that trespass against us. And lead us not into temptation, But deliver us from evil. For Thine is the kingdom, the power, and the glory, For ever and ever. Amen.

Then likewise shall the Minister shall or sing,
O LORD, open Thou our lips.
Answer. And our mouth shall show forth Thy praise.
Priest. O God, ✠ make speed to save us.
Answer. O Lord, make haste to help us.

Here all standing up, the Priest shall say,
GLORY be to the Father, and to the Son, and to the Holy Ghost;
Answer. As it was in the beginning, is now, and ever shall be, world without end. Amen.
Priest. Praise ye the Lord.
Answer. The Lord's Name be praised.

THE MINISTRATION OF THE WORD.

Then shall be said or sung this Psalm following: Except it be on Christmas-day, Easter-Day, Ascension-Day, and Whitsunday, and their Octaves, for which days Proper Anthems are appointed to be used; and on the nineteenth day of every month it is not to be read here, but in the ordinary course of the Psalms. And at the appointed times, the Invitatories set forth for use may be said or sung before the said Psalm and after the Gloria Patri thereafter following, except it be during Passiontide when Gloria Patri is not used.

DIVINE OFFICE

VENITE, EXULTEMUS DOMINO. *Psalm 95.*

O COME, let us sing unto the Lord; / let us heartily rejoice in the strength of our salvation. Let us come before His presence with thanksgiving, / and shew ourselves glad in Him with psalms. For the Lord is a great God, / and a great King above all gods. In His hand are all the corners of the earth, / and the strength of the hills is His also. The sea is His, and He made it; / and His hands prepared the dry land. O come, let us worship, and fall down, / and kneel before the Lord our Maker. For He is the Lord our God, / and we are the people of His pasture, and the sheep of His hand. To-day if ye will hear His voice: / Harden not your hearts as in the provocation, and as in the day of temptation in the wilderness; When your fathers tempted me, / proved me, and saw my works. Forty years long was I grieved with this generation, and said, / It is a people that do err in their hearts, for they have not known my ways. Unto whom I sware in my wrath / that they should not enter into my rest.

GLORY be to the Father, and to the Son / and to the Holy Ghost:
As it was in the beginning, is now, and ever shall be, / world without end. Amen.

Then shall follow the Psalms in order as they are appointed. And at the end of every Psalm throughout the Year, and likewise at the end of every Canticle, shall be repeated,
GLORY be to the Father, and to the Son, / and to the Holy Ghost;
Answer. As it was in the beginning, is now, and ever shall be, / world without end. Amen.

And here let it be noted, that during the seasons of Lent and Advent the appointed Prose Anthem shall be sung or said in the place of Venite Exultemus Domino *if they be not used as the Anthem after the Office.*

Then shall be read distinctly and clearly the First Lesson, taken out of the Old Testament, as is appointed in the Calendar, except there be proper Lessons assigned for that day: He that readeth so standing and turning himself, as he may best be heard of all such as are present.

And before every Lesson the Minister shall say, The Lesson is taken from *such* a Chapter of *such* a Book, beginning at *such* a Verse: *And after every Lesson shall be said,* Here endeth the *First, or* the *Second* Lesson: This is the Word of the Lord; *to which the people shall respond, saying,* Thanks be to God.

And after the First Lesson is ended, Te Deum Laudamus *shall be sung or said as hereafter followeth; but from Septuagesima Sunday until Passion Sunday, and on Rogation Sunday and the three Rogation-Days, on Whitsunday and throughout Whitsuntide, and at Harvest Thanksgiving, the Canticle* Benedicite Omnia Opera *may be used in the place of* Te Deum Laudamus.

TE DEUM LAUDAMUS.

WE praise Thee, O God, we acknowledge Thee to be the Lord. / All the earth doth worship Thee, the Father everlasting. To Thee all angels cry aloud, the heavens and all the powers therein. / To Thee Cherubim and Seraphim continually do cry, / Holy, Holy, Holy, Lord God of hosts; / Heaven and earth are full of the Majesty of Thy glory. / The glorious company of the Apostles praise Thee. / The goodly fellowship of the Prophets praise Thee. / The noble army of Martyrs praise Thee. / The holy Church throughout all the world doth acknowledge Thee: / The Father of an infinite Majesty; / Thine honourable, true, and only Son; / Also the Holy Ghost the Comforter.

Thou art the King of glory, O Christ. / Thou art the everlasting Son of the Father. / When Thou tookest upon Thee to deliver man, Thou didst not abhor the Virgin's womb. / When Thou hadst overcome the sharpness of death, Thou didst open the kingdom of heaven to all believers. / Thou sittest at the right hand of God, in the glory of the Father. / We believe that Thou shalt come to be our Judge. / We therefore pray Thee, help Thy servants, whom Thou hast redeemed with Thy precious Blood. / Make them to be numbered with Thy Saints in glory everlasting.

O Lord, save Thy people, and bless Thine heritage. / Govern them, and lift them up forever. / Day by day we magnify Thee; And we worship Thy Name ever world without end. / Vouchsafe, O Lord, to keep us this day without sin. / O Lord, have mercy upon us, have mercy upon us. / O Lord, let Thy mercy lighten upon us, as our trust is in Thee. / O Lord, in Thee have I trusted, let me never be confounded. / Amen.

Or this,

BENEDICITE, OMNIA OPERA. *The Song of the Three Children.*

O ALL ye works of the Lord, bless ye the Lord; O ye Angels of the Lord, bless ye the Lord; O ye Heavens, bless ye the Lord: / Praise Him and magnify Him forever. O ye Waters that be above the Firmament, bless ye the Lord; O all ye powers of the Lord, bless ye the Lord; O ye Sun and Moon, bless ye the Lord: / Praise Him and magnify Him forever. O ye Stars of Heaven, bless ye the Lord; O ye Showers and Dew, bless ye the Lord; O ye Winds of God, bless ye the Lord: / Praise Him and magnify Him forever. O ye Fire and Heat, bless ye the Lord; O ye Winter and Summer, bless ye the Lord; O ye Dews and Frosts, bless ye the Lord: / Praise Him and magnify Him forever. O ye Frost and Cold, bless ye the Lord; O ye Ice and Snow, bless ye the Lord; O ye Nights and Days, bless ye the Lord: / Praise Him and magnify Him forever. O ye Light and Darkness, bless ye the Lord; O ye Lightnings and Cloud, bless ye the Lord; O let the earth bless the Lord: / Praise Him and magnify Him forever. O ye Mountains and Hills, bless ye the Lord; O all ye Green things upon the Earth, bless ye the Lord; O ye Wells, bless ye the Lord: / Praise Him and magnify Him forever. O ye Seas and Floods, bless ye the Lord; O ye Whales, and all that move in the Waters, bless ye the Lord; O all ye Fowls of the Air, bless ye the Lord: / Praise Him and magnify Him forever. O all ye Beasts and Cattle, bless ye the Lord: / Praise Him and magnify Him forever. O ye Children of Men, bless ye the Lord; O let Israel bless the Lord; O ye Priests of the Lord, bless ye the Lord: / Praise Him and magnify Him forever. O ye Servants of the Lord, bless ye the Lord; O ye Spirits and Souls of the Righteous, bless ye the Lord; O ye holy and humble Men of heart, bless ye the Lord: / Praise Him and magnify Him forever. O Ananias, Azarias, and Misael, bless ye the Lord: / Praise Him and Magnify Him forever.

GLORY be to the Father, and to the Son, / and to the Holy Ghost;
As it was in the beginning, is now, and ever shall be, / world without end. Amen.

Then shall be read in like manner the Second Lesson, taken out of the New Testament. And after that Jubilate Deo *may be sung or said; but from Advent Sunday to Christmas-Day, and from the Epiphany until Septuagesima, and upon the Feasts of Saint John the Baptist, the Canticle* Benedictus *may be used in the place of* Jubilate Deo. *The* Beatitudes *may also be said or sung throughout Lent in the place of* Jubilate Deo *and* Benedictus.

JUBILATE DEO. *Psalm* 100.

O BE joyful in the Lord, all ye lands: / serve the Lord with gladness, and come before His presence with a song. Be ye sure that the Lord, He is God; / it is He that hath made us, and not we ourselves; we are His people, and the sheep of His pasture. O go your way into His gates with thanksgiving, and into His courts with praise; / be thankful unto Him, and speak good of His Name. For the Lord is gracious, His mercy is everlasting; / and His truth endureth from generation to generation.

GLORY be to the Father, and to the Son, / and to the Holy Ghost;
As it was in the beginning, is now, and ever shall be, / world without end. Amen.

Or this,

BENEDICTUS. *Saint Luke* 1. 68.

BLESSED be the Lord God of Israel; / for He hath visited and redeemed His people; / and hath raised up a mighty salvation for us, / in the house of His servant David; / As He spake by the mouth of His holy Prophets, / which have been since the world began; / that we should be saved from our enemies, / and from the hands of all that hate us; / To perform the mercy promised to our forefathers, / and to remember His holy covenant; / to perform the oath which He sware to our forefather Abraham, / that He would give us; / That we being delivered out of the hands of our enemies / might serve Him without fear, / in holiness and righteousness before Him, / all the days of our life.

GLORY be to the Father, and to the Son, / and to the Holy Ghost;
As it was in the beginning, is now, and ever shall be, / world without end. Amen.

Or else this,

THE BEATITUDES. *Saint Matthew* 5. 3-10.

BLESSED are the poor in spirit, / for theirs is the kingdom of heaven. Blessed are they that mourn, / for they shall be comforted. Blessed are the meek, / for they shall inherit the earth. Blessed are they that do hunger and thirst after righteousness, / for they shall be filled. Blessed are the merciful, / for they shall obtain mercy. Blessed are the pure in heart, / for they shall see God. Blessed are the peace-makers, / for they shall be called the children of God. Blessed are they which are persecuted for righteousness sake, / for theirs is the kingdom of heaven. Blessed are ye, when men shall revile you, and persecute you, / and shall say all manner of evil against you falsely, for my sake. Rejoice, and be exceeding glad, for great is your reward in heaven; / for so persecuted they the prophets which were before you.

GLORY be to the Father, and to the Son, / and to the Holy Ghost;
As it was in the beginning, is now, and ever shall be, / world without end. Amen.

THE PRAYERS.

Then shall be sung or said the Apostle's Creed, by the Minister and the people standing:
Except only upon such days as the Creed of Saint Athanasius is appointed to be used in its place.

THE APOSTLES' CREED.

I BELIEVE in God the Father Almighty, Maker of heaven and earth: And in (*Here everyone shall reverently bow his head.*) **Jesus Christ** His only Son our Lord, Who was conceived by the Holy Ghost, born of the Virgin Mary, suffered under Pontius Pilate, was crucified, dead, and buried; He descended into hell; the third day He rose again from the dead; He ascended into heaven, and sitteth on the right hand of God the Father Almighty; from thence He shall come to judge the quick and the dead. I believe in the Holy Ghost; The holy Catholic Church; The Communion of Saints; The Forgiveness of sins; ✠ The Resurrection of the body, and the Life everlasting. Amen.

And here, let it be noted that whensoever the Creed shall be said or sung at any time during Divine Service, the Minister and the people shall all turn to face the Lord's Table.

And after that these Prayers following shall be said or sung, all devoutly kneeling:
the Priest first pronouncing with a loud voice,

DIVINE OFFICE

THE Lord be with you.
Answer. And with thy spirit.

Minister. Let us pray.

Lord, have mercy upon us.
Christ, have mercy upon us.
Lord, have mercy upon us.

Then the Priest, Clerks, and people shall say or sing the Lord's Prayer.

OUR Father, which art in heaven, hallowed be Thy Name. Thy kingdom come. Thy will be done in earth, as it is in heaven. Give us this day our daily bread. And forgive us our trespasses, as we forgive them that trespass against us. And lead us not into temptation, but deliver us from evil. Amen.

And standing up, the Priest shall say or sing,

O LORD, shew Thy mercy upon us;
   Answer. And grant us Thy salvation.
Priest. O Lord, save the Queen;
   Answer. And mercifully hear us when we call upon Thee.
Priest. Endue Thy Ministers with righteousness;
   Answer. And make Thy chosen people joyful.
Priest. O Lord, save Thy people;
   Answer. And bless Thine inheritance.
Priest. Give peace in our time, O Lord;
   Answer. And evermore mightily defend us.
Priest. O God, make clean our hearts within us;
   Answer. And take not Thy Holy Spirit from us.

And if it should be that the Minister be not a Priest, he shall not say the Mutual Salutation, nor shall he stand for the Lesser Litany and the Collects, but shall remain kneeling with the people.

Then shall follow three Collects: The first of the day, which shall be the same that is appointed at the Eucharist; The second for Peace; The third for Grace to live well. And the two last Collects shall never alter, but daily be said or sung at Morning Prayer throughout all the Year, as followeth, the people all still kneeling as before.

The second Collect, for Peace.

O GOD, Who art the Author of peace and Lover of concord, in knowledge of Whom standeth our eternal life, Whose service is perfect freedom: Defend us Thy humble servants in all assaults of our enemies; that we, surely trusting in Thy defence, may not fear the power of any adversaries, through the might of Jesus Christ our Lord. *Amen.*

The third Collect, for Grace.

O LORD, our heavenly Father, Almighty and everlasting God, Who hast safely brought us to the beginning of this day: Defend us in the same with Thy mighty power; and grant that this day we fall into no sin, neither run into any kind of danger; but that all our doings may be ordered by Thy governance, to do always that is righteous in Thy sight; through Jesus Christ our Lord. *Amen.*

In Quires and Places where they sing, the Anthem shall follow here.

DIVINE OFFICE

*Or else, when necessity shall so require, and in Parish Churches or Chapels,
a hymn may be sung here before the Prayers and Intercessions are read.*

*Then these Prayers in order following shall be read here, except when
the Great Litany is appointed to be sung or said.*

A Prayer for the Queen's Majesty.

O LORD our heavenly Father, high and mighty, King of kings, Lord of lords, the only Ruler of princes, Who dost from Thy throne behold all the dwellers upon earth: Most heartily we beseech Thee with Thy favour to behold our most gracious Sovereign Lady, Queen *ELIZABETH*; and so replenish her with the grace of Thy Holy Spirit, that she may alway incline to Thy will, and walk in Thy way: Endue her plenteously with heavenly gifts; grant her in health and wealth long to live; strengthen her that she may vanquish and overcome all her enemies, and finally after this life she may attain everlasting joy and felicity; through Jesus Christ our Lord. *Amen.*

A Prayer for the Royal Family.

ALMIGHTY God, the Fountain of all goodness, we humbly beseech Thee to bless *Philip* Duke of Edinburgh, *Charles* Prince of Wales, *William* Duke of Cambridge, Prince *George* of Cambridge, and all the Royal Family: Endue them with Thy Holy Spirit; enrich them with Thy heavenly grace; prosper them with all happiness; and bring them to Thine everlasting kingdom; through Jesus Christ our Lord. *Amen.*

A Prayer for all who are set in Authority.

LORD of all power and mercy, we beseech Thee to assist with Thy favour the Governor-General of this Dominion, the Lieutenant-Governors of the Provinces, and all those in this land who are set in authority under our Queen. Cause them, we pray Thee, always to walk before Thee in truth and righteousness; and to use their office and power to Thy glory, and the good of all Thy people; through Jesus Christ our Lord. *Amen.*

Or this,

O LORD God Almighty, Who rulest the nations of the earth, we humbly beseech Thee with Thy favour to behold our Sovereign Lady Queen *ELIZABETH*, that in all things she may be led by Thy guidance and protected by Thy power. We pray Thee also to bless *Philip* Duke of Edinburgh, *Charles* Prince of Wales, *William* Duke of Cambridge, Prince *George* of Cambridge, and all the Royal Family. Endue with wisdom the Governor-General, and the Prime Minister of this Dominion; the Lieutenant-Governors, Commissioners, and Premiers of the Provinces and Territories; and all who are set in authority over us under our Queen; that all things may be so ordered and settled by their endeavours upon the best and surest Christian foundations, that peace and happiness, truth and justice, religion and piety, may be established among us for all generations; through Jesus Christ our Lord. *Amen.*

A Prayer for the Clergy and people.

ALMIGHTY and everlasting God, from Whom cometh every good and perfect gift: Send down upon our Bishops and Clergy, and all Congregations committed to their charge, the healthful Spirit of Thy grace; and that they may truly please Thee, pour upon them the continual dew of Thy blessing. Grant this, O Lord, for the honour of our Advocate and Mediator, Jesus Christ. *Amen.*

And on all Sundays other than those which fall in Advent or Lent, or at any other time when the Great Litany shall be sung or said immediately before the Holy Eucharist, and on Wednesdays, and Fridays, instead of the foregoing Prayers, the Great Litany aforesaid shall be sung or said, and at any other such times as it shall be commanded by the Ordinary.

And when the Prayer following shall be used, the Minister may say, Let us pray for..., *and then shall be announced by the Minister the particular intentions for which the Congregation shall be bidden to pray. And likewise before the Prayer of General Thanksgiving, the Minister may say,* Let us give thanks for..., *and appropriate thanks and praise shall be offered up to Almighty God.*

The Minister shall say,
Let us pray.

A Prayer for all Conditions of men.

O GOD, the Creator and Preserver of all mankind, we humbly beseech Thee for all sorts and conditions of men; that Thou wouldest be pleased to make Thy ways known unto them, Thy saving health unto all nations. More especially we pray for the good estate of the Catholic Church; that it may be so guided and governed by Thy good Spirit, that all who profess and call themselves Christians may be led into the way of truth, and hold the Faith in unity of spirit, in the bond of peace, and in righteousness of life. Finally, we commend to Thy fatherly goodness all those, who are any ways afflicted, or distressed, in mind, body, or estate, *especially those for whom our prayers are desired;* that it may please Thee to comfort and relieve them, according to their several necessities, giving them patience under their sufferings, and a happy issue out of all their afflictions. And this we beg for Jesus Christ His sake. *Amen.*

Then shall be said this General Thanksgiving following either by the Minister alone, or by the Minister and people together.

A General Thanksgiving.

ALMIGHTY God, Father of all mercies, we Thine unworthy servants do give Thee most humble and hearty thanks for all Thy goodness and loving kindness to us, and to all men; *particularly to those who desire now to offer up their praises and thanksgivings unto Thee, O Lord.* We bless Thee for our creation, preservation, and all the blessings of this life; but above all, for Thine inestimable love in the redemption of the world by our Lord Jesus Christ; for the means of grace, and for the hope of glory. And, we beseech Thee, give us that due sense of all Thy mercies, that our hearts may be unfeignedly thankful, and that we shew forth Thy praise, not only with our lips, but in our lives; by giving up ourselves to Thy service, and by walking before Thee in holiness and righteousness all our days; through Jesus Christ our Lord, to Whom with Thee and the Holy Ghost be all honour and glory, world without end. *Amen.*

Then shall be said the Prayer of Saint Chrysostom and the Grace.

A Prayer of Saint Chrysostom.

ALMIGHTY God, Who hast given us grace at this time with one accord to make our common supplications unto Thee; and dost promise that when two or three are gathered together in Thy Name, Thou wilt grant their requests: Fulfill now, O Lord, the desires and petitions of Thy servants, as may be most expedient for them; granting us in this world knowledge of Thy truth, and in the world to come, life everlasting. *Amen.*

II *Corinthians* xiii. 14.

✠ T㏂ grace of our Lord Jesus Christ, and the love of God, and the fellowship of the Holy Ghost, be with us all evermore. *Amen.*

And here a Sermon may be preached or a Homily read.

And whensoever the Holy Eucharist be not celebrated following Morning Prayer, the Sermon or Homily ended, the Tithes, Offerings, and other Oblations and Gifts of the Faithful may be received, and presented before the Lord, in the appointed manner.

The Offertory ended, the Minister, standing before the Lord's Table, shall say one or more of the Collects, Prayers, or Thanksgivings set forth hereafter to be used, as he shall deem appropriate in his discretion, before the Benediction be said.

And if the Bishop or a Priest be present, he shall say,

N㎝ unto God's gracious mercy and protection we commit you. ✠ The Lord bless you, and keep you. The Lord make His face to shine upon you, and be gracious unto you. The Lord lift up His countenance upon you, and give you peace, both now and evermore. *Amen.*

Otherwise, the Minister shall say this Benediction following.

T㏊ God of peace, that brought again from the dead our Lord Jesus, that great Shepherd of the sheep, through the Blood of the everlasting Covenant: Make you perfect in every good work to do His will, working in you that which is well-pleasing in His sight, through Jesus Christ; to Whom be glory for ever and ever. *Amen.*

Here endeth the O㎜㏈ of M㎝㎜㏌g PㄖⱯㄧㄹ throughout the YㄷⱯㄖ.

T㏊ Cㄖㄷㄷㄉ of SⱯ㏌㏔ A㏔㏊Ɐ㎘Ɪ㎩Ɪ

Upon these Feasts: Christmas-Day, the Epiphany-Day, Easter-Day, Ascension-Day, Whitsunday, and Trinity Sunday, shall be said or sung at Morning Prayer, instead of the Apostles' Creed, and upon Trinity Sunday at the Holy Eucharist instead of the Nicene Creed, this Confession of our Christian Faith, commonly called the Creed of Saint Athanasius, by the Minister and people standing.

Q㎁㏌㎝㎁㎜㎖㎁㏝ V㎁㎐㏔.

W㏊㎝㎙Ⱡⱬ would be saved needeth before all things to hold fast the Catholic Faith. Which Faith except a man keep whole and undefiled, without doubt, he will perish eternally.

Now the Catholic Faith is this, that we worship One God in Trinity, and the Trinity in Unity; neither confusing the Persons, nor dividing the Substance. For there is one Person of the Father, another of the Son, another of the Holy Ghost; but the Godhead of the Father, and of the Son, and of the Holy Ghost is all One, the Glory equal, the Majesty co-eternal. Such as the Father is, such is the Son, and such is the Holy Ghost. The Father uncreated, the Son uncreated, the Holy Ghost uncreated; The Father infinite, the Son infinite, the Holy Ghost infinite; The Father eternal, the Son eternal, the Holy Ghost eternal. And yet there are not three eternals, but One Eternal; As also there are not three uncreated, nor three infinites, but One Infinite, and One Uncreated. So likewise the Father is almighty, the Son almighty, the Holy Ghost almighty; And yet there are not three almighties, but One Almighty. So the Father is God, the Son God, the Holy Ghost God; and yet there are not three Gods, but One God. So the Father is Lord, the Son Lord, the Holy Ghost Lord; And yet there are not three Lords, but One Lord. For like as we are compelled by the Christian verity to confess each Person by Himself to be both God and Lord; So are we forbidden by the Catholic Religion to speak of three Gods or three Lords. The Father is made of none, nor created, nor begotten. The Son is of the Father alone; not made, nor created, but begotten. The Holy Ghost is of the Father and the Son; not made, nor created, nor begotten, but proceeding. There is therefore one Father, not three Fathers; one Son, not three Sons; one Holy Ghost, not three Holy Ghosts. And in this Trinity there is no before or after, no greater or less; But all three Persons are co-eternal together and co-equal. So that in all ways, as is aforesaid, both the Trinity is to be worshipped in Unity, and the Unity in Trinity. He therefore that would be saved, let him thus think of the Trinity.

Furthermore, it is necessary to eternal salvation, that he also believe faithfully the Incarnation of our Lord JESUS CHRIST. Now the right faith is that we believe and confess that our Lord JESUS CHRIST, the Son of God, is both God and Man. He is God, of the substance of the Father, begotten before the worlds; and He is Man, of the substance of His Mother, born in the world; Perfect God, perfect Man, of reasoning soul and human flesh subsisting; Equal to the Father as touching His Godhead; less than the Father as touching His Manhood. Who although He be God and Man, yet He is not two, but is one Christ; One however, not by conversion of Godhead into flesh, but by taking Manhood into God; One altogether; not by confusion of substance, but by unity of Person. For as reasoning soul and flesh is one man, so God and Man is one Christ; Who suffered for our salvation, descended into hell, rose again from the dead; Ascended into heaven, sat down at the right hand of the Father; from whence He shall come to judge the quick and the dead. At Whose coming all men must rise again with their bodies, and shall give account for their own deeds. And they that have done good will go into life eternal, and they that have done evil into eternal fire.

This is the Catholic Faith, which except a man do faithfully and steadfastly believe, he cannot be saved.

GLORY be to the Father, and to the Son, and to the Holy Ghost;
As it was in the beginning, is now, and ever shall be, world without end. Amen.

Here endeth the CREED OF SAINT ATHANASIUS.

THE GREAT LITANY

O GOD the Father of heaven: have mercy upon us.
O God the Father of heaven: have mercy upon us.

O God the Son, Redeemer of the world: have mercy upon us.
O God the Son, Redeemer of the world: have mercy upon us.

O God the Holy Ghost, proceeding from the Father and the Son: have mercy upon us.
O God the Holy Ghost, proceeding from the Father and the Son: have mercy upon us.

O holy, blessed, and glorious Trinity, three Persons and one God: have mercy upon us.
O holy, blessed, and glorious Trinity, three Persons and one God: have mercy upon us.

REMEMBER not, Lord, our offences, nor the offences of our forefathers; neither take Thou vengeance of our sins: Spare us, good Lord, spare Thy people, whom Thou hast redeemed with Thy most precious Blood, and be not angry with us for ever.
Spare us, good Lord.

FROM all evil and mischief; from sin; from the crafts and assaults of the devil; from Thy wrath, and from everlasting condemnation,
Good Lord, deliver us.

From all blindness of heart; from pride, vain-glory, and hypocrisy; from envy, hatred, and malice, and all uncharitableness,
Good Lord, deliver us.

From fornication and adultery, and all other deadly sin; from all uncleanness in thought, word, and deed; and from all the deceits of the world, the flesh, and the devil,
Good Lord, deliver us.

From lightning and tempest; from earthquake, fire, and flood; from plague, pestilence, and famine; from battle and murder; and from sudden death,
Good Lord, deliver us.

From all sedition, conspiracy, and rebellion; from all false doctrine, heresy, and schism; from hardness of heart, and contempt of Thy Word and Commandment,
Good Lord, deliver us.

BY the mystery of Thy holy Incarnation; by Thy blessed Nativity and Circumcision; by Thy Baptism, Fasting, and Temptation,
Good Lord, deliver us.

By Thine Agony and bloody Sweat; by Thy saving Cross and Passion; by Thy precious Death and Burial,
Good Lord, deliver us.

By Thy glorious Resurrection and Ascension; by Thy sending of the Holy Ghost; by Thine everlasting Priesthood; and by Thy coming again in glory,
Good Lord, deliver us.

In all time of our tribulation; in all time of our wealth; in the hour of death, and in the day of judgement,
Good Lord, deliver us.

WE sinners do beseech Thee to hear us, O Lord God; and that it may please Thee to rule and govern Thy holy Church universal in the right way,
We beseech Thee, good Lord.

To lead all nations in the way of righteousness; and so to guide and direct their governors and rulers, that Thy people may enjoy the blessings of freedom and peace,
We beseech Thee, good Lord.

To keep and strengthen in the true worshipping of Thee, in righteousness and holiness of life, and in devotion to her people, Thy chosen Servant *ELIZABETH*, our most gracious Queen and Governor,
We beseech Thee, good Lord.

To rule and govern her heart in Thy faith, fear, and love, that in all her thoughts, words, and works, she may ever seek Thy honour and glory,
We beseech Thee, good Lord.

To be her Defender and Keeper, giving her the victory over all her enemies,
We beseech Thee, good Lord.

To bless and preserve *Philip* Duke of Edinburgh, *Charles* Prince of Wales, *William* Duke of Cambridge, Prince *George* of Cambridge, and all the Royal Family,
We beseech Thee, good Lord.

To bless all the Bishops of Thy Church; to endue them with Thy Holy Spirit; and to fill them with Thy heavenly grace; that they may govern and feed the flock committed to their care, according to Thy will,
We beseech Thee, good Lord.

To pour out Thy Spirit upon all the Clergy; and to illuminate them with true knowledge and understanding of Thy Word, and that both by their preaching and living, they may set it forth, and shew it accordingly,
We beseech Thee, good Lord.

16

To bless all who minister in Thy Name; that each, according to his calling, may execute his office, to Thy honour and glory, and the edifying of Thy people,
We beseech Thee, good Lord.

To send forth labourers into Thy harvest; to prosper their work by Thy Holy Spirit; to make Thy saving health known unto all nations; and to hasten Thy kingdom,
We beseech Thee, good Lord.

To bless, protect, and prosper the people of this Dominion, and of all the Realms and Countries of our Commonwealth; and to endue those who are set in authority under our Queen with grace, wisdom, and understanding,
We beseech Thee, good Lord.

To bless and guide the Judges and Magistrates, giving them grace to execute justice, and to maintain truth,
We beseech Thee, good Lord.

To bless and keep the Queen's forces by sea, and land, and air; to defend them from the craft and power of the enemy; and to shield them in all dangers and adversities,
We beseech Thee, good Lord.

To give to all nations unity, peace, and concord, that Thy people may serve Thee without fear,
We beseech Thee, good Lord.

To bless and keep all Thy people,
We beseech Thee, good Lord.

To give to all Thy people an heart to love and dread Thee, and to seek Thy will; and to follow Thy Word and Commandments,
We beseech Thee, good Lord.

To give to all Thy people increase of grace to hear meekly Thy Word, and to receive it with pure affection; and to bring forth the fruits of the Spirit,
We beseech Thee, good Lord.

To bring into the way of truth all such as have erred, and are deceived; and save us from all delusion, that we may believe no lies,
We beseech Thee, good Lord.

To strengthen such as do stand; to comfort and help the weak-hearted; to raise up those who fall; and finally to beat down Satan under our feet,
We beseech Thee, good Lord.

To succour, help, and comfort, all that are in danger, necessity, or tribulation,
We beseech Thee, good Lord.

To preserve all that travel; all women labouring of child, all sick persons, and young children; and to shew Thy pity upon all prisoners and captives,
We beseech Thee, good Lord.

To defend, and provide for, all widows and orphans, and all who are desolate and oppressed,
We beseech Thee, good Lord.

To have mercy upon all men,
We beseech Thee, good Lord.

To forgive our enemies, persecutors, and slanderers, and to turn their hearts,
We beseech Thee, good Lord.

To give and preserve to our use the kindly fruits of the earth, so that in due time we may enjoy them,
We beseech Thee, good Lord.

To give us true repentance; to forgive us all our sins, negligences, and ignorances; and to endue us with the grace of Thy Holy Spirit, to amend our lives according to Thy Word,
We beseech Thee, good Lord.

SON of God, we beseech Thee to hear us.
Son of God, we beseech Thee to hear us.

O Lamb of God, that takest away the sins of the world;
Have mercy upon us.

O Lamb of God, that takest away the sins of the world;
Grant us Thy peace.

O Christ, hear us.
O Christ, hear us.

Then shall be said or sung the Collect of the Day.

THE SUPPLICATIONS AND PRAYERS

Minister. Lord, have mercy upon us.
Answer. Christ, have mercy upon us.
Minister. Lord, have mercy upon us.

Minister. O Lord, deal not with us according to our sins;
Answer. Neither reward us according to our iniquities.

Minister. Let us pray.

O GOD, merciful Father, Who despisest not the sighing of a contrite heart, nor the desire of such as be sorrowful: Mercifully assist our prayers that we make before Thee in all our troubles and adversities, whensoever they oppress us; and vouchsafe graciously to hear us, that those evils, which the craft and subtilty of the devil or man worketh against us, be brought to nought; and that by the providence of Thy goodness they may be dispersed; that we Thy servants, being hurt by no persecutions, may evermore give thanks unto Thee in Thy holy Church; through Jesus Christ our Lord. *Amen.*

Minister and people.
O Lord, arise, help us, and deliver us for Thy Name's sake.

Minister.
O GOD, we heard with our ears, and our fathers have declared unto us, the noble works that Thou didst in their days, and in the old time before them.

Minister and people.
O Lord, arise, help us, and deliver us for Thine honour.

Minister. Glory be to the Father, and to the Son, and to the Holy Ghost;
Answer. As it was in the beginning, is now, and ever shall be, world without end. Amen.

Minister. From our enemies defend us, O Christ;
Answer. Graciously look upon our afflictions.
Minister. Pitifully behold the sorrows of our hearts;
Answer. And mercifully forgive the sins of Thy people.
Minister. Favourably with mercy, hear our prayers;
Answer. O Son of David, have mercy upon us.
Minister. Both now and ever vouchsafe to hear us, O Christ;
Answer. Graciously hear us, O Christ; graciously hear us, O Lord Christ.
Minister. O Lord, let Thy mercy be shewn upon us;
Answer. As we do put our trust in Thee.
Minister. O Lord, hear our prayer;
Answer. And let our cry come unto Thee.

Minister. Let us pray.

WE humbly beseech Thee, O Father, mercifully to look upon our infirmities; and for the glory of Thy Name turn from us all those evils that we have most justly deserved; and grant that, in all our troubles, we may put our whole trust and confidence in Thy mercy, and evermore serve Thee in holiness and pureness of living, to Thy honour and glory; through Jesus Christ our Lord. *Amen.*

And here may be sung or said one or two of the Prayers and Thanksgivings
upon several occasions as are appointed to be used.

A General Thanksgiving to be used at the discretion of the Minister.
ALMIGHTY God, Father of all mercies, we Thine unworthy servants do give Thee most humble and hearty thanks for all Thy goodness and loving kindness to us, and to all men; *particularly to those who desire now to offer up their praises and thanksgivings unto Thee, O Lord.* We bless Thee for our creation, preservation, and all the blessings of this life; but above all, for Thine inestimable love in the redemption of the world by our Lord Jesus Christ; for the means of grace, and for the hope of glory. And, we beseech Thee, give us that due sense of all Thy mercies, that our hearts may be unfeignedly thankful, and that we shew forth Thy praise, not only with our lips, but in our lives; by giving up ourselves to Thy service, and by walking before Thee in holiness and righteousness all our days; through Jesus Christ our Lord, to Whom with Thee and the Holy Ghost be all honour and glory, world without end. *Amen.*

A Prayer of Saint Chrysostom
Then shall be said or sung this Prayer of Saint Chrysostom following.

ALMIGHTY God, Who hast given us grace at this time with one accord to make our common supplications unto Thee; and dost promise that, when two or three are gathered together in Thy Name, Thou wilt grant their requests: Fulfill now, O Lord, the desires and petitions of Thy servants, as may be most expedient for them; granting us in this world knowledge of Thy truth, and in the world to come life everlasting. *Amen.*

II *Corinthians xiii.*

✠ THE grace of our Lord Jesus Christ, and the love of God, and the fellowship of the Holy Ghost, be with us all evermore. *Amen.*

Here endeth the GREAT LITANY.

PRAYERS AT MID-DAY

When the Prayers at Mid-day are said openly in the Church, it is fitting that the Church bell should be rung according to custom, thrice at each Sentence of holy Scripture that precedeth the Collect following.

✠ IN the Name of the Father, and of the Son,
and of the Holy Ghost. Amen.

OUR Father, which art in heaven, hallowed be Thy Name. Thy kingdom come. Thy will be done, in earth as it is in heaven. Give us this day our daily bread. And forgive us our trespasses, As we forgive them that trespass against us. And lead us not into temptation, But deliver us from evil. For Thine is the kingdom, the power, and the glory, For ever and ever. Amen.

And I, if I be lifted up from the earth,
will draw all men unto me. *Saint John* 12. 32.

BLESSED Saviour, Who at this hour didst hang upon the Cross, stretching out Thy loving arms: Grant that all mankind may look unto Thee and be saved; Who livest and reignest with the Father and the Holy Ghost, ever one God, world without end. *Amen.*

At mid-day, O king, I saw in the way a light from heaven,
above the brightness of the sun. *Acts* 26. 13.

ALMIGHTY Saviour, Who at mid-day didst call Thy servant Saint Paul to be an Apostle to the Gentiles: We beseech Thee to illuminate the world with the radiance of Thy glory, that all nations may come and worship Thee, Who with the Father and the Holy Ghost art the only God, world without end. *Amen.*

Peter went up upon the house-top to pray,
about the sixth hour. *Acts* 10. 9.

O FATHER of all mercies, Who had respect unto the faith of our forefather Abraham in the offering of his beloved son Isaac, and did Thyself provide instead thereof the sacrificial ram for the burnt offering; and Who hast in like manner provided for the redemption of all mankind by the sacrifice of Thine own beloved Son Jesus Christ: Forgive, we pray Thee, our unbelief; and so enlarge our hearts, and enkindle our zeal, that we may fervently desire the salvation of souls, and with more ready diligence labour to make known the Gospel of Thy Son unto all men; for His sake, even the same our Saviour Jesus Christ. *Amen.*

GLORY be to the Father, and to the Son, and to the Holy Ghost;
As it was in the beginning, is now, and ever shall be, world without end. Amen.

*Additional Prayers and Thanksgivings set forth in this Book
may be used at the discretion of the Minister.*

THE ORDER FOR
EVENING PRAYER
DAILY THROUGHOUT THE YEAR.

The daily Office of Evening Prayer, commonly called Evensong, shall be said or sung in the accustomed place of the Church, Chapel, or Chancel; except it shall be otherwise determined by the Ordinary of the Place. And at the beginning of Evening Prayer, the Minister shall stand in the place of the Church, Chapel, or Chancel appointed for the saying or singing of the Divine Office; and, turning himself to the people, he shall call them to worship, reading in a loud voice some one or more of these Sentences of the holy Scriptures following, the first according to the Season, and then those of Worship and Penitence that follow thereafter, as he shall determine in his discretion.

THE CALL TO WORSHIP AND PREPARATION.

Advent. Repent ye; for the kingdom of heaven is at hand. *Saint Matthew* 3. 2.

Christmastide. Behold, I bring you good tidings of great joy which shall be to all people. For unto you is born this day in the city of David a Saviour, which is Christ the Lord. *Saint Luke* 2. 10-11.

Epiphanytide. The earth shall be filled with the knowledge of the glory of the Lord, as the waters cover the sea. *Habakkuk* 2. 14.

Lent. The sacrifices of God are a broken spirit: a broken and contrite heart, O God, Thou wilt not despise. *Psalm* 51. 17.

Rend your heart, and not your garments, and turn unto the Lord your God; for He is gracious and merciful, slow to anger, and of great kindness, and repenteth Him of the evil. *Joel* 2. 13.

Passiontide. God commendeth His love toward us, in that, while we were yet sinners, Christ died for us. *Romans* 5. 8.

Palm Sunday. Hosanna to the Son of David: Blessed is He that cometh in the Name of the Lord; Hosanna in the highest. *Saint Matthew* 21. 9.

Good Friday. All we like sheep have gone astray; we have turned everyone to his own way; and the Lord hath laid on Him the iniquity of us all. *Isaiah* 53. 6.

Easter-Even. For Christ also hath once suffered for sins, the just for the unjust, that He might bring us to God. I *Saint Peter* 3. 18.

Eastertide. The Lord is risen indeed. *Saint Luke* 24. 34.

Thanks be to God, which giveth us the victory through our Lord Jesus Christ. I *Corinthians* 15. 57.

Rogationtide. The Lord is nigh unto all them that call upon Him, to all that call upon Him in truth. *Psalm* 145. 18.

Ascensiontide. Seeing then that we have a great high Priest that is passed into the heavens, Jesus the Son of God, let us come boldly unto the throne of grace, that we may obtain mercy, and find grace to help in time of need. *Hebrews* 4. 14,16.

Whitsuntide. It shall come to pass in the last days, saith God, I will pour out of my Spirit upon all flesh. *Acts* 2. 17.

Trinity Sunday. God is love; and he that abideth in love abideth in God, and God in him. I *Saint John* 4. 16.

Saints' Days. Wherefore seeing we also are compassed about with so great a cloud of witnesses, let us lay aside every weight, and the sin which doth so easily beset us, and let us run with patience the race that is set before us, looking unto Jesus the Author and Finisher of our faith. *Hebrews* 12. 1-2.

National Occasions. Blessed is the nation whose God is the Lord, and the people whom He hath chosen for His own inheritance. *Psalm* 33. 12.

Of Evening Prayer. Let my prayer be set forth in Thy sight, O Lord, as the incense, and the lifting up of my hands as an evening sacrifice. *Psalm* 141. 2.

Of Worship. The Lord is in His holy temple: let all the earth keep silence before Him. *Habakkuk* 2. 20.

O worship the Lord in the beauty of holiness, let the whole earth stand in awe of Him. *Psalm* 96. 9.

Thus saith the high and lofty One that inhabiteth eternity, Whose Name is Holy: I dwell in the high and holy place, with him also that is of a contrite and humble spirit. *Isaiah* 57. 15.

I was glad when they said unto me, Let us go into the house of the Lord. *Psalm* 122. 1.

The hour cometh, and now is, when the true worshippers shall worship the Father in spirit and in truth; for the Father seeketh such to worship Him. *Saint John* 4. 23.

Of Penitence. I will arise and go to my Father, and will say unto Him, Father, I have sinned against heaven, and before Thee, and am no more worthy to be called Thy son. *Saint Luke* 15. 18-19.

If we say that we have no sin, we deceive ourselves, and the truth is not in us: but if we confess our sins, He is faithful and just to forgive us our sins, and to cleanse us from all unrighteousness. I *Saint John* 1. 8-9.

The sacrifices of God are a broken spirit; a broken and a contrite heart, O God, Thou wilt not despise. *Psalm* 51. 17.

Enter not into judgement with Thy servant, O Lord; for in Thy sight shall no man living be justified. *Psalm* 143. 2.

O Lord, correct me, but with judgement: not in Thine anger, lest Thou bring me to nothing. *Jeremiah* 10. 24.

When the wicked man turneth away from his wickedness that he hath committed, and doeth that which is lawful and right, he shall save his soul alive. *Ezekiel* 18. 27.

To the Lord our God belong mercies and forgivenesses, though we have rebelled against Him: neither have we obeyed the voice of the Lord our God, to walk in His laws which He set before us. *Daniel* 9. 9-10.

Seek ye the Lord while He may be found, call ye upon Him while He is near: let the wicked forsake his way and the unrighteous man his thoughts; and let him return unto the Lord, and He will have mercy upon him; and to our God, for He will abundantly pardon. *Isaiah* 55. 6-7.

The Minister, still facing the people, shall say the Exhortation as followeth. However, from time to time, at the discretion of the Minister (it not being a Sunday in Christmastide, Eastertide, or Whitsuntide) the second Exhortation may be read instead.

DEARLY beloved brethren, the Scripture moveth us in sundry places to acknowledge and confess our manifold sins and wickedness; and that we should not dissemble nor cloak them before the face of Almighty God our heavenly Father; but confess them with an humble, lowly, penitent, and obedient heart; to the end that we may obtain forgiveness of the same, by His infinite goodness and mercy. And although we ought, at all times, humbly to acknowledge our sins before God; yet ought we chiefly so to do, when we assemble and meet together to render thanks for the great benefits that we have received at His hands, to set forth His most worthy praise, to hear His most holy Word, and to ask those things which are requisite and necessary, as well for the body as the soul. Wherefore I pray and beseech you, as many as are here present, to accompany me with a pure heart, and humble voice, unto the throne of the heavenly grace, saying after me:

Or this.

DEARLY beloved brethren, at this evening hour, we are come together into the presence of Almighty God our heavenly Father; and, as endeth this day which He hath made, to make unto Him confession of all our sins, and to ask His pardon; to hear His holy Word; to offer, through our Lord Jesus Christ, our glad service of worship, praise, and thanksgiving; to pray, as well for others as for ourselves, that we may know more truly the greatness of God's love for us, and shew forth in our lives the fruits of His grace; and to ask on behalf of all men all such things as their well-being and eternal salvation may require. Wherefore, my brethren, let us now confess our sins unto Almighty God, and with pure hearts, and humble voices, come before the throne of the heavenly grace, saying after me:

A general Confession to be said of the whole Congregation after the Minister,
all meekly and devoutly kneeling upon their knees.

ALMIGHTY and most merciful Father, We have erred, and strayed from Thy ways like lost sheep, We have followed too much the devices and desires of our own hearts, We have offended against Thy holy laws, We have left undone those things which we ought to have done, And we have done those things which we ought not to have done, And there is no health in us: But thou, O Lord, have mercy upon us, miserable offenders; Spare Thou them, O God, which confess their faults, Restore Thou them that are penitent, According to Thy promises declared unto mankind in Christ Jesu our Lord: And grant, O most merciful Father, for His sake, That we may hereafter live a godly, righteous, and sober life, To the glory of Thy holy Name. Amen.

Then shall this Prayer for Absolution be said by the Minister alone, still kneeling.

ALMIGHTY God, Father of our Lord Jesus Christ, Who desirest not the death of a sinner, but rather that he may turn from his wickedness and live; and pardonest and absolvest all them that truly repent, and unfeignedly believe Thy holy Gospel: We beseech Thee to grant us true repentance, and Thy Holy Spirit; that those things may please Thee which we do at this present, and that the rest of our life hereafter may be pure and holy; so that at the last we may come to Thine eternal joy; through Jesus Christ our Lord.

The people shall answer here, and at the end of all common prayers,

Amen.

If the Bishop or a Priest be present, he shall stand up;
and turning himself to the people, he shall pronounce this Absolution following.

MAY the Almighty and most merciful Lord God grant unto you pardon, ✠ absolution, and remission of all your sins; give you time for amendment of life, and the grace and comfort of His Holy Spirit; deliver you from all evil; preserve and strengthen you in all goodness; and bring you finally to everlasting life; through Jesus Christ our Lord. *Amen.*

Then shall the Minister, together with the people, say or sing the Lord's Prayer.

OUR Father, which art in heaven, hallowed be Thy Name. Thy kingdom come. Thy will be done in earth, as it is in heaven. Give us this day our daily bread. And forgive us our trespasses, As we forgive them that trespass against us. And lead us not into temptation, But deliver us from evil. For Thine is the kingdom, the power, and the glory, For ever and ever. Amen.

Then likewise shall the Minister shall or sing,

O LORD, open Thou our lips.
Answer. And our mouth shall show forth Thy praise.
Priest. O God, ✠ make speed to save us.
Answer. O Lord, make haste to help us.

Here all standing up, the Priest shall say,

GLORY be to the Father, and to the Son, and to the Holy Ghost;
Answer. As it was in the beginning, is now, and ever shall be, world without end. Amen.
Priest. Praise ye the Lord.
Answer. The Lord's Name be praised.

THE MINISTRATION OF THE WORD.

Then shall be said or sung this Psalm following: Except it be on Christmas-day, Easter-Day, Ascension-Day, and Whitsunday, and their Octaves, for which days Proper Anthems are appointed to be used; and on the twelfth day of every month it is not to be read here, but in the ordinary course of the Psalms. And at the appointed times, the Invitatories set forth for use may be said or sung before the said Psalm and after the Gloria Patri thereafter following, except it be during Passiontide when Gloria Patri is not used. And here let it be noted, that during the seasons of Lent and Advent the appointed Prose Anthem shall be sung or said in the place of Deus Misereatur if they be not used as the Anthem after the Office.

DEUS MISEREATUR. *Psalm 67.*

GOD be merciful unto us, and bless us; / and shew us the light of His countenance, and be merciful unto us. That Thy way may be known upon earth, / Thy saving health among all nations. Let the people praise Thee, O God; / yea, let all the people praise Thee. O let the nations rejoice, and be glad; / for Thou shalt judge the folk righteously, and govern the nations upon earth. Let the people praise Thee, O God; / yea, let all the people praise Thee. Then shall the earth bring forth her increase; / and God, even our own God, shall give us His blessing. God shall bless us, / and all the ends of the world shall fear Him.

GLORY be to the Father, and to the Son, / and to the Holy Ghost;
As it was in the beginning, is now, and ever shall be, / world without end. Amen.

Then shall follow the Psalms in order as they are appointed. And at the end of every Psalm throughout the Year, and likewise at the end of every Canticle, shall be repeated,
GLORY be to the Father, and to the Son, / and to the Holy Ghost;
Answer. As it was in the beginning, is now, and ever shall be, / world without end. Amen.

Then shall be read distinctly and clearly the First Lesson, taken out of the Old Testament, as is appointed in the Kalendar, except there be proper Lessons assigned for that day: He that readeth so standing and turning himself, as he may best be heard of all such as are present.

And before every Lesson the Minister shall say, The Lesson is taken from *such* a Chapter of *such* a Book, beginning at *such* a Verse: *And after every Lesson shall be said,* Here endeth the *First, or* the *Second* Lesson. This is the Word of the Lord; *to which the people shall respond, saying,* Thanks be to God.

And after the First Lesson is ended, the Canticle Magnificat *shall be sung or said as hereafter followeth; but from Septuagesima until the Saturday before Passion Sunday,* Cantate Domino *may be used; and from Passion Sunday until Holy Saturday, the Canticle* Salvator Mundi *may be used in the place of* Magnificat.

MAGNIFICAT. *Saint Luke* 1. 46.

✠ MY soul doth magnify the Lord, / and my spirit hath rejoiced in God my Saviour. For He hath regarded / the lowliness of His handmaiden. For behold, from henceforth, / all generations shall call me blessed. For He that is mighty hath magnified me; / and holy is His Name. And His mercy is on them that fear Him, / throughout all generations. He hath shewed strength with His arm; / he hath scattered the proud in the imagination of their hearts. He hath put down the mighty from their seat, / and hath exalted the humble and meek. He hath filled the hungry with good things; / and the rich He hath sent empty away. He remembering His mercy / hath holpen His servant Israel; as He promised to our forefathers, / Abraham and his seed forever.

GLORY be to the Father, and to the Son, / and to the Holy Ghost;
As it was in the beginning, is now, and ever shall be, / world without end. Amen.

Or this,

CANTATE DOMINO. *Psalm* 98.

O SING unto the Lord a new song, / for He hath done marvellous things. With His own right hand, and with His holy arm, / hath He gotten Himself the victory. The Lord declared His salvation, / His righteousness hath He openly shewed in the sight of the heathen. He hath remembered His mercy and truth towards the house of Israel, / and all the ends of the world have seen the salvation of our God. Shew yourselves joyful unto the Lord all ye lands; / sing, rejoice, and give thanks. Praise the Lord upon the harp; / sing unto the harp with a psalm of thanksgiving. With trumpets also, and with shawms; / O shew yourselves joyful before the Lord the King. Let the sea make a noise, and all that therein is; / the round world, and they that dwell therein. Let the floods clap their hands, and let the hills be joyful together before the Lord: / for He cometh to judge the earth. With righteousness shall He judge the world, / and the people with equity.

GLORY be to the Father, and to the Son, / and to the Holy Ghost;
As it was in the beginning, is now, and ever shall be, / world without end. Amen.

Or else this,

SALVATOR MUNDI.

O SAVIOUR of the world, Who by Thy Cross and precious Death hast redeemed us: / Save us, and help us, we humbly beseech Thee, O Lord. Thou didst hear Thy disciples when ready to perish: / Hear us, and save us, we humbly beseech Thee, O Lord. Let the pitifulness of Thy great mercy loose us from our sins, / we humbly beseech Thee, O Lord. Make it appear that Thou art our Saviour and mighty Deliverer: / O save us that we may praise Thee, we humbly beseech Thee. Draw near according to Thy promise from the throne of Thy glory: / Look down and hear our crying, we humbly beseech Thee, O Lord. Come again, and dwell with us, O Lord Christ Jesus: / Abide with us forever, we humbly beseech Thee. And when Thou shalt appear with power and great glory, / may we be made like unto Thee, in Thy glorious kingdom, we humbly beseech Thee, O Lord.

GLORY be to the Father, and to the Son, / and to the Holy Ghost;

As it was in the beginning, is now, and ever shall be, / world without end. Amen.

Then shall be read in like manner the Second Lesson, taken out of the New Testament. And after that Nunc Dimittis *shall be sung or said; or else during Christmastide, Eastertide, and Whitsuntide, the Canticle* Surge Illuminare *may be sung or said in the place of* Nunc Dimittis.

NUNC DIMITTIS. *Saint Luke* 2. 29.

LORD, now lettest Thou Thy servant depart in peace, / according to Thy Word. For mine eyes have seen Thy salvation, / which Thou hast prepared before the face of all people; to be a Light to lighten the Gentiles, / and to be the glory of Thy people Israel.

GLORY be to the Father, and to the Son, / and to the Holy Ghost;

As it was in the beginning, is now, and ever shall be, world without end. Amen.

Or this,

SURGE, ILLUMINARE. *Isaiah* 60. 1.

ARISE, shine, for thy light is come, / and the glory of the Lord is risen upon thee. / For, behold, the darkness shall cover the earth, / and gross darkness the people. / But the Lord shall arise upon thee, / and His glory shall be seen upon thee. / And the Gentiles shall come to thy light, / and kings to the brightness of thy rising. / Thy gates shall be open continually; / they shall not be shut day nor night. / The sons also of them that afflicted thee / shall come bending unto thee; / And all they that despised thee / shall bow themselves down at the soles of thy feet. / And they shall call thee the City of the Lord, / the Sion of the Holy One of Israel. / Violence shall no more be heard in thy land, / wasting nor destruction within thy borders. / But thou shalt call thy walls Salvation, / and thy gates Praise. / The sun shall be no more thy light by day, / neither for brightness shall the moon give light unto thee; / But the Lord shall be unto thee an everlasting light, / and thy God thy glory.

GLORY be to the Father, and to the Son, / and to the Holy Ghost;

As it was in the beginning, is now, and ever shall be, / world without end. Amen.

THE PRAYERS.

Then shall be sung or said the Apostle's Creed, by the Minister and the people standing:
Except only upon such days as the Creed of Saint Athanasius is appointed to be used in its place.

The Apostles' Creed.

I BELIEVE in God the Father Almighty, Maker of heaven and earth: And in (*Here everyone shall reverently bow his head.*) **Jesus Christ** His only Son our Lord, Who was conceived by the Holy Ghost, born of the Virgin Mary, suffered under Pontius Pilate, was crucified, dead, and buried; He descended into hell; the third day He rose again from the dead; He ascended into heaven, and sitteth on the right hand of God the Father Almighty; from thence He shall come to judge the quick and the dead. I believe in the Holy Ghost; The holy Catholic Church; The Communion of Saints; The Forgiveness of sins; ✠ The Resurrection of the body, and the Life everlasting. Amen.

And here, let it be noted that whensoever the Creed shall be said or sung at any time during Divine Service, the Minister and the people shall all turn to face the Lord's Table.

And after that these Prayers following shall be said or sung, all devoutly kneeling: the Priest first pronouncing with a loud voice,

THE Lord be with you.

Answer. And with thy spirit.

Minister. Let us pray.

Lord, have mercy upon us.

Christ, have mercy upon us.

Lord, have mercy upon us.

Then the Priest, Clerks, and people shall say or sing the Lord's Prayer.

OUR Father, which art in heaven, hallowed be Thy Name. Thy kingdom come. Thy will be done in earth, as it is in heaven. Give us this day our daily bread. And forgive us our trespasses, As we forgive them that trespass against us. And lead us not into temptation, But deliver us from evil. Amen.

And standing up, the Priest shall say or sing,

O LORD, shew Thy mercy upon us;

Answer. And grant us Thy salvation.

Priest. O Lord, save the Queen;

Answer. And mercifully hear us when we call upon Thee.

Priest. Endue Thy Ministers with righteousness;

Answer. And make Thy chosen people joyful.

Priest. O Lord, save Thy people;

Answer. And bless Thine inheritance.

Priest. Give peace in our time, O Lord;

Answer. And evermore mightily defend us.

Priest. O God, make clean our hearts within us;

Answer. And take not Thy Holy Spirit from us.

And if it should be that the Minister be not a Priest, he shall not say the Mutual Salutation, nor shall he stand for the Lesser Litany and the Collects, but shall remain kneeling with the people.

Then shall follow three Collects: The first being the Collect of the Day, which shall be the same that is appointed at the Holy Eucharist; the second for Peace; and the third for Aid against all Perils. And the two last Collects shall never alter, but shall be daily said or sung at Evening Prayer throughout all the Year, as followeth, the people all still kneeling as before.

The Second Collect for Peace.

O GOD, from Whom all holy desires, all good counsels, and all just works do proceed: Give unto Thy servants that peace which the world cannot give; that our hearts may be set to obey Thy commandments, and also that by Thee we being defended from the fear of our enemies may pass our time in rest and quietness; through the merits of Jesus Christ our Saviour. *Amen.*

The Third Collect for Aid against all Perils.

LIGHTEN our darkness, we beseech Thee, O Lord; and by Thy great mercy defend us from all perils and dangers of this night; for the love of Thine only Son, our Saviour Jesus Christ. *Amen.*

In Quires and Places where they sing, the Anthem shall follow here.

Or else, when necessity shall so require, and in Parish Churches or Chapels, a hymn may be sung here before the Prayers and Intercessions are read.

Then these Prayers in order following may be read here, except when the Intercessions appointed for Eventide are used instead.

A Prayer for the Queen's Majesty.

O LORD our heavenly Father, high and mighty, King of kings, Lord of lords, the only Ruler of princes, Who dost from Thy throne behold all the dwellers upon earth: Most heartily we beseech Thee with Thy favour to behold our most gracious Sovereign Lady, Queen *ELIZABETH*; and so replenish her with the grace of Thy Holy Spirit, that she may alway incline to Thy will, and walk in Thy way: Endue her plenteously with heavenly gifts; grant her in health and wealth long to live; strengthen her that she may vanquish and overcome all her enemies, and finally after this life she may attain everlasting joy and felicity; through Jesus Christ our Lord. *Amen.*

A Prayer for the Royal Family.

ALMIGHTY God, the Fountain of all goodness, we humbly beseech Thee to bless *Philip* Duke of Edinburgh, *Charles* Prince of Wales, *William* Duke of Cambridge, Prince *George* of Cambridge, and all the Royal Family: Endue them with Thy Holy Spirit; enrich them with Thy heavenly grace; prosper them with all happiness; and bring them to Thine everlasting kingdom; through Jesus Christ our Lord. *Amen.*

A Prayer for all who are set in Authority.

LORD of all power and mercy, we beseech Thee to assist with Thy favour the Governor-General of this Dominion, the Lieutenant-Governors of the Provinces, and all those in this land who are set in authority under our Queen. Cause them, we pray Thee, always to walk before Thee in truth and righteousness; and to use their office and power to Thy glory, and the good of all Thy people; through Jesus Christ our Lord. *Amen.*

Or this,

O LORD God Almighty, Who rulest the nations of the earth, we humbly beseech Thee with Thy favour to behold our Sovereign Lady Queen *ELIZABETH*, that in all things she may be led by Thy guidance and protected by Thy power. We pray Thee also to bless *Philip* Duke of Edinburgh, *Charles* Prince of Wales, *William* Duke of Cambridge, Prince *George* of Cambridge, and all the Royal Family. Endue with wisdom the Governor-General, and the Prime Minister of this Dominion; the Lieutenant-Governors, Commissioners, and Premiers of the Provinces and Territories; and all who are set in authority over us under our Queen; that all things may be so ordered and settled by their endeavours upon the best and surest Christian foundations, that peace and happiness, truth and justice, religion and piety, may be established among us for all generations; through Jesus Christ our Lord. *Amen.*

A Prayer for the Clergy and people.

ALMIGHTY and everlasting God, from Whom cometh every good and perfect gift: Send down upon our Bishops and Clergy, and all Congregations committed to their charge, the healthful Spirit of Thy grace; and that they may truly please Thee, pour upon them the continual dew of Thy blessing. Grant this, O Lord, for the honour of our Advocate and Mediator, Jesus Christ. *Amen.*

And on any Sunday or Holy-Day, at the discretion of the Minister, the Intercessions at Eventide may be used in the place of the foregoing Prayers. And whensoever the Intercession aforesaid shall be used, the Minister shall end the Service of Evening Prayer with the General Thanksgiving, the Prayer of Saint Chrysostom, and the Grace, the people throughout all humbly and devoutly kneeling.

And when the Prayer following shall be used, the Minister may say, Let us pray for..., *and then shall be announced by the Minister the particular intentions for which the Congregation shall be bidden to pray. And likewise before the Prayer of General Thanksgiving, the Minister may say,* Let us give thanks for..., *and appropriate thanks and praise shall be offered up to Almighty God.*

The Minister shall say,
Let us pray.

A Prayer for all Conditions of men.

O GOD, the Creator and Preserver of all mankind, we humbly beseech Thee for all sorts and conditions of men; that Thou wouldest be pleased to make Thy ways known unto them, Thy saving health unto all nations. More especially we pray for the good estate of the Catholic Church; that it may be so guided and governed by Thy good Spirit, that all who profess and call themselves Christians may be led into the way of truth, and hold the Faith in unity of spirit, in the bond of peace, and in righteousness of life. Finally, we commend to Thy fatherly goodness all those, who are any ways afflicted, or distressed, in mind, body, or estate, *especially those for whom our prayers are desired*; that it may please Thee to comfort and relieve them, according to their several necessities, giving them patience under their sufferings, and a happy issue out of all their afflictions. And this we beg for Jesus Christ His sake. *Amen.*

Then shall be said this General Thanksgiving following either by the Minister alone,
or by the Minister and people together.

A General Thanksgiving.

ALMIGHTY God, Father of all mercies, we Thine unworthy servants do give Thee most humble and hearty thanks for all Thy goodness and loving kindness to us, and to all men; *particularly to those who desire now to offer up their praises and thanksgivings unto Thee, O Lord.* We bless Thee for our creation, preservation, and all the blessings of this life; but above all, for Thine inestimable love in the redemption of the world by our Lord Jesus Christ; for the means of grace, and for the hope of glory. And, we beseech Thee, give us that due sense of all Thy mercies, that our hearts may be unfeignedly thankful, and that we shew forth Thy praise, not only with our lips, but in our lives; by giving up ourselves to Thy service, and by walking before Thee in holiness and righteousness all our days; through Jesus Christ our Lord, to Whom with Thee and the Holy Ghost be all honour and glory, world without end. *Amen.*

Then shall be said the Prayer of Saint Chrysostom and the Grace.

A Prayer of Saint Chrysostom.

ALMIGHTY God, Who hast given us grace at this time with one accord to make our common supplications unto Thee; and dost promise that when two or three are gathered together in Thy Name, Thou wilt grant their requests: Fulfill now, O Lord, the desires and petitions of Thy servants, as may be most expedient for them; granting us in this world knowledge of Thy truth, and in the world to come, life everlasting. *Amen.*

II *Corinthians* xiii. 14.

✠ THE grace of our Lord Jesus Christ, and the love of God, and the fellowship of the Holy Ghost, be with us all evermore. *Amen.*

And here a Sermon may be preached or a Homily read.

And the Sermon or Homily ended, the Tithes, Offerings, and other Oblations and Gifts of the Faithful may be received and presented before the Lord in the appointed manner.

The Offertory ended, the Minister, standing before the Lord's Table, shall say one or more of the Collects, Prayers, or Thanksgivings set forth hereafter to be used, as he shall deem appropriate in his discretion, before the Benediction be said.

And if the Bishop or a Priest be present, he shall say,

NOW unto God's gracious mercy and protection we commit you. ✠ The Lord bless you, and keep you. The Lord make His face to shine upon you, and be gracious unto you. The Lord lift up His countenance upon you, and give you peace, both now and evermore. *Amen.*

Otherwise, the Minister shall say this Benediction following.

THE God of peace, that brought again from the dead our Lord Jesus, that great Shepherd of the sheep, through the Blood of the everlasting Covenant: Make you perfect in every good work to do His will, working in you that which is well-pleasing in His sight, through Jesus Christ; to Whom be glory for ever and ever. *Amen.*

Here endeth the ORDER OF EVENING PRAYER THROUGHOUT THE YEAR.

INTERCESSIONS AT EVENTIDE

In the place of the Intercessory Prayers appointed to be used after the Anthem at Evening Prayer, on Sundays and Holy-days these Intercessions following may instead be used.

Let us pray for the Queen, and for all those who are set in authority under her.

Minister. The Queen shall rejoice in Thy strength, O Lord;
Answer. Exceeding glad shall she be of Thy salvation.

ALMIGHTY God, the Fountain of all goodness, we humbly beseech Thee to bless and guide our most gracious Sovereign Lady Queen *ELIZABETH*, the Councils and Parliaments of the Commonwealth, and all who are set in authority; that they may order all things in wisdom, righteousness, and peace, to the honour of Thy holy Name, and the good of Thy Church and people; through Jesus Christ our Lord. *Amen.*

Let us pray for the peace of the Church,
and for the restoration of true unity amongst all Christian people.

Minister. Behold, how good and joyful a thing it is;
Answer. For brethren to dwell together in unity.

O MOST gracious Lord God, we humbly beseech Thee for Thy one holy Catholic Church: fill it with all truth; in all truth, with all peace. Where it is corrupt, purify it; where it is in error, direct it; where anything is amiss, reform it; where it is right, strengthen and confirm it; where it is in want, furnish it; where it is divided and rent asunder, make it whole again; through Jesus Christ our Lord. *Amen.*

Let us pray for the spread of the Gospel, and
for the extension of Christ's kingdom, throughout the world.

Minister. How beautiful are the feet of them that preach the gospel of peace;
Answer. And bring glad tidings of good things.

O GOD our heavenly Father, Who didst manifest Thy love by sending Thine only-begotten Son into the world that all might live through Him: Pour out Thy Spirit upon Thy holy Church, that it may fulfil His command to make disciples of all the nations; and send forth, we beseech Thee, labourers into Thy harvest, and hasten the time when the fullness of the Gentiles shall be gathered in, and all Israel shall be saved; through the same Thy Son Jesus Christ our Lord and Saviour. *Amen.*

Minister. Desire of me, and I shall give thee the heathen for thine inheritance;
Answer. And the utmost parts of the earth for thy possession.

O GOD, Who hast made of one blood all nations of men for to dwell on all the face of the earth, and didst send Thy blessed Son Jesus Christ to preach peace to them that are afar off and to them that are nigh: Grant that all those peoples who still sit in darkness and the shadow of death may feel after Thee and find Thee; and hasten, O Lord, the fulfilment of Thy promise to pour out Thy Spirit upon all flesh; through Jesus Christ our Lord. *Amen.*

Let us pray for the sick, and for all who suffer.

Minister. He healeth those that are broken in heart;
Answer. And giveth medicine to heal their sickness.

ALMIGHTY and immortal Lord God, the Giver of life and health: We beseech Thee to hear our prayers for Thy servants for whom we implore Thy mercy; that by Thy blessing upon them, and upon those who minister to them of Thy healing gifts, they may be restored, if it be Thy gracious will, to soundness of health in body, mind, and spirit, and give thanks to Thee in Thy holy Church; through Jesus Christ our Lord. *Amen.*

Let us remember before God all the faithful departed.

Minister. The souls of the righteous are in the hand of God;
Answer. And there shall no torment touch them.

O ETERNAL Lord God, Who holdest all souls in life: We beseech Thee to shed forth upon all the faithful departed the bright beams of Thy light, and fill them with all heavenly comfort; and grant that they, and we with them, by Thy mercy, may be made partakers of the resurrection of Thy blessed Son, and attain unto the joys of Thy kingdom; through the same Jesus Christ our Lord and Saviour. *Amen.*

Let us pray in blessed hope for the return of the Lord.

HASTEN, O God, the time when Thou shalt send from Thy right hand Him Whom Thou wilt send; at Whose appearing the saints departed shall be raised, and we which are alive and remain shall be caught up to meet Him, and so shall we ever be with our Lord. Keep us, we beseech Thee, O Father, unto that day; and grant that at His coming, we may, as One Body, be presented with exceeding joy before the Presence of His glory, holy and unspotted, prepared as a Bride adorned for her Husband; through the same Thy Son Jesus Christ our Lord. *Amen.*

Minister. Surely, I come quickly.
Answer. Amen. Even so, come, Lord Jesus.

THE SETTING FORTH OF
THE BLESSED SACRAMENT

At Evensong on Sundays and Holy-days, after the Anthem is ended or at other times according to custom or as permitted by the Ordinary, the Blessed Sacrament of the Holy Eucharist may be set before the Lord upon His Table in the sight of His people, and shall so remain until the Benediction is pronounced. And after the Service is ended, the Minister shall reverently remove the Blessed Sacrament from the Altar, and place the same again in the Tabernacle or Aumbry appointed for its reservation.

AT THE SETTING FORTH OF THE SACRAMENT

And whensoever the Blessed Sacrament is to be set forth before the Lord upon His Table, the Minister shall reverently remove the Blessed Sacrament from the Tabernacle or Aumbry, and shall place the same upon the Altar. And when the Minister hath so set the Blessed Sacrament upon the Altar, he shall kneel down and say this Prayer following.

O LORD God Almighty, our heavenly Father, we come before the throne of Thy glorious Majesty, and set before Thee and Thy people this visible Sacrament of the real Presence of Thine only-begotten Son, in the midst of the Congregation of Thy Church. Have respect, O Lord, unto His one, perfect, and sufficient Sacrifice, oblation, and satisfaction, made and offered for the sins of the whole world; and let His eternal high priestly Intercession at Thy right hand, on behalf of all Thy whole Church and all Thy creatures, ever ascend up before Thee; to the everlasting honour and glory of Thy Name, and the salvation of all the world; through the same Thy Son Jesus Christ our Lord. *Amen.*

A PRAYER BEFORE THE BLESSED SACRAMENT.

And at such times when the Blessed Sacrament shall be set forth before the Lord, this Collect following shall be said after any Devotions or Intercessions. And this Prayer, and that which followeth, may be said by the Minister in his discretion whensoever the Blessed Sacrament is present upon the Lord's Table.

HASTEN, O God, the time when Thou shalt send from Thy right hand Him Whom Thou wilt send; at Whose appearing the saints departed shall be raised, and we which are alive and remain to His coming shall be caught up to meet Him in the air, and so ever be with our Lord. And though under the veil of earthly things we have communion with Him now; grant unto us that, when He cometh, we may then behold Him with unveiled face, rejoicing in His glory, and be made like unto Him in the glory of His perfection; and that by Him we, with all Thy Church, holy and without blemish, prepared as a bride adorned for her husband, may be presented with exceeding joy before the Presence of Thy glory. Hear us, O heavenly Father, and grant this for His sake, to Whom, with Thee, and the Holy Ghost, the One living and true God, be all honour and glory, throughout all ages, world without end. *Amen.*

Then shall the Minister say or sing,
THOU gavest them Bread from heaven.
Answer. Containing in itself all sweetness.

Minister. Let us pray.

O GOD, Who in this wonderful Sacrament hast left unto us a memorial of Thy Passion: Grant us, we beseech Thee, so to venerate the sacred mysteries of Thy Body and Blood, that we may evermore perceive within ourselves the fruit of Thy redemption; Who livest and reignest with the Father and the Holy Ghost, ever one God, world without end. *Amen.*

The foregoing Prayer ended, Laudate Dominum *may then be sung or said.*

LAUDATE DOMINUM. *Psalm* 117.

O PRAISE the Lord all ye heathen; / praise Him all ye nations. For His merciful kindness is ever more and more / towards us; And the truth of the Lord endureth forever. / Praise the Lord.

GLORY be to the Father, and to the Son, / and to the Holy Ghost:

As it was in the beginning, is now, and ever shall be, world without end. Amen.

AT THE REMOVING OF THE SACRAMENT
And before the Blessed Sacrament is removed from the Altar, and returned to
the Tabernacle or Aumbry, the Minister shall first kneel down, and say this Prayer following.

O LORD, we draw near unto Thine Altar, to remove from this Thy Table the holy Sacrament of the Presence of Thy whole Person: Thy Body, Thy Blood, Thy Soul, and Thy Divinity. Thou hast vouchsafed unto us herein Thy Presence; and in this Blessed Sacrament Thou dost nourish us, and we are sustained by Thee, Thou Who art unseen by the world which doth not know Thee and cannot receive Thee. We worship not the outward form which we perceive with our earthly eyes, but Thee, O Lord and Saviour, Who art unseen, and Who art only to be perceived inwardly as yet by faith; and through Thee we glorify the Father, and the Holy Ghost, Who with Thee are forever Three Persons and One Almighty and Eternal Lord God, world without end. *Amen.*

And the Minister and people then shall stand, and say together,

WE worship Thee, O Lord Jesus Christ, and we praise Thee, for all Thy mercies; and in Thy Presence we rejoice. Hasten Thou, O Lord our Redeemer, the time when our joy shall be fulfilled, and we shall see Thee as Thou art. Amen.

Then shall the Minister reverently remove the Blessed Sacrament from the Altar,
and shall place the same in the Tabernacle or Aumbry.

THE PROPER ANTHEMS

FOR THE THREE

GREAT FESTIVAL SEASONS

appointed to be used at
Mattins and Evensong before the Psalms.

THE ANTHEMS FOR CHRISTMAS-DAY, AND ITS OCTAVE.

THEREFORE the Lord Himself shall give you a sign: A virgin shall conceive and bear a son, / and shall call His name Immanuel. Unto us a child is born, / unto us a son is given. In this was manifested the love of God toward us, / because that God sent his only-begotten Son into the world that we might live through Him. Blessed be the God and Father of our Lord Jesus Christ, / who hath blessed us with all spiritual blessings in heavenly places in Christ.

GLORY be to the Father, and to the Son, / and to the Holy Ghost;
As it was in the beginning, is now, and ever shall be, / world without end. Amen.

THE ANTHEMS FOR EASTER-DAY, AND ITS OCTAVE.

CHRIST our Passover is sacrificed for us: therefore let us keep the feast; Not with the old leaven, nor with the leaven of malice and wickedness; / but with the unleavened bread of sincerity and truth. Christ being raised from the dead dieth no more; / death hath no more dominion over Him. For in that He died, He died unto sin once: but in that He liveth, He liveth unto God. Likewise reckon ye also yourselves to be dead indeed unto sin, / but alive unto God, through Jesus Christ our Lord. Christ is risen from the dead, / and become the first-fruits of them that slept. For since by man came death, / by man came also the resurrection of the dead. For as in Adam all die, / even so in Christ shall all be made alive.

GLORY be to the Father, and to the Son, / and to the Holy Ghost;
As it was in the beginning, is now, and ever shall be, / world without end. Amen.

THE ANTHEMS FOR WHITSUNDAY, AND ITS OCTAVE.

O SING unto the Lord a new song; / for He hath done marvellous things. Christ, being by the right hand of God exalted, and having received of the Father the promise of the Holy Ghost, / hath shed forth this, which ye now see and hear. And because ye are sons, / God hath sent forth the Spirit of His Son into our hearts, crying, Abba, Father. We all, with open face / beholding as in a glass the glory of the Lord, Are changed into the same image from glory to glory, / even as by the Spirit of the Lord.

GLORY be to the Father, and to the Son, / and to the Holy Ghost;
As it was in the beginning, is now, and ever shall be, / world without end. Amen.

THE PROSE ANTHEMS
FOR THE TWO
GREAT PENITENTIAL SEASONS
appointed to be used at Mattins and Evensong
on all the Sundays and Week-days thereof.

THE ADVENT PROSE.

DROP down, ye heavens, from above, and let the skies pour forth righteousness; / let the earth be fruitful, and bring forth a Saviour. Be not very angry, O Lord, / neither remember our iniquity for ever. Thy holy cities are a wilderness, Jerusalem a desolation; / our holy and our beautiful house, where our fathers praised Thee. Drop down, ye heavens, from above, and let the skies pour forth righteousness; / let the earth be fruitful, and bring forth a Saviour.

We have sinned, and are as an unclean thing, and we all do fade as a leaf; / our iniquities, like the wind, have taken us away. Thou hast hid Thy face from us, and hast consumed us, / because of our iniquities. Drop down, ye heavens, from above, and let the skies pour forth righteousness; / let the earth be fruitful, and bring forth a Saviour.

Ye are my witnesses, saith the Lord, and my servant whom I have chosen; / that ye may know me and believe me. I, even I, am the Lord, and beside me there is no Saviour; / and there is none that can deliver out of my hand. Drop down, ye heavens, from above, and let the skies pour forth righteousness; / let the earth be fruitful, and bring forth a Saviour.

Comfort ye, comfort ye my people, my salvation shall not tarry; / I have blotted out as a thick cloud thy transgressions. Fear not, for I will save thee; / for I am the Lord thy God, the holy One of Israel, thy Redeemer. Drop down, ye heavens, from above, and let the skies pour forth righteousness; / let the earth be fruitful, and bring forth a Saviour.

Amen.

THE LENTEN PROSE.

HEAR us, O Lord, have mercy upon us, / for we have sinned against Thee. To Thee, Redeemer, on Thy throne of glory, / lift we our weeping eyes in holy pleadings: Listen, O Jesu, / to our supplications. Hear us, O Lord, have mercy upon us, / for we have sinned against Thee.

O Thou chief Cornerstone, Right hand of the Father, / Way of salvation, Gate of life celestial: Cleanse Thou our sinful souls / from all defilement. Hear us, O Lord, have mercy upon us, / for we have sinned against Thee.

O God, we implore Thee, in Thy glory seated, / bow down and hearken to Thy weeping children: Pity and pardon / all our grievous trespasses. Hear us, O Lord, have mercy upon us, / for we have sinned against Thee.

Sins oft committed, now we lay before Thee, / with true contrition, now no more we veil them: Grant us, Redeemer, / loving absolution. Hear us, O Lord, have mercy upon us, / for we have sinned against Thee.

Innocent Captive, taken unresisting, / falsely accused, and for us sinners sentenced: Save us, we pray Thee, / Jesu, our Redeemer. Hear us, O Lord, have mercy upon us, / for we have sinned against Thee.

Amen.

THE GREAT ANTIPHONS
OF THE ADVENT NOVENA

The following Antiphons are appointed to be sung or said at Morning Prayer before and after the Canticle Benedictus, *and at Evening Prayer before and after the Canticle* Magnificat, *each one on its own day during the Eight Days before Christmas-Day.*

O SAPIENTIA. *16 December.*

O WISDOM, which camest forth out of the mouth of the Most High, and reachest from one end of the world to the other, mightily and sweetly ordering all things: Come and teach us the way of prudence.

O ADONAI. *17 December.*

O LORD and Ruler of the House of Israel, Who didst appear unto Moses in a flame of fire in the burning bush, and gavest unto him the Law of Sinai: Come redeem us with an outstretched arm.

O RADIX JESSE. *18 December.*

O ROOT OF JESSE, Who standest for an ensign of the people, before Whom kings of the earth shall shut their mouths, and unto Whom the Gentiles shall pray: Come and deliver us, and tarry not.

O CLAVIS DAVID. *19 December.*

O KEY OF DAVID, and Sceptre of the House of Israel, Thou that openest and no man shutteth; and shuttest, and no man openeth: Come, and loose the prisoner from the prison house, and him that sitteth in darkness from the shadow of death.

O ORIENS. *20 December.*

O ORIENT, Thou brightest Star of the Eternal Light, and Sun of Righteousness: Come and lighten them that sit in darkness and in the shadow of death.

O REX GENTIUM. *21 December.*

O KING OF THE GENTILES, and their Desire, and the Corner-stone that makest them both to be One : Come and save man, whom Thou hast made from the dust of the earth.

O EMMANUEL. *22 December.*

O EMMANUEL, our King and Lawgiver, the great Desire of all nations, and their Saviour: Come and save us, O Lord our God.

O VIRGO VIRGINUM. *23 December.*

O VIRGIN OF VIRGINS, how shall this be? For neither before thee was there any like unto thee, nor shall there be any that cometh after thee. O Daughters of Jerusalem, why marvel ye at me? This thing that ye behold is a Divine mystery that surpasseth knowledge.

THE INVITATORY ANTIPHONS
APPOINTED FOR USE WITH THE PSALMS
AT MATTINS AND EVENSONG

*These Invitatories may be said or sung at Morning and Evening Prayer,
before and after the Proper Psalms appointed to be used.*

Advent. Our King and Saviour draweth nigh: O come, let us worship.

Christmastide. Unto us a Child is born, unto us a Son is given: O come, let us worship.

Epiphanytide. The Lord hath manifested forth His glory: O come, let us worship.

Lent. The goodness of God leadeth to repentance: O come, let us worship.

Annunciation. The Word was made flesh: O come, let us worship.

Passiontide. Christ our Lord became obedient unto death: O come, let us worship.

Eastertide. Christ our Lord is risen indeed: O come, let us worship.

Ascensiontide. Christ our Lord is ascended into heaven: O come, let us worship.

Whitsuntide. God hath sent forth the Spirit of His Son: O come, let us worship.

Trinitytide. The Lord God omnipotent reigneth: O come, let us worship.

Corpus Christi. Thou gavest them Bread from heaven: O come, let us worship.

Saints' Days. The Lord is glorious in His Saints: O come, let us worship.

The Blessed Virgin Mary. And blessed is she that believed: O come, let us worship.

Dedication Festival. The Lord is in His holy temple: O come, let us worship.

PRAYERS AND THANKSGIVINGS
UPON SEVERAL OCCASIONS

PRAYERS

FOR THE CHURCH.

For the good Estate of the Catholic Church.

MOST gracious Lord God, we humbly beseech Thee for Thy holy Catholic Church. Fill it with all truth; in all truth with all peace. Where it is corrupt, purify it; where it is in error, direct it; where anything is amiss, reform it; where it is right, strengthen and confirm it; where it is in want, furnish it; where it is divided and rent asunder, make it whole again; through Jesus Christ our Lord. *Amen.*

For the Mission of the Catholic Church.

O GOD of unchangeable power and eternal light: Look favourably upon Thy one holy Catholic Church, that wonderful and sacred mystery which is the living Body of Thy Son; and, by the tranquil operation of Thy perpetual Providence, carry out the work of men's salvation; that things which were cast down may be raised up, and that all things may return into unity through Him by Whom all things were made, even the same Thy Son Jesus Christ our Lord. *Amen.*

For the Peace and Unity of the Church.

O LORD Jesu Christ, Who didst say unto Thine Apostles, Peace I leave with you, my peace I give unto you: Regard not our sins, but the faith of Thy Church, and grant unto it that peace and unity which is agreeable to Thy will; Who livest and reignest with the Father and the Holy Ghost, ever One God, world without end. *Amen.*

For the Restoration of the visible Unity of the Church.

O GOD the Father of our Lord Jesus Christ our only Saviour and the Prince of Peace: Give us grace seriously to lay to heart the great dangers that we are in by our unhappy divisions. Take away from us all enmity, pride, and prejudice, and whatsoever else may hinder us from godly union and concord; and that as there is but only one Body and one Spirit, and one hope of our calling, one Lord, one Faith, one Baptism, one God and Father of us all, so grant unto us that we may henceforth be all of one heart and of one mind, united in one holy bond of Truth, full of faith, hope, and charity, within the communion and fellowship of Thy one holy Catholic Church; and so may we with one mind and one mouth glorify Thee, to the honour and glory of Thy Name, and the edifying of Thy people; through Jesus Christ our Lord. *Amen.*

For the Extension of the Church.

O ALMIGHTY God, Who by Thy blessed Son Jesus Christ didst give commandment to Thine Apostles that they should go into all the world, and preach the Gospel to every living creature: Grant to us Whom thou hast called into Thy holy Church, a ready will to obey Thy Word; and fill us with an hearty desire to make Thy way known upon earth, Thy saving health among all nations; through Jesus Christ our Lord. *Amen.*

For the Spread of the Gospel.
O GOD, Who hast made of one blood all nations of men for to dwell on the face of the earth, and didst send Thy blessed Son Jesus Christ to preach peace to them that are afar off and to them that are nigh: Grant that all peoples of the world may feel after Thee and find Thee; and hasten, O Lord, the fulfilment of Thy promise to pour out Thy Spirit upon all flesh; through the same Thy Son Jesus Christ our Lord. *Amen.*

For the Conversion of the Heathen.
O GOD our heavenly Father, Who didst say that repentance and forgiveness of sins should be preached in the Name of Jesus Christ among all nations, beginning at Jerusalem: Grant that all men everywhere may seek after Thee, and find Thee; bring the nations into Thy fold, and add the heathen to Thine inheritance; and shortly, we pray Thee, accomplish the number of Thine elect, and hasten Thy kingdom; through the same Thy Son Jesus Christ our Lord, Who with Thee and the Holy Ghost, liveth and reigneth, one God, world without end. *Amen.*

For the Conversion of the Jews.
ALMIGHTY and merciful Lord God, Who hast made all men, and hatest nothing that Thou hast made, nor wouldest the death of a sinner, but rather that he should be converted and live: Have mercy upon the Jews, and upon all descendants of Thy people Israel who reject and deny Thy Son; take from them all ignorance, hardness of heart, and contempt of Thy Word; and so fetch them home, O Blessed Lord, to Thy fold, that they may be saved among the remnant of the true Israelites, and be made together with them one flock under one Shepherd, even Jesus Christ our Lord and Saviour, Who liveth and reigneth with Thee and the Holy Ghost, one God, world without end. *Amen.*

For the Salvation of the Jews.
O GOD of Abraham, Isaac, and Jacob, Who didst choose Israel to be Thy people and Thine inheritance: Look, we beseech Thee, with compassion upon all those of Thine ancient people who have not believed the testimony of Thy Son, particularly those of the nation of Judah; open their hearts and minds that they may know and confess Jesus of Nazareth to be Thy Son and their true Messiah; and, believing, grant unto them life through His Name. Remove the veil that covereth their eyes and hearts, and take away from them all pride and prejudice that may hinder their understanding of the Gospel; and hasten the time, O Father, when all Israel shall be saved; through the same Thy Son Jesus Christ our Lord, the Son of David, the Messiah long foretold, and the Glory of Thy people Israel. *Amen.*

For those in Darkness and Error.
ALMIGHTY God, our heavenly Father, Who in Thy goodness hast caused the light of the Gospel to shine throughout the world: Extend Thy mercy, we beseech Thee, to those who still walk in darkness and error. Pour out Thy Spirit upon them, and enlighten them with the knowledge of Thy truth; grant that the great Gospel of salvation may be known in all lands, and that the hearts of all peoples may be turned unto Thee; through Jesus Christ our Lord. Amen.

For Missionaries.
O GOD, Who willest that all men should be saved and come to the knowledge of Thy truth: Prosper, we pray Thee, all those who labour for the Gospel here at home and in distant lands; protect them in all perils, and support them in loneliness and in every trial; give them Thy grace to

bear faithful witness unto Thee; and endue them with burning zeal and love, that they may turn many souls unto righteousness; through Jesus Christ our Lord. *Amen*

For Missionary Societies.

ALMIGHTY Saviour, Who, being exalted by the right hand of God, didst receive gifts for men: Send down the grace of Thy Holy Spirit upon Thy people, and grant that they may give both cheerfully and generously of their substance for the evangelising of the world. Bless all those who are banded together for the spread of the Gospel [*especially...*]; make them faithful and true witnesses in proclaiming Thy glorious Name; and prosper the work of their hands upon them, that the light of Thy truth may shine into the darkest corners of the earth. Hear us, O merciful Saviour, Who with the Father and the Holy Ghost livest and reignest, ever one God, world without end. *Amen.*

For the Synods and Convocations of the Church.

ALMIGHTY and everlasting God, Who by Thy Holy Spirit didst preside in the Council of the blessed Apostles, and hast promised, through Thy Son Jesus Christ, to be with Thy Church even unto the end of the world: We humbly beseech Thee to be present with the *National Synod* [or *the Convocation of this Province*, or *the Synod of this Diocese*] now [or *about to be*] assembled in Thy Name. Save its members from all error, ignorance, pride, and prejudice; and of Thy great mercy vouchsafe so to direct, govern, and sanctify them in their deliberations by Thy Holy Spirit, that through Thy blessing the Gospel of Christ may be faithfully preached and obeyed, the order and discipline of Thy Church maintained, and the kingdom of our Lord and Saviour enlarged and extended. Grant this, we beseech Thee, through the merits and mediation of the same Jesus Christ our Lord. *Amen.*

Or this,

GUIDE, we beseech Thee, Almighty God, by the light of Thy Holy Spirit, all the counsels and deliberations of the *Bishop*[*s*], Clergy, and Laity at this time assembled together in *National* [or *Diocesan*] Synod; that Thy Church may dwell in peace, and fulfil all the mind of Him Who loved it and gave Himself for it, even Thy Son our Saviour Jesus Christ. *Amen.*

For the Diocese.

ALMIGHTY and everlasting God, Who dost govern all things in heaven and in earth: Mercifully hear our prayers, and grant unto this *Diocese* [*of N.*] all things needful for its spiritual welfare [*ministers to labour in this portion of Thy vineyard, churches complete in the beauty of holiness*]. Strengthen and confirm the faithful; protect and guide the children; visit and relieve the sick; turn and soften the wicked; arouse the careless; recover the fallen; restore the penitent. Remove all hindrances to the advancement of Thy truth; and bring us all to be of one heart and mind within the fold of Thy one holy Catholic Church, to the honour and glory of Thy blessed Name; through Jesus Christ our Lord. *Amen.*

For a Parish, Congregation, or Mission of the Diocese.

O GOD the Holy Ghost, Sanctifier of the faithful: Sanctify this *Parish* by Thine abiding presence. Bless those who minister in holy things. Enlighten the minds of Thy people more and more with the light of the everlasting Gospel. Bring erring souls to the knowledge of God our Saviour; and those who are walking in the way of life, keep steadfast unto the end. Give patience to the sick and afflicted, and renew them in body and soul. Guard from forgetfulness of Thee those who are strong and prosperous. Increase in us Thy manifold gifts of grace, and make us all to be fruitful in good works; O blessed Spirit, Whom with the Father and the Son together we worship and glorify, one God, world without end. *Amen.*

During the Vacancy of a See.

ALMIGHTY God, the Giver of all good gifts: Grant Thy blessing, we humbly beseech Thee, to the *Bishops,* Clergy and Laity *about to assemble* for the election of a Bishop for this See and *Diocese,* give unto them wisdom and understanding, right judgment and discernment, that a chief Pastor may be chosen who shall minister before Thee to the honour and glory of Thy Name, the godly oversight and good government of the flock committed to his charge, and the welfare of all Thy holy Church; through Jesus Christ our Lord. *Amen.*

For the Increase of the Ministry.

WE beseech Thee, Almighty God, to call many to the Ministry of Thy Church; and to those Whom Thou dost call, give Thy grace that they may hear and answer Thy voice; through Jesus Christ our Lord. *Amen.*

For those studying for the sacred Ministry.

O HEAVENLY Father, Whose blessed Son Jesus Christ did command His disciples to proclaim the glad tidings of Thy saving love to all mankind: Pour out Thy Holy Spirit, we beseech Thee, upon all who are now studying in preparation for admission by ordination into the sacred Ministry of thy Church; make them to be modest, humble, and constant in their labours, and to have a ready will to obey all spiritual discipline; so that they may become faithful ministers of Thy holy Word and Sacraments; through the same Jesus Christ our Lord. *Amen.*

For those who are to be admitted to any Ministry.

ALMIGHTY God, the Giver of all good gifts, Who of Thy Divine Providence hast appointed divers Orders in Thy holy Church: Give Thy grace, we humbly beseech Thee, to all those who are to be called to any office and administration in the same; and so replenish them with the truth of Thy doctrine, and endue them with innocency of life, that they may faithfully and diligently serve Thee, to the honour and glory of Thy Name, and to the benefit of all Thy holy Church; through Jesus Christ our Lord. *Amen.*

For those who are to be admitted to Holy Orders.

ALMIGHTY God, our heavenly Father, Who hast purchased to Thyself an universal Church by the precious Blood of Thy dear Son: Mercifully look upon the same, and *at this time* so guide and govern the minds of Thy servants the Bishops, the successors of the Apostles in the office of oversight and the Pastors of thy flock, that they may lay hands suddenly on no man, but faithfully and wisely make choice of fit persons to serve in the sacred Ministry of Thy holy Church. And to those who shall be admitted to any Order of Ministry, give them Thy grace, and pour upon them Thy heavenly benediction; that both by their life and doctrine they may set forth Thy glory, and set forward the salvation of all men; through Jesus Christ our Lord. *Amen.*

For those who are to be Admitted to the sacred Priesthood.

BLESS, O Lord, we humbly beseech Thee, all those who are to be ordained *at this time* to the sacred Priesthood of Thy Son our Saviour Jesus Christ; and grant that, by Thy grace, they may always so dispense and minister Thy holy Word and Sacraments by their faithful ministrations and due diligence, that Thou wilt be thereby glorified, Thy people edified, and Thy kingdom enlarged and extended; through the same Jesus Christ our Lord. *Amen.*

For Christian Schools.

ALMIGHTY God, Who hast taught us to train up our children in the way that they should go, so that, when they are old, they shall not depart from it; and hast committed to Thy holy Church the care and nurture of all Thy children: Enlighten with Thy wisdom all those who teach, and all those who learn; that, rejoicing in the knowledge of Thy truth, they may walk only in the way of Christ, and serve and worship Thee acceptably all the days of their life; and grant that our children may increase in wisdom, knowledge, and true godliness, and bear good fruit each one as a righteous branch; through the same Thy Son Jesus Christ our Lord. *Amen.*

For Christian Schools, Academies, Colleges, and Universities.

ALMIGHTY God, of Whose only gift cometh wisdom and understanding: We beseech Thee with Thy gracious favour to behold our Christian schools, academies, colleges, and universities, that true knowledge may be increased among us, and all good and sound learning flourish and abound. Bless all those who teach, and all those who learn; and grant that in humility of heart they may ever seek after the truth, and find the same in Thy Son Jesus Christ, Who is the Way, the Truth, and the Life; in Whose Name we pray unto Thee, O Father, and Who with Thee and the Holy Ghost liveth and reigneth, ever one God, world without end. *Amen.*

For Christian Seminaries.

ALMIGHTY Father, grant that our seminaries may be homes of faith and fruitful study; and that all those who are students therein may so learn truth as to bear its light along their ways, and so learn Christ as to be found in Him; through the same Thy Son Jesus Christ our Lord, Who liveth and reigneth with Thee and the Holy Ghost, ever one God, world without end. *Amen.*

For those being prepared for Confirmation.

O GOD, Who through the teaching of Thy Son Jesus Christ didst prepare the disciples for the coming of the Comforter: Make ready, we beseech Thee, the hearts and minds of all those who *at this time* are seeking the gifts of the Holy Spirit through Anointing and the Laying on of hands; that, drawing near with penitent and faithful hearts, they may be filled with His power; through the same Jesus Christ our Lord. *Amen.*

For those who are to be Confirmed.

O ALMIGHTY God, without Whom nothing is strong, nothing is holy: We humbly commend unto Thee those who are about to renew, before the face of Thy Church, the solemn vows of their Baptism, and to seek Thy heavenly grace in the Sacrament of Confirmation. Guard them from the temptations of the world, the flesh, and the devil; and give them grace to devote themselves wholly unto Thee, in body, soul, and spirit; through Jesus Christ our Lord. *Amen.*

For the Right Observance of Sunday.

ALMIGHTY God, Who hast given a day of rest to Thy people, and, through Thy Holy Spirit in the Church, hast consecrated the first day of the week to be a perpetual memorial of Thy Son's Resurrection, and the Christian's sabbath-day: Grant, we beseech Thee, that we may so use Thy gift of rest that, refreshed and strengthened in soul and body, we may serve Thee faithfully all the days of our life; through the same Jesus Christ our Lord. *Amen.*

DIVINE OFFICE

FOR THE NATION.

For the Queen.

ALMIGHTY and everlasting God, we are taught by Thy holy Word, that the hearts of Kings are in Thy rule and governance, and that Thou dost dispose and turn them as it seemeth best to Thy godly wisdom: We humbly beseech Thee so to dispose and govern the heart of Thy servant *ELIZABETH*, our Queen and Governor, that in all her thoughts, words, and works, she may ever seek Thy honour and glory, and study to preserve Thy people committed to her charge, in wealth, peace, and godliness: Grant this, O merciful Father, for Thy dear Son's sake, Jesus Christ our Lord. *Amen.*

For the Royal Family.

ALMIGHTY God, the Fountain of all goodness, we humbly beseech Thee to bless our most gracious Sovereign Lady, Queen *ELIZABETH, Philip* Duke of Edinburgh, *Charles* Prince of Wales, *William* Duke of Cambridge, Prince *George* of Cambridge, and all the Royal Family: Endue them with thy Holy Spirit; enrich them with thy heavenly grace; prosper them with all happiness; and finally bring them all unto Thine everlasting kingdom; through Jesus Christ our Lord *Amen.*

For the Commonwealth.

ETERNAL God, Who rulest in the kingdoms of men: Grant, we most humbly beseech Thee, honour, health, and safety, to our Sovereign Lady, Queen *ELIZABETH;* peace throughout the Commonwealth of her peoples; promotion of true religion; encouragement to learning and godly living; a patient service to the concord of the world; and, by all these, glory to Thy holy Name; for His sake to Whom Thou hast given all power in heaven and earth, our Lord and Saviour Jesus Christ. *Amen.*

For the Governor-General of Canada.

O GOD our King and our heavenly Father, Who hast ordered all things, and appointed men to have dominion over Thy creation: We humbly beseech Thee for the Governor-General of this Dominion who hath been duly appointed to be the representative and steward of our Sovereign Lady the Queen in this land. Send down Thy blessing upon *him,* and grant unto *him* wisdom and right judgement; protect *him* from all evil; give unto *him* the grace necessary faithfully and loyally to execute *his* office, and to fulfill *his* duties to Thy glory, the honour of our Queen, and the good of our Nation; through Jesus Christ our Lord. *Amen.*

For the Prime Minister and the Premiers.

LORD of all power and mercy, we beseech Thee to bless and guide the Prime Minister of this Dominion, and the Premiers of the Provinces and Territories. Give unto them grace, wisdom, and understanding, sound judgement, and right discernment; and we pray thee, grant that they may always walk before Thee in truth and righteousness, and endeavour to fulfil their office to Thy glory and the public good; through Jesus Christ our Lord. *Amen.*

For Civic Authorities.

ALMIGHTY God, our heavenly Father, send forth, we beseech Thee, upon Thy servants who bear office in this *City* the spirit of prudence, charity, and justice; that they may in all things walk before Thee with righteous and steadfast purpose and a single heart, and faithfully serve in their several offices; through Jesus Christ our Lord. *Amen.*

DIVINE OFFICE

In the time of an Election.

ALMIGHTY God, the Source of all power, and the Giver of all wisdom: Guide, inspire, and direct, we most humbly beseech Thee, the minds and hearts of all those in this *Dominion* who are called upon at this time to elect fit persons to represent them in the government thereof. Grant that, in the exercise of their choice, they may be given grace to elect those who shall promote Thy honour and glory, and the maintenance of Thy laws; so that peace, order, and good government may prevail in this land, and our people may dwell together in righteousness, unity, concord, and safety; through Jesus Christ our Lord. *Amen.*

For those who serve in the Queen's Forces.

O LORD of hosts, stretch forth, we pray Thee, Thine almighty arm to strengthen and defend the Queen's forces in every peril of sea, and land, and air; shelter them in the day of battle, and ever keep them safe from all evil; endue them with loyalty and courage; and grant that in all things they may serve as seeing Thee Who art invisible; through Jesus Christ our Lord. *Amen.*

In the time of War and Tumults.

O ALMIGHTY Lord God, King of all kings, and Governor of all things, Whose power no creature is able to resist, to Whom it belongeth justly to punish sinners, and to be merciful to them that truly repent: Save and deliver us, we humbly beseech Thee, from the hands of our enemies; abate their pride, assuage their malice, and confound their devices; that we, being armed with Thy defence, may be preserved evermore from all perils, to glorify Thee, Who art the only Giver of all victory; through the Merits of Thine only Son Jesus Christ our Lord. *Amen.*

A Prayer for the Parliament of Canada, the Provincial and Territorial Legislatures, and the Legislatures of the Commonwealth; to be read during their session.

MOST gracious Lord God, we humbly beseech Thee, as for this Dominion of Canada in general, so especially for the High Court of Parliament [or *the Legislature of this Province,* or *Legislature of this Territory*] in particular; and for all the Parliaments and Legislatures of the Commonwealth under our most religious and gracious Queen *at this time assembled:* That thou wouldest be pleased to direct and prosper all their consultations to the advancement of Thy glory, the good of Thy Church, and the safety, honour, and welfare of our Sovereign, and her Dominions; that all things may be so ordered and settled by their endeavours, upon the best and surest Christian foundations, that peace and happiness, truth and justice, religion and piety, may be established among us for all generations. These and all other necessaries, for them, for us, and Thy whole Church, we humbly beg in the Name and through the Mediation of Jesus Christ our Lord. *Amen.*

For the whole People of God, to be said in time of Danger.

O GOD our Father, Who didst raise up Thy servant Queen Esther to be unto Thy people both a defender and an advocate, and didst appoint her righteous kinsman Mordecai to be unto her as her father, and her close counsellor; and Who, when the wicked Haman had devised the destruction of Thy people who dwelt in the lands subject to the King of Persia, and to that end deceived him in his grants, didst move Mordecai to pray for his people: Hear us, who likewise now pray unto Thee, O Father Almighty, Maker and Sustainer of all things, King of all creation, for the whole world is upheld by Thee and subject to Thy power; and if it be that Thou hast appointed to save Israel, there is no man nor power that can work against Thee: for Thou hast made heaven and earth, and all the wondrous things therein, both seen and unseen. Thou art Lord of all, and there is no man nor power that can resist Thee, for alone Thou art the Lord. Thou seest all things, O Lord, and knowest that it is neither in contempt nor pride, nor for any desire of glory, that we do not bow down before the ungodly; for if it would prosper Thy chosen people, we would be content with good will for the salvation of our people to kiss the soles of their feet. But we do not, that we might not prefer the glory of any man or nation above the glory of God: neither will we worship any but Thee, O God, and neither will we do it in pride. And so now, O Lord our God and King, Father of Israel, we beseech Thee, spare us Thy people, spare Thy people whom Thou hast redeemed with the most precious Blood of Thy Son Jesus Christ, shed for us upon the Cross; and bring us not unto destruction nor confusion: for the eyes of the ungodly are upon us to bring us to nought; yea, they desire to destroy the inheritance that hath been Thine from the beginning of the world. Despise not the portion which Thou hast delivered out of Egypt for Thine own self. Hear our prayer, O God, and be Thou merciful unto Thine inheritance: turn our sorrow into joy, that we may live, O Lord, and praise Thy Name; and destroy not the mouths of them that praise Thee. And this our supplication and prayer we make unto Thee, O Father in heaven, in the Name of the same Thy Son Jesus Christ our Lord, our Saviour and Redeemer, the true Shepherd of Israel, and the Hope of all mankind. *Amen.*

FOR AGRICULTURE, FISHERIES, AND INDUSTRY.

For Agriculture.

ALMIGHTY and merciful God, from Whom cometh every good and perfect gift: Bless, we beseech Thee, the labours of Thy people, and cause the earth to bring forth all her fruits abundantly in their season, that we may with grateful hearts again give thanks to Thee for the same; through Jesus Christ our Lord, Who liveth and reigneth with Thee and the Holy Spirit, one God, world without end. *Amen.*

For Farmers and Agricultural Labourers.

ALMIGHTY God, Who hast blessed the earth and, despite the consequences of man's fall, hast yet ordained that it should be fruitful and bring forth abundantly whatsoever is needful for the life of man: Prosper, we beseech Thee, O Lord, the work of our farmers and those who labour in the fields; and grant such seasonable weather that all may gather in the fruits of the earth, and proclaim Thy great goodness with thanksgiving; through Jesus Christ our Lord. *Amen.*

For a blessing on Fisheries.

O ALMIGHTY God, Who hast made the sea, and all that move therein: Bestow Thy blessing upon the harvest of the waters, that it may be abundant in its season, and upon our sailors and fishermen, that they may be safe in every peril of the deep; so that we all with thankful hearts may acknowledge Thee, Who art Lord of the sea and of the dry land; through Jesus Christ our Lord. *Amen.*

For fruitful Seasons and on Rogation Days.

O ALMIGHTY Lord God, Who hast created the earth for man, and man for Thy glory: Mercifully hear the supplications of Thy people, and be mindful of Thy covenant; that the earth may yield her increase, and the good seed of Thy Word may bring forth abundantly in our hearts, to the honour and glory of Thy Name; through Jesus Christ our Lord. *Amen.*

For Rain.

O GOD, our heavenly Father, Who through Thy Son Jesus Christ hast promised to all them that seek first Thy kingdom and righteousness all things necessary to their bodily sustenance: Send us, we beseech Thee, in this our necessity, such moderate rain and showers that we may receive the fruits of the earth to our comfort, and to Thine honour; through the same Jesus Christ our Lord. *Amen.*

For Fair Weather.

O ALMIGHTY Lord God, Who for the sins of mankind didst once drown all the world, except Noah and his family, and thereafter of Thy great mercy didst promise never to destroy it so again: We humbly beseech Thee, that although we for our iniquities have worthily deserved a plague of rain and waters yet, upon our true repentance, Thou wilt send us such weather as that we may receive the fruits of the earth in due season; and learn both by Thy punishment to amend our lives, and for Thy clemency to give Thee praise and glory; through Jesus Christ our Lord. *Amen.*

In Time of Dearth and Famine.

O GOD, our heavenly Father, Whose gift it is, that the rain doth fall, the earth is fruitful, beasts increase, and fishes do multiply: Behold, we beseech Thee, the afflictions of Thy people; and grant that the scarcity and dearth, which we do now most justly suffer for our sins and iniquities, may through Thy goodness be mercifully turned into abundance and plenty, and that we may find relief; increase for us, O Lord, the fruits of the earth; and grant that we, receiving Thy bountiful liberality, may use the same to Thy honour and glory, the relief of those who are in need, and our own comfort; for the love of Thine only Son Jesus Christ our Lord, to Whom, with Thee and the Holy Ghost, be all honour and glory, now and for ever. *Amen.*

For Industry.

O LORD Jesus Christ, Who in Thine earthly life didst share man's toil, and hallow the labour of his hands: Prosper our brethren who maintain the industries of this land, and give to all who labour pride in their work, a just reward for their labours, and joy both in supplying need and in serving Thee; Who with the Father and the Holy Ghost livest and reignest, ever one God, world without end. *Amen.*

For Right Relations in Industry.

O GOD, Who hast ordained that men should live and work together as brethren: We beseech Thee to bless the industries of this land, that there be no strife among those who are engaged in the varied tasks of industry and commerce. Grant that all, seeking only what is right, may ever continue in brotherly union and concord, to their own well-being and the good of their fellow men; through Jesus Christ our Lord. *Amen.*

For Workmen and the Employers of Labour.

O LORD God Almighty, Who in Thy providence hast appointed to every man his work, and Whose blessed Son didst share in His earthly life our toil, and didst thereby hallow the labour of our hands: We humbly beseech Thee, O merciful Lord, to put away all strife and contention between those who are engaged in the labours of industry, and those who employ their labour; deliver them from all greed and covetousness; and grant that they, seeking only that which is equitable and just, may live and work together in brotherly union and concord, to Thine honour and glory, and the well-being and prosperity of all the people of this Dominion, and all the Realms and Countries of our Commonwealth; through the same Thy Son Jesus Christ our Lord. *Amen.*

DIVINE OFFICE

FOR GENERAL INTENTIONS.

For Travellers.

O GOD, our heavenly Father, Who art present in Thy power at every time, and in every place: Preserve, we beseech Thee, all our brethren who travel by land, water, or air, or above and beyond the bounds of earth; surround them with Thy loving care; uphold them, and protect them from every danger and adversity; send ministering angels to help and defend them; and finally bring them all in perfect safety to their journey's end; through Jesus Christ our Lord. *Amen.*

In the Time of any common Plague or Sickness.

O ALMIGHTY God, Who in Thy wrath didst send a plague upon Thine own people in the wilderness, for their obstinate rebellion against Moses and Aaron; and also, in the time of King David, didst slay with the plague of pestilence threescore and ten thousand of Thy people, and yet, remembering Thy mercy, didst save the rest: Have pity upon us miserable sinners, who now are visited with great sickness and mortality; that like as Thou didst then accept of King David an atonement, and didst command the destroying Angel to cease from punishing, so it may now please Thee, O Lord, to withdraw from us this plague and grievous sickness; through Jesus Christ our Saviour. *Amen.*

For Healing Ministries.

ALMIGHTY God, Whose blessed Son Jesus Christ went about doing good, and healing all manner of sickness and disease, among the people: Continue, we beseech Thee, this His gracious work among us; cheer, heal, strengthen, and sanctify the sick and infirm; grant to the physicians, surgeons, and nurses wisdom and skill, sympathy and patience; and send down Thy blessing upon all who labour to prevent suffering, and to forward Thy merciful purposes of love; through Jesus Christ our Lord. *Amen.*

For the Recovery of a Sick Person.

ALMIGHTY and immortal God, the Giver of life and health: We beseech thee to hear our prayers for Thy *servant N.*, for whom we implore Thy mercy, that by Thy blessing upon *him* and upon those who minister to *him* of Thy healing gifts, *he* may be restored, according to Thy gracious will, to health of body and mind, and give thanks to Thee in thy holy Church; through Jesus Christ our Lord. *Amen.*

For the Faithful Departed.

ALMIGHTY God, with Whom do live the spirits of them that depart hence in the Lord, and with Whom the souls of the faithful, after they are delivered from the burden of the flesh and just punishments for sin, are in joy and felicity: We praise and magnify Thy holy Name for all Thy servants who have finished their course in Thy faith and fear; and we humbly beseech Thee to grant that at the day of the coming of Thy Son Jesus Christ in His perfect majesty, with power and great glory, when the dead shall be raised, and all the world shall be judged, we and they may be set altogether at His right hand, and there hear that His most joyful voice, saying unto all them that have believed in Him, Come, ye blessed of my Father, inherit the kingdom prepared for you from the foundation of the world. Grant this, O merciful Father, for the sake of Jesus Christ Thine only Son our Lord and Saviour. *Amen.*

49

O GOD our heavenly Father, in Whom do rest the souls of the faithful departed as they await their resurrection from the dead: We humbly beseech Thee, through Thy mercy, to grant unto them refreshment, rest, and peace; let light perpetual shine upon them, and may they awake, at the coming of the kingdom of the Lord, to a joyful resurrection; through the same Thy Son our Lord and Saviour Jesus Christ. *Amen.*

O GOD of the spirits of all flesh, we praise and magnify Thy holy Name for all Thy servants who have finished their course in Thy faith and fear [*especially Thy* servant *N.*]; beseeching Thee to grant unto them refreshment, rest and peace; and we pray that we, encouraged by their examples, strengthened by their fellowship, and assisted by their prayers, may with them be found meet to be partakers of the inheritance of the Saints in Light; through the Merits of Thy Son our Saviour Jesus Christ our Lord. *Amen.*

A Prayer to ask the Prayers of the Saints.

O GRACIOUS Lord God, and heavenly Father, Who art glorified in Thy Saints, and art pleased always to receive their prayers: Grant us, we humbly beseech Thee, a share in the prayers of the most blessed Virgin Mary, Mother of Thy dearly-beloved Son, and the prayers of all Thy Saints; and grant, O Lord, that they whose memory we devoutly preserve on earth may ever vouchsafe to intercede for us in heaven; through the same Thy Son Jesus Christ our Lord and Saviour. *Amen.*

A General Intercession.

BE mindful, O Lord, of Thy people bowed before Thee, and of those who are absent from us through age, sickness, infirmity, or carelessness. Protect the infants and children, guide the young, support the aged, strengthen the infirm, help the afflicted, encourage the faint-hearted, collect the scattered, mend the broken, and bring the wandering into Thy fold. Travel with the voyager, defend the widow, comfort the bereaved, support the orphan, deliver the captive, prosper the virtuous, shield the warrior, and heal the sick. Succour all who are in tribulation, necessity, or distress. Remember for good all those who love us, all those who hate us, and all those who have desired us (unworthy though we be) to pray for them. And those whom we have forgotten, do Thou, O Lord, remember: For Thou art the Helper of the helpless, the Saviour of the lost, the Refuge of the wanderer, the Healer of the sick; and do Thou, Who knowest the needs of all, and hearest every believer's prayer, grant unto each according to Thy merciful loving-kindness, and Thine eternal love; through Jesus Christ our Lord. *Amen.*

For Perseverance.

TEACH us, good Lord, to serve Thee as Thou deservest; to give, and not to count the cost; to fight, and not to heed the wounds; to toil, and not to seek for rest; to labour, and not to seek any reward, save that of knowing that we do Thy will; through Jesus Christ our Lord. *Amen.*

For greater Devotion.

THANKS be to Thee, O Lord Jesus Christ, for all the benefits which Thou hast given us; and for all the countless pains and insults which Thou hast borne for us. O Thou most merciful Redeemer, Friend, and Brother, grant that we may, day by day, come to know Thee more clearly, love Thee more dearly, and follow Thee more nearly; Who with the Father and the Holy Ghost livest and reignest ever one God, world without end. *Amen.*

For Worthiness.

REMEMBER, O Lord, that which Thou hast wrought in us, and not that which we deserve; and as Thou hast called us to Thy service, make us, we beseech Thee, worthy of our calling, and always ready to do Thy will; through Jesus Christ our Lord. *Amen.*

A Prayer at Eventide.

O LORD, support us all the day-long of this troublous life, until the shadows lengthen and the evening come, the busy world is hushed, the fever of life is over, and our work is done; then, Lord, in Thy mercy, grant us safe lodging, an holy rest, and peace at the last; through Jesus Christ our Lord. *Amen.*

THANKSGIVINGS

For Rain.

O GOD, our heavenly Father, Who by Thy gracious providence dost cause the former and the latter rain to descend upon the earth, that it may bring forth fruit to the use of man: We give Thee humble thanks that it hath pleased Thee, in our great necessity, to send us at the last a joyful rain upon Thine inheritance, and to refresh it when it was dry, to the great comfort of us, Thine unworthy servants; through Thy mercies in Jesus Christ our Lord. *Amen.*

For Fair Weather.

O LORD God, Who hast justly humbled us by sending this late plague of immoderate rain and waters, and in Thy mercy hast relieved and comforted our souls by this seasonable and blessed change of weather: We praise and glorify Thy holy Name for this Thy mercy, and will always declare Thy loving-kindness from generation to generation; through Jesus Christ our Lord. *Amen.*

For Plenty.

O MOST merciful Father, Who of Thy gracious goodness hast heard the devout prayers of Thy Church, and turned our dearth and scarcity into abundance and plenty: We give Thee humble thanks for this Thy special bounty; beseeching Thee to continue Thy loving-kindness unto us, that our land may yield us her fruits of increase, to Thy glory and our comfort; through Jesus Christ our Lord. Amen.

For Peace and Deliverance from our Enemies.

O ALMIGHTY God, Who art a strong Tower of defence unto Thy servants against the face of their enemies: We yield Thee praise and thanksgiving for our deliverance from these great and apparent dangers wherewith we were compassed round about, and we acknowledge it to be only of Thy great goodness that we were not delivered over as a prey unto our enemies; and we beseech Thee still to continue Thy mercy towards us, and to defend us and protect us from those who fight against us; that all the world may know that Thou art our Saviour, and mighty Deliverer; through Jesus Christ our Lord. Amen.

For Victory.

O ALMIGHTY God, the Sovereign Commander of all the world, in Whose hand is power and might which none is able to withstand: We bless and magnify Thy great and glorious Name for this happy Victory, the whole glory whereof we do ascribe unto Thee, Who art the only Giver of Victory. And, we beseech Thee, give us grace to improve this great mercy to Thy glory, the advancement of Thy

Gospel, the honour of our Sovereign, and, as much as in us lieth, the good of all mankind. And, we beseech Thee, give us such a sense of this great mercy, as may engage us to a true thankfulness, such as may appear in our lives by an humble, holy, and obedient walking before Thee all our days; through Jesus Christ our Lord, to Whom with Thee and the Holy Ghost, as for all Thy mercies, so in particular for this Victory and Deliverance, be all glory and honour, world without end. *Amen.*

For restoring Public Peace at Home.

O ETERNAL God, our heavenly Father, Who alone makest men to be of one mind in a house, and stillest the outrage of a violent and unruly people: We bless Thy holy Name, that it hath pleased Thee to appease the seditious tumults which have been lately raised up amongst us; and we most humbly beseech Thee to grant to all of us grace, that we may henceforth obediently walk in the way of Thy Commandments; and, leading a quiet and peaceable life in all godliness and honesty, may continually offer unto Thee our sacrifice of praise and thanksgiving for these Thy mercies towards us; through Jesus Christ our Lord. *Amen.*

For Deliverance from Plague, or other common Sickness.

O LORD God Almighty, Who hast justly wounded us for our sins, and consumed us for our transgressions, by Thy late heavy and dreadful visitation; and now, in the midst of judgement remembering mercy, hast redeemed our souls from the jaws of death: We offer unto Thy fatherly goodness ourselves, our souls, and bodies, which Thou hast delivered, to be a living sacrifice unto Thee, always praising and magnifying Thy mercies in the midst of Thy Church; through Jesus Christ our Lord. *Amen.*

For Recovery from Sickness.

MOST gracious God and heavenly Father, we render unto Thee our hearty thanks for the restoration to health of Thy *servant N.,* for whom we lately besought Thy loving-kindness and implored Thy mercy; and joyfully do we confess that, as Thy power is infinite, so also is Thy mercy toward them that call upon Thee for help in the Name of Thy Son Jesus Christ our only Lord and Saviour, through Whom we give our thanks to Thee. *Amen.*

For the Church in Canada.

WE thank Thee, most merciful Father, that it hath pleased Thee to establish and build Thy Church in this good land of Canada. We praise Thee for the light of the Gospel, the many labours of Thy servants, and the ministrations of Thy Bishops, Clergy, and Missionaries. We also bless Thy holy Name for all those who have lived, and suffered, and died for Thy sake; beseeching Thee to give us grace so to follow their good examples, that with them we may at last attain Thy heavenly promises; through Jesus Christ our Lord. *Amen.*

VESTRY PRAYERS

PRAYERS WHICH MAY BE SAID BEFORE AND AFTER WORSHIP.

Before the Divine Office.

O LORD our God, Who knowest all hearts: Be merciful to us sinners, and graciously assist us in our ministrations before Thee; that we may so offer our Service unto Thee that all we do may be pleasing and acceptable in Thy sight; through Jesus Christ our Lord. *Amen.*

After the Divine Office.

MERCIFULLY behold us, Thy servants, O Lord, who have now performed this Service in Thy holy House, and pardon all that which hath been amiss; forgive us, O God, if in our worship here our hearts and minds went far from Thee, and suffer us not when we leave Thy House to lose Thy Presence. And grant unto us, O Lord, as we go forth from this holy place: in thought, faith; in word, wisdom; in deed, courage; and in our daily life, joyful service to Thee and to our fellow man; through Jesus Christ our Lord. *Amen.*

Before the Divine Liturgy.

MOST gracious God, incline Thy merciful ears to our prayers, and enlighten our hearts by the grace of Thy Holy Spirit; that we may worthily approach the Mysteries of Thy holy Table, and love Thee with an everlasting love; through Jesus Christ our Lord. *Amen.*

After the Divine Liturgy.

O GOD, Who in a wonderful Sacrament hast left unto us a memorial of Thy Passion: Grant us, we beseech Thee, so to venerate the sacred Mysteries of Thy Body and Blood, that we may ever more perceive within ourselves the fruit of Thy redemption; Who livest and reignest with the Father and the Holy Ghost, ever One God, world without end. *Amen.*

After any Act of Worship.

✠ BLESSED, praised, and adored, be Jesus Christ on His Throne of glory in heaven, in the most holy Sacrament of the Altar, and in the hearts of His faithful people. *Amen.*

An Order of Service at Night

WHICH IS CALLED

Compline

A Late Night Service.

This Service may be said at some convenient time after the saying or singing of Evening Prayer, but may not at any time be used as a substitution therefor.

The Minister shall first say,
✠ In the Name of the Father, and of the Son, and of the Holy Ghost. *Amen.*

The Lord God Almighty grant us a quiet night, and at the last a perfect end.

Then shall he invite the people to confess their sins, saying,
Let us humbly confess our sins to Almighty God.

Then shall the Minister and people together say this Confession of sin following, all devoutly kneeling.
We confess to God Almighty, the Father, the Son, and the Holy Ghost, that we, each one of us, have sinned in thought, word, and deed, through our fault, through our own fault, through our own most grievous fault. Wherefore we pray Almighty God to have mercy upon us, forgive us our sins, confirm and strengthen us in all goodness, and finally bring us to everlasting life; through Jesus Christ our Lord. Amen.

And if a Priest be present, he shall stand and pronounce the following Absolution, saying,
The Almighty and most merciful Lord grant unto you pardon, ✠ absolution, and remission of all your sins, time and opportunity for amendment of life, and the grace and comfort of His Holy Spirit; through Christ our Lord. *Amen.*

Then shall the Minister say or sing,
O Lord, open Thou our lips.
Answer. And our mouth shall shew forth Thy praise.

Then this Hymn following may be sung.

Before the ending of the day,
Creator of the world we pray,
That with Thy wonted favour Thou
Wouldst be our Guard and Keeper now.

From all ill dreams defend our eyes,
From nightly fears and fantasies;
Tread under foot our ghostly foe,
That no pollution we may know.

O Father, that we ask be done,
Through Jesus Christ, Thine only Son,
Who, with the Holy Ghost and Thee,
Doth live and reign eternally. Amen.

Minister. Keep me as the apple of an eye.
Answer. Hide me under the shadow of Thy wings.

*Then shall be said or sung Psalm 91, or some other suitable Psalm
or portion thereof, at the discretion of the Minister.*

THE SHORT LESSON.

BRETHREN, be sober, be vigilant; because your adversary the devil, as a roaring lion, walketh about, seeking whom he may devour; whom resist, steadfast in the faith. I *Saint Peter 5.* 8-9.

Minister. Into Thy hands, O Lord, I commend my spirit.
  Answer. For Thou hast redeemed me, O Lord, Thou God of truth.
Minister. Preserve us, O Lord, waking, and guard us while sleeping;
  Answer. That awake we may watch with Christ, and asleep we may rest in peace.

LORD, have mercy upon us.
Christ, have mercy upon us.
Lord, have mercy upon us.

Then shall the Lord's Prayer be said or sung by all, as followeth.

OUR Father, which art in heaven, hallowed be thy name. Thy kingdom come. Thy will be done, in earth as it is in heaven. Give us this day our daily bread. And forgive us our trespasses, As we forgive them that trespass against us. And lead us not into temptation, But deliver us from evil. Amen.

Minister. Blessed art Thou, Lord God of our fathers;
  Answer. To be praised and glorified above all forever.
Minister. Let us bless the Father, the Son, and the Holy Ghost;
  Answer. Let us praise Him and magnify Him forever.
Minister. Blessed art Thou, O Lord, in the firmament of heaven;
  Answer. To be praised and glorified above all forever.
Minister. May the Almighty and most merciful Lord guard us;
  Answer. And give us His blessing.
Minister. O Lord, hear our prayer;
  Answer. And let our cry come unto Thee.

Minister. Let us pray.

BE present, O merciful God, and protect us through the silent hours of this night, so that we who are wearied by the changes and chances of this fleeting world, may repose upon Thine eternal changelessness; through Jesus Christ our Lord. *Amen.*

The Minister.

MAY the Lord bless us all this night long, preserve us and keep us from all evil, and bring us finally unto everlasting life. ✠ And may the souls of the faithful departed, through the mercy of God, rest in peace, and awake to a joyful resurrection. *Amen.*

Here endeth an ORDER FOR COMPLINE.

A BIDDING PRAYER

Before Sermons, Lectures, and Homilies, delivered outside Divine Service, and at other such times when no other Intercessions are used, the Preacher, or some other Minister, may move the people to join with him in Prayer according to this form hereafter following.

LET us pray for the one holy Catholic and Apostolic Church of God; that is, for the whole Body of faithful Christian people dispersed throughout the world; that it may please God to confirm and strengthen His Church in purity of faith, in holiness of life, and in perfectness of love, and to restore to it that witness of visible unity agreeable to His will; and especially let us pray for that portion of the Church to which we ourselves belong; that in all things it may work according to God's will, serve Him faithfully, and worship Him acceptably.

And herein let us pray for all Christian Kings, Princes, and Governors, especially for our own most gracious Sovereign Lady *ELIZABETH*, by the grace of God of the United Kingdom of Great Britain and Northern Ireland, Canada, and all other her Realms and Territories, Queen, Head of the Commonwealth, Defender of the Faith. Let us also pray for *Philip* Duke of Edinburgh, *Charles* Prince of Wales, *William* Duke of Cambridge, Prince *George* of Cambridge, and all the Royal Family.

Let us also pray for all those set in authority under our Queen in this Dominion: the Governor-General; the *Lieutenant-Governor* of this *Province*; and the *Mayor* of this *City*; and all those who assist them in the execution of their office. Let us pray for the Queen's Privy Council, and all her Courts of Justice, as well as for all the Judges and Magistrates of this Dominion; for the Parliament of Canada, the Legislative Assembly of this *Province*; and the Council of this *City*; and for all who bear any office in this Realm: that all of them, each according to his calling, may truly serve and duly execute his office to the honour and glory of God, the protection and safety of His Church, and the peaceable ordering and well-governing of this nation; remembering always their duty, and the strict and solemn account which they must one day give before the judgement-seat of Christ.

Let us pray for all Ministers of Christ's Church: for all the Patriarchs, Primates, Archbishops, and Bishops, as well as for all the Priests and Deacons, and for all Deaconesses; for all orders of Lay-ministers; and likewise for all spiritual and pastoral teachers, advisers, and counsellors; that all may serve truly, faithfully, and wisely, and in all things adorn the doctrine of God our Saviour.

And that there may never be wanting a supply of good persons duly qualified to serve God both in Church and State, let us implore His blessing upon all schools, universities, and seminaries of religious and useful learning; that in these, and all such places set apart for God's honour and service, true religion, and sound learning, may for ever flourish.

Let us pray for all the people of this Dominion, and for all the Realms and Countries of our Commonwealth, that they may live and dwell together in the true faith and fear of God, in humble obedience to the Queen, and in brotherly charity one to another; and particularly for all Christian people who travel by land, water, or air; for all prisoners and captives; for all who are in sorrow, need, sickness, or any other adversity; for all who have fallen into heresy or schism, or into any grievous or deadly sin; for all who, through temptation, ignorance, helplessness, grief, trouble, dread, or the near approach of death, specially need our prayers.

Finally, let us yield unto God our Father most high praise and hearty thanks for all those who are departed from out of this life in the faith and fear of Jesus Christ; and for the wonderful grace and virtue declared in all His Saints, who have been the chosen vessels of His grace, and lights of the world in their several generations; and let us pray unto God our Father that we may all have grace to direct our lives after their good example, and that this life ended we may be partakers with them of His everlasting kingdom.

All these prayers and praises let us now humbly offer up before the throne of heaven, in the words which our Saviour Christ Himself hath taught us, saying:

OUR Father, which art in heaven, hallowed be Thy Name. Thy kingdom come. Thy will be done, in earth as it is in heaven. Give us this day our daily bread. And forgive us our trespasses, As we forgive them that trespass against us. And lead us not into temptation, But deliver us from evil. For Thine is the kingdom, the power, and the glory, For ever and ever. Amen.

Here endeth a BIDDING PRAYER.

A FORM OF BLESSING BY A BISHOP

*This Form of Blessing following may be said by the Bishop at any time in his discretion
in the place of any other forms of Blessing that may be prescribed in this Book.*

The Bishop shall say,
LET us bless the Lord.
Answer. Thanks be to God.

Bishop. The Lord bless you, and keep you.
Answer. Amen.

Bishop. The Lord make His face to shine upon you,
and be gracious unto you.
Answer. Amen.

Bishop. The Lord lift up His countenance upon you,
and give you peace.
Answer. Amen

The Bishop.
AND the blessing of God Almighty, ✠ the Father, the Son, and the Holy Ghost,
rest upon you, and remain with you all, both now and for evermore. *Amen.*

A FORM OF DISMISSAL

*This Form of Dismissal following may be used after any Prayers or Thanksgivings
when no other Benediction or Form of Dismissal is ordered to be used.*
MAY the Almighty and Merciful Lord God, ✠ the Father, the Son, and the Holy Ghost,
bless us, protect us, preserve us, and keep, both now and for evermore. *Amen.*

ACTS OF PRAISE

Ephesians 3. 20 & 21.

NOW unto Him that is able to do exceeding abundantly above all that we ask or think, according to the power that worketh in us, unto Him be glory in the Church and in Christ Jesus, throughout all ages, world without end. *Amen.*

Jude 24 & 25.

NOW unto Him that is able to keep us from falling and to present us faultless before the presence of His glory with exceeding joy; to the only wise God our Saviour be glory and majesty, dominion and power, both now and ever. *Amen.*

I *Timothy* 1. 17.

NOW unto the King eternal, immortal, invisible, the only wise God, be honour and glory, for ever and ever. *Amen.*

Revelation 1. 5 & 6.

UNTO Him that loved us, and washed us from our sins in His own Blood, and hath made us kings and priests unto God and His Father, to Him be glory and dominion for ever and ever. *Amen.*

TRISAGION

This Devotion following may be said or sung before the Lord's Supper,
except at such times when the Great Litany shall be sung or said, and during Passiontide.

✠ IN the Name of the Father, and of the Son, and of the Holy Ghost. Amen.

O GOD our heavenly King, O God our Comforter, O God our Saviour, and Lord of all truth: Thou Who art present in all places, and fillest all which Thou hast made; O Thou Treasury of all good things, and Giver of all life: Come and dwell in us; cleanse us from every stain of sin; and save our souls from death; O most gracious Lord and God Almighty. *Amen.*

> HOLY God, Holy and Mighty, Holy and Immortal:
> *Have mercy on us.*
> Holy God, Holy and Mighty, Holy and Immortal:
> *Have mercy on us.*
> Holy God, Holy and Mighty, Holy and Immortal:
> *Have mercy on us.*

MOST Holy, Blessed, and Glorious Trinity, three Persons and one God, have mercy on us. O Lord our God, cleanse us from our sins. O Lord our God, pardon our iniquities. O Lord our God, visit and heal our infirmities for Thy Name's sake. *Amen.*

> GLORY be to the Father, and to the Son, and to the Holy Ghost:
> *As it was in the beginning, is now, and ever shall be, world without end.* Amen.

Here endeth the Devotion called TRISAGION, or THRICE HOLY.

THE DIVINE LITURGY

The Great Litany
AS IT IS APPOINTED TO BE SUNG OR SAID BEFORE
The Holy Eucharist

Here followeth the GREAT LITANY as it is appointed to be used before the Lord's Supper on the Lord's Day during the seasons of Advent and Lent, as well as during Rogationtide, and at such other times of Penitence or Solemn Prayer when it shall be commanded by the Ordinary.

O GOD the Father of heaven: have mercy upon us.
O God the Father of heaven: have mercy upon us.

O God the Son, Redeemer of the world: have mercy upon us.
O God the Son, Redeemer of the world: have mercy upon us.

O God the Holy Ghost, proceeding from the Father and the Son: have mercy upon us.
O God the Holy Ghost, proceeding from the Father and the Son: have mercy upon us.

O holy, blessed, and glorious Trinity, three Persons and one God: have mercy upon us.
O holy, blessed, and glorious Trinity, three Persons and one God: have mercy upon us.

REMEMBER not, Lord, our offences, nor the offences of our forefathers; neither take Thou vengeance of our sins: Spare us, good Lord, spare Thy people, whom Thou hast redeemed with Thy most precious Blood, and be not angry with us for ever.
Spare us, good Lord.

FROM all evil and mischief; from sin; from the crafts and assaults of the devil; from Thy wrath, and from everlasting condemnation,
Good Lord, deliver us.

From all blindness of heart; from pride, vain-glory, and hypocrisy; from envy, hatred, and malice, and all uncharitableness,
Good Lord, deliver us.

From fornication and adultery, and all other deadly sin; from all uncleanness in thought, word, and deed; and from all the deceits of the world, the flesh, and the devil,
Good Lord, deliver us.

From lightning and tempest; from earthquake, fire, and flood; from plague, pestilence, and famine; from battle and murder; and from sudden death,
Good Lord, deliver us.

From all sedition, conspiracy, and rebellion; from all false doctrine, heresy, and schism; from hardness of heart, and contempt of Thy Word and Commandment,
Good Lord, deliver us.

BY the mystery of Thy holy Incarnation; by Thy blessed Nativity and Circumcision; by Thy Baptism, Fasting, and Temptation,
Good Lord, deliver us.

By Thine Agony and bloody Sweat; by Thy saving Cross and Passion; by Thy precious Death and Burial,
Good Lord, deliver us.

By Thy glorious Resurrection and Ascension; by Thy sending of the Holy Ghost; by Thine everlasting Priesthood; and by Thy coming again in glory,
Good Lord, deliver us.

In all time of our tribulation; in all time of our wealth; in the hour of death, and in the day of judgement,
Good Lord, deliver us.

WE sinners do beseech Thee to hear us, O Lord God; and that it may please Thee to rule and govern Thy holy Church universal in the right way,
We beseech Thee, good Lord.

To lead all nations in the way of righteousness; and so to guide and direct their governors and rulers, that Thy people may enjoy the blessings of freedom and peace,
We beseech Thee, good Lord.

To keep and strengthen in the true worshipping of Thee, in righteousness and holiness of life, and in devotion to her people, Thy chosen Servant *ELIZABETH*, our most gracious Queen and Governor,
We beseech Thee, good Lord.

To rule and govern her heart in Thy faith, fear, and love, that in all her thoughts, words, and works, she may ever seek Thy honour and glory,
We beseech Thee, good Lord.

To be her Defender and Keeper, giving her the victory over all her enemies,
We beseech Thee, good Lord.

To bless and preserve *Philip* Duke of Edinburgh, *Charles* Prince of Wales, *William* Duke of Cambridge, Prince *George* of Cambridge, and all the Royal Family,
We beseech Thee, good Lord.

To bless all the Bishops of Thy Church; to endue them with Thy Holy Spirit; and to fill them with Thy heavenly grace; that they may govern and feed the flock committed to their care, according to Thy will,
We beseech Thee, good Lord.

To pour out Thy Spirit upon all the Clergy; and to illuminate them with true knowledge and understanding of Thy Word, and that both by their preaching and living, they may set it forth, and shew it accordingly,
We beseech Thee, good Lord.

To bless all who minister in Thy Name; that each, according to his calling, may execute his office, to Thy honour and glory, and the edifying of Thy people,
We beseech Thee, good Lord.

To send forth labourers into Thy harvest; to prosper their work by Thy Holy Spirit; to make Thy saving health known unto all nations; and to hasten Thy kingdom,
We beseech Thee, good Lord.

To bless, protect, and prosper the people of this Dominion, and of all the Realms and Countries of our Commonwealth; and to endue those who are set in authority under our Queen with grace, wisdom, and understanding,
We beseech Thee, good Lord.

To bless and guide the Judges and Magistrates, giving them grace to execute justice, and to maintain truth,
We beseech Thee, good Lord.

To bless and keep the Queen's forces by sea, and land, and air; to defend them from the craft and power of the enemy; and to shield them in all dangers and adversities,
We beseech Thee, good Lord.

To give to all nations unity, peace, and concord, that Thy people may serve Thee without fear,
We beseech Thee, good Lord.

To bless and keep all Thy people,
We beseech Thee, good Lord.

To give to all Thy people an heart to love and dread Thee, and to seek Thy will; and to follow Thy Word and Commandments,
We beseech Thee, good Lord.

To give to all Thy people increase of grace to hear meekly Thy Word, and to receive it with pure affection; and to bring forth the fruits of the Spirit,
We beseech Thee, good Lord.

To bring into the way of truth all such as have erred, and are deceived; and to save us from all delusion, that we may believe no lies,
We beseech Thee, good Lord.

To strengthen such as do stand; to comfort and help the weak-hearted; to raise up those who fall; and finally to beat down Satan under our feet,
We beseech Thee, good Lord.

To succour, help, and comfort, all that are in danger, necessity, or tribulation,
We beseech Thee, good Lord.

To preserve all that travel; all women labouring of child, all sick persons, and young children; and to shew Thy pity upon all prisoners and captives,
We beseech Thee, good Lord.

To defend, and provide for, all widows and orphans, and all who are desolate and oppressed,
We beseech Thee, good Lord.

THE GREAT LITANY

To have mercy upon all men,
We beseech Thee, good Lord.

To forgive our enemies, persecutors, and slanderers, and to turn their hearts,
We beseech Thee, good Lord.

To give and preserve to our use the kindly fruits of the earth, so that in due time we may enjoy them,
We beseech Thee, good Lord.

To give us true repentance; to forgive us all our sins, negligences, and ignorances; and to endue us with the grace of Thy Holy Spirit, to amend our lives according to Thy Word,
We beseech Thee, good Lord.

SON of God, we beseech Thee to hear us.
Son of God, we beseech Thee to hear us.

O Lamb of God, that takest away the sins of the world;
Have mercy upon us.

O Lamb of God, that takest away the sins of the world;
Grant us Thy peace.

O Christ, hear us.
O Christ, hear us.

And when the Great Litany is said or sung by some Minister other than the Priest, when it is ended, the Priest himself shall then proceed directly to the Lord's Prayer and the Collect for Purity, beginning first with the Mutual Salutation, as followeth.

*And turning himself to face the people,
the Priest shall say,*
THE Lord be with you.
Answer. And with thy spirit.

Priest. Let us pray.

*And turning himself to face the Lord's Table, the Priest shall say the Lord's Prayer
with the Collect for Purity following, the people all devoutly kneeling.*

OUR Father, which art in heaven, hallowed be Thy Name. Thy kingdom come. Thy will be done, in earth as it is in heaven. Give us this day our daily bread. And forgive us our trespasses, As we forgive them that trespass against us. And lead us not into temptation, But deliver us from evil. Amen.

ALMIGHTY God, unto Whom all hearts be open, all desires known, and from Whom no secrets are hid: Cleanse the thoughts of our hearts by the inspiration of Thy Holy Spirit, that we may perfectly love Thee, and worthily magnify Thy holy Name; through Christ our Lord. *Amen.*

Then shall be said or sung the Psalm appointed for the Introit.

The Order for the Administration of
The Lord's Supper,
or
Holy Communion,
which is called
The Holy Eucharist
and also called
The Mass

The Lord's Supper, or Holy Communion, the Administration whereof is called the Holy Eucharist and also called the Mass, was instituted by our Lord and Saviour Jesus Christ Himself at the Last Supper with His disciples on the night in which He was betrayed, for the continual remembrance and the shewing forth of His saving death and sacrifice, until His coming again; and this same Holy Eucharist is the principal and highest act of Christian worship, and the source and summit of the Christian life: and for this reason, the Holy Eucharist shall be celebrated in every Cathedral and Collegiate Church, and in every Parish Church or Chapel where there is a Priest, on every Lord's Day and Holy-day for which provision is made, except there be reasonable cause to the contrary.

It is the duty of every confirmed person, after due preparation, to communicate at Easter, Whitsun, and Christmas, at the least, and more frequently throughout the year if it may be at all possible for him so to do.

It is convenient that so many as shall intend to be partakers of the Holy Communion should signify their names unto the Parish Priest at least some time the day before; and if any person, after due examination, perceive himself not to be in a state of grace to receive the Holy Communion, he is to confess himself to the Priest and receive Absolution, and by the due performance of the penance imposed upon him to make satisfaction for his sins, before partaking of that holy Sacrament.

If any person be an open and notorious sinner or evil liver, or have done any wrong to his neighbours by word or by deed, so that the Congregation of Christ's faithful be thereby offended; the Priest, having knowledge thereof, shall call him and advertise him, that in any wise he presume not to come to the Lord's Table, until he have openly declared himself to have truly repented and amended his former sinful life, confessed himself to the Priest, received Absolution, and performed the penance required of him.

And the same order shall the Priest use with those betwixt whom he shall perceive malice and hatred to reign; not suffering them to be partakers of the Lord's Table, until he know them to be reconciled. And if one of the parties so at variance be content to forgive from the bottom of his heart all that the other hath trespassed against him, and to make amends for that in which he himself hath offended; and the other party will not be persuaded to a godly unity, but will remain still in his frowardness and malice: the Priest in that case ought to admit the penitent person to the Holy Communion, and not him that is obstinate. Provided that every Priest so repelling any, as is specified in this, or the next precedent paragraph, shall be obliged to give an account of the same to the Ordinary within fourteen days after at the farthest. And the Ordinary shall proceed against the offending person according to the Canon.

And there shall be no celebration of the Eucharist, except there be at least one person present to communicate with the Priest, unless it be for some just and lawful cause and with the explicit permission of the Ordinary.

The Lord's Table, being the Altar whereon the Sacrifice of the Death of our Lord and Saviour Jesus Christ is shewn forth, and offered up to God the Father in the celebration of the Supper of the Lord, shall stand in the east in the Sanctuary in the uppermost part of the Chancel or Chapel. And the Lord's Table, at the time of the said Administration, and whensoever else the Communion may be ministered to the faithful, shall have a fair white linen cloth upon it.

THE HOLY EUCHARIST

*This Form of Preparation following may be used in the Church
before the celebration of the Lord's Supper.*

THE PREPARATION

The Priest, standing at the Altar steps, shall say,
✠ IN the Name of the Father, and of the Son, and of the Holy Ghost. *Amen.*

Then shall the Priest say,
I WILL go unto the altar of God,
Answer. Even unto the God of my joy and gladness.

Then shall the Priest say,
GIVE sentence with me, O God, and defend my cause against the ungodly people; O deliver me from the deceitful and wicked man.
People. For Thou art the God of my strength; why hast Thou put me from Thee? and why go I so heavily while the enemy oppresseth me?
Priest. O send out Thy light and Thy truth, that they may lead me, and bring me unto Thy holy hill, and to Thy dwelling.
People. And that I may go unto the altar of God, even unto the God of my joy and gladness; and upon the harp will I give thanks unto Thee, O God, my God.
Priest. Why art thou so heavy, O my soul, and why art thou so disquieted within me?
People. O put thy trust in God, for I will yet give Him thanks, which is the Help of my countenance, and my God.

And the Priest shall say,
GLORY be to the Father, and to the Son, and to the Holy Ghost;
People. As it was in the beginning, is now, and ever shall be, world without end. Amen.

Then shall the Priest say,
I WILL go unto the altar of God,
Answer. Even unto the God of my joy and gladness.

Priest. Our help standeth in the Name of the Lord;
Answer. Who hath made heaven and earth.
Priest. Wilt Thou not turn again and quicken us, O God;
Answer. That Thy people may rejoice in Thee?
Priest. O Lord, shew Thy mercy upon us;
Answer. And grant us Thy salvation.
Priest. O Lord, hear our prayer;
Answer. And let our cry come unto Thee.

And turning to the people, the Priest shall say,
THE Lord be with you.
Answer. And with thy spirit.
Priest. Let us pray.

And the Priest, facing the Lord's Table, shall begin the Lord's Supper saying in an audible voice the Lord's Prayer, after which he shall say the Collect following, the people all humbly and devoutly kneeling.

OUR Father, which art in heaven, hallowed be Thy Name. Thy kingdom come. Thy will be done, in earth as it is in heaven. Give us this day our daily bread. And forgive us our trespasses, As we forgive them that trespass against us. And lead us not into temptation, But deliver us from evil. Amen.

ALMIGHTY God, unto Whom all hearts be open, all desires known, and from Whom no secrets are hid: Cleanse the thoughts of our hearts by the inspiration of Thy Holy Spirit, that we may perfectly love Thee, and worthily magnify Thy holy Name; through Christ our Lord. *Amen.*

Then shall the Priest proceed in the celebration of the Holy Eucharist.

THE LITURGY OF THE WORD OF GOD

THE INTROIT.
Then shall be said or sung the Psalm or portion of a Psalm appointed to be used that day for the Introit, at which time the Priest shall proceed up to the Lord's Table. And at high and solemn celebrations, the Holy Table may be censed during the singing of the Introit.

THE GREETING.
The Introit ended, the Priest shall reverently kiss the Lord's Table; and, standing there, the Priest shall turn himself to the people, and shall greet them in the Name of the Lord, saying,
GRACE be unto you, and peace, from God our Father, and the Lord Jesus Christ.
Answer. And with thy spirit.

THE COMMANDMENTS.
Then shall the Priest, still facing the people, rehearse the Ten Commandments, or else our Blessed Lord's Summary of the Law; provided always that the Ten Commandments shall be read on all Sundays in Advent and Lent, on Days of Fasting, Abstinence, and Solemn Prayer, and throughout the rest of the year on one Sunday every month.
HEAR the Law of God which was given to Israel in old time. God spake these words, and said, I AM THE LORD THY GOD, which brought thee out of the land of Egypt, out of the house of bondage: Thou shalt have none other gods but me.

People. Lord, have mercy upon us, and incline our hearts to keep this law.

Priest. Thou shalt not make to thyself any graven image, nor the likeness of any thing that is in heaven above, or in the earth beneath, or in the water under the earth. Thou shalt not bow down to them, nor worship them: for I the LORD thy God am a jealous God, and visit the sins of the fathers upon the children unto the third and fourth generation of them that hate me, and shew mercy unto thousands in them that love me, and keep my commandments.

People. Lord, have mercy upon us, and incline our hearts to keep this law.

Priest. Thou shalt not take the Name of the LORD thy God in vain: for the LORD will not hold him guiltless that taketh His Name in vain.

People. Lord, have mercy upon us, and incline our hearts to keep this law.

Priest. Remember that thou keep holy the Sabbath day. Six days shalt thou labour, and do all that thou hast to do; but the seventh day is the Sabbath of the LORD thy God. In it thou shalt do no manner of work, thou, and thy son, and thy daughter, thy man-servant, and thy maid-servant, thy cattle, and the stranger that is within thy gates. For in six days the LORD made heaven and earth, the sea, and all that in them is, and rested the seventh day: wherefore the LORD blessed the Sabbath day, and hallowed it.

People. Lord, have mercy upon us, and incline our hearts to keep this law.

Priest. Honour thy father and thy mother; that thy days may be long in the land which the LORD thy God giveth thee.

People. Lord, have mercy upon us, and incline our hearts to keep this law.

Priest. Thou shalt do no murder.

People. Lord, have mercy upon us, and incline our hearts to keep this law.

Priest. Thou shalt not commit adultery.

People. Lord, have mercy upon us, and incline our hearts to keep this law.

Priest. Thou shalt not steal.

People. Lord, have mercy upon us, and incline our hearts to keep this law.

Priest. Thou shalt not bear false witness against thy neighbour.

People. Lord, have mercy upon us, and incline our hearts to keep this law.

Priest. Thou shalt not covet thy neighbour's house; thou shalt not covet thy neighbour's wife, nor his servant, nor his maid, nor his ox, nor his ass, nor anything that is his.

People. Lord, have mercy upon us, and write all these Thy laws in our hearts, we beseech Thee.

THE SUMMARY OF THE LAW.
Or else, instead of the Ten Commandments, the Priest may rehearse
our Blessed Lord's Summary of the Law, as followeth.

OUR Lord Jesus Christ said: Hear, O Israel, THE LORD OUR GOD IS ONE LORD; and thou shalt love the LORD thy God with all thy heart, and with all thy soul, and with all thy mind, and with all thy strength. This is the first and great Commandment. And the second is like unto it, Thou shalt love thy neighbour as thyself. On these two Commandments hang all the Law and the Prophets.

People. Lord, have mercy upon us, and write both these Thy laws in our hearts, we beseech Thee.

KYRIE ELEISON.
Then shall be said or sung in either English or in Greek,
LORD, have mercy upon us. / Kyrie, eleison.
Christ, have mercy upon us. / Christe, eleison.
Lord, have mercy upon us. / Kyrie, eleison.

GLORIA IN EXCELSIS.
Then here at certain times may be said or sung by all standing,

GLORY be to God on high, and in earth peace, good will towards men. We praise Thee, we bless Thee, (*Here all shall bow.*) **we worship Thee**, we glorify Thee, we give thanks to Thee for Thy great glory, O Lord God, heavenly King, God the Father Almighty.

O Lord, the only-begotten Son, (*And here all shall reverently bow.*) **Jesu Christ**; O Lord God, Lamb of God, Son of the Father, that takest away the sins of the world, have mercy upon us. Thou that takest away the sins of the world, (*And here all shall bow again.*) **receive our prayer**. Thou that sittest at the right hand of God the Father, have mercy upon us.

For Thou only art holy, Thou only art the Lord, Thou only, O Christ, with the Holy Ghost, ✠ art most high in the glory of God the Father. Amen.

And here it is to be noted, that when Gloria in Excelsis *is said or sung here,*
the people shall remain standing for the Collects that follow thereafter.

HOLY EUCHARIST

THE COLLECTS.
Then shall the Priest turn himself to the people,
and shall say or sing,
THE Lord be with you.
Answer. And with thy spirit.

Priest. Let us pray.

Then shall the Priest turn again to the Lord's Table,
and shall say or sing this Collect for the Queen's Majesty following.
ALMIGHTY God, Whose kingdom is everlasting, and power infinite: Have mercy upon Thy people in this Dominion, and all the Realms and Countries of our Commonwealth; and so rule the heart of Thy chosen servant *ELIZABETH*, our Queen and Governor, that she (knowing Whose minister she is) may above all things seek Thy honour and glory: and grant that we, and all her subjects (duly considering Whose authority she hath) may faithfully serve, honour, and humbly obey her, in Thee, and for Thee, according to Thy blessed Word and ordinance; through Jesus Christ our Lord, Who with Thee and the Holy Ghost liveth and reigneth, ever one God, world without end. *Amen.*

Then shall be said or sung the Collect or Collects appointed to be used that day.

THE EPISTLE.
Then, the people being seated, the Priest, or some other Minister, shall read the Epistle or Lesson appointed for that day, first saying, The Epistle [or *The Lesson appointed for the Epistle*] is written in the....chapter of....beginning at the....verse. *And the Epistle or Lesson ended, the Minister shall say,* Here endeth the Epistle [or *Lesson*]: This is the Word of the Lord.

And all shall answer saying,
Thanks be to God.

A hymn may be sung before the Gradual.

THE GRADUAL.
Then shall all the people stand, and the Psalm or portion thereof
appointed to be used for the Gradual shall be said or sung.

THE GOSPEL.
Then shall the Deacon or Priest read the Gospel
appointed for that day, the people all still standing as before.

And the Minister that shall read the Gospel shall first say,
THE Lord be with you.
Answer. And with thy spirit.

Then shall the Minister announce that portion of
the Gospel which is to be read, saying,
✠ THE holy Gospel is written in the....chapter of the Gospel according to Saint....beginning at the....verse.

Then shall be said or sung,
GLORY be to Thee, O Lord.

Then shall the Gospel be read.

HOLY EUCHARIST

And the reading of the holy Gospel ended, all shall then together in like manner as before say or sing,
PRAISE be to Thee, O Christ.

Then shall the Minister say,
AND through the Words of the Gospel
may our sins be blotted out.

THE NICENE CREED.
*Then shall be said or sung the Nicene Creed as followeth,
the Priest and people still standing.*

I BELIEVE in one God the Father Almighty, Maker of heaven and earth, And of all things visible and invisible.

And in one Lord (*And here all shall bow their heads.*) **Jesus Christ**, the only-begotten Son of God, Begotten of His Father before all worlds : God, of God; Light, of Light; Very God, of very God; Begotten, not made; Being of one substance with the Father; Through Whom all things were made: (*And here all shall devoutly kneel or bow.*) **Who for us men and for our salvation came down from heaven, And was incarnate by the Holy Ghost of the Virgin Mary, AND WAS MADE MAN**, (*And here all shall rise.*) And was crucified also for us under Pontius Pilate. He suffered and was buried, And the third day He rose again according to the Scriptures, And ascended into heaven, And sitteth on the right hand of the Father. And He shall come again with glory to judge both the quick and the dead: Whose kingdom shall have no end.

And I believe in the Holy Ghost, The Lord and Giver of Life, Who proceedeth from the Father and the Son, Who with the Father and the Son together (*And here all shall bow.*) **is worshipped and glorified**, Who spake by the Prophets. And I believe One Holy Catholic and Apostolic Church. I acknowledge one Baptism for the remission of sins. And I look for the ✠ Resurrection of the dead, And the Life of the world to come. Amen.

And here on the Lord's Day, the Priest himself, or some other appointed Minister, shall declare unto the people what Holy-days, Days of Fasting or Abstinence, and Days of Penitence or Solemn Prayer, are ordered to be observed in the Week following.

And then also (if occasion be) shall notice be given of the Lord's Supper, or else one of the Exhortations read out, as well as any Briefs, Citations, and Excommunications. And nothing shall be proclaimed or published in the Church during the time of Divine Service, but by the Priest himself, or by some other Minister duly appointed by him; nor by him anything but what is allowed or prescribed by the Rubrics and the Canons of the Church, or else enjoined by the Queen, or by the Ordinary of the place.

THE SERMON

*And here at the principal Eucharist upon the Lord's Day and greater Holy-days,
a Sermon shall be preached or an Homily read out to the faithful.*

THE OFFERTORY

*Then shall the Priest return to the Lord's Table,
and shall begin the Offertory, before which he may say,*
LET us present our offerings and oblations to the Lord
with reverence and godly fear.

HOLY EUCHARIST

Then shall the Priest say or sing one or more of these Sentences following,
as he thinketh most convenient in his discretion.

AND they came every one whose heart stirred him up, and every one whom his spirit made willing, and they brought the Lord's offering. *Exodus xxxv.*

Offer unto God the sacrifice of thanksgiving, and pay thy vows unto the Most High. *Psalm l.*

Give unto the Lord the honour due unto His Name; bring an offering and come into His courts. *Psalm xcvi.*

I will offer to Thee the sacrifice of thanksgiving, and will call upon the Name of the Lord; I will pay my vow unto the Lord in the sight of all His people. *Psalm cxvi.*

These Sentences following may also be used.

Advent. As we have opportunity, let us do good unto all men; and especially unto them that are of the household of faith. *Galatians vi.*

Christmastide. Brethren, you know the grace of our Lord Jesus Christ, that, though He was rich, yet for your sakes He became poor, that you through His poverty might become rich. *II Corinthians viii.*

Epiphanytide. Let your light so shine before men, that they may see your good works, and glorify your Father which is in heaven. *Saint Matthew v.*

Lent. I beseech you, brethren, by the mercies of God, that you present your bodies a living sacrifice, holy, acceptable unto God, which is your reasonable service. *Romans xii.*

Passiontide. Walk in love, as Christ also hath loved us, and hath given Himself for us an offering and a sacrifice to God. *Ephesians v.*

Maundy Thursday. Our Lord Jesus Christ saith, A new commandment I give unto you, that ye love one another; even as I have loved you, that ye also love one another. *Saint John xiii.*

Eastertide. Worthy is the Lamb that was slain to receive power, and riches, and wisdom, and strength, and honour, and glory, and blessing. *Revelation v.*

Ascensiontide. Lay not up for yourselves treasure upon earth; where the rust and moth doth corrupt, and where thieves break through and steal: but lay up for yourselves treasure in heaven; where neither rust nor moth doth corrupt, and where thieves do not break through and steal; for where your treasure is, there shall your heart be also. *Saint Matthew vi.*

Rogation and Harvest. He that soweth little shall reap little; and he that soweth plenteously shall reap plenteously. Let every man do according as he is disposed in his heart, not grudging, or of necessity; for God loveth a cheerful giver. II *Corinthians ix.*

Whitsuntide. Whatsoever ye would that men should do unto you, even so do unto them; for this is the Law and the Prophets. *Saint Matthew vii.*

Trinitytide. Not every one that saith unto me, Lord, Lord, shall enter the kingdom of heaven; but he that doeth the will of my Father which is in heaven. *Saint Matthew vii.*

Corpus Christi. Melchizedek King of Salem brought forth bread and wine: and he was the Priest of the most high God. *Genesis xiv.*

Saints' Days. All Thy works praise Thee, O Lord: and Thy saints give thanks unto Thee. *Psalm cxlv.*

Of Tithing. Honour the Lord with thy substance, and with the first fruits of all thine increase; so shall thy barns be filled with plenty, and thy presses shall burst forth with new wine. *Proverbs iii.*

Bring ye all the tithes into the storehouse, that there may be meat in my house, and prove me now herewith, saith the Lord of hosts, if I will not open up the windows of heaven and pour you out a blessing, so that there shall not be room enough to receive it. *Malachi iii.*

Do ye not know, that they who minister about holy things live of the sacrifice; and they who wait at the altar are partakers with the altar? Even so hath the Lord also ordained, that they who preach the Gospel should live of the Gospel. I *Corinthians ix.*

Let him that is taught in the Word minister unto him that teacheth, in all good things. Be not deceived, God is not mocked: for whatsoever a man soweth that shall he reap. *Galatians vi.*

Of Almsgiving. Blessed is he that considereth the poor and needy: the Lord shall deliver him in the time of trouble. *Psalm xli.*

Charge them who are rich in this world, that they be ready to give, and glad to distribute; laying up in store for themselves a good foundation against the time to come, that they may attain eternal life. I *Timothy vi.*

Whoso hath this world's good, and seeth his brother have need, and shutteth up his compassion from him, how dwelleth the love of God in him? I *Saint John iii.*

Remember the words of the Lord Jesus, how He said, It is more blessed to give than to receive. *Acts xx.*

And on Sundays and Holy-days, whilst these Sentences are in reading or during the singing of the Offertory Hymn when such shall be sung, the Tithes and Offerings of the people shall be collected by the Deacons, Churchwardens, Sidesmen, or other fit persons appointed by the Priest, and put into a decent bason provided for that purpose, and shall be brought to the Priest, who shall humbly present them before the Lord's Table and then place them, or else cause them to be placed, on the table near to the Altar set apart for that use.

And when the Tithes and Offerings are presented, the following may be said or sung,
BLESSED be Thou, O Lord God of Israel, forever and ever. All that is in the heaven and in the earth is Thine. All things come of Thee; and of Thine own have we given Thee. Amen.

Or else this,
ALL things come of Thee, O Lord;
and of Thine own have we given Thee. Amen.

And when there is a celebration of the Lord's Supper, at the time of the Offertory, the Priest shall place upon the Lord's Table so much Bread and Wine as he shall think sufficient. And the Bread shall be the best and purest unleavened wheat bread; and the Wine pure grape wine, with which a little water shall be mingled. And at high and solemn celebrations, the Lord's Table may then be censed by the Priest.

HOLY EUCHARIST

The Intercession.

*When the Great Litany is said or sung before the Eucharist, and at such other times when necessity may require,
the Priest may simply bid the Prayers of the people instead of saying the Prayer of Intercession.*

*And when the Prayer of Intercession is said,
the Priest shall first turn to face the people, and shall say,*
Let us pray for Christ's holy Catholic Church.

Then shall the Priest turn again to face the Altar, and shall say this Prayer following.

ALMIGHTY and everliving God, Who by Thy holy Apostle hast taught us to make prayers, and supplications, and to give thanks, for all men: We humbly beseech Thee most mercifully *to accept our alms and oblations, and* to receive these our prayers, which we offer unto Thy Divine Majesty; beseeching Thee to inspire continually the universal Church with the spirit of truth, unity, and concord: And grant that all they that do confess Thy holy Name may agree in the truth of Thy holy Word, and live in unity and godly love.

We beseech Thee also to save and defend all Christian Kings, Princes, and Governors; and especially Thy servant *ELIZABETH* our Queen; that under her we may be godly and quietly governed: And grant unto her whole Council, and to all that are put in authority under her, that they may truly and impartially minister justice, to the punishment of wickedness and vice, and to the maintenance of Thy true religion and virtue.

Give grace, O heavenly Father, to all Bishops, Priests, and Deacons, *and specially to Thy servant N. our Bishop,* that they may both by their life and doctrine set forth Thy true and living Word, and rightly and duly administer Thy holy Sacraments. And we beseech Thee also to bless all others who minister in Thy Name; that every one according to his calling and ministry may truly and godly serve Thee, to Thy honour and glory, and the edifying of Thy holy Church.

And to all Thy people give Thy heavenly grace; and specially to this congregation here present; that, with meek heart and due reverence, they may hear and receive Thy holy Word, truly serving Thee in holiness and righteousness all the days of their life. And we most humbly beseech Thee of Thy goodness, O Lord, to comfort and succour all them who, in this transitory life, are in trouble, sorrow, need, sickness, or any other adversity, *especially those for whom our prayers are desired.*

✠ We remember before Thee, O Lord, and commend to Thy gracious keeping, all Thy servants departed this life in Thy faith and fear, *especially Thy* servant *N.;* and we bless Thy holy Name for all who in life and death have glorified Thee, remembering chiefly the Blessed Virgin Mary, Mother of Thy Son Jesus Christ our Lord; together with blessed Joseph, her Spouse; blessed John the Baptist, Forerunner of our Lord, and all who served Thee before His coming; Thy blessed Apostles Peter and Paul, and all Thy blessed Apostles, Prophets, Evangelists, Pastors and Doctors; Thy blessed Martyrs and Confessors, Virgins, Widows, and Matrons; *and especially Thy blessed Saint N. whom we remember before Thee this day;* and all Thy blessed Saints, in every place, and in every age: beseeching Thee to give us grace that, rejoicing in their fellowship, and assisted by their prayers, we may follow their good examples, and with them be partakers of Thy heavenly kingdom. Grant this, O Father, for Jesus Christ's sake, our only Mediator and Advocate, to Whom, with Thee and the Holy Ghost, be all honour and glory, world without end. *Amen.*

*And here, when there is a Communion, all those who are not baptised,
and those who are excommunicate, shall withdraw from the Congregation.*

73

HOLY EUCHARIST

The Liturgy of the Supper of the Lord

The Preparation of the Faithful

Then shall the Priest or one of the Ministers invite the faithful to the Lord's Table, saying,

YE that do truly and earnestly repent you of your sins, and are in love and charity with your neighbours, and intend to lead a new life, following the commandments of God, and walking from henceforth in His holy ways: Draw near with faith, and take this holy Sacrament to your comfort; and make your humble confession to Almighty God, meekly kneeling upon your knees.

Then shall this general Confession be made by all that are minded to receive the Holy Communion, both the Priest and people together, all humbly kneeling upon their knees, and saying,

ALMIGHTY God, Father of our Lord Jesus Christ, Maker of all things, Judge of all men: We acknowledge and confess our manifold sins and wickedness, Which we from time to time most grievously have committed, By thought, word, and deed, Against Thy Divine Majesty, Provoking most justly Thy wrath and indignation against us. We do earnestly repent, And are heartily sorry for these our misdoings; The remembrance of them is grievous unto us; The burden of them is intolerable. Have mercy upon us; have mercy upon us, most merciful Father; For Thy Son our Lord Jesus Christ's sake, Forgive us all that is past; And grant that we may ever hereafter Serve and please Thee In newness of life, To the honour and glory of Thy Name; Through Jesus Christ our Lord. Amen.

Then shall the Priest (or the Bishop, if he be present,) stand up, and turning himself to the people, pronounce this Absolution following.

ALMIGHTY God, our heavenly Father, Who of His great mercy hath promised forgiveness of sins to all them that with hearty repentance and true faith turn unto Him: Have mercy upon you; ✠ pardon and deliver you from all your sins; confirm and strengthen you in all goodness; and bring you to everlasting life; through Jesus Christ our Lord. *Amen.*

Then shall the Priest say,
Hear what comfortable words our Saviour Christ saith
unto all that truly turn to Him.

COME unto me all that travail and are heavy laden, and I will refresh you. *Saint Matthew xi.*

So God loved the world, that He gave His only-begotten Son, to the end that all that believe in Him should not perish, but have everlasting life. *Saint John iii.*

Hear also what Saint Paul saith.
This is a true saying, and worthy of all men to be received, That Christ Jesus came into the world to save sinners. I *Timothy i.*

Hear also what Saint John saith.
If any man sin, we have an Advocate with the Father, Jesus Christ the righteous; and He is the propitiation for our sins. I *Saint John ii.*

74

HOLY EUCHARIST

THE PREPARATION OF THE LORD'S TABLE

The Priest shall turn to face the people, and shall say or sing,
THE peace of the Lord be always with you.
Answer. And with thy spirit.

*Then shall the Priest turn again to the Lord's Table, and shall prepare and
set in order all the Bread and Wine which is to be consecrated.*

The Priest shall first take the Bread into his hands, and shall say,
BLESSED art Thou, O Lord our God, Maker and King of heaven and earth; for from Thy bounty we have received this Bread, which we offer unto Thee: Fruit of the earth and the work of men's hands, from which shall be made for us the Bread of eternal life.

Answer. Blessed be God forever.

Then shall the Priest pour a little Water into the Wine, saying,
O GOD, Who didst wonderfully create, and even yet more wonderfully renew, the dignity of our nature: Grant that, by the mystery of this Water and Wine, we may come to share in the divinity of Christ, Who humbled Himself to partake of our humanity. *Amen.*

Then shall the Priest take the Chalice into his hands, and shall say,
BLESSED art Thou, O Lord our God, Maker and King of heaven and earth; for from Thy bounty we have received this Wine, which we offer unto Thee: Fruit of the vine and the work of men's hands, from which shall be made for us the Cup of everlasting salvation.

Answer. Blessed be God forever.

Then shall the Priest say this Prayer following.
IN a spirit of humility, and with a contrite heart, may we be accepted of Thee, O Lord; and may our sacrifice be so made in Thy sight this day as to be pleasing unto Thee, O Lord our God. *Amen.*

Then shall the Priest wash his hands, saying,
I WILL wash my hands in innocency, O Lord, and so will I go to Thine altar; that I may shew the voice of thanksgiving, and tell of all Thy wondrous works. Lord, I have loved the habitation of Thy house, and the place where Thine honour dwelleth.

THE EXHORTATION TO THE FAITHFUL.

*And when the Bread and Wine have been prepared and set in order upon the Lord's Table,
the people shall rise; and the Priest, turning himself to face the people, shall say,*
PRAY, brethren, that this shewing forth of the death of our Lord Jesus Christ, which is my sacrifice and yours, may be acceptable to God the Father Almighty.

And the Congregation shall answer,
MAY the Lord receive the sacrifice at thy hands, to the praise and glory of His Name, and for our good also, and that of all His holy Church. Amen.

*Then shall the Priest turn himself again towards the Altar,
and he and the people shall pray quietly for a space.*

HOLY EUCHARIST

The Consecration of the Eucharist

Then shall the Priest begin the Preface to the Consecration of the Eucharist,
and turning himself to face the people, he shall say,

THE Lord be with you.

Answer. And with thy spirit.

Priest. Lift up your hearts.

Answer. We lift them up unto the Lord.

Priest. Let us give thanks unto our Lord God.

Answer. It is meet and right so to do.

Then shall the Priest turn himself again to face the Lord's Table, and say,

IT is very meet, right, and our bounden duty, that we should at all times, and in all places, give thanks unto Thee, Holy Lord, Almighty Father, Everlasting God, Maker and Preserver of all things.

Here shall follow the Proper Preface, if any be specially appointed, after which shall be sung or said,

THEREFORE with Angels and Archangels, and with all the company of heaven, we laud and magnify Thy glorious Name; evermore praising Thee, and saying,

And the Priest and people together shall say or sing,

HOLY, Holy, Holy, Lord God of hosts, Heaven and earth are full of Thy glory: Glory be to Thee, O Lord most high. ✠ Blessed is He that cometh in the Name of the Lord: Hosanna in the highest.

Then shall all devoutly and reverently kneel down upon their knees.

And when the Priest, standing before the Altar, hath so ordered the Bread and Wine, that he may with the more readiness and decency break the Bread, and take the Cup into his hands; he shall say the Prayer of Consecration and the Oblation of the Eucharist, as followeth.

ALL blessing, glory, and thanksgiving be unto Thee, Almighty God, our heavenly Father, Who of Thy tender mercy didst give Thine only Son Jesus Christ to take our nature upon Him, and to suffer Death upon the Cross for our redemption; Who made there, by His one Oblation of Himself once offered, a full, perfect, and sufficient Sacrifice, Oblation, and Satisfaction, for the sins of the whole world; and did institute, and in His holy Gospel command us to continue, a perpetual memory of that His precious Death and Sacrifice, until His coming again:

   Hear us, O merciful Father, we most humbly beseech Thee; and vouchsafe to send down Thy Holy Spirit upon us, and upon these Thy creatures of Bread and Wine which we set apart, according to Thy Son our Saviour Jesus Christ's holy institution, in remembrance of His Death and Passion, that they may become for us His most blessed Body and Blood, and be received by us as He hath commanded: Who, in the same night that He was betrayed, (*Here the Priest is to take the Paten into his hands.*) took Bread; and, when He had given thanks, (*And here the Priest is to make the sign of the Cross over all the Bread which is to be consecrated.*) He blessed it, (*And here the Priest is to break the Bread.*) and brake it; and gave it to His disciples, saying, (*And here the Priest is to lay his hands upon all the Bread.*) Take, eat;

This is my Body which is given for you:
Do this in remembrance of me.

Likewise, after Supper, (*Here the Priest is to take the Chalice into his hands.*) He took the Cup; and, when He had given thanks, (*And here the Priest is to make the sign of the Cross over every vessel (be it Chalice or Flagon)*)

in which there is any Wine to be consecrated.) He blessed it, and gave it to them, saying, (*And here the Priest is to lay his hands upon every vessel in which there is any Wine to be consecrated.*) Drink ye all of this;

**For this is my Blood of the New Testament,
which is shed for you and for many for the remission of sins:
Do this, as oft as ye shall drink it, in remembrance of me.**

Then the Priest may say or sing,
The Mystery of Faith:

After which, the Priest and people shall say or sing,
CHRIST was dead;
Christ is risen;
Christ will come again.

Or else this,
As often as we eat this Bread, and drink this Cup,
we do shew Thy Death, O Lord, till Thou shalt come.

Then shall the Priest proceed with the Oblation of the Eucharist, as followeth.

WHEREFORE, O Father, Lord of heaven and earth, according to the institution of Thy dearly beloved Son our Saviour Jesus Christ, we Thy humble servants, in union with all Thy holy Church, do celebrate, and make here before the sight of Thy Divine Majesty, with these Thy holy gifts of the Bread of eternal life, and the Cup of everlasting salvation, which we now offer unto Thee, that memory of His blessed Passion and precious Death which in His Gospel He hath commanded us to make; and having also in remembrance His mighty Resurrection and glorious Ascension, and looking for His Coming again in glory, we render unto Thee most high praise and hearty thanks for all the benefits procured unto us by the same.

And we entirely desire Thy fatherly goodness mercifully to accept this our sacrifice of praise and thanksgiving; most humbly beseeching Thee to grant, that by the Merits and Death of Thy Son Jesus Christ which we plead here before Thee, and through faith in His Blood, we and all Thy whole Church may obtain remission of our sins, and all other benefits of His Passion.

And as we here shew forth, O heavenly Father, that one, full, perfect, and sufficient Sacrifice, Oblation, and Satisfaction, made once and for all by Thy Son Jesus Christ for the sins of the whole world, so also we offer and present unto Thee, O Lord, ourselves, our souls and bodies, to be a reasonable, holy, and living sacrifice unto Thee; humbly beseeching Thee to grant, that all we, who are partakers of this holy Communion, may worthily receive the same, and be fulfilled with Thy grace and heavenly benediction and preserved both in body and soul unto everlasting life.

And although we be unworthy, through our manifold sins, to offer unto Thee any sacrifice, yet we beseech Thee to accept this our bounden duty and service, not weighing our merits, but pardoning our offences; through Jesus Christ our Lord: by Whom, and with Whom, in the unity of the Holy Ghost, all honour and glory be unto Thee, O Father Almighty, world without end.

*And the Priest and people together
shall say or sing,*
AMEN.

HOLY EUCHARIST

Then shall the Priest say or sing,
Let us pray.

As our Saviour Christ hath commanded and taught us, we are bold to say:

And the Priest and people together shall then say or sing the Lord's Prayer, as followeth.
OUR Father, which art in heaven, hallowed be Thy Name. Thy kingdom come. Thy will be done, in earth as it is in heaven. Give us this day our daily bread. And forgive us our trespasses, As we forgive them that trespass against us. And lead us not into temptation, But deliver us from evil. For Thine is the kingdom, the power, and the glory, For ever and ever. Amen.

Then shall silence be kept for a space.

*Then shall the Priest break the consecrated Bread. And as the Priest
breaketh the consecrated Bread, he shall say,*
O LORD Jesu Christ, Who didst say to Thine Apostles, Peace I leave with you, my peace I give unto you: Regard not our sins, but the faith of Thy Church; and grant unto it that peace and unity which is agreeable to Thy will; Who livest and reignest with the Father and the Holy Ghost, ever one God, world without end. *Amen.*

THE PREPARATION FOR HOLY COMMUNION

*And the Holy Sacrament being ready for distribution,
the Priest shall then say or sing,*
CHRIST our Passover is sacrificed for us, therefore let us keep the feast: Not with the old leaven, neither with the leaven of malice and wickedness; but with the unleavened bread of sincerity and truth.

*Then shall the Priest, together with all them that shall receive the Holy Communion,
humbly say this Prayer of humble access to the Lord's Table, as followeth.*
WE do not presume to come to this Thy Table, O merciful Lord, Trusting in our own righteousness, But in Thy manifold and great mercies. We are not worthy So much as to gather up the crumbs under Thy Table. But Thou art the same Lord, Whose property is always to have mercy: Grant us therefore, gracious Lord, So to eat the Flesh of Thy dear Son Jesus Christ, And to drink His Blood, That our sinful bodies may be made clean by His Body, And our souls washed through His most precious Blood, And that we may evermore dwell in Him, And He in us. Amen.

Then shall be said or sung,
O LAMB of God, that takest away the sins of the world,
have mercy upon us.
O Lamb of God, that takest away the sins of the world,
have mercy upon us.
O Lamb of God, that takest away the sins of the world,
grant us Thy peace.

Then shall the Priest first receive the Holy Communion in both kinds himself; and then he shall proceed to deliver the same to the Bishops, Priests, and Deacons, in like manner (if any be present), and then after that to the people also in order, all meekly and devoutly kneeling upon their knees; but if anyone cannot receive the Holy Communion kneeling, either due to age or infirmity, he may stand to receive the Blessed Sacrament.

HOLY EUCHARIST

THE MINISTRATION OF HOLY COMMUNION

And when the Priest himself hath received the Holy Communion, before he shall proceed to deliver the same to anyone, he shall first take the consecrated Bread and Wine into his hands, and turning himself unto the people, and shewing them the Holy Sacrament, he shall invite them to partake of the Lord's Supper, saying,

BEHOLD, the Lamb of God; behold Him that taketh away the sin of the world: Blessed are they which are called unto the marriage supper of the Lamb.

And all they that shall receive the Holy Communion shall say,

Lord, I am not worthy that Thou shouldest come under my roof; but speak the word only, and my soul shall be healed.

Then shall the faithful come forward to receive the Holy Communion.

And when the Priest delivereth the consecrated Bread to any one, he shall say,

✠ THE Body of our Lord Jesus Christ, which was given for thee, preserve thy body and soul unto everlasting life: Take and eat this in remembrance that Christ died for thee, and feed on Him in thy heart by faith with thanksgiving.

And every one that receiveth the consecrated Bread shall answer, saying,

AMEN.

And the Minister that delivereth the Cup to any one shall say,

✠ THE Blood of our Lord Jesus Christ, which was shed for thee, preserve thy body and soul unto everlasting life: Drink this in remembrance that Christ's Blood was shed for thee, and be thankful.

And every one that receiveth the Cup shall answer, saying,

AMEN.

And it is hereby ordered that, except for reasons of sickness or infirmity, the Holy Communion of the Body and Blood of our Lord Jesus Christ shall be received by all the Communicants humbly and reverently kneeling upon their knees at the Communion rail, or for just cause in some other convenient place appointed by the Ordinary.

And here it is also ordered that in the ministering of Holy Communion, the Priest shall place the consecrated Bread either directly into the mouth of each Communicant, or else into his right hand; and the Minister shall not at any time release his hold of the Chalice, but the faithful shall only touch the Chalice with their hands, and guide the same to their mouths; and this is appointed to be done so that no disorder or profanation may ensue at any time in the ministration of the Holy Communion of Christ's Body and Blood.

When all have communicated, the Priest shall return to the Lord's Table, and reverently place upon it what remaineth of the consecrated Elements, covering the same with a fair linen cloth. And if any of the consecrated Bread or Wine is to be reserved by the Priest, the same he shall reverently place inside the Tabernacle or Aumbry appointed for that purpose, and the door thereof shall be securely locked, and covered with a white cloth to indicate the Real Presence of our Lord Jesus Christ in the Blessed Sacrament therein reserved.

THE THANKSGIVING AFTER HOLY COMMUNION

Then shall the Priest turn to the people, and say,
THE Lord be with you.
Answer. And with thy spirit.

Priest. Let us pray.

HOLY EUCHARIST

Then shall the Priest turn again to face the Altar, and say,

ALMIGHTY and everliving God, we most heartily thank Thee, for that Thou dost vouchsafe to feed us, who have duly received these Holy Mysteries, with the spiritual food of the most precious Body and Blood of Thy Son our Saviour Jesus Christ; and dost assure us thereby of Thy favour and goodness towards us; and that we are very members incorporate in the mystical Body of Thy Son, which is the blessed company of all faithful people; and are also heirs through hope of Thy everlasting kingdom, by the Merits of His most precious Death and Passion. And we most humbly beseech Thee, O heavenly Father, so to assist us with Thy grace, that we may continue in that holy fellowship, and do all such good works as Thou hast prepared for us to walk in; through Jesus Christ our Lord, to Whom, with Thee and the Holy Ghost, be all honour and glory, world without end. *Amen.*

And here may follow any Post-Communion Collect appointed for use.

And Gloria in Excelsis *shall be sung or said here, except at such times when it shall be sung or said before the Collect for the Queen's Majesty; provided always that it may be omitted altogether on the Sundays and week-days in Advent and Lent and on Days of Penitence, and at any celebrations for the Dead. And whensoever* Gloria in Excelsis *shall be sung or said before the Collect for the Queen's Majesty, and at all such times when it is omitted, one of the appointed Dismissal Anthems shall here be sung or said instead.*

GLORIA IN EXCELSIS.

GLORY be to God on high, and in earth peace, good will towards men. We praise Thee, we bless Thee, (*Here all shall bow.*) **we worship Thee**, we glorify Thee, we give thanks to Thee for Thy great glory, O Lord God, heavenly King, God the Father Almighty.

O Lord, the only-begotten Son, (*And here all shall reverently bow.*) **Jesu Christ**; O Lord God, Lamb of God, Son of the Father, that takest away the sins of the world, have mercy upon us. Thou that takest away the sins of the world, (*And here all shall bow again.*) **receive our prayer.** Thou that sittest at the right hand of God the Father, have mercy upon us.

For Thou only art holy, Thou only art the Lord, Thou only, O Christ, with the Holy Ghost, ✠ art most high in the glory of God the Father. Amen.

THE BLESSING.
Then the Priest (or the Bishop if he be present) shall let them depart
with this Blessing, the people all devoutly kneeling.

THE peace of God, which passeth all understanding, keep your hearts and minds in the knowledge and love of God, and of His Son Jesus Christ our Lord: And the blessing of God Almighty, ✠ the Father, the Son, and the Holy Ghost, be amongst you and remain with you always. *Amen.*

THE DISMISSAL.
Then shall the Priest say,
THE Lord be with you.
Answer. And with thy spirit.
Priest. Let us depart in peace.
Answer. In the Name of the Lord.
Amen.

The Proper Prefaces, Post-Communion Collects, and Dismissal Anthems
Appointed for Use According to the Season and at Other Times of the Year

ADVENT

The Preface.

WHOSE grace that bringeth salvation hath appeared unto all men, and Who hath taught us to deny ungodliness and worldly lusts, and that we should live soberly, righteously, and godly, in this present world; looking for that blessed hope, and the glorious appearing of the great God and our Saviour Jesus Christ. Therefore with Angels, &c.

The Collect after Communion.

O LORD Jesu Christ our God and King, Who hast ordained this holy Sacrament to be the continual memory of the atoning sacrifice of Thy precious Death, until Thy coming again: Grant, we humbly beseech Thee, that all we who have partaken of these holy Mysteries may be enabled, through Thy strength and comfort, to endure steadfastly unto the day of Thine appearing; and to lift up our heads with joy, in the knowledge that our redemption draweth nigh; Who, with the Father and the Holy Ghost, livest and reignest, forever One God, world without end. *Amen.*

The Dismissal Anthem.

DROP down, ye heavens, from above, / and let the skies pour down righteousness: Let the earth open, and let them bring forth salvation; / And let righteousness spring up together; I the Lord have created it. And in mercy shall the throne be established: / and he shall sit upon it in truth in the tabernacle of David, judging, and seeking judgment, and hastening righteousness.

GLORY be to the Father, and to the Son, / and to the Holy Ghost;

As it was in the beginning, is now, and ever shall be, / world without end. Amen.

CHRISTMAS AND CHRISTMASTIDE

The Preface.

BECAUSE Thou didst give Jesus Christ Thine only Son to be born *as at this time* for us: Who, by the operation of the Holy Ghost, was made very man of the substance of the Virgin Mary His Mother: and that without spot of sin, to make us clean from all sin. Therefore with Angels, &c.

The Collect after Communion.

O GOD, Who hast given us grace at this time to celebrate the Incarnation and Nativity of our most Blessed Lord and Saviour Jesus Christ: We laud and magnify Thy glorious Name for the countless blessings which He hath procured and brought unto us by the same; and we humbly beseech Thee to grant that we may evermore set forth Thy praise in our joyful obedience to Thy will, doing all such good works as Thou wouldst have us do; through the same Thy Son Jesus Christ our Lord. *Amen.*

HOLY EUCHARIST

THE DISMISSAL ANTHEM.

O PRAISE God in His holiness; / praise Him in the firmament of His power. Praise Him in His noble acts; / praise Him according to His excellent greatness. Praise Him in the sound of the trumpet; / praise Him upon the lute and harp. Praise Him in the cymbals and dances; / praise Him upon the strings and pipe. Praise Him upon the well-tuned cymbals; / praise Him upon the loud cymbals. Let everything that hath breath, / praise the Lord.

GLORY be to the Father, and to the Son, and to the Holy Ghost;
As it was in the beginning, is now, and ever shall be, world without end. Amen.

THE EPIPHANY AND ITS OCTAVE

THE PREFACE.

THROUGH Jesus Christ our Lord, Who in the substance of our mortal flesh manifested forth His glory: that He might bring all men out of darkness, and into His own marvellous light. Therefore with Angels, &c.

THE COLLECT AFTER COMMUNION.

ALMIGHTY God, Who didst manifest to the Gentiles the glorious Godhead of Thy blessed Son our Lord and Saviour Jesus Christ: Grant, we beseech thee, that the brightness of His presence may shine forever in our hearts, and His glory be manifested and shewn forth in the godly living of our lives; through the same Jesus Christ our Lord. *Amen.*

THE DISMISSAL ANTHEM.

THE people that walked in darkness have seen a great light: they that dwell in the land of the shadow of death, upon them hath the light shined. There is sprung up a light for the righteous: / and joyful gladness for such as are true-hearted. Rejoice in Lord, ye righteous; / and give thanks for a remembrance of His holiness.

GLORY be to the Father, and to the Son, / and to the Holy Ghost;
As it was in the beginning, is now, and ever shall be, / world without end. Amen.

EPIPHANYTIDE

THE PREFACE.

WHO with Thine only-begotten Son and Holy Ghost proceeding art One God and One Lord, in Trinity of Persons and in Unity of Substance: For that which we believe of Thy glory, O Father, the same we believe of the Son, and of the Holy Ghost. Therefore with Angels, &c.

THE COLLECT AFTER COMMUNION.

HASTEN, O God, the time when Thou shalt send from Thy right hand Him Whom Thou wilt send; at Whose appearing the saints departed shall be raised, and we which are alive and remain shall be caught up to meet Him, and so shall we ever be with our Lord. Keep us, we beseech Thee, O Father, unto that day; and grant that at His coming, we may, as One Body, be presented with exceeding joy before the Presence of His glory, holy and unspotted, prepared as a Bride adorned for her Husband; through the same Thy Son Jesus Christ our Lord. *Amen.*

HOLY EUCHARIST

The Dismissal Anthem.

For the Lord hath chosen Sion to be an habitation for Himself; / He hath longed for her. This shall be my rest for ever: / here will I dwell, for I have a delight therein. I will bless her provisions with increase: / and will satisfy her poor with bread. I will deck her priests with salvation, / and her saints shall rejoice and sing.

Glory be to the Father, and to the Son, / and to the Holy Ghost;
As it was in the beginning, is now, and ever shall be, / world without end. Amen.

Shrovetide

The Preface.

Who with Thine only-begotten Son and Holy Ghost proceeding art One God and One Lord, in Trinity of Persons and in Unity of Substance: For that which we believe of Thy glory, O Father, the same we believe of the Son, and of the Holy Ghost. Therefore with Angels, &c.

The Collect after Communion.

Hasten, O God, the time when Thou shalt send from Thy right hand Him Whom Thou wilt send; at Whose appearing the saints departed shall be raised, and we which are alive and remain shall be caught up to meet Him, and so shall we ever be with our Lord. Keep us, we beseech Thee, O Father, unto that day; and grant that at His coming, we may, as One Body, be presented with exceeding joy before the Presence of His glory, holy and unspotted, prepared as a Bride adorned for her Husband; through the same Thy Son Jesus Christ our Lord. *Amen.*

The Dismissal Anthem.

The Lord is King, be the people never so impatient: / He sitteth between the cherubim, be the earth never so unquiet. The Lord is great in Sion, / and high above all people. They shall give thanks unto Thy Name, / which is great, and wonderful, and holy.

Glory be to the Father, and to the Son, / and to the Holy Ghost;
As it was in the beginning, is now, and ever shall be, / world without end. Amen.

Lent

The Preface.

Because that by abstinence and fasting Thou dost curb our sinfulness, Thou dost raise our minds from things of earth, Thou dost renew our strength, and reward us with manifold blessings. Therefore with Angels, &c.

The Collect after Communion.

O most merciful Father, Who hast so wonderfully constituted Thy Church that the whole body doth participate in the honour, joy, and strength, or suffering, sorrow, and weakness, of every member thereof: Grant, we humbly beseech Thee, that through the partaking of these holy Mysteries, Thy whole Church may receive increase of life, and be renewed in all the gifts and graces of Thy Holy Spirit, to the glory of Thy holy Name; through Jesus Christ our Lord. *Amen.*

The Dismissal Anthem.

Bless the Lord, O my soul: and all that is within me, bless His holy Name. Bless the Lord, O my soul, / and forget not all His benefits. Who forgiveth all thine iniquities, / Who healeth all thy diseases; Who satisfieth thy mouth with good things: / so that thy youth is renewed like the eagle's.

HOLY EUCHARIST

GLORY be to the Father, and to the Son, / and to the Holy Ghost;
As it was in the beginning, is now, and ever shall be, / world without end. Amen.

PASSIONTIDE

THE PREFACE.
FOR the redemption of the world by the Death and Passion of our Saviour Christ, both God and Man; Who did humble Himself, even to the death of the Cross for us sinners, Who lay in darkness and the shadow of death; that He might make us the children of God, and exalt us to everlasting life. Therefore with Angels, &c.

THE COLLECT AFTER COMMUNION.
O GOD our heavenly Father, Who by the Cross and Passion of Thy dear Son Jesus Christ hast saved and delivered Thine elect: We humbly beseech Thee to grant that, by steadfast faith in the merits of that same Sacrifice, all we who are called by His Name may find help and salvation, and receive grace to triumph in the power of His mighty victory; through the same Thy blessed Son Jesus Christ our Lord. *Amen.*

THE DISMISSAL ANTHEM.
THOU hast redeemed us from the curse; / with Thine own most precious Blood. Nailed to the Cross, pierced with the spear, / Thou hast restored immortality to man. We worship Thee, Who died for us, / O blessed Lord and Saviour. Glory be to Thee, O Lord: / glory be to Thee, O Christ.

EASTER AND EASTERTIDE

THE PREFACE.
BUT chiefly are we bound to praise Thee for the glorious Resurrection of Thy Son Jesus Christ our Lord: For He is the very Paschal Lamb, which was offered for us, and hath taken away the sins of the world; Who by His death hath destroyed death, and by His rising to life again hath restored unto us everlasting life. Therefore with Angels, &c.

THE COLLECT AFTER COMMUNION.
O LORD God Almighty, Whose blessed Son our Saviour Jesus Christ did on the third day rise again triumphant over death: Raise us, we beseech Thee, from the death of sin unto the life of righteousness; and pour out abundantly upon us the Spirit of adoption, that we may always seek those things which are above, where He sitteth on Thy right hand in glory; and this we beg for the sake of the same Thy Son Jesus Christ our Lord. *Amen.*

THE DISMISSAL ANTHEM.
O PRAISE God in His holiness; / praise Him in the firmament of His power. Praise Him in His noble acts; / praise Him according to His excellent greatness. Praise Him in the sound of the trumpet; / praise Him upon the lute and harp. Praise Him in the cymbals and dances; / praise Him upon the strings and pipe. Praise Him upon the well-tuned cymbals; / praise Him upon the loud cymbals. Let everything that hath breath, / praise the Lord.
GLORY be to the Father, and to the Son, and to the Holy Ghost;
As it was in the beginning, is now, and ever shall be, world without end. Amen.

HOLY EUCHARIST

The Ascension and Ascensiontide

The Preface.

THROUGH Thy most dearly beloved Son Jesus Christ our Lord, Who after His most glorious Resurrection manifestly appeared to all His Apostles; and in their sight ascended up into heaven to prepare a place for us, and whence He shall come again in glory to judge both the quick and the dead; that where He is, thither we might also ascend, and reign with Him in glory. Therefore with Angels, &c.

The Collect after Communion.

ALMIGHTY God, Whose blessed Son our Saviour Jesus Christ ascended far above all the heavens that He might fill all things: Mercifully give us faith to perceive that, according to His promise, He abideth ever with His Church on earth, even unto the end of the world; through the same Jesus Christ our Lord. *Amen.*

The Dismissal Anthem.

LET not your heart be troubled: / ye believe in God, believe also in me. In my Father's house are many mansions: / if it were not so, I would have told you. I go to prepare a place for you. / And if I go and prepare a place for you, / I will come again, and receive you unto myself; That where I am, / there ye may be also.

GLORY be to the Father, and to the Son, / and to the Holy Ghost;

As it was in the beginning, is now, and ever shall be, / world without end. Amen.

Whitsunday and Whitsuntide

The Preface.

THROUGH Jesus Christ our Lord, Who after that He was ascended up far above all the heavens, and was set down at the right hand of Thy Majesty on high, did, according to His most true promise, send forth the Holy Ghost with a sudden great sound, as it had been a rushing mighty wind, in the likeness of fiery tongues, lighting upon the Apostles, to teach them, and to lead them into all truth; giving them both the gift of divers languages, and also boldness with fervent zeal constantly to preach the Gospel unto all nations; whereby we have been brought out of darkness and error into the clear light and true knowledge of Thee, and of Thy Son Jesus Christ. Therefore with Angels, &c.

The Collect after Communion.

ALMIGHTY God our heavenly Father, Who at this time didst send the Comforter to abide in thy Church: Bestow upon us, we beseech Thee, Thy manifold gifts of grace; that with minds enlightened by Thy truth, and hearts purified by Thy presence, we may daily be strengthened and comforted in the inward man; through Jesus Christ our Lord. *Amen.*

The Dismissal Anthem.

BEHOLD, how good and joyful a thing it is, / brethren, to dwell together in unity! It is like the precious ointment upon the head, that ran down unto the beard, / even unto Aaron's beard, and went down to the skirts of his clothing. Like as the dew of Hermon, / which fell upon the hill of Sion. For there the Lord promised His blessing, / and life for evermore.

GLORY be to the Father, and to the Son, and to the Holy Ghost; /

As it was in the beginning, is now, and ever shall be, / world without end. Amen.

HOLY EUCHARIST

TRINITY SUNDAY

THE PREFACE.
WHO with Thine only-begotten Son and Holy Ghost proceeding art One God and One Lord, in Trinity of Persons and in Unity of Substance: For that which we believe of Thy glory, O Father, the same we believe of the Son, and of the Holy Ghost. Therefore with Angels, &c.

THE COLLECT AFTER COMMUNION.
O GRACIOUS Lord and King Eternal, Immortal, Invisible, the only wise God, the mysteries of Whose Being are unsearchable: Accept, we beseech Thee, our praises for the revelation which Thou hast made of Thyself to be Father, Son, and Holy Ghost, three Persons and one Almighty God; and mercifully grant that ever holding and professing this faith, we may magnify Thy glorious Name, and lay hold on everlasting life; Who livest and reignest, ever one God, world without end. *Amen.*

THE DISMISSAL ANTHEM.
O PRAISE God in His holiness; / praise Him in the firmament of His power. Praise Him in His noble acts; / praise Him according to His excellent greatness. Praise Him in the sound of the trumpet; / praise Him upon the lute and harp. Praise Him in the cymbals and dances; / praise Him upon the strings and pipe. Praise Him upon the well-tuned cymbals; / praise Him upon the loud cymbals. Let everything that hath breath, / praise the Lord.
GLORY be to the Father, and to the Son, and to the Holy Ghost;
As it was in the beginning, is now, and ever shall be, world without end. Amen.

TRINITYTIDE

THE PREFACE.
WHO with Thine only-begotten Son and the Holy Ghost proceeding art One God and One Lord, in Trinity of Persons and in Unity of Substance: For that which we believe of Thy glory, O Father, the same we believe of the Son, and of the Holy Ghost. Therefore with Angels, &c.

THE COLLECT AFTER COMMUNION.
HASTEN, O God, the time when Thou shalt send from Thy right hand Him Whom Thou wilt send; at Whose appearing the saints departed shall be raised, and we which are alive and remain shall be caught up to meet Him, and so shall we ever be with our Lord. Keep us, we beseech Thee, O Father, unto that day; and grant that at His coming, we may, as One Body, be presented with exceeding joy before the Presence of His glory, holy and unspotted, prepared as a Bride adorned for her Husband; through the same Thy Son Jesus Christ our Lord. *Amen.*

THE DISMISSAL ANTHEM.
FOR the Lord hath chosen Sion to be an habitation for Himself; / He hath longed for her. This shall be my rest for ever: / here will I dwell, for I have a delight therein. I will bless her victuals with increase: / and will satisfy her poor with bread. I will deck her priests with salvation, / and her saints shall rejoice and sing.
GLORY be to the Father, and to the Son, / and to the Holy Ghost;
As it was in the beginning, is now, and ever shall be, / world without end. Amen.

HOLY EUCHARIST

MICHAELMAS AND MICHAELMASTIDE

THE PREFACE.

THROUGH Jesus Christ our Lord, Whom the Angels and Archangels praise, the Thrones, Principalities, and Dominions adore, the Powers and Virtues fear, and the Cherubim and Seraphim laud, with ceaseless exultation; with whom, we beseech Thee, O Father, to grant, that our own voices here on earth may be admitted; and that we might join in that never-ending hymn of praise with all the heavenly host before Thy Throne. Therefore with Angels, &c.

THE COLLECT AFTER COMMUNION.

VISIT, we beseech Thee, O Lord, the dwellings of all Thy people, especially those of us who have partaken of this holy Table, and drive far from us all the snares of the enemy; let Thy holy Angels dwell therein to preserve us in peace; and may Thy blessing be upon us evermore; through Christ our Lord. *Amen.*

THE DISMISSAL ANTHEM.

AND I beheld, and I heard the voice of many angels / round about the throne and the beasts and the elders: And the number of them was ten thousand times ten thousand, / and thousands of thousands; Saying with a loud voice, / Worthy is the Lamb that was slain: To receive power, and riches, and wisdom, / and strength, and honour, and glory, and blessing.
GLORY be to the Father, and to the Son, / and to the Holy Ghost;
As it was in the beginning, is now, and ever shall be, / world without end. Amen.

ALL SAINTS AND HALLOWMASTIDE AND SAINTS' DAYS

THE PREFACE.

WHO in the multitude of Thy blessed Saints hast compassed us about with so great a cloud of witnesses that we, rejoicing in their fellowship, may run with patience the race that is set before us, and together with them may receive the crown of glory that fadeth not away. Therefore with Angels, &c.

THE COLLECT AFTER COMMUNION.

O GOD, the King of all Saints, we praise and magnify Thy holy Name for all Thy servants who have finished their earthly course in Thy faith and fear; and we beseech Thee that, encouraged by their examples, strengthened by their fellowship, and assisted by their prayers, we may with them attain unto everlasting life in the glory of the resurrection of Thy Son Jesus Christ our Lord, for Whose sake and in Whose Name alone we pray. *Amen.*

THE DISMISSAL ANTHEM.

PRAISE ye the Lord. Sing unto the Lord a new song: / and His praise in the congregation of saints. Let Israel rejoice in Him that made him: / let the children of Sion be joyful in their King. For the Lord taketh pleasure in His people; / He will beautify the meek with salvation. Let the saints be joyful in glory: / let them sing aloud upon their beds.
GLORY be to the Father, and to the Son, / and to the Holy Ghost;
As it was in the beginning, is now, and ever shall be, / world without end. Amen.

HOLY EUCHARIST

FEASTS OF THE BLESSED VIRGIN MARY

THE PREFACE.

AND that *upon this day*, we should praise, bless, and tell forth the wonders of Thy love made known to all mankind in the most glorious and ever blessed Virgin Mary, the Mother of Thy Son Jesus Christ our Lord and God, by whose obedience to Thy Word salvation came into the world; and that we should thank Thee, O Father, that in her purity and faithfulness, we can perceive the perfection of Thy redemption. Therefore with Angels, *&c.*

THE DISMISSAL ANTHEM.

HAIL, thou that art highly favoured, / the Lord is with thee: / Blessed art thou among women; / and blessed is the Fruit of thy womb. And blessed is she that believed: / for there shall be a performance of those things which were told her from the Lord.

GLORY be to the Father, and to the Son, / and to the Holy Ghost;

As it was in the beginning, is now, and ever shall be, / world without end. Amen.

FEASTS OF THE APOSTLES

THE PREFACE.

AND also that we should humbly beseech Thee, O Lord, the everlasting Shepherd, never to forsake Thy flock; but through the witness and teaching of Thy blessed Apostles ever to keep Thy Church in the true faith and knowledge of Thy Son Jesus Christ, until the day of His appearing. Therefore with Angels, *&c.*

THE COLLECT AFTER COMMUNION.

O GOD, the King of all Saints, we praise and magnify Thy holy Name for all Thy servants who have finished their earthly course in Thy faith and fear; and we beseech Thee that, encouraged by their examples, strengthened by their fellowship, and assisted by their prayers, we may with them attain unto everlasting life in the glory of the resurrection of the same Thy Son Jesus Christ our Lord, for Whose sake and in Whose Name alone we pray. *Amen.*

THE DISMISSAL ANTHEM.

PRAISE ye the Lord. Sing unto the Lord a new song: / and His praise in the congregation of saints. Let Israel rejoice in Him that made him: / let the children of Sion be joyful in their King. For the Lord taketh pleasure in His people; / He will beautify the meek with salvation. Let the saints be joyful in glory: / let them sing aloud upon their beds.

GLORY be to the Father, and to the Son, / and to the Holy Ghost;

As it was in the beginning, is now, and ever shall be, / world without end. Amen.

CORPUS CHRISTI

THE PREFACE.

THROUGH Jesus Christ our Lord, Who having loved His own that were in the world loved them unto the end; and Who, on the night before He suffered, while sitting at meat with His disciples, did institute, and command us to continue to celebrate, these Holy Mysteries, until He shall come again; so that we, being worthy partakers of this blessed Sacrament, might be preserved both in body and soul unto everlasting life, and at the last be raised up and made partakers of His heavenly kingdom. Therefore with Angels, *&c.*

HOLY EUCHARIST

THE FAITHFUL DEPARTED

THE PREFACE.

THROUGH Jesus Christ our Lord, in Whom hath shone forth unto us the blessed hope of a joyful resurrection; that they who now mourn the certain condition of their mortality may be consoled by the sure promise of new and everlasting life in the world to come; for unto us, Thy faithful people, life is only changed, and not taken away; and at the dissolution of this earthly tabernacle, a perfect dwelling-place shall be made for us, not made by mortal hands, but made for us by Thee, eternal in the heavens. Therefore with Angels, &c.

THE DISMISSAL ANTHEM.

I HEARD a voice from heaven, saying unto me, / Write, From henceforth blessed are the dead which die in the Lord: Even so, saith the Spirit, for they rest from their labours; / and their works do follow them. O death, where is thy sting? O grave, where is thy victory? / Thanks be to God, which giveth us the victory, through our Lord Jesus Christ.
THE Lord gave, and the Lord hath taken away: /
Blessed be the Name of the Lord.

FERIAL DAYS

THE COLLECT AFTER COMMUNION.

HASTEN, O God, the time when Thou shalt send from Thy right hand Him Whom Thou wilt send; at Whose appearing the saints departed shall be raised, and we which are alive and remain shall be caught up to meet Him, and so shall we ever be with our Lord. Keep us, we beseech Thee, O Father, unto that day; and grant that at His coming, we may, as One Body, be presented with exceeding joy before the Presence of His glory, holy and unspotted, prepared as a Bride adorned for her Husband; through the same Thy Son Jesus Christ our Lord. *Amen.*

THE DISMISSAL ANTHEM

ALL glory, thanks and praise be unto Thee, / O God our heavenly Father, For this holy Supper in which the memorial of the Passion of Thy Son is renewed, / and His Testament proclaimed; Wherein He feeds us with His Presence, / and our souls are filled with grace; And a pledge of future glory is given unto us, / with the hope of everlasting life in Him. And so be given unto Thee, O Lord our God most high, / for all Thy many mercies to us, and to all Thy holy Church, all glory, thanks, and praise, for evermore.
GLORY be to the Father, and to the Son, / and to the Holy Ghost;
As it was in the beginning, is now, and ever shall be, / world without end. Amen.

THE ORDER FOR
A SECOND CONSECRATION

If the consecrated Bread or Wine be all spent before all have communicated,
the Priest shall consecrate more in both kinds, according to this Form of Consecration following.

HEAR us, O merciful Father, we most humbly beseech Thee; and vouchsafe to send down Thy Holy Spirit upon us, and upon these Thy creatures of Bread and Wine which we also set apart, according to Thy Son our Saviour Jesus Christ's holy institution, in remembrance of His Death and Passion, that they may become for us His most blessed Body and Blood, and be received by us as He hath commanded: Who, in the same night that He was betrayed, (*Here the Priest is to take the Paten into his hands.*) took Bread; and, when He had given thanks, (*And here the Priest is to make the sign of the Cross over all the Bread to be consecrated.*) He blessed it, (*And here the Priest is to break the Bread.*) and brake it; and gave it to His disciples, saying, (*And here the Priest is to lay his hands upon all the Bread.*) Take, eat;

This is my Body which is given for you:
Do this in remembrance of me.

Likewise, after Supper, (*Here the Priest is to take the Chalice into his hands.*) He took the Cup; and, when He had given thanks, (*And here the Priest is to make the sign of the Cross over every vessel (be it Chalice or Flagon) in which there is any Wine to be consecrated.*) He blessed it, and gave it to them, saying, (*And here the Priest is to lay his hands upon every vessel in which there is any Wine to be consecrated.*) Drink ye all of this;

For this is my Blood of the New Testament,
which is shed for you and for many for the remission of sins:
Do this, as oft as ye shall drink it, in remembrance of me.

Then shall the Priest continue, saying,

WHEREFORE, O Father, Lord of heaven and earth, according to the institution of Thy dearly beloved Son our Saviour Jesus Christ, we Thy humble servants, with all Thy holy Church, do celebrate, and make here before the sight of Thy Divine Majesty, with these Thy holy gifts of the Bread of eternal life, and the Cup of everlasting salvation, which we now offer unto Thee, that memory of His blessed Passion and precious Death which in His Gospel He hath commanded us to make; and having also in remembrance His mighty Resurrection and glorious Ascension, and looking for His Coming again in glory, we render unto Thee most high praise and hearty thanks for all the benefits procured unto us by the same. And we humbly beseech Thee to grant, that all we, who shall be partakers of this holy Communion, may worthily receive the same, and be fulfilled with Thy grace and heavenly benediction and preserved both in body and soul unto everlasting life; through the same Thy Son Jesus Christ our Lord. *Amen.*

Then shall the Priest proceed to continue to minister
the Holy Communion in the prescribed manner.

HOLY EUCHARIST

PERMISSIBLE VARIATIONS AND ADDITIONS

THE KYRIE ELEISON.

The Invocation of God the Most Holy Trinity for His mercy to be shewn upon His people, which is called the Kyrie Eleison, *may be said or sung in this portion of Christ's holy Church at any celebration of the Lord's Supper in any language spoken by the people; provided always that at all such times the* Kyrie Eleison *shall also be said or sung in part in English. Notwithstanding, the* Kyrie Eleison *when said or sung in Greek shall have no other language used therewith. And the* Kyrie Eleison *may at any time be said or sung in its three-fold, six-fold, or nine-fold forms.*

THE INTERCESSION.

At the principal celebration of the Lord's Supper on the Lord's Day, and on the greater Festivals and Holy-days, the Prayer of Intercession may be said immediately following the Consecration and Oblation of the Eucharist before the Lord's Prayer.

A PRAYER AT THE OFFERTORY.

This Prayer following may be said in an audible voice by the Priest immediately before the Preface to the Consecration of the Holy Eucharist.

ALMIGHTY and most merciful Father, we offer unto Thee this Bread and this Wine, which Thou hast given unto us of Thy bounty; for Thou art our God, and we are Thy people; all that is in the heaven and the earth is Thine, and of the gifts of Thy creation only have we anything to offer unto Thee. We are not worthy, dear Lord, through our manifold sins and trespasses, to offer unto Thee any sacrifice; and yet Thou hast commanded us in Thy Gospel to shew forth the Death of Thy Son our Saviour Jesus Christ until His coming again, which is both our only Sacrifice and our reasonable service. Wherefore we humbly beseech Thee, O Father, to accept this our sacrifice of praise and thanksgiving; and grant that all we who celebrate this holy Supper may be made partakers of the benefits which our Saviour Christ hath procured unto us by His Death and Passion. Have respect unto the faith and prayers of Thy Church, O Lord; and impute not unto us our former sins, but confirm, ratify, and make effectual, the words and acts which we, Thine unworthy servants, in obedience to Thy will, shall here speak and do in Thy Name; through the same Thy Son Jesus Christ our Lord, to Whom with Thee and the Holy Ghost, be all honour and glory, throughout all ages, world without end. *Amen.*

A PRAYER AFTER HOLY COMMUNION.

This Prayer following may be said by the Priest at the time of the consuming of that which remaineth of the holy Sacrament not to be reserved, and the Ablutions of the Communion vessels.

O GOD our Father, Who in these holy Mysteries hast vouchsafed to feed us with the Body and Blood of Thine only-begotten Son Jesus Christ: We beseech Thee that all who have faithfully partaken of the same may grow up in the communion and fellowship of His Body the Church, and attain unto the glory of His Resurrection; and so be made partakers of His heavenly kingdom; through the same Jesus Christ our Lord, Who liveth and reigneth with Thee, in the unity of the Holy Ghost, ever One God, world without end. *Amen.*

The Dismissal Collects

The Collects following are appointed to be said by the Minister after the Biddings or Intercession before the Dismissal when there is no Communion. And these Collects may also be said, as often as occasion shall so serve, before the Prayer of Saint Chrysostom at Divine Service or the Great Litany, at the discretion of the Minister.

ASSIST us mercifully, O Lord, in these our supplications and prayers, and dispose the way of Thy servants towards the attainment of everlasting salvation; that, among all the changes and chances of this mortal life, they may ever be defended by Thy most gracious and ready help; through Jesus Christ our Lord. *Amen.*

O ALMIGHTY Lord, and everlasting God, vouchsafe, we beseech Thee, to direct, sanctify, and govern, both our hearts and bodies, in the ways of Thy laws, and in the works of Thy commandments; that through Thy most mighty protection, both here and ever, we may be preserved in body and soul; through our Lord and Saviour Jesus Christ. *Amen.*

GRANT, we beseech Thee, Almighty God, that the words, which we have heard this day with our outward ears, may through Thy grace be so grafted inwardly in our hearts, that they may bring forth in us the fruit of good living, to the honour and praise of Thy Name; through Jesus Christ our Lord. *Amen.*

PREVENT us, O Lord, in all our doings with Thy most gracious favour, and further us with Thy continual help; that in all our works begun, continued, and ended in Thee, we may glorify Thy holy Name, and finally by Thy mercy obtain everlasting life; through Jesus Christ our Lord. *Amen.*

ALMIGHTY God, the Fountain of all wisdom, Who knowest our necessities before we ask, and our ignorance in asking: We beseech Thee to have compassion upon our infirmities; and those things, which for our unworthiness we dare not, and for our blindness we cannot ask, vouchsafe to give us, for the worthiness of Thy Son Jesus Christ our Lord. *Amen.*

ALMIGHTY God, Who hast promised to hear the petitions of them that ask in Thy Son's Name: We beseech Thee mercifully to incline Thine ears to us that have now made our prayers and supplications unto Thee; and grant, that those things, which we have faithfully asked according to Thy will, may effectually be obtained, to the relief of our necessity, and to the setting forth of Thy glory; through Jesus Christ our Lord. *Amen.*

WE humbly beseech Thee, O Father, mercifully to look upon our infirmities; and for the glory of Thy Name turn from us all those evils that we have most justly deserved; and grant that, in all our troubles, we may put our whole trust and confidence only in Thy mercy, and evermore serve Thee in holiness and pureness of living, to Thy honour and glory; through Jesus Christ our Lord. *Amen.*

O GOD, Whose nature and property is ever to have mercy and to forgive: Receive our humble petitions, we beseech Thee, O heavenly Father; and though we be tied and bound with the chain of our sins, yet let the pitifulness of Thy great mercy loose us, and let our prayers and supplications rise up before Thee; for the honour of Jesus Christ, Thy beloved Son and our only Saviour. *Amen.*

HOLY EUCHARIST

ADDITIONAL RUBRICS

THE VESTURE OF THE MINISTERS.

And here it is to be noted, that every Minister that shall celebrate or assist in the celebration of the Eucharist shall be vested in the proper Vesture appointed for his office and ministration. That is to say, that every Bishop or Priest who shall celebrate the Eucharist shall be vested in the Albe with its Amice and Cincture, and shall have upon him the Stole and the Chasuble. However, when circumstances are such that the proper vestments may not be had, it shall suffice for the Bishop to celebrate the Eucharist vested in his Rochet and Cope, or his Rochet and Chimere, with the Stole; and for a Priest to celebrate vested in his Surplice only with the Cope and Stole, or with the Stole alone if necessity so require.

Likewise, any Deacon who shall assist the Bishop or Priest in the celebration of the Eucharist shall be vested in the Albe with its Amice and Cincture, and shall have upon him the Stole worn Deacon-wise and the Dalmatic; or, if necessity so require, he may be vested in his Surplice, and shall have upon him the Stole worn Deacon-wise. And any Subdeacon who shall assist in the celebration of the Eucharist shall also be vested in the Albe with its Amice and Cincture, and shall have upon himself the Tunicle; or, if necessity so require, he may be vested with his full Surplice only.

And any Bishop who presideth at the Eucharist (but shall not himself be the celebrant thereof) shall be vested in his Rochet, and shall have upon him the Stole and the Cope; or, if necessity so require, he may be vested in his Rochet and Chimere, and shall wear the Stole. And any Bishop who shall celebrate or preside at the Eucharist may wear the Mitre, and may either himself carry, or else have borne before him, his Crosier. And whensoever any Bishop shall make Deacons, order Priests, or consecrate a Bishop or an Archbishop, he may be vested also with the Dalmatic worn under his Chasuble.

And any Bishop who shall be present at a celebration of the Eucharist (but shall not himself thereat preside) shall be vested in his Rochet and Chimere, and shall wear the Stole. But if any Bishop shall assist at the Eucharist and not preside thereat, he shall be vested in his Rochet, and shall wear the Stole and Cope; or else if necessity so require, he may wear the Rochet and Chimere and be vested only with the Stole.

And likewise any Priest who shall assist in the celebration of the Eucharist shall be vested in his Surplice, and shall wear the Stole, with which he may also wear the Cope. And if any Priest be present at the Eucharist (but shall not assist therein) he shall be vested in his Surplice and Stole. And any Deacon who shall be present at a celebration of the Eucharist (but shall not assist therein) shall be vested in his Surplice and wear the Stole worn Deacon-wise. And any Clerk who may assist at the Eucharist shall be vested with the short Surplice only.

And in the saying or singing of Divine Service, wherein there is no administration of any of the Sacraments, the Bishop shall be vested in his Rochet and Chimere, with his clerical Hood, and Tippet or Scarf; the Priests in their Surplices, with their clerical Hoods, and Tippets or Scarves; the Deacons in their Surplices, with their clerical Hoods; and all other Ministers in their Surplices only. And let it here be noted that all Subdeacons and Lay-Readers are permitted to wear the full Surplice at all times of Divine Service, and in the singing and saying of the Litanies, and at the Burial of the Dead.

THE RESERVATION OF THE BLESSED SACRAMENT.

It was ever the custom in the undivided Church from the earliest times, for the Priest to reserve at the Lord's Supper so much of the Sacrament of the Body and Blood of our Blessed Saviour as might be required for the Communion of the Sick and of such other persons as were, for just and lawful reasons, unable to be present thereat. Therefore, in all Cathedral and Collegiate Churches, and in all such Parish Churches and Chapels where it is practicable, a portion of the consecrated Elements shall be reserved by the Priest after the principal celebration of the Eucharist on the Lord's Day, the same always being kept secure in a Tabernacle or Aumbry, or in some other suitable receptacle approved by the Ordinary. And wheresoever it may conveniently be done, the consecrated Elements so reserved shall be kept for seven days, and renewed every Lord's Day.

HOLY EUCHARIST

THE EXHORTATIONS

TO COMMUNICANTS BEFORE THE GREATER FESTIVALS.

When the Priest giveth warning for the celebration of the Lord's Supper (which he shall always do upon the Lord's Day next before Christmas-Day, Easter-Day, Whitsunday, Michaelmas-Day, and All Saints' Day), either before or else after the Sermon or the Homily ended, he shall read this exhortation following.

DEARLY beloved in the Lord, on......day, I purpose, through God's assistance, to celebrate the Supper of the Lord, and to administer to all such as shall be religiously and devoutly disposed the most comfortable Sacrament of the Body and Blood of Christ; to be by them received in remembrance of His meritorious Cross and Passion, whereby alone we obtain remission of our sins, and are made partakers of the Kingdom of heaven.

Wherefore it is our duty to render most humble and hearty thanks to Almighty God our heavenly Father, for that He hath given His Son our Saviour Jesus Christ, not only to die for us, but also to be our spiritual Food and sustenance in that most Holy Sacrament of His Body and Blood. Which being so divine and comfortable a thing to them who receive it worthily, and so dangerous to them that will presume to receive it unworthily; my duty is to exhort you in the mean season to consider the dignity of that Holy Mystery, and the great peril of the unworthy receiving thereof; and so to search and examine your own consciences, and that not lightly, and after the manner of dissemblers with God: but so that ye may come holy and clean to such an heavenly Feast, in the marriage-garment required by God in Holy Scripture, and be received as worthy partakers of that Holy Table.

Now the way and means thereto is this: First, to examine your lives and conversations by the rule of God's commandments; and whereinsoever ye shall perceive yourselves to have offended, either by will, word, or deed, there to bewail your own sinfulness, and to confess yourselves to Almighty God, with full purpose of amendment of life. And if ye shall perceive your offences to be such as are not only against God, but also against your neighbours, then ye shall reconcile yourselves unto them, being ready to make restitution and satisfaction, according to the uttermost of your powers, for all injuries and wrongs done by you to any other; and being likewise ready to forgive others that have offended you, as ye would have forgiveness of your own offences at God's hand; for otherwise the receiving of the Holy Communion doth nothing else but increase your condemnation.

Therefore if any of you be a blasphemer of God, an hinderer or slanderer of His Word, an adulterer or fornicator, or be in malice, or envy, or in any other grievous crime, repent ye of your sins, or else come not to that Holy Table; lest, after the taking of that Holy Sacrament, the devil enter into you, as he entered into Judas, and fill you full of all iniquities, and bring you to destruction both of body and soul.

And because it is requisite that no man should come to the Holy Communion but with a full trust in God's mercy, and with a quiet conscience; therefore if there be any of you, who by this means cannot quiet his own conscience herein, but thinketh that he be fallen into deadly sin, let him come unto me, or to some other discreet and learned Minister of God's Word and Sacraments, and open his grief; that by the ministry of God's holy Word he may receive the benefit of Absolution, together with spiritual counsel and advice, to the quieting of his conscience, and avoiding of all scruple and doubtfulness.

WHEN PEOPLE ARE NEGLIGENT TO RECEIVE THE HOLY COMMUNION.

Or, in case he shall see the people negligent to come to the Holy Communion, instead of the former, the Priest shall use this Exhortation following.

DEARLY beloved brethren, who by the grace of Almighty God have been born anew of Water and of the Holy Ghost, and who are invited by Him to be partakers of the blessed Sacrament of the Body and Blood of His most dearly beloved Son our Saviour Jesus Christ, I bid you all in His Name, and I beseech you, that ye will not refuse to come to His Holy Table, who are so lovingly called and bidden by God Himself.

Ye know how grievous and unkind a thing it is, when a man hath prepared a rich feast, decked his table with all kinds of provision, so that there lacketh nothing but the guests to sit down; and yet they who are called (without any cause) most unthankfully refuse to come. Which of you in such a case would not be moved? Who would not think a great injury and wrong done unto him? Wherefore, most dearly beloved in Christ, take ye good heed, lest ye, withdrawing yourselves from this Holy Supper, provoke God's indignation against you. It is an easy thing for a man to say, I will not communicate, because I am otherwise hindered with worldly business. But such excuses are not so easily accepted and allowed before God. If any man say, I am a grievous sinner, and therefore am afraid to come: wherefore then do ye not repent and amend? When God calleth you, are ye not ashamed to say that ye will not come? When ye should return unto God, will ye excuse yourselves, and say ye are not ready? Consider therefore earnestly with yourselves how little such feigned excuses will avail before God. They that refused the feast in the Gospel, because they had bought a farm, or would try their yokes of oxen, or because they were married, were not so excused, but counted unworthy of the heavenly feast.

I, for my part, am ready to communicate; and, according to mine Office, I bid you in the Name of God, I call you in Christ's behalf, I exhort you, as ye love your own salvation, that ye also will be ready to be partakers of this Holy Communion. And as the Son of God did vouchsafe to yield up His soul by death upon the Cross for your salvation; so it is your duty to receive the Holy Communion in remembrance of the Sacrifice of His Death, as He Himself hath commanded; which, if ye shall neglect to do, consider with yourselves how great an injury ye do unto God, and how sore punishment hangeth over your heads for the same; when ye wilfully abstain from the Lord's Table, and separate yourselves from your brethren, who come to feed on the banquet of that most heavenly Food. These things if ye earnestly consider, ye will by God's grace return to a better mind; and know ye that for the obtaining whereof we shall not cease to make our humble petitions unto Almighty God our heavenly Father.

FOR THE WORTHY RECEIVING OF HOLY COMMUNION.

At the time of the celebration of the Lord's Supper, either immediately before the Sermon or Homily, or else immediately before the faithful are invited to partake of the Lord's Table, the Priest may say this Exhortation following, the people all standing. And this Exhortation shall always be read out on the First Sunday in Advent and First Sunday in Lent; and whensoever the Priest shall be moved in his discretion to exhort the people to the worthy receiving of the Holy Communion (it not being any Sunday within Christmastide, Epiphanytide, Eastertide, Ascensiontide, or Whitsuntide, or on any of the Greater Holy-Days), he may read to them this Exhortation following.

DEARLY beloved in the Lord, ye that mind to come to the Holy Communion of the Body and Blood of our Saviour Christ, must consider what Saint Paul the Apostle writeth to the Corinthians; how he exhorteth all persons diligently to try and examine themselves before they presume to eat of that Bread and drink of that Cup.

For as the benefit is great, if with a true penitent heart and lively faith, we receive that holy Sacrament; (for then we spiritually eat the Flesh of Christ and drink His Blood; then we dwell in Christ, and Christ in us; then we are one with Christ, and Christ with us); so is the danger great, if we receive the same unworthily. For then we are guilty of the Body and Blood of Christ our Saviour; we eat and drink our own damnation, not discerning the Lord's Body; we kindle God's wrath against us; we provoke Him to plague us with divers diseases, and sundry kinds of death.

Judge therefore yourselves, brethren, that ye be not judged of the Lord; repent you truly for sins past; have a lively and steadfast faith in Christ our Saviour; amend your lives, and be in perfect charity with all men; so shall ye be meet partakers of those Holy Mysteries.

And above all things ye must give most humble and hearty thanks to God, the Father, the Son, and the Holy Ghost, for the redemption of the world by the Death and Passion of our Saviour Christ, both God and man; Who did humble Himself, even to the death upon the Cross, for us, miserable sinners, who lay in darkness and the shadow of death; that He might make us the children of God, and exalt us to everlasting life.

And to the end that we should always remember the exceeding great love of our Master and only Saviour, Jesus Christ, thus dying for us, and the innumerable benefits which by His precious Blood-shedding He hath obtained to us; He hath instituted and ordained Holy Mysteries, as pledges of His love, and for a continual remembrance of His death, to our great and endless comfort. To Him therefore, with the Father and the Holy Ghost, let us give (as we are most bounden) continual thanks; submitting ourselves wholly to His holy will and pleasure, and studying to serve Him in true holiness and righteousness all the days of our life. *Amen.*

A DECLARATION REGARDING
THE REAL PRESENCE OF CHRIST IN THE EUCHARIST

AND HERE IT IS TO BE NOTED, that the outward and visible Signs (or *Accidents*, as they are called,) of the consecrated Bread and Wine of the Blessed Sacrament of the Lord's Supper remain still very much in their natural forms, and may not therefore as such be adored or worshipped (for to worship the *Accidents* of Bread and Wine were Idolatry, to be abhorred of all faithful Christians): Howbeit, the inward and spiritual part of the Blessed Sacrament of the Lord's Supper, that is to say, the true and real *Substance* thereof, is the most precious Body and Blood of our Lord and Saviour Jesus Christ which, altogether with and inseparable from His very Soul and Divinity, are truly and really present under the outward and visible Signs of the consecrated Bread and Wine; and the same Body and Blood of our Lord and Saviour Jesus Christ, altogether with and inseparable from His very Soul and Divinity, are verily and indeed offered up and given, and taken and received, in the Sacrament of the Lord's Supper. Wherefore, it is hereby declared that in the Sacrament of the Lord's Supper, the whole and perfect *Substance* of the Person of our Lord and Saviour Jesus Christ, in His Body and Blood, Soul and Divinity, is truly and really present under the outward and visible Signs of the consecrated Elements of Bread and Wine; and that the Lord Jesus Christ is there rightly and properly to be worshipped and adored by all faithful Christians.

THE INTROITS AND GRADUALS,
COLLECTS, EPISTLES AND GOSPELS
APPOINTED TO BE USED AT
THE EUCHARIST
THROUGHOUT
THE CHRISTIAN YEAR

The Collect or Collects appointed for any Sunday or Holy-day shall be used at the Evening Service next before, except in the case of Easter-Day. And the Propers of that Sunday shall serve all the week after, except when other provision is made; however, on any weekday that is not a Holy-day and for which no special Propers are appointed, the Priest may use the Propers which are provided for lesser commemorations and weekdays, in accordance with the directions given.

The Collect appointed for any Holy-day may be said after the Sunday Collect or Collects during the seven days following; and the Propers appointed for any Holy-day which hath an Octave may be used on any day in the Octave for which no special provision hath been made.

Any Holy-day falling on a Sunday in Advent or Lent, or on Ash Wednesday or the Ascension-Day, shall be transferred to the following Tuesday. Any Holy-day falling between Palm Sunday and Low Sunday shall be transferred to the Tuesday after Low Sunday; and one falling between Whitsunday and Trinity Sunday shall be transferred to the Tuesday after Trinity Sunday. If any such Tuesday be not free, the Holy-day shall be transferred to some convenient day following.

But in the case of any Holy-day falling on a Sunday after Christmas, Epiphany, and Trinity, and from the Second Sunday after Easter to Rogation Sunday: The Propers of the Holy-day shall be used, the Collect of the Sunday being said after the Collect of the Holy-day.

In the case of Holy-days falling on Septuagesima, Sexagesima, or Quinquagesima Sundays: The Propers of the Purification of Saint Mary the Virgin shall be used on the Sunday, the Collect of the Sunday being said after that of the Feast; but the Conversion of Saint Paul, and Saint Matthias, shall be transferred to the following Tuesday.

Any Holy-day falling on a Monday (except the Holy-days from Christmas to Epiphany) may be transferred to the following Tuesday.

In the singing or saying of the Introit Psalm, except during Passiontide, the Gloria Patri shall always follow the Psalm, and one of the verses may be used before and after the Psalm as an Antiphon.

In reading any Collect ending with the words, through Jesus Christ our Lord, *the Priest may add the ascription,* Who liveth and reigneth with Thee and the Holy Ghost, one God, world without end. Amen.

In the singing or saying of the Gradual Psalm, except during Advent and Lent and other penitential times, the Alleluias shall be sung or said according to custom with two Alleluias preceding the Psalm and one Alleluia following the Psalm.

Except where it shall be otherwise noted, the sequence of Liturgical Colours used at the Divine Liturgy shall follow the customary usages of the English Church.

Advent Sunday is always the nearest Sunday to the Feast of Saint Andrew, whether before or after.

THE FIRST SUNDAY OF ADVENT
COMMONLY CALLED
ADVENT SUNDAY

THE INTROIT. *Psalm* 25. 1-7.

UNTO Thee, O Lord, will I lift up my soul; my God, I have put my trust in Thee: / O let me not be confounded, neither let mine enemies triumph over me. For all they that hope in Thee shall not be ashamed; / but such as transgress without a cause shall be put to confusion. Shew me Thy ways, O Lord, / and teach me Thy paths. Lead me forth in Thy truth, and teach me, / for Thou art the God of my salvation; in Thee hath been my hope all the day long. Call to remembrance, O Lord, Thy tender mercies, / and Thy loving-kindnesses, which have been ever of old. O remember not the sins and offences of my youth; / but according to Thy mercy think Thou upon me, O Lord, for Thy goodness. Gracious and righteous is the Lord: / therefore will He teach sinners in the way.

GLORY be to the Father, and to the Son, / and to the Holy Ghost;

As it was in the beginning, is now, and ever shall be, / world without end. Amen.

THE COLLECT.

ALMIGHTY God, give us grace that we may cast away the works of darkness, and put upon us the armour of light, now in the time of this mortal life in which Thy Son Jesus Christ came to visit us in great humility; that in the last day, when He shall come again in His glorious majesty to judge both the quick and the dead, we may rise to the life immortal; through Him Who liveth and reigneth with Thee and the Holy Ghost, one God, now and for ever. *Amen.*

THE EPISTLE. *Romans* 13. 8-14.

OWE no man anything, but to love one another: for he that loveth another hath fulfilled the Law. For this, Thou shalt not commit adultery, Thou shalt not kill, Thou shalt not steal, Thou shalt not bear false witness, Thou shalt not covet; and if there be any other commandment, it is briefly comprehended in this saying, namely, Thou shalt love thy neighbour as thyself. Love worketh no ill to his neighbour: therefore love is the fulfilling of the Law. And that, knowing the time, that now it is high time to awake out of sleep: for now is our salvation nearer than when we believed. The night is far spent, the day is at hand: let us therefore cast off the works of darkness, and let us put on the armour of light. Let us walk honestly, as in the day; not in rioting and drunkenness, not in chambering and wantonness, not in strife and envying. But put ye on the Lord Jesus Christ, and make not provision for the flesh, to fulfil the lusts thereof.

THE GRADUAL. *Psalm* 85. 4-7.

TURN us then, O God our Saviour, / and let Thine anger cease from us. Wilt Thou be displeased at us for ever? / and wilt Thou stretch out Thy wrath from one generation to another? Wilt Thou not turn again, and quicken us, / that Thy people may rejoice in Thee? O Lord, shew Thy mercy upon us, / and grant us Thy salvation.

THE GOSPEL. *Saint Matthew* 21. 1-13.

WHEN they drew nigh unto Jerusalem, and were come to Bethphage, unto the mount of Olives, then sent Jesus two disciples, saying unto them, Go into the village over against you, and straightway ye shall find a donkey tied, and a colt with her: loose them, and bring them unto me. And if any man say ought unto you, ye shall say, The Lord hath need of them; and straightway he will send them. All this was done, that it might be fulfilled which was spoken by the prophet, saying, Tell ye the daughter of Sion, Behold, thy King cometh unto thee, meek, and sitting upon a donkey, and a colt the foal of a donkey. And the disciples went, and did as Jesus commanded them; and brought the donkey, and the colt, and put on them their clothes, and they set Him thereon. And a very great multitude spread their garments in the way; others cut down branches from the trees, and strawed them in the way. And the multitudes that went before, and that followed, cried, saying, Hosanna to the son of David: Blessed is He that cometh in the Name of the Lord; Hosanna in the highest. And when He was come into Jerusalem, all the city was moved, saying, Who is this? And the multitude said, This is Jesus the prophet of Nazareth of Galilee. And Jesus went into the temple of God, and cast out all them that sold and bought in the temple, and overthrew the tables of the money-changers, and the seats of them that sold doves, and said unto them, It is written, My house shall be called the house of prayer; but ye have made it a den of thieves.

THE SECOND SUNDAY IN ADVENT

THE INTROIT. *Psalm* 80. 1-7.
HEAR, O Thou Shepherd of Israel, Thou that leadest Joseph like a sheep; / shew Thyself also, Thou that sittest upon the cherubim. Before Ephraim, Benjamin, and Manasses, / stir up Thy strength, and come, and help us. Turn us again, O God; / shew the light of Thy countenance, and we shall be whole. O Lord God of hosts, / how long wilt Thou be angry with Thy people that prayeth? Thou feedest them with the bread of tears, / and givest them plenteousness of tears to drink. Thou hast made us a very strife unto our neighbours, / and our enemies laugh us to scorn. Turn us again, Thou God of hosts; / shew the light of Thy countenance, and we shall be whole.

GLORY be to the Father, and to the Son, / and to the Holy Ghost;
As it was in the beginning, is now, and ever shall be, / world without end. Amen.

THE COLLECT.
O BLESSED Lord, Who hast caused all Holy Scriptures to be written for our learning: Grant that we may in such wise hear them, read, mark, learn, and inwardly digest them, that by patience and comfort of Thy holy Word, we may embrace, and ever hold fast, the blessed hope of everlasting life, which Thou hast given us in our Saviour Jesus Christ. *Amen.*

ALMIGHTY God, give us grace that we may cast away the works of darkness, and put upon us the armour of light, now in the time of this mortal life in which Thy Son Jesus Christ came to visit us in great humility; that in the last day, when He shall come again in His glorious majesty to judge both the quick and the dead, we may rise to the life immortal; through Him Who liveth and reigneth with Thee and the Holy Ghost, one God, now and for ever. *Amen.*

THE EPISTLE. *Romans* 15. 4-13.
WHATSOEVER things were written aforetime were written for our learning, that we through patience and comfort of the Scriptures might have hope. Now the God of patience and consolation grant you to be likeminded one toward another according to Christ Jesus: that ye may with one mind and one mouth glorify God, even the Father of our Lord Jesus Christ. Wherefore receive ye one another, as Christ also received us to the glory of God. Now I say that Jesus Christ was a minister of the circumcision for the truth of God, to confirm the promises made unto the fathers: and that the Gentiles might glorify God for His mercy; as it is written, For this cause I will confess to Thee among

the Gentiles, and sing unto Thy Name. And again He saith, Rejoice, ye Gentiles, with His people. And again, Praise the Lord, all ye Gentiles; and laud Him, all ye people. And again, Esaias saith, There shall be a root of Jesse, and He that shall rise to reign over the Gentiles; in Him shall the Gentiles trust. Now the God of hope fill you with all joy and peace in believing, that ye may abound in hope, through the power of the Holy Ghost.

THE GRADUAL. *Psalm* 50. 1-4.

THE Lord, even the most mighty God, hath spoken; / and called the world, from the rising up of the sun unto the going down thereof. Out of Sion hath God appeared / in perfect beauty. Our God shall come, and shall not keep silence; / there shall go before Him a consuming fire, and a mighty tempest shall be stirred up round about Him. He shall call the heaven from above; / and the earth, that He may judge His people.

THE GOSPEL. *Saint Luke* 21. 25-33.

AT that time Jesus said unto them: There shall be signs in the sun, and in the moon, and in the stars; and upon the earth distress of nations, with perplexity; the sea and the waves roaring; men's hearts failing them for fear, and for looking after those things which are coming on the earth: for the powers of heaven shall be shaken. And then shall they see the Son of Man coming in a cloud with power and great glory. And when these things begin to come to pass, then look up, and lift up your heads; for your redemption draweth nigh. And He spake to them a parable, Behold the fig tree, and all the trees; when they now shoot forth, ye see and know of your own selves that summer is now nigh at hand. So likewise ye, when ye see these things come to pass, know ye that the kingdom of God is nigh at hand. Verily I say unto you, This generation shall not pass away, till all be fulfilled. Heaven and earth shall pass away: but my words shall not pass away.

THE THIRD SUNDAY IN ADVENT

THE INTROIT. *Psalm* 33. 1-6.

I WILL magnify Thee, O Lord, for Thou hast set me up, / and not made my foes to triumph over me. O Lord my God, I cried unto Thee, / and Thou hast healed me. Thou, Lord, hast brought my soul out of hell; / Thou hast kept my life from them that go down to the pit. Sing praises unto the Lord, O ye saints of His, / and give thanks unto Him for a remembrance of His holiness. For His wrath endureth but the twinkling of an eye, and in His pleasure is life; / heaviness may endure for a night, but joy cometh in the morning. And in my prosperity I said, I shall never be removed; / Thou, Lord, of Thy goodness hast made my hill so strong.

GLORY be to the Father, and to the Son, / and to the Holy Ghost;
As it was in the beginning, is now, and ever shall be, / world without end. Amen.

THE COLLECT.

O LORD Jesu Christ, Who at Thy first coming didst send Thy messenger to prepare Thy way before Thee: Grant that Thy Ministers, the Stewards of Thy mysteries, may likewise so prepare and make ready Thy way, by turning the hearts of the disobedient to the wisdom of the just, that, at Thy second coming to judge the world, we may be found an acceptable people in Thy sight, Who livest and reignest with the Father and the Holy Spirit, ever one God, world without end. *Amen.*

ALMIGHTY God, give us grace that we may cast away the works of darkness, and put upon us the armour of light, now in the time of this mortal life in which Thy Son Jesus Christ came to visit us in great humility; that in the last day, when He shall come again in His glorious majesty to judge both the quick and the dead, we may rise to the life immortal; through Him Who liveth and reigneth with Thee and the Holy Ghost, one God, now and for ever. *Amen.*

THE EPISTLE. I *Corinthians* 4. 1-5.

LET a man so account of us, as of the ministers of Christ, and stewards of the mysteries of God. Moreover it is required in stewards, that a man be found faithful. But with me it is a very small thing that I should be judged of you, or of man's judgement: yea, I judge not mine own self. For I know nothing by myself; yet am I not hereby justified: but He that judgeth me is the Lord. Therefore judge nothing before the time, until the Lord come, Who both will bring to light the hidden things of darkness, and will make manifest the counsels of the hearts: and then shall every man have praise of God.

THE GRADUAL. *Psalm* 80. 1-3.

HEAR, O Thou Shepherd of Israel, Thou that leadest Joseph like a sheep; / shew Thyself also, Thou that sittest upon the cherubim. Before Ephraim, Benjamin, and Manasses, / stir up Thy strength, and come, and help us. Turn us again, O God; / shew the light of Thy countenance, and we shall be whole.

THE GOSPEL. *Saint Matthew* 11. 2-10.

NOW when John had heard in the prison the works of Christ, he sent two of his disciples, and said unto Him, Art Thou He that should come, or do we look for another? Jesus answered and said unto them, Go and shew John again those things which ye do hear and see: the blind receive their sight, and the lame walk, the lepers are cleansed, and the deaf hear, the dead are raised up, and the poor have the gospel preached to them. And blessed is
he, whosoever shall not be offended in me. And as they departed, Jesus began to say unto the multitudes concerning John, What went ye out into the wilderness to see? A reed shaken with the wind? But what went ye out for to see? A man clothed in soft raiment? behold, they that wear soft clothing are in kings' houses. But what went ye out for to see? A prophet? yea, I say unto you, and more than a prophet. For this is he, of whom it is written, Behold, I send my messenger before Thy face, which shall prepare Thy way before Thee.

THE FOURTH SUNDAY IN ADVENT

THE INTROIT. *Psalm* 19. 1-8.

THE heavens declare the glory of God, / and the firmament sheweth His handy-work. One day telleth another, / and one night certifieth another. There is neither speech nor language; / but their voices are heard among them. Their sound is gone out into all lands, / and their words into the ends of the world. In them hath He set a tabernacle for the sun, / which cometh forth as a bridegroom out of his chamber, and rejoiceth as a giant to run his course. It goeth forth from the uttermost part of the heaven, and runneth about unto the end of it again, / and there is nothing hid from the heat thereof. The Law of the Lord is an undefiled Law, converting the soul; / the testimony of the Lord is sure, and giveth wisdom unto the simple. The statutes of the Lord are right, and rejoice the heart; / the commandment of the Lord is pure, and giveth light unto the eyes.

THE PROPERS OF THE YEAR

G<small>LORY</small> be to the Father, and to the Son, / and to the Holy Ghost;
As it was in the beginning, is now, and ever shall be, / world without end. Amen.

T<small>HE</small> C<small>OLLECT</small>.

R<small>AISE</small> up, we beseech Thee, O Lord, Thy power, and come among us; and with great might succour us; that whereas, through our sins and wickedness, we are sore let and hindered in running the race that is set before us, Thy bountiful grace and mercy may speedily help and deliver us; through the satisfaction of Thy Son our Lord, to Whom with Thee and the Holy Ghost be all honour and glory, world without end. *Amen.*

A<small>LMIGHTY</small> God, give us grace that we may cast away the works of darkness, and put upon us the armour of light, now in the time of this mortal life in which Thy Son Jesus Christ came to visit us in great humility; that in the last day, when He shall come again in His glorious majesty to judge both the quick and the dead, we may rise to the life immortal; through Him Who liveth and reigneth with Thee and the Holy Ghost, one God, now and for ever. *Amen.*

T<small>HE</small> E<small>PISTLE</small>. *Philippians* 4. 4-8.

R<small>EJOICE</small> in the Lord always: and again I say, Rejoice. Let your moderation be known unto all men. The Lord is at hand. Be careful for nothing; but in everything by prayer and supplication with thanksgiving let your requests be made known unto God. And the peace of God, which passeth all understanding, shall keep your hearts and minds through Christ Jesus. Finally, brethren, whatsoever things are true, whatsoever things are honest, whatsoever things are just, whatsoever things are pure, whatsoever things are lovely, whatsoever things are of good report; if there be any virtue, and if there be any praise, think on these things. Those things, which ye have both learned, and received, and heard, and seen in me, do: and the God of peace shall be with you.

T<small>HE</small> G<small>RADUAL</small>. *Psalm* 145. 18-21.

T<small>HE</small> Lord is righteous in all His ways, / and holy in all His works. The Lord is nigh unto all them that call upon Him; / yea, all such as call upon Him faithfully. He will fulfil the desire of them that fear Him; / He also will hear their cry, and will help them. The Lord preserveth all them that love Him, / but scattereth abroad all the ungodly. My mouth shall speak the praise of the Lord, / and let all flesh give thanks unto His holy Name for ever and ever.

T<small>HE</small> G<small>OSPEL</small>. *Saint John* 1. 19-34.

T<small>HIS</small> is the record of John, when the Jews sent priests and Levites from Jerusalem to ask him, Who art thou? And he confessed, and denied not; but confessed, I am not the Christ. And they asked him, What then? Art thou Elias? And he saith, I am not. Art thou that Prophet? And he answered, No. Then said they unto him, Who art thou? that we may give an answer to them that sent us. What sayest thou of thyself? He said, I am the voice of one crying in the wilderness, Make straight the way of the Lord, as said the Prophet Esaias. And they which were sent were of the Pharisees. And they asked him, and said unto him, Why baptisest thou then, if thou be not that Christ, nor Elias, neither that Prophet? John answered them, saying, I baptise with water: but there standeth One among you, Whom ye know not; He it is, Who coming after me is preferred before me, Whose shoe's latchet I am not worthy to unloose. These things were done in Bethabara beyond Jordan, where John was baptising. The next day John seeth Jesus coming unto him, and saith, Behold the Lamb of God, which taketh away the sin of the world. This is He of Whom I said, After me cometh a man which is preferred before me: for He was before me. And I knew Him not: but that He should be made manifest to Israel, therefore am I come baptising with water. And John bare record, saying, I saw the Spirit descending from heaven like a dove, and it abode upon Him. And I knew Him not: but He that sent me to baptise with water, the same said unto me, Upon Whom thou shalt see the Spirit descending, and remaining on Him, the same is He which baptiseth with the Holy Ghost. And I saw, and bare record that this is the Son of God.

CHRISTMAS

A DEVOTION.

*This Devotion following may be used before the Holy Eucharist
at Midnight on Christmas-Eve and before each Mass of Christmas-Day.*

*Standing at the Door of the Church,
the Priest shall first read these Sentences of Scripture following.*

THEREFORE the Lord Himself shall give you a sign: Behold, a Virgin shall conceive, and bear a Son, and shall call His Name Emmanuel. *Isaiah* 7. 14.

The people that sat in darkness have seen a great light: they that dwell in the land of the shadow of death, upon them hath the light shined. *Isaiah* 9. 2.

For unto us a Child is born, unto us a Son is given: and the government shall be upon His shoulder: and His Name shall be called Wonderful, Counsellor, The mighty God, the everlasting Father, the Prince of Peace. Of the increase of His government and peace there shall be no end, upon the Throne of David, and upon His kingdom, to order it, and to establish it with judgement and with justice from henceforth even forever. The zeal of the Lord of hosts will perform this. *Isaiah* 9. 6-7.

Then shall all stand for the reading of the Holy Gospel, as followeth.

THE ANNUNCIATION. *Saint Luke* 1. 26-35.

AND in the sixth month the angel Gabriel was sent from God unto a city of Galilee named Nazareth, to a Virgin espoused to a man whose name was Joseph, of the house of David; and the Virgin's name was Mary. And the angel came in unto her, and said, Hail, thou that art highly favoured, the Lord is with thee. And she was troubled at this saying, and cast in her mind what manner of salutation this should be. And the angel said unto her, Fear not, Mary; for thou hast found favour with God. And behold, thou shalt conceive in thy womb, and bring forth a Son, and shalt call His Name Jesus. He shall be great, and shall be called the Son of the Highest; and the Lord God shall give unto Him the throne of His father David. And He shall reign over the house of Jacob forever; and of His kingdom there shall be no end. Then said Mary unto the angel, How shall this be, seeing I know not a man? And the angel answered and said unto her, The Holy Ghost shall come upon thee, and the power of the Highest shall overshadow thee: Therefore also that holy thing which shall be born of thee shall be called the Son of God.

Then shall the Priest say,
Let us pray.

O GOD, Who makest us glad with the yearly remembrance of the birth of Thine only Son Jesus Christ: Grant that as we joyfully receive Him for our Redeemer, so we may with sure confidence behold Him when He shall come again to be our Judge; through the same Thy blessed Son our Lord, Who with Thee and the Holy Ghost liveth and reigneth, ever one God, world without end. *Amen.*

Then shall the Priest begin the celebration of the Holy Eucharist.

THE NATIVITY OF OUR LORD JESUS CHRIST
WHICH IS CALLED
CHRISTMAS-DAY
[25 December]

THE FIRST EUCHARIST OF CHRISTMAS

THE INTROIT. *Psalm* 96. 10-13.
TELL it out among the heathen, that the Lord is King: / and that it is He Who hath made the round world so fast that it cannot be moved; and how that He shall judge the people righteously. Let the heavens rejoice, and let the earth be glad; / let the sea make a noise, and all that therein is. Let the field be joyful, and all that is in it: / then shall all the trees of the wood rejoice before the Lord. For He cometh, for He cometh to judge the earth; / and with righteousness to judge the world, and the people with His truth.

GLORY be to the Father, and to the Son, / and to the Holy Ghost;

As it was in the beginning, is now, and ever shall be, / world without end. Amen.

THE COLLECT.
ALMIGHTY God, Who hast given us Thine only-begotten Son to take our nature upon Him, and as at this time to be born of a pure Virgin: Grant that we being regenerate, and made Thy children by adoption and grace, may daily be renewed by Thy Holy Spirit; through the same our Lord Jesus Christ, Who liveth and reigneth with Thee and the same Spirit, ever one God, world without end. *Amen.*

THE EPISTLE. *Hebrews* 1. 1-12.
GOD, Who at sundry times and in divers manners spake in time past unto the fathers by the prophets, hath in these last days spoken unto us by His Son, Whom He hath appointed Heir of all things, by Whom also He made the worlds; Who being the brightness of His glory, and the express Image of His Person, and upholding all things by the word of His power, when He had by Himself purged our sins, sat down on the right hand of the Majesty on high: being made so much better than the angels, as He hath by inheritance obtained a more excellent Name than they. For unto which of the angels said He at any time, Thou art my Son, this day have I begotten Thee? And again, I will be to him a Father, and He shall be to me a Son? And again, when He bringeth in the First-begotten into the world, He saith, And let all the angels of God worship Him. And of the angels He saith, Who maketh His angels spirits, and His ministers a flame of fire. But unto the Son He saith, Thy throne, O God, is for ever and ever: a sceptre of righteousness is the sceptre of Thy kingdom. Thou hast loved righteousness, and hated iniquity; therefore God, even Thy God, hath anointed Thee with

the oil of gladness above Thy fellows. And, Thou, Lord, in the beginning hast laid the foundation of the earth; and the heavens are the works of Thine hands: they shall perish; but Thou remainest; and they all shall wax old as doth a garment; and as a vesture shalt Thou fold them up, and they shall be changed: but Thou art the same, and Thy years shall not fail.

THE GRADUAL. *Psalm* 98. 1-4.

ALLELUIA, Alleluia. O Sing unto the Lord a new song, / for He hath done marvellous things. With His own right hand, and with His holy arm, / hath He gotten himself the victory. The Lord declared His salvation, / His righteousness hath He openly shewed in the sight of the heathen. He hath remembered His mercy and truth toward the house of Israel, / and all the ends of the world have seen the salvation of our God. Alleluia.

THE GOSPEL. *Saint Luke* 2. 1-20.

NOW it came to pass in those days, that there went out a decree from Caesar Augustus, that all the world should be taxed. (And this taxing was first made when Cyrenius was governor of Syria.) And all went to be taxed, every one into his own city. And Joseph also went up from Galilee, out of the city of Nazareth, into Judaea, unto the city of David, which is called Bethlehem (because he was of the house and lineage of David;) to be taxed with Mary his espoused wife, being great with child. And so it was, that while they were there, the days were accomplished that she should be delivered. And she brought forth her first-born Son, and wrapped Him in swaddling clothes, and laid Him in a manger; because there was no room for them in the inn. And there were in the same country shepherds abiding in the field, keeping watch over their flock by night. And, lo, the angel of the Lord came upon them, and the glory of the Lord shone round about them: and they were sore afraid. And the angel said unto them, Fear not: for, behold, I bring you good tidings of great joy, which shall be to all people. For unto you is born this day in the city of David a Saviour, which is Christ the Lord. And this shall be a sign unto you: Ye shall find the babe wrapped in swaddling clothes, lying in a manger. And suddenly there was with the angel a multitude of the heavenly host praising God, and saying, Glory to God in the highest, and on earth peace, good will toward men. And it came to pass, as the angels were gone away from them into heaven, the shepherds said one to another, Let us now go even unto Bethlehem, and see this thing which is come to pass, which the Lord hath made known unto us. And they came with haste, and found Mary, and Joseph, and the babe lying in a manger. And when they had seen it, they made known abroad the saying which was told them concerning this child. And all they that heard it wondered at those things which were told them by the shepherds. But Mary kept all these things, and pondered them in her heart. And the shepherds returned, glorifying and praising God for all the things that they had heard and seen, as it was told unto them.

THE SECOND EUCHARIST OF CHRISTMAS

And if there be a Second Eucharist celebrated on Christmas-Day,
the following Introit, Collect, Epistle, Gradual, Gospel, and Preface shall be used.

THE INTROIT. *Psalm* 2. 7-8.

I WILL tell of the decree of the Lord, wherein He hath said unto me, / Thou art my Son, this day have I begotten Thee. Desire of me, and I shall give Thee the nations for thine inheritance, / and the utmost parts of the earth for Thy possession.

105

GLORY be to the Father, and to the Son, / and to the Holy Ghost;
As it was in the beginning, is now, and ever shall be, / world without end. Amen.

THE COLLECT.

O GOD, Who makest us glad with the yearly remembrance of the Birth of Thine only-begotten Son Jesus Christ: Grant that as we joyfully receive Him as our Redeemer, we may with sure confidence behold Him when He shall come again to be our Judge; through the same our Lord Jesus Christ, Who liveth and reigneth with Thee and the Holy Ghost, ever one God, world without end. *Amen.*

THE EPISTLE. *Titus* 2. 11-15.

THE grace of God that bringeth salvation hath appeared to all men, teaching us that, denying ungodliness and worldly lusts, we should live soberly, righteously, and godly, in this present world; looking for that blessed hope, and the glorious appearing of the great God and our Saviour Jesus Christ; Who gave Himself for us, that He might redeem us from all iniquity, and purify unto Himself a peculiar people, zealous of good works. These things speak; and exhort, and rebuke with all authority. Let no man despise thee.

THE GRADUAL. *Psalm* 98. 6-8.

ALLELUIA, Alleluia. Shew yourselves joyful unto the Lord, all ye lands; / sing, rejoice, and give thanks. Praise the Lord upon the harp; / sing to the harp with a psalm of thanksgiving. With trumpets also and shawms; / O shew yourselves joyful before the Lord the King. Alleluia.

THE GOSPEL. *Saint John* 1. 1-14.

IN the beginning was the Word, and the Word was with God, and the Word was God. The same was in the beginning with God. All things were made by Him; and without Him was not anything made that was made. In Him was Life; and the Life was the Light of men. And the Light shineth in darkness; and the darkness comprehended it not. There was a man sent from God, whose name was John. The same came for a witness, to bear witness of the Light, that all men through him might believe. He was not that Light, but was sent to bear witness of that Light. That was the true Light, which lighteth every man that cometh into the world. He was in the world, and the world was made by Him, and the world knew Him not. He came unto His own, and His own received Him not. But as many as received Him, to them gave He power to become the sons of God, even to them that believe on His name: which were born, not of blood, nor of the will of the flesh, nor of the will of man, but of God. And the Word was made flesh, and dwelt among us, (and we beheld His glory, the glory as of the only-begotten of the Father,) full of grace and truth.

SAINT STEPHEN THE FIRST MARTYR
[26 December]

THE INTROIT. *Psalm* 119. 17-22.

O DO well unto Thy servant, / that I may live, and keep Thy word. Open Thou mine eyes, / that I may see the wondrous things of Thy Law. I am a stranger upon earth: / O hide not Thy commandments from me. My soul breaketh out for the very fervent desire, / that it hath alway unto Thy judgements. Thou hast rebuked the proud, / and cursed are they that do err from Thy commandments. O turn from me shame and rebuke, / for I have kept Thy testimonies.

THE PROPERS OF THE YEAR

G<small>LORY</small> be to the Father, and to the Son, / and to the Holy Ghost;
As it was in the beginning, is now, and ever shall be, / world without end. Amen.

THE COLLECT.

G<small>RANT</small>, we beseech Thee, O Lord, that, in all our sufferings here upon earth for the testimony of Thy truth, we may steadfastly look up to heaven, and by faith behold the glory that shall be revealed; and, being filled with the Holy Ghost, may learn to love and bless our persecutors according to the example of Thy first Martyr Saint Stephen, who prayed for his murderers unto Thee, O blessed Jesus, Who standest at the right hand of God to succour all those that suffer for Thee, our only Mediator. *Amen.*

FOR THE EPISTLE. *Acts* 7. 55-60.

S<small>TEPHEN</small>, being full of the Holy Ghost, looked up steadfastly into heaven, and saw the glory of God, and Jesus standing on the right hand of God, and said, Behold, I see the heavens opened, and the Son of Man standing on the right hand of God. Then they cried out with a loud voice, and stopped their ears, and ran upon him with one accord, and cast him out of the city, and stoned him: and the witnesses laid down their clothes at a young man's feet, whose name was Saul. And they stoned Stephen, calling upon God, and saying, Lord Jesus, receive my spirit. And he kneeled down, and cried with a loud voice, Lord, lay not this sin to their charge. And when he had said this, he fell asleep.

THE GRADUAL. *Psalm* 119. 161-168.

A<small>LLELUIA</small>, Alleluia. Princes have persecuted me without a cause; / but my heart standeth in awe of Thy word. I am as glad of Thy word, / as one that findeth great spoils. As for lies, I hate and abhor them; / but Thy Law do I love. Seven times a day do I praise Thee / because of Thy righteous judgements. Great is the peace that they have who love Thy Law, / and they are not offended at it. Lord, I have looked for Thy saving health, / and done after Thy commandments. My soul hath kept Thy testimonies, / and loved them exceedingly. I have kept Thy commandments and testimonies, / for all my ways are before Thee. Alleluia.

THE GOSPEL. *Saint Matthew* 23. 34-39.

A<small>T</small> that time Jesus said unto them: Behold, I send unto you prophets, and wise men, and scribes: and some of them ye shall kill and crucify; and some of them shall ye scourge in your synagogues, and persecute them from city to city: that upon you may come all the righteous blood shed upon the earth, from the blood of righteous Abel unto the blood of Zacharias son of Barachias, whom ye slew between the temple and the altar. Verily I say unto you, All these things shall come upon this generation. O Jerusalem, Jerusalem, thou that killest the prophets, and stonest them which are sent unto thee, how often would I have gathered thy children together, even as a hen gathereth her chickens under her wings, and ye would not! Behold, your house is left unto you desolate. For I say unto you, Ye shall not see me henceforth, till ye shall say, Blessed is He that cometh in the Name of the Lord.

Saint John the Apostle and Evangelist

[27 December]

The Introit. *Psalm* 92. 1-5.

It is a good thing to give thanks unto the Lord, / and to sing praises unto Thy Name, O Thou Most High; To tell of Thy loving-kindness early in the morning, / and of Thy truth in the night-season; Upon an instrument of ten strings, and upon the lute; / upon a loud instrument, and upon the harp. For Thou, Lord, hast made me glad through Thy works, / and I will rejoice in giving praise for the operations of Thy hands. O Lord, how glorious are Thy works: / Thy Thoughts are very deep.

Glory be to the Father, and to the Son, / and to the Holy Ghost;

As it was in the beginning, is now, and ever shall be, / world without end. Amen.

The Collect.

Merciful Lord, we beseech Thee to cast Thy bright beams of light upon Thy Church, that it being enlightened by the doctrine of Thy blessed Apostle and Evangelist Saint John may so walk in the light of Thy truth, that it may at length attain to the light of everlasting life; through Jesus Christ our Lord. *Amen.*

The Epistle. I *Saint John* 1. 1-10.

That which was from the beginning, which we have heard, which we have seen with our eyes, which we have looked upon, and our hands have handled, of the Word of Life; (for the Life was manifested, and we have seen it, and bear witness, and shew unto you that eternal Life, which was with the Father, and was manifested unto us;) that which we have seen and heard declare we unto you, that ye also may have fellowship with us: and truly our fellowship is with the Father, and with His Son Jesus Christ. And these things write we unto you, that your joy may be full. This then is the message which we have heard of Him, and declare unto you, that God is Light, and in Him is no darkness at all. If we say that we have fellowship with Him, and walk in darkness, we lie, and do not the truth: but if we walk in the light, as He is in the light, we have fellowship one with another, and the Blood of Jesus Christ His Son cleanseth us from all sin. If we say that we have no sin, we deceive ourselves, and the truth is not in us. If we confess our sins, He is faithful and just to forgive us our sins, and to cleanse us from all unrighteousness. If we say that we have not sinned, we make Him a liar, and His Word is not in us.

The Gradual. *Psalm* 92. 11-14.

Alleluia, Alleluia. The righteous shall flourish like a palm-tree, / and shall spread abroad like a cedar in Libanus. Such as are planted in the house of the Lord / shall flourish in the courts of the house of our God. They also shall bring forth more fruit in their age, / and shall be fat and well-liking. That they may shew how true the Lord my Strength is, / and that there is no unrighteousness in Him. Alleluia.

The Gospel. *Saint John* 21. 19-25.

Jesus said unto Peter, Follow me. Then Peter, turning about, seeth the disciple whom Jesus loved following; which also leaned on his breast at supper, and said, Lord, which is he that betrayeth Thee? Peter seeing him saith to Jesus, Lord, and what shall this man do? Jesus saith unto him, If I will that he tarry till I come, what is that to thee? follow thou me. Then went this saying abroad among the brethren, that that disciple should not die: yet Jesus said not unto him, He shall not die; but, If I will that he tarry till I come, what is that to thee? This is the disciple which testifieth of these things, and wrote these things: and we know that his testimony is true. And there are also many other things which Jesus did, the which, if they should be written every one, I suppose that even the world itself could not contain the books that should be written. Amen.

THE HOLY INNOCENTS
[28 December]

THE INTROIT. *Psalm* 15. 1-7.

LORD, who shall dwell in Thy tabernacle, / or who shall rest upon Thy holy hill? Even he that leadeth an uncorrupt life, / and doeth the thing which is right, and speaketh the truth from his heart. He that hath used no deceit in his tongue, nor done evil to his neighbour, / and hath not slandered his neighbour. He that setteth not by himself, but is lowly in his own eyes, / and maketh much of them that fear the Lord. He that sweareth unto his neighbour, and disappointeth him not, / though it were to his own hindrance. He that hath not given his money upon usury, / nor taken reward against the innocent. Whoso doeth these things / shall never fall.

GLORY be to the Father, and to the Son, / and to the Holy Ghost;
As it was in the beginning, is now, and ever shall be, / world without end. Amen.

THE COLLECT.

O ALMIGHTY God, Who out of the mouths of babes and sucklings hast ordained strength, and madest Infants and little Children to glorify Thee by their deaths: Mortify and kill all vices in us; and so strengthen us by Thy grace, that by the innocency of our lives, and the constancy of our faith even unto death, we may glorify Thy holy Name; through Jesus Christ our Lord. *Amen.*

FOR THE EPISTLE. *Revelation* 14. 1-5.

AND I looked, and, lo, a Lamb stood on the mount Sion, and with Him an hundred forty and four thousand, having His Father's Name written in their foreheads. And I heard a voice from heaven, as the voice of many waters, and as the voice of a great thunder: and I heard the voice of harpers harping with their harps: and they sung as it were a new song before the throne, and before the four beasts, and the elders: and no man could learn that song but the hundred and forty and four thousand, which were redeemed from the earth. These are they which were not defiled with women; for they are virgins. These are they which follow the Lamb whithersoever He goeth. These were redeemed from among men, being the first-fruits unto God and to the Lamb. And in their mouth was found no guile: for they are without fault before the throne of God.

THE GRADUAL. *Psalm* 8. 1-2.

ALLELUIA, Alleluia. O Lord our Governor, how excellent is Thy Name in all the world, / Thou that hast set Thy glory above the heavens! Out of the mouth of very babes and sucklings hast Thou ordained strength, because of Thine enemies, / that Thou mightest still the enemy and the avenger. Alleluia.

THE GOSPEL. *Saint Matthew* 2. 13-18.

THE angel of the Lord appeareth to Joseph in a dream, saying, Arise, and take the young Child and His Mother, and flee into Egypt, and be thou there until I bring thee word: for Herod will seek the young Child to destroy Him. When he arose, he took the young Child and His mother by night, and departed into Egypt: and was there until the death of Herod: that it might be fulfilled which was spoken of the Lord by the Prophet, saying, Out of Egypt have I called my Son. Then Herod, when he saw that he was mocked of the wise men, was exceeding wroth, and sent forth, and slew all the children that were in Bethlehem, and in all the coasts thereof, from two years old and under, according to the time which he had diligently enquired of the wise men. Then was fulfilled that which was spoken by Jeremy the Prophet, saying, In Ramah was there a voice heard, lamentation, and weeping, and great mourning, Rachel weeping for her children, and would not be comforted, because they are not.

And if there be any further Week-days, the Introit, Collect, Epistle,
Gradual, Gospel, and Preface for Christmas-Day shall be used.

THE SUNDAY AFTER CHRISTMAS-DAY

THE INTROIT. *Psalm* 93. 1-6.

THE Lord is King, and hath put on glorious apparel; / the Lord hath put on His apparel, and girded Himself with strength. He hath made the round world so sure, / that it cannot be moved. Ever since the world began hath Thy seat been prepared; / Thou art from everlasting. The floods are risen, O Lord, the floods have lift up their voice; / the floods lift up their waves. The waves of the sea are mighty, and rage horribly; / but yet the Lord, Who dwelleth on high, is mightier. Thy testimonies, O Lord, are very sure; / holiness becometh Thine house for ever.

GLORY be to the Father, and to the Son, / and to the Holy Ghost;

As it was in the beginning, is now, and ever shall be, / world without end. Amen.

THE COLLECT.

ALMIGHTY God, Who hast given us Thine only-begotten Son to take our nature upon Him, and as at this time to be born of a pure Virgin: Grant that we being regenerate, and made Thy children by adoption and grace, may daily be renewed by Thy Holy Spirit; through the same our Lord Jesus Christ, Who liveth and reigneth with Thee and the same Spirit, ever one God, world without end. *Amen.*

THE EPISTLE. *Galatians* 4. 1-7.

NOW I say, that the heir, as long as he is a child, differeth nothing from a servant, though he be lord of all; but is under tutors and governors until the time appointed of the father. Even so we, when we were children, were in bondage under the elements of the world: but when the fullness of the time was come, God sent forth His Son, made of a woman, made under the Law, to redeem them that were under the Law, that we might receive the adoption of sons. And because ye are sons, God hath sent forth the Spirit of His Son into your hearts, crying, Abba, Father. Wherefore thou art no more a servant, but a son; and if a son, then an heir of God through Christ.

THE GRADUAL. *Psalm* 110. 1-4.

ALLELUIA, Alleluia. The Lord said unto my Lord, / Sit Thou on my right hand, until I make Thine enemies Thy footstool. The Lord shall send the rod of Thy power out of Sion: / be Thou ruler, even in the midst among Thine enemies. In the day of Thy power shall the people offer Thee free-will offerings with an holy worship: / the dew of Thy birth is of the womb of the morning. The Lord sware, and will not repent, / Thou art a priest for ever after the order of Melchizedek. Alleluia.

THE GOSPEL. *Saint Matthew* 1. 18-25.

NOW the birth of Jesus Christ was on this wise: When as His Mother Mary was espoused to Joseph, before they came together, she was found with Child of the Holy Ghost. Then Joseph her husband, being a just man, and not willing to make her a public example, was minded to put her away privily. But while he thought on these things, behold, the angel of the Lord appeared unto him in a dream, saying, Joseph, thou son of David, fear not to take unto thee Mary thy wife: for that which is conceived in her is of the Holy Ghost. And she shall bring forth a Son, and thou shalt call His Name Jesus: for He shall save His people from their sins. Now all this was done, that it might be fulfilled which was spoken of the Lord by the prophet, saying, Behold, a Virgin shall be with Child, and shall bring forth a Son, and they shall call His Name Emmanuel, which being interpreted is, God with us. Then Joseph being raised from sleep did as the angel of the Lord had bidden him, and took unto him his wife: and knew her not till she had brought forth her firstborn Son: and he called His Name JESUS.

THE CIRCUMCISION OF OUR LORD JESUS CHRIST
[1 January]

THE INTROIT. *Psalm* 8. 1-5 *and* 9.

O LORD our Governor, how excellent is Thy Name in all the world, / Thou that hast set Thy glory above the heavens! Out of the mouth of very babes and sucklings hast Thou ordained strength, because of Thine enemies, / that Thou mightest still the enemy and the avenger. When I consider Thy heavens, even the works of Thy fingers; / the moon and the stars, which Thou hast ordained; What is man, that Thou art mindful of him, / and the son of man, that Thou visitest him? Thou madest him a little lower than the angels, / and hast crowned him with glory and worship.

GLORY be to the Father, and to the Son, / and to the Holy Ghost;

As it was in the beginning, is now, and ever shall be, / world without end. Amen.

THE COLLECTS.

Of Christmastide.

ALMIGHTY God, Who hast given us Thine only-begotten Son to take our nature upon Him, and as at this time to be born of a pure Virgin: Grant that we being regenerate, and made Thy children by adoption and grace, may daily be renewed by Thy Holy Spirit; through the same our Lord Jesus Christ, Who liveth and reigneth with Thee and the same Spirit, ever one God, world without end. *Amen.*

Of the Circumcision of our Lord.

ALMIGHTY God, Who madest Thy blessed Son to be circumcised, and obedient to the Law for man: Grant unto us the true Circumcision of the Spirit; that, our hearts, and all our members, being mortified from all worldly and carnal lusts, we may in all things obey Thy blessed will; through the same Thy Son Jesus Christ our Lord. *Amen.*

Of the Holy Name.

ALMIGHTY God, who by Thy blessed Apostle hast taught us that there is none other name given among men whereby we must be saved, but only the Name of our Lord Jesus Christ: Grant, we beseech Thee, that we may ever glory in His holy Name, and strive to make Thy salvation known unto all mankind; through the same Jesus Christ our Lord, Who liveth and reigneth with Thee and the Holy Ghost, one God, for ever and ever. *Amen.*

THE EPISTLE. *Romans* 4. 8-14.

BLESSED is the man to whom the Lord will not impute sin. Cometh this blessedness then upon the circumcision only, or upon the uncircumcision also? for we say that faith was reckoned to Abraham for righteousness. How was it then reckoned? when he was in circumcision, or in uncircumcision? Not in circumcision, but in uncircumcision. And he received the sign of circumcision, a seal of the righteousness of the faith which he had yet being uncircumcised: that he might be the father of all them that believe, though they be not circumcised; that righteousness might be imputed unto them also: and the father of circumcision to them who are not of the circumcision only, but who also walk in the steps of that faith of our father Abraham, which he had being yet uncircumcised. For the promise, that he should be the heir of the world, was not to Abraham, or to his seed, through the Law, but through the righteousness of faith. For if they which are of the Law be heirs, faith is made void, and the promise made of none effect.

THE GRADUAL. *Psalm* 145. 17-21.

ALLELUIA, Alleluia. The Lord is righteous in all His ways, / and holy in all His works. The Lord is nigh unto all them that call upon Him; / yea, all such as call upon Him faithfully. He will fulfil the desire of them that fear Him; / He also will hear their cry, and will help them. The Lord preserveth all them that love Him, / but scattereth abroad all the ungodly. My mouth shall speak the praise of the Lord, / and let all flesh give thanks unto His holy Name, for ever and ever. Alleluia.

THE GOSPEL. *Saint Luke* 2. 15-21.

AND it came to pass, as the angels were gone away from them into heaven, the shepherds said one to another, Let us now go even unto Bethlehem, and see this thing which is come to pass, which the Lord hath made known unto us. And they came with haste, and found Mary, and Joseph, and the Babe lying in a manger. And when they had seen it, they made known abroad the saying which was told them concerning this Child. And all they that heard it wondered at those things which were told them by the shepherds. But Mary kept all these things, and pondered them in her heart. And the shepherds returned, glorifying and praising God for all the things that they had heard and seen, as it was told unto them. And when eight days were accomplished for the circumcising of the Child, His Name was called JESUS, which was so named of the angel before He was conceived in the womb.

THE EPIPHANY OF OUR LORD JESUS CHRIST
OR
THE MANIFESTATION OF THE SON OF GOD
TO THE GENTILES
[6 January]

THE INTROIT. *Psalm* 72. 1-7.

GIVE the King Thy judgements, O God, / and Thy righteousness unto the King's son. Then shall He judge Thy people according unto right, / and defend the poor. The mountains also shall bring peace, / and the little hills righteousness unto the people. He shall keep the simple folk by their right, / defend the children of the poor, and punish the wrong-doer. They shall fear Thee, as long as the sun and moon endureth; / from one generation to another. He shall come down like the rain into a fleece of wool, / even as the drops that water the earth. In His time shall the righteous flourish; / yea, and abundance of peace, so long as the moon endureth.

GLORY be to the Father, and to the Son, / and to the Holy Ghost;

As it was in the beginning, is now, and ever shall be, / world without end. Amen.

THE COLLECT.

O GOD, Who by the leading of a star didst manifest Thine only-begotten Son Jesus Christ to the Gentiles: Mercifully grant, that we, who know Thee now by faith, may be led onward through this earthly life, until we see the vision of Thy heavenly glory; through the same Thy Son Jesus Christ our Lord, Who with Thee and the Holy Ghost liveth and reigneth, ever one God, world without end. *Amen.*

THE EPISTLE. *Ephesians* 3. 1-12.

FOR this cause I Paul, the prisoner of Jesus Christ for you Gentiles, if ye have heard of the dispensation of the grace of God which is given me to you-ward: how that by revelation He made known unto me the mystery; (as I wrote afore in few words, whereby, when ye read, ye may understand my knowledge in the mystery of Christ) which in other ages was not made known unto the sons of men, as it is now revealed unto His holy Apostles and Prophets by the Spirit; that the Gentiles should be fellow-heirs, and of the same body, and partakers of His promise in Christ by the Gospel: whereof I was made a minister, according to the gift of the grace of God given unto me by the effectual working of His power. Unto me, who am less than the least of all saints, is this grace given, that I should preach among the Gentiles the unsearchable riches of Christ; and to make all men see what is the fellowship of the mystery, which from the beginning of the world hath been hid in God, Who created all things by Jesus Christ: to the intent that now unto the principalities and powers in heavenly places might be known by the Church the manifold wisdom of God, according to the eternal purpose which He purposed in Christ Jesus our Lord: in Whom we have boldness and access with confidence by the faith of Him.

THE GRADUAL. *Psalm* 72. 8-11.

ALLELUIA, Alleluia. His dominion shall be also from sea to sea, / and from the river unto the world's end. They that dwell in the wilderness shall kneel before Him; / His enemies shall lick the dust. The kings of Tharsis and of the isles shall give presents; / the kings of Arabia and Seba shall bring gifts. All kings shall fall down before Him, / all nations shall do Him service. Alleluia.

THE GOSPEL. *Saint Matthew* 2. 1-12.

WHEN Jesus was born in Bethlehem of Judaea in the days of Herod the king, behold, there came wise men from the east to Jerusalem, saying, Where is He that is born King of the Jews? for we have seen His star in the east, and are come to worship Him. When Herod the king had heard these things, he was troubled, and all Jerusalem with him. And when he had gathered all the chief priests and scribes of the people together, he demanded of them where the Christ should be born. And they said unto him, In Bethlehem of Judaea: for thus it is written by the Prophet, And thou Bethlehem, in the land of Judah, art not the least among the princes of Judah: for out of thee shall come a Governor, that shall rule my people Israel. Then Herod, when he had privily called the wise men, enquired of them diligently what time the star appeared. And he sent them to Bethlehem, and said, Go and search diligently for the young Child; and when ye have found Him, bring me word again, that I may come and worship Him also. When they had heard the king, they departed; and, lo, the star, which they saw in the east, went before them, till it came and stood over where the young Child was. When they saw the star, they rejoiced with exceeding great joy. And when they were come into the house, they saw the young Child with Mary His Mother, and fell down, and worshipped Him: and when they had opened their treasures, they presented unto Him gifts; gold, and frankincense and myrrh. And being warned of God in a dream that they should not return to Herod, they departed into their own country another way.

THE BAPTISM OF OUR LORD JESUS CHRIST

THE INTROIT. *Psalm* 98. 1-4.

O SING unto the Lord a new song, / for He hath done marvellous things. With His own right hand, and with His holy arm, / hath He gotten himself the victory. The Lord declared His salvation, / His righteousness hath He openly shewed in the sight of the heathen. He hath remembered His mercy and truth toward the house of Israel, / and all the ends of the world have seen the salvation of our God.

GLORY be to the Father, and to the Son, / and to the Holy Ghost;
As it was in the beginning, is now, and ever shall be, / world without end. Amen.

THE COLLECT.

O HEAVENLY Father, Whose blessed Son Jesus Christ did take our nature upon Him, and was baptised for our sakes in the river Jordan: Mercifully grant that we being regenerate, and made Thy children by adoption and grace, may also be partakers of Thy Holy Spirit; through Him Whom Thou didst send to be our Saviour and Redeemer, even the same Thy Son Jesus Christ our Lord. *Amen.*

FOR THE EPISTLE. *Isaiah* 42. 1-8.

BEHOLD my Servant, Whom I uphold; mine Elect, in Whom my soul delighteth; I have put my Spirit upon Him: He shall bring forth judgement to the Gentiles. He shall not cry, nor lift up, nor cause His voice to be heard in the street. A bruised reed shall He not break, and the smoking flax shall He not quench: He shall bring forth judgement unto truth. He shall not fail nor be discouraged, till He have set judgement in the earth: and the isles shall wait for His Law. Thus saith God the Lord, He that created the heavens, and stretched them out; He that spread forth the earth, and that which cometh out of it; He that giveth breath unto the people upon it, and spirit to them that walk therein: I the Lord have called Thee in righteousness, and will hold Thine hand, and will keep Thee, and give Thee for a covenant of the people, for a Light of the Gentiles; to open the blind eyes, to bring out the prisoners from the prison, and them that sit in darkness out of the prison house. I am the Lord: that is my Name: and my glory will I not give to another, neither my praise to graven images.

THE GRADUAL. *Psalm* 98. 8-10.

ALLELUIA, Alleluia. Let the sea make a noise, and all that therein is; / the round world, and they that dwell therein. Let the floods clap their hands, and let the hills be joyful together before the Lord, / for He is come to judge the earth. With righteousness shall He judge the world, / and the people with equity. Alleluia.

THE GOSPEL. *Saint Mark* 1. 1-11.

THE beginning of the Gospel of Jesus Christ, the Son of God; as it is written in the Prophets, Behold, I send my messenger before Thy face, which shall prepare Thy way before Thee. The voice of one crying in the wilderness, Prepare ye the way of the Lord, make His paths straight. John did baptise in the wilderness, and preach the baptism of repentance for the forgiveness of sins. And there went out unto him all the land of Judaea, and they of Jerusalem, and were all baptised of him in the river of Jordan, confessing their sins. And John was clothed with camel's hair, and with a girdle of a skin about his loins; and he did eat locusts and wild honey; and preached, saying, There cometh one mightier than I after me, the latchet of Whose shoes I am not worthy to stoop down and unloose. I indeed have baptised you with water: but He shall baptise you with the Holy Ghost. And it came to pass in those days, that Jesus came from Nazareth of Galilee, and was baptised of John in Jordan. And straightway coming up out of the water, he saw the heavens opened, and the Spirit like a dove descending upon Him: and there came a voice from heaven, saying, Thou art my beloved Son, in Whom I am well pleased.

This Introit, Collect, Epistle, Gradual, Gospel, and Preface may be used on
any Week-day in the Octave of the Epiphany, or as a second Service on the Epiphany.

THE FIRST SUNDAY AFTER THE EPIPHANY

THE INTROIT. *Psalm* 100.

O BE joyful in the Lord, all ye lands; / serve the Lord with gladness, and come before His presence with a song. Be ye sure that the Lord He is God: / it is He that hath made us, and not we ourselves; we are His people, and the sheep of His pasture. O go your way into His gates with thanksgiving, and into His courts with praise; / be thankful unto Him, and speak good of His Name. For the Lord is gracious, His mercy is everlasting; / and His truth endureth from generation to generation.

GLORY be to the Father, and to the Son, / and to the Holy Ghost;
As it was in the beginning, is now, and ever shall be, / world without end. Amen.

THE COLLECT.

O LORD, we beseech Thee mercifully to receive the prayers of Thy people which call upon Thee; and grant that they may both perceive and know what things they ought to do, and also may have grace and power faithfully to fulfil the same; through Jesus Christ our Lord. *Amen.*

THE EPISTLE. *Romans* 12. 1-5.

I BESEECH you therefore, brethren, by the mercies of God, that ye present your bodies a living sacrifice, holy, acceptable unto God, which is your reasonable service. And be not conformed to this world: but be ye transformed by the renewing of your mind, that ye may prove what is that good, and acceptable, and perfect, will of God. For I say, through the grace given unto me, to every man that is among you, not to think of himself more highly than he ought to think; but to think soberly, according as God hath dealt to every man the measure of faith. For as we have many members in one body, and all members have not the same office: so we, being many, are one body in Christ, and every one members one of another.

THE GRADUAL. *Psalm* 84. 1-4.

ALLELUIA, Alleluia. O how amiable are Thy dwellings, / Thou Lord of hosts! My soul hath a desire and longing to enter into the courts of the Lord; / my heart and my flesh rejoice in the living God.

Yea, the sparrow hath found her an house, and the swallow a nest where she may lay her young: / even Thine altars, O Lord of hosts, my King and my God. Blessed are they that dwell in Thy house: / they will be alway praising Thee. Alleluia.

THE GOSPEL. *Saint Luke* 2. 41-52.

NOW Jesus' parents went to Jerusalem every year at the feast of the Passover. And when He was twelve years old, they went up to Jerusalem after the custom of the feast. And when they had fulfilled the days, as they returned, the Child Jesus tarried behind in Jerusalem; and Joseph and His Mother knew not of it. But they, supposing Him to have been in the company, went a day's journey; and they sought Him among their kinsfolk and acquaintance. And when they found Him not, they turned back again to Jerusalem, seeking Him. And it came to pass, that after three days they found Him in the temple, sitting in the midst of the doctors, both hearing them, and asking them questions. And all that heard Him were astonished at His understanding and answers. And when they saw Him, they were amazed: and His Mother said unto Him, Son, why hast Thou thus dealt with us? behold, Thy father and I have sought Thee sorrowing. And He said unto them, How is it that ye sought me? wist ye not that I must be about my Father's business? And they understood not the saying which He spake unto them. And He went down with them, and came to Nazareth, and was subject unto them: but His Mother kept all these sayings in her heart. And Jesus increased in wisdom and stature, and in favour with God and man.

THE SECOND SUNDAY AFTER THE EPIPHANY

THE INTROIT. *Psalm* 66. 1-4.

O BE joyful in God, all ye lands, / sing praises unto the honour of His Name, make His praise to be glorious. Say unto God, O how wonderful art Thou in Thy works; / through the greatness of Thy power shall Thine enemies be found liars unto Thee. For all the world shall worship Thee, / sing of Thee, and praise Thy Name. O come hither, and behold the works of God, / how wonderful He is in His doing toward the children of men.

GLORY be to the Father, and to the Son, / and to the Holy Ghost;
As it was in the beginning, is now, and ever shall be, / world without end. Amen.

THE COLLECT.

ALMIGHTY and everlasting God, Who dost govern all things in heaven and earth: Mercifully hear the supplications of Thy people, and grant us Thy peace all the days of our life; through Jesus Christ our Lord. *Amen.*

THE EPISTLE. *Romans* 12. 6-16.

HAVING then gifts differing according to the grace that is given to us, whether prophecy, let us prophesy according to the proportion of faith; or ministry, let us wait on our ministering: or he that teacheth, on teaching; or he that exhorteth, on exhortation: he that giveth, let him do it with simplicity; he that ruleth, with diligence; he that sheweth mercy, with cheerfulness. Let love be without dissimulation. Abhor that which is evil; cleave to that which is good. Be kindly affectioned one to another with brotherly love; in honour preferring one another; not slothful in business; fervent in spirit; serving the Lord; rejoicing in hope; patient in tribulation; continuing instant in prayer; distributing to the necessity of saints; given to hospitality. Bless them which persecute you: bless, and curse not. Rejoice with them that do rejoice, and weep with them that weep. Be of the same mind one toward another. Mind not high things, but condescend to men of low estate.

THE GRADUAL. Psalm 107. 8-9.

ALLELUIA, Alleluia. O that men would therefore praise the Lord for His goodness, / and declare the wonders that He doeth for the children of men! For He satisfieth the empty soul, / and filleth the hungry soul with goodness. Alleluia.

THE GOSPEL. Saint John 2. 1-11.

AND the third day there was a marriage in Cana of Galilee; and the Mother of Jesus was there: and both Jesus was called, and His disciples, to the marriage. And when they wanted wine, the Mother of Jesus saith unto Him, They have no wine. Jesus saith unto her, Woman, what is that to me and to thee? mine hour is not yet come. His mother saith unto the servants, Whatsoever He saith unto you, do it. And there were set there six water-pots of stone, after the manner of the purifying of the Jews, containing two or three firkins apiece. Jesus saith unto them, Fill the water-pots with water. And they filled them up to the brim. And He saith unto them, Draw out now, and bear unto the governor of the feast. And they bare it. When the ruler of the feast had tasted the water that was made wine, and knew not whence it was: (but the servants which drew the water knew;) the governor of the feast called the bridegroom, and saith unto him, Every man at the beginning doth set forth good wine; and when men have well drunk, then that which is worse: but thou hast kept the good wine until now. This beginning of miracles did Jesus in Cana of Galilee, and manifested forth His glory; and His disciples believed on Him.

THE THIRD SUNDAY AFTER THE EPIPHANY

THE INTROIT. Psalm 148. 1-6.

O PRAISE the Lord of heaven: / praise Him in the height. Praise Him, all ye angels of His: / praise Him, all His host. Praise Him, sun and moon: / praise Him, all ye stars and light. Praise Him, all ye heavens, / and ye waters that are above the heavens. Let them praise the Name of the Lord; / for He spake the word, and they were made; He commanded, and they were created. He hath made them fast for ever and ever: / He hath given them a Law which shall not be broken.

GLORY be to the Father, and to the Son, / and to the Holy Ghost;
As it was in the beginning, is now, and ever shall be, / world without end. Amen.

THE COLLECT.

ALMIGHTY and everlasting God, mercifully look upon our infirmities; and in all our dangers and necessities stretch forth Thy right hand to help and defend us; through Jesus Christ our Lord. Amen.

THE EPISTLE. Romans 12. 16-21.

BE not wise in your own conceits. Recompense to no man evil for evil. Provide things honest in the sight of all men. If it be possible, as much as lieth in you, live peaceably with all men. Dearly beloved, avenge not yourselves, but rather give place unto wrath: for it is written, Vengeance is mine; I will repay, saith the Lord. Therefore if thine enemy hunger, feed him; if he thirst, give him drink: for in so doing thou shalt heap coals of fire on his head. Be not overcome of evil, but overcome evil with good.

THE GRADUAL. *Psalm* 102. 15-18.

ALLELUIA, Alleluia. The heathen shall fear Thy Name, O Lord, / and all the kings of the earth Thy majesty; When the Lord shall build up Sion, / and when His glory shall appear; When He turneth Him unto the prayer of the poor destitute, / and despiseth not their desire. This shall be written for those that come after, / And the people which shall be born shall praise the Lord. Alleluia.

THE GOSPEL. *Saint Matthew* 8. 1-13.

WHEN Jesus was come down from the mountain, great multitudes followed Him. And, behold, there came a leper and worshipped Him, saying, Lord, if Thou wilt, Thou canst make me clean. And Jesus put forth His hand, and touched him, saying, I will; be thou clean. And immediately his leprosy was cleansed. And Jesus saith unto him, See thou tell no man; but go thy way, shew thyself to the priest, and offer the gift that Moses commanded, for a testimony unto them. And when Jesus was entered into Capernaum, there came unto Him a centurion, beseeching Him, and saying, Lord, my servant lieth at home sick of the palsy, grievously tormented. And Jesus saith unto him, I will come and heal him. The centurion answered and said, Lord, I am not worthy that Thou shouldest come under my roof: but speak the word only, and my servant shall be healed. For I am a man under authority, having soldiers under me: and I say to this man, Go, and he goeth; and to another, Come, and he cometh; and to my servant, Do this, and he doeth it. When Jesus heard it, He marvelled, and said to them that followed, Verily I say unto you, I have not found so great faith, no, not in Israel. And I say unto you, That many shall come from the east and west, and shall sit down with Abraham, and Isaac, and Jacob, in the kingdom of heaven. But the children of the kingdom shall be cast out into outer darkness: there shall be weeping and gnashing of teeth. And Jesus said unto the centurion, Go thy way; and as thou hast believed, so be it done unto thee. And his servant was healed in the selfsame hour.

THE FOURTH SUNDAY AFTER THE EPIPHANY

THE INTROIT. *Psalm* 98. 1-7.

O SING unto the Lord a new song, / for He hath done marvellous things. With His own right hand, and with His holy arm, / hath He gotten himself the victory. The Lord declared His salvation, / His righteousness hath He openly shewed in the sight of the heathen. He hath remembered His mercy and truth toward the house of Israel, / and all the ends of the world have seen the salvation of our God. Shew yourselves joyful unto the Lord, all ye lands; / sing, rejoice, and give thanks. Praise the Lord upon the harp; / sing to the harp with a psalm of thanksgiving. With trumpets also and shawms; / O shew yourselves joyful before the Lord the King.

GLORY be to the Father, and to the Son, / and to the Holy Ghost;
As it was in the beginning, is now, and ever shall be, / world without end. Amen.

THE COLLECT.

O GOD, Who knowest us to be set in the midst of so many and great dangers, that by reason of the frailty of our nature we cannot always stand upright: Grant unto us such strength and protection, as may support us in all dangers, and carry us through all temptations; through Jesus Christ our Lord. *Amen.*

THE EPISTLE. *Romans* 13. 1-7.

LET every soul be subject unto the higher powers. For there is no power but of God: the powers that be are ordained of God. Whosoever therefore resisteth the power, resisteth the ordinance of God: and they that resist shall receive to themselves damnation. For rulers are not a terror to good works, but to the evil. Wilt thou then not be afraid of the power? do that which is good, and thou shalt have praise of the same: For he is the minister of God to thee for good. But if thou do that which is evil, be afraid; for he beareth not the sword in vain: for he is the minister of God, a revenger to execute wrath upon him that doeth evil. Wherefore ye must needs be subject, not only for wrath, but also for conscience' sake. For this cause pay ye tribute also: for they are God's ministers, attending continually upon this very thing. Render therefore to all their dues: tribute to whom tribute is due; custom to whom custom; fear to whom fear; honour to whom honour.

THE GRADUAL. *Psalm* 98. 8-10.

ALLELUIA, Alleluia. Let the sea make a noise, and all that therein is; / the round world, and they that dwell therein. Let the floods clap their hands, and let the hills be joyful together before the Lord, / for He is come to judge the earth. With righteousness shall He judge the world / and the people with equity. Alleluia.

THE GOSPEL. *Saint Matthew* 8. 23-34.

AND when Jesus was entered into a ship, His disciples followed Him. And, behold, there arose a great tempest in the sea, insomuch that the ship was covered with the waves: but He was asleep. And His disciples came to Him, and awoke Him, saying, Lord, save us, we perish. And He saith unto them, Why are ye fearful, O ye of little faith? Then He arose, and rebuked the winds and the sea; and there was a great calm. But the men marvelled, saying, What manner of man is this, that even the winds and the sea obey Him! And when He was come to the other side into the country of the Gergesenes, there met Him two possessed with devils, coming out of the tombs, exceeding fierce, so that no man might pass by that way. And, behold, they cried out, saying, What have we to do with Thee, Jesus, Thou Son of God? art Thou come hither to torment us before the time? And there was a good way off from them an herd of many swine feeding. So the devils besought him, saying, If Thou cast us out, suffer us to go away into the herd of swine. And He said unto them, Go. And when they were come out, they went into the herd of swine: and, behold, the whole herd of swine ran violently down a steep place into the sea, and perished in the waters. And they that kept them fled, and went their ways into the city, and told everything, and what was befallen to the possessed of the devils. And, behold, the whole city came out to meet Jesus: and when they saw Him, they besought Him that He would depart out of their coasts.

THE FIFTH SUNDAY AFTER THE EPIPHANY

THE INTROIT. *Psalm* 97. 1-6.

THE Lord is King, the earth may be glad thereof; / yea, the multitude of the isles may be glad thereof. Clouds and darkness are round about Him; / righteousness and judgement are the habitation of His seat. There shall go a fire before Him, / and burn up His enemies on every side. His lightnings gave shine unto the world; / the earth saw it, and was afraid. The hills melted like wax at the presence of the Lord; / at the presence of the Lord of the whole earth. The heavens have declared His righteousness, / and all the people have seen His glory.

THE PROPERS OF THE YEAR

GLORY be to the Father, and to the Son, / and to the Holy Ghost;
As it was in the beginning, is now, and ever shall be, / world without end. Amen.

THE COLLECT.

O LORD, we beseech Thee to keep Thy Church and household continually in Thy true religion; that they who do lean only upon the hope of Thy heavenly grace may evermore be defended by Thy mighty power; through Jesus Christ our Lord. *Amen.*

THE EPISTLE. *Colossians* 3. 12-17.

PUT on therefore, as the elect of God, holy and beloved, the tenderest of mercies, kindness, humbleness of mind, meekness, longsuffering; forbearing one another, and forgiving one another, if any man have a quarrel against any: even as Christ forgave you, so also do ye. And above all these things, put on charity, which is the bond of perfectness. And let the peace of God rule in your hearts, to the which also ye are called in one body; and be ye thankful. Let the word of Christ dwell in you richly in all wisdom; teaching and admonishing one another in psalms and hymns and spiritual songs, singing with grace in your hearts to the Lord. And whatsoever ye do in word or deed, do all in the name of the Lord Jesus, giving thanks to God and the Father by Him.

THE GRADUAL. *Psalm* 126. 5-7.

ALLELUIA, Alleluia. Turn our captivity, O Lord, / as the rivers in the south. They that sow in tears, / shall reap in joy. He that now goeth on his way weeping, and beareth forth good seed, / shall doubtless come again with joy, and bring his sheaves with him. Alleluia.

THE GOSPEL. *Saint Matthew* 13. 24-35.

AT that time Jesus said unto them: The kingdom of heaven is likened unto a man which sowed good seed in his field: but while men slept, his enemy came and sowed tares among the wheat, and went his way. But when the blade was sprung up, and brought forth fruit, then appeared the tares also. So the servants of the householder came and said unto him, Sir, didst not thou sow good seed in thy field? from whence then hath it tares? He said unto them, An enemy hath done this. The servants said unto him, Wilt thou then that we go and gather them up? But he said, Nay; lest while ye gather up the tares, ye root up also the wheat with them. Let both grow together until the harvest: and in the time of harvest I will say to the reapers, Gather ye together first the tares, and bind them in bundles to burn them: but gather the wheat into my barn. Another parable put He forth unto them, saying, The kingdom of heaven is like to a grain of mustard seed, which a man took, and sowed in his field: which indeed is the least of all seeds: but when it is grown, it is the greatest among herbs, and becometh a tree, so that the birds of the air come and lodge in the branches thereof. Another parable spake He unto them; The kingdom of heaven is like unto leaven, which a woman took, and hid in three measures of meal, till the whole was leavened. All these things spake Jesus unto the multitude in parables; and without a parable spake He not unto them: that it might be fulfilled which was spoken by the Prophet, saying, I will open my mouth in parables; I will utter things which have been kept secret from the foundation of the world.

THE SIXTH SUNDAY AFTER THE EPIPHANY

THE INTROIT. *Psalm* 99. 1-5

THE Lord is King, be the people never so unpatient; / He sitteth between the cherubim, be the earth never so unquiet. The Lord is great in Sion, / and high above all people. They shall give thanks unto Thy Name / which is great, wonderful, and holy. The King's power loveth judgement; Thou hast prepared equity; / Thou hast executed judgement and righteousness in Jacob. O magnify the Lord our God, / and fall down before His footstool, for He is holy.

GLORY be to the Father, and to the Son, / and to the Holy Ghost;
As it was in the beginning, is now, and ever shall be, / world without end. Amen.

THE COLLECT.

O GOD, Whose blessed Son was manifested that He might destroy the works of the devil, and make us the sons of God, and heirs of eternal life: Grant us, we beseech Thee, that, having this hope, we may purify ourselves, even as He is pure; that, when He shall appear again with power and great glory, we may be made like unto Him in His eternal and glorious kingdom; where with Thee, O Father, and Thee, O Holy Ghost, He liveth and reigneth, ever one God, world without end, and in Whose holy Name we pray. *Amen.*

THE EPISTLE. I *Saint John* 3. 1-8.

BEHOLD, what manner of love the Father hath bestowed upon us, that we should be called the sons of God: therefore the world knoweth us not, because it knew Him not. Beloved, now are we the sons of God, and it doth not yet appear what we shall be: but we know that, when He shall appear, we shall be like Him; for we shall see Him as He is. And every man that hath this hope in Him purifieth himself, even as He is pure. Whosoever committeth sin transgresseth also the Law: for sin is the transgression of the Law. And ye know that He was manifested to take away our sins; and in Him is no sin. Whosoever abideth in Him sinneth not: whosoever sinneth hath not seen Him, neither known Him. Little children, let no man deceive you: he that doeth righteousness is righteous, even as He is righteous. He that committeth sin is of the devil; for the devil sinneth from the beginning. For this purpose the Son of God was manifested, that He might destroy the works of the devil.

THE GRADUAL. *Psalm* 99. 6-9.

ALLELUIA, Alleluia. Moses and Aaron among His priests, and Samuel among such as call upon His Name: / these called upon the Lord, and He heard them. He spake unto them out of the cloudy pillar, / for they kept His testimonies, and the Law that He gave them. Thou heardest them, O Lord our God; / Thou forgavest them, O God, and punishedst their own inventions. O magnify the Lord our God, and worship Him upon His holy hill, / for the Lord our God is holy. Alleluia.

THE GOSPEL. *Saint Matthew* 24. 23-31.

AT that time Jesus said unto them: Then if any man shall say unto you, Lo, here is Christ, or there; believe it not. For there shall arise false Christs, and false prophets, and shall shew great signs and wonders; insomuch that, if it were possible, they shall deceive the very elect. Behold, I have told you before. Wherefore if they shall say unto you, Behold, he is in the desert; go not forth: behold, he is in the secret chambers; believe it not. For as the lightning cometh out of the east, and shineth even unto the west; so shall also the coming of the Son of Man be. For wheresoever the carcase is, there will the eagles be gathered together. Immediately after the tribulation of those days shall the sun be darkened, and the moon shall not give her light, and the stars shall fall from heaven, and the powers of the heavens shall be shaken: And then shall appear the sign of the Son of Man in heaven: and then shall all the tribes of the earth mourn, and they shall see the Son of Man coming in the clouds of heaven with power and great glory. And He shall send His angels with a great sound of a trumpet, and they shall gather together His elect from the four winds, from one end of heaven to the other.

THE THIRD SUNDAY BEFORE LENT
WHICH IS CALLED
SEPTUAGESIMA SUNDAY

THE INTROIT. *Psalm* 18. 1-6.

I WILL love Thee, O Lord, my Strength; / the Lord is my stony Rock, and my Defence, / My Saviour, my God, and my Might, / in Whom I will trust, my Buckler, the Horn also of my Salvation, and my Refuge. I will call upon the Lord, Who is worthy to be praised; / so shall I be safe from mine enemies. The sorrows of death compassed me, / and the overflowings of ungodliness made me afraid. The pains of hell came about me, / the snares of death overtook me. In my trouble I will call upon the Lord, / and complain unto my God. So shall He hear my voice out of His holy temple, / and my complaint shall come before Him, it shall enter even into His ears.

GLORY be to the Father, and to the Son, / and to the Holy Ghost;
As it was in the beginning, is now, and ever shall be, / world without end. Amen.

THE COLLECT.

O LORD, we beseech Thee favourably to hear the prayers of Thy people; that we, who are justly punished for our offences, may be mercifully delivered by Thy goodness, for the glory of Thy Name; through Jesus Christ our Saviour, Who liveth and reigneth with Thee and the Holy Ghost, ever one God, world without end. *Amen.*

This Lesson following shall be read before the Epistle.

THE LESSON. *Genesis* 1. 1–2. 3.

IN the beginning God created the heaven and the earth. And the earth was without form, and void; and darkness was upon the face of the deep. And the Spirit of God moved upon the face of the waters. And God said, Let there be light: and there was light. And God saw the light, that it was good: and God divided the light from the darkness. And God called the light Day, and the darkness He called Night. And the evening and the morning were the first day. And God said, Let there be a firmament in the midst of the waters, and let it divide the waters from the waters. And God made the firmament, and divided the waters which were under the firmament from the waters which were above the firmament: and it was so. And God called the firmament Heaven. And the evening and the morning were the second day. And God said, Let the waters under the heaven be gathered together unto one place, and let the dry land appear: and it was so. And God called the dry land Earth; and the gathering together of the waters called He Seas: and God saw that it was good. And God said, Let the earth bring forth grass, the herb yielding seed, and the fruit tree yielding fruit after his kind, whose seed is in itself, upon the earth: and it was so. And the earth brought forth grass, and herb yielding seed after his kind, and the tree yielding fruit, whose seed was in itself, after his kind: and God saw that it was good. And the evening and the morning were the third day. And God said, Let there be lights in the firmament of the heaven to divide the day from the night; and let them be for signs, and for seasons, and for days, and years: and let them be for lights in the firmament of the heaven to give light upon the earth: and it was so. And God made two great lights; the greater light to rule the day, and the lesser light to rule the night: He made the stars also. And God set them in the firmament of the heaven to give light upon the earth, and to rule over the day and over the night, and to divide the light from the darkness: and God saw that it was good. And the evening and the morning were the fourth day. And God said, Let the waters bring forth abundantly the moving creature that hath life, and fowl that may fly above the earth in the open firmament of heaven. And God created great whales, and every living creature that moveth, which the waters brought forth abundantly, after their kind, and every winged fowl after his kind: and God saw that it was good. And God blessed them, saying, Be fruitful, and multiply, and fill the waters in the seas, and let fowl multiply in the earth. And the evening and the morning were the fifth day. And God said, Let the earth bring forth the living creature after his kind, cattle, and creeping thing, and beast of the earth after his kind: and it was so. And God made the beast of the earth after his kind, and cattle after their kind, and everything that creepeth upon the earth after his kind: and God saw that it was good. And God said, Let us make man in our image, after our likeness: and let them have dominion over the fish of the sea, and over the fowl of the air, and over the cattle, and over all the earth, and over every creeping thing that creepeth upon the earth. So God created man in His own image, in the image of God created He him; male and female created He them. And God blessed them, and God said unto them, Be fruitful, and multiply, and replenish the earth, and subdue it: and have dominion over the fish of the sea, and over the fowl of the air, and over every living thing that moveth upon the earth. And God said, Behold, I have given you every herb bearing seed, which is upon the face of all the earth, and every tree, in the which is the fruit of a tree yielding seed; to you it shall be for meat. And to every beast of the earth, and to every fowl of the air, and to everything that creepeth upon the earth, wherein there is life, I have given every green herb for meat: and it was so. And God saw everything that He had made, and, behold, it was very good. And the evening and the morning were the sixth day. Thus the heavens and the earth were finished, and all the host of them. And on the seventh day God ended His work which He had made; and He rested on the seventh day from all His work which He had made. And God blessed the seventh day, and sanctified it: because that in it He had rested from all His work which God created and made.

Then shall be sung or said Benedicite, Omnia Opera,
or the Song of the Three Children, as followeth.

BENEDICITE, OMNIA OPERA. *The Song of the Three Children.*
O ALL ye works of the Lord, bless ye the Lord; O ye Angels of the Lord, bless ye the Lord; O ye Heavens, bless ye the Lord: / Praise Him, and magnify Him forever. O ye Waters that be above the Firmament, bless ye the Lord; O all ye powers of the Lord, bless ye the Lord; O ye Sun and Moon, bless ye the Lord: / Praise Him, and magnify Him forever. O ye Stars of Heaven, bless ye the Lord; O ye Showers and Dew, bless ye the Lord; O ye Winds of God, bless ye the Lord: / Praise Him, and magnify Him forever. O ye Fire and Heat, bless ye the Lord; O ye Winter and Summer, bless ye the Lord; O ye Dews and Frosts, bless ye the Lord: / Praise Him, and magnify Him forever. O ye Frost and Cold, bless ye the Lord; O ye Ice and Snow, bless ye the Lord; O ye Nights and Days, bless ye the Lord: / Praise Him, and magnify Him forever. O ye Light and Darkness, bless ye the Lord; O ye Lightnings and Cloud, bless ye the Lord; O let the earth bless the Lord: / Praise Him, and magnify Him forever. O ye Mountains and Hills, bless ye the Lord; O all ye Green things upon the Earth, bless ye the Lord; O ye Wells, bless ye the Lord: / Praise Him, and magnify Him forever. O ye Seas and Floods, bless ye the Lord; O ye Whales, and all

that move in the Waters, bless ye the Lord; O all ye Fowls of the Air, bless ye the Lord: / Praise Him, and magnify Him forever. O all ye Beasts and Cattle, bless ye the Lord: / Praise Him, and magnify Him forever. O ye Children of Men, bless ye the Lord; O let Israel bless the Lord; O ye Priests of the Lord, bless ye the Lord: / Praise Him, and magnify Him forever. O ye Servants of the Lord, bless ye the Lord; O ye Spirits and Souls of the Righteous, bless ye the Lord; O ye holy and humble Men of heart, bless ye the Lord: / Praise Him, and magnify Him forever. O Ananias, Azarias, and Misael, bless ye the Lord: / Praise Him, and magnify Him forever.

GLORY be to the Father, and to the Son, / and to the Holy Ghost;

As it was in the beginning, is now, and ever shall be, / world without end. Amen.

THE EPISTLE. I *Corinthians* 9. 24-27.

KNOW ye not that they which run in a race run all, but one receiveth the prize? So run, that ye may obtain. And every man that striveth for the mastery is temperate in all things. Now they do it to obtain a corruptible crown; but we an incorruptible. I therefore so run, not as uncertainly; so fight I, not as one that beateth the air: but I keep under my body, and bring it into subjection: lest that by any means, when I have preached to others, I myself should be a cast-away.

THE GRADUAL. *Psalm* 119. 25-32.

MY soul cleaveth to the dust, / O quicken Thou me, according to Thy word. I have acknowledged my ways, and Thou heardest me; / O teach me Thy statutes. Make me to understand the way of Thy commandments, / and so shall I talk of Thy wondrous works. My soul melteth away for very heaviness; / comfort Thou me according to Thy word. Take from me the way of lying, / and cause Thou me to make much of Thy Law. I have chosen the way of truth, / and Thy judgements have I laid before me. I have stuck unto Thy testimonies: / O Lord, confound me not. I will run the way of Thy commandments, / when Thou hast set my heart at liberty.

THE GOSPEL. *Saint Matthew* 20. 1-16.

AT that time Jesus said unto them: The kingdom of heaven is like unto a man that is an householder, which went out early in the morning to hire labourers into his vineyard. And when he had agreed with the labourers for a penny a day, he sent them into his vineyard. And he went out about the third hour, and saw others standing idle in the marketplace, and said unto them, Go ye also into the vineyard, and whatsoever is right I will give you. And they went their way. Again he went out about the sixth and ninth hour, and did likewise. And about the eleventh hour he went out, and found others standing idle, and saith unto them, Why stand ye here all the day idle? They say unto him, Because no man hath hired us. He saith unto them, Go ye also into the vineyard; and whatsoever is right, that shall ye receive. So when even was come, the lord of the vineyard saith unto his steward, Call the labourers, and give them their hire, beginning from the last unto the first. And when they came that were hired about the eleventh hour, they received every man a penny. But when the first came, they supposed that they should have received more; and they likewise received every man a penny. And when they had received it, they murmured against the goodman of the house, saying, These last have wrought but one hour, and thou hast made them equal unto us, which have borne the burden and heat of the day. But he answered one of them, and said, Friend, I do thee no wrong: didst not thou agree with me for a penny? Take that thine is, and go thy way: I will give unto this last, even as unto thee. Is it not lawful for me to do what I will with mine own? Is thine eye evil, because I am good? So the last shall be first, and the first last: for many be called, but few chosen.

The Second Sunday before Lent

WHICH IS CALLED

Sexagesima Sunday

The Introit. *Psalm* 44. 1-8.

WE have heard with our ears, O God, our fathers have told us, / what Thou hast done in their time of old; How Thou hast driven out the heathen with Thy hand, and planted them in; / how Thou hast destroyed the nations and cast them out. For they gat not the land in possession through their own sword, / neither was it their own arm that helped them; But Thy right hand, and Thine arm, and the light of Thy countenance, / because Thou hadst a favour unto them. Thou art my King, O God: / send help unto Jacob. Through Thee will we overthrow our enemies; / and in Thy Name will we tread them under, that rise up against us. For I will not trust in my bow: / it is not my sword that shall help me; But it is Thou that savest us from our enemies, / and puttest them to shame that hate us.

GLORY be to the Father, and to the Son, / and to the Holy Ghost;

As it was in the beginning, is now, and ever shall be, / world without end. Amen.

The Collect.

O LORD God, Who seest that we put not our trust in anything that we do: Mercifully grant that by Thy power we may be defended against all adversity; through Jesus Christ our Lord. *Amen.*

The Epistle. II *Corinthians* 11. 21-31.

WHEREINSOEVER any is bold, (I speak foolishly,) I am bold also. Are they Hebrews? so am I. Are they Israelites? so am I. Are they the seed of Abraham? so am I. Are they ministers of Christ? (I speak as a fool) I am more; in labours more abundant, in stripes above measure, in prisons more frequent, in deaths oft. Of the Jews five times received I forty stripes save one. Thrice was I beaten with rods, once was I stoned, thrice I suffered shipwreck, a night and a day I have been in the deep; in journeyings often, in perils of waters, in perils of robbers, in perils by mine own countrymen, in perils by the heathen, in perils in the city, in perils in the wilderness, in perils in the sea, in perils among false brethren; in weariness and painfulness, in watchings often, in hunger and thirst, in fastings often, in cold and nakedness. Beside those things that are without, that which cometh upon me daily, the care of all the churches. Who is weak, and I am not weak? who is offended, and I burn not? If I must needs glory, I will glory of the things which concern mine infirmities. The God and Father of our Lord Jesus Christ, which is blessed for evermore, knoweth that I lie not.

The Gradual. *Psalm* 17. 6-8.

I HAVE called upon Thee, O God, for Thou shalt hear me; / incline Thine ear to me, and hearken unto my words. Shew Thy marvellous loving-kindness, Thou that art the Saviour of them which put their trust in Thee, / from such as resist Thy right hand. Keep me as the apple of an eye; / hide me under the shadow of Thy wings.

The Gospel. *Saint Luke* 8. 4-15.

WHEN much people were gathered together, and were come to Jesus out of every city, He spake by a parable: A sower went out to sow his seed: and as he sowed, some fell by the way side; and it was trodden down, and the fowls of the air devoured it. And some fell upon a rock; and as soon as it was sprung up, it withered away, because it lacked moisture. And some fell among thorns; and the thorns sprang up with it, and choked it. And other fell on good ground, and sprang up, and bare fruit an hundredfold. And when He had said these things, He cried, He that hath ears to hear, let him hear. And His disciples asked Him, saying, What might this parable be? And He said, Unto you it is given to know the mysteries of the kingdom of God: but to others in parables; that seeing they might not see, and hearing they might not understand. Now the parable is this: The seed is the Word of God. Those by the way side are they that hear; then cometh the devil, and taketh away the Word out of their hearts, lest they should believe and be saved. They on the rock are they, which, when they hear, receive the Word with joy; and these have no root, which for a while believe, and in time of temptation fall away. And that which fell among thorns are they, which, when they have heard, go forth, and are choked with cares and riches and pleasures of this life, and bring no fruit to perfection. But that on the good ground are they, which in an honest and good heart, having heard the Word, keep it, and bring forth fruit with patience.

THE SUNDAY NEXT BEFORE LENT
WHICH IS CALLED
QUINQUAGESIMA SUNDAY

THE INTROIT. *Psalm* 31. 1-6.

IN Thee, O Lord, have I put my trust: / let me never be put to confusion, deliver me in Thy righteousness. Bow down Thine ear to me; / make haste to deliver me. And be Thou my strong Rock, and House of Defence, / that Thou mayest save me. For Thou art my strong Rock, and my Castle: / be Thou also my Guide, and lead me for Thy Name's sake. Draw me out of the net that they have laid privily for me, / for Thou art my Strength. Into Thy hands I commend my spirit; / for Thou hast redeemed me, O Lord, Thou God of truth.

GLORY be to the Father, and to the Son, / and to the Holy Ghost;
As it was in the beginning, is now, and ever shall be, / world without end. Amen.

THE COLLECT.

O LORD, Who hast taught us that all our doings without charity are nothing worth: Send down Thy Holy Spirit upon us, and pour into our hearts that most excellent gift of charity, the very bond of peace and of all virtues, without which whosoever liveth is counted dead before Thee; grant this for Thine only Son Jesus Christ's sake. *Amen.*

THE EPISTLE. I *Corinthians* 13. 1-13.

THOUGH I speak with the tongues of men and of angels, and have not charity, I am become as sounding brass, or a tinkling cymbal. And though I have the gift of prophecy, and understand all mysteries, and all knowledge; and though I have all faith, so that I could remove mountains, and have not charity, I am nothing. And though I bestow all my goods to feed the poor, and though I give my body to be burned, and have not charity, it profiteth me nothing. Charity suffereth long, and is kind; charity envieth not; charity vaunteth not itself, is not puffed up, doth not behave itself unseemly, seeketh not her own, is not easily provoked, thinketh no evil; rejoiceth not in iniquity, but rejoiceth in the truth; beareth all things, believeth all things, hopeth all things, endureth all things. Charity never faileth: but whether there be prophecies, they shall fail; whether there be tongues, they shall cease; whether there be knowledge, it shall vanish away. For we know in part, and we prophesy in part. But when that which is perfect is come, then that which is in part shall be done away. When I was a child, I spake as a child, I understood as a child, I thought as a child: but when I became a man, I put away childish things. For now we see through a glass, darkly; but then face to face: now I know in part; but then shall I know even as also I am known. And now abideth faith, hope, charity, these three; but the greatest of these is charity.

THE GRADUAL. *Psalm* 31. 21-24.

O HOW plentiful is Thy goodness, which Thou hast laid up for them that fear Thee; / and that Thou hast prepared for them that put their trust in Thee, even before the sons of men! Thou shalt hide them privily by Thine own presence from the provoking of all men; / Thou shalt keep them secretly in Thy tabernacle from the strife of tongues. Thanks be to the Lord, / for He hath shewed me marvellous great kindness in a strong city.

THE GOSPEL. *Saint Luke* 18. 31-43.

THEN Jesus took unto Him the twelve, and said unto them, Behold, we go up to Jerusalem, and all things that are written by the Prophets concerning the Son of Man shall be accomplished. For He shall be delivered unto the Gentiles, and shall be mocked, and spitefully entreated, and spitted on: and they shall scourge Him, and put Him to death: and the third day He shall rise again. And they understood none of these things: and this saying was hid from them, neither knew they the things which were spoken. And it came to pass, that as He was come nigh unto Jericho, a certain blind man sat by the way side begging: and hearing the multitude pass by, he asked what it meant. And they told him, that Jesus of Nazareth passeth by. And he cried, saying, Jesus, Thou Son of David, have mercy on me. And they which went before rebuked him, that he should hold his peace: but he cried so much the more, Thou Son of David, have mercy on me. And Jesus stood, and commanded him to be brought unto Him: and when he was come near, He asked him, saying, What wilt thou that I shall do unto thee? And he said, Lord, that I may receive my sight. And Jesus said unto him, Receive thy sight: thy faith hath saved thee. And immediately he received his sight, and followed Him, glorifying God: and all the people, when they saw it, gave praise unto God.

THE FIRST DAY OF LENT
WHICH IS CALLED
ASH WEDNESDAY

THE BLESSING AND IMPOSITION OF ASHES

THE SENTENCES.

JESUS came into Galilee, preaching the Gospel of God, and saying, The time is fulfilled, and the kingdom of God is at hand; repent ye, and believe the Gospel. *Saint Mark* 1. 14-15.

All that the Father giveth me shall come to me; and him that cometh to me I will in no wise cast out. *Saint John* 6. 37.

Come unto me all ye that labour, and are heavy laden, and I will give you rest. Take my yoke upon you, and learn of me; for I am meek and lowly in heart; and ye shall find rest for your souls. For my yoke is easy, and my burden is light. *Saint Matthew* 11. 28-30.

I will arise, and go to my Father, and will say unto him, Father, I have sinned against heaven, and before Thee, and am no more worthy to be called Thy son. *Saint Luke* 15. 18-19.

If we say that we have no sin, we deceive ourselves, and the truth is not in us; but if we confess our sins, He is faithful and just to forgive us our sins, and to cleanse us from all unrighteousness. I *Saint John* 1. 8-9.

Then may be sung a penitential hymn.

THE EXHORTATION.
BRETHREN, it hath been the custom of holy Mother Church, from the Apostles' time, to observe with great devotion the days of our Lord's Passion, Death, and Resurrection; and also, from the earliest times, to prepare for the same by a season of forty days of penitence, abstinence, fasting, and self-denial; and to mark the first day thereof by the Blessing and Imposition of Ashes upon the heads of the Christian faithful.

This holy season of Lent is also a time in which adult converts to the Faith are prepared for holy Baptism; and the faithful themselves are exhorted to have in their remembrance the solemn vows and promises that were made at their own Baptisms, and which they did vow and promise again to fulfill and keep when they were confirmed.

Lent is also a time when such persons as have, by reason of notorious sin, been separated from the body of the Church, are reconciled and restored to the full fellowship and communion of the same; whereby the whole Congregation is put in mind of the wonderful message of pardon and forgiveness contained in the Gospel of Christ our Saviour, and of the need, which all Christians continually have, of a renewal of repentance and faith.

I invite you, therefore, in the name of holy Mother Church, to the observance of a holy Lent, by self-examination and repentance, by prayer, fasting, and self-denial, and by reading and meditating upon God's holy Word.

THE LESSON. *Joel 2.* 12-18.
THEREFORE also now, saith the Lord, turn ye even unto me with all your heart, and with fasting, and with weeping, and with mourning; and rend your hearts, and not your garments, and turn unto the Lord your God: for He is gracious and merciful, slow to anger, and of great kindness, and repenteth Him of the evil. Who knoweth if he will return, and repent, and leave a blessing behind him; even a meat offering and a drink offering unto the Lord your God? Blow the trumpet in Sion, sanctify a fast, call a solemn assembly: gather the people, sanctify the congregation, assemble the elders, gather the children and infants: let the bridegroom go forth out of his chamber, and the bride out of her closet. Let the priests, the ministers of the Lord, weep between the porch and the altar, and let them say, Spare Thy people, O Lord, and give not Thine heritage to reproach, that the heathen should rule over them: wherefore should they say among the people, Where is their God? Then will the Lord be jealous for His land, and pity His people.

THE PENITENTIAL PSALM. *Psalm* 51. *Miserere Mei, Deus.*
HAVE mercy upon me, O God, after Thy great goodness; / according to the multitude of Thy mercies do away mine offences. Wash me thoroughly from my wickedness, / and cleanse me from my sin. For I acknowledge my faults, / and my sin is ever before me. Against Thee only have I sinned, and done that which is evil in Thy sight; / that Thou mightest be justified when Thou speakest, and clear when Thou dost judge. Behold, I was shapen in wickedness, / and in sin hath my mother conceived me. But lo, Thou requirest truth in the inward parts, / and shalt make me to understand wisdom secretly. Thou shalt purge me with hyssop, and I shall be clean; / Thou

shalt wash me, and I shall be whiter than snow. Thou shalt make me hear of joy and gladness, / that the bones which Thou hast broken may rejoice. Turn Thy face from my sins, / and put out all my misdeeds. Make me a clean heart, O God, / and renew a right spirit within me. Cast me not away from Thy presence, / and take not Thy Holy Spirit from me. O give me the comfort of Thy help again, / and stablish me with Thy free Spirit. Then shall I teach Thy ways unto the wicked, / and sinners shall be converted unto Thee. Deliver me from blood-guiltiness, O God, Thou that art the God of my health; / and my tongue shall sing of Thy righteousness. Thou shalt open my lips, O Lord, / and my mouth shall shew forth Thy praise. For Thou desirest no sacrifice, else would I give it Thee; / but Thou delightest not in burnt offerings. The sacrifice of God is a troubled spirit ; / a broken and contrite heart, O God, shalt Thou not despise. O be favourable and gracious unto Sion; / build Thou the walls of Jerusalem. Then shalt Thou be pleased with the sacrifices of righteousness, with the burnt-offerings and oblations; / then shall they offer young bullocks upon Thine altar.

GLORY be to the Father, and to the Son, / and to the Holy Ghost;
As it was in the beginning, is now, and ever shall be, world without end. Amen.

Then shall the Priest say,
THE Lord be with you.
Answer. And with thy spirit.

Priest. Let us pray.

Lord, have mercy upon us.
Christ, have mercy upon us.
Lord, have mercy upon us.

Then shall the Priest and People together say the Lord's Prayer, as followeth.
OUR Father which art in heaven, hallowed be Thy Name. Thy kingdom come. Thy will be done, in earth as it is in heaven. Give us this day our daily bread. And forgive us our trespasses, As we forgive them that trespass against us. And lead us not into temptation; But deliver us from evil. Amen.

Then shall the Priest say,
O LORD, save us Thy servants,
 Answer. That put our trust in Thee.
Priest. Send unto us help from above,
 Answer. And evermore mightily defend us.
Priest. O Lord, hear our prayer;
 Answer. And let our cry come unto Thee.

The Priest.
O LORD, we beseech Thee, mercifully to hear our prayers, and spare all them that confess their sins unto Thee; that they, whose consciences by sin are accused, by Thy merciful pardon may be absolved; through Jesus Christ our Lord. *Amen.*

O MOST mighty God, and merciful Father, Who hast compassion upon all men, and hatest nothing that Thou hast made; Who wouldest not the death of a sinner, but that he should rather turn from his sin, and be saved: Mercifully forgive us our trespasses; receive and comfort us, who are grieved and wearied with the burden of our sins. Thy property is always to have mercy; and to Thee only it appertaineth to forgive sins. Spare us, O Lord, spare Thy people, whom Thou hast redeemed with Thy most precious Blood; enter not into judgement with Thy servants, who truly repent us of our faults; but so make haste to help us in this world, that we may ever live with Thee in the world to come; through Jesus Christ our Lord. *Amen.*

Then shall the Priest and people say together,
Turn Thou us, O good Lord, and so shall we be turned. Be favourable, O Lord, be favourable to Thy people, who turn to Thee in weeping, fasting, and praying. For Thou art a merciful God, full of compassion, long-suffering, and of great pity. Thou sparest when we deserve punishment, and in Thy wrath Thou thinkest upon mercy. Spare Thy people, good Lord, spare them, and let not Thine heritage be brought to confusion. Hear us, O Lord, for Thy mercy is great; and according to the multitude of Thy mercies look upon us; through the Merits of our only Mediator, Thy blessed Son Jesus Christ our Lord. *Amen.*

Then shall the Priest proceed to bless the Ashes.

The Blessing of the Ashes

Almighty and everlasting God, spare Thou them that are penitent, be favourable unto them that call upon Thee; and vouchsafe to ✠ bless these Ashes, that they may be unto all such as shall receive them a sign of humility, a wholesome medicine for the healing of their consciences, and a sure safeguard and protection of their bodies, souls, and spirits from the consequences and ravages of sin; through Jesus Christ our Lord. *Amen.*

Then shall the Priest and people say together,
Lord, for Thy tender mercies' sake, lay not our sins to our charge; but forgive us all that is past, and give us grace to amend our sinful lives; grant that we may decline from sin, and incline unto virtue, and walk with perfect hearts before Thee, from this time forth, and for evermore; through Christ our Lord. *Amen.*

The Imposition of the Ashes

And when the Priest shall set the Ashes upon the head of any one, he shall say,
Remember, O man, that dust thou art, and unto dust thou shall return.
Answer. Lord, have mercy upon us.

And when all have received the Ashes, the Priest shall say,
The Lord be with you.
Answer. And with thy spirit.

Priest. Let us pray.

Almighty and everlasting God, Who didst forgive the people of Nineveh when they repented in sackcloth and ashes: Mercifully grant that we, truly repenting of our sins, may obtain of Thee perfect pardon and release; through Jesus Christ our Lord. *Amen.*

O God our Father, Who makest Thy sun to rise upon the evil and the good, and sendest rain upon the just and upon the unjust: Help us to love our enemies, and to forgive them that trespass against us; that we may receive of Thee the forgiveness of our sins, and be made Thy children in spirit and in truth; through Jesus Christ our Lord, Who liveth and reigneth with Thee and the Holy Ghost, ever one God, world without end. *Amen.*

LORD of all power and might, Who art the Author and Giver of all good things: Graft in our hearts the love of Thy Name; increase in us true religion; nourish us with all goodness; and of Thy great mercy ever keep us in the same; through Jesus Christ our Lord. *Amen.*

AT THE EUCHARIST

THE INTROIT. *Psalm 57. 1-6.*

BE MERCIFUL unto me, O God, be merciful unto me, for my soul trusteth in Thee; / and under the shadow of Thy wings shall be my refuge, until this tyranny be over-past. I will call unto the most high God: / even unto the God that shall perform the cause which I have in hand. He shall send from heaven, / and save me from the reproof of him that would eat me up.
GLORY be to the Father, and to the Son, / and to the Holy Ghost;
As it was in the beginning is now, and ever shall be, / world without end. Amen.

THE COLLECT.

ALMIGHTY and everlasting God, Who hatest nothing that Thou hast made, and dost forgive the sins of all them that are penitent: Create and make in us new and contrite hearts, that we, worthily lamenting our sins, and acknowledging our wretchedness, may obtain of Thee, the God of all mercy, perfect remission and forgiveness; through Jesus Christ our Lord. *Amen.*

THE EPISTLE. *Saint James 4. 6-11.*

GOD bestoweth abundant grace; wherefore the Scripture saith, God resisteth the proud, but giveth grace unto the humble. Submit yourselves therefore unto God. Resist the devil, and he will flee from you. Draw nigh unto God, and He will draw nigh unto you. Cleanse your hands, ye sinners; and purify your hearts, ye double-minded. Be afflicted, mourn, and weep: let your laughter be turned to mourning, and your joy to heaviness. Humble yourselves in the sight of the Lord, and He shall lift you up. Speak not evil one of another, brethren.

THE GRADUAL. *Psalm 103. 8-14.*

THE Lord is full of compassion and mercy, / long-suffering, and of great goodness. He will not always be chiding: / neither keepeth He His anger forever. He hath not dealt with us after our sins, / nor rewarded us according to our wickednesses. For look how high the heaven is in comparison of the earth, / so great is His mercy also toward them that fear Him. Look how wide also the east is from the west, / so far hath He set our sins from us. Yea, like as a father pitieth his own children, / even so is the Lord merciful unto them that fear Him. For He knoweth whereof we are made: / He remembereth that we are but dust.

THE GOSPEL. *Saint Matthew 6. 16-21.*

AT that time Jesus spake unto His disciples, saying: Moreover when ye fast, be not, as the hypocrites, of a sad countenance: for they disfigure their faces, that they may appear unto men to fast. Verily, I say unto you, They have their reward. But thou, when thou fastest, anoint thine head, and wash thy face, that thou appear not unto men to fast, but unto thy Father which is in secret; and thy Father, which seeth in secret, shall recompense thee. Lay not up for yourselves treasures upon earth, where moth and rust doth corrupt, and where thieves break through and steal: but lay up for yourselves treasures in heaven, where neither moth nor rust doth corrupt, and where thieves do not break through and steal: for where your treasure is, there will your heart be also.

THE FIRST SUNDAY IN LENT

THE INTROIT. *Psalm* 91. 1-8.

WHOSO dwelleth under the defence of the most High / shall abide under the shadow of the Almighty. I will say unto the Lord, Thou art my Hope, and my Stronghold; / my God, in Him will I trust. For He shall deliver thee from the snare of the hunter, / and from the noisome pestilence. He shall defend thee under His wings, and thou shalt be safe under His feathers; / His faithfulness and truth shall be thy shield and buckler. Thou shalt not be afraid for any terror by night, / nor for the arrow that flieth by day; for the pestilence that walketh in darkness, / nor for the sickness that destroyeth in the noon-day. A thousand shall fall beside thee, and ten thousand at thy right hand; / but it shall not come nigh thee. Yea, with thine eyes shalt thou behold, / and see the reward of the ungodly.

GLORY be to the Father, and to the Son, / and to the Holy Ghost;
As it was in the beginning, is now, and ever shall be, / world without end. Amen.

THE COLLECTS.

O LORD, Who for our sake didst fast forty days and forty nights: Give us grace to use such abstinence, that, our flesh being subdued to the Spirit, we may ever obey Thy godly motions in righteousness, and true holiness, to Thy honour and glory, Who livest and reignest with the Father and the same Holy Ghost, one God, world without end. *Amen.*

ALMIGHTY and everlasting God, Who hatest nothing that Thou hast made, and dost forgive the sins of all them that are penitent: Create and make in us new and contrite hearts, that we, worthily lamenting our sins, and acknowledging our wretchedness, may obtain of Thee, the God of all mercy, perfect remission and forgiveness; through Jesus Christ our Lord. *Amen.*

THE EPISTLE. II *Corinthians* 6. 1-10.

WE then, as workers together with Him, beseech you also that ye receive not the grace of God in vain. (For He saith, I have heard thee in a time accepted, and in the day of salvation have I succoured thee: Behold, now is the accepted time; behold, now is the day of salvation.) Giving no offence in anything, that the ministry be not blamed: but in all things approving ourselves as the ministers of God, in much patience, in afflictions, in necessities, in distresses, in stripes, in imprisonments, in tumults, in labours, in watchings, in fastings; by pureness, by knowledge, by long suffering, by kindness, by the Holy Ghost, by love unfeigned, by the word of truth, by the power of God, by the armour of righteousness on the right hand and on the left, by honour and dishonour, by evil report and good report: as deceivers, and yet true; as unknown, and yet well known; as dying, and, behold, we live; as chastened, and not killed; as sorrowful, yet alway rejoicing; as poor, yet making many rich; as having nothing, and yet possessing all things.

THE GRADUAL. *Psalm* 91. 9-16.

FOR Thou, Lord, art my Hope; / Thou hast set Thine house of defence very high. There shall no evil happen unto thee, / neither shall any plague come nigh thy dwelling. For He shall give His angels charge over thee, / to keep thee in all thy ways. They shall bear thee in their hands, / that thou hurt not thy foot against a stone. Thou shalt go upon the lion and adder, / the young lion and the dragon shalt thou tread under thy feet. Because he hath set his love upon Me, therefore will I deliver him; / I will set him up, because he hath known My Name. He shall call upon Me, and I will hear him; / yea, I am with him in trouble; I will deliver him, and bring him to honour. With long life will I satisfy him, / and shew him My salvation.

THE GOSPEL. *Saint Matthew* 4. 1-11.

THEN was Jesus led up of the Spirit into the wilderness to be tempted of the devil. And when He had fasted forty days and forty nights, He was afterward an-hungered. And when the tempter came to Him, he said, If Thou be the Son of God, command that these stones be made bread. But He answered and said, It is written, Man shall not live by bread alone, but by every word that proceedeth out of the mouth of God. Then the devil taketh Him up into the holy city, and setteth Him on a pinnacle of the temple, and saith unto Him, If Thou be the Son of God, cast Thyself down: for it is written, He shall give His angels charge concerning Thee: and in their hands they shall bear Thee up, lest at any time Thou dash Thy foot against a stone. Jesus said unto him, It is written again, Thou shalt not tempt the Lord thy God. Again, the devil taketh Him up into an exceeding high mountain, and sheweth Him all the kingdoms of the world, and the glory of them; and saith unto Him, All these things will I give Thee, if Thou wilt fall down and worship me. Then saith Jesus unto him, Get thee hence, Satan: for it is written, Thou shalt worship the Lord thy God, and Him only shalt thou serve. Then the devil leaveth Him, and, behold, angels came and ministered unto Him.

THE SECOND SUNDAY IN LENT

THE INTROIT. *Psalm* 25. 1-7.

UNTO Thee, O Lord, will I lift up my soul; my God, I have put my trust in Thee: / O let me not be confounded, neither let mine enemies triumph over me. For all they that hope in Thee shall not be ashamed; / but such as transgress without a cause shall be put to confusion. Shew me Thy ways, O Lord, / and teach me Thy paths. Lead me forth in Thy truth, and learn me, / for Thou art the God of my salvation; in Thee hath been my hope all the day long. Call to remembrance, O Lord, Thy tender mercies / and Thy loving-kindnesses, which have been ever of old. O remember not the sins and offences of my youth; / but according to Thy mercy think Thou upon me, O Lord, for Thy goodness. Gracious and righteous is the Lord; / therefore will He teach sinners in the way.

GLORY be to the Father, and to the Son, / and to the Holy Ghost;

As it was in the beginning, is now, and ever shall be, / world without end. Amen.

THE COLLECTS.

ALMIGHTY God, Who seest that we have no power of ourselves to help ourselves: Keep us both outwardly in our bodies, and inwardly in our souls; that we may be defended from all adversities which may happen to the body, and from all evil thoughts which may assault and hurt the soul; through Jesus Christ our Lord. *Amen.*

ALMIGHTY and everlasting God, Who hatest nothing that Thou hast made, and dost forgive the sins of all them that are penitent: Create and make in us new and contrite hearts, that we, worthily lamenting our sins, and acknowledging our wretchedness, may obtain of Thee, the God of all mercy, perfect remission and forgiveness; through Jesus Christ our Lord. *Amen.*

THE EPISTLE. I *Thessalonians* 4. 1-8.

WE beseech you, brethren, and exhort you by the Lord Jesus, that as ye have received of us how ye ought to walk and to please God, so ye would abound more and more. For ye know what commandments we gave you by the Lord Jesus. For this is the will of God, even your sanctification, that ye should abstain from fornication: that every one of you should know how to possess his vessel in sanctification and honour; not in the lust of concupiscence, even as the Gentiles which know not God: that no man go beyond and defraud his brother in any matter: because that the Lord is the avenger of all such, as we also have forewarned you and testified. For God hath not called us unto uncleanness, but unto holiness. He therefore that despiseth, despiseth not man, but God, Who hath also given unto us His Holy Spirit.

THE GRADUAL. *Psalm* 123. 1-2.

UNTO Thee lift I up mine eyes / O Thou that dwellest in the heavens. Behold, even as the eyes of servants look unto the hand of their masters, and as the eyes of a maiden unto the hand of her mistress, / even so our eyes wait upon the Lord our God, until He have mercy upon us.

THE GOSPEL. *Saint Matthew* 15. 21-28.

AND, behold, a woman of Canaan came out of the same coasts, and cried unto Him, saying, Have mercy on me, O Lord, Thou son of David; my daughter is grievously vexed with a devil. But He answered her not a word. And His disciples came and besought Him, saying, Send her away; for she crieth after us. But He answered and said, I am not sent but unto the lost sheep of the house of Israel. Then came she and worshipped Him, saying, Lord, help me. But He answered and said, It is not meet to take the children's bread, and to cast it to dogs. And she said, Truth, Lord: yet the dogs eat of the crumbs which fall from their masters' table. Then Jesus answered and said unto her, O woman, great is thy faith: be it unto thee even as thou wilt. And her daughter was made whole from that very hour.

THE THIRD SUNDAY IN LENT

THE INTROIT. *Psalm* 25. 8-15.

THEM that are meek shall He guide in judgement; / and such as are gentle, them shall He teach His way. All the paths of the Lord are mercy and truth / unto such as keep His covenant and His testimonies. For Thy Name's sake, O Lord / be merciful unto my sin, for it is great. What man is he that feareth the Lord? / him shall He teach in the way that He shall choose. His soul shall dwell at ease, / and his seed shall inherit the land. The secret of the Lord is among them that fear Him; / and He will shew them His covenant. Mine eyes are ever looking unto the Lord, / for He shall pluck my feet out of the net. Turn Thee unto me, and have mercy upon me, / for I am desolate and in misery.

GLORY be to the Father, and to the Son, / and to the Holy Ghost;
As it was in the beginning, is now, and ever shall be, / world without end. Amen.

THE COLLECT.

WE beseech Thee, Almighty God, look upon the hearty desires of Thy humble servants, and stretch forth the right hand of Thy Majesty, to be our defence against all our enemies; through Jesus Christ our Lord. *Amen.*

THE PROPERS OF THE YEAR

ALMIGHTY and everlasting God, Who hatest nothing that Thou hast made, and dost forgive the sins of all them that are penitent: Create and make in us new and contrite hearts, that we, worthily lamenting our sins, and acknowledging our wretchedness, may obtain of Thee, the God of all mercy, perfect remission and forgiveness; through Jesus Christ our Lord. *Amen.*

THE EPISTLE. *Ephesians 5. 1-14.*

BE ye therefore followers of God, as dear children; and walk in love, as Christ also hath loved us, and hath given Himself for us an offering and a sacrifice to God for a sweet-smelling savour. But fornication, and all uncleanness, or covetousness, let it not be once named among you, as becometh saints; neither filthiness, nor foolish talking, nor jesting, which are not convenient: but rather giving of thanks. For this ye know, that no whoremonger, nor unclean person, nor covetous man, who is an idolater, hath any inheritance in the kingdom of Christ and of God. Let no man deceive you with vain words: for because of these things cometh the wrath of God upon the children of disobedience. Be not ye therefore partakers with them. For ye were sometimes darkness, but now are ye light in the Lord: walk as children of light: (for the fruit of the Spirit is in all goodness and righteousness and truth;) proving what is acceptable unto the Lord. And have no fellowship with the unfruitful works of darkness, but rather reprove them. For it is a shame even to speak of those things which are done of them in secret. But all things that are reproved are made manifest by the light: for whatsoever doth make manifest is light. Wherefore He saith, Awake thou that sleepest, and arise from the dead, and Christ shall give thee light.

THE GRADUAL. *Psalm 25. 16-22.*

THE sorrows of my heart are enlarged: / O bring Thou me out of my troubles. Look upon my adversity and misery, / and forgive me all my sin. Consider mine enemies, how many they are, / and they bear a tyrannous hate against me. O keep my soul, and deliver me; / let me not be confounded, for I have put my trust in Thee. Let perfectness and righteous dealing wait upon me, / for my hope hath been in Thee. Deliver Israel, O God / out of all his troubles.

THE GOSPEL. *Saint Luke 11. 14-28.*

JESUS was casting out a devil, and it was dumb. And it came to pass, when the devil was gone out, the dumb spake; and the people wondered. But some of them said, He casteth out devils through Beelzebub the chief of the devils. And others, tempting Him, sought of Him a sign from heaven. But He, knowing their thoughts, said unto them, Every kingdom divided against itself is brought to desolation; and a house divided against a house falleth. If Satan also be divided against himself, how shall his kingdom stand? because ye say that I cast out devils through Beelzebub. And if I by Beelzebub cast out devils, by whom do your sons cast them out? therefore shall they be your judges. But if I with the finger of God cast out devils, no doubt the kingdom of God is come upon you. When a strong man armed keepeth his palace, his goods are in peace: but when a stronger than he shall come upon him, and overcome him, he taketh from him all his armour wherein he trusted, and divideth his spoils. He that is not with me is against me: and he that gathereth not with me scattereth. When the unclean spirit is gone out of a man, he walketh through dry places, seeking rest; and finding none, he saith, I will return unto my house whence I came out. And when he cometh, he findeth it swept and garnished. Then goeth he, and taketh to him seven other spirits more wicked than himself; and they enter in, and dwell there: and the last state of that man is worse than the first. And it came to pass, as He spake these things, a certain woman of the company lifted up her voice, and said unto Him, Blessed is the womb that bare Thee, and the breasts which Thou hast sucked. But He said, Yea rather, blessed are they that hear the word of God, and keep it.

135

The Fourth Sunday in Lent
COMMONLY CALLED
Mothering Sunday

INTROIT. *Psalm* 122.

I WAS glad when they said unto me, / We will go into the house of the Lord. Our feet shall stand in thy gates, / O Jerusalem. Jerusalem is built as a city / that is at unity in itself. For thither the tribes go up, even the tribes of the Lord, / to testify unto Israel, to give thanks unto the Name of the Lord. For there is the seat of judgement, / even the seat of the house of David. O pray for the peace of Jerusalem; / they shall prosper that love thee. Peace be within thy walls, / and plenteousness within thy palaces. For my brethren and companions' sakes / I will wish thee prosperity. Yea, because of the house of the Lord our God / I will seek to do thee good.

GLORY be to the Father, and to the Son, / and to the Holy Ghost;
As it was in the beginning, is now, and ever shall be, / world without end. Amen.

THE COLLECTS.

GRANT, we beseech Thee, Almighty God, that we, who for our evil deeds do worthily deserve to be punished, by the comfort of Thy grace may mercifully be relieved; through our Lord and Saviour Jesus Christ. *Amen.*

ALMIGHTY and everlasting God, Who hatest nothing that Thou hast made, and dost forgive the sins of all them that are penitent: Create and make in us new and contrite hearts, that we, worthily lamenting our sins, and acknowledging our wretchedness, may obtain of Thee, the God of all mercy, perfect remission and forgiveness; through Jesus Christ our Lord. *Amen.*

THE EPISTLE. *Galatians* 4. 21-31.

TELL me, ye that desire to be under the Law, do ye not hear the Law? For it is written, that Abraham had two sons, the one by a bondmaid, the other by a freewoman. But he who was of the bondwoman was born after the flesh; but he of the freewoman was by promise. Which things are an allegory: for these are the two covenants; the one from the mount Sinai, which gendereth to bondage, which is Agar. For this Agar is mount Sinai in Arabia, and answereth to Jerusalem which now is, and is in bondage with her children. But Jerusalem which is above is free, which is the mother of us all. For it is written, Rejoice, thou barren that bearest not; break forth and cry, thou that travailest not: for the desolate hath many more children than she which hath an husband. Now we, brethren, as Isaac was, are the children of promise. But as then he that was born after the flesh persecuted him that was born after the Spirit, even so it is now. Nevertheless what saith the Scripture? Cast out the bondwoman and her son: for the son of the bondwoman shall not be heir with the son of the freewoman. So then, brethren, we are not children of the bondwoman, but of the free.

THE GRADUAL. *Psalm* 125. 1-5.

THEY that put their trust in the Lord shall be even as the mount Sion / which may not be removed, but standeth fast for ever. The hills stand about Jerusalem, / even so standeth the Lord round about His people, from this time forth for evermore. For the rod of the ungodly cometh not into the lot of the righteous, / lest the righteous put their hand unto wickedness. Do well, O Lord, / unto those that are good and true of heart. As for such as turn back unto their own wickedness, / the Lord shall lead them forth with the evil-doers; but peace shall be upon Israel.

THE GOSPEL. *Saint John* 6. 1-14.

JESUS went over the sea of Galilee, which is the sea of Tiberias. And a great multitude followed Him, because they saw His miracles which He did on them that were diseased. And Jesus went up into a mountain, and there He sat with His disciples. And the Passover, a feast of the Jews, was nigh. When Jesus then lifted up His eyes, and saw a great company come unto Him, He saith unto Philip, Whence shall we buy bread, that these may eat? And this He said to prove him: for He Himself knew what He would do. Philip answered Him, Two hundred pennyworth of bread is not sufficient for them, that every one of them may take a little. One of His disciples, Andrew, Simon Peter's brother, saith unto Him, There is a lad here, which hath five barley loaves, and two small fishes: but what are they among so many? And Jesus said, Make the men sit down. Now there was much grass in the place. So the men sat down, in number about five thousand. And Jesus took the loaves; and when He had given thanks, He distributed to the disciples, and the disciples to them that were set down; and likewise of the fishes as much as they would. When they were filled, He said unto His disciples, Gather up the fragments that remain, that nothing be lost. Therefore they gathered them together, and filled twelve baskets with the fragments of the five barley loaves, which remained over and above unto them that had eaten. Then those men, when they had seen the miracle that Jesus did, said, This is of a truth that Prophet that should come into the world.

THE FIFTH SUNDAY IN LENT
WHICH IS CALLED
PASSION SUNDAY

From Passion Sunday until Maundy Thursday inclusive, and at all Masses for the Dead,
the Preparation before the celebration of the Holy Eucharist shall not be said.

THE INTROIT. *Psalm* 43.

GIVE sentence with me, O God, and defend my cause against the ungodly people; / O deliver me from the deceitful and wicked man. For Thou art the God of my strength, why hast Thou put me from Thee, / and why go I so heavily, while the enemy oppresseth me? O send out Thy light and Thy truth, that they may lead me, / and bring me unto Thy holy hill, and to Thy dwelling. And that I may go unto the altar of God, even unto the God of my joy and gladness; / and upon the harp will I give thanks unto Thee, O God, my God. Why art thou so heavy, O my soul, / and why art thou so disquieted within me? O put thy trust in God; / for I will yet give Him thanks, which is the help of my countenance, and my God.

THE COLLECTS.

WE beseech Thee, Almighty God, mercifully to look upon Thy people; that by Thy great goodness they may be governed and preserved evermore, both in body and soul; through Jesus Christ our Lord. *Amen.*

ALMIGHTY and everlasting God, Who hatest nothing that Thou hast made, and dost forgive the sins of all them that are penitent: Create and make in us new and contrite hearts, that we, worthily lamenting our sins, and acknowledging our wretchedness, may obtain of Thee, the God of all mercy, perfect remission and forgiveness; through Jesus Christ our Lord. *Amen.*

THE EPISTLE. *Hebrews* 9. 1-15.

THEN verily the first covenant had also ordinances of Divine service, and a worldly sanctuary. For there was a tabernacle made; the first, wherein was the candlestick, and the table, and the shew-bread; which is called the Sanctuary. And after the second veil, the tabernacle which is called the Holy of Holies; which had the golden censer, and the ark of the covenant overlaid round about with gold, wherein was the golden pot that had manna, and Aaron's rod that budded, and the tables of the covenant; and over it the cherubims of glory shadowing the mercy-seat; of which we cannot now speak particularly. Now when these things were thus ordained, the priests went always into the first tabernacle, accomplishing the service of God. But into the second went the high priest alone once every year, not without blood, which he offered for himself, and for the errors of the people: the Holy Ghost this signifying, that the way into the Holy of Holies was not yet made manifest, while as the first tabernacle was yet standing: which was a figure for the time then present, in which were offered both gifts and sacrifices, that could not make him that did the service perfect, as pertaining to the conscience; which stood only in meats and drinks, and divers washings, and carnal ordinances imposed on them until the time of reformation. But Christ being come an High Priest of good things to come, by a greater and more perfect Tabernacle, not made with hands, that is to say, not of this building; neither by the blood of goats and calves, but by His own Blood He entered in once into the Holy Place, having obtained eternal redemption for us. For if the blood of bulls and of goats, and the ashes of an heifer sprinkling the unclean, sanctifieth to the purifying of the flesh: how much more shall the Blood of Christ, Who through the eternal Spirit offered Himself without spot to God, purge your conscience from dead works to serve the living God? And for this cause He is the Mediator of the New Testament, that by means of death, for the redemption of the transgressions that were under the First Testament, they which are called might receive the promise of eternal inheritance.

THE GRADUAL. *Psalm* 143. 1-6.

HEAR my prayer, O Lord, and consider my desire; / hearken unto me for Thy truth and righteousness' sake. And enter not into judgement with Thy servant; / for in Thy sight shall no man living be justified. For the enemy hath persecuted my soul; he hath smitten my life down to the ground; / he hath laid me in the darkness, as the men that have been long dead. Therefore is my spirit vexed within me, / and my heart within me is desolate. Yet do I remember the time past; I muse upon all Thy works; / yea, I exercise myself in the works of Thy hands. I stretch forth my hands unto Thee, / my soul gaspeth unto Thee as a thirsty land.

THE GOSPEL. *Saint John* 8. 46-59.

JESUS said unto them: Which of you convinceth me of sin? And if I say the truth, why do ye not believe me? He that is of God heareth God's words: ye therefore hear them not, because ye are not of God. Then answered the Jews, and said unto him, Say we not well that Thou art a Samaritan, and hast a devil? Jesus answered, I have not a devil; but I honour my Father, and ye do dishonour me. And I seek not mine own glory: there is One that seeketh and judgeth. Verily, verily, I say unto you, If a man keep my saying, he shall never see death. Then said the Jews unto Him, Now we know that Thou hast a devil. Abraham is dead, and the prophets; and Thou sayest, If a man keep my saying, he shall never taste of death. Art Thou greater than our father Abraham, which is dead? and the prophets are dead: whom makest Thou Thyself? Jesus answered, If I honour myself, my honour is nothing: it is my Father that honoureth me; of Whom ye say, that He is your God: yet ye have not known Him; but I know Him: and if I should say, I know Him not, I shall be a liar like unto you: but I know Him, and keep His saying. Your father Abraham rejoiced to see my day: and he saw it, and was glad. Then said the Jews unto Him, Thou art not yet fifty years old, and hast Thou seen Abraham? Jesus said unto them, Verily, verily, I say unto you, Before Abraham was, I am. Then took they up stones to cast at Him: but Jesus hid Himself, and went out of the temple, going through the midst of them, and so passed by.

THE SUNDAY NEXT BEFORE EASTER
WHICH IS CALLED
PALM SUNDAY

THE BLESSING OF THE PALMS

The Blessing of the Palms shall take place in some convenient location outside the Church itself, whether it be in the Narthex or in a Chapel adjacent to the Church, or in some other suitable setting.

When all is ready, the Priest shall say,
✠ Blessed is He that cometh in the Name of the Lord:
    Answer. Hosanna in the highest.

Then shall the Priest proceed to bless the Palms according to this form following.

OUR help standeth in the Name of the Lord;
    Answer. Who hath made heaven and earth.
    Priest. Lord, hear our prayer.
    Answer. And let our cry come unto Thee.
    Priest. The Lord be with you.
    Answer. And with thy spirit.

    Priest. Let us pray.

WE beseech Thee, O Lord, increase the faith, hope, and charity of them that put their trust in Thee, and graciously regard the prayers of Thy people: And vouchsafe to send down Thy blessing upon these branches of *palm* which we now set apart to Thy honour; and grant that we who bear them in our hands, in remembrance of the triumphal entry of Thy beloved Son into the holy City, may, with true faith and good works, joyfully go forth to meet Him when He shall come again in power and glory to establish His kingdom; and there with Him enter into everlasting gladness; through the same Thy Son Jesus Christ our Lord. *Amen.*

BLESS, O Lord, we humbly beseech Thee, these branches of *palm*, and vouchsafe to grant unto us that as we Thy people outwardly do Thee service, so inwardly we may honour Thee with purity and true devotion; and finally by Thy mercy attain unto everlasting life; through Jesus Christ our Lord. *Amen.*

O GOD, Who didst send forth Thine only Son Jesus Christ our Lord into the world for our salvation, that He might humble Himself to be made like unto us, and to call us back unto Thee; and before Whom, at His coming into Jerusalem, for the fulfilling of the Scriptures, the multitude strawed their raiment and branches in the way: Vouchsafe, we beseech Thee, so to fill us with such faith, and all godly and holy virtues, that every stone of stumbling and rock of offence may be done away, and our good works blossom before Thee as branches of true righteousness, so that we may be found worthy to be counted amongst the number of Thy chosen and elect people; through the same Thy Son Jesus Christ our Lord, Who with Thee and the Holy Ghost, liveth and reigneth ever one God, world without end. *Amen.*

THE DISTRIBUTION OF THE PALMS

Then shall one or more of these Anthems following be sung or said as the Priest giveth the blessed Palms to the Ministers, and the Ministers distribute to the people.

THE FIRST ANTHEM.

AND a very great multitude spread their garments in the way; / others cut down branches from the trees, and strawed them in the way. And the multitudes that went before, and that followed, cried, saying, Hosanna to the son of David: / Blessed is He that cometh in the Name of the Lord; Hosanna in the highest. *Saint Matthew* 21. 8-9.

Hosanna: Blessed is the King of Israel / that cometh in the name of the Lord. *Saint John* 12. 13.

Blessed be the kingdom of our father David, / that cometh in the Name of the Lord: Hosanna in the highest. *Saint Mark* 11. 10.

THE SECOND ANTHEM.

LIFT up your heads, O ye gates, and be ye lift up, ye everlasting doors, / and the King of glory shall come in. Who is the King of glory? / it is the Lord strong and mighty, even the Lord mighty in battle. Lift up your heads, O ye gates, and be ye lift up, ye everlasting doors, / and the King of glory shall come in. Who is the King of glory? / even the Lord of hosts, He is the King of glory. *Psalm* 24. 7-10.

Hosanna: Blessed is the King of Israel / that cometh in the name of the Lord. *Saint John* 12. 13.

Blessed be the kingdom of our father David, / that cometh in the Name of the Lord: Hosanna in the highest. *Saint Mark* 11. 10.

THE THIRD ANTHEM.

AND I beheld, and I heard the voice of many angels round about the throne and the beasts and the elders: / and the number of them was ten thousand times ten thousand, and thousands of thousands; Saying with a loud voice, / Worthy is the Lamb that was slain to receive power, and riches, and wisdom, and strength, and honour, and glory, and blessing. And every creature which is in heaven, and on the earth, and under the earth, and such as are in the sea, and all that are in them, / heard I saying, Blessing, and honour, and glory, and power, be unto Him that sitteth upon the throne, and unto the Lamb for ever and ever.
Revelation 5. 11-13.

Hosanna: Blessed is the King of Israel / that cometh in the name of the Lord. *Saint John* 12. 13.

Blessed be the kingdom of our father David, / that cometh in the Name of the Lord: Hosanna in the highest. *Saint Mark* 11. 10.

And when all have received the blessed Palms,
the Priest or Deacon shall read the Gospel appointed for Palm Sunday.

THE HOLY GOSPEL

The Minister.
THE Lord be with you.
Answer. And with thy spirit.

The Minister.
The holy Gospel is written in the Twenty-first Chapter of the Gospel
according to Saint Matthew, beginning at the first verse.

The Minister and people.
GLORY be to Thee, O Lord.

WHEN they drew nigh unto Jerusalem, and were come to Bethphage, unto the mount of Olives, then sent Jesus two disciples, saying unto them, Go into the village over against you, and straightway ye shall find a donkey tied, and a colt with her: loose them, and bring them unto me. And if any man say ought unto you, ye shall say, The Lord hath need of them; and straightway he will send them. All this was done, that it might be fulfilled which was spoken by the Prophet, saying, Tell ye the daughter of Sion, Behold, thy King cometh unto thee, meek, and sitting upon a donkey, and a colt the foal of a donkey. And the disciples went, and did as Jesus commanded them; and brought the donkey, and the colt, and put on them their clothes, and they set Him thereon. And a very great multitude spread their garments in the way; others cut down branches from the trees, and strawed them in the way. And the multitudes that went before, and that followed, cried, saying, Hosanna to the son of David: Blessed is He that cometh in the Name of the Lord; Hosanna in the highest. And when He was come into Jerusalem, all the city was moved, saying, Who is this? And the multitude said, This is Jesus the Prophet of Nazareth of Galilee. And Jesus went into the temple of God, and cast out all them that sold and bought in the temple, and overthrew the tables of the money-changers, and the seats of them that sold doves, and said unto them, It is written, My house shall be called the house of prayer; but ye have made it a den of thieves.

The Minister.
This is the Gospel of the Lord.

The Minister and people.
PRAISE be to Thee, O Christ.

The Minister.
AND through the words of the Gospel may our sins be blotted out.

The Gospel ended, the Priest and Ministers,
together with the people, shall set the Procession in order.

THE PROPERS OF THE YEAR

THE PROCESSION TO THE ALTAR

And before they proceed into the Church,
the Priest shall say or sing,
✠ LET us go forth in peace.
Answer. In the Name of Christ. Amen.

Then shall the Priest, Ministers, and people proceed into the Church
for the celebration of the Lord's Supper.

During the Procession to the Altar suitable hymns may be sung.

And when the Procession is come into the Sanctuary, and the Priest is come to the Altar,
having made due reverence, he shall turn to the people, and say,
THE Lord be with you.
Answer. And with thy spirit.

Priest. Let us pray.

O LORD Jesu Christ, our King and Redeemer, to Whose honour we have sung our solemn praises, bearing in our hands these branches of *palm*: Mercifully grant that whithersoever these branches may be carried, there the grace of Thy benediction may descend, and all the wickedness and craft of the devil be put to flight; and by the power of Thy right hand protect and defend all those whom Thou hast redeemed; Who with the Father and the Holy Ghost we worship and glorify, ever one God, world without end. *Amen.*

Then shall the Priest begin the celebration of the Lord's Supper
with the Lord's Prayer and Collect for Purity

AT THE EUCHARIST

THE INTROIT. *Psalm* 118. 19-29.
OPEN me the gates of righteousness, / that I may go into them, and give thanks unto the Lord. This is the gate of the Lord: / the righteous shall enter into it. I will thank Thee, for Thou hast heard me, / and art become my Salvation. The same stone which the builders refused / is become the head-stone in the corner. This is the Lord's doing, / and it is marvellous in our eyes. This is the day which the Lord hath made: / we will rejoice and be glad in it. Help me now, O Lord: / O Lord, send us now prosperity. Blessed be He that cometh in the Name of the Lord: / we have blessed you out of the house of the Lord. God is the Lord Who hath shewed us light: / bind the sacrifice with cords, yea, even unto the horns of the altar. Thou art my God, and I will thank Thee: / Thou art my God, and I will praise Thee. O give thanks unto the Lord, for He is gracious; / and His mercy endureth for ever.

THE COLLECT.
ALMIGHTY and everlasting God, Who, of Thy tender love towards mankind, hast sent Thy Son, our Saviour Jesus Christ, to take upon Him our flesh, and to suffer death upon the Cross, that all mankind should follow the example of His great humility: Mercifully grant, that we may both follow the example of His patience, and also be made partakers of His resurrection; through the same Jesus Christ our Lord. *Amen.*

And this Collect is appointed to be used every day until Good Friday.

THE EPISTLE. *Philippians* 2. 5-11.

LET this mind be in you, which was also in Christ Jesus: Who, being in the form of God, thought it not robbery to be equal with God: but made Himself of no reputation, and took upon Him the form of a servant, and was made in the likeness of men: and being found in fashion as a man, He humbled Himself, and became obedient unto death, even the death of the Cross. Wherefore God also hath highly exalted Him, and given Him a Name which is above every name: that at the Name of Jesus every knee should bow, of things in heaven, and things in earth, and things under the earth; and that every tongue should confess that Jesus Christ is Lord, to the glory of God the Father.

THE GRADUAL. *Psalm* 22. 12-19.

MANY oxen are come about me; / fat bulls of Bashan close me in on every side. They gape upon me with their mouths, / as it were a ramping and a roaring lion. I am poured out like water, and all my bones are out of joint; / my heart also in the midst of my body is even like melting wax. My strength is dried up like a potsherd, and my tongue cleaveth to my gums; / and Thou shalt bring me into the dust of death. For many dogs are come about me, / and the council of the wicked layeth siege against. They pierced my hands and my feet; I may tell all my bones; / they stand staring and looking upon me. They part my garments among them, / and cast lots upon my vesture. But be not Thou far from me, O Lord: / Thou art my succour, haste Thee to help me.

THE PASSION OF OUR LORD JESUS CHRIST
ACCORDING TO SAINT MATTHEW.

THE GOSPEL. *Saint Matthew* 27. 1-54.

WHEN the morning was come, all the chief priests and elders of the people took counsel against Jesus to put Him to death: and when they had bound Him, they led Him away, and delivered Him to Pontius Pilate the governor. Then Judas, which had betrayed Him, when he saw that He was condemned, repented himself, and brought again the thirty pieces of silver to the chief priests and elders, saying, I have sinned in that I have betrayed the innocent Blood. And they said, What is that to us? see thou to that. And he cast down the pieces of silver in the temple, and departed, and went and hanged himself. And the chief priests took the silver pieces, and said, It is not lawful for to put them into the treasury, because it is the price of blood. And they took counsel, and bought with them the potter's field, to bury strangers in. Wherefore that field was called, The Field of Blood, unto this day. Then was fulfilled that which was spoken by Jeremy the Prophet, saying, And they took the thirty pieces of silver, the price of Him that was valued, Whom they of the children of Israel did value; and gave them for the potter's field, as the Lord appointed me. And Jesus stood before the governor: and the governor asked Him, saying, Art Thou the King of the Jews? And Jesus said unto him, Thou sayest. And when He was accused of the chief priests and elders, He answered nothing. Then said Pilate unto Him, Hearest Thou not how many things they witness against Thee? And He answered him to never a word; insomuch that the governor marvelled greatly. Now at that feast the governor was wont to release unto the people a prisoner, whom they would. And they had then a notable prisoner, called Barabbas. Therefore when they were gathered together, Pilate said unto them, Whom will ye that I release unto you? Barabbas, or Jesus which is called Christ? For he knew that for envy they had delivered Him. When he was set down on the judgement seat, his wife sent unto him, saying, Have thou nothing to do with that just man: for I have suffered many things this day in a dream because of Him. But the chief priests and elders persuaded the multitude that they should ask Barabbas, and destroy Jesus. The governor answered and said unto them, Whether of the twain will ye that I release unto you? They said, Barabbas. Pilate saith unto them, What shall I do then with Jesus which is called Christ? They all say unto him, Let Him be crucified. And the governor said, Why, what evil hath He done? But they cried out the more, saying, Let Him be crucified. When Pilate saw that he could prevail nothing, but that rather a tumult was made, he took water, and washed his hands before the multitude, saying, I am innocent of the Blood of this just person: see ye to it. Then answered all the people, and said, His Blood be on us, and on our children. Then released he Barabbas unto them: and when he had scourged Jesus, he delivered Him to be crucified. Then the soldiers of the governor took Jesus into the common hall, and gathered unto Him the whole band of soldiers. And they stripped Him, and put on Him a scarlet robe. And when they had platted a crown of thorns, they put it upon His head, and a reed in His right hand: and they bowed the knee before Him, and mocked Him, saying, Hail, King of the Jews! And they spit upon Him, and took the reed, and smote Him on the head. And after that they had mocked Him, they took the robe off from Him, and put His own raiment on Him, and led Him away to crucify Him. And as they came out, they found a man of Cyrene, Simon by name: him they compelled to bear His Cross. And when they were come unto a place called Golgotha, that is to say, a place of a skull, they gave Him vinegar to drink mingled with gall: and when He had tasted thereof, He would not drink. And they crucified Him, and parted His garments, casting lots: that it might be fulfilled which was spoken by the Prophet, They parted my garments among them, and upon my vesture did they cast lots. And sitting down they watched Him there; and set up over His head His accusation written, This is Jesus the King of the Jews. Then were there two thieves crucified with Him, one on the right hand, and another on the left. And they that passed by reviled Him, wagging their heads, and saying, Thou that destroyest the temple, and buildest it in three days, save Thyself. If Thou be the Son of God, come down from the Cross. Likewise also the chief priests mocking Him, with the scribes and elders, said, He saved others; Himself He cannot save. If He be the King of Israel, let Him now come down from the Cross, and we will believe Him. He trusted in God; let Him deliver Him now, if He will have Him: for He said, I am the Son of God. The thieves also, which were crucified with Him, cast the same in his teeth. Now from the sixth hour there was darkness over all the land unto the ninth hour. And about the ninth hour Jesus cried with a loud voice, saying, Eli, Eli, lama sabachthani? that is to say, My God, my God, why hast Thou forsaken me? Some of them that stood there, when they heard that, said, This man calleth for Elias. And straightway one of them ran, and took a sponge, and filled it with vinegar, and put it on a reed, and gave Him to drink. The rest said, Let be, let us see whether Elias will come to save Him. Jesus, when He had cried again with a loud voice, yielded up the ghost. (*Here all shall kneel and, after a short space, shall rise again.*) And, behold, the veil of the temple was rent in twain from the top to the bottom; and the earth did quake, and the rocks rent; and the graves were opened; and many bodies of the saints which slept arose, and came out of the graves after His resurrection, and went into the holy City, and appeared unto many. Now when the centurion, and they that were with him, watching Jesus, saw the earthquake, and those things that were done, they feared greatly, saying, Truly this was the Son of God.

Monday in Holy Week

The Introit. *Psalm* 35. 1-3.

PLEAD Thou my cause, O Lord, with them that strive with me, / and fight Thou against them that fight against me. Lay hand upon the shield and buckler, / and stand up to help me. Bring forth the spear, and stop the way against them that persecute me; / say unto my soul, I am Thy salvation.

The Collect.

ALMIGHTY and everlasting God, Who, of Thy tender love towards mankind, hast sent Thy Son, our Saviour Jesus Christ, to take upon Him our flesh, and to suffer death upon the Cross, that all mankind should follow the example of His great humility: Mercifully grant, that we may both follow the example of His patience, and also be made partakers of His resurrection; through the same Jesus Christ our Lord. *Amen.*

For the Epistle. *Isaiah* 63. 1-19.

WHO is this that cometh from Edom, with dyed garments from Bozrah? this that is glorious in his apparel, travelling in the greatness of his strength? I that speak in righteousness, mighty to save. Wherefore art thou red in thine apparel, and thy garments like him that treadeth in the winefat? I have trodden the winepress alone; and of the people there was none with me: for I will tread them in mine anger, and trample them in my fury; and their blood shall be sprinkled upon my garments, and I will stain all my raiment. For the day of vengeance is in mine heart, and the year of my redeemed is come. And I looked, and there was none to help; and I wondered that there was none to uphold: therefore mine own arm brought salvation unto me; and my fury, it upheld me. And I will tread down the people in mine anger, and make them drunk in my fury, and I will bring down their strength to the earth. I will mention the loving-kindnesses of the Lord, and the praises of the Lord, according to all that the Lord hath bestowed on us, and the great goodness toward the house of Israel, which he hath bestowed on them according to His mercies, and according to the multitude of His loving-kindnesses. For He said, Surely they are my people, children that will not lie: so He was their Saviour. In all their affliction He was afflicted, and the angel of His presence saved them: in His love and in His pity He redeemed them; and He bare them, and carried them all the days of old. But they rebelled, and vexed His Holy Spirit: therefore He was turned to be their enemy, and He fought against them. Then He remembered the days of old, Moses, and His people, saying, Where is He that brought them up out of the sea with the shepherd of His flock? where is He that put His Holy Spirit within him? That led them by the right hand of Moses with His glorious arm, dividing the water before them, to make Himself an everlasting Name? That led them through the deep, as an horse in the wilderness, that they should not stumble? As a beast goeth down into the valley, the Spirit of the Lord caused him to rest: so didst Thou lead Thy people, to make Thyself a glorious name. Look down from heaven, and behold from the habitation of Thy holiness and of Thy glory: where is Thy zeal and Thy strength, the sounding of Thy pity and of Thy mercies toward me? are they restrained? Doubtless Thou art our Father, though Abraham be ignorant of us, and Israel acknowledge us not: Thou, O Lord, art our Father, our Redeemer; Thy Name is from everlasting. O Lord, why hast Thou made us to err from Thy ways, and hardened our heart from Thy fear? Return for Thy servants' sake, the tribes of Thine inheritance. The people of Thy holiness have possessed it but a little while: our adversaries have trodden down Thy sanctuary. We are Thine: Thou never barest rule over them; they were not called by Thy Name.

THE PROPERS OF THE YEAR

THE GRADUAL. *Psalm* 79. 8-10.

O REMEMBER not our old sins, but have mercy upon us, and that soon: / for we are come to great misery. Help us, O God of our salvation, for the glory of Thy Name; / O deliver us, and be merciful unto our sins, for Thy Name's sake. Wherefore do the heathen say, / Where is now their God?

THE BEGINNING OF THE PASSION OF OUR LORD JESUS CHRIST
ACCORDING TO SAINT MARK.

THE GOSPEL. *Saint Mark* 14. 1-72.

AFTER two days was the feast of the Passover, and of unleavened bread: and the chief priests and the scribes sought how they might take Jesus by craft, and put Him to death. But they said, Not on the feast day, lest there be an uproar of the people. And being in Bethany in the house of Simon the leper, as He sat at meat, there came a woman having an alabaster box of ointment of spikenard very precious; and she brake the box, and poured it on His head. And there were some that had indignation within themselves, and said, Why was this waste of the ointment made? For it might have been sold for more than three hundred pence, and have been given to the poor. And they murmured against her. And Jesus said, Let her alone; why trouble ye her? she hath wrought a good work on me. For ye have the poor with you always, and whensoever ye will ye may do them good: but me ye have not always. She hath done what she could: she is come aforehand to anoint my body to the burying. Verily I say unto you, Wheresoever this Gospel shall be preached throughout the whole world, this also that she hath done shall be spoken of for a memorial of her. And Judas Iscariot, one of the twelve, went unto the chief priests, to betray Him unto them. And when they heard it, they were glad, and promised to give him money. And he sought how he might conveniently betray Him. And the first day of unleavened bread, when they killed the Passover, His disciples said unto Him, Where wilt Thou that we go and prepare that Thou mayest eat the Passover? And He sendeth forth two of His disciples, and saith unto them, Go ye into the city, and there shall meet you a man bearing a pitcher of water: follow him. And wheresoever he shall go in, say ye to the goodman of the house, The Master saith, Where is the guest-chamber, where I shall eat the Passover with my disciples? And he will shew you a large upper room furnished and prepared: there make ready for us. And His disciples went forth, and came into the city, and found as He had said unto them: and they made ready the Passover. And in the evening He cometh with the twelve. And as they sat and did eat, Jesus said, Verily I say unto you, one of you which eateth with me shall betray me. And they began to be sorrowful, and to say unto Him one by one, Is it I? and another said, Is it I? And He answered and said unto them, It is one of the twelve, that dippeth with me in the dish. The Son of Man indeed goeth, as it is written of Him: but woe to that man by whom the Son of Man is betrayed! good were it for that man if he had never been born. And as they did eat, Jesus took bread, and blessed, and brake it, and gave to them, and said, Take, eat: this is my body. And He took the cup, and when He had given thanks, He gave it to them: and they all drank of it. And He said unto them, This is my Blood of the New Testament, which is shed for many. Verily I say unto you, I will drink no more of the fruit of the vine, until that day that I drink it new in the kingdom of God. And when they had sung an hymn, they went out into the mount of Olives. And Jesus saith unto them, All ye shall be offended because of me this night: for it is written, I will smite the Shepherd, and the sheep shall be scattered. But after that I am risen, I will go before you into Galilee. But Peter said unto Him, Although all shall be offended, yet will not I. And Jesus saith unto him, Verily I say unto thee, that this day, even in this night, before the cock crow twice, thou shalt deny me thrice. But he spake the more vehemently, If I should die with Thee, I will not deny

Thee in any wise. Likewise also said they all. And they came to a place which was named Gethsemane: and He saith to His disciples, Sit ye here, while I shall pray. And He taketh with Him Peter and James and John, and began to be sore amazed, and to be very heavy; and saith unto them, My soul is exceeding sorrowful unto death: tarry ye here, and watch. And He went forward a little, and fell on the ground, and prayed that, if it were possible, the hour might pass from Him. And He said, Abba, Father, all things are possible unto Thee; take away this cup from me: nevertheless not what I will, but what Thou wilt. And He cometh, and findeth them sleeping, and saith unto Peter, Simon, sleepest thou? couldest not thou watch one hour? Watch ye and pray, lest ye enter into temptation. The spirit truly is ready, but the flesh is weak. And again He went away, and prayed, and spake the same words. And when He returned, He found them asleep again, (for their eyes were heavy,) neither wist they what to answer Him. And He cometh the third time, and saith unto them, Sleep on now, and take your rest: it is enough, the hour is come; behold, the Son of Man is betrayed into the hands of sinners. Rise up, let us go; lo, he that betrayeth me is at hand. And immediately, while He yet spake, cometh Judas, one of the twelve, and with him a great multitude with swords and staves, from the chief priests and the scribes and the elders. And he that betrayed Him had given them a token, saying, Whomsoever I shall kiss, that same is He; take Him, and lead Him away safely. And as soon as he was come, he goeth straightway to Him, and saith, Master, Master; and kissed Him. And they laid their hands on Him, and took Him. And one of them that stood by drew a sword, and smote a servant of the high priest, and cut off his ear. And Jesus answered and said unto them, Are ye come out, as against a thief, with swords and with staves to take me? I was daily with you in the temple teaching, and ye took me not: but the Scriptures must be fulfilled. And they all forsook Him, and fled. And there followed Him a certain young man, having a linen cloth cast about his naked body; and the young men laid hold on him: and he left the linen cloth, and fled from them naked. And they led Jesus away to the high priest: and with him were assembled all the chief priests and the elders and the scribes. And Peter followed Him afar off, even into the palace of the high priest: and he sat with the servants, and warmed himself at the fire. And the chief priests and all the council sought for witness against Jesus to put Him to death; and found none. For many bare false witness against Him, but their witness agreed not together. And there arose certain, and bare false witness against Him, saying, We heard Him say, I will destroy this temple that is made with hands, and within three days I will build another made without hands. But neither so did their witness agree together. And the high priest stood up in the midst, and asked Jesus, saying, Answerest Thou nothing? what is it which these witness against Thee? But He held His peace, and answered nothing. Again the high priest asked Him, and said unto Him, Art Thou the Christ, the Son of the Blessed? And Jesus said, I am: and ye shall see the Son of Man sitting on the right hand of power, and coming in the clouds of heaven. Then the high priest rent his clothes, and saith, What need we any further witnesses? Ye have heard the blasphemy: what think ye? And they all condemned him to be guilty of death. And some began to spit on Him, and to cover His face, and to buffet Him, and to say unto Him, Prophesy: and the servants did strike Him with the palms of their hands. And as Peter was beneath in the palace, there cometh one of the maids of the high priest: and when she saw Peter warming himself, she looked upon him, and said, And thou also wast with Jesus of Nazareth. But he denied, saying, I know not, neither understand I what thou sayest. And he went out into the porch; and the cock crew. And a maid saw him again, and began to say to them that stood by, This is one of them. And he denied it again. And a little after, they that stood by said again to Peter, Surely thou art one of them: for thou art a Galilaean, and thy speech agreeth thereto. But he began to curse and to swear, saying, I know not this man of Whom ye speak.

And the second time the cock crew. And Peter called to mind the word that Jesus said unto him, Before the cock crow twice, thou shalt deny me thrice. And when he thought thereon, he wept.

TUESDAY IN HOLY WEEK

THE INTROIT. *Psalm* 69. 17-22.

SAVE me, O God, / for the waters are come in, even unto my soul. I stick fast in the deep mire, where no ground is; / I am come into deep waters, so that the floods run over me. I am weary of crying; my throat is dry; / my sight faileth me for waiting so long upon my God. They that hate me without a cause are more than the hairs of my head; / they that are mine enemies, and would destroy me guiltless, are mighty. I paid them the things that I never took; / God, Thou knowest my simpleness, and my faults are not hid from Thee. Let not them that trust in Thee, O Lord God of hosts, be ashamed for my cause; / let not those that seek Thee be confounded through me, O Lord God of Israel. And why? for Thy sake have I suffered reproof; / shame hath covered my face.

THE COLLECT.

ALMIGHTY and everlasting God, Who, of Thy tender love towards mankind, hast sent Thy Son, our Saviour Jesus Christ, to take upon Him our flesh, and to suffer death upon the Cross, that all mankind should follow the example of His great humility: Mercifully grant, that we may both follow the example of His patience, and also be made partakers of His resurrection; through the same Jesus Christ our Lord. *Amen.*

FOR THE EPISTLE. *Isaiah* 50. 5-11.

THE Lord God hath opened mine ear, and I was not rebellious, neither turned away back. I gave my back to the smiters, and my cheeks to them that plucked off the hair: I hid not my face from shame and spitting. For the Lord God will help me; therefore shall I not be confounded: therefore have I set my face like a flint, and I know that I shall not be ashamed. He is near that justifieth me; who will contend with me? let us stand together: who is mine adversary? let him come near to me. Behold, the Lord God will help me; who is he that shall condemn me? lo, they all shall wax old as a garment; the moth shall eat them up. Who is among you that feareth the Lord, that obeyeth the voice of His servant, that walketh in darkness, and hath no light? let him trust in the Name of the Lord, and stay upon his God. Behold, all ye that kindle a fire, that compass yourselves about with sparks: walk in the light of your fire, and in the sparks that ye have kindled. This shall ye have of mine hand; ye shall lie down in sorrow.

THE GRADUAL. *Psalm* 35. 11-16.

FALSE witnesses did rise up; / they laid to my charge things that I knew not. They rewarded me evil for good, / to the great discomfort of my soul. Nevertheless, when they were sick, I
put on sackcloth, and humbled my soul with fasting; / and my prayer shall turn into mine own bosom. I behaved myself as though it had been my friend or my brother; / I went heavily, as one that mourneth for his mother. But in mine adversity they rejoiced, and gathered themselves together; / yea, the very abjects came together against me unawares, making mouths at me, and ceased not. With the flatterers were busy mockers / who gnashed upon me with their teeth.

THE PROPERS OF THE YEAR

THE CONTINUATION OF THE PASSION OF OUR LORD JESUS CHRIST ACCORDING TO SAINT MARK.

THE GOSPEL. *Saint Mark* 15. 1-39.

AND straightway in the morning the chief priests held a consultation with the elders and scribes and the whole council, and bound Jesus, and carried Him away, and delivered Him to Pilate. And Pilate asked Him, Art Thou the King of the Jews? And He answering said unto them, Thou sayest it. And the chief priests accused Him of many things: but He answered nothing. And Pilate asked Him again, saying, Answerest Thou nothing? behold how many things they witness against Thee. But Jesus yet answered nothing; so that Pilate marvelled. Now at that feast he released unto them one prisoner, whomsoever they desired. And there was one named Barabbas, which lay bound with them that had made insurrection with him, who had committed murder in the insurrection. And the multitude crying aloud began to desire him to do as he had ever done unto them. But Pilate answered them, saying, Will ye that I release unto you the King of the Jews? For he knew that the chief priests had delivered Him for envy. But the chief priests moved the people, that he should rather release Barabbas unto them. And Pilate answered and said again unto them, What will ye then that I shall do unto Him whom ye call the King of the Jews? And they cried out again, Crucify Him. Then Pilate said unto them, Why, what evil hath He done? And they cried out the more exceedingly, Crucify Him. And so Pilate, willing to content the people, released Barabbas unto them, and delivered Jesus, when he had scourged Him, to be crucified. And the soldiers led Him away into the hall, called Praetorium; and they call together the whole band. And they clothed Him with purple, and platted a crown of thorns, and put it about His head, and began to salute Him, Hail, King of the Jews! And they smote Him on the head with a reed, and did spit upon Him, and bowing their knees worshipped Him. And when they had mocked Him, they took off the purple from Him, and put His own clothes on Him, and led Him out to crucify Him. And they compel one Simon a Cyrenian, who passed by, coming out of the country, the father of Alexander and Rufus, to bear His Cross. And they bring Him unto the place Golgotha, which is, being interpreted, The Place of a Skull. And they gave Him to drink wine mingled with myrrh: but He received it not. And when they had crucified Him, they parted His garments, casting lots upon them, what every man should take. And it was the third hour, and they crucified Him. And the superscription of His accusation was written over, The King of the Jews. And with Him they crucify two thieves; the one on His right hand, and the other on His left. And the Scripture was fulfilled, which saith, And He was numbered with the transgressors. And they that passed by railed on Him, wagging their heads, and saying, Ah, Thou that destroyest the temple, and buildest it in three days, save Thyself, and come down from the Cross. Likewise also the chief priests mocking said among themselves with the scribes, He saved others; Himself He cannot save. Let Christ the King of Israel descend now from the Cross, that we may see and believe. And they that were crucified with Him reviled Him. And when the sixth hour was come, there was darkness over the whole land until the ninth hour. And at the ninth hour Jesus cried with a loud voice, saying, Eloi, Eloi, lama sabachthani? which is, being interpreted, My God, my God, why hast Thou forsaken me? And some of them that stood by, when they heard it, said, Behold, He calleth Elias. And one ran and filled a sponge full of vinegar, and put it on a reed, and gave Him to drink, saying, Let alone; let us see whether Elias will come to take Him down. And Jesus cried with a loud voice, and gave up the ghost. (*Here all shall kneel and, after a short space, shall rise again.*) And the veil of the temple was rent in twain from the top to the bottom. And when the centurion, which stood over against Him, saw that He so cried out, and gave up the ghost, he said, Truly this man was the Son of God.

WEDNESDAY IN HOLY WEEK

THE INTROIT. *Psalm* 102. 1-11.

HEAR my prayer, O Lord, / and let my cry come unto Thee. Hide not Thy face from me in the time of my trouble; / incline Thine ear unto me when I call; O hear me, and that right soon. For my days are consumed away like smoke, / and my bones are burnt up as it were a firebrand. My heart is smitten down, and withered like grass, / so that I forget to eat my bread. For the voice of my groaning / my bones will scarce cleave to my flesh. I am become like a pelican in the wilderness, / and like an owl that is in the desert. I have watched, and am even as it were a sparrow / that sitteth alone upon the house-top. Mine enemies revile me all the day long; / and they that are mad upon me are sworn together against me. For I have eaten ashes as it were bread, / and mingled my drink with weeping; And that because of Thine indignation and wrath; / for Thou hast taken me up, and cast me down. My days are gone like a shadow, / and I am withered like grass.

THE COLLECT.

ALMIGHTY and everlasting God, Who, of Thy tender love towards mankind, hast sent Thy Son, our Saviour Jesus Christ, to take upon Him our flesh, and to suffer death upon the Cross, that all mankind should follow the example of His great humility: Mercifully grant, that we may both follow the example of His patience, and also be made partakers of His resurrection; through the same Jesus Christ our Lord. *Amen.*

THE EPISTLE. *Hebrews* 9. 15-28.

AND for this cause Christ is the Mediator of the New Testament, that by means of death, for the redemption of the transgressions which were under the First Testament, they which are called might receive the promise of an eternal inheritance. For where a testament is, there must also of necessity be the death of the testator. For a testament is of force after men are dead: otherwise it is of no strength at all while the testator liveth. Whereupon neither the First Testament was dedicated without blood. For when Moses had spoken every precept to all the people according to the Law, he took the blood of calves and of goats, with water, and scarlet wool, and hyssop, and sprinkled both the book, and all the people, saying, This is the blood of the testament which God hath enjoined unto you. Moreover he sprinkled with blood both the tabernacle, and all the vessels of the ministry. And almost all things are by the Law purged with blood; and without shedding of blood is no remission. It was therefore necessary that the patterns of things in the heavens should be purified with these; but the heavenly things themselves with better sacrifices than these. For Christ is not entered into the holy places made with hands, which are the figures of the true; but into heaven itself, now to appear in the presence of God for us: nor yet that He should offer Himself often, as the high priest entereth into the holy place every year with blood of others; for then must He often have suffered since the foundation of the world: but now once in the end of the world hath He appeared to put away sin by the sacrifice of Himself. And as it is appointed unto men once to die, but after this the judgement: so Christ was once offered to bear the sins of many; and unto them that look for Him shall He appear the second time without sin unto salvation.

THE GRADUAL. *Psalm* 55. 12-15.

FOR it is not an open enemy, that hath done me this dishonour: / for then I could have borne it. Neither was it mine adversary, that did magnify himself against me: / for then peradventure I would have hid myself from him. But it was even thou, my companion, / my guide, and mine own familiar friend. We took sweet counsel together, / and walked in the house of God as friends.

THE PASSION OF OUR LORD JESUS CHRIST
ACCORDING TO SAINT LUKE.

THE GOSPEL. Saint Luke 22. 63-23. 49.

AND the men that held Jesus mocked Him, and smote Him. And when they had blindfolded Him, they struck Him on the face, and asked Him, saying, Prophesy, who is it that smote Thee? And many other things blasphemously spake they against Him. And as soon as it was day, the elders of the people and the chief priests and the scribes came together, and led Him into their council, saying, Art Thou the Christ? tell us. And He said unto them, If I tell you, ye will not believe: and if I also ask you, ye will not answer me, nor let me go. Hereafter shall the Son of Man sit on the right hand of the power of God. Then said they all, Art Thou then the Son of God? And He said unto them, Ye say that I am. And they said, What need we any further witness? for we ourselves have heard of His own mouth. The whole multitude of them arose, and led Him unto Pilate. And they began to accuse Him, saying, We found this fellow perverting the nation, and forbidding to give tribute to Caesar, saying that He Himself is Christ a King. And Pilate asked Him, saying, Art Thou the King of the Jews? And He answered Him and said, Thou sayest it. Then said Pilate to the chief priests and to the people, I find no fault in this man. And they were the more fierce, saying, He stirreth up the people, teaching throughout all Jewry, beginning from Galilee to this place. When Pilate heard of Galilee, he asked whether the man were a Galilaean. And as soon as he knew that He belonged unto Herod's jurisdiction, he sent Him to Herod, who himself also was at Jerusalem at that time. And when Herod saw Jesus, he was exceeding glad: for he was desirous to see Him of a long season, because he had heard many things of Him; and he hoped to have seen some miracle done by Him. Then he questioned with Him in many words; but He answered him nothing. And the chief priests and scribes stood and vehemently accused Him. And Herod with his men of war set Him at nought, and mocked Him, and arrayed Him in a gorgeous robe, and sent Him again to Pilate. And the same day Pilate and Herod were made friends together: for before they were at enmity between themselves. And Pilate, when he had called together the chief priests and the rulers and the people, said unto them, Ye have brought this man unto me, as one that perverteth the people: and, behold, I, having examined Him before you, have found no fault in this man touching those things whereof ye accuse Him: No, nor yet Herod: for I sent you to him; and, lo, nothing worthy of death is done unto Him. I will therefore chastise Him, and release Him. (For of necessity he must release one unto them at the feast.) And they cried out all at once, saying, Away with this man, and release unto us Barabbas: (Who for a certain sedition made in the city, and for murder, was cast into prison.) Pilate therefore, willing to release Jesus, spake again to them. But they cried, saying, Crucify Him, crucify Him. And he said unto them the third time, Why, what evil hath He done? I have found no cause of death in Him: I will therefore chastise Him, and let Him go. And they were instant with loud voices, requiring that He might be crucified. And the voices of them and of the chief priests prevailed. And Pilate gave sentence that it should be as they required. And he released unto them him that for sedition and murder was cast into prison, whom they had desired; but he delivered Jesus to their will. And as they led Him away, they laid hold upon one Simon, a Cyrenian, coming out of the country, and on him they laid the Cross, that he might bear it after Jesus. And there followed Him a great company of people, and of women, which also bewailed and lamented Him. But Jesus turning unto them said, Daughters of Jerusalem, weep not for me, but weep for yourselves, and for your children. For, behold, the days are coming, in the which they shall say, Blessed are the barren, and the wombs that never bare, and the paps which never gave suck. Then shall they begin to say to the mountains, Fall on us; and to the hills, Cover us. For if they do these things in a green tree, what shall be done in the dry? And there were also two other, malefactors, led with Him to be put to death. And when they were come to the place, which is called Calvary, there they crucified Him, and the malefactors, one on the right hand, and the other on the left. Then said Jesus, Father, forgive them; for they know not what they do. And they parted His raiment, and cast lots. And the people stood beholding. And the rulers also with them derided Him, saying, He saved others; let Him save Himself, if He be Christ, the Chosen of God. And the soldiers also mocked Him, coming to Him, and offering Him vinegar, and saying, If Thou be the King of the Jews, save Thyself. And a superscription also was written over Him in letters of Greek, and Latin, and Hebrew, This is the King of the Jews. And one of the malefactors which were hanged railed on Him, saying, If Thou be Christ, save Thyself and us. But the other answering rebuked him, saying, Dost not Thou fear God, seeing Thou art in the same condemnation? And we indeed justly; for we receive the due reward of our deeds: but this man hath done nothing amiss. And he said unto Jesus, Lord, remember me when Thou comest into Thy kingdom. And Jesus said unto him, Verily I say unto thee, to-day shalt thou be with me in paradise. And it was about the sixth hour, and there was a darkness over all the earth until the ninth hour. And the sun was darkened, and the veil of the temple was rent in the midst. And when Jesus had cried with a loud voice, He said, Father, into Thy hands I commend my spirit: and having said thus, He gave up the ghost. (*Here all shall kneel and, after a short space, shall rise again.*) Now when the centurion saw what was done, he glorified God, saying, Certainly this was a righteous man. And all the people that came together to that sight, beholding the things which were done, smote their breasts, and returned. And all His acquaintance, and the women that followed Him from Galilee, stood afar off, beholding these things.

THURSDAY IN HOLY WEEK
WHICH IS CALLED
MAUNDY THURSDAY

THE INTROIT. *Psalm* 145. 7-17.

THE memorial of Thine abundant kindness shall be shewed, / and men shall sing of Thy righteousness. The Lord is gracious and merciful, / long-suffering and of great goodness. The Lord is loving unto every man, / and His mercy is over all His works. All Thy works praise Thee, O Lord; / and Thy saints give thanks unto Thee. They shew the glory of Thy kingdom, / and talk of Thy power; That Thy power, Thy glory, and mightiness of Thy kingdom, / might be known unto men. Thy kingdom is an everlasting kingdom, / and Thy dominion endureth throughout all ages. The Lord upholdeth all such as fall, / and lifteth up all those that are down. The eyes of all wait upon Thee, O Lord, / and Thou givest them their meat in due season. Thou openest Thine hand, / and fillest all things living with plenteousness. The Lord is righteous in all His ways, / and holy in all His works.

THE COLLECT.

O GOD, Who in a wonderful Sacrament hast left unto us a memorial of Thy Passion: Grant us so to venerate the sacred mysteries of Thy Body and Blood, that we may ever more perceive within ourselves the fruit of Thy redemption; Who livest and reignest with the Father and the Holy Ghost, ever one God, world without end. *Amen.*

THE EPISTLE. I *Corinthians* 11. 23-29.

FOR I have received of the Lord that which also I delivered unto you, That the Lord Jesus the same night in which He was betrayed took bread: and when He had given thanks, He brake it, and said, Take, eat; this is my Body, which is broken for you: This do in remembrance of me. After the same manner also He took the Cup, when He had supped, saying, This Cup is the New Testament in my Blood: This do ye, as oft as ye drink it, in remembrance of me. For as often as ye eat this Bread, and drink this Cup, ye do shew the Lord's death till He come. Wherefore whosoever shall eat this Bread, or drink this Cup of the Lord, unworthily, shall be guilty of the Body and Blood of the Lord. But let a man examine himself, and so let him eat of that Bread, and Drink of that Cup. For he that eateth and drinketh unworthily, eateth and drinketh damnation to himself, not discerning the Lord's Body.

THE GRADUAL. *Psalm* 116. 11-19.

WHAT reward shall I give unto the Lord / for all the benefits that He hath done unto me? I will receive the Cup of salvation, / and call upon the Name of the Lord. I will pay my vows now in the presence of all His people: / right dear in the sight of the Lord is the death of His saints. Behold, O Lord, how that I am Thy servant: / I am Thy servant, and the son of Thy handmaid; Thou hast broken my bonds in sunder. I will offer unto Thee the sacrifice of thanksgiving, / and will call upon the Name of the Lord. I will pay my vows unto the Lord, in the sight of all His people; / in the courts of the Lord's house, even in the midst of thee, O Jerusalem. Praise the Lord.

THE GOSPEL. *Saint John* 6. 47-69.

AT that time Jesus said unto the Jews: Verily, verily, I say unto you, He that believeth on me hath everlasting life. I am that Bread of life. Your fathers did eat manna in the wilderness, and are dead. This is that Bread which cometh down from heaven, that a man may eat thereof, and not die. I am the living Bread which came down from heaven: if any man eat of this Bread, he shall live forever: and the Bread that I will give is my Flesh, which I will give for the life of the world. The Jews therefore strove among themselves, saying, How can this man give us His Flesh to eat? Then Jesus said unto them, Verily, verily, I say unto you, Except ye eat the Flesh of the Son of Man, and drink His Blood, ye have no life in you. Whoso eateth my Flesh, and drinketh my Blood, hath eternal life; and I will raise him up at the last day. For my Flesh is meat indeed, and my Blood is drink indeed. He that eateth my Flesh, and drinketh my Blood, dwelleth in me, and I in him. As the living Father hath sent me, and I live by the Father: so he that eateth me, even he shall live by me. This is that Bread which came down from heaven: not as your fathers did eat manna, and are dead: for he that eateth of this Bread shall live forever. These things said He in the synagogue, as He taught in Capernaum. Many therefore of His disciples, when they had heard this, said, This is an hard saying; who can hear it? When Jesus knew in Himself that His disciples murmured at it, He said unto them, Doth this offend you? What and if ye shall see the Son of Man ascend up where He was before? It is the Spirit that quickeneth; the flesh profiteth nothing: the words that I speak unto you, they are spirit, and they are life. But there are some of you that believe not. For Jesus knew from the beginning who they were that believed not, and who should betray Him. And He said, Therefore said I unto you, that no man can come unto me, except it were given unto him of my Father. From that time many of His disciples went back, and walked no more with Him. Then said Jesus unto the twelve, Will ye also go away? Then Simon Peter answered Him, Lord to whom shall we go? Thou hast the words of eternal life. And we believe and are sure that Thou art that Christ, the Son of the living God.

The Creed shall be omitted on Maundy Thursday.

THE PROPER PREFACE.
THROUGH Jesus Christ our Lord, Who having loved His own that were in the world loved them unto the end; and Who, on this very night before He suffered, whilst sitting at meat with His disciples, did institute, and command them to continue to celebrate, these Holy Mysteries, until He shall come again; so that they, and all we who believe their testimony, and being worthy partakers of this blessed Sacrament, might be preserved both in body and soul unto everlasting life, and at the last be raised up and made partakers of His heavenly kingdom. Therefore with Angels, &c.

And in the Prayer of Consecration, the Priest shall say,
Who, as on this very night in which He was betrayed, took bread, &c.

THE COLLECT AFTER COMMUNION.
ALMIGHTY Father, Whose blessed Son Jesus Christ, on this night in which He was betrayed, and handed over to suffer death for our redemption, did institute at the Last Supper with His disciples the most blessed Sacrament of His Body and Blood: Mercifully grant unto us that we may always worthily and thankfully receive the same, and be preserved thereby both in body and soul unto everlasting life; through the same Thy Son Jesus Christ our Lord. *Amen.*

THE ANTHEM AFTER COMMUNION.
WITH desire I have desired to eat this Passover with you, / before I suffered. For I say unto you, I will not eat anymore thereof, / until it be fulfilled in the kingdom of God. Peace I leave with you: / my peace I give unto you. Not as the world giveth, give I unto you: / Let not your heart be troubled, neither let it be afraid. All glory be to God on high; all praise be unto God. Amen.

THE RESERVATION OF THE BLESSED SACRAMENT

And if the Blessed Sacrament is to be reserved for the Communion of the Faithful at the Liturgy the next day, when the Lord's Supper is ended, the Priest shall cover all of the consecrated Elements, which are to be reserved for the Ministration of Holy Communion the day next following, with a fair linen cloth. And the Blessed Sacrament so reserved shall remain upon the Lord's Table until such time as it is translated to the Place or Altar of Repose.

Devotions may be sung or said before the Blessed Sacrament reserved upon the Lord's Table.

When all is ready, the Priest and Ministers shall then proceed to the place appointed for the Washing of Feet. And as the Priest and Ministers proceed thereunto, a hymn may be sung.

THE LITURGY OF THE MAUNDY

THE WASHING OF FEET

The persons chosen by the Priest for the washing of Feet shall be placed conveniently near unto the Chancel steps; and a bowl of water and a pitcher shall be made ready for the Washing of Feet.

The Priest shall first put off the Chasuble, and shall then take unto himself a towel.

THE PROPERS OF THE YEAR

And standing where he shall wash feet, the Priest shall say to the people,

BRETHREN, throughout the Church of God, since the Last Supper of our blessed Lord with His disciples, it hath ever been the custom of the Ministers of the Lord on this night to wash the feet of their brethren, after the Lord's own example as set forth for us in His holy Gospel. Wherefore, let us now be attentive, and hear the Word of the Lord.

Then shall this Gospel following be read.

THE GOSPEL. *Saint John* 13. 1-15.

BEFORE the feast of the Passover, when Jesus knew that His hour was come that He should depart out of this world unto the Father, having loved His own which were in the world, He loved them unto the end. And supper being ended, the devil having now put into the heart of Judas Iscariot, Simon's son, to betray Him: Jesus knowing that the Father had given all things into His hands, and that He was come from God, and went to God: He riseth from supper, and laid aside His garments: and took a towel, and girded Himself. After that He poureth water into a bason, and began to wash the disciples' feet, and to wipe them with the towel wherewith He was girded. Then cometh Simon Peter. And Peter saith unto Him, Lord, dost Thou wash my feet also? Jesus answered and said unto him, What I do thou knowest not now; but thou shalt know hereafter. Peter saith unto Him, Thou shalt never wash my feet. Jesus answered him, If I wash thee not, thou hast no part with Me. Simon Peter saith unto Him, Lord, not my feet only, but also my hands and my head. Jesus saith unto him, He that is washed needeth not save to wash his feet, but is clean every whit. And ye are clean, but not all. (For He knew who should betray Him; therefore He said, Ye are not all clean.) So after He had washed their feet, and had taken His garments, and was set down again, He said unto them, Know ye what I have done to you? Ye call me Master and Lord: and ye say well, for so I am. If I, then, your Lord and Master, have washed your feet; ye ought also to wash one another's feet. For I have given you an example, that ye should do as I have done to you.

Then shall these Anthems following be said or sung as
the Priest washeth the feet of the faithful.

THE RESPONSORY ANTHEM. *Ubi caritas.*

The Cantor, or some other Minister, shall sing or say,

A NEW commandment I give unto you, That ye love one another, as I have loved you, saith the Lord. Blessed are those that are undefiled in the way, and walk in the Law of the Lord. By this shall all men know that ye are my disciples, if ye have love one to another.

Answer. Where charity and love are, there is God.

Minister. The love of Christ hath gathered us together into one. Let us rejoice and be glad in Him. Let us fear and love the living God; and love one another in sincerity of heart.

Answer. Where charity and love are, there is God.

Minister. When therefore we are gathered together into one, take we heed that we be not divided in mind. Let malicious quarrels, let contentions, cease. And let Christ our God be in the midst of us.

Answer. Where charity and love are, there is God.

Minister. So may we also, with all the Blessed, see in glory Thy countenance, O Christ, our God: joy that is infinite and undefiled, for ever and for evermore.

Then shall the Priest say,
The Lord be with you.
Answer. And with thy spirit.

Priest. Let us pray.

Lord, have mercy upon us.
Christ, have mercy upon us.
Lord, have mercy upon us.

Then shall the Priest and people say together,

OUR Father, which art in heaven, hallowed be Thy Name. Thy kingdom come. Thy will be done, in earth as it is in heaven. Give us this day our daily bread. And forgive us our trespasses, As we forgive them that trespass against us. And lead us not into temptation, But deliver us from evil. Amen.

Priest. Thou didst wash the feet of Thy Disciples:
Answer. Do Thou, O Lord, wash us from our secret sins.

ASSIST us, we beseech Thee, our dearest Lord Jesus Christ, in this our bounden duty and most solemn service: And as Thou wast pleased in humility to wash the feet of Thy beloved disciples, despise not the works of Thine own hands which Thou hast bidden us to follow; that as here our outward stains are from us washed away, so also may all our secret sins be washed away by Thee; Who livest and reignest with the Father and the Holy Ghost, ever one God world without end. *Amen.*

THE TRANSLATION OF THE BLESSED SACRAMENT

The Washing of Feet ended, if the Blessed Sacrament is to be reserved, it shall then be translated from the Lord's Table to the Altar or Place of Repose. And when the consecrated Elements have been securely placed within the Tabernacle or Aumbry appointed for its reservation, the Priest and Ministers shall then proceed to strip the Lord's Table.

THE STRIPPING OF THE ALTAR

*Whilst the Altar is being stripped, the following Psalm shall be
said or sung by all devoutly kneeling upon their knees.*

PSALM 22. 1-27. *Deus, Deus meus.*

MY GOD, my God, look upon me; why hast Thou forsaken me, / and art so far from my health, and from the words of my complaint? O my God, I cry in the day-time, but Thou hearest not; / and in the night-season also I take no rest. And Thou continuest holy, / O Thou worship of Israel. Our fathers hoped in Thee; / they trusted in Thee, and Thou didst deliver them. They called upon Thee, and were holpen; / they put their trust in Thee, and were not confounded. But as for me, I am a worm, and no man: / a very scorn of men, and the outcast of the people. All they that see me laugh me to scorn; / they shoot out their lips, and shake their heads, saying, 'He trusted in God, that He would deliver Him; / let Him deliver Him, if He will have Him'. But Thou art He

156

that took me out of my mother's womb; / Thou wast my hope, when I hanged yet upon my mother's breasts. I have been left unto Thee ever since I was born; / Thou art my God, even from my mother's womb. O go not from me, for trouble is hard at hand, / and there is none to help me. Many oxen are come about me; / fat bulls of Bashan close me in on every side. They gape upon me with their mouths, / as it were a ramping and a roaring lion. I am poured out like water, and all my bones are out of joint; / my heart also in the midst of my body is even like melting wax. My strength is dried up like a potsherd, and my tongue cleaveth to my gums; / and Thou shalt bring me into the dust of death. For many dogs are come about me, / and the council of the wicked layeth siege against me. They pierced my hands and my feet; I may tell all my bones; / they stand staring and looking upon me. They part my garments among them, / and cast lots upon my vesture. But be not Thou far from me, O Lord: / Thou art my succour, haste Thee to help me. Deliver my soul from the sword, / my life from the power of the dog. Save me from the lion's mouth; / Thou hast heard me also from among the horns of the unicorns. I will declare Thy Name unto my brethren; / in the midst of the congregation will I praise Thee. O praise the Lord, ye that fear Him; / magnify Him, all ye of the seed of Jacob, and fear Him, all ye seed of Israel. For He hath not despised, nor abhorred, the low estate of the poor; / He hath not hid His face from him, but when he called unto Him He heard him. My praise is of Thee in the great congregation; / my vows will I perform in the sight of them that fear Him. The poor shall eat and be satisfied; / they that seek after the Lord shall praise Him; your heart shall live for ever. All the ends of the world shall remember themselves, and be turned unto the Lord; / and all the kindreds of the nations shall worship before Him.

And when the stripping of the Altars is ended,
then shall this Gospel following be read for the Last Gospel.

And all shall stand for the reading of the Last Gospel.

THE LAST GOSPEL. *Saint Luke* 22. 31-62.

AND the Lord said, Simon, Simon, behold, Satan hath desired to have you, that he may sift you as wheat: but I have prayed for thee, that thy faith fail not: and when thou art converted, strengthen thy brethren. And he said unto Him, Lord, I am ready to go with Thee, both into prison, and to death. And He said, I tell thee, Peter, the cock shall not crow this day, before that thou shalt thrice deny that thou knowest me. And He said unto them, When I sent you without purse, and scrip, and shoes, lacked ye anything? And they said, Nothing. Then said He unto them, But now, he that hath a purse, let him take it, and likewise his scrip: and he that hath no sword, let him sell his garment, and buy one. For I say unto you, that this that is written must yet be accomplished in me, And He was reckoned among the transgressors: for the things concerning me have an end. And they said, Lord, behold, here are two swords. And He said unto them, It is enough. And He came out, and went, as He was wont, to the mount of Olives; and His disciples also followed Him. And when He was at the place, He said unto them, Pray that ye enter not into temptation. And He was withdrawn from them about a stone's cast, and kneeled down, and prayed, saying, Father, if Thou be willing, remove this cup from me: nevertheless not my will, but Thine, be done. And there appeared an angel unto Him from heaven, strengthening Him. And being in an agony He prayed more earnestly: and His sweat was as it were great drops of blood falling down to the ground. And when He rose up from prayer, and was come to His disciples, He found them sleeping for sorrow, and said unto them, Why sleep ye? rise and pray, lest ye enter into temptation. And while He yet spake, behold a multitude, and he that was called Judas, one of the twelve, went before them, and drew near unto

Jesus to kiss Him. But Jesus said unto him, Judas, betrayest thou the Son of Man with a kiss? When they which were about Him saw what would follow, they said unto Him, Lord, shall we smite with the sword? And one of them smote the servant of the high priest, and cut off his right ear. And Jesus answered and said, Suffer ye thus far. And He touched his ear, and healed him. Then Jesus said unto the chief priests, and captains of the temple, and the elders, which were come to him, Be ye come out, as against a thief, with swords and staves? When I was daily with you in the temple, ye stretched forth no hands against me: but this is your hour, and the power of darkness. Then took they Him, and led Him, and brought Him into the high priest's house. And Peter followed afar off. And when they had kindled a fire in the midst of the hall, and were set down together, Peter sat down among them. But a certain maid beheld him as he sat by the fire, and earnestly looked upon him, and said, This man was also with Him. And he denied Him, saying, Woman, I know Him not. And after a little while another saw him, and said, Thou art also of them. And Peter said, Man, I am not. And about the space of one hour after another confidently affirmed, saying, Of a truth this fellow also was with Him: for he is a Galilæan. And Peter said, Man, I know not what thou sayest. And immediately, while he yet spake, the cock crew. And the Lord turned, and looked upon Peter. And Peter remembered the word of the Lord, how He had said unto him, Before the cock crow, thou shalt deny me thrice. And Peter went out, and wept bitterly.

THE PASSION OF OUR LORD JESUS CHRIST
WHICH IS CALLED
GOOD FRIDAY

THE LITURGY OF THE PASSION

*The Minister, and all those Ministers who shall assist him in the Liturgy,
shall enter the Church and proceed to the Chancel in silence.*

MATTINS

And coming to the Chancel steps, the Minister shall turn himself to the people, and say,
ALL we like sheep have gone astray; we have turned every one to his own way; and the Lord hath laid on Him the iniquity of us all. *Isaiah 53. 6.*

Then shall the Minister say to the people,
DEARLY beloved brethren, on this day, when our Saviour Christ was crucified, and by His Death and Passion purchased for us our salvation: Let us now come before the throne of heaven with penitent and contrite hearts, and make our humble confession unto God of all our sins and trespasses, for which He did send His only Son to make atonement, that we might be forgiven through Him. Wherefore I beseech you, my brethren, to accompany me, and make together our humble confession to Almighty God, and saying,

*Then shall all kneel down, and this Confession following
shall be said of the whole Congregation together after the Minister,*
ALMIGHTY and most merciful Father, We have erred and strayed from Thy ways like lost sheep, We have followed too much the devices and desires of our own hearts, We have offended against Thy holy laws, We have left undone those things which we ought to have done, And we have done

those things which we ought not to have done, And there is no health in us: But Thou, O Lord, have mercy upon us miserable offenders; Spare Thou them, O God, which confess their faults, Restore Thou them that are penitent, According to Thy promises declared unto mankind in Christ Jesu our Lord: And grant, O most merciful Father, for His sake, That we may hereafter live a godly, righteous, and sober life, To the glory of Thy holy Name. Amen.

Then shall this Prayer for Absolution, or Remission of sins, be said by the Minister alone.

ALMIGHTY God, Father of our Lord Jesus Christ, Who desirest not the death of a sinner, but rather that he may turn from his wickedness and live; and dost pardon and absolve all them that truly repent, and unfeignedly believe Thy holy Gospel: We beseech to grant us true repentance and Thy Holy Spirit; that those things may please Thee which we do at this present, and that the rest of our life hereafter may be pure and holy; so that, at the last, we may come to Thine eternal joy; through Jesus Christ our Lord. *Amen.*

Absolution is not given.

Then shall be said or sung this Psalm following,
all still devoutly kneeling upon their knees.

THE PENITENTIAL PSALM. *Psalm* 22. 1-32.

MY God, my God, look upon me; why hast Thou forsaken me, / and art so far from my health, and from the words of my complaint? O my God, I cry in the day-time, but Thou hearest not; / and in the night-season also I take no rest. And Thou continuest holy, / O Thou worship of Israel. Our fathers hoped in Thee; / they trusted in Thee, and Thou didst deliver them. They called upon Thee, and were holpen; / they put their trust in Thee, and were not confounded. But as for me, I am a worm, and no man: / a very scorn of men, and the outcast of the people. All they that see me laugh me to scorn; / they shoot out their lips, and shake their heads, saying, 'He trusted in God, that He would deliver Him; / let Him deliver Him, if He will have Him'. But Thou art He that took me out of my mother's womb; / Thou wast my hope, when I hanged yet upon my mother's breasts. I have been left unto Thee ever since I was born; / Thou art my God, even from my mother's womb. O go not from me, for trouble is hard at hand, / and there is none to help me. Many oxen are come about me; / fat bulls of Bashan close me in on every side. They gape upon me with their mouths, / as it were a ramping and a roaring lion. I am poured out like water, and all my bones are out of joint; / my heart also in the midst of my body is even like melting wax. My strength is dried up like a potsherd, and my tongue cleaveth to my gums; / and Thou shalt bring me into the dust of death. For many dogs are come about me, / and the council of the wicked layeth siege against me. They pierced my hands and my feet; I may tell all my bones; / they stand staring and looking upon me. They part my garments among them, / and cast lots upon my vesture. But be not Thou far from me, O Lord: / Thou art my succour, haste Thee to help me. Deliver my soul from the sword, / my life from the power of the dog. Save me from the lion's mouth; / Thou hast heard me also from among the horns of the unicorns. I will declare Thy Name unto my brethren; / in the midst of the congregation will I praise Thee. O praise the Lord, ye that fear Him; / magnify Him, all ye of the seed of Jacob, and fear Him, all ye seed of Israel. For He hath not despised, nor abhorred, the low estate of the poor; / He hath not hid His face from him, but when he called unto Him He heard him. My praise is of Thee in the great congregation; / my vows will I perform in the sight of them that fear Him. The poor shall eat and be satisfied; / they that seek after the Lord shall praise Him; your heart shall live for ever. All the ends of the world shall remember themselves, and be turned unto the Lord; / and all the kindreds of the nations shall worship before Him. For the kingdom is the Lord's, / and He is the Governor among the people. Surely to Him shall all the proud of the earth bow down; / and before Him shall kneel all that go down into the dust, and he that cannot keep his soul alive. My seed shall serve Him; / they shall be counted unto the Lord for a generation. They shall come, and the heavens shall declare His righteousness / unto a people that shall be born, whom the Lord hath made.

Then shall the this Lesson following be read for the First Lesson.

THE FIRST LESSON. *Genesis* 22. 1-18.

AND it came to pass after these things, that God did tempt Abraham, and said unto him, Abraham: and he said, Behold, here I am. And He said, Take now thy son, thine only son Isaac, whom thou lovest, and get thee into the land of Moriah; and offer him there for a burnt offering upon one of the mountains which I will tell thee of. And Abraham rose up early in the morning, and saddled his donkey, and took two of his young men with him, and Isaac his son, and clave the wood for the burnt offering, and rose up, and went unto the place of which God had told him. Then on the third day Abraham lifted up his eyes, and saw the place afar off. And Abraham said unto his young men, Abide ye here with the donkey; and I and the lad will go yonder and worship, and come again to you. And Abraham took the wood of the burnt offering, and laid it upon Isaac his son; and he took the fire in his hand, and a knife; and they went both of them together. And Isaac spake unto Abraham his father, and said, My father: and he said, Here am I, my son. And he said, Behold the fire and the wood: but where is the lamb for a burnt offering? And Abraham said, My son, God will provide Himself a lamb for a burnt offering: so they went both of them together. And they came to the place which God had told him of; and Abraham built an altar there, and laid the wood in order, and bound Isaac his son, and laid him on the altar upon the wood. And Abraham stretched forth his hand, and took the knife to slay his son. And the angel of the Lord called unto him out of heaven, and said, Abraham, Abraham: and he said, Here am I. And He said, Lay not thine hand upon the lad, neither do thou anything unto him: for now I know that thou fearest God, seeing thou hast not withheld thy son, thine only son from me. And Abraham lifted up his eyes, and looked, and behold behind him a ram caught in a thicket by his horns: and Abraham went and took the ram, and offered him up for a burnt offering in the stead of his son. And Abraham called the name of that place Jehovah-jireh: as it is said to this day, In the mount of the Lord it shall be seen. And the angel of the Lord called unto Abraham out of heaven the second time, and said, By Myself have I sworn, saith the Lord, for because thou hast done this thing, and hast not withheld thy son, thine only son: That in blessing I will bless thee, and in multiplying I will multiply thy seed as the stars of the heaven, and as the sand which is upon the sea shore; and thy seed shall possess the gate of his enemies; and in thy seed shall all the nations of the earth be blessed; because thou hast obeyed My voice.

Then shall be said or sung this Psalm following.

THE GRADUAL PSALM. *Psalm* 88. 1-18.

O LORD God of my salvation, / I have cried day and night before Thee. O let my prayer enter into Thy presence: / incline Thine ear unto my calling. For my soul is full of troubles, / and my life draweth nigh unto the grave. I am counted as one of them that go down into the pit; / I am even as a man that hath no strength; Like one cast forth among the dead, like the slain that lie in the grave, / whom Thou rememberest no more, and they are cut off from Thy hand. Thou hast

THE PROPERS OF THE YEAR

laid me in the lowest pit, / in places of darkness, and in the deeps. Thine indignation lieth hard upon me, / and Thou hast vexed me with all Thy storms. Thou hast put away mine acquaintance far from me, / and hast made me to be abhorred of them. I am so fast in prison that I cannot get forth; / my sight faileth for very trouble. Lord, I have called daily upon Thee: / I have stretched forth my hands unto Thee. Dost Thou shew wonders for the dead? / or shall the dead rise up and praise Thee? Shall Thy loving-kindness be declared in the grave, / or Thy faithfulness in Destruction? Shall Thy wondrous works be known in the dark, / and Thy righteousness in the land where all things are forgotten? Unto Thee have I cried, O Lord; / and early shall my prayer come before Thee. Lord, why abhorrest Thou my soul, / and hidest Thou Thy face from me? From my youth up I am in misery and ready to die; / Thy terrors have I suffered with a troubled mind. Thy wrathful displeasure goeth over me, / and the fear of Thee hath undone me. They came round about me like water all the day long, / and compassed me together on every side. My lovers and friends hast Thou put away from me, / and hid mine acquaintance out of my sight.

Then shall be read this Lesson for the Second Lesson.

THE SECOND LESSON. *Exodus* 12. 1-14.

AND the Lord spake unto Moses and Aaron in the land of Egypt saying, This month shall be unto you the beginning of months: it shall be the first month of the year to you. Speak ye unto all the congregation of Israel, saying, In the tenth day of this month they shall take to them every man a lamb, according to the house of their fathers, a lamb for an house: And if the household be too little for the lamb, let him and his neighbour next unto his house take it according to the number of the souls; every man according to his eating shall make your count for the lamb. Your lamb shall be without blemish, a male of the first year: ye shall take it out from the sheep, or from the goats; and ye shall keep it up until the fourteenth day of the same month; and the whole assembly of the congregation of Israel shall kill it in the evening. And they shall take of the blood, and strike it on the two side posts and on the upper door-post of the houses, wherein they shall eat it. And they shall eat the flesh in that night, roast with fire, and unleavened bread; and with bitter herbs they shall eat it. Eat not of it raw, nor sodden at all with water, but roast with fire; his head with his legs, and with the purtenance thereof. And ye shall let nothing of it remain until the morning; and that which remaineth of it until the morning ye shall burn with fire. And thus shall ye eat it; with your loins girded, your shoes on your feet, and your staff in your hand; and ye shall eat it in haste: it is the Lord's Passover. For I will pass through the land of Egypt this night, and will smite all the firstborn in the land of Egypt, both man and beast; and against all the gods of Egypt I will execute judgement: I am the Lord. And the blood shall be to you for a token upon the houses where ye are: and when I see the blood, I will pass over you, and the plague shall not be upon you to destroy you, when I smite the land of Egypt. And this day shall be unto you for a memorial; and ye shall keep it a feast to the Lord throughout your generations; ye shall keep it a feast by an ordinance for ever.

And if the Lord's Table be bare, here it shall be covered with a fair linen cloth, during which time a suitable hymn may be sung.

Then shall be said or sung the Great Litany, or General Supplication.

161

THE PROPERS OF THE YEAR

THE GREAT LITANY

O GOD the Father of heaven: have mercy upon us.
O God the Father of heaven: have mercy upon us.

O God the Son, Redeemer of the world: have mercy upon us.
O God the Son, Redeemer of the world: have mercy upon us.

O God the Holy Ghost, proceeding from the Father and the Son: have mercy upon us.
O God the Holy Ghost, proceeding from the Father and the Son: have mercy upon us.

O holy, blessed, and glorious Trinity, three Persons and one God: have mercy upon us.
O holy, blessed, and glorious Trinity, three Persons and one God: have mercy upon us.

REMEMBER not, Lord, our offences, nor the offences of our forefathers; neither take Thou vengeance of our sins: Spare us, good Lord, spare Thy people, whom Thou hast redeemed with Thy most precious Blood, and be not angry with us for ever.
Spare us, good Lord.

From all evil and mischief; from sin; from the crafts and assaults of the devil; from Thy wrath, and from everlasting condemnation,
Good Lord, deliver us.

From all blindness of heart; from pride, vain-glory, and hypocrisy; from envy, hatred, and malice, and all uncharitableness,
Good Lord, deliver us.

From fornication and adultery, and all other deadly sin; from all uncleanness in thought, word, and deed; and from all the deceits of the world, the flesh, and the devil,
Good Lord, deliver us.

From lightning and tempest; from earthquake, fire, and flood; from plague, pestilence, and famine; from battle and murder; and from sudden death,
Good Lord, deliver us.

From all sedition, conspiracy, and rebellion; from all false doctrine, heresy, and schism; from hardness of heart, and contempt of Thy Word and Commandment,
Good Lord, deliver us.

BY the mystery of Thy holy Incarnation; by Thy blessed Nativity and Circumcision; by Thy Baptism, Fasting, and Temptation,
Good Lord, deliver us.

By Thine Agony and bloody Sweat; by Thy saving Cross and Passion; by Thy precious Death and Burial,
Good Lord, deliver us.

By Thy glorious Resurrection and Ascension; by Thy sending of the Holy Ghost; by Thine everlasting Priesthood; and by Thy coming again in glory,
Good Lord, deliver us.

162

In all time of our tribulation; in all time of our wealth; in the hour of death, and in the day of judgement,
Good Lord, deliver us.

WE sinners do beseech Thee to hear us, O Lord God; and that it may please Thee to rule and govern Thy holy Church universal in the right way,
We beseech Thee, good Lord.

To lead all nations in the way of righteousness; and so to guide and direct their governors and rulers, that Thy people may enjoy the blessings of freedom and peace,
We beseech Thee, good Lord.

To keep and strengthen in the true worshipping of Thee, in righteousness and holiness of life, and in devotion to her people, Thy chosen Servant *ELIZABETH*, our most gracious Queen and Governor,
We beseech Thee, good Lord.

To rule and govern her heart in Thy faith, fear, and love, that in all her thoughts, words, and works, she may ever seek Thy honour and glory,
We beseech Thee, good Lord.

To be her Defender and Keeper, giving her the victory over all her enemies,
We beseech Thee, good Lord.

To bless and preserve *Philip* Duke of Edinburgh, *Charles* Prince of Wales, *William* Duke of Cambridge, Prince *George* of Cambridge, and all the Royal Family,
We beseech Thee, good Lord.

To bless all the Bishops of Thy Church; to endue them with Thy Holy Spirit; and to fill them with Thy heavenly grace; that they may govern and feed the flock committed to their care, according to Thy will,
We beseech Thee, good Lord.

To pour out Thy Spirit upon all the Clergy; and to illuminate them with true knowledge and understanding of Thy Word, and that both by their preaching and living, they may set it forth, and shew it accordingly,
We beseech Thee, good Lord.

To bless all who minister in Thy Name; that each, according to his calling, may execute his office, to Thy honour and glory, and the edifying of Thy people,
We beseech Thee, good Lord.

To send forth labourers into Thy harvest; to prosper their work by Thy Holy Spirit; to make Thy saving health known unto all nations; and to hasten Thy kingdom,
We beseech Thee, good Lord.

To bless, protect, and prosper the people of this Dominion, and of all the Realms and Countries of our Commonwealth; and to endue those who are set in authority under our Queen with grace, wisdom, and understanding,

THE PROPERS OF THE YEAR

We beseech Thee, good Lord.

To bless and guide the Judges and Magistrates, giving them grace to execute justice, and to maintain truth,
We beseech Thee, good Lord.

To bless and keep the Queen's forces by sea, and land, and air; to defend them from the craft and power of the enemy; and to shield them in all dangers and adversities,
We beseech Thee, good Lord.

To give to all nations unity, peace, and concord, that Thy people may serve Thee without fear,
We beseech Thee, good Lord.

To bless and keep all Thy people,
We beseech Thee, good Lord.

To give to all Thy people an heart to love and dread Thee; to seek Thy will; and to follow Thy Commandments,
We beseech Thee, good Lord.

To give to all Thy people increase of grace to hear meekly Thy Word, and to receive it with pure affection; and to bring forth the fruits of the Spirit,
We beseech Thee, good Lord.

To bring into the way of truth all such as have erred, and are deceived; and to save us from all delusion, that we may believe no lies,
We beseech Thee, good Lord.

To strengthen such as do stand; to comfort and help the weak-hearted; to raise up those who fall; and finally to beat down Satan under our feet,
We beseech Thee, good Lord.

To succour, help, and comfort, all that are in danger, necessity, or tribulation,
We beseech Thee, good Lord.

To preserve all that travel; all women labouring of child, all sick persons, and young children; and to shew Thy pity upon all prisoners and captives,
We beseech Thee, good Lord.

To defend, and provide for, all widows and orphans, and all who are desolate and oppressed,
We beseech Thee, good Lord.

To have mercy upon all men,
We beseech Thee, good Lord.

To forgive our enemies, persecutors, and slanderers, and to turn their hearts,
We beseech Thee, good Lord.

To give and preserve to our use the kindly fruits of the earth, so that in due time we may enjoy them,

We beseech Thee, good Lord.

To give us true repentance; to forgive us all our sins, negligences, and ignorances; and to endue us with the grace of Thy Holy Spirit, to amend our lives according to Thy Word,
We beseech Thee, good Lord.

SON of God, we beseech Thee to hear us.
Son of God, we beseech Thee to hear us.

O Lamb of God, that takest away the sins of the world;
Have mercy upon us.

O Lamb of God, that takest away the sins of the world;
Grant us Thy peace.

O Christ, hear us.
O Christ, hear us.

Minister.
Let us pray.

Then shall be said or sung this Prayer of Saint Chrysostom following.

ALMIGHTY God, Who hast given us grace at this time with one accord to make our common supplications unto Thee; and dost promise that, when two or three are gathered together in Thy Name, Thou wilt grant their requests: Fulfill now, O Lord, the desires and petitions of Thy servants, as may be most expedient for them; granting us in this world knowledge of Thy truth, and in the world to come life everlasting. *Amen.*

II *Corinthians xiii.*

✠ THE grace of our Lord Jesus Christ, and the love of God, and the fellowship of the Holy Ghost, be with us all evermore. *Amen.*

The Great Litany ended, the Minister may set upon the Lord's Table a plain Cross of wood.

A hymn may be sung as the Cross is set upon the Lord's Table.

THE VENERATION OF THE CROSS

And when all is ready, then shall the Minister say or sing,
BEHOLD the Cross, whereon was hanged the Salvation of the world.
Answer. O come, let us worship.

Behold the Cross, whereon was hanged the Salvation of the world.
Answer. O come, let us worship.

Behold the Cross, whereon was hanged the Salvation of the world.
Answer. O come, let us worship.

Then shall the Reproaches following be said or sung.

O MY people, what have I done unto thee? or wherein have I wearied thee? Testify against me. Because I brought thee forth from the land of Egypt, thou hast prepared a Cross for thy Saviour.

Answer. O Lord most holy, O God most mighty, O holy and most merciful Saviour, have mercy upon us.

Minister. Because I led thee through the desert forty years, and did feed thee with manna, and brought thee into a land exceeding good, thou hast prepared a Cross for thy Saviour.

Answer. O Lord most holy, O God most mighty, O holy and most merciful Saviour, have mercy upon us.

Minister. What more could I have done unto thee, that I have not done? I did plant thee, indeed, O my most beautiful vineyard, with exceeding fair fruit, and thou art become very bitter unto me; for in my thirst thou gavest me vinegar to drink, mingled with gall; and with a lance hast thou pierced the side of thy Saviour.

Answer. O Lord most holy, O God most mighty, O holy and most merciful Saviour, have mercy upon us.

Minister. I did scourge Egypt with her first-born for thy sake: and thou hast scourged me and delivered me up.

Answer. O my people, what have I done unto thee? or wherein have I wearied thee? Testify against me.

Minister. I did lead thee forth out of Egypt, drowning Pharaoh in the Red Sea, and thou hast delivered me up to the chief priests.

Answer. O my people, what have I done unto thee? or wherein have I wearied thee? Testify against me.

Minister. I did open the sea before thee, and thou hast opened my side with a spear.

Answer. O my people, what have I done unto thee? or wherein have I wearied thee? Testify against me.

Minister. I did go before thee in a pillar of cloud, and thou hast led me into the judgement hall of Pilate.

Answer. O my people, what have I done unto thee? or wherein have I wearied thee? Testify against me.

Minister. I fed thee with manna in the wilderness, and thou hast stricken me with blows and scourges.

Answer. O my people, what have I done unto thee? or wherein have I wearied thee? Testify against me.

Minister. I did give thee to drink the water of salvation from the rock, and thou hast given me gall and vinegar to drink.

Answer. O my people, what have I done unto thee? or wherein have I wearied thee? Testify against me.

Minister. I did strike the kings of the Canaanites for thy sake, and thou hast smitten my head with a reed.

Answer. O my people, what have I done unto thee? or wherein have I wearied thee? Testify against me.

Minister. I did give thee a royal sceptre, and thou hast given unto my head a crown of thorns.

   Answer. O my people, what have I done unto thee? or wherein have I wearied thee? Testify against me.

Minister. I did raise thee on high with great power, and thou hast hanged me upon the gibbet of the Cross.

   Answer. O my people, what have I done unto thee? or wherein have I wearied thee? Testify against me.

Then shall the Minister say or sing,
WE adore Thee, O Christ, and we bless Thee;
   Answer. Because by Thy holy Cross, Thou hast redeemed the world.

Then shall the Priest and people say or sing together,
WE adore Thee, O Christ, and we bless Thee; / because by Thy holy Cross Thou hast redeemed the world. Through the tree we were made slaves, / and by the holy Cross we are set free: The fruit of the tree betrayed us, / but the Son of God redeemed us. O Saviour of the world, Who by Thy Cross and precious Blood hast redeemed us: / Save us, and help us, we humbly beseech Thee, O Lord.

And again, the Minister shall say or sing,
WE adore Thee, O Christ, and we bless Thee;
   Answer. Because by Thy holy Cross, Thou hast redeemed the world.

The Veneration of the Cross ended, the officiating Minister and his assistant Ministers shall then proceed to the Chancel for the Liturgy of the Word of God; and, if there be also the ministration of Communion from the Reserved Sacrament, then for the Communion of the Faithful.

A hymn may be sung as the Ministers proceed to the Chancel.

THE LITURGY OF THE WORD OF GOD
AND
THE COMMUNION OF THE FAITHFUL

These Anthems following shall be said or sung as the Ministers proceed to the Altar.

THE ANTHEMS.
BEHOLD the Lamb of God, which taketh away the sin of the world. *Saint John* 1. 29.

He was wounded for our transgressions, He was bruised for our iniquities: the chastisement of our peace was upon Him; and with His stripes we are healed. *Isaiah* 53. 5.

Herein is love, not that we loved God, but that He loved us, and sent His Son to be the propitiation for our sins. *I Saint John* 4. 10.

Worthy is the Lamb that was slain to receive power, and riches, and wisdom, and strength, and honour, and glory, and blessing. *Revelation* 5. 12.

THE PROPERS OF THE YEAR

THE GREETING.

And when the Priest is come to the Altar, he shall bow,
and reverently kiss the Altar, and then turn to the people, and say,
GRACE be unto you, and peace,
from God our Father and the Lord Jesus Christ.
Answer. And with thy spirit.

THE SUMMARY OF THE LAW.

Then shall the officiating Minister rehearse our Blessed Lord's Summary of the Law, as followeth.
OUR Lord Jesus Christ said: Hear, O Israel, THE LORD OUR GOD IS ONE LORD; and thou shalt love the LORD thy God with all thy heart, and with all thy soul, and with all thy mind, and with all thy strength. This is the first and great Commandment. And the second is like unto it, Thou shalt love thy neighbour as thyself. On these two Commandments hang all the Law and the Prophets.
People. Lord, have mercy upon us, and write both these Thy laws in our hearts, we beseech Thee.

KYRIE ELEISON.

Then shall be said or sung in either English or in Greek,
LORD, have mercy upon us. / Kyrie, eleison.
Christ, have mercy upon us. / Christe, eleison.
Lord, have mercy upon us. / Kyrie, eleison.

THE GREAT COLLECTS.

Then shall the Priest say,
THE Lord be with you.
Answer. And with thy spirit.

Priest. Let us pray.

After a brief silence, the Priest shall say or sing these seven Collects following.

FOR THE CATHOLIC CHURCH.

Let us pray that our Lord God, Who cannot behold sin, may yet deign to look upon us: and regarding not our sins, but rather our faith; neither weighing our merits, but pardoning our offences; by the Blood of His only Son poured out for us upon the Cross, we may find mercy and favour in His sight.

And the Priest or Minister shall say,
LET us bend the knee.

And after a short space, the Deacon
or other Minister shall say,
ARISE.

ALMIGHTY God, we beseech Thee graciously to behold this Thy family, for whom our Lord Jesus Christ was contented to be betrayed, and given up into the hands of wicked men, and to suffer death upon the Cross; Who now liveth and reigneth with Thee and the Holy Ghost, ever one God, world without end. *Amen.*

THE PROPERS OF THE YEAR

FOR THE QUEEN'S MAJESTY.

Let us pray for our Most Gracious Sovereign Lady *ELIZABETH* the Second, by the grace of God of the United Kingdom of Great Britain and Northern Ireland, Canada, and all other Her Realms and Territories, Queen, Head of the Commonwealth, Defender of the Faith; that our Lord God would vouchsafe to bless and defend her, and all her subject peoples.

And the Priest or Minister shall say,
LET us bend the knee.

And after a short space, the Deacon
or other Minister shall say,
ARISE.

ALMIGHTY God, Whose kingdom is everlasting, and power infinite: Have mercy upon Thy people in this Dominion, and all the Realms and Countries of our Commonwealth; and so rule the heart of Thy chosen servant *ELIZABETH* our Queen and Governor, that she (knowing Whose minister she is) may above all things seek Thy honour and glory: and grant that we, and all her subjects (duly considering Whose authority she hath) may faithfully serve, honour, and humbly obey her, in Thee, and for Thee, according to Thy blessed Word and ordinance; through Jesus Christ our Lord, Who with Thee and the Holy Ghost liveth and reigneth, ever one God, world without end. *Amen.*

FOR THE BISHOPS AND MINISTERS OF THE CHURCH.

Let us pray for the Bishops of the Church of God, the Successors of the Apostles in the Office of Pastor and Overseer of the flock of Christ: let us pray for all the Patriarchs, Primates, Archbishops, and Bishops of the Church; for *N.* our own Primate, and for *N.* the Bishop of this Diocese; for all the Clergy; and for all who minister, each one according to his own calling in Christ.

And the Priest or Minister shall say,
LET us bend the knee.

And after a short space, the Deacon
or other Minister shall say,
ARISE.

ALMIGHTY and everlasting God, from Whom cometh every good and perfect gift: Send down upon our Bishops and Clergy, and all Congregations committed to their charge, the healthful Spirit of Thy grace; and that they may truly please Thee, pour upon them the continual dew of Thy blessing. Grant this, O Lord, for the honour of our Advocate and Mediator, Jesus Christ. *Amen.*

FOR ALL ESTATES OF THE FAITHFUL.

Let us pray for all estates of Christ's Faithful: for all the Bishops, Priests, and Deacons; for all the Subdeacons, Lectors, and Acolytes; for all the Deaconesses, Virgins, and Widows; for all the Catechists, Porters, Singers, and Musicians; and for all the holy people of God.

And the Priest or Minister shall say,
LET us bend the knee.

And after a short space, the Deacon
or other Minister shall say,
ARISE.

ALMIGHTY and everlasting God, by Whose blessed Spirit the whole body of the Church is governed and sanctified: Receive our supplications and prayers, which we offer before Thee, for all estates of the faithful within Thy holy Church; that every member of the same, in his vocation and ministry, may truly and godly serve Thee; through our Lord and Saviour Jesus Christ. *Amen.*

FOR CATECHUMENS.

Let us pray for all Catechumens preparing for Baptism, and for those preparing for Confirmation, that our Lord God would open their eyes that they may see, and their ears that they may hear, and their minds that they may understand, and their hearts that they may truly believe, the Gospel of Jesus Christ; and that they may be enabled thereby to become very members of Christ, children of God, and inheritors of the kingdom of heaven.

And the Priest or Minister shall say,
LET us bend the knee.

*And after a short space, the Deacon
or other Minister shall say,*
ARISE.

ALMIGHTY and everlasting God, Whose mercies cannot be numbered: We humbly beseech to look mercifully, and with Thy favour, upon all Catechumens who are seeking remission of sins and spiritual regeneration through the Sacrament of Baptism, and upon those who are being prepared to receive the Gifts of the Holy Ghost through the Sacrament of Confirmation; wash them, we pray Thee, in the precious Blood of Thy Son our Saviour Jesus Christ, and sanctify them with Thy Holy Spirit; that they, being delivered from Thy wrath, may be received into the ark of Christ's Church; and being steadfast in faith, joyful through hope, and rooted in charity, may so pass the waves of this troublesome world, that they may come to the land of everlasting life, there to reign with Thee world without end; through the same Jesus Christ our Lord. *Amen.*

FOR THE CONVERSION OF THE JEWS.

Let us pray for the Jews, and for all descendants of Israel who reject and deny Jesus Christ; that our Lord God will remove from them the stubbornness and the faithlessness which do veil their hearts, that they may come to true repentance and faith in Him by Whom alone all Israel shall be saved.

Priest or Minister.
Let us pray.

ALMIGHTY and merciful Lord God, Who hast made all men, and hatest nothing that Thou hast made, nor wouldest the death of a sinner, but rather that he should be converted and live: Have mercy upon the Jews, and upon all descendants of Israel who may reject and deny Thy Son; and take from them all ignorance, hardness of heart, and contempt of Thy Word; and so fetch them home, O Blessed Lord, to Thy fold, that they may be saved among the remnant of the true Israelites, and be made together with them one flock, under one Shepherd, even Jesus Christ our only Lord and Saviour, Who liveth and reigneth with Thee and the Holy Spirit, one God, world without end. *Amen.*

THE PROPERS OF THE YEAR

Let us pray for all Schismatics, Heretics, and Infidels, and for all followers of False prophets and teachers of Errors, that our Lord God will give them grace to see and acknowledge their ignorance, heresies, and errors, and so repent, and come to hold the true Faith within the fold and unity of the One Holy Catholic and Apostolic Church of God.

And the Priest or Minister shall say,
LET us bend the knee.

And after a short space, the Deacon
or other Minister shall say,
ARISE.

ALMIGHTY God, Who willest that all men should be saved and come to the knowledge of Thy truth: Save, we beseech Thee, and enlighten by the mighty working of Thy power, the minds and hearts of all heretics and infidels; that they may be converted unto the truth of Thy Gospel, and so receive the fulfillment of the promise of life everlasting in the joys of Thy kingdom; through Jesus Christ our Lord. *Amen.*

FOR THE CONVERSION OF THE HEATHEN.

Let us pray for the Heathen, and for all those who are enslaved by the darkness of sin, lust, and superstition; that our Lord God would remove from them all the iniquities of their hearts, and that they may put away their idols, and all residue of filthiness, and be converted unto Him, the One True and Only God.

And the Priest or Minister shall say,
LET us bend the knee.

And after a short space, the Deacon
or other Minister shall say,
ARISE.

ALMIGHTY and everlasting God, Who desirest not the eternal death of any son of Adam, but rather that he should turn from his wickedness and live: Mercifully hear our prayers which we make before Thee for all the heathen and those of reprobate mind; that they, being delivered from the darkness of sin, the lusts of the flesh, and the worship of devils and their idols, may be saved through Christ Thy Son, and ingrafted into His Body the Church as living members of the same; through the same Jesus Christ our Lord and Saviour. *Amen.*

The Collects ended, this Lesson following shall be read.

THE LESSON. *Isaiah* 53. 1-12.

WHO hath believed our report? and to whom is the arm of the Lord revealed? For He shall grow up before Him as a tender plant, and as a root out of a dry ground: He hath no form nor comeliness; and when we shall see Him, there is no beauty that we should desire Him. He is despised and rejected of men; a man of sorrows, and acquainted with grief: and we hid as it were our faces from Him; He was despised, and we esteemed Him not. Surely He hath borne our griefs, and carried our sorrows: yet we did esteem Him stricken, smitten of God, and afflicted. But He was wounded for our transgressions, He was bruised for our iniquities: the chastisement of our peace was upon Him; and with His stripes we are healed. All we like sheep have gone astray; we have turned every one to his own way; and the Lord hath laid on Him the iniquity of us all. He was oppressed, and He was afflicted, yet He opened not His mouth: He is brought as a lamb to the slaughter, and as a sheep before her shearers is dumb, so He openeth not His mouth. He was taken from prison and from judgement: and who shall declare His generation? for He was cut off out of the land of the living: for the transgression of my people was He stricken. And He made His grave with the wicked, and with the rich in His death; because He had done no violence, neither was any deceit in His mouth. Yet it pleased the Lord to bruise Him; He hath put Him to grief: when Thou shalt make His soul an offering for sin, He shall see His seed, He shall prolong His days, and the pleasure of the Lord shall prosper in His hand. He shall see of the travail of His soul, and shall be satisfied: by His knowledge shall my righteous servant justify many; for He shall bear their iniquities. Therefore will I divide Him a portion with the great, and He shall divide the spoil with the strong; because He hath poured out His soul unto death: and He was numbered with the transgressors; and He bare the sin of many, and made intercession for the transgressors.

THE LESSER GRADUAL. *Psalm* 135. 13-14.

THY Name, O Lord, endureth for ever: / so doth Thy memorial, O Lord, from one generation to another. For the Lord will avenge His people: / and be gracious unto His servants.

THE EPISTLE. *Hebrews* 10. 1-25.

THE Law of Moses, having as it were a shadow of good things which were to come, but not the very image of those things, can never with those sacrifices which they offered continually, year by year, make the comers thereunto perfect; for then would they not have ceased to be offered? since the worshippers, once they had been purified, should have had no more consciousness of sins. But in those sacrifices a remembrance of sins is made over again every year. For it is not possible that the blood of bulls and of goats should take away sins. Wherefore, when He cometh into the world, He saith, Sacrifice and offering Thou wouldest not, but a Body hast Thou prepared me: In burnt-offerings and sacrifices for sin Thou hast had no pleasure: Then said I, Lo, I come (In the volume of the Book it is written of me) To do Thy will, O God. Above when He said, Sacrifice and offering and burnt-offerings and offering for sin Thou wouldest not, neither hadst pleasure therein, (which are offered according to the Law;) then said He, Lo, I come to do Thy will, O God: He taketh away the first, that He may establish the second. By the which will we are sanctified, through the offering of the Body of Jesus Christ once for all. And every priest standeth daily in his ministry offering many times those same sacrifices which can never take away sins; but this Man, after He had offered one sacrifice for sins for ever, sat down at the right hand of God, waiting from henceforth till His enemies be made His footstool. For by one single offering He hath perfected for ever those who are sanctified; whereof the Holy Ghost also is a witness to us. For after saying, This is the covenant that I will make with them: After those days, saith the Lord, I will put my laws into their hearts, And in their minds will I write them; then saith He, And their sins and iniquities will I remember no more. Now where remission of these is, there is no more offering for sin. Having therefore, brethren, boldness to enter into the holiest by the Blood of Jesus, by a new and living Way, which He hath consecrated for us, through the veil, that is to say, His Flesh; and having an High Priest over the house of God: let us draw near with a true heart, in full assurance of faith, having our hearts sprinkled from an evil conscience, and our bodies washed with pure water. Let us hold fast the profession of our faith without wavering; (for He is faithful that promised;) and let us consider one another to provoke unto love, and to good works; not forsaking the assembling of ourselves together, as the manner of some is; but exhorting one another: and so much the more, as ye see the day approaching.

THE GREATER GRADUAL. *Psalm* 54. 1-3.

SAVE me, O God, for Thy Name's sake, / and avenge me in Thy strength. Hear my prayer, O God, / and hearken unto the words of my mouth. For strangers are risen up against me; / and tyrants, who have not God before their eyes, seek after my soul.

A hymn may be sung here as the Gradual Hymn before the reading of Passion.

Then shall be sung or said the Passion of our Lord
according to Saint John as followeth, the Minister and people all standing.

THE PASSION OF OUR LORD JESUS CHRIST
ACCORDING TO SAINT JOHN.

THE GOSPEL. *Saint John* 18. 33-19. 42.

THEN Pilate entered into the judgement-hall again, and called Jesus, and said unto Him, Art Thou the King of the Jews? Jesus answered him, Sayest thou this thing of thyself, or did others tell it thee of me? Pilate answered, Am I a Jew? Thine own nation and the chief priests have delivered Thee unto me: what hast Thou done? Jesus answered, My kingdom is not of this world: if my kingdom were of this world, then would my servants fight, that I should not be delivered to the Jews: but now my kingdom is not from hence. Pilate therefore said unto Him, Art Thou a king then? Jesus answered, Thou sayest that I am a king: to this end was I born and came into the world, that I should witness to the truth: every one that is of the truth heareth my voice. Pilate saith unto Him, What is truth? And when he had said this, he went out again unto the Jews, and saith unto them, I find in Him no fault at all; but ye have a custom, that I should release unto you one at the Passover: will ye therefore that I release unto you the King of the Jews? Then cried they all again, saying, Not this man, but Barabbas. Now Barabbas was a robber. Then Pilate therefore took Jesus, and scourged Him. And the soldiers platted a crown of thorns, and put it on His head, and they put on Him a purple robe, and came unto Him, and said, Hail, King of the Jews: and they smote Him with their hands. Pilate therefore went forth again, and saith unto them, Behold, I bring Him forth to you, that ye may know that I find no fault in Him. Then came Jesus forth, wearing the crown of thorns, and the purple robe. And Pilate saith unto them, Behold the man! When the chief priests therefore and officers saw Him, they cried out, saying, Crucify Him, crucify Him. Pilate saith unto them, Take ye Him, and crucify Him: for I find no fault in Him. The Jews answered him, We have a law, and by our law He ought to die, because He made Himself the Son of God. When Pilate therefore heard that saying, he was the more afraid; and went again into the judgement-hall, and saith unto Jesus, Whence art Thou? But Jesus gave him no answer. Then saith Pilate unto Him, Speakest Thou not unto me? knowest Thou not that I have power to crucify Thee, and have power to release Thee? Jesus answered, Thou couldest have no power at all against me, except it were given thee from above: therefore he that delivered me unto thee hath the greater sin. And from thenceforth Pilate sought to release Him: but the Jews cried out, saying, If thou let this man go, thou art not Caesar's friend: whosoever maketh himself a king speaketh against Caesar. When Pilate therefore heard that saying, he brought Jesus forth, and sat down in the judgement-seat, in a place that is called the Pavement, but in the Hebrew, Gabbatha. And it was the preparation of the Passover, and about the sixth hour: and he saith unto the Jews, Behold your King! But they cried out, Away with Him, away with Him, crucify Him. Pilate saith unto them, Shall I crucify your King? The chief priests answered, We have no king but Caesar. Then delivered he Him therefore unto them to be crucified: and they took Jesus, and led Him away. And He, bearing His Cross, went forth into a place called the place of a skull, which is called in the Hebrew Golgotha: where they crucified Him, and two other with Him, on either side one, and Jesus in the midst. And Pilate wrote a title, and put it on the Cross; and the writing was, Jesus of Nazareth the King of the Jews. This title then read many of the Jews: for the place where Jesus was crucified was nigh to the city: and it was written in Hebrew, and Greek, and Latin. Then said the chief priests of the Jews to Pilate, Write not, The King of the Jews; but that He said, I am the King of the Jews. Pilate answered, What I have written, I have written. Then the soldiers, when they had crucified Jesus, took His garments, and made four parts, to every soldier a part; and also His coat: now the coat was without seam, woven from the top throughout. They said therefore among themselves, Let us not rend it, but cast lots for it, whose it shall be: that the Scripture might be fulfilled, which saith, 'They parted my raiment among them, And for my vesture they did cast lots'. These things therefore the soldiers did. Now there stood by the Cross of Jesus, His Mother, and His Mother's sister, Mary the wife of Clopas, and Mary Magdalene. When Jesus therefore saw His Mother, and the disciple standing by, whom He loved, He saith unto His Mother, Woman, behold thy son. Then saith He to the disciple, Behold thy Mother. And from that hour that disciple took her unto his own home. After this, Jesus, knowing that all things were now accomplished, that the Scripture might be fulfilled, saith, I thirst. Now there was set a vessel full of vinegar: and they filled a sponge with vinegar, and put it upon hyssop, and put it to His mouth. When Jesus therefore had received the vinegar, He said, It is finished: and He bowed His head, and gave up the ghost. (*Here all shall devoutly kneel and, after a short space, shall rise again.*) The Jews therefore, because it was the preparation, that the bodies should not remain upon the Cross on the Sabbath-Day, (for that Sabbath-Day was an high day,) besought Pilate that their legs might be broken, and that they might be taken away. The soldiers, therefore, came and brake the legs of the first, and of the other which was crucified with Him. But when they came to Jesus, and saw that He was dead already, they brake not His legs. But one of the soldiers with a spear pierced His side, and forthwith came there out Blood and Water. And he that saw it bore witness, and his witness is true: and he knoweth that he saith true, that ye might believe. For these things were done that the Scripture should be fulfilled, A bone of Him shall not be broken. And again another Scripture saith, They shall look on Him Whom they pierced. And after this Joseph of Arimathaea, being a disciple of Jesus, but secretly for fear of the Jews, besought Pilate that he might take away the body of Jesus: and Pilate gave him leave. He came therefore, and took the body of Jesus. And there came also Nicodemus, which at the first came to Jesus by night, and brought a mixture of myrrh and aloes, about an hundred pound weight. Then took they the body of Jesus, and wound it in linen clothes with the spices, as the manner of the Jews is to bury. Now in the place where he was crucified there was a garden; and in the garden a new sepulchre, wherein was never man yet laid. There laid they Jesus therefore because of the Jews' preparation day; for the sepulchre was nigh at hand.

Then shall be said or sung the Nicene Creed by all still standing, after which a Sermon may be preached or an Homily read. And if there be no Communion, the officiating Minister shall say one or two of the Dismissal Collects appointed for use, and may close the Service with a suitable hymn for the Dismissal Hymn. The Service ended, the Minister and assistant Ministers shall depart in silence and in dignified haste and with a reverent disorder.

The Communion of the Faithful

If the Communion is to be ministered to the Faithful, then the Priest shall convey the consecrated Elements from their place of repose to the Lord's Table. During this Translation of the Blessed Sacrament, suitable anthems and hymns may be sung.

And when the Blessed Sacrament is placed upon the Lord's Table, and all is ready for the Ministration of the Holy Communion, this Anthem following shall be sung or said before the Priest shall begin the Office for the Ministration of the Holy Communion of the Body and Blood of Christ from that which had been reserved from the Lord's Supper of Maundy Thursday the evening before.

An Anthem.

WE adore Thee, O Christ, and we bless Thee, / because by Thy holy Cross Thou hast redeemed the world. Through the tree we were made slaves, / and by the holy Cross we are set free: The fruit of the tree betrayed us, / but the Son of God redeemed us. O Saviour of the world, Who by Thy Cross and precious Blood hast redeemed us: / Save us, and help us, we humbly beseech Thee, O Lord.

*Then shall the Priest proceed to minister the Holy Communion
to the Faithful according to the Form prescribed.*

*When all have communicated, and the Prayer of Thanksgiving after Holy Communion is ended,
the Priest and assistant Ministers shall depart in silence in dignified haste and with a reverent disorder.*

HOLY SATURDAY

The Order for Mattins and the Liturgy of the Word of God only shall be said or sung on Holy Saturday, and the Liturgy itself shall end with the Prayer of Intercession and the Collects appointed to be used.

The Liturgy of the Word of God shall begin with the Lord's Prayer and the Collect for Purity.

The Introit. *Psalm 42. 1-7.*

LIKE as the hart desireth the water-brooks, / so longeth my soul after Thee, O God. My soul is a-thirst for God; yea, even for the living God: / when shall I come to appear before the presence of God? My tears have been my meat day and night / while they daily say unto me, Where is now thy God? Now when I think thereupon, I pour out my heart by myself; / for I went with the multitude, and brought them forth into the house of God; In the voice of praise and thanksgiving, / among such as keep holy-day. Why art thou so full of heaviness, O my soul, / and why art thou so disquieted within me? Put thy trust in God; / for I will yet give Him thanks for the help of His countenance.

The Collect.

GRANT, O Lord, that as we are baptised into the death of Thy blessed Son our Saviour Jesus Christ, so by the continual mortifying of our corrupt affections we may be buried with Him; and that through the grave, and gate of death, we may pass to our joyful resurrection; for His Merits, Who died, and was buried, and rose again for us, Thy Son Jesus Christ our Lord. *Amen.*

The Epistle. *I Saint Peter 3. 17-22.*

IT is better, if the will of God be so, that ye suffer for well doing, than for evil doing. For Christ also hath once suffered for sins, the just for the unjust, that He might bring us to God, being put to death in the flesh, but quickened by the Spirit: by which also He went and preached unto the spirits in prison; which sometime were disobedient, when once the long-suffering of God waited in the days of Noah, while the ark was a preparing, wherein few, that is, eight souls were saved by water. The like figure whereunto even baptism doth also now save us (not the putting away of the filth of the flesh, but the answer of a good conscience toward God,) by the resurrection of Jesus Christ: Who is gone into heaven, and is on the right hand of God; angels and authorities and powers being made subject unto Him.

THE GRADUAL. *Psalm* 42. 8-14.

MY God, my soul is vexed within me; / therefore will I remember Thee concerning the land of Jordan, and the little hill of Hermon. One deep calleth another, because of the noise of the water-spouts; / all Thy waves and storms are gone over me. The Lord hath granted His loving-kindness in the day-time; / and in the night-season did I sing of Him, and made my prayer unto the God of my life. I will say unto the God of my strength, Why hast Thou forgotten me; / why go I thus heavily, while the enemy oppresseth me? My bones are smitten asunder as with a sword; / while mine enemies that trouble me cast me in the teeth; Namely, while they say daily unto me, / Where is now thy God? Why art thou so vexed, O my soul, / and why art thou so disquieted within me? O put thy trust in God; / for I will yet thank Him, which is the help of my countenance, and my God.

THE GOSPEL. *Saint Matthew* 27. 57-66.

WHEN the even was come, there came a rich man of Arimathaea, named Joseph, who also himself was Jesus' disciple: he went to Pilate, and begged the body of Jesus. Then Pilate commanded the body to be delivered. And when Joseph had taken the body, he wrapped it in a clean linen cloth, and laid it in his own new tomb, which he had hewn out in the rock: and he rolled a great stone to the door of the sepulchre, and departed. And there was Mary Magdalene, and the other Mary, sitting over against the sepulchre. Now the next day, that followed the day of the preparation, the chief priests and Pharisees came together unto Pilate, saying, Sir, we remember that that deceiver said, while He was yet alive, After three days I will rise again. Command therefore that the sepulchre be made sure until the third day, lest His disciples come by night, and steal Him away, and say unto the people, He is risen from the dead: so the last error shall be worse than the first. Pilate said unto them, Ye have a watch: go your way, make it as sure as ye can. So they went, and made the sepulchre sure, sealing the stone, and setting a watch.

EASTER-EVE

THE LITURGY OF THE PASCHAL VIGIL

THE BLESSING OF THE NEW FIRE

The ensuing Order shall be used after sundown before the First Mass of Easter-Day.

When all is ready for the celebration of the Liturgy of the Paschal Vigil,
the Priest shall first address the Congregation, saying,

DEARLY beloved, on this most holy night, in which our Saviour Christ passed from death to life, holy Mother Church biddeth her children, dispersed throughout the world, to gather together in vigil and prayer; for this night is truly the Passover of the Lord, in which we hear again the story of our deliverance from sin and death; we renew the vows of our profession; and celebrate anew our redemption and hope in Christ, Who, at the end of this night, rose in triumph from the grave, and giveth new and everlasting life to all who believe in Him.

Then shall the Priest kindle and bless the New Fire, saying,

O GOD, Who through Thy blessed Son Jesus Christ hast bestowed upon Thy faithful people the fire of Thy brightness: Sanctify, we beseech Thee, this New Fire, to be profitable to our use; and grant unto us that, by our celebration of this Paschal Feast, we may be so inflamed with heavenly desires, that we may with pure hearts and minds attain unto the feast of Thine eternal brightness; through the same Jesus Christ our Lord. *Amen.*

THE BLESSING OF THE PASCHAL CANDLE

The Priest shall then mark the Paschal Candle with a Cross; and thereafter with the Greek letter Alpha above the Cross, and the Greek letter Omega below the Cross; and in each quadrant of the Cross, the Priest shall mark one numeral of the present Year of the Incarnation, beginning first in the upper corner to the Priest's left.

As the Priest marketh the Candle, he shall say,

CHRIST yesterday, and to-day: the Beginning, and the End: the Alpha and the Omega: His are the times, and the ages: to Him be glory and dominion: through all the ages of eternity. *Amen.*

Then the Priest shall mark the Cross at each end and in the middle, saying,

THROUGH His holy: and glorious wounds: may Christ our Lord: guard us: and keep us. *Amen.*

Then shall the Priest light the Paschal Candle with a flame taken from the New Fire, saying,

MAY the light of Christ in glory rising dispel the darkness of our hearts and minds. *Amen.*

Then shall the Priest bless the Paschal Candle, saying,

WE beseech Thee, Almighty God, to pour down the abundance of Thy blessing upon this Candle; and do Thou, our Regenerator, Thyself unseen, vouchsafe to regard this nocturnal brilliance; and grant that not only the sacrifice, which is offered on this night unto Thee, be illumined by the secret mingling of Thy light, but that into whatsoever place this same light shall be carried from this mystery here sanctified, the wickedness and crafts of the devil may be driven forth and put to flight, and the power and glory of Thy majesty be present; through Jesus Christ our Lord. *Amen.*

THE PROCESSION TO THE CHANCEL

Then shall the Procession be set in order, and the Minister shall carry the Paschal Candle into the Church. As the procession moveth towards the place where the Exsultet and Paschal Praeconium shall be proclaimed, the company shall stop three times; and each time the Minister shall hold up the Candle for all to see, and shall say or sing,

THE Light of Christ!

*And each time all shall devoutly kneel, and
rise again, whilst singing or saying,*
Thanks be to God.

During the Procession, the candles of the faithful shall be lighted from the flame of the Paschal Candle. And when the Minister reacheth the place where the Exsultet and Paschal Praeconium are to be proclaimed, he shall fix the Paschal Candle in its stand; and by the light of the same he shall first sing or say the Exsultet as followeth.

And when the preceding Order for the Lighting of the New Fire and Blessing of the Paschal Candle is used before the celebration of the Holy Eucharist on Easter-Day, all that followeth hereafter shall be omitted.

THE EXSULTET

The Minister shall first say,

✠ MAY the Lord be in my mind, and on my lips, and in my heart, that I may worthily and meetly proclaim His Paschal praises. *Amen.*

Then shall the Minister sing or say the Exsultet, as followeth.

REJOICE, ye hosts of heaven! Sing, ye choirs of angels! With greatest exultation, rejoice before the throne of God! For the King that cometh with victory, sound forth the trumpet of salvation!

Let the earth also be glad, illumined by the radiancy of heaven, and enlightened by the splendour of its mighty King.

Rejoice, O Mother Church! Exult in glory, adorned with the brightness of so great a light! And let this temple now resound with the triumphant voices of God's chosen people!

Wherefore, dearly beloved brethren, I call upon all ye who are here present in the wondrous clearness of this holy light, that you might join with me in calling upon the mercy of Almighty God; that He, Who hath been pleased, for no merit of mine own, to admit me to the number of His Levites, may pour upon me the brightness of His light, and make me worthy to proclaim His Paschal praises, and the praises of this most holy night; through Jesus Christ our Lord, our Mediator, our Advocate, and our great Redeemer, Who with the Father and the Holy Ghost, liveth and reigneth, ever one God, world without end. *Amen.*

And here shall pause be made for silent prayer.

Then shall the Minister sing or say,

THE Lord be with you.

Answer. And with thy spirit.

Deacon. Lift up your hearts.

Answer. We lift them up unto the Lord.

Deacon. Let us give thanks unto our Lord God.

Answer. It is meet and right so to do.

And the Minister shall continue with the Paschal Praeconium, singing or saying,

IT is very meet, right, and our bounden duty, that we should at all times, and in all places, give thanks unto Thee, Holy Lord, Almighty Father, Everlasting God, Creator and Preserver of all things; through Jesus Christ, our Lord and Saviour, Who paid for us to Thee, Eternal Father, the debt of Adam's first transgression; and with His own most precious Blood hath washed away our sins.

Now therefore we, Thy people, redeemed by Him, Who is our Passover, Thy Son, the very Lamb of God, slain to take away the sins of the world, remember before Thee all Thy wondrous works; Who on this very night didst save our forefathers, passing over the homes of all them whose door-posts and lintels were marked by the blood of the slaughtered lamb; and didst lead them forth out of the land of Egypt, and brought them dry-shod through the parted sea.

Yea, this is the night when Thy people Israel, led forth by the pillar of cloud by day and of fire by night, were saved from the might of Pharaoh and his army; and when the sea was closed again, the Egyptians were drowned and cast about the shore.

This is the night when all who believe in Christ, scattered over the face of all the earth, delivered from this wicked world, and brought forth from out the shadow of death, are renewed unto grace, and the promise of eternal life.

THE PROPERS OF THE YEAR

This is the night wherein the bonds of death were loosed, and Christ arose from death, harrowing hell in the triumph of His risen life. For why should man be born into this world, save that, being born, he might be redeemed?

How wonderful, then, O God, is Thy loving-kindness unto us Thy children! Behold, what is the depth and greatness of Thy love, that, to redeem a sinful race, Thou didst give Thine only Son to suffer for our sins!

O happy fault, which was counted worthy to have such and so great a Redeemer! O truly necessary sin of Adam, which by the death of Christ was forever put away! O night, truly blessed, when our Saviour Christ rose triumphant from the grave!

The sanctifying power therefore of this night putteth to flight the deeds of darkness, purgeth away sin, restoreth innocence to the fallen, and giveth gladness to them that mourn; casteth out hatred, bringeth peace to all mankind, and humbleth earthly pride.

This is the night, truly blessed by Thee, when heaven is wedded to earth, and man is reconciled with his Creator. Therefore, O Father, on this holy night, vouchsafe to accept this our sacrifice of praise, which Thy Church now offereth unto Thee. Accept this lighted Candle, its flame divided and yet undimmed, a pillar of fire that burneth to Thy honour. O night truly blessed! O night wherein things of heaven are joined to things of earth, and things human unto things Divine.

We therefore pray Thee, gracious Lord, that this Candle, consecrated to the honour of Thy Name, may continue burning without ceasing to vanquish the darkness of this night.

May the light of this bright Candle mingle with the lights of heaven, and be accepted for a sweet-smelling savour pleasing unto Thee.

May the Morning-star find it burning as night giveth way to day, that Morning-star which knoweth not His going down; even Jesus Christ, that Morning-star, Who rising from the dead steadfastly giveth light to all mankind; and in Whose Name we make our prayers and glorify Thee, O Father Almighty, that same Jesus Christ Thy Son our Lord Who liveth and reigneth with Thee, in the unity of the Holy Ghost, to Whom be all honour and glory, throughout all ages, world without end. *Amen.*

THE GREAT LESSONS

The Minister shall then read this that followeth.

DEARLY beloved in the Lord, as we keep vigil on this most holy night, let us devoutly attend to God's holy Word; and let us hear how that He did save our father Noah and his family from the waters of the flood, prefiguring thereby the salvation of mankind within the ark of Christ's Church; and how God saved His people Israel from the power of Pharaoh and the might of the Egyptians, and led them all as on dry ground through the midst of the sea, prefiguring thereby the salvation of mankind in the waters of Baptism and our new life in Jesus Christ. Herein we are reminded how God hath ever saved His chosen people; and how, in His mighty acts of old, He hath foretold the coming of our Lord Jesus Christ, and by Him the establishing of the New Testament of grace, which is life, and health, and salvation to them that believe. Through the Sacrament of Baptism, we are grafted into Christ's holy Church, and made very members incorporate of His mystical Body, outside of which there is no salvation. As God saved Noah and his family, and also His people Israel, so He likewise saveth His Church to-day. To Him, therefore, may thanks and praise be given unto Him by all faithful Christian people, the ingrafted and spiritual Israel, for this, His unspeakable gift.

Then shall be read this Lesson following.

THE PROPERS OF THE YEAR

THE FIRST LESSON. *Genesis* 6. 5-22.

AND God saw that the wickedness of man was great in the earth, and that every imagination of the thoughts of his heart was only evil continually. And it repented the Lord that He had made man on the earth, and it grieved Him at His heart. And the Lord said, I will destroy man whom I have created from the face of the earth; both man, and beast, and the creeping thing, and the fowls of the air; for it repenteth Me that I have made them. But Noah found grace in the eyes of the Lord. These are the generations of Noah: Noah was a just man and perfect in his generations, and Noah walked with God. And Noah begat three sons, Shem, Ham, and Japheth. The earth also was corrupt before God, and the earth was filled with violence. And God looked upon the earth, and, behold, it was corrupt; for all flesh had corrupted his way upon the earth. And God said unto Noah, The end of all flesh is come before Me; for the earth is filled with violence through them; and, behold, I will destroy them with the earth. Make thee an ark of gopher wood; rooms shalt thou make in the ark, and shalt pitch it within and without with pitch. And this is the fashion which thou shalt make it of: the length of the ark shall be three hundred cubits, the breadth of it fifty cubits, and the height of it thirty cubits. A window shalt thou make to the ark, and in a cubit shalt thou finish it above; and the door of the ark shalt thou set in the side thereof; with lower, second, and third storeys shalt thou make it. And, behold, I, even I, do bring a flood of waters upon the earth, to destroy all flesh, wherein is the breath of life, from under heaven; and everything that is in the earth shall die. But with thee will I establish My covenant; and thou shalt come into the ark, thou, and thy sons, and thy wife, and thy sons' wives with thee. And of every living thing of all flesh, two of every sort shalt thou bring into the ark, to keep them alive with thee; they shall be male and female. Of fowls after their kind, and of cattle after their kind, of every creeping thing of the earth after his kind, two of every sort shall come unto thee, to keep them alive. And take thou unto thee of all food that is eaten, and thou shalt gather it to thee; and it shall be for food for thee, and for them. Thus did Noah; according to all that God commanded him, so did he.

Then shall this Psalm following be sung or said.

THE GRADUAL. *Psalm* 46. 1-11.

GOD is our Hope and Strength, / a very present help in trouble. Therefore will we not fear, though the earth be moved, / and though the hills be carried into the midst of the sea; Though the waters thereof rage and swell, / and though the mountains shake at the tempest of the same. The rivers of the flood thereof shall make glad the city of God, / the holy place of the tabernacle of the Most High. God is in the midst of her, therefore shall she not be removed; / God shall help her, and that right early. The heathen make much ado, and the kingdoms are moved; / but God hath shewed His voice, and the earth shall melt away. The Lord of hosts is with us; / the God of Jacob is our Refuge. O come hither, and behold the works of the Lord, / what destruction He hath brought upon the earth. He maketh wars to cease in all the world; / He breaketh the bow, and snappeth the spear in sunder, and burneth the chariots in the fire. Be still then, and know that I am God; / I will be exalted among the heathen, and I will be exalted in the earth. The Lord of hosts is with us; / the God of Jacob is our Refuge.

Then shall this Lesson following be read.

THE SECOND LESSON. *Exodus* 14. 1-31.

AND the Lord spake unto Moses, saying, Speak unto the children of Israel, that they turn and encamp before Pi-hahiroth, between Migdol and the sea, over against Baal-zephon: before it shall ye encamp by the sea. For Pharaoh will say of the children of Israel, They are entangled in the land, the wilderness hath shut them in. And I will harden Pharaoh's heart, that he shall follow after them; and I will be honoured upon Pharaoh, and upon all his host; that the Egyptians may know that I am the Lord. And they did so. And it was told the king of Egypt that the people fled: and the heart of Pharaoh and of his servants was turned against the people, and they said, Why have we done this, that we have let Israel go from serving us? And he made ready his chariot, and took his people with him: and he took six hundred chosen chariots, and all the chariots of Egypt, and captains over every one of them. And the Lord hardened the heart of Pharaoh king of Egypt, and he pursued after the children of Israel: and the children of Israel went out with an high hand. But the Egyptians pursued after them, all the horses and chariots of Pharaoh, and his horsemen, and his army, and overtook them encamping by the sea, beside Pi-hahiroth, before Baal-zephon. And when Pharaoh drew nigh, the children of Israel lifted up their eyes, and, behold, the Egyptians marched after them; and they were sore afraid: and the children of Israel cried out unto the Lord. And they said unto Moses, Because there were no graves in Egypt, hast thou taken us away to die in the wilderness? wherefore hast thou dealt thus with us, to carry us forth out of Egypt? Is not this the word that we did tell thee in Egypt, saying, Let us alone, that we may serve the Egyptians? For it had been better for us to serve the Egyptians, than that we should die in the wilderness. And Moses said unto the people, Fear ye not, stand still, and see the salvation of the Lord, which He will shew to you to-day: for the Egyptians whom ye have seen to-day, ye shall see them again no more for ever. The Lord shall fight for you, and ye shall hold your peace. And the Lord said unto Moses, Wherefore criest thou unto Me? speak unto the children of Israel, that they go forward: but lift thou up thy rod, and stretch out thine hand over the sea, and divide it: and the children of Israel shall go on dry ground through the midst of the sea. And I, behold, I will harden the hearts of the Egyptians, and they shall follow them: and I will get Me honour upon Pharaoh, and upon all his host, upon his chariots, and upon his horsemen. And the Egyptians shall know that I am the Lord, when I have gotten Me honour upon Pharaoh, upon his chariots, and upon his horsemen. And the angel of God, which went before the camp of Israel, removed and went behind them; and the pillar of the cloud went from before their face, and stood behind them: and it came between the camp of the Egyptians and the camp of Israel; and it was a cloud and darkness to them, but it gave light by night to these: so that the one came not near the other all the night. And Moses stretched out his hand over the sea; and the Lord caused the sea to go back by a strong east wind all that night, and made the sea dry land, and the waters were divided. And the children of Israel went into the midst of the sea upon the dry ground: and the waters were a wall unto them on their right hand, and on their left. And the Egyptians pursued, and went in after them to the midst of the sea, even all Pharaoh's horses, his chariots, and his horsemen. And it came to pass, that in the morning watch the Lord looked unto the host of the Egyptians through the pillar of fire and of the cloud, and troubled the host of the Egyptians, and took off their chariot wheels, that they drave them heavily: so that the Egyptians said, Let us flee from the face of Israel; for the Lord fighteth for them against the Egyptians. And the Lord said unto Moses, Stretch out thine hand over the sea, that the waters may come again upon the Egyptians, upon their chariots, and upon their horsemen. And Moses stretched forth his hand over the sea, and the sea returned to his strength when the morning appeared; and the Egyptians fled against it; and the Lord overthrew the Egyptians in the midst of the sea. And the waters returned, and covered the chariots, and the horsemen, and all the host of Pharaoh that came into the sea after them; there remained not so much as one of them. But the children of Israel walked upon dry land in the midst of the sea; and the waters were a wall unto them on their right hand, and on their left. Thus the Lord saved Israel that day out of the hand of the Egyptians; and Israel saw the Egyptians dead upon the sea shore.

And Israel saw that great work which the Lord did upon the Egyptians: and the people feared the Lord, and believed the Lord, and His servant Moses.

When the Lessons are ended, the Priest and Ministers shall proceed to the Baptismal Font for the blessing of the Baptismal Water, and the renewal of Baptismal Vows, at which time the first portion of the Great Litany shall be sung or said.

THE PROCESSION TO THE FONT

O GOD the Father of heaven: have mercy upon us.
O God the Father of heaven: have mercy upon us.

O God the Son, Redeemer of the world: have mercy upon us.
O God the Son, Redeemer of the world: have mercy upon us.

O God the Holy Ghost, proceeding from the Father and the Son: have mercy upon us.
O God the Holy Ghost, proceeding from the Father and the Son: have mercy upon us.

O holy, blessed, and glorious Trinity, three Persons and one God: have mercy upon us.
O holy, blessed, and glorious Trinity, three Persons and one God: have mercy upon us.

REMEMBER not, Lord, our offences, nor the offences of our forefathers; neither take Thou vengeance of our sins: Spare us, good Lord, spare Thy people, whom Thou hast redeemed with Thy most precious Blood, and be not angry with us for ever.
Spare us, good Lord.

FROM all evil and mischief; from sin; from the crafts and assaults of the devil; from Thy wrath, and from everlasting condemnation,
Good Lord, deliver us.

From all blindness of heart; from pride, vain-glory, and hypocrisy; from envy, hatred, and malice, and all uncharitableness,
Good Lord, deliver us.

From fornication and adultery, and all other deadly sin; from all uncleanness in thought, word, and deed; and from all the deceits of the world, the flesh, and the devil,
Good Lord, deliver us.

From lightning and tempest; from earthquake, fire, and flood; from plague, pestilence, and famine; from battle and murder; and from sudden death,
Good Lord, deliver us.

From all sedition, conspiracy, and rebellion; from all false doctrine, heresy, and schism; from hardness of heart, and contempt of Thy Word and Commandment,
Good Lord, deliver us.

BY the mystery of Thy holy Incarnation; by Thy blessed Nativity and Circumcision; by Thy Baptism, Fasting, and Temptation,
Good Lord, deliver us.

By Thine Agony and bloody Sweat; by Thy saving Cross and Passion; by Thy precious Death and Burial,
Good Lord, deliver us.

By Thy glorious Resurrection and Ascension; by Thy sending of the Holy Ghost; by Thine everlasting Priesthood; and by Thy coming again in glory,
Good Lord, deliver us.

By the intercession of Blessed Mary, the Virgin Mother of Jesus Christ our Lord and God; by the intercession of Blessed Joseph, her Spouse; by the intercession of Blessed John the Baptist, Forerunner of the Lord; by the intercession of the Blessed Apostles Peter and Paul, and all Thy blessed Apostles and Prophets, Evangelists, Doctors and Pastors, Martyrs and Confessors, Virgins, Widows and Matrons, and all Thy blessed Saints in every place and in every age,
Good Lord, deliver us.

By the intercession of the blessed Archangels, holy Michael, holy Gabriel, and holy Raphael, and all the blessed holy Archangels and Angels, the Cherubim and Seraphim, Thrones, Dominions, Virtues, Powers, and Principalities, and all orders of blessed spirits,
Good Lord, deliver us.

In all time of our tribulation; in all time of our wealth; in the hour of death, and in the day of judgement,
Good Lord, deliver us.

When they are come to the Baptismal Font, one of the Ministers
shall then fill the Font with pure, clean water.

Then shall the Priest say,
O LORD, hear our prayer;
Answer. And let our cry come unto Thee.

Priest. Let us pray.

ALMIGHTY and everlasting God, be present, we humbly beseech Thee, in the Sacraments of Thy Church, those sacred pledges which Thou hast ordained unto as means of grace; and grant that those same outward and visible signs of imparted inward and spiritual grace, appointed by Thee for the sanctification of Thy people, may work effectually to the great and endless comfort of all who shall receive them; through Jesus Christ our Lord. *Amen.*

THE BLESSING OF THE BAPTISMAL WATER

Then shall the Priest sing or say,
THE Lord be with you.
Answer. And with thy spirit.
Priest. Lift up your hearts.
Answer. We lift them up unto the Lord.
Priest. Let us give thanks unto our Lord God.
Answer. It is meet and right so to do.

THE PROPERS OF THE YEAR

Then shall the Priest proceed to bless the Baptismal Water, singing or saying,

IT is very meet, right, and our bounden duty, that we should at all times, and in all places, give thanks unto Thee, Holy Lord, Almighty Father, Everlasting God, Creator and Preserver of all things; Who by the invisible working of Thy power dost wondrously give effect to the working of Thy Sacraments; and although we be unworthy to perform mysteries so great, yet Thou dost not leave us destitute of the gifts of Thy grace, but mercifully inclinest Thine ear unto the supplications and prayers of Thy people.

And we who have received the Sacrament of Baptism, which Thou hast appointed for the salvation of all them that believe in Thy blessed Son Jesus Christ, do give Thee thanks for the new life which Thou hast given us by Water and the Holy Ghost; and that, by this means of grace, we have been made very members of Christ, Thy children by adoption, and inheritors of Thy heavenly kingdom.

Hear us, O merciful Father, we most humbly beseech Thee, and regard the prayers and supplications of Thy Church: and sanctify this Water to the mystical washing away of sin; and at Thy command, let every unclean spirit depart, and drive from hence all the craft and wickedness of the devil; let no power of the enemy have any place or portion herein, neither let the evil one ensnare us, or compass us around, nor waylay us in secret, or taint us with corruption. Grant that this creature of Water may be purified and hallowed by the power of the Holy Ghost. May this water be to all who receive it, as from the living fountain, water that doth regenerate, and a purifying stream. And vouchsafe to all who are baptised herein or who are blessed herewith, by the secret working of Thy grace, that they may be washed from all sin, and purified from every defilement of body and soul, unto eternal salvation.

Wherefore, O heavenly Father, vouchsafe we beseech Thee to bless this creature of Water, Thou Who art the true God, the living God, the one holy and Almighty Lord God, Whose Spirit in the beginning moved upon the face of the deep, and Who divided the land from the waters, and the day from night; Who in Eden made the waters to flow from the fountains of Paradise, to water the whole earth; Who in the desert bestowed sweetness upon the bitter waters that men might drink, and did bring forth water from the rock for to slake the thirst of Thy people. We beseech Thee, O Father, in the Name of Thy beloved Son Jesus Christ our Lord, to bless this Water; in the Name of Him Who did change the substance of water into wine at Cana of Galilee; Who did walk upon the water in the storm upon the sea; Who was baptised in the waters of the Jordan by John; Whose pierced side brought forth Water and Blood; and Who commanded His disciples that they should go forth into all the world, preaching the Gospel of salvation, and baptising men with Water In the Name of the Father, and of the Son, and of the Holy Ghost.

The Priest shall then breathe thrice upon the Water, and shall then continue, saying,

We beseech Thee, Almighty God, mercifully to hear the prayers of Thy people who strive to keep Thy commandments, and vouchsafe to breathe forth Thy Holy Spirit upon us, and so to give us life; and do Thou also, O Lord, with the breath of Thy mouth, bless this pure Water: that as by nature, having power to cleanse, and so made use of to cleanse; so also, by Thy grace, it may be effectual in purifying the souls and minds of men, for their regeneration in Christ by the washing away of sin; and so we humbly pray Thee, O Father:

The Priest shall then lower the Paschal Candle into the Font
three times, each time singing or saying,

May the power of the Holy Ghost descend upon the fullness of this Font;
May the power of the Holy Ghost descend upon the fullness of this Font;
May the power of the Holy Ghost descend upon the fullness of this Font.

THE PROPERS OF THE YEAR

And the Priest shall then continue, saying or singing,

And so, we beseech Thee, to make the whole substance of this Water to be fruitful unto regeneration and the remission of sins; and so here may the stains of every sin be washed away; here may man's nature, created in Thine own image, be restored by Thy grace to the honour of its first estate, and cleansed from all defilement contracted by the fall; that every person who cometh to this Sacrament of washing and regeneration may be born again unto the new childhood of true innocence; through Jesus Christ our Lord, Who shall come to judge the quick and the dead, and the world by fire.

And all shall say or sing,
AMEN.

Then, if there be any to be baptised, the Priest shall baptise them according to the manner prescribed, only omitting the Blessing of the Water, the Lord's Prayer, and the Blessing.

If there be none to be baptised, the Priest shall proceed to the Renewal of the Promises of Baptism.

Before the Renewal of the Baptismal Vows, this Canticle following shall first be sung or said.

CANTICLE. *Psalm 42. 1-2.*

LIKE as the hart desireth the water-brooks, / so longeth my soul after Thee, O God. My soul is a-thirst for the living God: / when shall I come to appear before the presence of God?

Then shall the Priest say,
O LORD, hear our prayer;
Answer. And let our cry come unto Thee.
Priest. Let us pray.

ALMIGHTY and everlasting God, look mercifully upon the devotions of Thy people whom Thou hast called to a new birth; and who, like the hart, desireth the fountains of Thy waters: Mercifully grant, that the thirst of their faith may, by the mystery of their Baptism, sanctify them both in body and soul unto everlasting life; through Jesus Christ our Lord. *Amen.*

Then shall the Priest proceed to the Renewal of Baptismal Vows.

THE RENEWAL OF BAPTISMAL VOWS

The Priest shall first say to the people,

DEARLY beloved in Christ, on this most holy night, holy mother Church keepeth vigil; and calling to mind the Death and Resurrection of her Blessed Lord and Saviour, she rendereth unto Him love for love; and celebrating His triumph over sin and death, she rejoiceth with great gladness.

Now since, as the Apostle teacheth, we have by Baptism been buried with Christ into His Death, so, just as He rose again from the dead, we must also walk in newness of Life; knowing that our old man hath been crucified with Christ, so that we may no longer be slaves unto sin. Let us, therefore, reckon ourselves dead indeed unto sin, but alive unto God in Christ Jesus our Lord.

Wherefore, dearly beloved, now that our Lenten exercises are done, let us renew the promises of our Baptism, by which we once renounced the devil and all his works, the vanity and wickedness of this present sinful world, and all that which is at enmity with God; and promised to serve God faithfully in His holy Catholic Church all the days of our life.

Now, therefore, I demand of you:

Do you renounce the devil and all his works, the vain pomp and glory of the world, with all the covetous desires of the same, and the carnal desires of the flesh, so that you will not follow, nor be led by them?

Answer. I renounce them all.

The Priest.

Do you believe in God the Father Almighty, Maker of heaven and earth? And do you believe in Jesus Christ His only-begotten Son our Lord? And that He was conceived by the Holy Ghost; born of the Virgin Mary; that He suffered under Pontius Pilate, was crucified, dead, and buried; that He went down into hell, and also did rise again the third day; that He ascended into heaven, and there sitteth at the right hand of God the Father Almighty; and from thence shall come again at the end of the world, to judge the quick and the dead? And do you believe in the Holy Ghost; the holy Catholic Church; the Communion of Saints; the Remission of sins; the Resurrection of the body; and everlasting Life after death?

Answer. All this I steadfastly believe.

The Priest.

Will you then obediently keep God's holy will and commandments, and walk in the same all the days of your life?

Answer. I will endeavour so to do, God being my Helper.

Then shall the Priest say,
Dearly beloved, let us pray.
As our Saviour Christ hath commanded and taught us,
we are bold to say,

And all shall say together,
Our Father, which art in heaven, hallowed be Thy Name. Thy kingdom come. Thy will be done, in earth as it is in heaven. Give us this day our daily bread. And forgive us our trespasses, As we forgive them that trespass against us. And lead us not into temptation, But deliver us from evil.

Then shall the Priest say,
Deliver us, we beseech Thee, O Lord, from every evil, past, present, and to come; and grant us peace in our days; and that, by the help of Thine availing mercy, we may be kept both free from sin, and safe from all distress, as we await the blessed hope, and the glorious appearing of the great God and our Saviour Jesus Christ.

And all shall then say or sing together,
For Thine is the kingdom, the power, and the glory, forever and ever.
Amen.

Asperges.

Then shall the Priest sprinkle the Ministers and people with the blessed Water.

A Psalm or hymn may be sung during the aspersing of the Ministers and people.

THE PROPERS OF THE YEAR

And when the Priest hath ended aspersing the people, he shall say,

AND may Almighty God, the Father of our Lord Jesus Christ, Who hath made us to be born again of Water and the Holy Ghost, and granted unto us forgiveness of all our sins, ever keep us by His grace in the same Christ Jesus, and finally bring us to everlasting life. *Amen.*

And when there is no celebration of the Holy Eucharist,
the Priest shall dismiss the people as followeth.

The Priest shall say,

✠ THE Lord bless you, and keep you. The Lord make His face to shine upon you, and be gracious unto you. The Lord lift up His countenance upon you, and give you peace, both now and evermore. *Amen.*

And when there shall be a celebration of the Holy Eucharist, the preceding Blessing shall not be said, but the Priest and Ministers shall proceed directly to the Chancel steps, at which time a hymn may be sung.

THE FIRST EUCHARIST OF EASTER-DAY

The Preparation shall not be said, but the Priest shall begin
the Lord's Supper with the Lord's Prayer and the Collect for Purity.

Then shall this Introit be sung or said as the Priest proceedeth
to the Altar for the celebration of the Holy Eucharist..

THE INTROIT. *Psalm* 139. 1-5.

O LORD, Thou hast searched me out and known me; / Thou knowest my down-sitting and mine up-rising, Thou understandest my thoughts long before. Thou art about my path, and about my bed, / and spiest out all my ways. For lo, there is not a word in my tongue, / but Thou, O Lord, knowest it altogether. Thou hast fashioned me behind and before, / and laid Thine hand upon me. Such knowledge is too wonderful and excellent for me: / I cannot attain unto it.

GLORY be to the Father, and to the Son, / and to the Holy Ghost;
As it was in the beginning, is now, and ever shall be, / world without end. Amen.

THE COLLECT.

O GOD, Who makest us glad with the yearly remembrance of the resurrection from the dead of Thine only Son Jesus Christ: Grant that we who celebrate this Paschal feast may die daily unto sin, and live with Him evermore in the glory of His endless life; through the same Jesus Christ our Lord. *Amen.*

THE EPISTLE. II *Timothy* 2. 8-14.

REMEMBER Jesus Christ, risen from the dead, of the seed of David, according to my gospel: wherein I suffer trouble as an evil doer, even unto bonds: but the Word of God is not bound. Therefore I endure all things for the elect's sake, that they also may obtain the salvation which is in Christ Jesus, with eternal glory. This is a faithful saying: For if we be dead with Him, we shall also live with Him. If we endure, we shall also reign with Him. If we deny Him, He also will deny us. If we believe not, yet He abideth faithful; He cannot deny Himself. Of these things put them in remembrance.

THE GRADUAL. *Psalm* 118. 22-25.

ALLELUIA, Alleluia. The same stone which the builders refused / is become the head-stone in the corner. This is the Lord's doing, / and it is marvellous in our eyes. This is the day which the Lord hath made: / we will rejoice and be glad in it. Help me now, O Lord: / O Lord, send us now prosperity. Alleluia.

THE GOSPEL. *Saint Mark* 16. 1-7.

WHEN the Sabbath was past, Mary Magdalene, and Mary the mother of James, and Salome, had bought sweet spices, that they might come and anoint Him. And very early in the morning the first day of the week, they came unto the sepulchre at the rising of the sun. And they said among themselves, Who will roll us away the stone from the door of the sepulchre? And when they looked, they saw that the stone was rolled away: for it was very great. And entering into the sepulchre, they saw a young man sitting on the right side, clothed in a long white garment; and they were affrighted. And he saith unto them, Be not affrighted: Ye seek Jesus of Nazareth, which was crucified: He is risen; He is not here: behold the place where they laid Him. But go your way, tell His disciples and Peter that He goeth before you into Galilee: there will ye see Him, as He said unto you.

THE RESURRECTION OF OUR LORD JESUS CHRIST
WHICH IS CALLED
EASTER-DAY

THE INTROIT. *Psalm* 30. 1-5.

I WILL magnify Thee, O Lord, for Thou hast set me up, / and not made my foes to triumph over me. O Lord my God, I cried unto Thee, / and Thou hast healed me. Thou, Lord, hast brought my soul out of hell; / Thou hast kept my life from them that go down to the pit. Sing praises unto the Lord, O ye saints of His, / and give thanks unto Him for a remembrance of His holiness. For His wrath endureth but the twinkling of an eye, and in His pleasure is life; / heaviness may endure for a night, but joy cometh in the morning.

GLORY be to the Father, and to the Son, / and to the Holy Ghost;
As it was in the beginning, is now, and ever shall be, / world without end. Amen.

THE COLLECT.

ALMIGHTY God, Who through Thine only-begotten Son Jesus Christ hast overcome death, and opened unto us the gate of everlasting life: We humbly beseech Thee, that, as by Thy special grace preparing the way before us, Thou dost put into our minds good desires, so by Thy continual help we may bring the same to good effect; through Jesus Christ our Lord, Who liveth and reigneth with Thee and the Holy Ghost, ever one God, world without end. *Amen.*

THE EPISTLE. *Colossians* 3. 1-7.

IF ye then be risen with Christ, seek those things which are above, where Christ sitteth on the right hand of God. Set your affection on things above, not on things on the earth. For ye are dead, and your life is hid with Christ in God. When Christ, Who is our life, shall appear, then shall ye also appear with Him in glory. Mortify therefore your members which are upon the earth; fornication, uncleanness, inordinate affection, evil concupiscence, and covetousness, which is idolatry: for which things' sake the wrath of God cometh on the children of disobedience: in the which ye also walked some time, when ye lived in them.

THE GRADUAL. *Psalm* 118. 22-25.

ALLELUIA, Alleluia. The same stone which the builders refused / is become the head-stone in the corner. This is the Lord's doing, / and it is marvellous in our eyes. This is the day which the Lord hath made: / we will rejoice and be glad in it. Help me now, O Lord: / O Lord, send us now prosperity. Alleluia.

THE GOSPEL. *Saint John* 20. 1-10.

THE first day of the week cometh Mary Magdalene early, when it was yet dark, unto the sepulchre, and seeth the stone taken away from the sepulchre. Then she runneth, and cometh to Simon Peter, and to the other disciple, whom Jesus loved, and saith unto them, They have taken away the Lord out of the sepulchre, and we know not where they have laid Him. Peter therefore went forth, and that other disciple, and came to the sepulchre. So they ran both together: and the other disciple did outrun Peter, and came first to the sepulchre. And he stooping down, and looking in, saw the linen clothes lying; yet went he not in. Then cometh Simon Peter following him, and went into the sepulchre, and seeth the linen clothes lie, and the napkin, that was about His head, not lying with the linen clothes, but wrapped together in a place by itself. Then went in also that other disciple, which came first to the sepulchre, and he saw, and believed. For as yet they knew not the Scripture, that He must rise again from the dead. Then the disciples went away again unto their own home.

MONDAY IN EASTER-WEEK

THE INTROIT. *Psalm* 105. 1-7.

O GIVE thanks unto the Lord, and call upon His Name; / tell the people what things He hath done. O let your songs be of Him, and praise Him, / and let your talking be of all His wondrous works. Rejoice in His holy Name; / let the heart of them rejoice that seek the Lord. Seek the Lord and His strength, / seek His face evermore. Remember the marvellous works that He hath done; / His wonders, and the judgements of His mouth; O ye seed of Abraham His servant: / ye children of Jacob His chosen. He is the Lord our God, / His judgements are in all the world.

GLORY be to the Father, and to the Son, / and to the Holy Ghost;

As it was in the beginning, is now, and ever shall be, / world without end. Amen.

THE COLLECT.

ALMIGHTY God, Who through Thine only-begotten Son Jesus Christ hast overcome death, and opened unto us the gate of everlasting life: We humbly beseech Thee, that, as by Thy special grace preparing the way before us, Thou dost put into our minds good desires, so by Thy continual help we may bring the same to good effect; through Jesus Christ our Lord, Who liveth and reigneth with Thee and the Holy Ghost, ever one God, world without end. *Amen.*

FOR THE EPISTLE. *Acts* 10. 34-43.

PETER opened his mouth, and said, Of a truth I perceive that God is no respecter of persons: But in every nation he that feareth Him, and worketh righteousness, is accepted with Him. The word which God sent unto the children of Israel, preaching peace by Jesus Christ: (He is Lord of all;) that word, I say, ye know, which was published throughout all Judaea, and began from Galilee, after the baptism which John preached; how God anointed Jesus of Nazareth with the Holy Ghost and with power: Who went about doing good, and healing all that were oppressed of the devil; for God was with Him. And we are witnesses of all things which He did both in the land of the Jews, and in Jerusalem; Whom they slew and hanged on a tree: Him God raised up the third day, and shewed Him openly; not to all the people, but unto witnesses chosen before God, even to us, who did eat and drink with Him after He rose from the dead. And He commanded us to preach unto the people, and to testify that it is He which was ordained of God to be the Judge of quick and dead. To Him give all the prophets witness, that through His Name whosoever believeth in Him shall receive remission of sins.

THE GRADUAL. *Psalm* 118. 22-25.

ALLELUIA, Alleluia. The same stone which the builders refused / is become the head-stone in the corner. This is the Lord's doing, / and it is marvellous in our eyes. This is the day which the Lord hath made: / we will rejoice and be glad in it. Help me now, O Lord: / O Lord, send us now prosperity. Alleluia.

THE GOSPEL. *Saint Luke* 24. 13-35.

BEHOLD, two of them went that same day to a village called Emmaus, which was from Jerusalem about threescore furlongs. And they talked together of all these things which had happened. And it came to pass, that, while they communed together and reasoned, Jesus Himself drew near, and went with them. But their eyes were holden that they should not know Him. And He said unto them, What manner of communications are these that ye have one to another, as ye walk, and are sad? And the one of them, whose name was Cleopas, answering said unto Him, Art thou only a stranger in Jerusalem, and hast not known the things which are come to pass there in these days? And He said unto them, What things? And they said unto Him, Concerning Jesus of Nazareth, which was a Prophet mighty in deed and word before God and all the people: and how the chief priests and our rulers delivered Him to be condemned to death, and have crucified Him. But we trusted that it had been He which should have redeemed Israel: and beside all this, to-day is the third day since these things were done. Yea, and certain women also of our company made us astonished, which were early at the sepulchre; and when they found not His body, they came, saying, That they had also seen a vision of angels, which said that He was alive. And certain of them which were with us went to the sepulchre, and found it even so as the women had said: but Him they saw not. Then He said unto them, O fools, and slow of heart to believe all that the prophets have spoken: ought not Christ to have suffered these things, and to enter into His glory? And beginning at Moses and all the prophets, He expounded unto them in all the Scriptures the things concerning Himself. And they drew nigh unto the village, whither they went: and He made as though He would have gone further. But they constrained Him, saying, Abide with us: for it is toward evening, and the day is far spent. And He went in to tarry with them. And it came to pass, as He sat at meat with them, He took bread, and blessed it, and brake, and gave to them. And their eyes were opened, and they knew Him; and He vanished out of their sight. And they said one to another, Did not our heart burn within us, while He talked with us by the way, and while He opened to us the Scriptures? And they rose up the same hour, and returned to Jerusalem, and found the eleven gathered together, and them that were with them, saying, The Lord is risen indeed, and hath appeared to Simon. And they told what things were done in the way, and how He was known of them in breaking of bread.

TUESDAY IN EASTER-WEEK

THE INTROIT. *Psalm* 106. 1-5.

O GIVE thanks unto the Lord, for He is gracious, / and His mercy endureth for ever. Who can express the noble acts of the Lord? / or shew forth all His praise? Blessed are they that alway keep judgement, / and do righteousness. Remember me, O Lord, according to the favour that Thou bearest unto Thy people: / O visit me with Thy salvation; That I may see the felicity of Thy chosen, / and rejoice in the gladness of Thy people, and give thanks with Thine inheritance.

GLORY be to the Father, and to the Son, / and to the Holy Ghost;

As it was in the beginning, is now, and ever shall be, / world without end. Amen.

THE COLLECT.

ALMIGHTY God, Who through Thine only-begotten Son Jesus Christ hast overcome death, and opened unto us the gate of everlasting life: We humbly beseech Thee, that, as by Thy special grace preparing the way before us, Thou dost put into our minds good desires, so by Thy continual help we may bring the same to good effect; through Jesus Christ our Lord, Who liveth and reigneth with Thee and the Holy Ghost, ever one God, world without end. *Amen.*

FOR THE EPISTLE. *Acts* 13. 26-41.

MEN and brethren, children of the stock of Abraham, and whosoever among you feareth God, to you is the word of this salvation sent. For they that dwell at Jerusalem, and their rulers, because they knew Him not, nor yet the voices of the prophets which are read every Sabbath-day, they have fulfilled them in condemning Him. And though they found no cause of death in Him, yet desired they Pilate that He should be slain. And when they had fulfilled all that was written of Him, they took Him down from the tree, and laid Him in a sepulchre. But God raised Him from the dead: and He was seen many days of them which came up with Him from Galilee to Jerusalem, who are His witnesses unto the people. And we declare unto you glad tidings, how that the promise which was made unto the fathers, God hath fulfilled the same unto us their children, in that He hath raised up Jesus again; as it is also written in the second psalm, Thou art my Son, this day have I begotten Thee. And as concerning that He raised Him up from the dead, now no more to return to corruption, He said on this wise, I will give you the sure mercies of David. Wherefore He saith also in another psalm, Thou shalt not suffer Thine Holy One to see corruption. For David, after he had served his own generation by the will of God, fell on sleep, and was laid unto his fathers, and saw corruption: but He, Whom God raised again, saw no corruption. Be it known unto you therefore, men and brethren, that through this Man is preached unto you the forgiveness of sins: and by Him all that believe are justified from all things, from which ye could not be justified by the Law of Moses. Beware therefore, lest that come upon you, which is spoken of in the prophets, Behold, ye despisers, and wonder, and perish: for I work a work in your days, a work which ye shall in no wise believe, though a man declare it unto you.

THE GRADUAL. *Psalm* 118. 22-25.

ALLELUIA, Alleluia. The same stone which the builders refused / is become the head-stone in the corner. This is the Lord's doing, / and it is marvellous in our eyes. This is the day which the Lord hath made: / we will rejoice and be glad in it. Help me now, O Lord: / O Lord, send us now prosperity. Alleluia.

THE GOSPEL. *Saint Luke* 24. 36-48.

JESUS Himself stood in the midst of them, and saith unto them, Peace be unto you. But they were terrified and affrighted, and supposed that they had seen a spirit. And He said unto them, Why are ye troubled? and why do thoughts arise in your hearts? Behold my hands and my feet, that it is I myself: handle me, and see; for a spirit hath not flesh and bones, as ye see me have. And when He had thus spoken, He shewed them His hands and His feet. And while they yet believed not for joy, and wondered, He said unto them, Have ye here any meat? And they gave Him a piece of a broiled fish, and of an honeycomb. And He took it, and did eat before them. And He said unto them, These are the words which I spake unto you, while I was yet with you, that all things must be fulfilled, which were written in the Law of Moses, and in the prophets, and in the psalms, concerning me. Then opened He their understanding, that they might understand the Scriptures, and said unto them, Thus it is written, and thus it behoved Christ to suffer, and to rise from the dead the third day: and that repentance and remission of sins should be preached in His name among all nations, beginning at Jerusalem. And ye are witnesses of these things.

THE FIRST SUNDAY AFTER EASTER
COMMONLY CALLED
LOW SUNDAY

THE INTROIT. *Psalm* 81. 1-4.

SING we merrily unto God our Strength; / make a cheerful noise unto the God of Jacob. Take the psalm, bring hither the tabret, / the merry harp with the lute. Blow up the trumpet in the new-moon, / even in the time appointed, and upon our solemn feast-day. For this was made a statute for Israel, / and a law of the God of Jacob.

GLORY be to the Father, and to the Son, / and to the Holy Ghost;
As it was in the beginning, is now, and ever shall be, / world without end. Amen.

THE COLLECT.

ALMIGHTY Father, Who hast given Thine only Son to die for our sins, and to rise again for our justification: Grant us so to put away the leaven of malice and wickedness, that we may alway serve Thee in pureness of living and truth; through the Merits of the same Thy Son Jesus Christ our Lord. *Amen.*

THE EPISTLE. I *Saint John* 5. 1-13.

WHOSOEVER believeth that Jesus is the Christ is born of God: and every one that loveth Him that begat loveth him also that is begotten of Him. By this we know that we love the children of God, when we love God, and keep His commandments. For this is the love of God, that we keep His commandments: and His commandments are not grievous. For whatsoever is born of God overcometh the world: and this is the victory that overcometh the world, even our faith. Who is he that overcometh the world, but he that believeth that Jesus is the Son of God? This is He that came by water and blood, even Jesus Christ; not by water only, but by water and blood. And it is the Spirit that beareth witness, because the Spirit is truth. For there are Three that bear record in heaven, the Father, the Word, and the Holy Ghost: and these Three are one. And there are three that bear witness in earth, the Spirit, and the water, and the blood: and these three agree in one. If we receive the witness of men, the witness of God is greater: for this is the witness of God which

He hath testified of His Son. He that believeth on the Son of God hath the witness in himself: he that believeth not God hath made him a liar; because he believeth not the record that God gave of His Son. And this is the record, that God hath given to us eternal life, and this life is in His Son. He that hath the Son hath life; and he that hath not the Son of God hath not life. These things have I written unto you that believe on the Name of the Son of God; that ye may know that ye have eternal life, and that ye may believe on the Name of the Son of God.

THE GRADUAL. *Psalm* 118. 22-25.

ALLELUIA, Alleluia. The same stone which the builders refused / is become the head-stone in the corner. This is the Lord's doing, / and it is marvellous in our eyes. This is the day which the Lord hath made: / we will rejoice and be glad in it. Help me now, O Lord: / O Lord, send us now prosperity. Alleluia.

THE GOSPEL. *Saint John* 20. 19-23.

THE same day at evening, being the first day of the week, when the doors were shut where the disciples were assembled for fear of the Jews, came Jesus and stood in the midst, and saith unto them, Peace be unto you. And when He had so said, He shewed unto them His hands and His side. Then were the disciples glad, when they saw the Lord. Then said Jesus to them again, Peace be unto you: as my Father hath sent me, even so send I you. And when He had said this, He breathed on them, and saith unto them, Receive ye the Holy Ghost: Whosesoever sins ye remit, they are remitted unto them; and whosesoever sins ye retain, they are retained.

THE SECOND SUNDAY AFTER EASTER
COMMONLY CALLED
GOOD SHEPHERD SUNDAY

THE INTROIT. *Psalm* 33. 1-9.

REJOICE in the Lord, O ye righteous, / for it becometh well the just to be thankful. Praise the Lord with harp; / sing praises unto Him with the lute, and instrument of ten strings. Sing unto the Lord a new song, / sing praises lustily unto Him with a good courage. For the word of the Lord is true, / and all His works are faithful. He loveth righteousness and judgement; / the earth is full of the goodness of the Lord. By the word of the Lord were the heavens made, / and all the hosts of them by the breath of His mouth. He gathereth the waters of the sea together, as it were upon an heap; / and layeth up the deep, as in a treasure-house. Let all the earth fear the Lord; / stand in awe of Him, all ye that dwell in the world. For He spake, and it was done; / He commanded, and it stood fast.

GLORY be to the Father, and to the Son, / and to the Holy Ghost;

As it was in the beginning, is now, and ever shall be, / world without end. Amen.

THE COLLECT.

ALMIGHTY God, Who hast given Thine only Son to be unto us both a Sacrifice for sin, and also an ensample of godly life: Give us grace that we may always most thankfully receive that His inestimable benefit, and also daily endeavour ourselves to follow the blessed steps of His most holy life; through the same Jesus Christ our Lord. *Amen.*

THE EPISTLE. I *Saint Peter* 2. 19-25.

THIS is thankworthy, if a man for conscience toward God endure grief, suffering wrongfully. For what glory is it, if, when ye be buffeted for your faults, ye shall take it patiently? but if, when ye do well, and suffer for it, ye take it patiently, this is acceptable with God. For even hereunto were ye called: because Christ also suffered for us, leaving us an example, that ye should follow His steps: Who did no sin, neither was guile found in His mouth: Who, when He was reviled, reviled not again; when He suffered, He threatened not; but committed Himself to Him that judgeth righteously: Who His own self bare our sins in His own Body on the tree, that we, being dead to sins, should live unto righteousness: by Whose stripes ye were healed. For ye were as sheep going astray; but are now returned unto the Shepherd and Bishop of your souls.

THE GRADUAL. *Psalm* 63. 1-5.

ALLELUIA, Alleluia. O God, Thou art my God: / early will I seek Thee. My soul thirsteth for Thee, my flesh also longeth after Thee, / in a barren and dry land where no water is. Thus have I looked for Thee in holiness, / that I might behold Thy power and glory. For Thy loving-kindness is better than the life itself; / my lips shall praise Thee. As long as I live will I magnify Thee on this manner, / and lift up my hands in Thy Name. Alleluia.

THE GOSPEL. *Saint John* 10. 11-16.

AT that time Jesus said: I am the good Shepherd: the good Shepherd giveth His life for the sheep. But he that is an hireling, and not the shepherd, whose own the sheep are not, seeth the wolf coming, and leaveth the sheep, and fleeth: and the wolf catcheth them, and scattereth the sheep. The hireling fleeth, because he is an hireling, and careth not for the sheep. I am the good Shepherd, and know my sheep, and am known of mine. As the Father knoweth me, even so know I the Father: and I lay down my life for the sheep. And other sheep I have, which are not of this fold: them also I must bring, and they shall hear my voice; and there shall be one fold, and one Shepherd.

THE THIRD SUNDAY AFTER EASTER

THE INTROIT. *Psalm* 66. 1-6.

O BE joyful in God, all ye lands, / sing praises unto the honour of His Name, make His praise to be glorious. Say unto God, O how wonderful art Thou in Thy works; / through the greatness of Thy power shall Thine enemies be found liars unto Thee. For all the world shall worship Thee, / sing of Thee, and praise Thy Name. O come hither, and behold the works of God, / how wonderful He is in His doing toward the children of men. He turned the sea into dry land, / so that they went through the water on foot; there did we rejoice thereof. He ruleth with His power for ever; His eyes behold the people, / and such as will not believe shall not be able to exalt themselves.

GLORY be to the Father, and to the Son, / and to the Holy Ghost;

As it was in the beginning, is now, and ever shall be, / world without end. Amen.

THE COLLECT.

ALMIGHTY God, Who shewest to them that be in error the light of Thy truth, to the intent that they may return into the way of righteousness: Grant unto all them that are admitted into the fellowship of Christ's religion, that they may eschew those things that are contrary to their profession, and follow all such things as are agreeable to the same; through our Lord Jesus Christ. *Amen.*

THE EPISTLE. I *Saint Peter* 2. 11-17.

DEARLY BELOVED, I beseech you as strangers and pilgrims, abstain from fleshly lusts, which war against the soul; having your conversation honest among the Gentiles: that, whereas they speak against you as evildoers, they may by your good works, which they shall behold, glorify God in the day of visitation. Submit yourselves to every ordinance of man for the Lord's sake: whether it be to the King, as supreme; or unto governors, as unto them that are sent by him for the punishment of evildoers, and for the praise of them that do well. For so is the will of God, that with well doing ye may put to silence the ignorance of foolish men: as free, and not using your liberty for a cloak of maliciousness, but as the servants of God. Honour all men. Love the brotherhood. Fear God. Honour the King.

THE GRADUAL. *Psalm* 66. 7-8.

ALLELUIA, Alleluia. O praise our God, ye people, / and make the voice of His praise to be heard; Who holdeth our soul in life, / and suffereth not our feet to slip. Alleluia.

THE GOSPEL. *Saint John* 16. 12-22.

JESUS said to His disciples, I have yet many things to say unto you, but ye cannot bear them now. Howbeit when He, the Spirit of truth, is come, He will guide you into all truth: for He shall not speak of Himself; but whatsoever He shall hear, that shall He speak: and He will shew you things to come. He shall glorify me: for He shall receive of mine, and shall shew it unto you. All things that the Father hath are mine: therefore said I, that He shall take of mine, and shall shew it unto you. A little while, and ye shall not see me: and again, a little while, and ye shall see me, because I go to the Father. Then said some of His disciples among themselves, What is this that He saith unto us, A little while, and ye shall not see me: and again, A little while, and ye shall see me: and, Because I go to the Father? They said therefore, What is this that He saith, A little while? we cannot tell what He saith. Now Jesus knew that they were desirous to ask Him, and said unto them, Do ye enquire among yourselves of that I said, A little while, and ye shall not see me: and again, A little while, and ye shall see me? Verily, verily, I say unto you, that ye shall weep and lament, but the world shall rejoice: and ye shall be sorrowful, but your sorrow shall be turned into joy. A woman when she is in travail hath sorrow, because her hour is come: but as soon as she is delivered of the child, she remembereth no more the anguish, for joy that a man is born into the world. And ye now therefore have sorrow: but I will see you again, and your heart shall rejoice, and your joy no man taketh from you.

THE FOURTH SUNDAY AFTER EASTER

THE INTROIT. *Psalm* 98. 1-4.

O SING unto the Lord a new song, / for He hath done marvellous things. With His own right hand, and with His holy arm, / hath He gotten Himself the victory. The Lord declared His salvation, / His righteousness hath He openly shewed in the sight of the heathen. He hath remembered His mercy and truth toward the house of Israel, / and all the ends of the world have seen the salvation of our God.

Glory be to the Father, and to the Son, / and to the Holy Ghost;
As it was in the beginning, is now, and ever shall be, / world without end. Amen.

THE COLLECT.

O ALMIGHTY God, Who alone canst order the unruly wills and affections of sinful men: Grant unto Thy people, that they may love the thing which Thou commandest, and desire that which Thou dost promise; that so, among the sundry and manifold changes of the world, our hearts may surely there be fixed, where true joys are to be found; through Jesus Christ our Lord. *Amen.*

THE EPISTLE. *Saint James* 1. 17-21.

EVERY good gift and every perfect gift is from above, and cometh down from the Father of lights, with Whom is no variableness, neither shadow of turning. Of His own will begat He us with the word of truth, that we should be a kind of first-fruits of His creatures. Wherefore, my beloved brethren, let every man be swift to hear, slow to speak, slow to wrath: For the wrath of man worketh not the righteousness of God. Wherefore lay apart all filthiness and residue of wickedness, and receive with meekness the engrafted Word, which is able to save your souls.

THE GRADUAL. *Psalm* 118. 15-16.

ALLELUIA, Alleluia. The voice of joy and health is in the dwellings of the righteous; / the right hand of the Lord bringeth mighty things to pass. The right hand of the Lord hath the pre-eminence; / the right hand of the Lord bringeth mighty things to pass. Alleluia.

THE GOSPEL. *Saint John* 16. 5-12.

JESUS said unto His disciples, Now I go my way to Him that sent me; and none of you asketh me, Whither goest Thou? But because I have said these things unto you, sorrow hath filled your heart. Nevertheless I tell you the truth; it is expedient for you that I go away: for if I go not away, the Comforter will not come unto you; but if I depart, I will send Him unto you. And when He is come, He will reprove the world of sin, and of righteousness, and of judgement: of sin, because they believe not on me; of righteousness, because I go to my Father, and ye see me no more; of judgement, because the prince of this world is judged. I have yet many things to say unto you, but ye cannot bear them now.

THE FIFTH SUNDAY AFTER EASTER
WHICH IS CALLED
ROGATION SUNDAY

THE INTROIT. *Psalm* 107. 1-9.

O GIVE thanks unto the Lord, for He is gracious, / and His mercy endureth for ever. Let them give thanks whom the Lord hath redeemed, / and delivered from the hand of the enemy; And gathered them out of the lands, from the east and from the west, / from the north and from the south. They went astray in the wilderness out of the way, / and found no city to dwell in; Hungry and thirsty, / their soul fainted in them. So they cried unto the Lord in their trouble, / and He delivered them from their distress. He led them forth by the right way, / that they might go to the city where they dwelt. O that men would therefore praise the Lord for His goodness, / and declare the wonders that He doeth for the children of men! For He satisfieth the empty soul, / and filleth the hungry soul with goodness.

GLORY be to the Father, and to the Son, / and to the Holy Ghost;

As it was in the beginning, is now, and ever shall be, / world without end. Amen.

THE PROPERS OF THE YEAR

THE COLLECT.

O LORD, from Whom all good things do come: Grant to us Thy humble servants, that by Thy holy inspiration we may think those things that be good, and by Thy merciful guiding may perform the same; through our Lord Jesus Christ. *Amen.*

THE EPISTLE. *Saint James* 1. 22-27.

BUT be ye doers of the word, and not hearers only, deceiving your own selves. For if any be a hearer of the word, and not a doer, he is like unto a man beholding his natural face in a glass: For he beholdeth himself, and goeth his way, and straightway forgetteth what manner of man he was. But whoso looketh into the perfect law of liberty, and continueth therein, he being not a forgetful hearer, but a doer of the work, this man shall be blessed in his deed. If any man among you seem to be religious, and bridleth not his tongue, but deceiveth his own heart, this man's religion is vain. Pure religion and undefiled before God and the Father is this, to visit the fatherless and widows in their affliction, and to keep himself unspotted from the world.

THE GRADUAL. *Psalm* 66. 14-18.

ALLELUIA, Alleluia. O come hither, and hearken, all ye that fear God, / and I will tell you what He hath done for my soul. I called unto Him with my mouth, / and gave Him praises with my tongue. If I incline unto wickedness with mine heart, / the Lord will not hear me. But God hath heard me / and considered the voice of my prayer. Praised be God Who hath not cast out my prayer, / nor turned His mercy from me. Alleluia.

THE GOSPEL. *Saint John* 16. 23-33.

AT that time Jesus said unto them: Verily, verily, I say unto you, Whatsoever ye shall ask the Father in my Name, He will give it you. Hitherto have ye asked nothing in my Name: ask, and ye shall receive, that your joy may be full. These things have I spoken unto you in proverbs: but the time cometh, when I shall no more speak unto you in proverbs, but I shall shew you plainly of the Father. At that day ye shall ask in my Name: and I say not unto you, that I will pray the Father for you: for the Father Himself loveth you, because ye have loved me, and have believed that I came out from God. I came forth from the Father, and am come into the world: again, I leave the world, and go to the Father. His disciples said unto Him, Lo, now speakest Thou plainly, and speakest no proverb. Now are we sure that Thou knowest all things, and needest not that any man should ask Thee: by this we believe that Thou camest forth from God. Jesus answered them, Do ye now believe? Behold, the hour cometh, yea, is now come, that ye shall be scattered, every man to his own, and shall leave me alone: and yet I am not alone, because the Father is with me. These things I have spoken unto you, that in me ye might have peace. In the world ye shall have tribulation: but be of good cheer; I have overcome the world.

THE ROGATION-DAYS
BEING THE THREE DAYS BEFORE
THE ASCENSION-DAY

THE INTROIT. *Psalm* 4. 1-6.

HEAR me when I call, O God of my righteousness: / Thou hast set me at liberty when I was in trouble; have mercy upon me, and hearken unto my prayer. O ye sons of men, how long will ye blaspheme mine honour, / and have such pleasure in vanity, and seek after falsehood? Know this also, that the Lord hath chosen to Himself the man that is godly; / when I call upon the Lord, He will hear me. Stand in awe, and sin not; / commune with your own heart, and in your chamber, and be still. Offer the sacrifice of righteousness, / and put your trust in the Lord.

GLORY be to the Father, and to the Son, / and to the Holy Ghost;
As it was in the beginning, is now, and ever shall be, / world without end. Amen.

THE COLLECT.

ALMIGHTY and merciful God, from Whom cometh every good and perfect gift: Hear, we beseech Thee, the devout prayers of Thy people, and bless the righteous labours of their hands; and vouchsafe to reward them according to Thy gracious loving-kindness, and cause the earth to bring forth her fruits abundantly in their season, that we may all with grateful hearts give thanks to Thee for the same; through Jesus Christ our Lord. *Amen.*

THE EPISTLE. I *Timothy* 2. 1-8.

I EXHORT therefore, that, first of all, supplications, prayers, intercessions, and giving of thanks, be made for all men; for kings, and for all that are in authority; that we may lead a quiet and peaceable life in all godliness and honesty. For this is good and acceptable in the sight of God our Saviour; Who will have all men to be saved, and to come unto the knowledge of the truth. For there is one God, and one Mediator between God and men, the Man Christ Jesus; Who gave Himself a ransom for all, to be testified in due time. Whereunto I am ordained a preacher, and an Apostle (I speak the truth in Christ, and lie not), a teacher of the Gentiles in faith and verity. I will therefore that men pray everywhere, lifting up holy hands, without wrath and doubting.

THE GRADUAL. *Palm* 23. 1-3.

ALLELUIA, Alleluia. The Lord is my Shepherd, / therefore can I lack nothing. He shall feed me in a green pasture, / and lead me forth beside the waters of comfort. He shall restore my soul, / and bring me forth in the paths of righteousness, for His Name's sake. Alleluia.

THE GOSPEL. *Saint Luke* 11. 1-10.

IT came to pass, that, as Jesus was praying in a certain place, when He ceased, one of His disciples said unto Him, Lord, teach us to pray, as John also taught his disciples. And He said unto them, When ye pray, say, Father, Hallowed be Thy Name. Thy kingdom come. Give us day by day our daily bread. And forgive us our sins; for we ourselves also forgive every one that is indebted to us. And bring us not into temptation. And He said unto them, Which of you shall have a friend, and shall go unto him at midnight, and say unto him, Friend, lend me three loaves; for a friend of mine in his journey is come to me, and I have nothing to set before him? And he from within shall answer and say, Trouble me not: the door is now shut, and my children are with me in bed; I cannot rise and give thee. I say unto you, Though he will not rise and give him, because he is his friend, yet because of his importunity he will rise and give him as many as he needeth. And I say unto you, Ask, and it shall be given you; seek, and ye shall find; knock, and it shall be opened unto you. For every one that asketh receiveth; and he that seeketh findeth; and to him that knocketh it shall be opened.

THE ASCENSION OF OUR LORD JESUS CHRIST
COMMONLY CALLED
HOLY THURSDAY

THE INTROIT. *Psalm* 47. 1-9.

CLAP your hands together, all ye people; / O sing unto God with the voice of melody. For the Lord is high, and to be feared; / He is the great King upon all the earth. He shall subdue the people under us, / and the nations under our feet. He shall choose out an heritage for us; / even the worship of Jacob, whom He loved. God is gone up with a merry noise; / and the Lord with the sound of the trump. O sing praises, sing praises unto our God: / O sing praises, sing praises unto our King. For God is the King of all the earth; / sing ye praises with understanding.

GLORY be to the Father, and to the Son, / and to the Holy Ghost;

As it was in the beginning, is now, and ever shall be, / world without end. Amen.

THE COLLECT.

GRANT, we beseech Thee, Almighty God, that like as we do believe Thine only-begotten Son our Saviour Jesus Christ to have ascended into the heavens; so we may also in heart and mind thither ascend, and with Him continually dwell; through the same Thy blessed Son our Lord, Who liveth and reigneth with Thee and the Holy Ghost, one God, world without end. *Amen.*

FOR THE EPISTLE. *Acts* 1. 1-11.

THE former treatise have I made, O Theophilus, of all that Jesus began both to do and teach, until the day in which He was taken up, after that He through the Holy Ghost had given commandments unto the Apostles whom He had chosen: to whom also He shewed Himself alive after His passion by many infallible proofs, being seen of them forty days, and speaking of the things pertaining to the kingdom of God: and, being assembled together with them, commanded them that they should not depart from Jerusalem, but wait for the promise of the Father, which, saith He, ye have heard of me. For John truly baptised with water; but ye shall be baptised with the Holy Ghost not many days hence. When they therefore were come together, they asked of Him, saying, Lord, wilt Thou at this time restore again the kingdom to Israel? And He said unto them, It is not for you to know the times or the seasons, which the Father hath put in His own power. But ye shall receive power, after that the Holy Ghost is come upon you: and ye shall be witnesses unto me both in Jerusalem, and in all Judaea, and in Samaria, and unto the uttermost part of the earth. And when He had spoken these things, while they beheld, He was taken up; and a cloud received Him out of their sight. (*And here the Paschal Candle shall be extinguished.*) And while they looked steadfastly toward heaven as He went up, behold, two men stood by them in white apparel; which also said, Ye men of Galilee, why stand ye gazing up into heaven? this same Jesus, which is taken up from you into heaven, shall so come in like manner as ye have seen Him go into heaven.

THE GRADUAL. *Psalm* 68. 17-20.

ALLELUIA, Alleluia. The chariots of God are twenty thousand, even thousands of angels, / and the Lord is among them, as in the holy place of Sinai. Thou art gone up on high, Thou hast led captivity captive, and received gifts for men; / yea, even for Thine enemies, that the Lord God might dwell among them. Praised be the Lord daily; / even the God Who helpeth us, and poureth His benefits upon us. He is our God, even the God of Whom cometh salvation; / God is the Lord, by Whom we escape death. Alleluia.

THE GOSPEL. *Saint Mark* 16. 14-20.

JESUS appeared unto the eleven as they sat at meat, and upbraided them with their unbelief and hardness of heart, because they believed not them which had seen Him after He was risen. And He said unto them, Go ye into all the world, and preach the Gospel to every creature. He that believeth and is baptised shall be saved; but he that believeth not shall be damned. And these signs shall follow them that believe: in my Name shall they cast out devils; they shall speak with new tongues; they shall take up serpents; and if they drink any deadly thing, it shall not hurt them; they shall lay hands on the sick, and they shall recover. So then after the Lord had spoken unto them, He was received up into heaven, and sat on the right hand of God. And they went forth, and preached everywhere, the Lord working with them, and confirming the word with signs following. Amen.

THE SUNDAY AFTER ASCENSION-DAY

THE INTROIT. *Psalm* 37. 3-11.

DELIGHT thou in the Lord, / and He shall give thee thy heart's desire. Commit thy way unto the Lord, and put thy trust in Him, / and He shall bring it to pass. He shall make thy righteousness as clear as the light, / and thy just dealing as the noon-day. Hold thee still in the Lord, and abide patiently upon Him; / but grieve not thyself at him whose way doth prosper, against the man that doeth after evil counsels. Leave off from wrath, and let go displeasure; / fret not thyself, else shalt thou be moved to do evil. Wicked doers shall be rooted out; / and they that patiently abide the Lord, those shall inherit the land. Yet a little while, and the ungodly shall be clean gone; / thou shalt look after his place, and he shall be away. But the meek-spirited shall possess the earth, / and shall be refreshed in the multitude of peace.

GLORY be to the Father, and to the Son, / and to the Holy Ghost;

As it was in the beginning, is now, and ever shall be, / world without end. Amen.

THE COLLECT.

O GOD the King of glory, Who hast exalted Thine only Son Jesus Christ with great triumph unto Thy kingdom in heaven: We beseech Thee, leave us not comfortless; but send to us Thy Holy Spirit to comfort us, and exalt us unto the same place whither our Saviour Christ is gone before; through the same Thy Son, Who liveth and reigneth with Thee and the Holy Ghost, ever one God, world without end. *Amen.*

THE EPISTLE. I *Saint Peter* 4. 7-11.

THE end of all things is at hand: be ye therefore sober, and watch unto prayer. And above all things have fervent charity among yourselves: for charity shall cover the multitude of sins. Use hospitality one to another without grudging. As every man hath received the gift, even so minister the same one to another, as good stewards of the manifold grace of God. If any man speak, let him speak as the oracles of God; if any man minister, let him do it as of the ability which God giveth: that God in all things may be glorified through Jesus Christ, to Whom be praise and dominion for ever and ever. Amen.

THE GRADUAL. *Psalm 47. 5-9.*

ALLELUIA, Alleluia. God is gone up with a merry noise; / and the Lord with the sound of the trump. O sing praises, sing praises unto our God: / O sing praises, sing praises unto our King. For God is the King of all the earth; / sing ye praises with understanding. God reigneth over the heathen; / God sitteth upon His holy seat. The princes of the people are joined unto the people of the God of Abraham; / for God, which is very high exalted, doth defend the earth, as it were with a shield. Alleluia.

THE GOSPEL. *Saint John* 15. 26-16. 4.

AT that time Jesus said unto them: When the Comforter is come, Whom I will send unto you from the Father, even the Spirit of truth, which proceedeth from the Father, He shall testify of me: and ye also shall bear witness, because ye have been with me from the beginning. These things have I spoken unto you, that ye should not be offended. They shall put you out of the synagogues: yea, the time cometh, that whosoever killeth you will think that he doeth God service. And these things will they do unto you, because they have not known the Father, nor me. But these things have I told you, that when the time shall come, ye may remember that I told you of them.

WHITSUN-EVE

The Great Litany shall be said or sung in the place of the Preparation.

INTROIT. *Psalm 32. 1-7.*

BLESSED is he whose unrighteousness is forgiven / and whose sin is covered. Blessed is the man unto whom the Lord imputeth no sin, / and in whose spirit there is no guile. For while I held my tongue / my bones consumed away through my daily complaining. For thy hand is heavy upon me day and night, / and my moisture is like the drought in summer. I will acknowledge my sin unto thee, / and mine unrighteousness have I not hid. I said, I will confess my sins unto the Lord, / and so thou forgavest the wickedness of my sin. For this shall every one that is godly make his prayer unto thee, in a time when thou mayest be found; / but in the great water-floods they shall not come nigh him.

GLORY be to the Father, and to the Son, / and to the Holy Ghost;
As it was in the beginning, is now, and ever shall be, / world without end. Amen.

THE COLLECT.

GRANT, we beseech Thee, Almighty God, that the splendour of Thy brightness may shine upon us, and that the light of Thy Holy Spirit may strengthen us who by Thy grace have been regenerated by the mighty working of His power; through our Lord Jesus Christ, Thine only-begotten Son, Who liveth and reigneth with Thee in the unity of the same Holy Ghost, ever one God, world without end. *Amen.*

FOR THE EPISTLE. *Acts* 19. 1-8.

AND it came to pass, that, while Apollos was at Corinth, Paul having passed through the upper coasts came to Ephesus: and finding certain disciples, He said unto them, Have ye received the

Holy Ghost since ye believed? And they said unto him, We have not so much as heard whether there be any Holy Ghost. And he said unto them, Unto what then were ye baptised? And they said, Unto John's baptism. Then said Paul, John verily baptised with the baptism of repentance, saying unto the people, that they should believe on him which should come after him, that is, on Christ Jesus. When they heard this, they were baptised in the name of the Lord Jesus. And when Paul had laid his hands upon them, the Holy Ghost came on them; and they spake with tongues, and prophesied. And all the men were about twelve. And he went into the synagogue, and spake boldly for the space of three months, disputing and persuading the things concerning the kingdom of God.

THE GRADUAL. *Psalm* 32. 8-9.

ALLELUIA, Alleluia. Thou art a place to hide me in, thou shalt preserve me from trouble, / thou shalt compass me about with songs of deliverance. I will inform thee, and teach thee in the way wherein thou shalt go, / and I will guide thee with mine eye. Alleluia.

THE GOSPEL. *Saint Matthew* 3. 1-17.

IN those days came John the Baptist, preaching in the wilderness of Judaea, and saying, Repent ye: for the kingdom of heaven is at hand. For this is he that was spoken of by the prophet Esaias, saying, The voice of one crying in the wilderness, Prepare ye the way of the Lord, make His paths straight. And the same John had his raiment of camel's hair, and a leathern girdle about his loins; and his meat was locusts and wild honey. Then went out to him Jerusalem, and all Judaea, and all the region round about Jordan, and were baptised of him in Jordan, confessing their sins. But when he saw many of the Pharisees and Sadducees come to his baptism, he said unto them, O generation of vipers, who hath warned you to flee from the wrath to come? Bring forth therefore fruits meet for repentance: and think not to say within yourselves, We have Abraham to our father: for I say unto you, that God is able of these stones to raise up children unto Abraham. And now also the axe is laid unto the root of the trees: therefore every tree which bringeth not forth good fruit is hewn down, and cast into the fire. I indeed baptise you with water unto repentance. but He that cometh after me is mightier than I, Whose shoes I am not worthy to bear: He shall baptise you with the Holy Ghost, and with fire: Whose fan is in His hand, and He will thoroughly purge His floor, and gather His wheat into the garner; but He will burn up the chaff with unquenchable fire. Then cometh Jesus from Galilee to Jordan unto John, to be baptised of him. But John forbade Him, saying, I have need to be baptised of Thee, and comest Thou to me? And Jesus answering said unto him, Suffer it to be so now: for thus it becometh us to fulfill all righteousness. Then he suffered Him. And Jesus, when He was baptised, went up straightway out of the water: and, lo, the heavens were opened unto Him, and He saw the Spirit of God descending like a dove, and lighting upon Him: and lo a voice from heaven, saying, This is my beloved Son, in Whom I am well pleased.

THE COLLECT AFTER COMMUNION.

ALMIGHTY GOD, Who hast caused the hearts of Thy people to desire and long for the anointing of Thy Holy Spirit: Grant unto us, we beseech Thee, to be enriched with His manifold gifts; that, patiently enduring through the darkness of this world, and filled with Divine grace, we may be found shining brightly, like burning lamps, in the Presence of our Lord Jesus Christ, when He cometh in power and glory into His kingdom. Hear us, we beseech Thee, O heavenly Father, for the sake of the same Thy Son Jesus Christ, our only Mediator and Redeemer. *Amen.*

THE DAY OF PENTECOST
COMMONLY CALLED
WHITSUNDAY

THE INTROIT. *Psalm* 122. 1-9.

I WAS glad when they said unto me, / We will go into the house of the Lord. Our feet shall stand in thy gates, / O Jerusalem. Jerusalem is built as a city / that is at unity in itself. For thither the tribes go up, even the tribes of the Lord, / to testify unto Israel, to give thanks unto the Name of the Lord. For there is the seat of judgement, / even the seat of the house of David. O pray for the peace of Jerusalem; / they shall prosper that love thee. Peace be within thy walls, / and plenteousness within thy palaces. For my brethren and companions' sakes, / I will wish thee prosperity. Yea, because of the house of the Lord our God, / I will seek to do thee good.

GLORY be to the Father, and to the Son, / and to the Holy Ghost;
As it was in the beginning, is now, and ever shall be, / world without end. Amen.

THE COLLECTS.

O GOD, Who as at this time didst teach the hearts of Thy faithful people, by the sending to them the light of Thy Holy Spirit: Grant us by the same Spirit to have a right judgement in all things, and evermore to rejoice in His holy comfort; through the Merits of Christ Jesus our Saviour, Who liveth and reigneth with Thee, in the unity of the same Spirit, ever one God, world without end. *Amen.*

And this Collect shall be repeated every day,
with the other Collects in Whitsuntide, until Trinity Sunday.

O HEAVENLY Father, Who makest us glad with the yearly remembrance of the coming of the Holy Ghost upon Thy disciples at Jerusalem: Grant that we who celebrate before Thee this Feast of Pentecost may continue Thine for ever, and daily increase in Thy Holy Spirit more and more, until we come to Thine eternal kingdom; through Jesus Christ our Lord. *Amen.*

FOR THE EPISTLE. *Acts* 2. 1-11.

WHEN the day of Pentecost was fully come, they were all with one accord in one place. And suddenly there came a sound from heaven as of a rushing mighty wind, and it filled all the house where they were sitting. And there appeared unto them cloven tongues like as of fire, and it sat upon each of them. And they were all filled with the Holy Ghost, and began to speak with other tongues, as the Spirit gave them utterance. And there were dwelling at Jerusalem Jews, devout men, out of every nation under heaven. Now when this was noised abroad, the multitude came together, and were confounded, because that every man heard them speak in his own language. And they were all amazed and marvelled, saying one to another, Behold, are not all these which speak Galilaeans? And how hear we every man in our own tongue, wherein we were born? Parthians, and Medes, and Elamites, and the dwellers in Mesopotamia, and in Judaea, and Cappadocia, in Pontus, and Asia, Phrygia, and Pamphylia, in Egypt, and in the parts of Libya about Cyrene, and strangers of Rome, Jews and proselytes, Cretes and Arabians, we do hear them speak in our tongues the wonderful works of God.

ALLELUIA, Alleluia. O God, when Thou wentest forth before the people, / when Thou wentest through the wilderness; The earth shook, and the heavens dropped at the presence of God, / even as Sinai also was moved at the presence of God, Who is the God of Israel. Thou, O God, sentest a gracious rain upon Thine inheritance, / and refreshedst it when it was weary. Alleluia.

THE GOSPEL. *Saint John* 14. 15-31.

JESUS said unto His disciples, If ye love me, keep my commandments. And I will pray the Father, and He shall give you another Comforter, that He may abide with you for ever; even the Spirit of truth; Whom the world cannot receive, because it seeth Him not, neither knoweth Him: but ye know Him; for He dwelleth with you, and shall be in you. I will not leave you comfortless: I will come to you. Yet a little while, and the world seeth me no more; but ye see me: because I live, ye shall live also. At that day ye shall know that I am in my Father, and ye in me, and I in you. He that hath my commandments, and keepeth them, he it is that loveth me: and he that loveth me shall be loved of my Father, and I will love him, and will manifest myself to him. Judas saith unto Him, (not Iscariot,) Lord, how is it that Thou wilt manifest Thyself unto us, and not unto the world? Jesus answered and said unto him, If a man love me, he will keep my words: and my Father will love him, and we will come unto him, and make our abode with him. He that loveth me not keepeth not my sayings: and the word which ye hear is not mine, but the Father's which sent me. These things have I spoken unto you, being yet present with you. But the Comforter, which is the Holy Ghost, Whom the Father will send in my Name, He shall teach you all things, and bring all things to your remembrance, whatsoever I have said unto you. Peace I leave with you, my peace I give unto you: not as the world giveth, give I unto you. Let not your heart be troubled, neither let it be afraid. Ye have heard how I said unto you, I go away, and come again unto you. If ye loved me, ye would rejoice, because I said, I go unto the Father: for my Father is greater than I. And now I have told you before it come to pass, that, when it is come to pass, ye might believe. Hereafter I will not talk much with you: for the prince of this world cometh, and hath nothing in me. But that the world may know that I love the Father; and as the Father gave me commandment, even so I do.

THE CONSECRATION OF CHRISM

In the Cathedral Church, and in such other places which have received a Faculty from the Bishop himself, at the time of the Celebration of the Lord's Supper, the Bishop (or the Priest authorised by him) shall consecrate the Oil of Chrism to be used in the Services of the Church throughout the year. And the Consecration of Chrism may take place at the principal Mass on Whitsunday, or else at the principal Mass on the Monday or Tuesday after Whitsunday, at the discretion of the Bishop. And the Communion ended, immediately after the Prayer of Thanksgiving after Holy Communion hath been said, the Bishop (or Priest) shall proceed to consecrate the Chrism according to the Form hereafter following.

THE FORM OF
CONSECRATION OF CHRISM

The Bishop shall say,
✠ IN the Name of the Father, and of the Son,
and of the Holy Ghost. *Amen.*

Let us pray.

Prevent us, O Lord, in all our doings, with Thy most gracious favour, and further us with Thy continual help; that in all our works, begun, continued, and ended in Thee, we may glorify Thy holy Name, and finally, by Thy mercy, obtain everlasting life; through Jesus Christ our Lord. *Amen.*

Then shall be sung or said by verses this hymn following
by all meekly and devoutly kneeling.

Veni, Creator Spiritus.
Come, Holy Ghost, our souls inspire,
And lighten with celestial fire.
Thou the anointing Spirit art,
Who dost Thy seven-fold gifts impart.

Thy blessed unction from above
Is comfort, life, and fire of love.
Enable with perpetual light
The dullness of our blinded sight.

Anoint and cheer our soilèd face
With the abundance of Thy grace.
Keep far our foes, give peace at home:
Where Thou art Guide, no ill can come.

Teach us to know the Father, Son,
And Thee, of Both, to be but One;
That, through the ages all along,
This may be our endless song:
Praise to Thine eternal merit,
Father, Son, and Holy Spirit. Amen.

And the Oil, having been mixed with Balsam and made ready, shall be set upon the Lord's Table,
and the Bishop shall proceed to bless and consecrate the Chrism Oil, as followeth.

The Bishop shall extend his hands over the Oil to be blessed, and shall say,
Cast out, we beseech Thee, O heavenly Father, in the Name of Jesus Christ, and by the power of the Holy Ghost, any evil which may be in, and around, this creature of Oil and Balm which we intend, by Thy grace, to set apart this day for use as Chrism in the service of Thy Church; through the same Thy Son Jesus Christ our Lord. *Amen.*

We pray Thee, O God, Who art the One True and Only God, the Almighty, Holy, and Immortal Lord God, One God in three Divine Persons: That Thou, O Father, wouldest be pleased to purify this creature of Oil and Balm, that it may be made meet and ready to receive the benediction of Thy Holy Spirit; through Thine only Son Jesus Christ our Lord. *Amen.*

Then shall the Bishop say this Prayer following over the Chrism Oil.
O God our heavenly Father, Who art pleased to set apart the good things of this earth for the use of Thy people in the Sacraments of Thy Church: vouchsafe, we beseech Thee, O Lord, to sanctify this creature of sweet and fragrant Oil, that it may become for us holy Chrism; to the end that unto all them who shall receive the same, it may be an outward sign of the sealing of the salvation and

new life which they have received in and through our Lord Jesus Christ. And as the waters of holy Baptism wash away the evil inherited from our forefather Adam, so do Thou grant, O Lord, that all they who are anointed with this holy Chrism may be filled with Thy Holy Spirit, and made temples of Thy glory, radiant with the goodness of that Life which hath its only source in Thee; through the same Thy Son Jesus Christ our Lord. *Amen.*

Then shall the Bishop bless and consecrate the Chrism Oil, saying,

WE bless, hallow, and consecrate this sweet and fragrant Oil, and set it apart for use as Chrism to anoint, Chrism to consecrate, and Chrism to seal all who are called by the Name of Jesus Christ in the fellowship of His Body the Church: In the Name of the Father, and of the Son, and of the Holy Ghost. *Amen.*

Then shall this Collect be said immediately before the Anthem.

HASTEN, O God, the time when Thou shalt send from Thy right hand Him Whom Thou wilt send; at Whose appearing the saints departed shall be raised, and we which are alive and remain shall be caught up to meet Him, and so shall we ever be with our Lord. Keep us, we beseech Thee, O Father, unto that day; and grant that at His coming, we may, as One Body, be presented with exceeding joy before the Presence of His glory, holy and unspotted, prepared as a Bride adorned for her Husband; through the same Thy Son Jesus Christ our Lord. *Amen.*

And the blessing of Chrism ended, this Psalm following
shall be said or sung as the Anthem in place of Gloria in Excelsis.

PSALM 133. *Ecce, quam bonum!*

BEHOLD, how good and joyful a thing it is, / brethren, to dwell together in unity! It is like the precious ointment upon the head, that ran down unto the beard, / even unto Aaron's beard, and went down to the skirts of his clothing. Like as the dew of Hermon, / which fell upon the hill of Sion. For there the Lord promised His blessing, / and life for evermore.

GLORY be to the Father, and to the Son, and to the Holy Ghost; /
As it was in the beginning, is now, and ever shall be, / world without end. Amen.

THE BLESSING.

Then shall the Bishop let them depart with this Blessing.

THE peace of God, which passeth all understanding, keep your hearts and minds in the knowledge and love of God, and of His Son Jesus Christ our Lord: And the blessing of God Almighty, ✠ the Father, the Son, and the Holy Ghost, be amongst you and remain with you always. *Amen.*

Here endeth the FORM OF CONSECRATION OF CHRISM.

Monday in Whitsun-Week

The Introit. *Psalm* 81. 13-17.

I AM the Lord thy God, who brought thee out of the land of Egypt: / open thy mouth wide, and I shall fill it. But my people would not hear my voice, / and Israel would not obey me. So I gave them up unto their own hearts' lusts, / and let them follow their own imaginations. O that my people would have hearkened unto me; / for if Israel had walked in my ways, I should soon have put down their enemies, / and turned my hand against their adversaries. The haters of the Lord should have been found liars; / but their time should have endured for ever. He should have fed them also with the finest wheat-flour, / and with honey out of the stony rock should I have satisfied thee.

GLORY be to the Father, and to the Son, / and to the Holy Ghost;
As it was in the beginning, is now, and ever shall be, / world without end. Amen.

The Collect.

O GOD, Who as at this time didst teach the hearts of Thy faithful people, by the sending to them the light of Thy Holy Spirit: Grant us by the same Spirit to have a right judgement in all things, and evermore to rejoice in His holy comfort; through the Merits of Christ Jesus our Saviour, Who liveth and reigneth with Thee, in the unity of the same Spirit, ever one God, world without end. *Amen.*

For the Epistle. *Acts* 10. 34-48.

THEN Peter opened his mouth, and said, Of a truth I perceive that God is no respecter of persons: but in every nation he that feareth Him, and worketh righteousness, is accepted with Him. The word which God sent unto the children of Israel, preaching peace by Jesus Christ: (He is Lord of all;) that word, I say, ye know, which was published throughout all Judaea, and began from Galilee, after the baptism which John preached; how God anointed Jesus of Nazareth with the Holy Ghost and with power: Who went about doing good, and healing all that were oppressed of the devil; for God was with Him. And we are witnesses of all things which He did both in the land of the Jews, and in Jerusalem; Whom they slew and hanged on a tree: Him God raised up the third day, and shewed Him openly; not to all the people, but unto witnesses chosen before God, even to us, who did eat and drink with Him after He rose from the dead. And He commanded us to preach unto the people, and to testify that it is He which was ordained of God to be the Judge of quick and dead. To Him give all the prophets witness, that through His Name whosoever believeth in Him shall receive remission of sins. While Peter yet spake these words, the Holy Ghost fell on all them which heard the word. And they of the circumcision which believed were astonished, as many as came with Peter, because that on the Gentiles also was poured out the gift of the Holy Ghost. For they heard them speak with tongues, and magnify God. Then answered Peter, Can any man forbid water, that these should not be baptised, which have received the Holy Ghost as well as we? And he commanded them to be baptised in the Name of the Lord. Then prayed they him to tarry certain days.

The Gradual. *Psalm* 104. 28-31.

ALLELUIA, Alleluia. These wait all upon Thee, / that Thou mayest give them meat in due season. When Thou givest it them they gather it; / and when Thou openest Thy hand they are filled with good. When Thou hidest Thy face they are troubled; / when Thou takest away their breath they die, and are turned again to their dust. When Thou lettest Thy breath go forth they shall be made, / and

Thou shalt renew the face of the earth. The glorious majesty of the Lord shall endure for ever; / the Lord shall rejoice in His works. Alleluia.

THE GOSPEL. *Saint John* 3. 16-21.

GOD so loved the world, that He gave His only-begotten Son, that whosoever believeth in Him should not perish, but have everlasting life. For God sent not His Son into the world to condemn the world; but that the world through Him might be saved. He that believeth on Him is not condemned: but he that believeth not is condemned already, because he hath not believed in the Name of the only-begotten Son of God. And this is the condemnation, that light is come into the world, and men loved darkness rather than light, because their deeds were evil. For every one that doeth evil hateth the light, neither cometh to the light, lest his deeds should be reproved. But he that doeth truth cometh to the light, that his deeds may be made manifest, that they are wrought in God.

TUESDAY IN WHITSUN-WEEK

THE INTROIT. *Psalm* 78. 1-8.

HEAR my Law, O my people; / incline your ears unto the words of my mouth. I will open my mouth in a parable, / I will declare hard sentences of old; Which we have heard and known, / and such as our fathers have told us; That we should not hide them from the children of the generations to come, / but to shew the honour of the Lord, His mighty and wonderful works that He hath done. He made a covenant with Jacob, and gave Israel a Law, / which He commanded our forefathers to teach their children; That their posterity might know it, / and the children which were yet unborn; To the intent that when they came up, / they might shew their children the same; That they might put their trust in God, / and not to forget the works of God, but to keep His commandments;

GLORY be to the Father, and to the Son, / and to the Holy Ghost;

As it was in the beginning, is now, and ever shall be, / world without end. Amen.

THE COLLECT.

O GOD, Who as at this time didst teach the hearts of Thy faithful people, by the sending to them the light of Thy Holy Spirit: Grant us by the same Spirit to have a right judgement in all things, and evermore to rejoice in His holy comfort; through the Merits of Christ Jesus our Saviour, Who liveth and reigneth with Thee, in the unity of the same Spirit, ever one God, world without end. *Amen.*

FOR THE EPISTLE. *Acts* 8. 14-17.

WHEN the Apostles which were at Jerusalem heard that Samaria had received the Word of God, they sent unto them Peter and John: who, when they were come down, prayed for them, that they might receive the Holy Ghost: (for as yet He was fallen upon none of them; only they were baptised in the Name of the Lord Jesus). Then laid they their hands on them, and they received the Holy Ghost.

THE GRADUAL. *Psalm* 23. 1-5.

ALLELUIA, Alleluia. The Lord is my Shepherd, / therefore can I lack nothing. He shall feed me in a green pasture, / and lead me forth beside the waters of comfort. He shall restore my soul, / and bring me forth in the paths of righteousness, for His Name's sake. Yea, Though I walk through the valley of the shadow of death, I will fear no evil; / for Thou art with me; Thy rod and

Thy staff comfort me. Thou shalt prepare a table before me against them that trouble me; / Thou hast anointed my head with oil, and my cup shall be full. Alleluia.

THE GOSPEL. *Saint John* 10. 1-10.

AT that time Jesus said unto them: Verily, verily, I say unto you, He that entereth not by the door into the sheepfold, but climbeth up some other way, the same is a thief and a robber. But he that entereth in by the door is the shepherd of the sheep. To him the porter openeth; and the sheep hear his voice: and he calleth his own sheep by name, and leadeth them out. And when he putteth forth his own sheep, he goeth before them, and the sheep follow him: for they know his voice. And a stranger will they not follow, but will flee from him: for they know not the voice of strangers. This parable spake Jesus unto them: but they understood not what things they were which He spake unto them. Then said Jesus unto them again, Verily, verily, I say unto you, I am the Door of the sheep. All that ever came before me are thieves and robbers: but the sheep did not hear them. I am the Door: by me if any man enter in, he shall be saved, and shall go in and out, and find pasture. The thief cometh not, but for to steal, and to kill, and to destroy: I am come that they might have life, and that they might have it more abundantly.

TRINITY SUNDAY

THE INTROIT. *Psalm* 8. 1-5 & 9.

O LORD our Governor, how excellent is Thy Name in all the world, / Thou that hast set Thy glory above the heavens! Out of the mouth of very babes and sucklings hast Thou ordained strength, because of Thine enemies, / that Thou mightest still the enemy and the avenger. For when I consider Thy heavens, even the works of Thy fingers; / the moon and the stars, which Thou hast ordained; What is man, that Thou art mindful of him, / and the son of man, that Thou visitest him? Thou madest him a little lower than the angels, / and hast crowned him with glory and worship. O Lord our Governor, / how excellent is Thy Name in all the world!

GLORY be to the Father, and to the Son, / and to the Holy Ghost;

As it was in the beginning, is now, and ever shall be, / world without end. Amen.

THE COLLECT.

ALMIGHTY and everlasting God, Who hast given unto us Thy servants grace by the confession of a true Faith, to acknowledge the glory of the eternal Trinity, and in the power of the Divine Majesty to worship the Unity: We beseech Thee, that Thou wouldest keep us steadfast in this Faith, and evermore defend us from all adversities, Who livest and reignest, one God, world without end. *Amen.*

FOR THE EPISTLE. *Revelation* 4. 1-11.

AFTER this I looked, and, behold, a door was opened in heaven: and the first voice which I heard was as it were of a trumpet talking with me; which said, Come up hither, and I will shew thee things which must be hereafter. And immediately I was in the spirit: and, behold, a throne was set in heaven, and One sat on the throne. And He that sat was to look upon like a jasper and a sardine stone: and there was a rainbow round about the throne, in sight like unto an emerald. And round about the throne were four and twenty seats: and upon the seats I saw four and twenty elders sitting, clothed in white raiment; and they had on their heads crowns of gold. And out of the throne proceeded lightnings and thunderings and voices: and there were seven lamps of fire burning before the throne, which are the seven Spirits of God. And before the throne there was a sea of glass like unto crystal: and in the midst of the throne, and round about the throne, were four beasts full of eyes before and behind. And the first beast was like a lion, and the second beast like a calf, and the third beast had a face as a man, and the fourth beast was like a flying eagle. And the four beasts had each of them six wings about him; and they were full of eyes within: and they rest not day and night, saying, Holy, holy, holy, Lord God Almighty, which was, and is, and is to come. And when those beasts give glory and honour and thanks to Him that sat on the throne, Who liveth for ever and ever, the four and twenty elders fall down before Him that sat on the throne, and worship Him that liveth for ever and ever, and cast their crowns before the throne, saying, Thou art worthy, O Lord, to receive glory and honour and power: for Thou hast created all things, and for Thy pleasure they are and were created.

THE GRADUAL. *Psalm* 136. 1-3.

ALLELUIA, Alleluia. O give thanks unto the Lord, for He is gracious; / and His mercy endureth for ever. O give thanks unto the God of all gods / for His mercy endureth for ever. O thank the Lord of all Lords / for His mercy endureth for ever. Alleluia.

THE GOSPEL. *Saint John* 3. 1-15.

THERE was a man of the Pharisees, named Nicodemus, a ruler of the Jews: the same came to Jesus by night, and said unto Him, Rabbi, we know that Thou art a teacher come from God: for no man can do these miracles that Thou doest, except God be with Him. Jesus answered and said unto him, Verily, verily, I say unto thee, Except a man be born again, he cannot see the kingdom of God. Nicodemus saith unto Him, How can a man be born when he is old? can he enter the second time into his mother's womb, and be born? Jesus answered, Verily, verily, I say unto thee, Except a man be born of water and of the Spirit, he cannot enter into the kingdom of God. That which is born of the flesh is flesh; and that which is born of the Spirit is spirit. Marvel not that I said unto thee, Ye must be born again. The wind bloweth where it listeth, and thou hearest the sound thereof, but canst not tell whence it cometh, and whither it goeth: so is every one that is born of the Spirit. Nicodemus answered and said unto Him, How can these things be? Jesus answered and said unto him, Art thou a master of Israel, and knowest not these things? Verily, verily, I say unto thee, We speak that we do know, and testify that we have seen; and ye receive not our witness. If I have told you earthly things, and ye believe not, how shall ye believe, if I tell you of heavenly things? And no man hath ascended up to heaven, but He that came down from heaven, even the Son of Man which is in heaven. And as Moses lifted up the serpent in the wilderness, even so must the Son of Man be lifted up: that whosoever believeth in Him should not perish, but have eternal life.

CORPUS CHRISTI
[The Thursday after Trinity Sunday.]

THE INTROIT. *Psalm* 145. 7-17.

THE memorial of Thine abundant kindness shall be shewed, / and men shall sing of Thy righteousness. The Lord is gracious and merciful, / long-suffering and of great goodness. The Lord is loving unto every man, / and His mercy is over all His works. All Thy works praise Thee, O Lord; / and Thy saints give thanks unto Thee. They shew the glory of Thy kingdom, / and talk of Thy power; That Thy power, Thy glory, and mightiness of Thy kingdom, / might be known unto men. Thy kingdom is an everlasting kingdom, / and Thy dominion endureth throughout all ages. The

Lord upholdeth all such as fall, / and lifteth up all those that are down. The eyes of all wait upon Thee, O Lord, / and Thou givest them their meat in due season. Thou openest Thine hand, / and fillest all things living with plenteousness. The Lord is righteous in all His ways, / and holy in all His works.

GLORY be to the Father, and to the Son, / and to the Holy Ghost;
As it was in the beginning, is now, and ever shall be, / world without end. Amen.

THE COLLECT.

O GOD, Who in a wonderful Sacrament hast left unto us a memorial of Thy Passion: Grant us so to venerate the sacred mysteries of Thy Body and Blood, that we may evermore perceive within ourselves the fruit of Thy redemption; Who with the Father and the Holy Ghost livest and reignest ever one God, world without end. *Amen.*

THE EPISTLE. I *Corinthians* 11. 23-29.

FOR I have received of the Lord that which also I delivered unto you, That the Lord Jesus the same night in which He was betrayed took bread: and when He had given thanks, He brake it, and said, Take, eat; this is my Body, which is broken for you: This do in remembrance of me. After the same manner also He took the Cup, when He had supped, saying, This Cup is the New Testament in my Blood: This do ye, as oft as ye drink it, in remembrance of me. For as often as ye eat this Bread, and drink this Cup, ye do shew the Lord's death till He come. Wherefore whosoever shall eat this Bread, or drink this Cup of the Lord, unworthily, shall be guilty of the Body and Blood of the Lord. But let a man examine himself, and so let him eat of that Bread, and Drink of that Cup. For he that eateth and drinketh unworthily, eateth and drinketh damnation to himself, not discerning the Lord's Body.

THE GRADUAL. *Psalm* 116. 11-19.

ALLELUIA, Alleluia. What reward shall I give unto the Lord / for all the benefits that He hath done unto me? I will receive the Cup of salvation, / and call upon the Name of the Lord. I will pay my vows now in the presence of all His people: / right dear in the sight of the Lord is the death of His saints. Behold, O Lord, how that I am Thy servant: / I am Thy servant, and the son of Thy handmaid; Thou hast broken my bonds in sunder. I will offer unto Thee the sacrifice of thanksgiving, / and will call upon the Name of the Lord. I will pay my vows unto the Lord, in the sight of all His people; / in the courts of the Lord's house, even in the midst of thee, O Jerusalem. Praise the Lord. Alleluia.

THE GOSPEL. *Saint John* 6. 47-69.

AT that time Jesus said unto the Jews: Verily, verily, I say unto you, He that believeth on me hath everlasting life. I am that Bread of life. Your fathers did eat manna in the wilderness, and are dead. This is that Bread which cometh down from heaven, that a man may eat thereof, and not die. I am the living Bread which came down from heaven: if any man eat of this Bread, he shall live forever: and the Bread that I will give is my Flesh, which I will give for the life of the world. The Jews therefore strove among themselves, saying, How can this man give us His Flesh to eat? Then Jesus said unto them, Verily, verily, I say unto you, Except ye eat the Flesh of the Son of Man, and drink His Blood, ye have no life in you. Whoso eateth my Flesh, and drinketh my Blood, hath eternal life; and I will raise him up at the last day. For my Flesh is meat indeed, and my Blood is drink indeed. He that eateth my Flesh, and drinketh my Blood, dwelleth in me, and I in him. As the living Father hath sent me, and I live by the Father: so he that eateth me, even he shall live by me. This is that Bread which came down from heaven: not as your fathers did eat manna, and are dead: for he that eateth of this Bread shall live forever. These things said He in the synagogue, as He taught in Capernaum. Many therefore of His disciples, when they had heard this, said, This is an hard saying; who can hear it? When Jesus knew in Himself that His disciples murmured at it, He said unto them, Doth this offend you? What and if ye shall see the Son of Man ascend up where He was before? It is the Spirit that quickeneth; the flesh profiteth nothing: the words that I speak unto you, they are spirit, and they are life. But there are some of you that believe not. For Jesus knew from the beginning who they were that believed not, and who should betray Him. And He said, Therefore said I unto you, that no man can come unto me, except it were given unto him of my Father. From that time many of His disciples went back, and walked no more with Him. Then said Jesus unto the twelve, Will ye also go away? Then Simon Peter answered Him, Lord to whom shall we go? Thou hast the words of eternal life. And we believe and are sure that Thou art that Christ, the Son of the living God.

THE FIRST SUNDAY AFTER TRINITY

THE INTROIT. *Psalm* 13. 1-6.

HOW long wilt Thou forget me, O Lord, for ever; / how long wilt Thou hide Thy face from me? How long shall I seek counsel in my soul, and be so vexed in my heart; / how long shall mine enemies triumph over me? Consider, and hear me, O Lord my God; / lighten mine eyes, that I sleep not in death. Lest mine enemy say, I have prevailed against him; / for if I be cast down, they that trouble me will rejoice at it. But my trust is in Thy mercy, / and my heart is joyful in Thy salvation. I will sing of the Lord, because He hath dealt so lovingly with me; / yea, I will praise the Name of the Lord Most High.

GLORY be to the Father, and to the Son, / and to the Holy Ghost;
As it was in the beginning, is now, and ever shall be, / world without end. Amen.

THE COLLECT.

O GOD, the Strength of all them that put their trust in Thee: Mercifully accept our prayers; and because through the weakness of our mortal nature we can do no good thing without Thee, grant us the help of Thy grace, that in keeping of Thy commandments we may please Thee, both in will and deed; through Jesus Christ our Lord. *Amen.*

THE EPISTLE. I *Saint John* 4. 1-21.

BELOVED, believe not every spirit, but try the spirits whether they are of God: because many false prophets are gone out into the world. Hereby know ye the Spirit of God: Every spirit that confesseth that Jesus Christ is come in the flesh is of God: And every spirit that confesseth not that Jesus Christ is come in the flesh is not of God: and this is that spirit of antichrist, whereof ye have heard that it should come; and even now already is it in the world. Ye are of God, little children, and have overcome them: because greater is He that is in you, than he that is in the world. They are of the world: therefore speak they of the world, and the world heareth them. We are of God: he that knoweth God heareth us; he that is not of God heareth not us. Hereby know we the spirit of truth, and the spirit of error. Brethren, let us love one another: for love is of God; and every one that loveth is born of God, and knoweth God. He that loveth not knoweth not God; for God is love. In this was manifested the love of God toward us, because that God sent His only-begotten Son into the world, that we might live through Him. Herein is love, not that we loved God, but that He loved us, and sent His Son to be the propitiation for our sins. Beloved, if God so loved us, we ought also to love one another. No man hath seen God at any time. If we love one another, God dwelleth in us, and His love is perfected in us. Hereby know we that we dwell in Him, and He in us, because He hath given us of His Spirit. And we have seen and do testify that the Father sent the Son to be the Saviour of the world. Whosoever shall confess that Jesus is the Son of God, God dwelleth in him, and he in God. And we have known and believed the love that God hath to us. God is love; and he that dwelleth in love dwelleth in God, and God in him. Herein is our love made perfect, that we may have boldness in the day of judgement: because as He is, so are we in this world. There is no fear in love; but perfect love casteth out fear: because fear hath torment. He that feareth is not made perfect in love. We love Him, because He first loved us. If a man say, I love God, and hateth his brother, he is a liar: for he that loveth not his brother whom he hath seen, how can he love God Whom he hath not seen? And this commandment have we from Him, That he who loveth God love his brother also.

THE GRADUAL. *Psalm* 41. 1-2.
ALLELUIA, Alleluia. Blessed is he that considereth the poor and needy; / the Lord shall deliver him in the time of trouble. The Lord preserve him, and keep him alive, that he may be blessed upon earth; / and deliver not Thou him into the will of his enemies. Alleluia.

THE GOSPEL. *Saint Luke* 16. 19-31.
AT that time Jesus said unto them: There was a certain rich man, which was clothed in purple and fine linen, and fared sumptuously every day: and there was a certain beggar named Lazarus, which was laid at his gate, full of sores, and desiring to be fed with the crumbs which fell from the rich man's table: moreover the dogs came and licked his sores. And it came to pass, that the beggar died, and was carried by the angels into Abraham's bosom: the rich man also died, and was buried; and in hell he lift up his eyes, being in torments, and seeth Abraham afar off, and Lazarus in his bosom. And he cried and said, Father Abraham, have mercy on me, and send Lazarus, that he may dip the tip of his finger in water, and cool my tongue; for I am tormented in this flame. But Abraham said, Son, remember that thou in thy lifetime receivedst thy good things, and likewise Lazarus evil things: but now he is comforted, and thou art tormented. And beside all this, between us and you there is a great gulf fixed: so that they which would pass from hence to you cannot; neither can they pass to us, that would come from thence. Then he said, I pray thee therefore, Father, that thou wouldest send him to my father's house: for I have five brethren; that he may testify unto them, lest they also come into this place of torment. Abraham saith unto him, They have Moses and the Prophets; let them hear them. And he said, Nay, Father Abraham: but if one went unto them from the dead, they will repent. And he said unto him, If they hear not Moses and the Prophets, neither will they be persuaded, though one rose from the dead.

THE SECOND SUNDAY AFTER TRINITY

THE INTROIT. *Psalm* 18. 18-22.
THEY prevented me in the day of my trouble, / but the Lord was my Upholder. He brought me forth also into a place of liberty; / He brought me forth, even because He had a favour unto me. The Lord shall reward me after my righteous dealing, / according to the cleanness of my hands shall He recompense me. Because I have kept the ways of the Lord, / and have not forsaken my God, as the wicked doth. For I have an eye unto all His laws, / and will not cast out His commandments from me.

THE PROPERS OF THE YEAR

GLORY be to the Father, and to the Son, / and to the Holy Ghost;
As it was in the beginning, is now, and ever shall be, / world without end. Amen.

THE COLLECT.

O LORD, Who never failest to help and govern them whom Thou dost bring up in Thy steadfast fear and love: Keep us, we beseech Thee, under the protection of Thy good Providence, and make us to have a perpetual fear and love of Thy holy Name; through Jesus Christ our Lord. *Amen.*

THE EPISTLE. I *Saint John* 3. 13-24.

MARVEL not, my brethren, if the world hate you. We know that we have passed from death unto life, because we love the brethren. He that loveth not his brother abideth in death. Whosoever hateth his brother is a murderer: and ye know that no murderer hath eternal life abiding in him. Hereby perceive we the love of God, because He laid down His life for us: and we ought to lay down our lives for the brethren. But whoso hath this world's good, and seeth his brother have need, and shutteth up his depths of compassion from him, how dwelleth the love of God in him? My little children, let us not love in word, neither in tongue; but in deed and in truth. And hereby we know that we are of the truth, and shall assure our hearts before Him. For if our heart condemn us, God is greater than our heart, and knoweth all things. Beloved, if our heart condemn us not, then have we confidence toward God. And whatsoever we ask, we receive of Him, because we keep His commandments, and do those things that are pleasing in His sight. And this is His commandment, that we should believe on the Name of His Son Jesus Christ, and love one another, as He gave us commandment. And he that keepeth His commandments dwelleth in Him, and He in him. And hereby we know that He abideth in us, by the Spirit which He hath given us.

THE GRADUAL. *Psalm* 23. 4-6.

ALLELUIA, Alleluia. Yea, though I walk through the valley of the shadow of death, I will fear no evil; / for Thou art with me; Thy rod and Thy staff comfort me. Thou shalt prepare a table before me in the presence of them that trouble me; / Thou hast anointed my head with oil, and my cup shall be full. Surely Thy loving-kindness and mercy shall follow me all the days of my life, / and I will dwell in the house of the Lord for ever. Alleluia.

THE GOSPEL. *Saint Luke* 14. 16-24.

AT that time Jesus said unto them: A certain man made a great supper, and bade many: and sent his servant at supper time to say to them that were bidden, Come; for all things are now ready. And they all with one consent began to make excuse. The first said unto him, I have bought a piece of ground, and I must needs go and see it: I pray thee have me excused. And another said, I have bought five yoke of oxen, and I go to prove them: I pray thee have me excused. And another said, I have married a wife, and therefore I cannot come. So that servant came, and shewed his Lord these things. Then the master of the house being angry said to his servant, Go out quickly into the streets and lanes of the city, and bring in hither the poor, and the maimed, and the halt, and the blind. And the servant said, Lord, it is done as thou hast commanded, and yet there is room. And the Lord said unto the servant, Go out into the highways and hedges, and compel them to come in, that my house may be filled. For I say unto you, that none of those men which were bidden shall taste of my supper.

THE THIRD SUNDAY AFTER TRINITY

THE INTROIT. *Psalm* 25. 15-21.

TURN Thee unto me, and have mercy upon me, / for I am desolate and in misery. The sorrows of my heart are enlarged: / O bring Thou me out of my troubles. Look upon my adversity and misery, / and forgive me all my sin. Consider mine enemies, how many they are; / and they bear a tyrannous hate against me. O keep my soul, and deliver me; / let me not be confounded, for I have put my trust in Thee. Let perfectness and righteous dealing wait upon me, / for my hope hath been in Thee. Deliver Israel, O God / out of all his troubles.

GLORY be to the Father, and to the Son, / and to the Holy Ghost;
As it was in the beginning, is now, and ever shall be, / world without end. Amen.

THE COLLECT.

O LORD, we beseech Thee mercifully to hear us; and grant that we, to whom Thou hast given an hearty desire to pray, may by Thy mighty aid be defended and comforted in all dangers and adversities; through Jesus Christ our Lord. *Amen.*

THE EPISTLE. I *Saint Peter* 5. 5-11.

ALL of you be subject one to another, and be clothed with humility: for God resisteth the proud, and giveth grace to the humble. Humble yourselves therefore under the mighty hand of God, that He may exalt you in due time: casting all your care upon Him; for He careth for you. Be sober, be vigilant; because your adversary the devil, as a roaring lion, walketh about, seeking whom he may devour: whom resist steadfast in the faith, knowing that the same afflictions are accomplished in your brethren that are in the world. But the God of all grace, Who hath called us unto His eternal glory by Christ Jesus, after that ye have suffered a while, make you perfect, stablish, strengthen, settle you. To Him be glory and dominion for ever and ever. Amen.

THE GRADUAL. *Psalm* 7. 8-12.

ALLELUIA, Alleluia. The Lord shall judge the people; give sentence with me, O Lord, / according to my righteousness, and according to the innocency that is in me. O let the wickedness of the ungodly come to an end; / but guide Thou the just. For the righteous God / trieth the very hearts and reins. My help cometh of God, / Who preserveth them that are true of heart. God is a righteous Judge, strong and patient; / and God is provoked every day. If a man will not turn, He will whet His sword; / He hath bent His bow, and made it ready. Alleluia.

THE GOSPEL. *Saint Luke* 15. 1-10.

THEN drew near unto Jesus all the publicans and sinners for to hear Him. And the Pharisees and scribes murmured, saying, This man receiveth sinners, and eateth with them. And He spake this parable unto them, saying, What man of you, having an hundred sheep, if he lose one of them, doth not leave the ninety and nine in the wilderness, and go after that which is lost, until he find it? And when he hath found it, he layeth it on his shoulders, rejoicing. And when he cometh home, he calleth together his friends and neighbours, saying unto them, Rejoice with me; for I have found my sheep which was lost. I say unto you, that likewise joy shall be in heaven over one sinner that repenteth, more than over ninety and nine just persons, which need no repentance. Either what woman having ten pieces of silver, if she lose one piece, doth not light a candle, and sweep the house, and seek diligently till she find it? And when she hath found it, she calleth her friends and her neighbours together, saying, Rejoice with me; for I have found the piece which I had lost.

Likewise, I say unto you, there is joy in the presence of the angels of God over one sinner that repenteth.

The Fourth Sunday after Trinity

The Introit. *Psalm* 27. 1-7.

THE Lord is my Light and my Salvation; whom then shall I fear? / the Lord is the Strength of my life; of whom then shall I be afraid? When the wicked, even mine enemies and my foes, came upon me to eat up my flesh; / they stumbled and fell. Though an host of men were laid against me, yet shall not my heart be afraid; / and though there rose up war against me, yet will I put my trust in Him. One thing have I desired of the Lord, which I will require: / even that I may dwell in the house of the Lord all the days of my life, to behold the fair beauty of the Lord, and to visit His temple. For in the time of trouble He shall hide me in His tabernacle; / yea, in the secret place of His dwelling shall He hide me, and set me up upon a rock of stone. And now shall He lift up mine head / above mine enemies round about me. Therefore will I offer in His dwelling an oblation with great gladness; / I will sing, and speak praises unto the Lord.

GLORY be to the Father, and to the Son, / and to the Holy Ghost;

As it was in the beginning, is now, and ever shall be, / world without end. Amen.

The Collect.

O GOD, the Protector of all that trust in Thee, without Whom nothing is strong, nothing is holy: Increase and multiply upon us Thy mercy; that, Thou being our Ruler and Guide, we may so pass through things temporal, that we finally lose not the things eternal; grant this, O heavenly Father, for Jesus Christ's sake our Lord. *Amen.*

The Epistle. *Romans* 8. 18-23.

I RECKON that the sufferings of this present time are not worthy to be compared with the glory which shall be revealed in us. For the earnest expectation of the creature waiteth for the manifestation of the sons of God. For the creature was made subject to vanity, not willingly, but by reason of Him who hath subjected the same in hope, because the creature itself also shall be delivered from the bondage of corruption into the glorious liberty of the children of God. For we know that the whole creation groaneth and travaileth in pain together until now. And not only they, but ourselves also, which have the first-fruits of the Spirit, even we ourselves groan within ourselves, waiting for the adoption, to wit, the redemption of our body.

The Gradual. *Psalm* 9. 9-12.

ALLELUIA, Alleluia. The Lord also will be a defence for the oppressed, / even a refuge in due time of trouble. And they that know Thy Name will put their trust in Thee; / for Thou, Lord, hast never failed them that seek Thee. O praise the Lord which dwelleth in Sion; / shew the people of His doings. For when He maketh inquisition for blood, He remembereth them, / and forgetteth not the complaint of the poor. Alleluia.

The Gospel. *Saint Luke* 6. 36-42.

AT that time Jesus said unto them: Be ye therefore merciful, as your Father also is merciful. Judge not, and ye shall not be judged: condemn not, and ye shall not be condemned: forgive, and ye shall be forgiven: give, and it shall be given unto you; good measure, pressed down, and shaken together, and running over, shall men give into your bosom. For with the same measure that ye mete withal it shall be measured to you again. And He spake a parable unto them, Can the blind lead the blind? shall they not both fall into the ditch? The disciple is not above his master: but every one that is perfect shall be as his master. And why beholdest thou the mote that is in thy brother's eye, but perceivest not the beam that is in thine own eye? Either how canst thou say to thy brother, Brother, let me pull out the mote that is in thine eye, when thou thyself beholdest not the beam that is in thine own eye? Thou hypocrite, cast out first the beam out of thine own eye, and then shalt thou see clearly to pull out the mote that is in thy brother's eye.

THE FIFTH SUNDAY AFTER TRINITY

THE INTROIT. *Psalm* 27. 8-16.

Hearken unto my voice, O Lord, when I cry unto Thee; / have mercy upon me, and hear me. My heart hath talked of Thee, Seek ye my face: / Thy face, Lord, will I seek. O hide not Thou Thy face from me, / nor cast Thy servant away in displeasure. Thou hast been my succour; / leave me not, neither forsake me, O God of my salvation. When my father and my mother forsake me, / the Lord taketh me up. Teach me Thy way, O Lord, / and lead me in the right way, because of mine enemies. Deliver me not over into the will of mine adversaries, / for there are false witnesses risen up against me, and such as speak wrong. I should utterly have fainted; / but that I believe verily to see the goodness of the Lord in the land of the living. O tarry thou the Lord's leisure; / be strong, and He shall comfort thine heart ; and put thou thy trust in the Lord.

GLORY be to the Father, and to the Son, / and to the Holy Ghost;
As it was in the beginning, is now, and ever shall be, / world without end. Amen.

THE COLLECT.

GRANT, O Lord, we beseech Thee, that the course of this world may be so peaceably ordered by Thy governance, that Thy Church may joyfully serve Thee in all godly quietness; through Jesus Christ our Lord. *Amen.*

THE EPISTLE. I *Saint Peter* 3. 8-15.

FINALLY be ye all of one mind, having compassion one of another; love as brethren, be pitiful, be courteous: not rendering evil for evil, or railing for railing: but contrariwise blessing; knowing that ye are thereunto called, that ye should inherit a blessing. For he that will love life, and see good days, let him refrain his tongue from evil, and his lips that they speak no guile: let him eschew evil, and do good; let him seek peace, and ensue it. For the eyes of the Lord are over the righteous, and His ears are open unto their prayers: but the face of the Lord is against them that do evil. And who is he that will harm you, if ye be followers of that which is good? But and if ye suffer for righteousness' sake, happy are ye: and be not afraid of their terror, neither be troubled; but sanctify the Lord God in your hearts.

THE GRADUAL. *Psalm* 84. 8-13.

ALLELUIA, Alleluia. O Lord God of hosts, hear my prayer: / hearken, O God of Jacob. Behold, O God our Defender, / and look upon the face of Thine Anointed. For one day in Thy courts / is better than a thousand. I had rather be a door-keeper in the house of my God, / than to dwell in the tents of ungodliness. For the Lord God is a Light and Defence; / the Lord will give grace and worship, and no good thing shall He withhold from them that live a godly life. O Lord God of hosts, / blessed is the man that putteth his trust in Thee. Alleluia.

THE GOSPEL. *Saint Luke 5.* 1-11.

AND IT came to pass, that, as the people pressed upon Jesus to hear the Word of God, He stood by the lake of Gennesaret, and saw two ships standing by the lake: but the fishermen were gone out of them, and were washing their nets. And He entered into one of the ships, which was Simon's, and prayed him that he would thrust out a little from the land. And He sat down, and taught the people out of the ship. Now when He had left speaking, He said unto Simon, Launch out into the deep, and let down your nets for a draught. And Simon answering said unto Him, Master, we have toiled all the night, and have taken nothing: nevertheless at Thy word I will let down the net. And when they had this done, they inclosed a great multitude of fishes: and their net brake. And they beckoned unto their partners, which were in the other ship, that they should come and help them. And they came, and filled both the ships, so that they began to sink. When Simon Peter saw it, he fell down at Jesus' knees, saying, Depart from me; for I am a sinful man, O Lord. For he was astonished, and all that were with him, at the draught of the fishes which they had taken: and so was also James, and John, the sons of Zebedee, which were partners with Simon. And Jesus said unto Simon, Fear not; from henceforth thou shalt catch men. And when they had brought their ships to land, they forsook all, and followed Him.

THE SIXTH SUNDAY AFTER TRINITY

THE INTROIT. *Psalm* 28. 7-10.

PRAISED be the Lord, / for He hath heard the voice of my humble petitions. The Lord is my Strength and my Shield; my heart hath trusted in Him, and I am helped; / therefore my heart danceth for joy, and in my song will I praise Him. The Lord is my Strength, / and He is the wholesome Defence of His Anointed. O save Thy people, and give Thy blessing unto Thine inheritance; / feed them, and set them up for ever.

GLORY be to the Father, and to the Son, / and to the Holy Ghost;

As it was in the beginning, is now, and ever shall be, / world without end. Amen.

THE COLLECT.

O GOD, Who hast prepared for all them that love Thee such good things as pass man's understanding: Pour into our hearts, we beseech Thee, such love toward Thee, that we, loving Thee above all things, may obtain Thy promises, which exceed all that we can desire; through Jesus Christ our Lord. *Amen.*

THE EPISTLE. *Romans* 6. 1-11.

WHAT shall we say then? Shall we continue in sin, that grace may abound? God forbid. How shall we, that are dead to sin, live any longer therein? Know ye not, that so many of us as were baptised into Jesus Christ were baptised into His death? Therefore we are buried with Him by baptism into death: that like as Christ was raised up from the dead by the glory of the Father, even so we also should walk in newness of life. For if we have been planted together in the likeness of His death, we shall be also in the likeness of His resurrection: knowing this, that our old man is crucified with Him, that the body of sin might be destroyed, that henceforth we should not serve sin. For he that is dead is freed from sin. Now if we be dead with Christ, we believe that we shall also live with Him: knowing that Christ being raised from the dead dieth no more; death hath no more dominion over Him. For in that He died, He died unto sin once: but in that He liveth, He liveth unto God. Likewise reckon ye also yourselves to be dead indeed unto sin, but alive unto God through Jesus Christ our Lord.

THE GRADUAL. *Psalm* 90. 13-17.

ALLELUIA, Alleluia. Turn Thee again, O Lord, at the last, / and be gracious unto Thy servants. O satisfy us with Thy mercy, and that soon; / so shall we rejoice and be glad all the days of our life. Comfort us again now after the time that Thou hast plagued us, / and for the years wherein we have suffered adversity. Shew Thy servants Thy work, / and their children Thy glory. And the glorious majesty of the Lord our God be upon us: / prosper Thou the work of our hands upon us; O prosper Thou our handy-work. Alleluia.

THE GOSPEL. *Saint Luke* 6. 27-38.

JESUS said, Love your enemies, do good to them which hate you, bless them that curse you, and pray for them which despitefully use you. And unto him that smiteth thee on the one cheek, offer also the other; and him that taketh away thy cloak, forbid not to take thy coat also. Give to every man that asketh of thee; and of him that taketh away thy goods, ask them not again. And as ye would that men should do to you, do ye also to them likewise. For if ye love them which love you, what thank have ye? for sinners also love those that love them. And if ye do good to them which do good to you, what thank have ye? for sinners also do even the same. And if ye lend to them of whom ye hope to receive, what thank have ye? for sinners also lend to sinners, to receive as much again. But love ye your enemies, and do good, and lend, hoping for nothing again; and your reward shall be great, and ye shall be the children of the Highest: for He is kind unto the unthankful, and to the evil. Be ye therefore merciful, as your Father also is merciful. Judge not, and ye shall not be judged: condemn not, and ye shall not be condemned: forgive, and ye shall be forgiven: give, and it shall be given unto you; good measure, pressed down, and shaken together, and running over, shall men give into your bosom. For with the same measure that ye mete withal it shall be measured to you again.

Or this.

THE GOSPEL. *Saint Matthew* 5. 20-26.

JESUS said unto His disciples, Except your righteousness shall exceed the righteousness of the Scribes and Pharisees, ye shall in no case enter into the kingdom of heaven. Ye have heard that it was said of them of old time, Thou shalt not kill; and whosoever shall kill shall be in danger of the judgement: but I say unto you, that whosoever is angry with his brother without a cause shall be in danger of the judgement: and whosoever shall say to his brother, Raca, shall be in danger of the council: but whosoever shall say, Thou fool, shall be in danger of hell fire. Therefore if thou bring thy gift to the altar, and there rememberest that thy brother hath ought against thee; leave there thy gift before the altar, and go thy way; first be reconciled to thy brother, and then come and offer thy gift. Agree with thine adversary quickly, whiles thou art in the way with him; lest at any time the adversary deliver thee to the judge, and the judge deliver thee to the officer, and thou be cast into prison. Verily I say unto thee, thou shalt by no means come out thence, till thou hast paid the uttermost farthing.

THE SEVENTH SUNDAY AFTER TRINITY

THE INTROIT. *Psalm* 47. 1-4.

CLAP your hands together, all ye people; / O sing unto God with the voice of melody. For the Lord is high, and to be feared; / He is the great King upon all the earth. He shall subdue the people under us, / and the nations under our feet. He shall choose out an heritage for us; / even the worship of Jacob, whom He loved.

GLORY be to the Father, and to the Son, / and to the Holy Ghost;
As it was in the beginning, is now, and ever shall be, / world without end. Amen.

THE COLLECT.

LORD of all power and might, Who art the Author and Giver of all good things: Graft in our hearts the love of Thy Name, increase in us true religion, nourish us with all goodness, and of Thy great mercy keep us in the same; through Jesus Christ our Lord. *Amen.*

THE EPISTLE. *Romans* 6. 12-23.

LET not sin therefore reign in your mortal body, that ye should obey it in the lusts thereof. Neither yield ye your members as instruments of unrighteousness unto sin: but yield yourselves unto God, as those that are alive from the dead, and your members as instruments of righteousness unto God. For sin shall not have dominion over you: for ye are not under the law, but under grace. What then? shall we sin, because we are not under the law, but under grace? God forbid. Know ye not, that to whom ye yield yourselves servants to obey, his servants ye are to whom ye obey; whether of sin unto death, or of obedience unto righteousness? But God be thanked, that ye were the servants of sin, but ye have obeyed from the heart that form of doctrine which was delivered you. Being then made free from sin, ye became the servants of righteousness. I speak after the manner of men because of the infirmity of your flesh: for as ye have yielded your members servants to uncleanness and to iniquity unto iniquity; even so now yield your members servants to righteousness unto holiness. For when ye were the servants of sin, ye were free from righteousness. What fruit had ye then in those things whereof ye are now ashamed? for the end of those things is death. But now being made free from sin, and become servants to God, ye have your fruit unto holiness, and the end everlasting life. For the wages of sin is death; but the gift of God is eternal life through Jesus Christ our Lord.

THE GRADUAL. *Psalm* 34. 12-15.

ALLELUIA, Alleluia. What man is he that lusteth to live, / and would fain see good days? Keep thy tongue from evil, / and thy lips, that they speak no guile. Eschew evil, and do good; / seek peace, and pursue it. The eyes of the Lord are over the righteous, / and His ears are open unto their prayers. Alleluia.

THE GOSPEL. *Saint Mark* 8. 1-9.

IN those days the multitude being very great, and having nothing to eat, Jesus called His disciples unto Him, and saith unto them, I have compassion on the multitude, because they have now been with me three days, and have nothing to eat: and if I send them away fasting to their own houses, they will faint by the way: for divers of them came from far. And His disciples answered Him, From whence can a man satisfy these men with bread here in the wilderness? And He asked them, How many loaves have ye? And they said, Seven. And He commanded the people to sit down on the ground: and He took the seven loaves, and gave thanks, and brake, and gave to His disciples to set before them; and they did set them before the people. And they had a few small fishes: and He blessed, and commanded to set them also before them. So they did eat, and were filled: and they took up of the broken meat that was left seven baskets. And they that had eaten were about four thousand: and He sent them away.

THE EIGHTH SUNDAY AFTER TRINITY

THE INTROIT. *Psalm* 48. 1-8.

GREAT is the Lord, and highly to be praised, / in the city of our God, even upon His holy hill. The hill of Sion is a fair place, / and the joy of the whole earth; upon the north-side lieth the city of the great King; God is well known in her palaces as a sure Refuge. For lo, the kings of the earth / are gathered, and gone by together. They marvelled to see such things; / they were astonished, and suddenly cast down. Fear came there upon them, and sorrow, / as upon a woman in her travail. Thou shalt break the ships of the sea / through the east-wind. Like as we have heard, / so have we seen in the city of the Lord of hosts, in the city of our God: God upholdeth the same for ever. We wait for Thy loving-kindness, O God, / in the midst of Thy temple.

GLORY be to the Father, and to the Son, / and to the Holy Ghost;

As it was in the beginning, is now, and ever shall be, / world without end. Amen.

THE COLLECT.

O GOD, Whose never-failing providence ordereth all things both in heaven and earth: We humbly beseech Thee to put away from us all hurtful things, and to give us those things which be profitable for us; through Jesus Christ our Lord. *Amen.*

THE EPISTLE. *Romans* 8. 12-17.

BRETHREN, we are debtors, not to the flesh, to live after the flesh. For if ye live after the flesh, ye shall die: but if ye through the Spirit do mortify the deeds of the body, ye shall live. For as many as are led by the Spirit of God, they are the sons of God. For ye have not received the spirit of bondage again to fear; but ye have received the Spirit of adoption, whereby we cry, Abba, Father. The Spirit Himself beareth witness with our spirit, that we are the children of God: and if children, then heirs; heirs of God, and joint-heirs with Christ; if so be that we suffer with Him, that we may be also glorified together.

THE GRADUAL. *Psalm* 48. 13-15.

ALLELUIA, Alleluia. Walk about Sion, and go round about her, / and tell the towers thereof. Mark well her bulwarks, set up her houses, / that ye may tell them that come after. For this God is our God for ever and ever; / He shall be our Guide unto death. Alleluia.

THE GOSPEL. *Saint Matthew* 7. 7-21.

AT that time Jesus said unto them: Ask, and it shall be given you; seek, and ye shall find; knock, and it shall be opened unto you: for every one that asketh receiveth; and he that seeketh findeth; and to him that knocketh it shall be opened. Or what man is there of you, whom if his son ask bread, will he give him a stone? Or if he ask a fish, will he give him a serpent? If ye then, being evil, know how to give good gifts unto your children, how much more shall your Father which is in heaven give good things to them that ask Him? Therefore all things whatsoever ye would that men should do to you, do ye even so to them: for this is the Law and the Prophets. Enter ye in at the strait gate: for wide is the gate, and broad is the way, that leadeth to destruction, and many there be which go in thereat: because strait is the gate, and narrow is the way, which leadeth unto life, and few there be that find it. Beware of false prophets, which come to you in sheep's clothing, but inwardly they are ravening wolves. Ye shall know them by their fruits. Do men gather grapes of thorns, or figs of thistles? Even so every good tree bringeth forth good fruit; but a corrupt tree bringeth forth evil fruit. A good tree cannot bring forth evil fruit, neither can a corrupt tree bring forth good fruit. Every tree that bringeth not forth good fruit is hewn down, and cast into the fire. Wherefore by their fruits ye shall know them. Not everyone that saith unto me, Lord, Lord, shall enter into the kingdom of heaven; but he that doeth the will of my Father which is in heaven.

THE NINTH SUNDAY AFTER TRINITY

THE INTROIT. *Psalm 54. 1-7.*

SAVE me, O God, for Thy Name's sake, / and avenge me in Thy strength. Hear my prayer, O God, / and hearken unto the words of my mouth. For strangers are risen up against me; / and tyrants, which have not God before their eyes, seek after my soul. Behold, God is my Helper; / the Lord is with them that uphold my soul. He shall reward evil unto mine enemies: / destroy Thou them in Thy truth. An offering of a free heart will I give Thee, and praise Thy Name, O Lord; / because it is so comfortable. For He hath delivered me out of all my trouble, / and mine eye hath seen His desire upon mine enemies.

GLORY be to the Father, and to the Son, / and to the Holy Ghost;
As it was in the beginning, is now, and ever shall be, / world without end. Amen.

THE COLLECT.

GRANT to us, Lord, we beseech Thee, the spirit to think and do always such things as be rightful; that we, who cannot do anything that is good without Thee, may by Thee be enabled to live according to Thy will; through Jesus Christ our Lord. *Amen.*

THE EPISTLE. I *Corinthians* 10. 1-13.

BRETHREN, I would not that ye should be ignorant, how that all our fathers were under the cloud, and all passed through the sea; and were all baptised unto Moses in the cloud and in the sea; and did all eat the same spiritual meat; and did all drink the same spiritual drink: for they drank of that spiritual Rock that followed them: and that Rock was Christ. But with many of them God was not well pleased: for they were overthrown in the wilderness. Now these things were our examples, to the intent we should not lust after evil things, as they also lusted. Neither be ye idolaters, as were some of them; as it is written, The people sat down to eat and drink, and rose up to play. Neither let us commit fornication, as some of them committed, and fell in one day three and twenty thousand. Neither let us tempt Christ, as some of them also tempted, and were destroyed of serpents. Neither murmur ye, as some of them also murmured, and were destroyed of the destroyer. Now all these things happened unto them for ensamples: and they are written for our admonition, upon whom the ends of the world are come. Wherefore let him that thinketh he standeth take heed lest he fall. There hath no temptation taken you but such as is common to man: but God is faithful, Who will not suffer you to be tempted above that ye are able; but will with the temptation also make a way to escape, that ye may be able to bear it.

THE PROPERS OF THE YEAR

THE GRADUAL. *Psalm* 105. 39-44.

ALLELUIA, Alleluia. At their desire He brought quails, / and He filled them with the bread of heaven. He opened the rock of stone, and the waters flowed out, / so that rivers ran in the dry places. For why? He remembered His holy promise, / and Abraham His servant. And He brought forth His people with joy/ and His chosen with gladness; And gave them the lands of the heathen, / and they took the labours of the people in possession; that they might keep His statutes, / and observe His laws. Alleluia.

THE GOSPEL. *Saint Luke* 16. 1-13.

JESUS said unto His disciples, There was a certain rich man, which had a steward; and the same was accused unto him that he had wasted his goods. And he called him, and said unto him, How is it that I hear this of thee? give an account of thy stewardship; for thou mayest be no longer steward. Then the steward said within himself, What shall I do? for my Lord taketh away from me the stewardship: I cannot dig; to beg I am ashamed. I am resolved what to do, that, when I am put out of the stewardship, they may receive me into their houses. So he called every one of his Lord's debtors unto him, and said unto the first, How much owest thou unto my Lord? And he said, An hundred measures of oil. And he said unto him, Take thy bill, and sit down quickly, and write fifty. Then said he to another, And how much owest thou? And he said, An hundred measures of wheat. And he said unto him, Take thy bill, and write fourscore. And the Lord commended the unjust steward, because he had done wisely: for the children of this world are in their generation wiser than the children of light. And I say unto you, Make to yourselves friends of the mammon of unrighteousness; that, when ye fail, they may receive you into everlasting habitations. He that is faithful in that which is least is faithful also in much: and he that is unjust in the least is unjust also in much. If therefore ye have not been faithful in the unrighteous mammon, who will commit to your trust the true riches? And if ye have not been faithful in that which is another man's, who shall give you that which is your own? No servant can serve two masters: for either he will hate the one, and love the other; or else he will hold to the one, and despise the other. Ye cannot serve God and mammon.

THE TENTH SUNDAY AFTER TRINITY

THE INTROIT. *Psalm* 137. 1-6.

BY the waters of Babylon we sat down and wept, / when we remembered thee, O Sion. As for our harps, we hanged them up / upon the trees that are therein. For they that led us away captive required of us then a song, and melody in our heaviness; / Sing us one of the songs of Sion. How shall we sing the Lord's song / in a strange land? If I forget thee, O Jerusalem, / let my right hand forget her cunning. If I do not remember thee, let my tongue cleave to the roof of my mouth; / yea, if I prefer not Jerusalem in my mirth.

GLORY be to the Father, and to the Son, / and to the Holy Ghost;
As it was in the beginning, is now, and ever shall be, / world without end. Amen.

THE COLLECT.

LET Thy merciful ears, O Lord, be open to the prayers of Thy humble servants; and that they may obtain their petitions make them to ask such things as shall please Thee; through Jesus Christ our Lord. *Amen.*

THE EPISTLE. I *Corinthians* 12. 1-11.

CONCERNING spiritual gifts, brethren, I would not have you ignorant. Ye know that ye were Gentiles, carried away unto these dumb idols, even as ye were led. Wherefore I give you to understand, that no man speaking by the Spirit of God calleth Jesus accursed: and that no man can say that Jesus is the Lord, but by the Holy Ghost. Now there are diversities of gifts, but the same Spirit. And there are differences of administrations, but the same Lord. And there are diversities of operations, but it is the same God which worketh all in all. But the manifestation of the Spirit is given to every man to profit withal. For to one is given by the Spirit the word of wisdom; to another the word of knowledge by the same Spirit; to another faith by the same Spirit; to another the gifts of healing by the same Spirit; to another the working of miracles; to another prophecy; to another discerning of spirits; to another divers kinds of tongues; to another the interpretation of tongues: but all these worketh that one and the selfsame Spirit, dividing to every man severally as He will.

THE GRADUAL. *Psalm* 55. 6-8 & 23.

ALLELUIA, Alleluia. And I said, O that I had wings like a dove; / for then would I flee away, and be at rest. Lo, then would I get me away far off, / and remain in the wilderness. I would make haste to escape, / because of the stormy wind and tempest. O cast thy burden upon the Lord, and He shall nourish thee, / and shall not suffer the righteous to fall for ever. Alleluia.

THE GOSPEL. *Saint Luke* 19. 41-47.

AND when Jesus was come near, He beheld the city, and wept over it, saying, If thou hadst known, even thou, at least in this thy day, the things which belong unto thy peace! but now they are hid from thine eyes. For the days shall come upon thee, that thine enemies shall cast a trench about thee, and compass thee round, and keep thee in on every side, and shall lay thee even with the ground, and thy children within thee; and they shall not leave in thee one stone upon another; because thou knewest not the time of thy visitation. And He went into the temple, and began to cast out them that sold therein, and them that bought, saying unto them, It is written, My house is the house of prayer: but ye have made it a den of thieves. And he taught daily in the temple.

THE ELEVENTH SUNDAY AFTER TRINITY

THE INTROIT. *Psalm* 111. 4-10.

THE merciful and gracious Lord hath so done His marvellous works, / that they ought to be had in remembrance. He hath given meat unto them that fear Him; / He shall ever be mindful of His covenant. He hath shewed His people the power of His works, / that He may give them the heritage of the heathen. The works of His hands are verity and judgement; / all His commandments are true. They stand fast for ever and ever, / and are done in truth and equity. He sent redemption unto His people; / He hath commanded His covenant for ever; holy and reverend is His Name. The fear of the Lord is the beginning of wisdom: / a good understanding have all they that do thereafter; the praise of it endureth for ever.

GLORY be to the Father, and to the Son, / and to the Holy Ghost;
As it was in the beginning, is now, and ever shall be, / world without end. Amen.

THE COLLECT.

O GOD our Father, Who declarest Thine almighty power most chiefly in shewing mercy and pity: Mercifully grant unto us such a measure of Thy grace, that we, running the way of Thy commandments, may obtain Thy gracious promises, and be made partakers of Thy heavenly treasure; through Jesus Christ our Lord. *Amen.*

THE EPISTLE. I *Corinthians* 15. 1-11.

BRETHREN, I declare unto you the Gospel which I preached unto you, which also ye have received, and wherein ye stand; by which also ye are saved, if ye keep in memory what I preached unto you, unless ye have believed in vain. For I delivered unto you first of all that which I also received, how that Christ died for our sins according to the Scriptures; and that He was buried, and that He rose again the third day according to the Scriptures: and that He was seen of Cephas, then of the twelve: after that, He was seen of above five hundred brethren at once; of whom the greater part remain unto this present, but some are fallen asleep. After that, He was seen of James; then of all the Apostles. And last of all He was seen of me also, as of one born out of due time. For I am the least of the Apostles, that am not meet to be called an Apostle, because I persecuted the Church of God. But by the grace of God I am what I am: and His grace which was bestowed upon me was not in vain; but I laboured more abundantly than they all: yet not I, but the grace of God which was with me. Therefore whether it were I or they, so we preach, and so ye believed.

THE GRADUAL. *Psalm* 51. 15-17.

ALLELUIA, Alleluia. O Lord, open Thou my lips; / and my mouth shall shew forth Thy praise. For Thou desirest no sacrifice, else would I give it Thee; / but Thou delightest not in burnt-offerings. The sacrifice of God is a troubled spirit; / a broken and contrite heart, O God, shalt Thou not despise. Alleluia.

THE GOSPEL. *Saint Luke* 18. 9-14.

JESUS spake this parable unto certain which trusted in themselves that they were righteous, and despised others: Two men went up into the temple to pray; the one a Pharisee, and the other a Publican. The Pharisee stood and prayed thus with himself, God, I thank Thee, that I am not as other men are, extortioners, unjust, adulterers, or even as this Publican. I fast twice in the week, I give tithes of all that I possess. And the Publican, standing afar off, would not lift up so much as his eyes unto heaven, but smote upon his breast, saying, God be merciful to me a sinner. I tell you, this man went down to his house justified rather than the other: for every one that exalteth himself shall be abased; and he that humbleth himself shall be exalted.

THE TWELFTH SUNDAY AFTER TRINITY

THE INTROIT. *Psalm* 70. 1-6.

HASTE Thee, O God, to deliver me; / make haste to help me, O Lord. Let them be ashamed and confounded that seek after my soul; / let them be turned backward and put to confusion that wish me evil. Let them for their reward be soon brought to shame / that cry over me, 'There, there'. But let all those that seek Thee be joyful and glad in Thee; / and let all such as delight in Thy salvation say alway, 'The Lord be praised'. As for me, I am poor and in misery: / haste Thee unto me, O God. Thou art my Helper and my Redeemer: / O Lord, make no long tarrying.

GLORY be to the Father, and to the Son, / and to the Holy Ghost;
As it was in the beginning, is now, and ever shall be, / world without end. Amen.

THE PROPERS OF THE YEAR

THE COLLECT.

ALMIGHTY and everlasting God, Who art always more ready to hear than we are to pray, and art wont to give more than either we desire, or deserve: Pour down upon us the abundance of Thy mercy; forgiving us those things whereof our conscience is afraid, and giving us those good things which we are not worthy to ask, but through the Merits and Mediation of Jesus Christ, Thy Son, our Lord. *Amen.*

THE EPISTLE. II *Corinthians* 3. 4-9.

SUCH trust have we through Christ to God-ward: not that we are sufficient of ourselves to think anything as of ourselves; but our sufficiency is of God; Who also hath made us able Ministers of the New Testament; not of the letter, but of the spirit: for the letter killeth, but the spirit giveth life. But if the ministration of death, written and engraven in stones, was glorious, so that the children of Israel could not steadfastly behold the face of Moses for the glory of his countenance; which glory was to be done away: how shall not the ministration of the Spirit be more glorious? For if the ministration of condemnation be glory, much more doth the ministration of righteousness exceed in glory.

THE GRADUAL. *Psalm* 34. 1-5.

ALLELUIA, Alleluia. I will alway give thanks unto the Lord; / His praise shall ever be in my mouth. My soul shall make her boast in the Lord; / the humble shall hear thereof, and be glad. O praise the Lord with me, / and let us magnify His Name together. I sought the Lord, and He heard me; / yea, He delivered me out of all my fear. They had an eye unto Him, and were lightened; / and their faces were not ashamed. Lo, the poor crieth, and the Lord heareth him; / yea, and saveth him out of all his troubles. The angel of the Lord tarrieth round about them that fear Him, / and delivereth them. Alleluia.

THE GOSPEL. *Saint Mark* 7. 14-37.

AND when He had called all the people unto Him, He said unto them, Hearken unto me every one of you, and understand: there is nothing from without a man, that entering into him can defile him: but the things which come out of him, those are they that defile the man. If any man have ears to hear, let him hear. And when He was entered into the house from the people, His disciples asked Him concerning the parable. And He saith unto them, Are ye so without understanding also? Do ye not perceive, that whatsoever thing from without entereth into the man, it cannot defile him; because it entereth not into his heart, but into the belly, and goeth out into the draught, purging all meats? And He said, That which cometh out of the man, that defileth the man. For from within, out of the heart of men, proceed evil thoughts, adulteries, fornications, murders, thefts, covetousness, wickedness, deceit, lasciviousness, an evil eye, blasphemy, pride, foolishness: All these evil things come from within, and defile the man. And from thence He arose, and went into the borders of Tyre and Sidon, and entered into an house, and would have no man know it: but He could not be hid. For a certain woman, whose young daughter had an unclean spirit, heard of Him, and came and fell at His feet: the woman was a Greek, a Syrophoenician by nation; and she besought Him that He would cast forth the devil out of her daughter. But Jesus said unto her, Let the children first be filled: for it is not meet to take the children's bread, and to cast it unto the dogs. And she answered and said unto Him, Yes, Lord: yet the dogs under the table eat of the children's crumbs. And He said unto her, For this saying go thy way; the devil is gone out of thy daughter. And when she was come to her house, she found the devil gone out, and her daughter laid upon the bed. And again, departing from the coasts of Tyre and Sidon, He came unto the sea of Galilee, through the midst of the coasts of Decapolis. And they bring unto Him one that was deaf, and had an impediment in his speech; and they beseech Him to put His hand upon him. And He took him aside from the multitude, and put His fingers into His ears, and He spit, and touched His tongue; and looking up to heaven, He sighed, and saith unto him, Ephphatha, that is, Be opened. And straightway his ears were opened, and the string of his tongue was loosed, and he spake plain. And He charged them that they should tell no man: but the more He charged them, so much the more a great deal they published it; and were beyond measure astonished, saying, He hath done all things well: He maketh both the deaf to hear, and the dumb to speak.

The Thirteenth Sunday after Trinity

The Introit. *Psalm* 90. 1-9.

LORD, Thou hast been our Refuge, / from one generation to another. Before the mountains were brought forth, or ever the earth and the world were made, / Thou art God from everlasting, and world without end. Thou turnest man to destruction, / and sayest, Return, ye children of men. For a thousand years in Thy sight are but as yesterday when it is past, / and as a watch in the night. As soon as Thou scatterest them, they are even as a sleep; / and fade away suddenly like the grass. In the morning it is green, and groweth up; / but in the evening it is cut down, dried up, and withered. For we consume away in Thy displeasure, / and are afraid at Thy wrathful indignation. Thou hast set our misdeeds before Thee, / and our secret sins in the light of Thy countenance. For when Thou art angry all our days are gone; / we bring our years to an end, as it were a tale that is told.

GLORY be to the Father, and to the Son, / and to the Holy Ghost;

As it was in the beginning, is now, and ever shall be, / world without end. Amen.

The Collect.

ALMIGHTY and merciful God, of Whose only gift it cometh that Thy faithful people do unto Thee true and laudable service: Grant, we beseech Thee, that we may so faithfully serve Thee in this life, that we fail not finally to attain Thy heavenly promises; through the Merits of Jesus Christ our Lord. *Amen.*

The Epistle. *Galatians* 3. 16-22.

NOW to Abraham and his Seed were the promises made. He saith not, And to seeds, as of many; but as of one, and to thy Seed, which is Christ. And this I say, that the covenant, that was confirmed before of God in Christ, the Law, which was four hundred and thirty years after, cannot disannul, that it should make the promise of none effect. For if the inheritance be of the Law, it is no more of promise: but God gave it to Abraham by promise. Wherefore then serveth the Law? It was added because of transgressions, till the Seed should come to Whom the promise was made; and it was ordained by angels in the hand of a Mediator. Now a mediator is not a mediator of one, but God is One. Is the Law then against the promises of God? God forbid: for if there had been a law given which could have given life, verily righteousness should have been by the Law. But the Scripture hath concluded all under sin, that the promise by faith of Jesus Christ might be given to them that believe.

The Gradual. *Psalm* 90. 10-12.

ALLELUIA, Alleluia. The days of our age are threescore years and ten; and though men be so strong that they come to fourscore years; / yet is their strength then but labour and sorrow; so soon passeth it away, and we are gone. But who regardeth the power of Thy wrath? / for even thereafter as a man feareth, so is Thy displeasure. So teach us to number our days, / that we may apply our hearts unto wisdom. Alleluia.

THE GOSPEL. *Saint Luke* 10. 23-37.

AT that time Jesus said unto them: Blessed are the eyes which see the things that ye see: for I tell you, that many prophets and kings have desired to see those things which ye see, and have not seen them; and to hear those things which ye hear, and have not heard them. And, behold, a certain lawyer stood up, and tempted Him, saying, Master, what shall I do to inherit eternal life? He said unto him, What is written in the Law? how readest thou? And he answering said, Thou shalt love the Lord thy God with all thy heart, and with all thy soul, and with all thy strength, and with all thy mind; and thy neighbour as thyself. And He said unto him, Thou hast answered right: this do, and thou shalt live. But he, willing to justify himself, said unto Jesus, And who is my neighbour? And Jesus answering said, A certain man went down from Jerusalem to Jericho, and fell among thieves, which stripped him of his raiment, and wounded him, and departed, leaving him half dead. And by chance there came down a certain Priest that way: and when he saw him, he passed by on the other side. And likewise a Levite, when he was at the place, came and looked on him, and passed by on the other side. But a certain Samaritan, as he journeyed, came where he was: and when he saw him, he had compassion on him, and went to him, and bound up his wounds, pouring in oil and wine, and set him on his own beast, and brought him to an inn, and took care of him. And on the morrow when he departed, he took out two-pence, and gave them to the host, and said unto him, Take care of him; and whatsoever thou spendest more, when I come again, I will repay thee. Which now of these three, thinkest thou, was neighbour unto him that fell among the thieves? And he said, He that shewed mercy on him. Then said Jesus unto him, Go, and do thou likewise.

THE FOURTEENTH SUNDAY AFTER TRINITY

THE INTROIT. *Psalm* 84. 1-7.

O HOW amiable are Thy dwellings, / Thou Lord of hosts! My soul hath a desire and longing to enter into the courts of the Lord; / my heart and my flesh rejoice in the living God. Yea, the sparrow hath found her an house, and the swallow a nest where she may lay her young: / even Thine altars, O Lord of hosts, my King and my God. Blessed are they that dwell in Thy house: / they will be alway praising Thee. Blessed is the man whose strength is in Thee, / in whose heart are Thy ways; Who going through the vale of misery use it for a well, / and the pools are filled with water. They will go from strength to strength; / and unto the God of gods appeareth every one of them in Sion.

GLORY be to the Father, and to the Son, / and to the Holy Ghost;
As it was in the beginning, is now, and ever shall be, / world without end. Amen.

THE COLLECT.

ALMIGHTY and everlasting God, give unto us the increase of faith, hope, and charity; and, that we may obtain that which Thou dost promise, make us to love that which Thou dost command; through Jesus Christ our Lord. *Amen.*

THE EPISTLE. *Galatians* 5. 16-26.

THIS I say then, walk in the Spirit, and ye shall not fulfil the lust of the flesh. For the flesh lusteth against the Spirit, and the Spirit against the flesh: and these are contrary the one to the other: so that ye cannot do the things that ye would. But if ye be led of the Spirit, ye are not under the Law. Now the works of the flesh are manifest, which are these: adultery, fornication, uncleanness, lasciviousness, idolatry, witchcraft, hatred, variance, emulations, wrath, strife, seditions, heresies, envyings, murders, drunkenness, revellings, and such like; of the which I tell you before, as I have also told you in time past, that they which do such things shall not inherit the kingdom of God. But the fruit of the Spirit is love, joy, peace, long-suffering, gentleness, goodness, faith, meekness, temperance: against such there is no law. And they that are Christ's have crucified the flesh with the affections and lusts. If we live in the Spirit, let us also walk in the Spirit. Let us not be desirous of vain glory, provoking one another, envying one another.

THE GRADUAL. *Psalm* 84. 10-13.

ALLELUIA, Alleluia. For one day in Thy courts / is better than a thousand. I had rather be a door-keeper in the house of my God, / than to dwell in the tents of ungodliness. For the Lord God is a Light and Defence; / the Lord will give grace and worship, and no good thing shall he withhold from them that live a godly life. O Lord God of hosts, / blessed is the man that putteth his trust in Thee. Alleluia.

THE GOSPEL. *Saint Luke* 17. 11-19.

AND it came to pass, as Jesus went to Jerusalem, that He passed through the midst of Samaria and Galilee. And as He entered into a certain village, there met Him ten men that were lepers, which stood afar off: and they lifted up their voices, and said, Jesus, Master, have mercy on us. And when He saw them, He said unto them, Go shew yourselves unto the priests. And it came to pass, that, as they went, they were cleansed. And one of them, when he saw that he was healed, turned back, and with a loud voice glorified God, and fell down on his face at His feet, giving Him thanks: and he was a Samaritan. And Jesus answering said, Were there not ten cleansed? but where are the nine? There are not found that returned to give glory to God, save this stranger. And He said unto him, Arise, go thy way: thy faith hath made thee whole.

THE FIFTEENTH SUNDAY AFTER TRINITY

THE INTROIT. *Psalm* 86. 1-7.

BOW down Thine ear, O Lord, and hear me, / for I am poor, and in misery. Preserve Thou my soul, for I am holy; / my God, save Thy servant that putteth his trust in Thee. Be merciful unto me, O Lord, / for I will call daily upon Thee. Comfort the soul of Thy servant; / for unto Thee, O Lord, do I lift up my soul. For Thou, Lord, art good and gracious, / and of great mercy unto all them that call upon Thee. Give ear, Lord, unto my prayer, / and ponder the voice of my humble desires. In the time of my trouble I will call upon Thee, / for Thou hearest me.

GLORY be to the Father, and to the Son, / and to the Holy Ghost;
As it was in the beginning, is now, and ever shall be, / world without end. Amen.

THE PROPERS OF THE YEAR

The Collect.

Keep, we beseech Thee, O Lord, Thy Church with Thy perpetual mercy; and, because the frailty of man without Thee cannot but fall, keep us ever by Thy help from all things hurtful, and lead us to all things profitable to our salvation; through Jesus Christ our Lord. *Amen.*

The Epistle. *Galatians* 6. 11-18.

Ye see how large a letter I have written unto you with mine own hand. As many as desire to make a fair shew in the flesh, they constrain you to be circumcised; only lest they should suffer persecution for the Cross of Christ. For neither they themselves who are circumcised keep the Law; but desire to have you circumcised, that they may glory in your flesh. But God forbid that I should glory, save in the Cross of our Lord Jesus Christ, by Whom the world is crucified unto me, and I unto the world. For in Christ Jesus neither circumcision availeth anything, nor uncircumcision, but a new creature. And as many as walk according to this rule, peace be on them, and mercy, and upon the Israel of God. From henceforth let no man trouble me: for I bear in my body the marks of the Lord Jesus. Brethren, the grace of our Lord Jesus Christ be with your spirit. Amen.

The Gradual. *Psalm* 92. 1-4.

Alleluia, Alleluia. It is a good thing to give thanks unto the Lord, / and to sing praises unto Thy Name, O Thou Most High; To tell of Thy loving-kindness early in the morning, / and of Thy truth in the night-season; Upon an instrument of ten strings, and upon the lute; / upon a loud instrument, and upon the harp. For Thou, Lord, hast made me glad through Thy works, / and I will rejoice in giving praise for the operations of Thy hands. Alleluia.

The Gospel. *Saint Matthew* 6. 24-34.

At that time Jesus said unto them: No man can serve two masters: for either he will hate the one, and love the other; or else he will hold to the one, and despise the other. Ye cannot serve God and mammon. Therefore I say unto you, take no thought for your life, what ye shall eat, or what ye shall drink; nor yet for your body, what ye shall put on. Is not the life more than meat, and the body than raiment? Behold the fowls of the air: for they sow not, neither do they reap, nor gather into barns; yet your heavenly Father feedeth them. Are ye not much better than they? Which of you by taking thought can add one cubit unto his stature? And why take ye thought for raiment? Consider the lilies of the field, how they grow; they toil not, neither do they spin: and yet I say unto you, that even Solomon in all his glory was not arrayed like one of these. Wherefore, if God so clothe the grass of the field, which today is, and tomorrow is cast into the oven, shall He not much more clothe you, O ye of little faith? Therefore take no thought, saying, What shall we eat? or, What shall we drink? or, Wherewithal shall we be clothed? (for after all these things do the Gentiles seek:) for your heavenly Father knoweth that ye have need of all these things. But seek ye first the kingdom of God, and His righteousness; and all these things shall be added unto you. Take therefore no thought for the morrow: for the morrow shall take thought for the things of itself. Sufficient unto the day is the evil thereof.

The Sixteenth Sunday after Trinity

The Introit. *Psalm* 146. 1-6.

PRAISE the Lord, O my soul; while I live will I praise the Lord; / yea, as long as I have any being, I will sing praises unto my God. O put not your trust in princes, nor in any child of man, / for there is no help in them. For when the breath of man goeth forth he shall turn again to his earth, / and then all his thoughts perish. Blessed is he that hath the God of Jacob for his Help, / and whose hope is in the Lord his God; Who made heaven and earth, the sea, and all that therein is; / Who keepeth His promise for ever; Who helpeth them to right that suffer wrong, / Who feedeth the hungry.

GLORY be to the Father, and to the Son, / and to the Holy Ghost;
As it was in the beginning, is now, and ever shall be, / world without end. Amen.

The Collect.

O LORD, we beseech Thee, let Thy continual pity cleanse and defend Thy Church; and, because it cannot continue in safety without Thy succour, preserve it evermore by Thy help and goodness; through Jesus Christ our Lord. *Amen.*

The Epistle. *Ephesians* 3. 13-21.

WHEREFORE I desire that ye faint not at my tribulations for you, which is your glory. For this cause I bow my knees unto the Father of our Lord Jesus Christ, of Whom the whole family in heaven and earth is named, that He would grant you, according to the riches of His glory, to be strengthened with might by His Spirit in the inner man; that Christ may dwell in your hearts by faith; that ye, being rooted and grounded in love, may be able to comprehend with all saints what is the breadth, and length, and depth, and height; and to know the love of Christ, which passeth knowledge, that ye might be filled with all the fullness of God. Now unto Him that is able to do exceeding abundantly above all that we ask or think, according to the power that worketh in us, unto Him be glory in the Church by Christ Jesus throughout all ages, world without end. Amen.

The Gradual. *Psalm* 146. 7-10.

ALLELUIA, Alleluia. The Lord looseth men out of prison; / the Lord giveth sight to the blind. The Lord helpeth them that are fallen; / the Lord careth for the righteous. The Lord careth for the strangers, He defendeth the fatherless and widow: / as for the way of the ungodly, He turneth it upside down. The Lord thy God, O Sion, shall be King for evermore, / and throughout all generations. Alleluia.

The Gospel. *Saint Luke* 7. 11-17.

AND it came to pass the day after, that Jesus went into a city called Nain; and many of His disciples went with Him, and much people. Now when He came nigh to the gate of the city, behold, there was a dead man carried out, the only son of his mother, and she was a widow: and much people of the city was with her. And when the Lord saw her, He had compassion on her, and said unto her, Weep not. And He came and touched the bier: and they that bare him stood still. And He said, Young man, I say unto thee, Arise. And he that was dead sat up, and began to speak. And He delivered him to his mother. And there came a fear on all: and they glorified God, saying, That a great Prophet is risen up among us; and, That God hath visited His people. And this rumour of Him went forth throughout all Judaea, and throughout all the region round about.

THE SEVENTEENTH SUNDAY AFTER TRINITY

THE INTROIT. *Psalm* 119. 137-144.

RIGHTEOUS art Thou, O Lord, / and true is Thy judgement. The testimonies that Thou hast commanded / are exceeding righteous and true. My zeal hath even consumed me, / because mine enemies have forgotten Thy words. Thy word is tried to the uttermost, / and Thy servant loveth it. I am small, and of no reputation; / yet do I not forget Thy commandments. Thy righteousness is an everlasting righteousness, / and Thy Law is the truth. Trouble and heaviness have taken hold upon me; / yet is my delight in Thy commandments. The righteousness of Thy testimonies is everlasting: / O grant me understanding, and I shall live.

GLORY be to the Father, and to the Son, / and to the Holy Ghost;
As it was in the beginning, is now, and ever shall be, / world without end. Amen.

THE COLLECT.

LORD, we pray Thee that Thy grace may always prevent and follow us, and make us continually to be given to all good works; through Jesus Christ our Lord. *Amen.*

THE EPISTLE. *Ephesians* 4. 1-6.

I THEREFORE, the prisoner of the Lord, beseech you that ye walk worthy of the vocation wherewith ye are called, with all lowliness and meekness, with long-suffering, forbearing one another in love; endeavouring to keep the unity of the Spirit in the bond of peace. There is one body, and one Spirit, even as ye are called in one hope of your calling; one Lord, one Faith, one Baptism, one God and Father of all, Who is above all, and through all, and in you all.

THE GRADUAL. *Psalm* 131. 1-4.

ALLELUIA, Alleluia. Lord, I am not high-minded, / I have no proud looks. I do not exercise myself in great matters / which are too high for me. But I refrain my soul, and keep it low, like as a child that is weaned from his mother; / yea, my soul is even as a weaned child. O Israel, trust in the Lord, / from this time forth for evermore. Alleluia.

THE GOSPEL. *Saint Luke* 14. 1-11.

AND it came to pass, as Jesus went into the house of one of the chief Pharisees to eat bread on the Sabbath-day, that they watched Him. And, behold, there was a certain man before Him which had the dropsy. And Jesus answering spake unto the lawyers and Pharisees, saying, Is it lawful to heal on the Sabbath-day? And they held their peace. And He took him, and healed him, and let him go; and answered them, saying, Which of you shall have an ass or an ox fallen into a pit, and will not straightway pull him out on the Sabbath-day? And they could not answer Him again to these things. And He put forth a parable to those which were bidden, when He marked how they chose out the chief seats; saying unto them, When thou art bidden of any man to a wedding, sit not down in the highest seat; lest a more honourable man than thou be bidden of him; and he that bade thee and him come and say to thee, Give this man place; and thou begin with shame to take the lowest place. But when thou art bidden, go and sit down in the lowest seat; that when he that bade thee cometh, he may say unto thee, Friend, go up higher: then shalt thou have worship in the presence of them that sit at meat with thee. For whosoever exalteth himself shall be abased; and he that humbleth himself shall be exalted.

The Eighteenth Sunday after Trinity

The Introit. *Psalm* 122. 1-5.

I WAS glad when they said unto me, / We will go into the house of the Lord. Our feet shall stand in thy gates, / O Jerusalem. Jerusalem is built as a city / that is at unity in itself. For thither the tribes go up, even the tribes of the Lord, / to testify unto Israel, to give thanks unto the Name of the Lord. For there is the seat of judgement, / even the seat of the house of David.

GLORY be to the Father, and to the Son, / and to the Holy Ghost;

As it was in the beginning, is now, and ever shall be, / world without end. Amen.

The Collect.

LORD, we beseech Thee, grant Thy people grace to withstand the temptations of the world, the flesh, and the devil; and with pure hearts and minds to follow Thee, the only God; through Jesus Christ our Lord. *Amen.*

The Epistle. I *Corinthians* 1. 3-10.

GRACE be unto you, and peace, from God our Father, and from the Lord Jesus Christ. I thank my God always on your behalf, for the grace of God which is given you by Jesus Christ; that in everything ye are enriched by Him, in all utterance, and in all knowledge; even as the testimony of Christ was confirmed in you: so that ye come behind in no gift; waiting for the coming of our Lord Jesus Christ, Who shall also confirm you unto the end, that ye may be blameless in the day of our Lord Jesus Christ. God is faithful, by whom ye were called unto the fellowship of his Son Jesus Christ our Lord. Now I beseech you, brethren, by the name of our Lord Jesus Christ, that ye all speak the same thing, and that there be no divisions among you; but that ye be perfectly joined together in the same mind and in the same judgement.

The Gradual. *Psalm* 122. 6-9.

ALLELUIA, Alleluia. O pray for the peace of Jerusalem; / they shall prosper that love thee. Peace be within thy walls, / and plenteousness within thy palaces. For my brethren and companions' sakes, / I will wish thee prosperity. Yea, because of the house of the Lord our God, / I will seek to do thee good. Alleluia.

The Gospel. *Saint Matthew* 22. 34.

WHEN the Pharisees had heard that He had put the Sadducees to silence, they were gathered together. Then one of them, which was a lawyer, asked Him a question, tempting Him, and saying, Master, which is the great commandment in the Law? Jesus said unto him, Thou shalt love the Lord thy God with all thy heart, and with all thy soul, and with all thy mind. This is the first and great commandment. And the second is like unto it, Thou shalt love thy neighbour as thyself. On these two commandments hang all the Law and the prophets. While the Pharisees were gathered together, Jesus asked them, saying, What think ye of Christ? Whose Son is He? They say unto Him, The Son of David. He saith unto them, How then doth David in spirit call Him Lord, saying, The Lord said unto my Lord, Sit Thou on my right hand, till I make Thine enemies Thy footstool? If David then call Him Lord, how is He his Son? And no man was able to answer Him a word, neither durst any man from that day forth ask Him any more questions.

The Nineteenth Sunday after Trinity

The Introit. *Psalm* 138. 1-8.

I WILL give thanks unto Thee, O Lord, with my whole heart; / even before the gods will I sing praise unto Thee. I will worship toward Thy holy temple, and praise Thy Name, because of Thy loving-kindness and truth: / for Thou hast magnified Thy Name and Thy word above all things. When I called upon Thee, Thou heardest me, / and enduedst my soul with much strength. All the kings of the earth shall praise Thee, O Lord; / for they have heard the words of Thy mouth. Yea, they shall sing in the ways of the Lord, / that great is the glory of the Lord. For though the Lord be high, yet hath He respect unto the lowly; / as for the proud, He beholdeth them afar off. Though I walk in the midst of trouble, yet shalt Thou refresh me; / Thou shalt stretch forth Thy hand upon the furiousness of mine enemies, and Thy right hand shall save me. The Lord shall make good His loving-kindness toward me; / yea, Thy mercy, O Lord, endureth for ever; despise not then the works of Thine own hands.

GLORY be to the Father, and to the Son, / and to the Holy Ghost;
As it was in the beginning, is now, and ever shall be, / world without end. Amen.

The Collect.

O GOD, forasmuch as without Thee we are not able to please Thee: Mercifully grant, that Thy Holy Spirit may in all things direct and rule our hearts; through Jesus Christ our Lord. *Amen.*

The Epistle. *Ephesians* 4. 17-32.

THIS I say therefore, and testify in the Lord, that ye henceforth walk not as other Gentiles walk, in the vanity of their mind, having the understanding darkened, being alienated from the life of God through the ignorance that is in them, because of the blindness of their heart: who being past feeling have given themselves over unto lasciviousness, to work all uncleanness with greediness. But ye have not so learned Christ; if so be that ye have heard Him, and have been taught by Him, as the truth is in Jesus: that ye put off, concerning the former conversation, the old man, which is corrupt according to the deceitful lusts; and be renewed in the spirit of your mind; and that ye put on the new man, which after God is created in righteousness and true holiness. Wherefore putting away lying, speak every man truth with his neighbour: for we are members one of another. Be ye angry, and sin not: let not the sun go down upon your wrath: neither give place to the devil. Let him that stole steal no more: but rather let him labour, working with his hands the thing which is good, that he may have to give to him that needeth. Let no corrupt communication proceed out of your mouth, but that which is good to the use of edifying, that it may minister grace unto the hearers. And grieve not the Holy Spirit of God, whereby ye are sealed unto the day of redemption. Let all bitterness, and wrath, and anger, and clamour, and evil speaking, be put away from you, with all malice: and be ye kind one to another, tender-hearted, forgiving one another, even as God for Christ's sake hath forgiven you.

The Gradual. *Psalm* 103. 1-5.

ALLELUIA, Alleluia. Praise the Lord, O my soul, / and all that is within me praise His holy Name. Praise the Lord, O my soul, / and forget not all His benefits; Who forgiveth all thy sin, / and healeth all thine infirmities; Who saveth thy life from destruction, / and crowneth thee with mercy and loving-kindness; Who satisfieth thy mouth with good things, / making thee young and lusty as an eagle. Alleluia.

THE GOSPEL. *Saint Matthew* 9. 1-8.

JESUS entered into a ship, and passed over, and came into His own city. And, behold, they brought to Him a man sick of the palsy, lying on a bed: and Jesus seeing their faith said unto the sick of the palsy, Son, be of good cheer; thy sins be forgiven thee. And, behold, certain of the scribes said within themselves, This man blasphemeth. And Jesus knowing their thoughts said, Wherefore think ye evil in your hearts? For whether is easier, to say, Thy sins be forgiven thee; or to say, Arise, and walk? But that ye may know that the Son of Man hath power on earth to forgive sins, (then saith He to the sick of the palsy,) Arise, take up thy bed, and go unto thine house. And he arose, and departed to his house. But when the multitudes saw it, they marvelled, and glorified God, which had given such power unto men.

THE TWENTIETH SUNDAY AFTER TRINITY

THE INTROIT. *Psalm* 145. 7-13.

THE memorial of Thine abundant kindness shall be shewed, / and men shall sing of Thy righteousness. The Lord is gracious and merciful, / long-suffering and of great goodness. The Lord is loving unto every man, / and His mercy is over all His works. All Thy works praise Thee, O Lord; / and Thy saints give thanks unto Thee. They shew the glory of Thy kingdom, / and talk of Thy power; That Thy power, Thy glory, and mightiness of Thy kingdom, / might be known unto men. Thy kingdom is an everlasting kingdom, / and Thy dominion endureth throughout all ages.

GLORY be to the Father, and to the Son, / and to the Holy Ghost;
As it was in the beginning, is now, and ever shall be, / world without end. Amen.

THE COLLECT.

O ALMIGHTY and most merciful God, of Thy bountiful goodness keep us, we beseech Thee, from all things that may hurt us; that we, being ready both in body and soul, may cheerfully accomplish all those things that Thou wouldest have done; through Jesus Christ our Lord. *Amen.*

THE EPISTLE. *Ephesians* 5. 15-33.

SEE then that ye walk circumspectly, not as fools, but as wise, redeeming the time, because the days are evil. Wherefore be ye not unwise, but understanding what the will of the Lord is. And be not drunk with wine, wherein is excess; but be filled with the Spirit; speaking to yourselves in psalms, and hymns, and spiritual songs, singing and making melody in your heart to the Lord; giving thanks always for all things unto God and the Father in the Name of our Lord Jesus Christ; submitting yourselves one to another in the fear of God. Wives, submit yourselves unto your own husbands, as unto the Lord. For the husband is the head of the wife, even as Christ is the Head of the Church: and He is the Saviour of the body. Therefore as the Church is subject unto Christ, so let the wives be to their own husbands in everything. Husbands, love your wives, even as Christ also loved the Church, and gave Himself for it; that He might sanctify and cleanse it with the washing of water by the word, that He might present it to Himself a glorious Church, not having spot, or wrinkle, or any such thing; but that it should be holy and without blemish. So ought men to love their wives as their own bodies. He that loveth his wife loveth himself. For no man ever yet hated his own flesh; but nourisheth and cherisheth it, even as the Lord the Church: for we are members of His body, of His flesh, and of His bones. For this cause shall a man leave his father and mother, and shall be joined unto his wife, and they two shall be one flesh. This is a great mystery: but I speak concerning Christ and the Church. Nevertheless let every one of you in particular so love his wife even as himself; and the wife see that she reverence her husband.

THE GRADUAL. *Psalm* 145. 18-21.

ALLELUIA, Alleluia. The Lord is nigh unto all them that call upon Him; / yea, all such as call upon Him faithfully. He will fulfil the desire of them that fear Him; / He also will hear their cry, and will help them. The Lord preserveth all them that love Him, / but scattereth abroad all the ungodly. My mouth shall speak the praise of the Lord, / and let all flesh give thanks unto His holy Name for ever and ever. Alleluia.

THE GOSPEL. *Saint Matthew* 22. 1-14.

AND Jesus answered and spake unto them again by parables, and said, The kingdom of heaven is like unto a certain king, which made a marriage for his son, and sent forth his servants to call them that were bidden to the wedding: and they would not come. Again, he sent forth other servants, saying, Tell them which are bidden, Behold, I have prepared my dinner: my oxen and my fatlings are killed, and all things are ready: come unto the marriage. But they made light of it, and went their ways, one to his farm, another to his merchandise: and the remnant took his servants, and entreated them spitefully, and slew them. But when the king heard thereof, he was wroth: and he sent forth his armies, and destroyed those murderers, and burned up their city. Then saith he to his servants, The wedding is ready, but they which were bidden were not worthy. Go ye therefore into the highways, and as many as ye shall find, bid to the marriage. So those servants went out into the highways, and gathered together all as many as they found, both bad and good: and the wedding was furnished with guests. And when the king came in to see the guests, he saw there a man which had not on a wedding garment: and he saith unto him, Friend, how camest thou in hither not having a wedding garment? And he was speechless. Then said the king to the servants, Bind him hand and foot, and take him away, and cast him into outer darkness, there shall be weeping and gnashing of teeth. For many are called, but few are chosen.

THE TWENTY-FIRST SUNDAY AFTER TRINITY

THE INTROIT. *Psalm* 119. 1-8.

BLESSED are those that are undefiled in the way, / and walk in the Law of the Lord. Blessed are they that keep His testimonies, / and seek Him with their whole heart. For they who do no wickedness / walk in His ways. Thou hast charged / that we shall diligently keep Thy commandments. O that my ways were made so direct, / that I might keep Thy statutes! So shall I not be confounded / while I have respect unto all Thy commandments. I will thank Thee with an unfeigned heart, / when I shall have learned the judgements of Thy righteousness. I will keep Thy ceremonies: / O forsake me not utterly.

GLORY be to the Father, and to the Son, / and to the Holy Ghost;
As it was in the beginning, is now, and ever shall be, / world without end. Amen.

THE COLLECT.

GRANT, we beseech Thee, merciful Lord, to Thy faithful people pardon and peace; that they may be cleansed from all their sins, and serve Thee with a quiet mind; through Jesus Christ our Lord. *Amen.*

THE EPISTLE. *Ephesians* 6. 10-20.

FINALLY my brethren, be strong in the Lord, and in the power of His might. Put on the whole armour of God, that ye may be able to stand against the wiles of the devil. For we wrestle not against flesh and blood, but against principalities, against powers, against the rulers of the darkness of this world, against spiritual wickedness in high places. Wherefore take unto you the whole armour of God, that ye may be able to withstand in the evil day, and having done all, to stand. Stand therefore, having your loins girt about with truth, and having on the breastplate of righteousness; and your feet shod with the preparation of the Gospel of peace; above all, taking the shield of faith, wherewith ye shall be able to quench all the fiery darts of the wicked. And take the helmet of salvation, and the sword of the Spirit, which is the Word of God: praying always with all prayer and supplication in the Spirit, and watching thereunto with all perseverance and supplication for all saints; and for me, that utterance may be given unto me, that I may open my mouth boldly, to make known the mystery of the Gospel, for which I am an ambassador in bonds: that therein I may speak boldly, as I ought to speak.

THE GRADUAL. *Psalm* 114. 1-8.

ALLELUIA, Alleluia. When Israel came out of Egypt, / and the house of Jacob from among the strange people, Judah was His sanctuary, / and Israel His dominion. The sea saw that, and fled; / Jordan was driven back. The mountains skipped like rams, / and the little hills like young sheep. What aileth thee, O thou sea, that thou fleddest; / and thou Jordan, that thou wast driven back? Ye mountains, that ye skipped like rams; / and ye little hills, like young sheep? Tremble, thou earth, at the presence of the Lord: / at the presence of the God of Jacob; Who turned the hard rock into a standing water, / and the flint-stone into a springing well. Alleluia.

THE GOSPEL. *Saint John* 4. 46-54.

SO Jesus came again into Cana of Galilee, where he made the water wine. And there was a certain nobleman, whose son was sick at Capernaum. When he heard that Jesus was come out of Judaea into Galilee, he went unto Him, and besought Him that He would come down, and heal his son: for he was at the point of death. Then said Jesus unto him, Except ye see signs and wonders, ye will not believe. The nobleman saith unto Him, Sir, come down ere my child die. Jesus saith unto him, Go thy way; thy son liveth. And the man believed the word that Jesus had spoken unto him, and he went his way. And as he was now going down, his servants met him, and told him, saying, Thy son liveth. Then enquired he of them the hour when he began to amend. And they said unto him, Yesterday at the seventh hour the fever left him. So the father knew that it was at the same hour, in the which Jesus said unto him, Thy son liveth: and himself believed, and his whole house. This is again the second miracle that Jesus did, when He was come out of Judaea into Galilee.

THE TWENTY-SECOND SUNDAY AFTER TRINITY

THE INTROIT. *Psalm* 130. 1-8.

OUT of the deep have I called unto Thee, O Lord: / Lord, hear my voice. O let Thine ears consider well / the voice of my complaint. If Thou, Lord, wilt be extreme to mark what is done amiss, / O Lord, who may abide it? For there is mercy with Thee; / therefore shalt Thou be feared. I look for the Lord; my soul doth wait for Him; / in His word is my trust. My soul fleeth unto the Lord, / before the morning watch, I say, before the morning watch. O Israel, trust in the

Lord, for with the Lord there is mercy; / and with Him is plenteous redemption. And He shall redeem Israel / from all his sins.

GLORY be to the Father, and to the Son, / and to the Holy Ghost;

As it was in the beginning, is now, and ever shall be, / world without end. Amen.

THE COLLECT.

LORD, we beseech Thee to keep Thy household the Church in continual godliness; that through Thy protection it may be free from all adversities, and devoutly given to serve Thee in all good works, to the glory of Thy Name; through Jesus Christ our Lord. *Amen.*

THE EPISTLE. *Philippians* 1. 3-11.

I THANK my God upon every remembrance of you, (always in every prayer of mine for you all making request with joy,) for your fellowship in the Gospel from the first day until now; being confident of this very thing, that He which hath begun a good work in you will perform it until the day of Jesus Christ: even as it is meet for me to think this of you all, because I have you in my heart; inasmuch as both in my bonds, and in the defence and confirmation of the Gospel, ye all are partakers of my grace. For God is my record, how greatly I long after you all in the deepest mercies of Jesus Christ. And this I pray, that your love may abound yet more and more in knowledge, and in all judgement; that ye may approve things that are excellent; that ye may be sincere, and without offence, till the day of Christ: being filled with the fruits of righteousness, which are by Jesus Christ, unto the glory and praise of God.

THE GRADUAL. *Psalm* 133. 1-4.

ALLELUIA, Alleluia. Behold, how good and joyful a thing it is, / brethren, to dwell together in unity! It is like the precious ointment upon the head, that ran down unto the beard, / even unto Aaron's beard, and went down to the skirts of his clothing. Like as the dew of Hermon, / which fell upon the hill of Sion. For there the Lord promised His blessing, / and life for evermore. Alleluia.

THE GOSPEL. *Saint Matthew* 18. 21-35.

PETER said unto Jesus, Lord, how oft shall my brother sin against me, and I forgive him? till seven times? Jesus saith unto him, I say not unto thee, Until seven times: but, Until seventy times seven. Therefore is the kingdom of heaven likened unto a certain king, which would take account of his servants. And when he had begun to reckon, one was brought unto him, which owed him ten thousand talents. But forasmuch as he had not to pay, his Lord commanded him to be sold, and his wife, and children, and all that he had, and payment to be made. The servant therefore fell down, and worshipped him, saying, Lord, have patience with me, and I will pay thee all. Then the Lord of that servant was moved with compassion, and loosed him, and forgave him the debt. But the same servant went out, and found one of his fellow-servants, which owed him an hundred pence: and he laid hands on him, and took him by the throat, saying, Pay me that thou owest. And his fellow-servant fell down at his feet, and besought him, saying, Have patience with me, and I will pay thee all. And he would not: but went and cast him into prison, till he should pay the debt. So when his fellow-servants saw what was done, they were very sorry, and came and told unto their Lord all that was done. Then his Lord, after that he had called him, said unto him, O thou wicked servant, I forgave thee all that debt, because thou desiredst me: shouldest not thou also have had compassion on thy fellow-servant, even as I had pity on thee? And his Lord was wroth, and delivered him to the tormentors, till he should pay all that was due unto him. So likewise shall my heavenly Father do also unto you, if ye from your hearts forgive not everyone his brother their trespasses.

THE TWENTY-THIRD SUNDAY AFTER TRINITY

THE INTROIT. *Psalm* 24. 7-10.

LIFT up your heads, O ye gates, and be ye lift up, ye everlasting doors; / and the King of glory shall come in. Who is the King of glory? / it is the Lord strong and mighty, even the Lord mighty in battle. Lift up your heads, O ye gates, and be ye lift up, ye everlasting doors, / and the King of glory shall come in. Who is the King of glory? / even the Lord of hosts, He is the King of glory.

GLORY be to the Father, and to the Son, / and to the Holy Ghost;

As it was in the beginning, is now, and ever shall be, / world without end. Amen.

THE COLLECT.

O GOD, our Refuge and Strength, Who art the Author of all godliness: Be ready, we beseech Thee, to hear the devout prayers of Thy Church; and grant that those things which we ask faithfully, we may obtain effectually; through Jesus Christ our Lord. *Amen.*

THE EPISTLE. *Philippians* 3. 17-21.

BRETHREN, be followers together of me, and mark them which walk so as ye have us for an ensample. (For many walk, of whom I have told you often, and now tell you even weeping, that they are the enemies of the Cross of Christ: whose end is destruction, whose God is their belly, and whose glory is in their shame, who mind earthly things.) For our conversation is in heaven; from whence also we look for the Saviour, the Lord Jesus Christ; Who shall change our vile body, that it may be fashioned like unto His glorious body, according to the working whereby He is able even to subdue all things unto Himself.

THE GRADUAL. *Psalm* 121. 1-4.

ALLELUIA, Alleluia. I will lift up mine eyes unto the hills; / from whence cometh my help? My help cometh even from the Lord, / Who hath made heaven and earth. He will not suffer thy foot to be moved; / and He that keepeth thee will not sleep. Behold, He that keepeth Israel / shall neither slumber nor sleep. Alleluia.

THE GOSPEL. *Saint Matthew* 22. 15-22.

THEN went the Pharisees, and took counsel how they might entangle Him in His talk. And they sent out unto Him their disciples with the Herodians, saying, Master, we know that Thou art true, and teachest the way of God in truth, neither carest Thou for any man: for Thou regardest not the person of men. Tell us therefore, What thinkest Thou? Is it lawful to give tribute unto Caesar, or not? But Jesus perceived their wickedness, and said, Why tempt ye me, ye hypocrites? Shew me the tribute money. And they brought unto Him a penny. And He saith unto them, Whose is this image and superscription? They say unto Him, Caesar's. Then saith He unto them, Render therefore unto Caesar the things which are Caesar's; and unto God the things that are God's. When they had heard these words, they marvelled, and left Him, and went their way.

THE TWENTY-FOURTH SUNDAY AFTER TRINITY

THE INTROIT. *Psalm* 147. 1-11.

O PRAISE the Lord, for it is a good thing to sing praises unto our God; / yea, a joyful and pleasant thing it is to be thankful. The Lord doth build up Jerusalem, / and gather together the out-casts of Israel. He healeth those that are broken in heart, / and giveth medicine to heal their sickness. He telleth the number of the stars, / and calleth them all by their names. Great is our Lord, and great is His power; / yea, and His wisdom is infinite. The Lord setteth up the meek, / and bringeth the ungodly down to the ground. O sing unto the Lord with thanksgiving, / sing praises upon the harp unto our God; Who covereth the heaven with clouds, and prepareth rain for the earth, / and maketh the grass to grow upon the mountains, and herb for the use of men; Who giveth fodder unto the cattle, / and feedeth the young ravens that call upon Him. He hath no pleasure in the strength of an horse, / neither delighteth He in any man's legs. But the Lord's delight is in them that fear Him, / and put their trust in His mercy.

GLORY be to the Father, and to the Son, / and to the Holy Ghost;
As it was in the beginning, is now, and ever shall be, / world without end. Amen.

THE COLLECT.

O LORD, we beseech Thee, absolve Thy people from their offences; that through Thy bountiful goodness we may all be delivered from the bands of those sins, which by our frailty we have committed; grant this, O heavenly Father, for Jesus Christ's sake, our Blessed Lord and Saviour. *Amen.*

THE EPISTLE. *Colossians* 1. 3-12.

WE give thanks to God and the Father of our Lord Jesus Christ, praying always for you, since we heard of your faith in Christ Jesus, and of the love which ye have to all the saints, for the hope which is laid up for you in heaven, whereof ye heard before in the word of the truth of the Gospel; which is come unto you, as it is in all the world; and bringeth forth fruit, as it doth also in you, since the day ye heard of it, and knew the grace of God in truth: as ye also learned of Epaphras our dear fellowservant, who is for you a faithful minister of Christ; who also declared unto us your love in the Spirit. For this cause we also, since the day we heard it, do not cease to pray for you, and to desire that ye might be filled with the knowledge of His will in all wisdom and spiritual understanding; that ye might walk worthy of the Lord unto all pleasing, being fruitful in every good work, and increasing in the knowledge of God; strengthened with all might, according to His glorious power, unto all patience and long-suffering with joyfulness; giving thanks unto the Father, which hath made us meet to be partakers of the inheritance of the saints in light.

THE GRADUAL. *Psalm* 147. 12-15.

ALLELUIA, Alleluia. Praise the Lord, O Jerusalem; / praise thy God, O Sion. For He hath made fast the bars of thy gates, / and hath blessed thy children within thee. He maketh peace in thy borders, / and filleth thee with the flour of wheat. He sendeth forth His commandment upon earth, / and His word runneth very swiftly. Alleluia.

THE GOSPEL. *Saint Matthew* 9. 18-26.

WHILE He spake these things unto them, behold, there came a certain ruler, and worshipped Him, saying, My daughter is even now dead: but come and lay Thy hand upon her, and she shall live. And Jesus arose, and followed him, and so did His disciples. And, behold, a woman, which was diseased with an issue of blood twelve years, came behind Him, and touched the hem of His garment: for she said within herself, If I may but touch His garment, I shall be whole. But Jesus turned Him about, and when He saw her, He said, Daughter, be of good comfort; thy faith hath made thee whole. And the woman was made whole from that hour. And when Jesus came into the ruler's house, and saw the minstrels and the people making a noise, He said unto them, Give place: for the maid is not dead, but sleepeth. And they laughed Him to scorn. But when the people were put forth, He went in, and took her by the hand, and the maid arose. And the fame hereof went abroad into all that land.

And if any more Sundays remain before the Sunday next before Advent, the proper Introit, Collect, Epistle, Gradual, and Gospel of those Sundays that were omitted after the Epiphany shall be taken to supply so many as may be wanting. And if there be fewer, the remainder may be omitted.

THE SUNDAY NEXT BEFORE ADVENT

THE INTROIT. *Psalm* 85. 1-7
LORD, Thou art become gracious unto Thy land; / Thou hast turned away the captivity of Jacob. Thou hast forgiven the offence of Thy people, / and covered all their sins. Thou hast taken away all Thy displeasure, / and turned Thyself from Thy wrathful indignation. Turn us then, O God our Saviour, / and let Thine anger cease from us. Wilt Thou be displeased at us for ever? / and wilt Thou stretch out Thy wrath from one generation to another? Wilt Thou not turn again, and quicken us, / that Thy people may rejoice in Thee? O Lord, shew Thy mercy upon us, / and grant us Thy salvation.

GLORY be to the Father, and to the Son, / and to the Holy Ghost;
As it was in the beginning, is now, and ever shall be, / world without end. Amen.

THE COLLECT.
STIR up, we beseech Thee, O Lord, the wills of Thy faithful people; that they, plenteously bringing forth the fruit of good works, may of Thee be plenteously rewarded; through Jesus Christ our Lord. *Amen.*

FOR THE EPISTLE. *Jeremiah* 23. 1-8.
WOE be unto the pastors that destroy and scatter the sheep of my pasture! saith the Lord. Therefore thus saith the Lord God of Israel against the pastors that feed my people; Ye have scattered my flock, and driven them away, and have not visited them: behold, I will visit upon you the evil of your doings, saith the Lord. And I will gather the remnant of my flock out of all countries whither I have driven them, and will bring them again to their folds; and they shall be fruitful and increase. And I will set up shepherds over them which shall feed them: and they shall fear no more, nor be dismayed, neither shall they be lacking, saith the Lord. Behold, the days come, saith the Lord, that I will raise unto David a righteous Branch, and a King shall reign and prosper, and shall execute judgement and justice in the earth. In His days Judah shall be saved, and Israel shall dwell safely: and this is His name whereby He shall be called, THE LORD OUR RIGHTEOUSNESS. Therefore, behold, the days come, saith the Lord, that they shall no more say, The Lord liveth, which brought up the children of Israel out of the land of Egypt; but, The Lord liveth, which brought up and which led the seed of the house of Israel out of the north country, and from all countries whither I had driven them; and they shall dwell in their own land.

THE GRADUAL. *Psalm* 85. 8-13.

ALLELUIA, Alleluia. I will hearken what the Lord God will say concerning me, / for He shall speak peace unto His people, and to His saints, that they turn not again. For His salvation is nigh them that fear Him, / that glory may dwell in our land. Mercy and truth are met together; / righteousness and peace have kissed each other. Truth shall flourish out of the earth, / and righteousness hath looked down from heaven. Yea, the Lord shall shew loving-kindness, / and our land shall give her increase. Righteousness shall go before Him, / and He shall direct his going in the way. Alleluia.

THE GOSPEL. *Saint John* 6. 5-14.

WHEN Jesus then lifted up His eyes, and saw a great company come unto Him, He saith unto Philip, Whence shall we buy bread, that these may eat? And this He said to prove him: for He Himself knew what He would do. Philip answered Him, Two hundred penny-worth of bread is not sufficient for them, that every one of them may take a little. One of His disciples, Andrew, Simon Peter's brother, saith unto Him, There is a lad here, which hath five barley loaves, and two small fishes: but what are they among so many? And Jesus said, Make the men sit down. Now there was much grass in the place. So the men sat down, in number about five thousand. And Jesus took the loaves; and when He had given thanks, He distributed to the disciples, and the disciples to them that were set down; and likewise of the fishes as much as they would. When they were filled, He said unto His disciples, Gather up the fragments that remain, that nothing be lost. Therefore they gathered them together, and filled twelve baskets with the fragments of the five barley loaves, which remained over and above unto them that had eaten. Then those men, when they had seen the miracle that Jesus did, said, This is of a truth that Prophet that should come into the world.

SAINT ANDREW THE APOSTLE
[30 November]

THE INTROIT. *Psalm* 92. 1-4.

IT is a good thing to give thanks unto the Lord, / and to sing praises unto Thy Name, O Thou Most High; To tell of Thy loving-kindness early in the morning, / and of Thy truth in the night-season; Upon an instrument of ten strings, and upon the lute, / upon a loud instrument, and upon the harp. For Thou, Lord, hast made me glad through Thy works, / and I will rejoice in giving praise for the operations of Thy hands.

GLORY be to the Father, and to the Son, / and to the Holy Ghost;

As it was in the beginning is now, and ever shall be, / world without end. Amen.

THE COLLECT.

ALMIGHTY God, Who didst give such grace unto Thy blessed Apostle Saint Andrew, the first to be called by Thy Son Jesus Christ, who readily obeyed that calling, and followed Him without delay: Grant unto us, that we, being called by Thy holy Word, may forthwith give up ourselves obediently to fulfil Thy Commandments, and walk steadfastly according to our calling; through the same Jesus Christ our Lord. *Amen.*

THE EPISTLE. *Romans* 10. 9-21.

IF thou shalt confess with thy mouth the Lord Jesus, and shalt believe in thine heart that God hath raised Him from the dead, thou shalt be saved. For with the heart man believeth unto righteousness; and with the mouth confession is made unto salvation. For the Scripture saith, Whosoever believeth on Him shall not be ashamed. For there is no difference between the Jew and the Greek: for the same Lord over all is rich unto all that call upon Him. For whosoever shall call upon the Name of the Lord shall be saved. How then shall they call on Him in Whom they have not believed? and how shall they believe in Him of Whom they have not heard? and how shall they hear without a preacher? and how shall they preach, except they be sent? as it is written, How beautiful are the feet of them that preach the Gospel of peace, and bring glad tidings of good things! But they have not all obeyed the Gospel. For Isaiah saith, Lord, who hath believed our report? So then faith cometh by hearing, and hearing by the word of God. But I say, Have they not heard? Yes verily, their sound went into all the earth, and their words unto the ends of the world. But I say, Did not Israel know? First Moses saith, I will provoke you to jealousy by them that are no people, and by a foolish nation I will anger you. But Isaiah is very bold, and saith, I was found of them that sought me not; I was made manifest unto them that asked not after me. But to Israel He saith, All day long I have stretched forth my hands unto a disobedient and gainsaying people.

THE GRADUAL. *Psalm* 92. 11-14.

ALLELUIA, Alleluia. The righteous shall flourish like a palm-tree, / and shall spread abroad like a cedar in Libanus. Such as are planted in the house of the Lord, / shall flourish in the courts of the house of our God. They also shall bring forth more fruit in their age, / and shall be fat and well-liking. That they may shew how true the Lord my Strength is, / and that there is no unrighteousness in him. Alleluia.

THE GOSPEL. *Saint Matthew* 4. 18-22.

JESUS, walking by the sea of Galilee, saw two brethren, Simon called Peter, and Andrew his brother, casting a net into the sea: for they were fishers. And he saith unto them, Follow me, and I will make you fishers of men. And they straightway left their nets, and followed Him. And going on from thence, He saw other two brethren, James the son of Zebedee, and John his brother, in a ship with Zebedee their father, mending their nets; and He called them. And they immediately left the ship and their father, and followed Him.

SAINT THOMAS THE APOSTLE
[21 December]

THE INTROIT. *Psalm* 139. 1-9.
O LORD, Thou hast searched me out and known me; / Thou knowest my down-sitting and mine up-rising, Thou understandest my thoughts long before. Thou art about my path, and about my bed, / and spiest out all my ways. For lo, there is not a word in my tongue, / but Thou, O Lord, knowest it altogether. Thou hast fashioned me behind and before, / and laid Thine hand upon me. Such knowledge is too wonderful and excellent for me: / I cannot attain unto it. Whither shall I go then from Thy Spirit, / or whither shall I go then from Thy presence? If I climb up into heaven, Thou art there; / if I go down to hell, Thou art there also. If I take the wings of the morning, / and remain in the uttermost parts of the sea; Even there also shall Thy hand lead me, / and Thy right hand shall hold me.

GLORY be to the Father, and to the Son, / and to the Holy Ghost;
As it was in the beginning is now, and ever shall be, / world without end. Amen.

THE COLLECT.
ALMIGHTY and everliving God, Who for the more confirmation of the faith didst suffer Thy blessed Apostle Saint Thomas to be doubtful in Thy Son's resurrection: Grant us so perfectly, and without all doubt, to believe in Thy Son Jesus Christ, that our faith in Thy sight may never be reproved. Hear us, O Lord, through the same Jesus Christ, to Whom with Thee and the Holy Ghost, be all honour and glory, now and fore evermore. *Amen.*

THE EPISTLE. *Ephesians* 2. 19-22.
NOW therefore ye are no more strangers and foreigners, but fellow-citizens with the saints, and of the household of God; and are built upon the foundation of the Apostles and Prophets, Jesus Christ Himself being the chief Corner-stone; in Whom all the building fitly framed together groweth unto an holy temple in the Lord: in Whom ye also are builded together for an habitation of God through the Spirit.

THE GRADUAL. *Psalm* 30. 1-5.
ALLELUIA, Alleluia. I will magnify Thee, O Lord, for Thou hast set me up, / and not made my foes to triumph over me. O Lord my God, I cried unto Thee, / and Thou hast healed me. Thou, Lord, hast brought my soul out of hell; / Thou hast kept my life from them that go down to the pit. Sing praises unto the Lord, O ye saints of His, / and give thanks unto Him for a remembrance of His holiness. For His wrath endureth but the twinkling of an eye, and in His pleasure is life; / heaviness may endure for a night, but joy cometh in the morning. Alleluia.

THE GOSPEL. *Saint John* 20. 24-31.
THOMAS, one of the twelve, called Didymus, was not with them when Jesus came. The other disciples therefore said unto him, We have seen the Lord. But he said unto them, Except I shall see

in His hands the print of the nails, and put my finger into the print of the nails, and thrust my hand into His side, I will not believe. And after eight days again His disciples were within, and Thomas with them: then came Jesus, the doors being shut, and stood in the midst, and said, Peace be unto you. Then saith He to Thomas, Reach hither thy finger, and behold my hands; and reach hither thy hand, and thrust it into my side: and be not faithless, but believing. And Thomas answered and said unto Him, My Lord and my God. Jesus saith unto him, Thomas, because thou hast seen me, thou hast believed: blessed are they that have not seen, and yet have believed. And many other signs truly did Jesus in the presence of His disciples, which are not written in this book: but these are written, that ye might believe that Jesus is the Christ, the Son of God; and that believing ye might have life through His Name.

THE CONVERSION OF
SAINT PAUL THE APOSTLE
[25 January]

THE INTROIT. *Psalm* 126. 1-7.

WHEN the Lord turned again the captivity of Sion, / then were we like unto them that dream. Then was our mouth filled with laughter, / and our tongue with joy. Then said they among the heathen, / The Lord hath done great things for them. Yea, the Lord hath done great things for us already; / whereof we rejoice. Turn our captivity, O Lord, / as the rivers in the south. They that sow in tears, / shall reap in joy. He that now goeth on his way weeping, and beareth forth good seed, / shall doubtless come again with joy, and bring his sheaves with him.

GLORY be to the Father, and to the Son, / and to the Holy Ghost;
As it was in the beginning is now, and ever shall be, / world without end. Amen.

THE COLLECT.

O GOD, Who, through the preaching of Thy blessed Apostle Saint Paul, hast caused the light of the Gospel to shine throughout the world: Grant, we beseech Thee, that we, having his wonderful conversion in remembrance, may shew forth our thankfulness unto Thee for the same, by following the holy doctrine which He taught; through Jesus Christ our Lord. *Amen.*

FOR THE EPISTLE. *Acts* 9. 1.

AND Saul, yet breathing out threatenings and slaughter against the disciples of the Lord, went unto the high priest, and desired of him letters to Damascus to the synagogues, that if he found any of this Way, whether they were men or women, he might bring them bound unto Jerusalem. And as he journeyed, he came near Damascus: and suddenly there shined round about him a light from heaven: and he fell to the earth, and heard a voice saying unto him, Saul, Saul, why persecutest thou me? And he said, Who art Thou, Lord? And the Lord said, I am Jesus Whom thou persecutest: it is hard for thee to kick against the pricks. And he trembling and astonished said, Lord, what wilt Thou have me to do? And the Lord said unto him, Arise, and go into the city, and it shall be told thee what thou must do. And the men which journeyed with him stood speechless, hearing a voice, but seeing no man. And Saul arose from the earth; and when his eyes were opened, he saw no man: but they led him by the hand, and brought him into Damascus. And he was three days without sight, and neither did eat nor drink. And there was a certain disciple at Damascus, named Ananias; and to him said the Lord in a vision, Ananias. And he said, Behold, I am here, Lord. And the Lord said unto him, Arise, and go into the street which is called Straight, and enquire in the house of Judas for one called Saul, of Tarsus: for, behold, he prayeth, and hath seen in a vision a man named Ananias coming in, and putting his hand on him, that he might receive his sight. Then Ananias answered, Lord, I have heard by many of this man, how much evil he hath done to thy saints at Jerusalem: and here he hath authority from the chief priests to bind all that call on Thy Name. But the Lord said unto him, Go thy way: for he is a chosen vessel unto me, to bear my name before the Gentiles, and kings, and the children of Israel: For I will shew him how great things he must suffer for my Name's sake. And Ananias went his way, and entered into the house; and putting his hands on him said, Brother Saul, the Lord, even Jesus, that appeared unto thee in the way as thou camest, hath sent me, that thou mightest receive thy sight, and be filled with the Holy Ghost. And immediately there fell from his eyes as it had been scales: and he received sight forthwith, and arose, and was baptised. And when he had received meat, he was strengthened. Then was Saul certain days with the disciples which were at Damascus. And straightway he preached Christ in the synagogues, that He is the Son of God. But all that heard him were amazed, and said, Is not this he that destroyed them which called on this Name in Jerusalem, and came hither for that intent, that he might bring them bound unto the chief priests? But Saul increased the more in strength, and confounded the Jews which dwelt at Damascus, proving that this is very Christ.

THE GRADUAL. *Psalm* 117. 1-2.

ALLELUIA, Alleluia. O praise the Lord, all ye heathen; / praise him, all ye nations. For His merciful kindness is ever more and more towards us: / and the truth of the Lord endureth for ever. Praise the Lord. Alleluia.

THE GOSPEL. *Saint Matthew* 19. 27.

PETER answered and said unto him, Behold, we have forsaken all, and followed Thee; what shall we have therefore? And Jesus said unto them, Verily I say unto you, That ye which have followed me, in the regeneration when the Son of Man shall sit in the throne of His glory, ye also shall sit upon twelve thrones, judging the twelve tribes of Israel. And every one that hath forsaken houses, or brethren, or sisters, or father, or mother, or wife, or children, or lands, for my Name's sake, shall receive an hundredfold, and shall inherit everlasting life. But many that are first shall be last; and the last shall be first.

THE PRESENTATION OF OUR LORD JESUS CHRIST IN THE TEMPLE AND THE PURIFICATION OF SAINT MARY THE VIRGIN

COMMONLY CALLED

CANDLEMAS-DAY

[2 February]

THE BLESSING OF THE CANDLES

The Priest shall first say this sentence of Scripture following.

THEN spake Jesus again unto them, saying, I am the Light of the world: he that followeth me shall not walk in darkness, but shall have the Light of life. *Saint John* 8. 12.

THE PROPERS OF THE YEAR

Then shall the Priest say,
OUR help standeth in the Name of the Lord.
    Answer. Who hath made heaven and earth.
Priest. O Lord, hear our prayer;
    Answer. And let our cry come unto Thee.
Priest. The Lord be with you.
    Answer. And with thy spirit.

Priest. Let us pray.

Then shall the Priest proceed to bless the Candles, as followeth.

BLESS, we beseech Thee, Almighty God, these Candles of wax to our use, and to the service of Thy House; that the light coming therefrom may be unto us a sign and token of the true Light which lighteth every man that cometh into the world, even our Lord Jesus Christ, Thy Son, in Whose blessed Name we make our prayers and supplications unto Thee. *Amen.*

ALMIGHTY and Everlasting God, Who as on this day, through the pious obedience of the Blessed Virgin Mary, and of blessed Saint Joseph her Spouse, to the ordinances of the Law of Moses, didst present Thine only-begotten Son our Saviour Jesus Christ in Thy holy temple at Jerusalem, to be received into the waiting arms of Thy just and devout servant Simeon: We humbly beseech Thee to bless, hallow, and consecrate these Candles, and to kindle them with the light of Thy perfect brightness; and grant that all they who behold them, or who receive them in honour of this holy day, may be inflamed with the fire of Thy love, and be made worthy to be presented in the holy temple of Thy heavenly glory; through the same Thy Son Jesus Christ our Lord, Who with Thee and the Holy Ghost liveth and reigneth, ever one God, world without end. *Amen.*

LIGHTEN our darkness, we beseech Thee, O Lord, and by Thy great mercy defend us from the perils and dangers of this present time; for the love of Thine only Son, our Saviour Jesus Christ. *Amen.*

AT THE EUCHARIST

Then shall the Priest proceed in the celebration of the Holy Eucharist
wherein these following shall be the Propers.

THE INTROIT. *Psalm* 48. 1-9.

GREAT is the Lord, and highly to be praised, / in the city of our God, even upon His holy hill. The hill of Sion is a fair place, and the joy of the whole earth; / upon the north-side lieth the city of the great King; God is well known in her palaces as a sure Refuge. For lo, the kings of the earth / are gathered, and gone by together. They marvelled to see such things; / they were astonished, and suddenly cast down. Fear came there upon them, and sorrow, / as upon a woman in her travail. Thou shalt break the ships of the sea / through the east-wind. Like as we have heard, so have we seen in the city of the Lord of hosts, in the city of our God: / God upholdeth the same for ever. We wait for Thy loving-kindness, O God, / in the midst of Thy temple. O God, according to Thy Name, so is Thy praise unto the world's end; / Thy right hand is full of righteousness.

GLORY be to the Father, and to the Son, / and to the Holy Ghost;
As it was in the beginning, is now, and ever shall be, / world without end. Amen.

THE PROPERS OF THE YEAR

The Collect.

ALMIGHTY and everliving God, we humbly beseech Thy Divine Majesty, that, as Thine only-begotten Son was this day presented in the Temple in substance of our flesh, so we may be presented unto Thee with pure and clean hearts; through the same Thy Son Jesus Christ our Lord. *Amen.*

FOR THE EPISTLE. *Malachi* 3. 1-5.

BEHOLD, I will send my messenger, and he shall prepare the way before me: and the Lord, Whom ye seek, shall suddenly come to His temple, even the Messenger of the Covenant, Whom ye delight in: behold, He shall come, saith the Lord of hosts. But who may abide the day of His coming? and who shall stand when He appeareth? for He is like a refiner's fire, and like fullers' soap: and He shall sit as a refiner and purifier of silver: and He shall purify the sons of Levi, and purge them as gold and silver, that they may offer unto the Lord an offering in righteousness. Then shall the offering of Judah and Jerusalem be pleasant unto the Lord, as in the days of old, and as in former years. And I will come near to you to judgement; and I will be a swift witness against the sorcerers, and against the adulterers, and against false swearers, and against those that oppress the hireling in his wages, the widow, and the fatherless, and that turn aside the stranger from his right, and fear not me, saith the Lord of hosts.

THE GRADUAL. *Psalm* 48. 10-13.

ALLELUIA, Alleluia. Let the mount Sion rejoice, and the daughters of Judah be glad, / because of Thy judgements. Walk about Sion, and go round about her, / and tell the towers thereof. Mark well her bulwarks, set up her houses, / that ye may tell them that come after. For this God is our God for ever and ever, / He shall be our Guide unto death. Alleluia.

THE GOSPEL. *Saint Luke* 2. 22-40.

AND when the days of her purification according to the Law of Moses were accomplished, they brought Him to Jerusalem, to present Him to the Lord; (as it is written in the Law of the Lord, Every male that openeth the womb shall be called holy to the Lord;) and to offer a sacrifice according to that which is said in the Law of the Lord, A pair of turtledoves, or two young pigeons. And, behold, there was a man in Jerusalem, whose name was Simeon; and the same man was just and devout, waiting for the consolation of Israel: and the Holy Ghost was upon him. And it was revealed unto him by the Holy Ghost, that he should not see death, before he had seen the Lord's Christ. And he came by the Spirit into the temple: and when the parents brought in the Child Jesus, to do for Him after the custom of the Law, then took he Him up in his arms, and blessed God, and said, Lord, now lettest Thou Thy servant depart in peace, according to Thy word: For mine eyes have seen Thy salvation, which Thou hast prepared before the face of all people; A light to lighten the Gentiles, and the glory of Thy people Israel. And Joseph and His mother marvelled at those things which were spoken of Him. And Simeon blessed them, and said unto Mary His mother, Behold, this Child is set for the fall and rising again of many in Israel; and for a sign which shall be spoken against; Yea, a sword shall pierce through thine own soul also, that the thoughts of many hearts may be revealed. And there was one Anna, a prophetess, the daughter of Phanuel, of the tribe of Asher: she was of a great age, and had lived with an husband seven years from her virginity; and she was a widow of about fourscore and four years, which departed not from the temple, but served God with fastings and prayers night and day. And she coming in that instant gave thanks likewise unto the Lord, and spake of Him to all them that looked for redemption in Jerusalem. And when they had performed all things according to the Law of the Lord, they returned into Galilee, to their own city Nazareth. And the Child grew, and waxed strong in spirit, filled with wisdom: and the grace of God was upon Him.

THE COLLECT AFTER COMMUNION.

O LORD, Who didst fulfill the expectation of just Simeon, that he should not see death before he had looked upon Thy Christ: We beseech Thee, fulfill also unto us Thy word of promise, made unto us by Thy Son; that all we, who have partaken of the Communion of His blessed Supper, may have our part in the glory of His Resurrection; through the same Jesus Christ our Lord and Saviour. *Amen.*

SAINT MATTHIAS THE APOSTLE
[24 February]

THE INTROIT. *Psalm* 16. 1-7.

PRESERVE me, O God, / for in Thee have I put my trust. O my soul, thou hast said unto the Lord, / Thou art my God, my goods are nothing unto Thee. All my delight is upon the saints, that are in the earth, / and upon such as excel in virtue. But they that run after another god / shall have great trouble. Their drink-offerings of blood will I not offer, / neither make mention of their names within my lips. The Lord Himself is the portion of mine inheritance, and of my cup: / Thou shalt maintain my lot. The lines are fallen unto me in pleasant places; / yea, I have a goodly heritage.

GLORY be to the Father, and to the Son, / and to the Holy Ghost;
As it was in the beginning, is now, and ever shall be, / world without end. Amen.

THE COLLECT.

O ALMIGHTY God, Who into the place of the traitor Judas didst choose Thy faithful servant Saint Matthias to be of the number of the Twelve Apostles: Grant that Thy Church, being alway preserved from false Apostles, may be ordered and guided by faithful and true pastors; through Jesus Christ our Lord. *Amen.*

FOR THE EPISTLE. *Acts* 1. 15-26.

IN those days Peter stood up in the midst of the disciples, and said, (the number of names together were about an hundred and twenty,) Men and brethren, this Scripture must needs have been fulfilled, which the Holy Ghost by the mouth of David spake before concerning Judas, which was guide to them that took Jesus. For he was numbered with us, and had obtained part of this Ministry. Now this man purchased a field with the reward of iniquity; and falling headlong, he burst asunder in the midst, and all his bowels gushed out. And it was known unto all the dwellers at Jerusalem; insomuch as that field is called in their proper tongue, Akeldama, that is to say, The Field of Blood. For it is written in the book of Psalms, Let his habitation be desolate, and let no man dwell therein: and his bishopric let another take. Wherefore of these men which have companied with us all the time that the Lord Jesus went in and out among us, beginning from the baptism of John, unto that same day that He was taken up from us, must one be ordained to be a witness with us of His resurrection. And they appointed two, Joseph called Barsabas, who was surnamed Justus, and Matthias. And they prayed, and said, Thou, Lord, which knowest the hearts of all men, shew whether of these two Thou hast chosen, that he may take part of this Ministry and Apostleship, from which Judas by transgression fell, that he might go to his own place. And they gave forth their lots; and the lot fell upon Matthias; and he was numbered with the eleven Apostles.

THE GRADUAL. *Psalm* 80. 8-9.

ALLELUIA, Alleluia. Thou hast brought a vine out of Egypt; / Thou hast cast out the heathen, and planted it. Thou madest room for it; / and when it had taken root it filled the land. Alleluia.

THE GOSPEL. *Saint Matthew* 11. 25.

AT that time Jesus answered and said, I thank Thee, O Father, Lord of heaven and earth, because Thou hast hid these things from the wise and prudent, and hast revealed them unto babes. Even so, Father: for so it seemed good in Thy sight. All things are delivered unto me of my Father: and no man knoweth the Son, but the Father; neither knoweth any man the Father, save the Son, and he to whomsoever the Son will reveal Him. Come unto me, all ye that labour and are heavy laden, and I will give you rest. Take my yoke upon you, and learn of me; for I am meek and lowly in heart: and ye shall find rest unto your souls. For my yoke is easy, and my burden is light.

SAINT JOSEPH OF NAZARETH
[19 March]

THE INTROIT. *Psalm* 1. 1-7.

BLESSED is the man that hath not walked in the counsel of the ungodly, nor stood in the way of sinners, / and hath not sat in the seat of the scornful. But his delight is in the Law of the Lord; / and in His Law doth he meditate day and night. And he shall be like a tree planted by the water-side, / that bringeth forth his fruit in due season, Whose leaf also doth not wither; / and look, whatsoever he doeth, it shall prosper. As for the ungodly, it is not so with them; / but they are like the chaff, which the wind scattereth away from the face of the earth. Therefore the ungodly shall not be able to stand in the judgement, / neither the sinners in the congregation of the righteous. For the Lord knoweth the way of the righteous; / but the way of the ungodly shall perish.

GLORY be to the Father, and to the Son, / and to the Holy Ghost;

As it was in the beginning, is now, and ever shall be, / world without end. Amen.

THE COLLECT.

O GOD Most High, Who from the family of Thy servant David didst raise up Saint Joseph the carpenter to be Protector and Spouse of the Blessed Virgin Mary, and Foster-father of our Lord Jesus Christ her Divine Son: Grant that we may so labour in our earthly vocations, that they may become labours of love and service offered unto Thee, our Father; through the same Jesus Christ our Lord, Who with Thee and the Holy Ghost liveth and reigneth, one God, for ever and ever. *Amen.*

FOR THE EPISTLE. *Wisdom* 4. 7-5. 5.

BUT though the righteous be prevented with death, yet shall he be in rest. For honourable age is not that which standeth in length of time, nor that is measured by number of years. But wisdom is the grey hair unto men, and an unspotted life is old age. He pleased God, and was beloved of him, so that living among sinners he was translated. Yea speedily was he taken away, lest that wickedness should alter his understanding, or deceit beguile his soul. For the bewitching of naughtiness doth obscure things that are honest; and the wandering of concupiscence doth undermine the simple mind. He, being made perfect in a short time, fulfilled a long time: for his soul pleased the Lord; therefore hasted he to take him away from among the wicked. This the people saw, and understood it not, neither laid they up this in their minds, that His grace and mercy is with His saints, and that He hath respect unto His chosen. Thus the righteous that is dead shall condemn the ungodly which are living; and youth that is soon perfected the many years and old age of the unrighteous. For they shall see the end of the wise, and shall not understand what God in His counsel hath decreed of him, and to what end the Lord hath set him in safety. They shall see him, and despise him; but God shall laugh them to scorn; and they shall hereafter be a vile carcase, and a reproach among the dead for evermore. For He shall rend them, and cast them down headlong, that they shall be speechless; and He shall shake them from the foundation; and they shall be utterly laid waste, and be in sorrow; and their memorial shall perish. And when they cast up the accounts of their sins, they shall come with fear; and their own iniquities shall convince them to their face. Then shall the righteous man stand in great boldness before the face of such as have afflicted him, and made no account of his labours. When they see it, they shall be troubled with terrible fear, and shall be amazed at the strangeness of his salvation, so far beyond all that they looked for. And they, repenting and groaning for anguish of spirit, shall say within themselves, This was he, whom we had sometimes in derision, and a proverb of reproach; we fools accounted his life madness, and his end to be without honour: How is he numbered among the children of God, and his lot is among the saints!

THE GRADUAL. *Psalm* 112. 4-9.
ALLELUIA, Alleluia. Unto the godly there ariseth up light in the darkness; / he is merciful, loving, and righteous. A good man is merciful, and lendeth, / and will guide his words with discretion. For he shall never be moved, / and the righteous shall be had in everlasting remembrance. He will not be afraid of any evil tidings, / for his heart standeth fast, and believeth in the Lord. His heart is established, and will not shrink, / until he see his desire upon his enemies. He hath dispersed abroad, and given to the poor, / and his righteousness remaineth for ever; his horn shall be exalted with honour. Alleluia.

THE GOSPEL. *Saint Matthew* 1. 18-25.
NOW the birth of Jesus Christ was on this wise: When as His Mother Mary was espoused to Joseph, before they came together, she was found with Child of the Holy Ghost. Then Joseph her husband, being a just man, and not willing to make her a public example, was minded to put her away privily. But while he thought on these things, behold, the Angel of the Lord appeared unto him in a dream, saying, Joseph, thou son of David, fear not to take unto thee Mary thy wife: for that which is conceived in her is of the Holy Ghost. And she shall bring forth a Son, and thou shalt call His Name Jesus, for He shall save His people from their sins. Now all this was done, that it might be fulfilled which was spoken of the Lord by the Prophet, saying, Behold, a Virgin shall be with Child, and shall bring forth a Son, and they shall call His Name Emmanuel, which being interpreted is, God with us. Then Joseph being raised from sleep did as the Angel of the Lord had bidden him, and took unto him his wife; and knew her not till she had brought forth her firstborn Son: and he called His Name JESUS.

THE ANNUNCIATION OF OUR LADY
COMMONLY CALLED
LADY-DAY
[25 March]

THE INTROIT. *Psalm* 45. 10-15.

KINGS' daughters were among thy honourable women; / upon thy right hand did stand the queen in a vesture of gold, wrought about with divers colours. Hearken, O daughter, and consider, incline thine ear ; / forget also thine own people, and thy father's house. So shall the King have pleasure in thy beauty; / for He is thy Lord God, and worship thou Him. And the daughter of Tyre shall be there with a gift, / like as the rich also among the people shall make their supplication before Thee. The King's daughter is all glorious within; / her clothing is of wrought gold. She shall be brought unto the King in raiment of needle-work; / the virgins that be her fellows shall bear her company, and shall be brought unto Thee.

GLORY be to the Father, and to the Son, / and to the Holy Ghost;
As it was in the beginning, is now, and ever shall be, / world without end. Amen.

THE COLLECT.

POUR forth, we beseech Thee, O Lord, Thy grace into our hearts; that, as we have known the Incarnation of Thy Son Jesus Christ by the message of an angel, so by His Cross and Passion we may be brought unto the glory of His Resurrection; through the same Jesus Christ our Lord. *Amen.*

FOR THE EPISTLE. *Isaiah* 7. 10-15.

MOREOVER, the Lord spake again unto Ahaz, saying, Ask thee a sign of the Lord thy God; ask it either in the depth, or in the height above. But Ahaz said, I will not ask, neither will I tempt the Lord. And he said, Hear ye now, O house of David; is it a small thing for you to weary men, but will ye weary my God also? Therefore the Lord Himself shall give you a sign; Behold, a virgin shall conceive, and bear a son, and shall call His name Immanuel. Butter and honey shall He eat, that He may know to refuse the evil, and choose the good.

THE GRADUAL. *Psalm* 131. 1-4.

ALLELUIA, Alleluia. Lord, I am not high-minded, / I have no proud looks. I do not exercise myself in great matters / which are too high for me. But I refrain my soul, and keep it low, like as a child that is weaned from his mother; / yea, my soul is even as a weaned child. O Israel, trust in the Lord, / from this time forth for evermore. Alleluia.

THE GOSPEL. *Saint Luke* 1. 26-38.

AND in the sixth month the angel Gabriel was sent from God unto a city of Galilee, named Nazareth, to a Virgin espoused to a man whose name was Joseph, of the house of David; and the Virgin's name was Mary. And the angel came in unto her, and said, Hail, thou that art highly favoured, the Lord is with thee: blessed art thou among women. And when she saw him, she was troubled at his saying, and cast in her mind what manner of salutation this should be. And the angel said unto her, Fear not, Mary: for thou hast found favour with God. And, behold, thou shalt conceive in thy womb, and bring forth a Son, and shalt call His name Jesus. He shall be great, and shall be called the Son of the Highest: and the Lord God shall give unto Him the throne of His father David: and He shall reign over the house of Jacob for ever; and of His kingdom there shall be no end. Then said Mary unto the angel, How shall this be, seeing I know not a man? And the angel answered and said unto her, The Holy Ghost shall come upon thee, and the power of the Highest shall overshadow thee: therefore also that holy thing which shall be born of thee shall be called the Son of God. And, behold, thy cousin Elisabeth, she hath also conceived a son in her old age: and this is the sixth month with her, who was called barren. For with God nothing shall be impossible. And Mary said, Behold the handmaid of the Lord; be it unto me according to thy word. And the angel departed from her.

SAINT MARK THE EVANGELIST
[25 April]

THE INTROIT. *Psalm* 45. 1-4.

MY heart is inditing of a good matter; / I speak of the things which I have made unto the King. My tongue is the pen / of a ready writer. Thou art fairer than the children of men; / full of grace are thy lips, because God hath blessed thee for ever. Gird Thee with Thy sword upon Thy thigh, O Thou most Mighty, / according to Thy worship and renown.

GLORY be to the Father, and to the Son, / and to the Holy Ghost;
As it was in the beginning, is now, and ever shall be, / world without end. Amen.

THE COLLECT.

O ALMIGHTY God, Who hast instructed Thy holy Church with the heavenly doctrine of Thine Evangelist Saint Mark: Give us grace, that, being not like children carried away with every blast of vain doctrine, we may be established in the truth of Thy holy Gospel; through Jesus Christ our Lord. *Amen.*

THE EPISTLE. *Ephesians* 4. 7-16.

BUT unto every one of us is given grace according to the measure of the gift of Christ. Wherefore He saith, When He ascended up on high, He led captivity captive, and gave gifts unto men. (Now that He ascended, what is it but that He also descended first into the lower parts of the earth? He that descended is the same also that ascended up far above all heavens, that He might fill all things.) And He gave some, Apostles; and some, Prophets; and some, Evangelists; and some, Pastors and Teachers; for the perfecting of the saints, for the work of the Ministry, for the edifying of the body of Christ: till we all come in the unity of the Faith, and of the knowledge of the Son of God, unto a perfect man, unto the measure of the stature of the fullness of Christ: that we henceforth be no more children, tossed to and fro, and carried about with every wind of doctrine, by the sleight of men, and cunning craftiness, whereby they lie in wait to deceive; but speaking the truth in love, may grow up into Him in all things, which is the head, even Christ: from Whom the whole body fitly joined together and compacted by that which every joint supplieth, according to the effectual working in the measure of every part, maketh increase of the body unto the edifying of itself in love.

THE GRADUAL. *Psalm* 119. 9-16.

ALLELUIA, Alleluia. Wherewithal shall a young man cleanse his way? / even by ruling himself after Thy Word. With my whole heart have I sought Thee: / O let me not go wrong out of Thy commandments. Thy words have I hid within my heart, / that I should not sin against Thee. Blessed art Thou, O Lord: / O teach me Thy statutes. With my lips have I been telling / of all the judgements of Thy mouth. I have had as great delight in the way of Thy testimonies, / as in all manner of riches. I will talk of Thy commandments, / and have respect unto Thy ways. My delight shall be in Thy statutes, / and I will not forget Thy word. Alleluia.

THE GOSPEL. *Saint John* 15. 1-11.

I AM the true vine, and my Father is the Husbandman. Every branch in me that beareth not fruit He taketh away: and every branch that beareth fruit, He purgeth it, that it may bring forth more fruit. Now ye are clean through the word which I have spoken unto you. Abide in me, and I in you. As the branch cannot bear fruit of itself, except it abide in the vine; no more can ye, except ye abide in me. I am the vine, ye are the branches: he that abideth in me, and I in him, the same bringeth forth much fruit: for without me ye can do nothing. If a man abide not in me, he is cast forth as a branch, and is withered; and men gather them, and cast them into the fire, and they are burned. If ye abide in me, and my words abide in you, ye shall ask what ye will, and it shall be done unto you. Herein is my Father glorified, that ye bear much fruit; so shall ye be my disciples. As the Father hath loved me, so have I loved you: continue ye in my love. If ye keep my commandments, ye shall abide in my love; even as I have kept my Father's commandments, and abide in His love. These things have I spoken unto you, that my joy might remain in you, and that your joy might be full.

SAINT PHILIP THE APOSTLE
AND SAINT JAMES THE APOSTLE
[1 May]

THE INTROIT. *Psalm* 33. 1-6.

REJOICE in the Lord, O ye righteous, / for it becometh well the just to be thankful. Praise the Lord with harp; / sing praises unto Him with the lute, and instrument of ten strings. Sing unto the Lord a new song, / sing praises lustily unto Him with a good courage. For the word of the Lord is true, / and all His works are faithful. He loveth righteousness and judgement; / the earth is full of the goodness of the Lord. By the word of the Lord were the heavens made, / and all the hosts of them by the breath of His mouth.

GLORY be to the Father, and to the Son, / and to the Holy Ghost;
As it was in the beginning, is now, and ever shall be, / world without end. Amen.

THE COLLECT.

O ALMIGHTY God, Whom truly to know is everlasting life: Grant us perfectly to know Thy Son Jesus Christ to be the Way, the Truth, and the Life; that, following the steps of Thy holy Apostles, Saint Philip and Saint James, we may steadfastly walk in the way that leadeth to eternal life; through the same thy Son Jesus Christ our Lord. *Amen.*

THE EPISTLE. *Saint James* 1. 1-12.

JAMES, a servant of God and of the Lord Jesus Christ, to the twelve tribes which are scattered abroad, greeting. My brethren, count it all joy when ye fall into divers temptations; knowing this, that the trying of your faith worketh patience. But let patience have her perfect work, that ye may be perfect and entire, wanting nothing. If any of you lack wisdom, let him ask of God, that giveth to all men liberally, and upbraideth not; and it shall be given him. But let him ask in faith, nothing wavering. For he that wavereth is like a wave of the sea driven with the wind and tossed. For let not that man think that he shall receive any thing of the Lord. A double minded man is unstable in all his ways. Let the brother of low degree rejoice in that he is exalted; but the rich, in that he is made low, because as the flower of the grass, he shall pass away. For the sun is no sooner risen with a burning heat, but it withereth the grass, and the flower thereof falleth, and the grace of the fashion of it perisheth: so also shall the rich man fade away in his ways. Blessed is the man that endureth temptation; for when he is tried, he shall receive the crown of life, which the Lord hath promised to them that love Him.

THE GRADUAL. *Psalm* 89. 5-8.

ALLELUIA, Alleluia. O Lord, the very heavens shall praise Thy wondrous works; / and Thy truth in the congregation of the saints. For who is he among the clouds / that shall be compared unto the Lord? And what is he among the gods / that shall be like unto the Lord? God is very greatly to be feared in the council of the saints, / and to be had in reverence of all them that are round about Him. Alleluia.

THE GOSPEL. *Saint John* 14. 1-17.

AND Jesus said unto His disciples, Let not your heart be troubled: ye believe in God, believe also in me. In my Father's house are many mansions: if it were not so, I would have told you. I go to prepare a place for you. And if I go and prepare a place for you, I will come again, and receive you unto myself; that where I am, there ye may be also. And whither I go ye know, and the way ye know. Thomas saith unto him, Lord, we know not whither Thou goest; and how can we know the way? Jesus saith unto him, I am the Way, the Truth, and the Life: no man cometh unto the Father, but by me. If ye had known me, ye should have known my Father also: and from henceforth ye know Him, and have seen Him. Philip saith unto Him, Lord, shew us the Father, and it sufficeth us. Jesus saith unto him, Have I been so long time with you, and yet hast thou not known me, Philip? he that hath seen me hath seen the Father; and how sayest thou then, Shew us the Father? Believest thou not that I am in the Father, and the Father in me? the words that I speak unto you I speak not of myself: but the Father that dwelleth in me, He doeth the works. Believe me that I am in the Father, and the Father in me: or else believe me for the very works' sake. Verily, verily, I say unto you, he that believeth on me, the works that I do shall he do also; and greater works than these shall he do; because I go unto my Father. And whatsoever ye shall ask in my Name, that will I do, that the Father may be glorified in the Son. If ye shall ask any thing in my Name, I will do it. If ye love me, keep my commandments. And I will pray the Father, and He shall give you another Comforter, that He may abide with you forever; even the Spirit of truth; Whom the world cannot receive, because it seeth Him not, neither knoweth Him: but ye know Him; for He dwelleth with you, and shall be in you.

SAINT BARNABAS THE APOSTLE
[11 June]

THE INTROIT. *Psalm* 112. 1-10.

BLESSED is the man that feareth the Lord: / he hath great delight in His commandments. His seed shall be mighty upon earth: / the generation of the faithful shall be blessed. Riches and plenteousness shall be in his house, / and his righteousness endureth for ever. Unto the godly there ariseth up light in the darkness; / He is merciful, loving, and righteous. A good man is merciful, and lendeth, / and will guide his words with discretion. For he shall never be moved, / and the righteous shall be had in everlasting remembrance. He will not be afraid of any evil tidings, / for his heart standeth fast, and believeth in the Lord. His heart is established, and will not shrink / until he see his desire upon his enemies. He hath dispersed abroad, and given to the poor, / and his righteousness remaineth for ever; his horn shall be exalted with honour. The ungodly shall see it, and it shall grieve him; / he shall gnash with his teeth, and consume away; the desire of the ungodly shall perish.

GLORY be to the Father, and to the Son, / and to the Holy Ghost;

As it was in the beginning, is now, and ever shall be, / world without end. Amen.

THE COLLECT.

O LORD God Almighty, Who didst endue Thy holy Apostle Barnabas with singular gifts of the Holy Ghost: Leave us not, we beseech thee, destitute of Thy manifold gifts, nor yet of grace to use them always to Thy honour and glory; through Jesus Christ our Lord. *Amen.*

FOR THE EPISTLE. *Acts* 11. 22-30.

TIDINGS of these things came unto the ears of the Church which was in Jerusalem: and they sent forth Barnabas, that he should go as far as Antioch. Who, when he came, and had seen the grace of God, was glad, and exhorted them all, that with purpose of heart they would cleave unto the Lord. For he was a good man, and full of the Holy Ghost and of faith: and much people was added unto the Lord. Then departed Barnabas to Tarsus, for to seek Saul: and when he had found him, he brought him unto Antioch. And it came to pass, that a whole year they assembled themselves with the Church, and taught much people. And the disciples were called Christians first in Antioch. And in these days came prophets from Jerusalem unto Antioch. And there stood up one of them named Agabus, and signified by the Spirit that there should be great dearth throughout all the world: which came to pass in the days of Claudius Caesar. Then the disciples, every man according to his ability, determined to send relief unto the brethren which dwelt in Judaea: which also they did, and sent it to the elders by the hands of Barnabas and Saul.

THE GRADUAL. *Psalm* 145. 8-13.

ALLELUIA, Alleluia. All Thy works praise Thee, O Lord; / and Thy saints give thanks unto Thee. They shew the glory of Thy kingdom, / and talk of Thy power; That Thy power, Thy glory, and mightiness of Thy kingdom, / might be known unto men. Thy kingdom is an everlasting kingdom, / and Thy dominion endureth throughout all ages. Alleluia.

THE GOSPEL. *Saint John* 15. 12-23.

THIS is my commandment, That ye love one another, as I have loved you. Greater love hath no man than this, that a man lay down his life for his friends. Ye are my friends, if ye do whatsoever I command you. Henceforth I call you not servants; for the servant knoweth not what his Lord doeth: but I have called you friends; for all things that I have heard of my Father I have made known unto you. Ye have not chosen me, but I have chosen you, and ordained you, that ye should go and bring forth fruit, and that your fruit should remain: that whatsoever ye shall ask of the Father in my Name, He may give it you. These things I command you, that ye love one another. If the world hate you, ye know that it hated me before it hated you. If ye were of the world, the world would love his own: but because ye are not of the world, but I have chosen you out of the world, therefore the world hateth you. Remember the word that I said unto you, The servant is not greater than his lord. If they have persecuted me, they will also persecute you; if they have kept my saying, they will keep yours also. But all these things will they do unto you for my name's sake, because they know not Him that sent me. If I had not come and spoken unto them, they had not had sin: but now they have no cloak for their sin. He that hateth me hateth my Father also.

THE NATIVITY OF SAINT JOHN THE BAPTIST
[24 June]

THE INTROIT. *Psalm* 46. 1-8.

GOD is our Hope and Strength, / a very present help in trouble. Therefore will we not fear, though the earth be moved, / and though the hills be carried into the midst of the sea; Though the waters thereof rage and swell, / and though the mountains shake at the tempest of the same. The rivers of the flood thereof shall make glad the city of God, / the holy place of the tabernacle of the Most High. God is in the midst of her, therefore shall she not be removed; / God shall help her, and that right early. The heathen make much ado, and the kingdoms are moved; / but God hath shewed His voice, and the earth shall melt away. The Lord of hosts is with us; / the God of Jacob is our Refuge.

GLORY be to the Father, and to the Son, / and to the Holy Ghost;
As it was in the beginning, is now, and ever shall be, / world without end. Amen.

THE COLLECT.

ALMIGHTY God, by Whose providence Thy servant Saint John the Baptist was wonderfully born, and sent to prepare the way of Thy Son our Saviour, by preaching of repentance: Make us so to follow his doctrine and holy life, that we may truly repent according to his preaching; and after his example constantly speak the truth, boldly rebuke vice, and patiently suffer for the truth's sake; through Jesus Christ our Lord. *Amen.*

FOR THE EPISTLE. *Isaiah* 40. 1-11.

COMFORT ye, comfort ye my people, saith your God. Speak ye comfortably to Jerusalem, and cry unto her, that her warfare is accomplished, that her iniquity is pardoned: for she hath received of the Lord's hand double for all her sins. The voice of him that crieth in the wilderness, Prepare ye the way of the Lord, make straight in the desert a highway for our God. Every valley shall be exalted, and every mountain and hill shall be made low: and the crooked shall be made straight, and the rough places plain: and the glory of the Lord shall be revealed, and all flesh shall see it together: for the mouth of the Lord hath spoken it. The voice said, Cry. And he said, What shall I cry? All flesh is grass, and all the goodliness thereof is as the flower of the field: the grass withereth, the flower fadeth: because the Spirit of the Lord bloweth upon it: surely the people is grass. The grass withereth, the flower fadeth: but the Word of our God shall stand for ever. O Sion, that bringest good tidings, get thee up into the high mountain; O Jerusalem, that bringest good tidings, lift up thy voice with strength; lift it up, be not afraid; say unto the cities of Judah, Behold your God! Behold, the Lord God will come with strong hand, and His arm shall rule for Him: behold, His reward is with Him, and His work before Him. He shall feed His flock like a shepherd: He shall gather the lambs with His arm, and carry them in His bosom, and shall gently lead those that are with young.

THE GRADUAL. *Psalm* 119. 161-168.

ALLELUIA, Alleluia. Princes have persecuted me without a cause; / but my heart standeth in awe of Thy word. I am as glad of Thy word, / as one that findeth great spoils. As for lies, I hate and abhor them; / but Thy Law do I love. Seven times a day do I praise Thee / because of Thy righteous judgements. Great is the peace that they have who love Thy Law, / and they are not offended at it. Lord, I have looked for Thy saving health, / and done after Thy commandments. My soul hath kept Thy testimonies, / and loved them exceedingly. I have kept Thy commandments and testimonies, / for all my ways are before Thee. Alleluia.

THE GOSPEL. *Saint Luke* 1. 57-80.

ELISABETH'S full time came that she should be delivered; and she brought forth a son. And her neighbours and her cousins heard how the Lord had shewed great mercy upon her; and they rejoiced with her. And it came to pass, that on the eighth day they came to circumcise the child; and they called him Zacharias, after the name of his father. And his mother answered and said, Not so; but he shall be called John. And they said unto her, There is none of thy kindred that is called by this name. And they made signs to his father, how he would have him called. And he asked for a writing table, and wrote, saying, His name is John. And they marvelled all. And his mouth was opened immediately, and his tongue loosed, and he spake, and praised God. And fear came on all that dwelt round about them: and all these sayings were noised abroad throughout all the hill country of Judaea. And all they that heard them laid them up in their hearts, saying, What manner of child shall this be! And the hand of the Lord was with him. And his father Zacharias was filled with the Holy Ghost, and prophesied, saying, Blessed be the Lord God of Israel; for He hath visited and redeemed His people, and hath raised up an horn of salvation for us in the house of His servant David; as He spake by the mouth of His holy prophets, which have been since the world began: that we should be saved from our enemies, and from the hand of all that hate us; to perform the mercy promised to our fathers, and to remember His holy covenant; the oath which He sware to our father Abraham, that He would grant unto us, that we being delivered out of the hand of our enemies might serve Him without fear, in holiness and righteousness before Him, all the days of our life. And thou, child, shalt be called the prophet of the Highest: for thou shalt go before the face of the Lord to prepare His ways; to give knowledge of salvation unto His people by the remission of their sins, through the tender mercy of our God; whereby the dayspring from on high hath visited us, to give light to them that sit in darkness and in the shadow of death, to guide our feet into the way of peace. And the child grew, and waxed strong in spirit, and was in the deserts till the day of his shewing unto Israel.

SAINT PETER THE APOSTLE
[29 June]

THE INTROIT. *Psalm* 87. 1-7.

HER foundations are upon the holy hills; / the Lord loveth the gates of Sion more than all the dwellings of Jacob. Very excellent things are spoken of thee, / thou city of God. I will think upon Rahab and Babylon / with them that know me. Behold ye the Philistines also, / and they of Tyre, with the Morians; lo, there was he born. And of Sion, it shall be said, This and that man was born in her: / and the Most High Himself shall establish her. The Lord shall count, when He writeth up the people, / that this man was born there. As well the singers as the players on instruments shall be there, / All my fresh springs shall be in thee.

GLORY be to the Father, and to the Son, / and to the Holy Ghost;

As it was in the beginning, is now, and ever shall be, / world without end. Amen.

THE COLLECT.

O ALMIGHTY God, Who by Thy Son Jesus Christ didst give to Thine Apostle Saint Peter many excellent gifts, and commandest him earnestly to feed Thy flock: Make, we beseech Thee, all Bishops and Pastors of Thy Church diligently to preach Thy holy Word, and the people obediently to follow the same, that they may receive the crown of everlasting glory; through Jesus Christ our Lord. *Amen.*

FOR THE EPISTLE. *Acts* 12. 1-11.

ABOUT that time Herod the king stretched forth his hands to vex certain of the Church. And he killed James the brother of John with the sword. And because he saw it pleased the Jews, he proceeded further to take Peter also. (Then were the days of unleavened bread.) And when he had apprehended him, he put him in prison, and delivered him to four quaternions of soldiers to keep him; intending after Easter to bring him forth to the people. Peter therefore was kept in prison: but prayer was made without ceasing of the Church unto God for him. And when Herod would have brought him forth, the same night Peter was sleeping between two soldiers, bound with two chains: and the keepers before the door kept the prison. And, behold, the angel of the Lord came upon him, and a light shined in the prison: and he smote Peter on the side, and raised him up, saying, Arise up quickly. And his chains fell off from his hands. And the angel said unto him, Gird thyself, and bind on thy sandals. And so he did. And he saith unto him, Cast thy garment about thee, and follow me. And he went out, and followed him; and wist not that it was true which was done by the angel; but thought he saw a vision. When they were past the first and the second ward, they came unto the iron gate that leadeth unto the city; which opened to them of his own accord: and they went out, and passed on through one street; and forthwith the angel departed from him. And when Peter was come to himself, he said, Now I know of a surety, that the Lord hath sent His angel, and hath delivered me out of the hand of Herod, and from all the expectation of the people of the Jews.

THE GRADUAL. *Psalm* 31. 1-4.

ALLELUIA, Alleluia. In Thee, O Lord, have I put my trust: / let me never be put to confusion, deliver me in Thy righteousness. Bow down Thine ear to me; / make haste to deliver me. And be Thou my strong Rock, and House of Defence, / that Thou mayest save me. For Thou art my strong Rock, and my Castle: / be Thou also my Guide, and lead me for Thy Name's sake. Alleluia.

THE GOSPEL. *Saint Matthew* 16. 13-19.

THEN Jesus came into the coasts of Caesarea Philippi, He asked His disciples, saying, Whom do men say that I, the Son of Man, am? And they said, Some say that Thou art John the Baptist: some, Elijah; and others, Jeremiah, or one of the Prophets. He saith unto them, But whom say ye that I am? And Simon Peter answered and said, Thou art the Christ, the Son of the living God. And Jesus answered and said unto him, Blessed art thou, Simon Bar-Jonah: for flesh and blood hath not revealed it unto thee, but my Father which is in heaven. And I say also unto thee, That thou art Peter, and upon this rock I will build my church; and the gates of hell shall not prevail against it. And I will give unto thee the keys of the kingdom of heaven: and whatsoever thou shalt bind on earth shall be bound in heaven: and whatsoever thou shalt loose on earth shall be loosed in heaven.

ALL HOLY APOSTLES
[14 July]

INTROIT. *Psalm* 56. 1-9.
BE merciful unto me, O God, for man goeth about to devour me: / he is daily fighting, and troubling me. Mine enemies are daily in hand to swallow me up; / for they be many that fight against me, O Thou most High. Nevertheless, though I am sometime afraid, / yet put I my trust in Thee. I will praise God, because of His Word: I have put my trust in God, / and will not fear what flesh can do unto me. They daily mistake my words: / all that they imagine is to do me evil. They hold all together, and keep themselves close, / and mark my steps, when they lay wait for my soul. Shall they escape for their wickedness? / Thou, O God, in Thy displeasure shalt cast them down. Thou tellest my flittings; put my tears into Thy bottle: / are not these things noted in Thy book? Whensoever I call upon Thee, then shall mine enemies be put to flight: / this I know; for God is on my side.

GLORY be to the Father, and to the Son, / and to the Holy Ghost;
As it was in the beginning, is now, and ever shall be, / world without end. Amen.

THE COLLECT.
O ALMIGHTY and Everliving God, our heavenly Father, Who through Thy Son Jesus Christ didst call and separate unto Thyself Apostles, sending them out to make disciples of every nation, baptising them, and teaching them to observe all things whatsoever the Lord had commanded them: Mercifully grant that all we who profess the truth which they taught, may faithfully follow their doctrine and ever remain in their fellowship, and so finally attain unto everlasting life in that blessed kingdom of Thy Son where those same holy Apostles shall be seated upon thrones judging the twelve tribes of Israel; through the same Thy Son Jesus Christ our Lord. *Amen.*

THE EPISTLE. *Acts* 5. 12-32.
AND by the hands of the Apostles were many signs and wonders wrought among the people; (and they were all with one accord in Solomon's porch. And of the rest durst no man join himself to them: but the people magnified them. And believers were the more added to the Lord, multitudes both of men and women.) Insomuch that they brought forth the sick into the streets, and laid them on beds and couches, that at the least the shadow of Peter passing by might overshadow some of them. There came also a multitude out of the cities round about unto Jerusalem, bringing sick folks, and them which were vexed with unclean spirits: and they were healed every one. Then the high priest rose up, and all they that were with him, (which is the sect of the Sadducees,) and were filled with indignation, and laid their hands on the Apostles, and put them in the common prison. But the angel of the Lord by night opened the prison doors, and brought them forth, and said, Go, stand and speak in the temple to the people all the words of this life. And when they heard that, they entered into the temple early in the morning, and taught. But the high priest came, and they that were with him, and called the council together, and all the senate of the children of Israel, and sent to the prison to have them brought. But when the officers came, and found them not in the prison, they returned, and told, saying, The prison truly found we shut with

all safety, and the keepers standing without before the doors: but when we had opened, we found no man within. Now when the high priest and the captain of the temple and the chief priests heard these things, they doubted of them whereunto this would grow. Then came one and told them, saying, Behold, the men whom ye put in prison are standing in the temple, and teaching the people. Then went the captain with the officers, and brought them without violence: for they feared the people, lest they should have been stoned. And when they had brought them, they set them before the council: and the high priest asked them, saying, Did not we straitly command you that ye should not teach in this Name? and, behold, ye have filled Jerusalem with your doctrine, and intend to bring this Man's Blood upon us. Then Peter and the other Apostles answered and said, We ought to obey God rather than men. The God of our fathers raised up Jesus, Whom ye slew and hanged on a tree. Him hath God exalted with His right hand to be a Prince and a Saviour, for to give repentance to Israel, and forgiveness of sins. And we are His witnesses of these things; and so is also the Holy Ghost, Whom God hath given to them that obey Him.

THE GRADUAL. *Psalm* 56. 10-13.

ALLELUIA, Alleluia. In God's word I will rejoice: / in the Lord's word will I comfort me. Yea, in God have I put my trust, I will not be afraid; / what man can do unto me? Unto Thee, O God, will I pay my vows; / unto Thee will I give thanks. For Thou hast delivered my soul from death, and my feet from falling, / that I may walk before God in the light of the living. Alleluia.

THE GOSPEL. *Saint Luke* 22. 24-30.

AND there was also a strife among them, which of them should be accounted the greatest. And He said unto them, The kings of the Gentiles exercise lordship over them; and they that exercise authority upon them are called benefactors. But ye shall not be so: but he that is greatest among you, let him be as the younger; and he that is chief, as he that doth serve. For whether is greater, he that sitteth at meat, or he that serveth? is not he that sitteth at meat? but I am among you as He that serveth. Ye are they which have continued with me in my temptations. And I appoint unto you a kingdom, as my Father hath appointed unto me; that ye may eat and drink at my table in my kingdom, and sit on thrones judging the twelve tribes of Israel.

THE COLLECT AFTER COMMUNION.

ALMIGHTY God, Who by Thy Son Jesus Christ didst give to Thy holy Apostles many excellent gifts, and didst charge them to feed Thy flock: Give Thy grace, we beseech Thee, to the Bishops, the Pastors of Thy Church, who succeed in their order from the Apostles in the particular oversight and government thereof, that they may ever diligently preach Thy Word, and faithfully follow and uphold their doctrine and example in the ministration of the same; and grant to the people, that they may all likewise obediently follow them; that all together may receive the crown of everlasting glory; through Jesus Christ our Lord. *Amen.*

SAINT MARY MAGDALENE

[22 July]

THE INTROIT. *Psalm* 139. 1-9.

O LORD, Thou hast searched me out and known me; / Thou knowest my down-sitting and mine up-rising, Thou understandest my thoughts long before. Thou art about my path, and about my bed, / and spiest out all my ways. For lo, there is not a word in my tongue, / but Thou, O Lord, knowest it altogether. Thou hast fashioned me behind and before, / and laid Thine hand upon me. Such knowledge is too wonderful and excellent for me: / I cannot attain unto it. Whither shall I go then from Thy Spirit, / or whither shall I go then from Thy presence? If I climb up into heaven, Thou art there; / if I go down to hell, Thou art there also. If I take the wings of the morning, / and remain in the uttermost parts of the sea; Even there also shall Thy hand lead me, / and Thy right hand shall hold me.

GLORY be to the Father, and to the Son, / and to the Holy Ghost;
As it was in the beginning, is now, and ever shall be, / world without end. Amen.

THE COLLECT.

O ALMIGHTY God, Whose blessed Son did sanctify Saint Mary Magdalene, and call her to be a witness to His resurrection: Mercifully grant that by Thy grace we may be healed of all our infirmities, and always serve Thee in the power of His endless life; who with Thee and the Holy Ghost liveth and reigneth, one God, world without end. *Amen.*

FOR THE EPISTLE. *Acts* 13. 27-31.

FOR those who dwell in Jerusalem, and their rulers, though they found no cause of death in Jesus, yet desired they Pilate that He should be slain. And when they had fulfilled all that was written of Him, they took Him down from the tree, and laid Him in a sepulchre. But God raised Him from the dead: and He was seen many days by them which came up with Him from Galilee to Jerusalem, who are His witnesses unto the people.

THE GRADUAL. *Psalm* 30. 1-5.

ALLELUIA, Alleluia. I will magnify Thee, O Lord, for Thou hast set me up, / and not made my foes to triumph over me. O Lord my God, I cried unto Thee, / and Thou hast healed me. Thou, Lord, hast brought my soul out of hell; / Thou hast kept my life from them that go down to the pit. Sing praises unto the Lord, O ye saints of His, / and give thanks unto Him for a remembrance of His holiness. For His wrath endureth but the twinkling of an eye, and in His pleasure is life; / heaviness may endure for a night, but joy cometh in the morning. Alleluia.

THE GOSPEL. *Saint John* 20. 11-19.

MARY stood without at the sepulchre weeping: and as she wept, she stooped down, and looked into the sepulchre, and seeth two angels in white sitting, the one at the head, and the other at the feet, where the body of Jesus had lain. And they say unto her, Woman, why weepest thou? She saith unto them, Because they have taken away my Lord, and I know not where they have laid Him. And when she had thus said, she turned herself back, and saw Jesus standing, and knew not that it was Jesus. Jesus saith unto her, Woman, why weepest thou? Whom seekest thou? She, supposing Him to be the gardener, saith unto Him, Sir, if thou have borne Him hence, tell me where thou hast laid Him, and I will take Him away. Jesus saith unto her, Mary. She turned herself, and saith unto Him, Rabboni; which is to say, Master. Jesus saith unto her, Touch me not; for I am not yet ascended to my Father: but go to my brethren, and say unto them, I ascend unto my Father, and your Father; and to my God, and your God. Mary Magdalene came and told the disciples that she had seen the Lord, and that He had spoken these things unto her.

SAINT JAMES THE APOSTLE
[25 July]

THE INTROIT. *Psalm* 15. 1-7.

LORD, who shall dwell in Thy tabernacle, / or who shall rest upon Thy holy hill? Even he that leadeth an uncorrupt life, / and doeth the thing which is right, and speaketh the truth from his heart. He that hath used no deceit in his tongue, nor done evil to his neighbour, / and hath not slandered his neighbour. He that setteth not by himself, but is lowly in his own eyes, / and maketh much of them that fear the Lord. He that sweareth unto his neighbour, and disappointeth him not, / though it were to his own hindrance. He that hath not given his money upon usury, / nor taken reward against the innocent. Whoso doeth these things / shall never fall.

GLORY be to the Father, and to the Son, / and to the Holy Ghost;

As it was in the beginning, is now, and ever shall be, / world without end. Amen.

THE COLLECT.

GRANT, O merciful God, that as Thy holy Apostle Saint James, leaving his father and all that he had, without delay was obedient unto the calling of Thy Son Jesus Christ, and followed Him; so we, forsaking all worldly and carnal affections, may be evermore ready to follow Thy holy commandments; through Jesus Christ our Lord. *Amen.*

FOR THE EPISTLE. *Acts* 11. 27-12. 3.

IN these days came prophets from Jerusalem unto Antioch. And there stood up one of them named Agabus, and signified by the Spirit that there should be great dearth throughout all the world: which came to pass in the days of Claudius Caesar. Then the disciples, every man according to his ability, determined to send relief unto the brethren which dwelt in Judaea: which also they did, and sent it to the elders by the hands of Barnabas and Saul. Now about that time Herod the king stretched forth his hands to vex certain of the Church. And he killed James the brother of John with the sword. And because he saw it pleased the Jews, he proceeded further to take Peter also.

THE GRADUAL. *Psalm* 149. 1-4.

ALLELUIA, Alleluia. O sing unto the Lord a new song: / let the congregation of saints praise Him. Let Israel rejoice in Him that made him: / and let the children of Sion be joyful in their King. Let them praise His Name in the dance: / let them sing praises unto Him with tabret and harp. For the Lord hath pleasure in His people, / and helpeth the meek-hearted. Alleluia.

THE GOSPEL. *Saint Matthew* 20. 20-28.

THEN came to Him the mother of Zebedee's children with her sons, worshipping Him, and desiring a certain thing of Him. And He said unto her, What wilt thou? She saith unto Him, Grant that these my two sons may sit, the one on Thy right hand, and the other on the left, in Thy kingdom. But Jesus answered and said, Ye know not what ye ask. Are ye able to drink of the cup that I shall drink of, and to be baptised with the baptism that I am baptised with? They say unto him, We are able. And He saith unto them, Ye shall drink indeed of my cup, and be baptised with the baptism that I am baptised with: but to sit on my right hand, and on my left, is not mine to give, but it shall be given to them for whom it is prepared of my Father. And when the ten heard it, they were moved with indignation against the two brethren. But Jesus called them unto Him, and said, Ye know that the princes of the Gentiles exercise dominion over them, and they that are great exercise authority upon them. But it shall not be so among you: but whosoever will be great among you, let him be your minister; and whosoever will be chief among you, let him be your servant: even as the Son of Man came not to be ministered unto, but to minister, and to give His life a ransom for many.

THE TRANSFIGURATION OF OUR LORD JESUS CHRIST
[6 August]

THE INTROIT. *Psalm* 84. 1-7.

O HOW amiable are Thy dwellings, / Thou Lord of hosts! My soul hath a desire and longing to enter into the courts of the Lord; / my heart and my flesh rejoice in the living God. Yea, the sparrow hath found her an house, and the swallow a nest where she may lay her young: / even Thine altars, O Lord of hosts, my King and my God. Blessed are they that dwell in Thy house: / they will be alway praising Thee. Blessed is the man whose strength is in Thee, / in whose heart are Thy ways. Who going through the vale of misery use it for a well, / and the pools are filled with water. They will go from strength to strength; / and unto the God of gods appeareth every one of them in Sion.

GLORY be to the Father, and to the Son, / and to the Holy Ghost;
As it was in the beginning, is now, and ever shall be, / world without end. Amen.

THE COLLECT.

O GOD, Who on the holy mount didst reveal to chosen witnesses Thy well-beloved Son wonderfully transfigured: Mercifully grant unto us such a vision of His Divine Majesty, that we, being purified and strengthened by Thy grace, may be transformed into His likeness from glory to glory; through the same Thy Son Jesus Christ our Lord. *Amen.*

THE EPISTLE. *II St Peter* 1. 16-21.

WE have not followed cunningly devised fables, when we made known unto you the power and coming of our Lord Jesus Christ, but were eyewitnesses of His majesty. For He received from God the Father honour and glory, when there came such a voice to Him from the excellent glory, This is my beloved Son, in Whom I am well pleased. And this voice which came from heaven we heard, when we were with Him in the holy mount. We have also a more sure word of prophecy; whereunto ye do well that ye take heed, as unto a light that shineth in a dark place, until the day dawn, and the day star arise in your hearts: knowing this first, that no prophecy of the Scripture is of any private interpretation. For the prophecy came not in old time by the will of man: but holy men of God spake as they were moved by the Holy Ghost.

THE GRADUAL. *Psalm* 84. 8-13.

ALLELUIA, Alleluia. O Lord God of hosts, hear my prayer: / hearken, O God of Jacob. Behold, O God our Defender, / and look upon the face of Thine Anointed. For one day in Thy courts / is better than a thousand. I had rather be a door-keeper in the house of my God, / than to dwell in the tents of ungodliness. For the Lord God is a Light and Defence; / the Lord will give grace and worship, and no good thing shall He withhold from them that live a godly life. O Lord God of hosts, / blessed is the man that putteth his trust in Thee. Alleluia.

THE GOSPEL. *Saint Matthew* 17. 1-9.

AFTER six days Jesus taketh Peter, James, and John his brother, and bringeth them up into an high mountain apart, and was transfigured before them: and His face did shine as the sun, and His raiment was white as the light. And behold, there appeared unto them Moses and Elijah talking with Him. Then answered Peter, and said unto Jesus, Lord, it is good for us to be here: if Thou wilt, let us make here three tabernacles; one for Thee, and one for Moses, and one for Elijah. While he yet spake, behold, a bright cloud overshadowed them: and behold a voice out of the cloud, which said, This is my beloved Son, in Whom I am well pleased; Hear ye Him. And when the disciples heard it, they fell on their face, and were sore afraid. And Jesus came and touched them, and said, Arise, and be not afraid. And when they had lifted up their eyes, they saw no man, save Jesus only. And as they came down from the mountain, Jesus charged them, saying, Tell the vision to no man, until the Son of Man be risen again from the dead.

THE FALLING ASLEEP, OR ASSUMPTION OF THE BLESSED VIRGIN MARY
[15 August]

THE INTROIT. *Psalm* 45. 10-13.

KINGS' daughters were among thy honourable women; / upon thy right hand did stand the queen in a vesture of gold, wrought about with divers colours. Hearken, O daughter, and consider, incline thine ear; / forget also thine own people, and thy father's house. So shall the King have pleasure in thy beauty; / for He is thy Lord God, and worship thou Him.

GLORY be to the Father, and to the Son, / and to the Holy Ghost;

As it was in the beginning, is now, and ever shall be, / world without end. Amen.

THE COLLECT.

O ALMIGHTY God, Who didst endue with singular grace the Blessed Virgin Mary, that she might be the Mother of Thy Son; and Who wast pleased, at the end of the course of her earthly life, to receive her unto Thyself: Give us grace, we beseech Thee, heavenly Father, to see in her obedience and humility a true model and pattern for our life; and grant that we with her may be found worthy to obtain the promises of her Son, which shall be ours in the glory of His Resurrection; through the same Thy Son Jesus Christ our Lord, Who with Thee and the Holy Ghost liveth and reigneth, ever one God, world without end. *Amen.*

THE EPISTLE. *Romans* 8. 1-11.

THERE is therefore now no condemnation to them which are in Christ Jesus, who walk not after the flesh, but after the Spirit. For the Law of the Spirit of life in Christ Jesus hath made me free from the law of sin and death. For what the Law could not do, in that it was weak through the flesh, God sending His own Son in the likeness of sinful flesh, and for sin, condemned sin in the flesh; that the righteousness of the Law might be fulfilled in us, who walk not after the flesh, but after the Spirit. For they that are after the flesh do mind the things of the flesh; but they that are after the Spirit, the things of the Spirit. For to be carnally minded is death; but to be spiritually minded is life and peace. Because the carnal mind is enmity against God; for it is not subject to the Law of God, neither indeed can be. So then they that are in the flesh cannot please God. But ye are not in the flesh, but in the Spirit, if so be that the Spirit of God dwell in you. Now if any man have not the Spirit of Christ, he is none of His. And if Christ be in you, the body is dead because of sin; but the Spirit is life because of righteousness. But if the Spirit of Him that raised up Jesus from the dead dwell in you, He that raised Christ up from the dead shall also quicken your mortal bodies by His Spirit that dwelleth in you.

THE GRADUAL. *Psalm* 45. 14-15.

ALLELUIA, Alleluia. The King's daughter is all glorious within; / her clothing is of wrought gold. She shall be brought unto the King in raiment of needle-work; / the virgins that be her fellows shall bear her company, and shall be brought unto Thee. Alleluia.

THE GOSPEL. *Saint Luke* 1. 39-49.

AND Mary arose in those days, and went into the hill country with haste, into a city of Judah; and entered into the house of Zacharias, and saluted Elizabeth. And it came to pass that, when Elizabeth heard the salutation of Mary, the babe leaped in her womb; and Elizabeth was filled with the Holy Ghost; and she spake with a loud voice, and said, Blessed art thou among women, and blessed is the Fruit of thy womb. And whence is this to me, that the Mother of my Lord should come to me? For lo, as soon as the voice of thy salutation sounded in mine ears, the babe leaped in my womb for joy. And blessed is she that believed; for there shall be a performance of those things which were told her from the Lord. And Mary said, My soul doth magnify the Lord, And my spirit hath rejoiced in God my Saviour, For He hath regarded the low estate of his handmaiden. For behold, from henceforth all generations shall call me blessed. For He that is mighty hath magnified me; and holy is His Name.

SAINT BARTHOLOMEW THE APOSTLE
[24 August]

THE INTROIT. *Psalm* 116. 11-18.

WHAT reward shall I give unto the Lord / for all the benefits that He hath done unto me? I will receive the cup of salvation, / and call upon the Name of the Lord. I will pay my vows now in the presence of all His people; / right dear in the sight of the Lord is the death of His saints. Behold, O Lord, how that I am Thy servant: / I am Thy servant, and the son of Thine handmaid; Thou hast broken my bonds in sunder. I will offer to Thee the sacrifice of thanksgiving, / and will call upon the Name of the Lord. I will pay my vows unto the Lord, in the sight of all His people, / in the courts of the Lord's house, even in the midst of thee, O Jerusalem. Praise the Lord.

GLORY be to the Father, and to the Son, / and to the Holy Ghost;
As it was in the beginning, is now, and ever shall be, / world without end. Amen.

THE COLLECT.

O ALMIGHTY and everlasting God, Who didst give unto Thine Apostle Saint Bartholomew, *whom we know also as Nathanael,* grace truly to believe and to preach Thy Word: Grant, we beseech Thee, unto Thy Church, to love that Word which he believed, and both to preach and receive the same; through Jesus Christ our Lord. *Amen.*

FOR THE EPISTLE. *Acts* 1. 6-14.

WHEN they therefore were come together, they asked of Him, saying, Lord, wilt Thou at this time restore again the kingdom to Israel? And He said unto them, It is not for you to know the times or the seasons, which the Father hath put in His own power. But ye shall receive power, after that the Holy Ghost is come upon you: and ye shall be witnesses unto me both in Jerusalem, and in all Judaea, and in Samaria, and unto the uttermost part of the earth. And when He had spoken these things, while they beheld, He was taken up; and a cloud received Him out of their sight. And while they looked steadfastly toward heaven as He went up, behold, two men stood by them in white apparel; which also said, Ye men of Galilee, why stand ye gazing up into heaven? this same Jesus, which is taken up from you into heaven, shall so come in like manner as ye have seen Him go into heaven. Then returned they unto Jerusalem from the mount called Olivet, which is from Jerusalem a sabbath day's journey. And when they were come in, they went up into an upper room, where abode both Peter, and James, and John, and Andrew, Philip, and Thomas, Bartholomew, and Matthew, James the son of Alphaeus, and Simon Zelotes, and Judas the brother of James. These all continued with one accord in prayer and supplication, with the women, and Mary the mother of Jesus, and with His brethren.

THE GRADUAL. *Psalm* 97. 7-10.
ALLELUIA, Alleluia. Confounded be all they that worship carved images, and that delight in vain gods: / worship Him, all ye gods. Sion heard of it, and rejoiced; / and the daughters of Judah were glad, because of Thy judgements, O Lord. For Thou, Lord, art higher than all that are in the earth; / Thou art exalted far above all gods. O ye that love the Lord, see that ye hate the thing which is evil; / the Lord preserveth the souls of His saints; He shall deliver them from the hand of the ungodly. Alleluia.

THE GOSPEL. *Saint Mark* 3. 13-19.
AND Jesus goeth up into a mountain, and calleth unto Him whom He would: and they came unto Him. And He ordained twelve, that they should be with Him, and that He might send them forth to preach, and to have power to heal sicknesses, and to cast out devils: and Simon He surnamed Peter; and James the son of Zebedee, and John the brother of James; and He surnamed them Boanerges, which is, The sons of thunder: and Andrew, and Philip, and Bartholomew, and Matthew, and Thomas, and James the son of Alphaeus, and Thaddaeus, and Simon the Canaanite, and Judas Iscariot, which also betrayed Him: and they went into an house.

Or this.

Saint John 1. 45-51.
PHILIP findeth Nathanael, and saith unto him, We have found Him, of Whom Moses in the law, and the prophets, did write, Jesus of Nazareth, the son of Joseph. And Nathanael said unto him, Can there any good thing come out of Nazareth? Philip saith unto him, Come and see. Jesus saw Nathanael coming to Him, and saith of him, Behold an Israelite indeed, in whom is no guile! Nathanael saith unto him, Whence knowest Thou me? Jesus answered and said unto him, Before that Philip called thee, when thou wast under the fig tree, I saw thee. Nathanael answered and saith unto Him, Rabbi, Thou art the Son of God; Thou art the King of Israel. Jesus answered and said unto him, Because I said unto thee, I saw thee under the fig tree, believest thou? thou shalt see greater things than these. And he saith unto him, Verily, verily, I say unto you, Hereafter ye shall see heaven open, and the angels of God ascending and descending upon the Son of man.

THE BEHEADING OF
SAINT JOHN THE BAPTIST
[29 August]

THE INTROIT. *Psalm* 46. 1-8.

GOD is our Hope and Strength, / a very present help in trouble. Therefore will we not fear, though the earth be moved, / and though the hills be carried into the midst of the sea; Though the waters thereof rage and swell, / and though the mountains shake at the tempest of the same. The rivers of the flood thereof shall make glad the city of God, / the holy place of the tabernacle of the Most High. God is in the midst of her, therefore shall she not be removed; / God shall help her, and that right early. The heathen make much ado, and the kingdoms are moved; / but God hath shewed His voice, and the earth shall melt away. The Lord of hosts is with us; / the God of Jacob is our Refuge.

GLORY be to the Father, and to the Son, / and to the Holy Ghost;
As it was in the beginning, is now, and ever shall be, / world without end. Amen.

THE COLLECT.

O GOD, Who didst send Thy messenger, John the Baptist, to be the Forerunner of the Lord, and to glorify Thee by his death: Grant that we, who have received the truth of Thy most holy Gospel, may bear our witness thereunto; and after his example constantly speak the truth, boldly rebuke vice, and patiently suffer for the truth's sake; through Jesus Christ our Lord. *Amen.*

FOR THE EPISTLE. *Isaiah* 40. 1-11.

COMFORT ye, comfort ye my people, saith your God. Speak ye comfortably to Jerusalem, and cry unto her, that her warfare is accomplished, that her iniquity is pardoned: for she hath received of the Lord's hand double for all her sins. The voice of him that crieth in the wilderness, Prepare ye the way of the Lord, make straight in the desert a highway for our God. Every valley shall be exalted, and every mountain and hill shall be made low: and the crooked shall be made straight, and the rough places plain: and the glory of the Lord shall be revealed, and all flesh shall see it together: for the mouth of the Lord hath spoken it. The voice said, Cry. And he said, What shall I cry? All flesh is grass, and all the goodliness thereof is as the flower of the field: the grass withereth, the flower fadeth: because the spirit of the Lord bloweth upon it: surely the people is grass. The grass withereth, the flower fadeth: but the Word of our God shall stand for ever. O Sion, that bringest good tidings, get thee up into the high mountain; O Jerusalem, that bringest good tidings, lift up thy voice with strength; lift it up, be not afraid; say unto the cities of Judah, Behold your God! Behold, the Lord God will come with strong hand, and His arm shall rule for Him: behold, His reward is with Him, and His work before Him. He shall feed His flock like a shepherd: He shall gather the lambs with His arm, and carry them in His bosom, and shall gently lead those that are with young.

THE GRADUAL. *Psalm* 119. 161-168.

ALLELUIA, Alleluia. Princes have persecuted me without a cause; / but my heart standeth in awe of Thy word. I am as glad of Thy word, / as one that findeth great spoils. As for lies, I hate and abhor them; / but Thy Law do I love. Seven times a day do I praise Thee / because of Thy righteous judgements. Great is the peace that they have who love Thy Law, / and they are not offended at it. Lord, I have looked for Thy saving health, / and done after Thy commandments. My soul hath kept

Thy testimonies, / and loved them exceedingly. I have kept Thy commandments and testimonies, / for all my ways are before Thee. Alleluia.

THE GOSPEL. *Saint Mark* 6. 17-29.

AND King Herod heard of him; (for his name was spread abroad:) and he said, That John the Baptist was risen from the dead, and therefore mighty works do shew forth themselves in him. Others said, That it is Elias. And others said, That it is a prophet, or as one of the prophets. But when Herod heard thereof, he said, It is John, whom I beheaded: he is risen from the dead. For Herod himself had sent forth and laid hold upon John, and bound him in prison for Herodias' sake, his brother Philip's wife: for he had married her. For John had said unto Herod, It is not lawful for thee to have thy brother's wife. Therefore Herodias had a quarrel against him, and would have killed him; but she could not: for Herod feared John, knowing that he was a just man and an holy, and observed him; and when he heard him, he did many things, and heard him gladly. And when a convenient day was come, that Herod on his birthday made a supper to his lords, high captains, and chief estates of Galilee; and when the daughter of the said Herodias came in, and danced, and pleased Herod and them that sat with him, the king said unto the damsel, Ask of me whatsoever thou wilt, and I will give it thee. And he sware unto her, Whatsoever thou shalt ask of me, I will give it thee, unto the half of my kingdom. And she went forth, and said unto her mother, What shall I ask? And she said, The head of John the Baptist. And she came in straightway with haste unto the king, and asked, saying, I will that thou give me by and by in a charger the head of John the Baptist. And the king was exceeding sorry; yet for his oath's sake, and for their sakes which sat with him, he would not reject her. And immediately the king sent an executioner, and commanded his head to be brought: and he went and beheaded him in the prison, and brought his head in a charger, and gave it to the damsel: and the damsel gave it to her mother. And when his disciples heard of it, they came and took up his corpse, and laid it in a tomb.

HOLY CROSS DAY
[14 September]

THE INTROIT. *Psalm* 57. 6-12.

SET up Thyself, O God, above the heavens; / and Thy glory above all the earth. They have laid a net for my feet, and pressed down my soul; / they have digged a pit before me, and are fallen into the midst of it themselves. My heart is fixed, O God, my heart is fixed: / I will sing, and give praise. Awake up, my glory; awake, lute and harp: / I myself will awake right early. I will give thanks unto Thee, O Lord, among the people, / and I will sing unto Thee among the nations. For the greatness of Thy mercy reacheth unto the heavens, / and Thy truth unto the clouds. Set up Thyself, O God, above the heavens; / and Thy glory above all the earth.

GLORY be to the Father, and to the Son, / and to the Holy Ghost;
As it was in the beginning, is now, and ever shall be, / world without end. Amen.

THE COLLECT.

O BLESSED Saviour, Who by Thy Cross and Passion hast given life unto the world: Grant, we beseech Thee, that we Thy servants may be given grace to take up the Cross daily and ever follow Thee through life and death; Whom with the Father and the Holy Ghost we worship and glorify, one God, for ever and ever. *Amen.*

THE EPISTLE. *Philippians* 2. 5-11.

LET this mind be in you, which was also in Christ Jesus: Who, being in the form of God, thought it not robbery to be equal with God; but made Himself of no reputation, and took upon Him the form of a servant, and was made in the likeness of men: and being found in fashion as a man, He humbled Himself, and became obedient unto death, even the death of the Cross. Wherefore God also hath highly exalted Him, and given Him a Name which is above every name: That at the Name of Jesus every knee should bow, of things in heaven, and things in earth, and things under the earth; and that every tongue should confess that Jesus Christ is Lord, to the glory of God the Father.

THE GRADUAL. *Psalm* 67. 1-4.

ALLELUIA, Alleluia. God be merciful unto us, and bless us, / and shew us the light of His countenance, and be merciful unto us; That Thy way may be known upon earth, / Thy saving health among all nations. Let the people praise Thee, O God; / yea, let all the people praise Thee. O let the nations rejoice and be glad, / for Thou shalt judge the folk righteously, and govern the nations upon earth. Alleluia.

THE GOSPEL. *Saint John* 12. 23-36.

AND Jesus answered them, saying, The hour is come, that the Son of Man should be glorified. Verily, verily, I say unto you, Except a corn of wheat fall into the ground and die, it abideth alone: but if it die, it bringeth forth much fruit. He that loveth his life shall lose it; and he that hateth his life in this world shall keep it unto life eternal. If any man serve me, let him follow me; and where I am, there shall also my servant be: if any man serve me, him will my Father honour. Now is my soul troubled; and what shall I say? Father, save me from this hour: but for this cause came I unto this hour. Father, glorify Thy Name. Then came there a voice from heaven, saying, I have both glorified it, and will glorify it again. The people therefore, that stood by, and heard it, said that it thundered: others said, An angel spake to Him. Jesus answered and said, This voice came not because of me, but for your sakes. Now is the judgement of this world: now shall the prince of this world be cast out. And I, if I be lifted up from the earth, will draw all men unto me. This He said, signifying what death He should die. The people answered Him, We have heard out of the Law that Christ abideth for ever: and how sayest Thou, The Son of Man must be lifted up? who is this Son of Man? Then Jesus said unto them, Yet a little while is the light with you. Walk while ye have the light, lest darkness come upon you: for he that walketh in darkness knoweth not whither he goeth. While ye have light, believe in the light, that ye may be the children of light. These things spake Jesus, and departed, and did hide Himself from them.

SAINT MATTHEW THE APOSTLE
AND EVANGELIST
[21 September]

THE INTROIT. *Psalm* 119. 65-72.

O LORD, Thou hast dealt graciously with Thy servant, / according unto Thy word. O teach me true understanding and knowledge, / for I have believed Thy commandments. Before I was troubled, I went wrong; / but now have I kept Thy word. Thou art good and gracious: / O teach me Thy statutes. The proud have imagined a lie against me; / but I will keep Thy commandments with my whole heart. Their heart is as fat as brawn; / but my delight hath been in Thy Law. It is good for me that I have been in trouble, / that I may learn Thy statutes. The Law of Thy mouth is dearer unto me / than thousands of gold and silver.

GLORY be to the Father, and to the Son, / and to the Holy Ghost;
As it was in the beginning, is now, and ever shall be, / world without end. Amen.

THE COLLECT.

O ALMIGHTY God, Who by Thy blessed Son didst call Saint Matthew from the receipt of custom to be an Apostle and Evangelist: Grant us grace to forsake all covetous desires, and inordinate love of riches, and to follow the same Thy Son Jesus Christ; through Him Who liveth and reigneth with Thee and the Holy Ghost, one God, world without end. *Amen.*

THE EPISTLE. II *Corinthians* 4. 1-6.

THEREFORE seeing we have this ministry, as we have received mercy, we faint not; but have renounced the hidden things of dishonesty, not walking in craftiness, nor handling the Word of God deceitfully; but by manifestation of the truth commending ourselves to every man's conscience in the sight of God. But if our Gospel be hid, it is hid to them that are lost; in whom the god of this world hath blinded the minds of them which believe not, lest the light of the glorious Gospel of Christ, Who is the image of God, should shine unto them. For we preach not ourselves, but Christ Jesus the Lord; and ourselves your servants for Jesus' sake. For God, who commanded the light to shine out of darkness, hath shined in our hearts, to give the light of the knowledge of the glory of God in the face of Jesus Christ.

THE GRADUAL. *Psalm* 119. 89-93.

ALLELUIA, Alleluia. O Lord, Thy word / endureth for ever in heaven. Thy truth also remaineth from one generation to another: / Thou hast laid the foundation of the earth, and it abideth. They continue this day according to Thine ordinance, / for all things serve Thee. If my delight had not been in Thy Law, / I should have perished in my trouble. I will never forget Thy commandments, / for with them Thou hast quickened me. Alleluia.

THE GOSPEL. *Saint Matthew* 9. 9-23.

AND as Jesus passed forth from thence, He saw a man, named Matthew, sitting at the receipt of custom: and He saith unto him, Follow me. And he arose, and followed Him. And it came to pass, as Jesus sat at meat in the house, behold, many publicans and sinners came and sat down with Him and His disciples. And when the Pharisees saw it, they said unto His disciples, Why eateth your Master with publicans and sinners? But when Jesus heard that, He said unto them, They that be whole need not a physician, but they that are sick. But go ye and learn what that meaneth, I will have mercy, and not sacrifice: for I am not come to call the righteous, but sinners to repentance.

SAINT MICHAEL AND ALL ANGELS
COMMONLY CALLED
MICHAELMAS-DAY
[29 September]

THE INTROIT. *Psalm* 103. 19-22.

THE Lord hath prepared His seat in heaven, / and His kingdom ruleth over all. O praise the Lord, ye angels of His, ye that excel in strength: / ye that fulfil His commandment, and hearken unto the voice of His words. O praise the Lord, all ye His hosts: / ye servants of His that do His pleasure. O speak good of the Lord, all ye works of His, in all places of His dominion: / praise thou the Lord, O my soul.

GLORY be to the Father, and to the Son, / and to the Holy Ghost;
As it was in the beginning, is now, and ever shall be, / world without end. Amen.

THE COLLECT.

O EVERLASTING God, Who hast ordained and constituted the services of Angels and men in a wonderful order: Mercifully grant, that as Thy holy Angels alway do Thee service in heaven, so by Thine appointment they may succour and defend us on earth; through Jesus Christ our Lord. *Amen.*

And this Collect shall be used throughout the Octave.

FOR THE EPISTLE. *Revelation* 12. 7-12.

THERE was war in heaven: Michael and his angels fought against the dragon; and the dragon fought and his angels, and prevailed not; neither was their place found any more in heaven. And the great dragon was cast out, that old serpent, called the devil, and Satan, which deceiveth the whole world: he was cast out into the earth, and his angels were cast out with him. And I heard a loud voice saying in heaven, Now is come salvation, and strength, and the kingdom of our God, and the power of His Christ: for the accuser of our brethren is cast down, which accused them before our God day and night. And they overcame him by the Blood of the Lamb, and by the word of their testimony; and they loved not their lives unto the death. Therefore rejoice, ye heavens, and ye that dwell in them. Woe to the inhabiters of the earth and of the sea! for the devil is come down unto you, having great wrath, because he knoweth that he hath but a short time.

THE GRADUAL. *Psalm* 148. 1-3.

ALLELUIA, Alleluia. O praise the Lord of heaven: / praise Him in the height. Praise Him, all ye angels of His: / praise Him, all His host. Praise Him, sun and moon: / praise Him, all ye stars and light. Alleluia.

THE GOSPEL. *Saint Matthew* 18. 1-10.

AT the same time came the disciples unto Jesus, saying, Who is the greatest in the kingdom of heaven? And Jesus called a little child unto Him, and set him in the midst of them, and said, Verily I say unto you, Except ye be converted, and become as little children, ye shall not enter into the kingdom of heaven. Whosoever therefore shall humble himself as this little child, the same is greatest in the kingdom of heaven. And whoso shall receive one such little child in my Name receiveth me. But whoso shall offend one of these little ones which believe in me, it were better for him that a millstone were hanged about his neck, and that he were drowned in the depth of the sea. Woe unto the world because of offences! for it must needs be that offences come; but woe to that man by whom the offence cometh! Wherefore if thy hand or thy foot offend thee, cut them off, and cast them from thee: it is better for thee to enter into life halt or maimed, rather than having two hands or two feet to be cast into everlasting fire. And if thine eye offend thee, pluck it out, and cast it from thee: it is better for thee to enter into life with one eye, rather than having two eyes to be cast into hell fire. Take heed that ye despise not one of these little ones; for I say unto you, That in heaven their angels do always behold the face of my Father which is in heaven.

SAINT LUKE THE EVANGELIST
[18 October]

THE INTROIT. *Psalm* 45. 1-4.
MY heart is inditing of a good matter; / I speak of the things which I have made unto the King. My tongue is the pen / of a ready writer. Thou art fairer than the children of men; / full of grace are thy lips, because God hath blessed thee for ever. Gird Thee with Thy sword upon Thy thigh, O Thou Most Mighty, / according to Thy worship and renown.
GLORY be to the Father, and to the Son, / and to the Holy Ghost;
As it was in the beginning, is now, and ever shall be, / world without end. Amen.

THE COLLECT.
ALMIGHTY God, Who didst call Saint Luke the Physician, whose praise is in the Gospel, to be an Evangelist, and Physician of the soul: Grant that by the wholesome medicines of the doctrine delivered by him, all the diseases of our souls may be healed; through the Merits of Thy Son Jesus Christ our Lord. *Amen.*

THE EPISTLE. II *Timothy* 4. 5-13.
WATCH thou in all things, endure afflictions, do the work of an evangelist, make full proof of thy ministry. For I am now ready to be offered, and the time of my departure is at hand. I have fought a good fight, I have finished my course, I have kept the Faith: henceforth there is laid up for me a crown of righteousness, which the Lord, the righteous Judge, shall give me at that day: and not to me only, but unto all them also that love His appearing. Do thy diligence to come shortly unto me: for Demas hath forsaken me, having loved this present world, and is departed unto Thessalonica; Crescens to Galatia, Titus unto Dalmatia. Only Luke is with me. Take Mark, and bring him with thee: for he is profitable to me for the ministry. And Tychicus have I sent to Ephesus. The cloak that I left at Troas with Carpus, when thou comest, bring with thee, and the books, but especially the parchments.

THE GRADUAL. *Psalm* 37. 31-32.
ALLELUIA, Alleluia. The mouth of the righteous is exercised in wisdom, / and his tongue will be talking of judgement. The Law of his God is in his heart, / and his goings shall not slide. Alleluia.

THE GOSPEL. *Saint Luke* 10. 1-11.
THE Lord appointed other seventy also, and sent them two and two before His face into every city and place, whither He Himself would come. Therefore said He unto them, The harvest truly is great, but the labourers are few: pray ye therefore the Lord of the harvest, that He would send forth

labourers into His harvest. Go your ways: Behold, I send you forth as lambs among wolves. Carry neither purse, nor scrip, nor shoes: and salute no man by the way. And into whatsoever house ye enter, first say, Peace be to this house. And if the son of peace be there, your peace shall rest upon it: if not, it shall turn to you again. And in the same house remain, eating and drinking such things as they give: for the labourer is worthy of his hire. Go not from house to house. And into whatsoever city ye enter, and they receive you, eat such things as are set before you: and heal the sick that are therein, and say unto them, The kingdom of God is come nigh unto you. But into whatsoever city ye enter, and they receive you not, go your ways out into the streets of the same, and say, Even the very dust of your city, which cleaveth on us, we do wipe off against you: notwithstanding be ye sure of this, that the kingdom of God is come nigh unto you.

SAINT SIMON THE APOSTLE
AND SAINT JUDE THE APOSTLE
[28 October]

THE INTROIT. *Psalm* 87. 1-7.

HER foundations are upon the holy hills; / the Lord loveth the gates of Sion more than all the dwellings of Jacob. Very excellent things are spoken of thee, / thou city of God. I will think upon Rahab and Babylon / with them that know me. Behold ye the Philistines also, / and they of Tyre, with the Morians; lo, there was he born. And of Sion, it shall be said, This and that man was born in her: / and the Most High Himself shall establish her. The Lord shall count, when He writeth up the people, / that this man was born there. As well the singers as the players on instruments shall be there, / All my springs be in thee.

GLORY be to the Father, and to the Son, / and to the Holy Ghost;
As it was in the beginning, is now, and ever shall be, / world without end. Amen.

THE COLLECT.

O ALMIGHTY God, Who hast built Thy Church upon the foundation of the Apostles and Prophets, such as were Thy blessed servants Saint Simon and Saint Jude *whom we also call Thaddaeus*, our Saviour Jesus Christ Himself being the head Corner-stone: Grant us all so to be joined together in unity of spirit by their doctrine, that we may be made an holy temple acceptable unto Thee; through Jesus Christ our Lord. *Amen.*

THE EPISTLE. *Saint Jude* 1. 1-8.

JUDE, the servant of Jesus Christ, and brother of James, to them that are sanctified by God the Father, and preserved in Jesus Christ, and called: Mercy unto you, and peace, and love, be multiplied. Beloved, when I gave all diligence to write unto you of the common salvation, it was needful for me to write unto you, and exhort you that ye should earnestly contend for the faith which was once delivered unto the saints. For there are certain men crept in unawares, who were before of old ordained to this condemnation, ungodly men, turning the grace of our God into lasciviousness, and denying the only Lord God, and our Lord Jesus Christ. I will therefore put you in remembrance, though ye once knew this, how that the Lord, having saved the people out of the land of Egypt, afterward destroyed them that believed not. And the angels which kept not their first estate, but left their own habitation, He hath reserved in everlasting chains under darkness unto the judgement of the great day. Even as Sodom and Gomorrah, and the cities about them in like manner, giving themselves over to fornication, and going after strange flesh, are set forth for an example, suffering the vengeance of eternal fire. Likewise also these filthy dreamers defile the flesh, despise dominion, and speak evil of dignities.

THE GRADUAL. *Psalm* 45. 16-17.

ALLELUIA, Alleluia. Instead of thy fathers thou shalt have children, / whom thou mayest make princes in all lands. I will remember Thy Name from one generation to another; / therefore shall the people give thanks unto Thee, world without end. Alleluia.

THE GOSPEL. *Saint John* 15. 17-27.

THESE things I command you, that ye love one another. If the world hate you, ye know that it hated me before it hated you. If ye were of the world, the world would love his own: but because ye are not of the world, but I have chosen you out of the world, therefore the world hateth you. Remember the word that I said unto you, The servant is not greater than his Lord. If they have persecuted me, they will also persecute you; if they have kept my saying, they will keep yours also. But all these things will they do unto you for my Name's sake, because they know not Him that sent me. If I had not come and spoken unto them, they had not had sin: but now they have no cloak for their sin. He that hateth me hateth my Father also. If I had not done among them the works which none other man did, they had not had sin: but now have they both seen and hated both me and my Father. But this cometh to pass, that the word might be fulfilled that is written in their law, They hated me without a cause. But when the Comforter is come, Whom I will send unto you from the Father, even the Spirit of truth, which proceedeth from the Father, He shall testify of me: And ye also shall bear witness, because ye have been with me from the beginning.

ALL SAINTS' DAY
ALSO CALLED
HALLOWMAS-DAY
[1 November]

THE INTROIT. *Psalm* 33. 1-5.

REJOICE in the Lord, O ye righteous, / for it becometh well the just to be thankful. Praise the Lord with harp; / sing praises unto Him with the lute, and instrument of ten strings. Sing unto the Lord a new song, / sing praises lustily unto Him with a good courage. For the word of the Lord is true, / and all His works are faithful. He loveth righteousness and judgement; / the earth is full of the goodness of the Lord.

GLORY be to the Father, and to the Son, / and to the Holy Ghost;
As it was in the beginning, is now, and ever shall be, / world without end. Amen.

THE COLLECT.

O ALMIGHTY God, Who hast knit together Thine elect in one communion and fellowship, in the mystical body of Thy Son Jesus Christ: Grant us grace so to follow Thy blessed Saints in all virtuous and godly living, that we may come to those unspeakable joys, which Thou hast prepared for all them that unfeignedly love Thee; through the same Jesus Christ our Lord. *Amen.*

And this Collect shall be used throughout the Octave.

THE PROPERS OF THE YEAR

FOR THE EPISTLE. *Revelation* 7. 9-17.

AFTER this I beheld, and lo, a great multitude, which no man could number, of all nations, and kindreds, and people, and tongues, stood before the throne, and before the Lamb, clothed with white robes, and palms in their hands; and cried with a loud voice, saying, Salvation to our God which sitteth upon the throne, and unto the Lamb. And all the angels stood round about the throne, and about the elders, and the four living creatures, and fell before the throne on their faces, and worshipped God, saying, Amen; Blessing, and glory, and wisdom, and thanksgiving, and honour, and power, and might, be unto our God for ever and ever. Amen. And one of the elders answered, saying unto me, What are these which are arrayed in white robes? and whence came they? And I said unto him, Sir, thou knowest. And he said to me, These are they which came out of great tribulation, and have washed their robes, and made them white in the blood of the Lamb. Therefore are they before the throne of God, and serve Him day and night in His temple: and He that sitteth on the throne shall dwell among them. They shall hunger no more, neither thirst anymore; neither shall the sun light on them, nor any heat. For the Lamb which is in the midst of the throne shall feed them, and shall lead them unto living fountains of waters: and God shall wipe away all tears from their eyes.

THE GRADUAL. *Psalm* 34. 7-10.

ALLELUIA, Alleluia. The angel of the Lord tarrieth round about them that fear Him, / and delivereth them. O taste, and see, how gracious the Lord is; / blessed is the man that trusteth in Him. O fear the Lord, ye that are His saints; / for they that fear Him lack nothing. Alleluia.

THE GOSPEL. *Saint Matthew* 5. 1-12.

JESUS, seeing the multitudes, went up into a mountain: and when He was set, His disciples came unto Him: And He opened His mouth, and taught them, saying, Blessed are the poor in spirit: for theirs is the kingdom of heaven. Blessed are they that mourn: for they shall be comforted. Blessed are the meek: for they shall inherit the earth. Blessed are they which do hunger and thirst after righteousness: for they shall be filled. Blessed are the merciful: for they shall obtain mercy. Blessed are the pure in heart: for they shall see God. Blessed are the peacemakers: for they shall be called the children of God. Blessed are they which are persecuted for righteousness' sake: for theirs is the kingdom of heaven. Blessed are ye, when men shall revile you, and persecute you, and shall say all manner of evil against you falsely, for my sake. Rejoice, and be exceeding glad: for great is your reward in heaven: for so persecuted they the prophets which were before you.

ALL SOULS' DAY
[2 November]

THE INTROIT. *Psalm* 65. 1-4.

THOU, O God, art praised in Sion, / and unto Thee shall the vow be performed in Jerusalem. Thou that hearest the prayer, / unto Thee shall all flesh come. My misdeeds prevail against me; / O be Thou merciful unto our sins. Blessed is the man whom Thou choosest, and receivest unto Thee; / he shall dwell in Thy court, and shall be satisfied with the pleasures of Thy house, even of Thy holy temple.

THE Lord gave, and the Lord hath taken away: /
Blessed be the Name of the Lord.

276

THE PROPERS OF THE YEAR

THE COLLECT.

MOST merciful God and loving Father of all mankind, Who hast been pleased to take unto Thyself the souls of our brethren departed: Forgive them their sins; purge away their guilt; and wash them in the Blood of that Immaculate Lamb that was slain to take away the sins of the world; that they may be presented pure and without spot before Thee; and grant unto us who are still in our earthly pilgrimage, and who walk as yet by faith, that having served thee faithfully in this world we may, with all redeemed and faithful souls, be joined hereafter to the company of Thine elect and blessed Saints, and be made partakers with them in the glory and joy of the resurrection of Thy Son Jesus Christ our Lord, Who with Thee and the Holy Ghost liveth and reigneth, ever one God, world without end. *Amen.*

FOR THE EPISTLE. *Wisdom* 3. 1-9.

THE souls of the righteous are in the hand of God, and there shall no torment touch them. In the sight of the unwise they seemed to die; and their departure is taken for misery, and their going from us to be utter destruction; but they are in peace. For though they be punished in the sight of men, yet is their hope full of immortality. And having been a little chastened, they shall be greatly rewarded; for God proved them and found them worthy for Himself. As gold in the furnace hath He tried them, and received them as a burnt-offering. And in the time of their visitation they shall shine, and run to and fro like sparks among the stubble; they shall judge the nations and have dominion over the people, and their Lord shall reign for ever and ever. They that put their trust in Him shall understand the truth: and such as be faithful in love shall abide with Him: for grace and mercy is to His saints, and He hath care for His elect.

THE GRADUAL. *Psalm* 112. 1-7.

BLESSED is the man that feareth the Lord: / he hath great delight in His commandments. His seed shall be mighty upon earth: / the generation of the faithful shall be blessed. Riches and plenteousness shall be in his house, / and his righteousness endureth for ever. Unto the godly there ariseth up light in the darkness; / he is merciful, loving, and righteous. A good man is merciful, and lendeth, / and will guide his words with discretion. For he shall never be moved, / and the righteous shall be had in everlasting remembrance. He will not be afraid of any evil tidings, / for his heart standeth fast, and believeth in the Lord.

THE GOSPEL. *Saint John* 10. 22-30.

IT was at Jerusalem, at the feast of the dedication, and it was winter; and Jesus walked in the temple in Solomon's porch. Then came the Jews round about Him, and said unto Him, How long dost Thou make us to doubt? If Thou be the Christ, tell us plainly. Jesus answered them, I told you, and ye believed not; the works that I do in my Father's Name, they bear witness of me. But ye believe not, because ye are not of my sheep, as I said unto you. My sheep hear my voice, and I know them, and they follow me: and I give them eternal life; and they shall never perish, neither shall any man pluck them out of my hand. My Father Who gave them to me is greater than all; and no man is able to pluck them out of my Father's hand. I and my Father are one.

COMMON OF THE BLESSED VIRGIN MARY
APPOINTED FOR USE ON THE FEASTS OF
THE CONCEPTION OF OUR LADY
AND
THE NATIVITY OF OUR LADY
AND ON OTHER COMMEMORATIONS OF
THE BLESSED VIRGIN MARY

THE INTROIT. *Psalm* 85. 8-11.

I WILL hearken what the Lord God will say concerning me, / for He shall speak peace unto His people, and to His saints, that they turn not again. For His salvation is nigh them that fear Him, / that glory may dwell in our land. Mercy and truth are met together; / righteousness and peace have kissed each other. Truth shall flourish out of the earth, / and righteousness hath looked down from heaven.

GLORY be to the Father, and to the Son, / and to the Holy Ghost;
As it was in the beginning, is now, and ever shall be, / world without end. Amen.

THE COLLECT.

O GOD Most High, Who didst endue with wonderful virtue and grace the Blessed Virgin Mary, the Mother of our Lord: Grant that we, who now call her blessed, may be made very members of the heavenly family of Him, Who was pleased to be called the first-born among many brethren; Who liveth and reigneth with Thee and the Holy Ghost, one God, world without end. *Amen.*

FOR THE EPISTLE. *Acts* 1. 12-14.

THEN the Apostles returned unto Jerusalem from the mount called Olivet, which is from Jerusalem a sabbath-day's journey. And when they were come in, they went up into an upper room, where abode Peter and James and John and Andrew, Philip and Thomas, Bartholomew and Matthew, James the son of Alphaeus and Simon the Zealot, and Jude the brother of James. These all continued with one accord in prayer and supplication, with the women, and Mary the Mother of Jesus, and with His brethren.

THE GRADUAL. *Psalm* 66. 12-17.

ALLELUIA, Alleluia. O come hither, and hearken, all ye that fear God, / and I will tell you what He hath done for my soul. I called unto Him with my mouth, / and gave Him praises with my tongue. If I had regarded wickedness in mine heart, / the Lord would not have heard me. Alleluia.

THE GOSPEL. *Saint Luke* 1. 39-49.

AND Mary arose in those days, and went into the hill country with haste, into a city of Judah; and entered into the house of Zacharias, and saluted Elisabeth. And it came to pass that, when Elisabeth heard the salutation of Mary, the babe leaped in her womb; and Elisabeth was filled with the Holy Ghost; and she spake with a loud voice, and said, Blessed art thou among women, and blessed is the Fruit of thy womb. And whence is this to me, that the Mother of my Lord should come to me? For lo, as soon as the voice of thy salutation sounded in mine ears, the babe leaped in my womb for joy. And blessed is she that believed; for there shall be a performance of those things which were told her from the Lord. And Mary said, My soul doth magnify the Lord, and my spirit hath rejoiced in God my Saviour, for He hath regarded the low estate of His handmaiden. For behold, from henceforth all generations shall call me blessed. For He that is mighty hath magnified me; and holy is His Name.

COMMON OF A MARTYR

THE INTROIT. *Psalm* 119. 161-168.

PRINCES have persecuted me without a cause; / but my heart standeth in awe of Thy Word. I am as glad of Thy Word, / as one that findeth great spoils. As for lies, I hate and abhor them; / but Thy Law do I love. Seven times a day do I praise Thee / because of Thy righteous judgements. Great is the peace that they have who love Thy Law, / and they are not offended at it. Lord, I have looked for Thy saving health, / and done after Thy commandments. My soul hath kept Thy testimonies, / and loved them exceedingly. I have kept Thy commandments and testimonies, / for all my ways are before Thee.

GLORY be to the Father, and to the Son, / and to the Holy Ghost;
As it was in the beginning, is now, and ever shall be, / world without end. Amen.

THE COLLECT.

ALMIGHTY God, by Whose grace and power Thy blessed Martyr Saint *N.* was enabled to witness to the truth, and to be faithful unto death: Grant that we, who now remember *him* before Thee, may be enabled by Thy grace likewise to bear witness unto Thee in this world; and, persevering to the end, may be found worthy to receive with *him* the crown of glory that fadeth not away; through Jesus Christ our Lord, Who with Thee and the Holy Ghost liveth and reigneth, one God, for ever and ever. *Amen.*

THE EPISTLE. I *Saint Peter* 4. 12-19.

BELOVED, think it not strange concerning the fiery trial which is to try you, as though some strange thing happened unto you; but rejoice, inasmuch as ye are partakers of the sufferings of Christ; that when His glory shall be revealed, ye may be glad also with exceeding joy. If ye be reproached for the Name of Christ, blessed are ye; for the Spirit of glory and of God resteth upon you; on their part He is evil spoken of, but on your part He is glorified. But let none of you suffer as a murderer, or as a thief, or as a busybody in other men's matters; but if any man suffer as a Christian, let him not be ashamed; but let him glorify God in this name. For the time is come that judgement must begin at the house of God; and if it first begin at us, what shall the end be of them that obey not the Gospel of God? And if the righteous scarcely be saved, where shall the ungodly and the sinner appear? Wherefore let them that suffer according to the will of God commit the keeping of their souls to Him, in well-doing, as unto a faithful Creator.

THE GRADUAL. *Psalm* 116. 11-15.

ALLELUIA, Alleluia. What reward shall I give unto the Lord / for all the benefits that He hath done unto me? I will receive the cup of salvation, / and call upon the Name of the Lord. I will pay my vows now in the presence of all His people; / right dear in the sight of the Lord is the death of His saints. Behold, O Lord, how that I am Thy servant: / I am Thy servant, and the son of Thine handmaid; Thou hast broken my bonds in sunder. I will offer to Thee the sacrifice of thanksgiving, / and will call upon the Name of the Lord. *Alleluia.*

Note that the Alleluias *of the Gradual shall be omitted during Advent and Lent, and other times of Penitence or Solemn Prayer.*

THE GOSPEL. *Saint Matthew* 16. 24-27.

THEN said Jesus unto His disciples, If any man will come after me, let him deny himself, and take up his cross, and follow me. For whosoever will save his life shall lose it; and whosoever will lose his life for my sake shall find it. For what is a man profited, if he shall gain the whole world, and lose his own soul? or what shall a man give in exchange for his soul? For the Son of Man shall come in the glory of His Father with his angels; and then shall He reward every man according to his works.

COMMON OF AN ARCHBISHOP OR BISHOP

THE INTROIT. *Psalm* 132. 11-18.

THE Lord hath made a faithful oath unto David, / and He shall not shrink from it: 'Of the fruit of thy body / shall I set upon thy seat. If thy children will keep my covenant, and my testimonies that I shall teach them, / their children also shall sit upon thy seat for evermore'. For the Lord hath chosen Sion to be an habitation for Himself; / He hath longed for her. This shall be my rest for ever; / here will I dwell, for I have a delight therein. I will bless her victuals with increase, / and will satisfy her poor with bread. I will deck her priests with health, / and her saints shall rejoice and sing. There shall I make the horn of David to flourish; / I have ordained a lantern for mine Anointed.

GLORY be to the Father, and to the Son, / and to the Holy Ghost;
As it was in the beginning, is now, and ever shall be, / world without end. Amen.

THE COLLECT.

O GOD, our heavenly Father, Who didst raise up Thy faithful servant Saint *N.* to be a Bishop in Thy holy Church, and to feed Thy flock: We beseech Thee to send down upon all Thy Bishops, the Pastors of Thy Church, the abundant gift of Thy Holy Spirit, that they, being endued with power from on high, and ever walking in the footsteps of Thy blessed Apostles, and continuing steadfast in their doctrine and fellowship, may minister before Thee in Thy household as true servants of Christ and stewards of Thy Divine Mysteries; through the same Jesus Christ our Lord, Who liveth and reigneth with Thee in the unity of the same Spirit, one God, world without end. *Amen.*

THE EPISTLE. I *Timothy* 6. 11-16.

BUT thou, O man of God, flee these things; and follow after righteousness, godliness, faith, love, patience, meekness. Fight the good fight of faith, lay hold on eternal life, whereunto thou art also called, and hast professed a good profession before many witnesses. I give thee charge in the sight of God, Who giveth life to all, and before Christ Jesus, Who before Pontius Pilate witnessed a good confession; that thou keep this commandment without spot, unrebukeable, until the appearing of our Lord Jesus Christ; which in His times He shall shew, Who is the blessed and only Sovereign, the King of kings and Lord of lords; Who alone hath immortality, dwelling in the light which no man can approach unto; Whom no man hath seen, nor can see; to Whom be honour and power everlasting. Amen.

THE GRADUAL. *Psalm* 135. 1-4.

ALLELUIA, Alleluia. O praise the Lord, laud ye the Name of the Lord; / praise it, O ye servants of the Lord; Ye that stand in the house of the Lord, / in the courts of the house of our God. O praise the Lord, for the Lord is gracious; / O sing praises unto His Name, for it is lovely. For why? the Lord hath chosen Jacob unto Himself, / and Israel for His own possession. Alleluia.

Note that the Alleluias *of the Gradual shall be omitted during Advent and Lent, and other times of Penitence or Solemn Prayer.*

THE GOSPEL. *Saint Luke* 12. 37-44.

BLESSED are those servants, whom their lord when he cometh shall find watching. Verily I say unto you, that he shall gird himself, and make them to sit down to meat, and will come forth and serve them. And if he shall come in the second watch, or come in the third watch, and find them so, blessed are those servants. And this know, that if the good-man of the house had known what hour the thief would come, he would have watched, and not have suffered his house to be broken through. Be ye therefore ready also; for the Son of Man cometh at an hour when ye think not. Then Peter said unto Him, Lord, speakest Thou this parable unto us, or even unto all? And the Lord said, Who then is that faithful and wise steward, whom his Lord shall make ruler over his household, to give them their food in due season? Blessed is that servant, whom his Lord when He cometh shall find so doing. Of a truth I say unto you, that He will make him ruler over all that He hath.

COMMON OF A MISSIONARY

THE INTROIT. *Psalm* 96. 1-9.

O SING unto the Lord a new song; / sing unto the Lord, all the whole earth. Sing unto the Lord, and praise His Name; / be telling of His salvation from day to day. Declare His honour unto the heathen, / and His wonders unto all people. For the Lord is great, and cannot worthily be praised; / He is more to be feared than all gods. As for all the gods of the heathen, they are but idols; / but it is the Lord that made the heavens. Glory and worship are before Him; / power and honour are in His sanctuary. Ascribe unto the Lord, O ye kindreds of the people, / ascribe unto the Lord worship and power. Ascribe unto the Lord the honour due unto His Name; / bring presents, and come into His courts. O worship the Lord in the beauty of holiness, / let the whole earth stand in awe of Him.

GLORY be to the Father, and to the Son, / and to the Holy Ghost;
As it was in the beginning, is now, and ever shall be, / world without end. Amen.

THE COLLECT.

O GOD, our heavenly Father, Who by Thy Son Jesus Christ didst call Thy blessed Apostles and send them forth to preach the Gospel of salvation unto all nations: We bless Thy holy Name for Thy *servant* Saint *N.*, whose life and labours we commemorate this day; and we pray thee, according to Thy holy Word, to send forth many labourers into Thy harvest; through the same Jesus Christ our Lord, Who liveth and reigneth with Thee and the Holy Ghost, one God, for ever and ever. *Amen.*

FOR THE EPISTLE. *Acts* 12. 24-13. 5.

NOW the Word of God grew and multiplied, and Barnabas and Saul returned from Jerusalem, when they had fulfilled their ministry, and took with them John, whose surname was Mark. And there were in the Church which was at Antioch certain prophets and teachers; as Barnabas, and Symeon that was called Niger, and Lucius of Cyrene, and Manaen the foster-brother of Herod the tetrarch, and Saul. And as they were ministering to the Lord, and fasting, the Holy Ghost said, Separate me Barnabas and Saul for the work whereunto I have called them; and when they had fasted and prayed and laid their hands upon them, they sent them away. And they, being sent forth by the Holy Ghost, departed unto Seleucia, and from thence they sailed to Cyprus. And when they were at Salamis, they preached the Word of God in the synagogues of the Jews: and they had also John to their minister.

THE GRADUAL. *Psalm* 96. 10-13.

ALLELUIA, Alleluia. Tell it out among the heathen, that the Lord is King: / and that it is He Who hath made the round world so fast that it cannot be moved; and how that He shall judge the people righteously. Let the heavens rejoice, and let the earth be glad; / let the sea make a noise, and all that therein is. Let the field be joyful, and all that is in it: / then shall all the trees of the wood rejoice before the Lord. For He cometh, for He cometh to judge the earth; / and with righteousness to judge the world, and the people with His truth. *Alleluia.*

Note that the Alleluias *of the Gradual shall be omitted during Advent and Lent, and other times of Penitence or Solemn Prayer.*

THE GOSPEL. *Saint Matthew* 4. 13-24.

AND Jesus left Nazareth, and came and dwelt in Capernaum, which is upon the sea-coast in the land of Zabulon and Naphtali, that it might be fulfilled which was spoken by Isaiah the Prophet, saying, Land of Zebulon and land of Naphtali, the way of the sea, beyond Jordan, Galilee of the Gentiles; the people which sat in darkness have seen a great light; to them which sat in the region and shadow of death, light is arisen. From that time, Jesus began to preach, and to say, Repent; for the kingdom of heaven is at hand. And Jesus, walking by the sea of Galilee, saw two brethren, Simon called Peter, and Andrew his brother, casting a net into the sea; for they were fishers. And He saith unto them, Follow me; and I will make you fishers of men. And they straightway left their nets, and followed Him. And going on from thence, He saw other two brethren, James the son of Zebedee, and John his brother, in a ship with Zebedee their father, mending their nets; and He called them. And they immediately left the ship and their father, and followed Him. And Jesus went about all Galilee, teaching in their synagogues, and preaching the Gospel of the kingdom, and healing all manner of sickness and all manner of disease among the people. And His fame went throughout all Syria.

COMMON OF A VIRGIN OR MATRON

THE INTROIT. *Psalm* 119. 1-8.

BLESSED are those that are undefiled in the way, / and walk in the Law of the Lord. Blessed are they that keep His testimonies, / and seek Him with their whole heart. For they who do no wickedness / walk in His ways. Thou hast charged / that we shall diligently keep Thy commandments. O that my ways were made so direct, / that I might keep Thy statutes! So shall I not be confounded / while I have respect unto all Thy commandments. I will thank Thee with an unfeigned heart, / when I shall have learned the judgements of Thy righteousness. I will keep Thy ceremonies: / O forsake me not utterly.

GLORY be to the Father, and to the Son, / and to the Holy Ghost;

As it was in the beginning, is now, and ever shall be, / world without end. Amen.

THE COLLECT.

O GOD Most High, the Creator of all mankind, we bless Thy holy Name for the virtue and grace which Thou hast given unto holy women in all ages, especially Thy handmaiden Saint *N.*; and we pray that the example of her faith, purity, and faithfulness unto death, may inspire many souls in this generation to look unto Thee, and to follow Thy blessed Son Jesus Christ our Saviour; Who with Thee and the Holy Ghost liveth and reigneth, one God, world without end. *Amen.*

FOR THE EPISTLE. *Acts* 9. 36-42.

NOW there was in Joppa a certain disciple named Tabitha, which by interpretation is called Dorcas; this woman was full of good works and alms-deeds which she did. And it came to pass in those days, that she was sick, and died; whom when they had washed, they laid her in an upper chamber. And forasmuch as Lydda was nigh to Joppa, and the disciples had heard that Peter was there, they sent unto him two men, desiring him that he would not delay to come to them. Then Peter arose and went with them; and when he was come, they brought him into the upper chamber; and all the widows stood by him weeping, and shewing the garments and cloaks which Dorcas had made while she was with them. And Peter put them out of the chamber, and kneeled down and prayed; and turning towards the body, he said, Tabitha, arise. And she opened her eyes; and when she saw Peter, she sat up; and he gave her his hand, and lifted her up; and when he had called the brethren and the widows, he presented her to them alive. And it was known throughout all Joppa, and many believed in the Lord.

THE GRADUAL. *Psalm* 34. 7-10.

ALLELUIA, Alleluia. The angel of the Lord tarrieth round about them that fear Him, / and delivereth them. O taste, and see, how gracious the Lord is; / blessed is the man that trusteth in Him. O fear the Lord, ye that are his saints, / for they that fear Him lack nothing. The lions do lack, and suffer hunger; / but they who seek the Lord shall want no manner of thing that is good. *Alleluia.*

Note that the Alleluias *of the Gradual shall be omitted during Advent and Lent, and other times of Penitence or Solemn Prayer.*

THE GOSPEL. *Saint Luke* 10. 38-42.

NOW it came to pass, as they went on their journey, that Jesus entered into a certain village; and a certain woman named Martha received Him into her house. And she had a sister called Mary, who was sitting at Jesus' feet and listening to His word. But Martha was cumbered about much serving; and she came up to Him and said, Lord, dost Thou not care that my sister hath left me alone to serve? Bid her therefore that she help me. And Jesus answered, and said unto her, Martha, Martha; thou art anxious and troubled about a multitude of things; one thing is needful; and Mary hath chosen the good portion, which shall not be taken away from her.

COMMON OF A DOCTOR, POET, OR SCHOLAR

THE INTROIT. *Psalm* 1. 1-4.

BLESSED is the man that hath not walked in the counsel of the ungodly, nor stood in the way of sinners, / and hath not sat in the seat of the scornful. But his delight is in the Law of the Lord; / and in His Law doth he meditate day and night. And he shall be like a tree planted by the water-side, / that bringeth forth his fruit in due season, Whose leaf also doth not wither; / and look, whatsoever he doeth, it shall prosper.

GLORY be to the Father, and to the Son, / and to the Holy Ghost;

As it was in the beginning, is now, and ever shall be, / world without end. Amen.

THE COLLECT.

O GOD, Who by Thy Holy Spirit hast given unto one man a word of wisdom, and to another a word of knowledge, and to another the gift of tongues: We praise Thy Name for the gifts of grace manifested in Thy *servant Saint N.*; and we pray that Thy Church may never be destitute of the same; through Jesus Christ our Lord. *Amen.*

FOR THE EPISTLE. *Daniel* 2. 17-24.

THEN Daniel went to his house, and made the thing known to Ananias, Azarias, and Misael, his companions; that they should seek mercies from the God of heaven concerning this mystery; that Daniel and his companions should not perish with the rest of the wise men of Babylon. Then was the mystery revealed unto Daniel in a vision of the night. Then Daniel blessed the God of heaven. Daniel answered and said, Blessed be the Name of God for ever and ever; for wisdom and might are His. And He changeth the times and the seasons; He removeth kings, and setteth up kings; He giveth wisdom unto the wise, and knowledge to them that know understanding; He revealeth the deep and secret things; He knoweth what is in darkness, and the light dwelleth with Him. I thank Thee and praise Thee, O Thou God of my fathers, Who hast given me wisdom and might, and hast made known unto me what we desired of Thee; for Thou hast made known unto us the king's matter. Therefore Daniel went in unto Arioch, whom the king had appointed to destroy the wise men of Babylon; he went in and said unto him, Destroy not the wise men of Babylon; bring me in before the king, and I will shew unto the king the interpretation.

THE GRADUAL. *Psalm* 34. 7-11.

ALLELUIA, Alleluia. The angel of the Lord tarrieth round about them that fear Him, / and delivereth them. O taste, and see, how gracious the Lord is; / blessed is the man that trusteth in Him. O fear the Lord, ye that are His saints, / for they that fear Him lack nothing. The lions do lack, and suffer hunger; / but they who seek the Lord shall want no manner of thing that is good. Come, ye children, and hearken unto me: / I will teach you the fear of the Lord. *Alleluia.*

Note that the Alleluias *of the Gradual shall be omitted during Advent and Lent, and other times of Penitence or Solemn Prayer.*

THE GOSPEL. *Saint Matthew* 13. 9.

JESUS said, He who hath ears to hear, let him hear. And His disciples came, and said unto Him, Why speakest Thou unto them in parables? He answered and said unto them, To you it is given to know the mysteries of the kingdom of heaven, but to them it is not given. For whosoever hath, to him shall be given, and he shall have in abundance; but whosoever hath not, from him shall be taken even that he hath. Therefore speak I unto them in parables, because they see and see not, and they hear and hear not, neither do they understand. And in them is fulfilled the prophecy of Isaiah which saith, Hearing, ye shall hear and shall not understand, and seeing, ye shall see and not perceive; for the heart of this people is become fat, and with their ears they hardly hear, and their eyes they have shut, lest they should see with their eyes, and hear with their ears, and understand with their heart, and should turn, and I should heal them. But blessed are your eyes, for they see; and your ears, for they hear. For verily I say unto you, that many prophets and righteous men have desired to see those things which ye see, and have not seen; and to hear those things which ye hear, and have not heard.

COMMON OF ANY SAINT

THE INTROIT. *Psalm* 145. 8-13.

THE Lord is gracious and merciful, / long-suffering and of great goodness. The Lord is loving unto every man, / and His mercy is over all His works. All Thy works praise Thee, O Lord; / and Thy saints give thanks unto Thee. They shew the glory of Thy kingdom, / and talk of Thy power; That Thy power, Thy glory, and mightiness of Thy kingdom, / might be known unto men. Thy kingdom is an everlasting kingdom, / and Thy dominion endureth throughout all ages.

GLORY be to the Father, and to the Son, / and to the Holy Ghost;
As it was in the beginning, is now, and ever shall be, / world without end. Amen.

THE COLLECT.

O ALMIGHTY God, Who willest to be glorified in Thy Saints, and didst raise up Thy *servant* Saint *N.* to shine as a light in the world: Shine, we pray Thee, in our hearts, that we also in our generation may shew forth Thy praises, who hast called us out of darkness into Thine own marvellous light; through Jesus Christ our Lord. *Amen.*

FOR THE EPISTLE. *Revelation* 5. 6-10.

I BEHELD, and lo, in the midst of the throne and of the four living creatures, and in the midst of the elders, stood a Lamb as it had been slain, having seven horns and seven eyes, which are the seven Spirits of God sent forth into all the earth. And He came and took the book out of the right hand of Him that sat upon the throne. And when He had taken the book, the four living creatures and four and twenty elders fell down before the Lamb, having every one of them harps and golden vials full of odours, which are the prayers of saints. And they sung a new song, saying, Thou art worthy to take the book, and to open the seals thereof: for thou wast slain, and hast redeemed us to God by Thy Blood out of every kindred, and tongue, and people, and nation; and hast made us unto our God kings and priests: and we shall reign on the earth.

THE GRADUAL. *Psalm* 92. 11-14.

ALLELUIA, Alleluia. The righteous shall flourish like a palm-tree, / and shall spread abroad like a cedar in Libanus. Such as are planted in the house of the Lord / shall flourish in the courts of the house of our God. They also shall bring forth more fruit in their age, / and shall be fat and well-liking. That they may shew how true the Lord my Strength is, / and that there is no unrighteousness in Him. *Alleluia.*

Note that the Alleluias *of the Gradual shall be omitted during Advent
and Lent, and other times of Penitence or Solemn Prayer.*

THE GOSPEL. *Saint Matthew* 25. 31-40.

WHEN the Son of Man shall come in his glory, and all the holy angels with Him, then shall He sit upon the throne of His glory: and before Him shall be gathered all nations: and He shall separate them one from another, as a shepherd divideth his sheep from the goats: and He shall set the sheep on his right hand, but the goats on the left. Then shall the King say unto them on His right hand, Come, ye blessed of my Father, inherit the kingdom prepared for you from the foundation of the world: for I was an-hungered, and ye gave me meat: I was thirsty, and ye gave me drink: I was a stranger, and ye took me in: naked, and ye clothed me: I was sick, and ye visited me: I was in prison, and ye came unto me. Then shall the righteous answer Him, saying, Lord, when saw we Thee an-hungered, and fed Thee? or thirsty, and gave Thee drink? When saw we Thee a stranger, and took Thee in? or naked, and clothed Thee? Or when saw we Thee sick, or in prison, and came unto Thee? And the King shall answer and say unto them, Verily I say unto you, Inasmuch as ye have done it unto one of the least of these my brethren, ye have done it unto me.

COMMON OF FOUNDERS, BENEFACTORS, MISSIONARIES, AND OTHER WORTHIES OF THE CHURCH IN CANADA

THE INTROIT. *Psalm* 89. 1-9.

MY song shall be alway of the loving-kindness of the Lord; / with my mouth will I ever be shewing Thy truth from one generation to another. For I have said, Mercy shall be set up for ever: / Thy truth shalt Thou stablish in the heavens. I have made a covenant with my chosen: / I have sworn unto David my servant, Thy seed will I stablish for ever, / and set up Thy throne from one generation to another. O Lord, the very heavens shall praise Thy wondrous works; / and Thy truth in the congregation of the saints. For who is he among the clouds / that shall be compared unto the Lord? And what is he among the gods / that shall be like unto the Lord? God is very greatly to be feared in the council of the saints, / and to be had in reverence of all them that are round about Him. O Lord God of hosts, Who is like unto Thee? / Thy truth, most mighty Lord, is on every side.

GLORY be to the Father, and to the Son, / and to the Holy Ghost;
As it was in the beginning, is now, and ever shall be, / world without end. Amen.

THE COLLECT.

ALMIGHTY God, our heavenly Father, we remember before Thee all Thy servants who have served Thee faithfully in their generation, and have entered into rest, [*especially Thy servant N.*]; beseeching Thee to give us grace so to follow in their steps, that with them we may be partakers of Thy heavenly kingdom; through Jesus Christ our Lord. *Amen.*

THE EPISTLE. *Hebrews* 11. 13-12. 1-2.

THESE all died in faith, not having received the promises, but having seen them afar off, and were persuaded of them, and embraced them, and confessed that they were strangers and pilgrims on the earth. For they that say such things declare plainly that they seek a country. And truly, if they had been mindful of that country from whence they came out, they might have had opportunity to have returned. But now they desire a better country, that is, an heavenly: wherefore God is not ashamed to be called their God: for He hath prepared for them a city. Wherefore seeing we also are compassed about with so great a cloud of witnesses, let us lay aside every weight, and the sin which doth so easily beset us, and let us run with patience the race that is set before us, looking unto Jesus the Author and Finisher of our Faith; Who for the joy that was set before Him endured the Cross, despising the shame, and hath sat down on the right hand of the throne of God.

THE GRADUAL. *Psalm* 126. 1-7.

ALLELUIA, Alleluia. When the Lord turned again the captivity of Sion, / then were we like unto them that dream. Then was our mouth filled with laughter, / and our tongue with joy. Then said they among the heathen, / 'The Lord hath done great things for them'. Yea, the Lord hath done great things for us already; / whereof we rejoice. Turn our captivity, O Lord, / as the rivers in the south. They that sow in tears, / shall reap in joy. He that now goeth on his way weeping, and beareth forth good seed, / shall doubtless come again with joy, and bring his sheaves with him. *Alleluia.*

Note that the Alleluias *of the Gradual shall be omitted during Advent and Lent, and other times of Penitence or Solemn Prayer.*

THE GOSPEL. *Saint John* 4. 32.-38.

JESUS said unto His disciples, I have food to eat that ye know not of. Therefore said the disciples one to another, Hath any man brought Him aught to eat? Jesus saith unto them, My food is to do the will of Him that sent me, and to finish His work. Say not ye, There are yet four months, and then cometh harvest? Behold, I say unto you, Lift up your eyes, and look on the fields; for they are white already to harvest. And he that reapeth receiveth wages, and gathereth fruit unto life eternal: that both he that soweth and he that reapeth may rejoice together. And herein is that saying true, One soweth, and another reapeth. I sent you to reap that whereon ye bestowed no labour: other men laboured, and ye have entered into their labours.

DEDICATION FESTIVAL

THE INTROIT. *Psalm* 84. 1-7.

O HOW amiable are Thy dwellings, / Thou Lord of hosts! My soul hath a desire and longing to enter into the courts of the Lord; / my heart and my flesh rejoice in the living God. Yea, the sparrow hath found her an house, and the swallow a nest where she may lay her young: / even Thine altars, O Lord of hosts, my King and my God. Blessed are they that dwell in Thy house: / they will be alway praising Thee. Blessed is the man whose strength is in Thee, / in whose heart are Thy ways. Who going through the vale of misery use it for a well, / and the pools are filled with water. They will go from strength to strength; / and unto the God of gods appeareth every one of them in Sion.

GLORY be to the Father, and to the Son, / and to the Holy Ghost;
As it was in the beginning, is now, and ever shall be, / world without end. Amen.

THE COLLECT.

O MOST blessed Saviour, Who didst vouchsafe Thy gracious presence at the Feast of Dedication: Be present with us at this time by Thy Holy Spirit; and so possess our souls by Thy grace, that we may be living temples, holy and acceptable unto Thee; Who livest and reignest with the Father and the Holy Ghost, one God, world without end. *Amen.*

THE EPISTLE. I *St Peter* 2. 1-10.

WHEREFORE, laying aside all malice, and all guile, and hypocrisies, and envies, and all evil-speaking, as new-born babes, desire the sincere milk of the word, that ye may grow thereby unto salvation; if so be that ye have tasted that the Lord is good; to Whom you come, as unto a living Stone, rejected indeed by men, but chosen by God and precious, and are built up yourselves as living stones into a spiritual house, to be a holy priesthood, to offer up spiritual sacrifices, acceptable unto God through Jesus Christ. Wherefore also it is contained in the Scripture, Behold, I lay in Sion a chief Corner-stone, elect, precious, and he who believeth on Him shall not be put to shame. To you therefore who believe, He is precious, but to them that are disobedient it saith, The Stone which the builders rejected, the same is made the Head of the corner; and, a Stone of stumbling, and a Rock of offence; for those who stumble at the word in their disobedience; whereunto also it was appointed. But you are a chosen generation, a royal priesthood, an holy nation, a people for His own possession; that ye should declare the praises of Him who called you out of darkness into His own marvellous light; which in times past were no people, but are now the people of God; which once had not obtained mercy, but have now obtained mercy.

THE GRADUAL. *Psalm* 138. 1-3.

ALLELUIA, Alleluia. I will give thanks unto Thee, O Lord, with my whole heart; / even before the gods will I sing praise unto Thee. I will worship toward Thy holy temple, and praise Thy Name, because of Thy loving-kindness and truth: / for Thou hast magnified Thy Name and Thy word above all things. When I called upon Thee, Thou heardest me, / and enduedst my soul with much strength. *Alleluia.*

Note that the Alleluias *of the Gradual shall be omitted during Advent and Lent, and other times of Penitence or Solemn Prayer.*

THE GOSPEL. *Saint Matthew* 21. 10-16.

AND when Jesus was come into Jerusalem all the city was moved, saying, Who is this? And the multitude said, This is Jesus the Prophet of Nazareth of Galilee. And Jesus went into the temple of God, and cast out all those who sold and bought in the temple; and overthrew the tables of the money-changers, and the seats of those who sold doves; and He said unto them, It is written, My house shall be called the house of prayer, but ye have made it a den of thieves. And the blind and the lame came to Him in the temple, and He healed them. And when the chief priests and the scribes saw the wonderful things that He did, and the children shouting in the temple, and saying, Hosanna to the son of David; they were sore displeased, and said unto Him, Hearest Thou what these say? And Jesus said unto them, Yea: have ye never read, Out of the mouth of babes and sucklings Thou hast perfected praise?

THANKSGIVING-DAY

THE INTROIT. *Psalm* 111. 1-10.

I WILL give thanks unto the Lord with my whole heart / secretly among the faithful, and in the congregation. The works of the Lord are great, / sought out of all of them that have pleasure therein. His work is worthy to be praised and had in honour, / and His righteousness endureth for ever. The merciful and gracious Lord hath so done His marvellous works, / that they ought to be had in remembrance. He hath given meat unto them that fear Him; / He shall ever be mindful of His covenant. He hath shewed His people the power of His works, / that He may give them the heritage of the heathen. The works of His hands are´ verity and judgement; / all His Commandments are true. They stand fast for ever and ever, / and are done in truth and equity. He sent redemption unto His people; / He hath commanded His covenant for ever; holy and reverend is His Name. The fear of the Lord is the beginning of wisdom: / a good understanding have all they that do thereafter; the praise of it endureth for ever.

GLORY be to the Father, and to the Son, / and to the Holy Ghost;

As it was in the beginning, is now, and ever shall be, / world without end. Amen.

THE COLLECT.

O MOST merciful Father, we humbly thank Thee for all Thy gifts so freely bestowed upon us; for life and health and safety; for power to work and leisure to rest; for all that is beautiful in creation and in the lives of men, we praise and magnify Thy holy Name; but above all we thank Thee for our spiritual mercies in Christ Jesus our Lord, for the means of grace, and for the hope of glory; fill our hearts with all joy and peace in believing; through the same Thy Son Jesus Christ, Who with Thee and the Holy Ghost liveth and reigneth, one God, for ever and ever. *Amen.*

FOR THE EPISTLE. *Deuteronomy* 8. 6-11.

THOU shalt keep the Commandments of the Lord thy God, to walk in His ways and to fear Him. For the Lord thy God bringeth thee into a good land, a land of brooks of water, of fountains and depths, that spring out of valleys and hills; a land of wheat and barley and vines and fig-trees and pomegranates; a land of oil-olive and honey; a land wherein thou shalt eat bread without scarceness; thou shalt not lack any thing in it; a land whose stones are iron, and out of whose hills thou mayest dig brass. When thou hast eaten and art full, then thou shalt bless the Lord thy God for the good land which He hath given thee. Beware that thou forget not the Lord thy God, in not keeping His Commandments and His Judgements and His Statutes, which I command thee this day.

THE GRADUAL. *Psalm* 75. 1-2.

ALLELUIA, Alleluia. Unto Thee, O God, do we give thanks; / yea, unto Thee do we give thanks. Thy Name also is so nigh, / and that do Thy wondrous works declare. Alleluia.

THE GOSPEL. *Saint Luke* 17. 11-19.

AND it came to pass, as Jesus went on His way to Jerusalem, that He passed through the midst of Samaria and Galilee. And as He entered into a certain village, there met Him ten men that were lepers, which stood afar off: and they lifted up their voices, and said, Jesus, Master, have mercy on us. And when He saw them, He said unto them, Go, shew yourselves unto the priests. And it came to pass that, as they went, they were cleansed. And one of them, when he saw that he was healed, turned back; and with a loud voice glorified God, and fell down on his face at His feet, giving Him thanks; and he was a Samaritan. And Jesus answering said, Were there not ten cleansed? but where are the nine? There are not found that returned to give glory to God, save only this stranger. And He said unto him, Arise, go thy way, thy faith hath made thee whole.

FOR THE SICK

THE INTROIT. *Psalm* 6. 1-9.

O LORD, rebuke me not in Thine indignation, / neither chasten me in Thy displeasure. Have mercy upon me, O Lord, for I am weak; / O Lord, heal me, for my bones are vexed. My soul also is sore troubled: / but Thou, O Lord, how long? Turn Thee, O Lord, and deliver my soul; / O save me for Thy mercy's sake. For in death no man remembereth Thee; / and who will give Thee thanks in the pit? I am weary of my groaning; / every night wash I my bed, and water my couch with my tears. My beauty is gone for very trouble, / and worn away because of all mine enemies. Away from me, all ye that work iniquity; / for the Lord hath heard the voice of my weeping. The Lord hath heard my petition; / the Lord will receive my prayer.

GLORY be to the Father, and to the Son, / and to the Holy Ghost;
As it was in the beginning, is now, and ever shall be, / world without end. Amen.

THE COLLECT.

O GOD of all grace and power: Behold, visit, and relieve this Thy *servant N.*; look upon *him* with the eyes of Thy mercy, give *him* comfort and sure confidence in Thee, defend *him* in all danger, and keep *him* in perpetual peace and safety; through Jesus Christ our Lord. *Amen.*

THE EPISTLE. I *Saint Peter 5.* 5-11.

MY brethren, God resisteth the proud, and giveth grace unto the humble. Humble yourselves, therefore, under the mighty hand of God, that He may exalt you in due time; casting all your care upon Him, for He careth for you. Be sober, be vigilant; because your adversary the devil goeth about like a roaring lion, seeking whom he may devour: whom resist steadfast in the faith, knowing that the same afflictions are accomplished in your brethren who are in the world. And the God of all grace, Who hath called you unto His eternal glory by Christ Jesus, after that ye have suffered a little, will Himself make you perfect, stablish, strengthen, settle you. To Him be glory and dominion for ever and ever. Amen.

THE GRADUAL. *Psalm* 28. 7-10

PRAISED be the Lord, / for He hath heard the voice of my humble petitions. The Lord is my Strength and my Shield; my heart hath trusted in Him, and I am helped; / therefore my heart danceth for joy, and in my song will I praise Him. The Lord is my Strength, / and He is the wholesome Defence of His Anointed.

THE GOSPEL. *Saint Matthew* 8. 13-17.

AND Jesus said unto the centurion, Go Thy way; and as Thou hast believed, so be it done unto Thee; and his servant was healed in the selfsame hour. And when Jesus was come into Peter's house, He saw his wife's mother lying sick of a fever. And He touched her hand, and the fever left her; and she arose and ministered unto them. And when the even was come, they brought unto Him many that were possessed of devils; and He cast out the spirits with His word, and healed all that were sick; that it might be fulfilled which was spoken by Isaiah the prophet, Himself took our infirmities, and bare our sicknesses.

AT A NATIONAL SYNOD, PROVINCIAL CONVOCATION, OR DIOCESAN SYNOD

THE INTROIT. *Psalm* 68. 7-11.

O GOD, when Thou wentest forth before the people, / when Thou wentest through the wilderness; The earth shook, and the heavens dropped at the presence of God, / even as Sinai also was moved at the presence of God, Who is the God of Israel. Thou, O God, sentest a gracious rain upon Thine inheritance, / and refreshedst it when it was weary. Thy congregation shall dwell therein; / for Thou, O God, hast of Thy goodness prepared for the poor. The Lord gave the word; / great was the company of the preachers.

GLORY be to the Father, and to the Son, / and to the Holy Ghost;
As it was in the beginning, is now, and ever shall be, / world without end. Amen.

THE COLLECT.

GUIDE, we beseech Thee, Almighty God, by the light of Thy Holy Spirit, the counsels of the *Archbishop, Bishop,* Clergy, and Laity who are at this time assembled together in *National Synod* or *Provincial Convocation,* or *Diocesan Synod;* that Thy Church may dwell in peace, and fulfil all the mind of Him Who loved it and gave Himself for it, even Thy Son our Saviour Jesus Christ. *Amen.*

Or this.

O LORD, we beseech Thee to keep Thy household the Church continually in Thy one true religion; that they who do lean only upon the hope of Thy heavenly grace may evermore be defended by Thy mighty power; through Jesus Christ our Lord, Who liveth and reigneth with Thee and the Holy Ghost, one God, world without end. *Amen.*

FOR THE EPISTLE. *Acts* 2. 38-47.

THEN Peter said unto them, Repent, and be baptised every one of you in the Name of Jesus Christ for the remission of sins; and ye shall receive the gift of the Holy Ghost. For the promise is unto you, and to your children, and to all that are afar off, even as many as the Lord our God shall call. And with many other words did he testify and exhort, saying, Save yourselves from this crooked generation. Then they that gladly received his word were baptised; and the same day there were added unto them about three thousand souls. And they continued steadfastly in the Apostles' doctrine and fellowship, and in the breaking of the bread, and in the prayers. And fear came upon every soul; and many wonders and signs were done by the Apostles. And all that believed were together, and had all things in common; and sold their possessions and goods, and parted them to all men as every man had need. And they continued daily with one accord in the temple, and breaking bread from house to house, did eat their food with gladness and singleness of heart, praising God, and having favour with all the people. And the Lord added to the Church daily such as should be saved.

ALLELUIA, Alleluia. Thy God hath sent forth strength for thee; / stablish the thing, O God, that Thou hast wrought in us; For Thy temple's sake at Jerusalem, / so shall kings bring presents unto Thee. *Alleluia.*

Note that the Alleluias *of the Gradual shall be omitted during Advent and Lent, and other times of Penitence or Solemn Prayer.*

THE GOSPEL. *Saint John* 16. 5-15.

JESUS said unto His disciples, Now I go my way to Him that sent me, and none of you asketh me, Whither goest Thou? But, because I have said these things unto you, sorrow hath filled your heart. Nevertheless, I tell you the truth: It is expedient for you that I go away; for if I go not away, the Comforter will not come unto you; but if I depart, I will send Him unto you. And when He is come, He will reprove the world of sin, and of righteousness, and of judgement: of sin, because they believe not on me; of righteousness, because I go to my Father, and ye see me no more; of judgement, because the prince of this world is judged. I have yet many things to say unto you, but ye cannot bear them now. Howbeit, when He, the Spirit of truth, is come, He will guide you into all truth: for He shall not speak of Himself; but whatsoever He shall hear, that shall He speak: and He will shew you things to come. He shall glorify me: for He shall receive of mine, and shall shew it unto you. All things that the Father hath are mine: therefore said I, that He shall take of mine, and shall shew it unto you.

AT A CONFERENCE OR RETREAT

THE INTROIT. *Psalm* 121. 1-8.

I WILL lift up mine eyes unto the hills; / from whence cometh my help? My help cometh even from the Lord, / Who hath made heaven and earth. He will not suffer thy foot to be moved; / and He that keepeth thee will not sleep. Behold, He that keepeth Israel / shall neither slumber nor sleep. The Lord himself is thy Keeper; / the Lord is thy Defence upon thy right hand; So that the sun shall not burn thee by day, / neither the moon by night. The Lord shall preserve thee from all evil; / yea, it is even He that shall keep thy soul. The Lord shall preserve thy going out, and thy coming in, / from this time forth for evermore.

GLORY be to the Father, and to the Son, / and to the Holy Ghost;
As it was in the beginning, is now, and ever shall be, / world without end. Amen.

THE COLLECT.

ALMIGHTY God, Who dost promise that when two or three are gathered together in Thy Name Thou wilt grant their requests: Grant the desires and petitions of Thy servants, as may be most expedient for them; through Christ our Lord. *Amen.*

THE EPISTLE. *Ephesians* 3. 14-21.

FOR this cause I bow my knees unto the Father, from Whom the whole family in heaven and earth is named, that He would grant you, according to the riches of His glory, to be strengthened with might by His Spirit in the inner man; that Christ may dwell in your hearts by faith; that ye, being rooted and grounded in love, may be able to comprehend with all saints, what is the breadth, and length, and depth, and height; and to know the love of Christ which passeth knowledge, that ye may be filled with all the fullness of God. Now unto Him that is able to do exceeding abundantly above all that we ask or think, according to the power that worketh in us, unto Him be glory in the Church and in Christ Jesus, throughout all ages, world without end. Amen.

THE GRADUAL. *Psalm* 123. 1-2.

ALLELUIA, Alleluia. Unto Thee lift I up mine eyes, / O Thou that dwellest in the heavens. Behold, even as the eyes of servants look unto the hand of their masters, and as the eyes of a maiden unto the hand of her mistress, / even so our eyes wait upon the Lord our God, until He have mercy upon us. *Alleluia.*

Note that the Alleluias *of the Gradual shall be omitted during Advent and Lent, and other times of Penitence or Solemn Prayer.*

THE GOSPEL. *Saint Matthew* 11. 25-30.

AT that time Jesus answered and said, I thank Thee, O Father, Lord of heaven and earth, because Thou hast hid these things from the wise and prudent, and hast revealed them unto babes. Even so, Father, for so it seemed good in Thy sight. All things are delivered unto me of my Father; and no man knoweth the Son but the Father; neither knoweth any man the Father, save the Son, and he to whomsoever the Son will reveal Him. Come unto me, all ye that labour and are heavy laden, and I will give you rest. Take my yoke upon you, and learn of me; for I am meek and lowly in heart; and ye shall find rest unto your souls. For my yoke is easy, and my burden is light.

FOR REPENTANCE AND RENEWAL

THE INTROIT. *Psalm* 51. 1-7.

HAVE mercy upon me, O God, after Thy great goodness; / according to the multitude of Thy mercies do away mine offences. Wash me thoroughly from my wickedness, / and cleanse me from my sin. For I acknowledge my faults, / and my sin is ever before me. Against Thee only have I sinned, and done this evil in Thy sight; / that Thou mightest be justified when Thou speakest, and clear when Thou dost judge. Behold, I was shapen in wickedness, / and in sin hath my mother conceived me. But lo, Thou requirest truth in the inward parts, / and shalt make me to understand wisdom secretly. Thou shalt purge me with hyssop, and I shall be clean; / Thou shalt wash me, and I shall be whiter than snow.

GLORY be to the Father, and to the Son, / and to the Holy Ghost;
As it was in the beginning, is now, and ever shall be, / world without end. Amen.

THE COLLECT.

STIR up, we beseech Thee, O mighty Lord, Thy power and come among us; that by Thy protection we may be rescued from the bondage of our sins, and saved by Thy mighty deliverance; Who with the Father and the Holy Ghost livest and reignest, one God, world without end. *Amen.*

THE EPISTLE. *Romans* 3. 19-26.

WHATSOEVER things the Law saith, it saith to them who are under the Law, that every mouth may be stopped, and all the world be made subject to the judgement of God; for no flesh shall be accounted righteous in His sight by the works of the Law; for by the Law cometh knowledge of sin; but now the righteousness of God hath been revealed apart from the Law, being witnessed to by the Law and the Prophets; even the righteousness of God, which is by faith in Jesus Christ for all them that believe. For there is no distinction made; for all have sinned, and come short of the glory of God, and are granted righteousness as a free gift through the redemption which is in Christ Jesus, Whom God hath set forth to be an atonement, through faith, by His Blood, to declare His righteousness for the remission of sins that are past, through the forbearance of God; to declare, I say, at this time, His righteousness: that He might be just, and the Justifier of him which believeth in Jesus.

THE GRADUAL. *Psalm* 51. 10-13.

MAKE me a clean heart, O God, / and renew a right spirit within me. Cast me not away from Thy presence, / and take not Thy Holy Spirit from me. O give me the comfort of Thy help again, / and stablish me with Thy free Spirit. Then shall I teach Thy ways unto the wicked, / and sinners shall be converted unto Thee.

THE GOSPEL. *Saint Luke* 15. 11-32.

AND He spake to them another parable, A certain man had two sons: and the younger of them said to his father, Father, give me the portion of goods that falleth to me. And he divided unto them his living. And not many days after, the younger son gathered all together, and took his journey into a far country, and there wasted his substance with riotous living. And when he had spent all, there arose a mighty famine in that land; and he began to be in want. And he went and joined himself to a citizen of that country; and he sent him into his fields to feed swine. And he would fain have filled his belly with the husks that the swine did eat: and no man gave unto him. And when he came to himself, he said, How many hired servants of my father's have bread enough and to spare, and I perish with hunger! I will arise and go to my father, and will say unto him, Father, I have sinned against heaven, and before thee, and am no more worthy to be called thy son: make me as one of thy hired servants. And he arose, and came to his father. But when he was yet a great way off, his father saw him, and had compassion, and ran, and fell on his neck, and kissed him. And the son said unto him, Father, I have sinned against heaven, and in thy sight, and am no more worthy to be called thy son. But the father said to his servants, Bring forth the best robe, and put it on him; and put a ring on his hand, and shoes on his feet: and bring hither the fatted calf, and kill it; and let us eat, and be merry: for this my son was dead, and is alive again; he was lost, and is found. And they began to be merry. Now his elder son was in the field: and as he came and drew nigh to the house, he heard music and dancing. And he called one of the servants, and asked what these things meant. And he said unto him, Thy brother is come; and thy father hath killed the fatted calf, because he hath received him safe and sound. And he was angry, and would not go in: therefore came his father out, and entreated him. And he answering said to his father, Lo, these many years do I serve thee, neither transgressed I at any time thy commandment: and yet thou never gavest me a kid, that I might make merry with my friends: but as soon as this thy son was come, which hath devoured thy living with harlots, thou hast killed for him the fatted calf. And he said unto him, Son, thou art ever with me, and all that I have is thine. It was meet that we should make merry, and be glad: for this thy brother was dead, and is alive again; and was lost, and is found.

FOR MISSIONARY WORK

THE INTROIT. *Psalm* 67. 1-5.

GOD be merciful unto us, and bless us, / and shew us the light of His countenance, and be merciful unto us; That Thy way may be known upon earth, / Thy saving health among all nations.

Let the people praise Thee, O God; / yea, let all the people praise Thee. O let the nations rejoice and be glad, / for Thou shalt judge the folk righteously, and govern the nations upon earth. Let the people praise Thee, O God; / let all the people praise Thee.

GLORY be to the Father, and to the Son, / and to the Holy Ghost;

As it was in the beginning, is now, and ever shall be, / world without end. Amen.

THE COLLECT.

ALMIGHTY and everlasting God, Who desirest not the death of sinners, but rather that they may turn unto Thee and live: Deliver the nations of the world from idolatry, superstition, and unbelief, and gather them all into Thy one holy Church, to the praise and glory of Thy Name; through Jesus Christ our Lord. *Amen.*

THE EPISTLE. *Romans* 10. 8-15.

WHAT saith the Scripture? Near is the word, in thy mouth and in thy heart, even the word which we proclaim. If thou shalt confess with thy mouth that Jesus is Lord, and shalt believe in thy heart that God raised Him from the dead, thou shalt be saved; for with the heart man believeth unto righteousness, and with the mouth confession is made unto salvation. For the Scripture saith, Whosoever believeth on Him shall not be put to shame. For there is no difference between Jew and Greek; for the same Lord of all is rich unto all that call upon Him; for whosoever shall call upon the Name of the Lord shall be saved. How then shall they call upon Him in Whom they have not believed? And how shall they believe in Him of Whom they have not heard? And how shall they hear without a preacher? And how shall they preach unless they be sent? As it is written, How beautiful are the feet of them that bring glad tidings of good things!

THE GRADUAL. *Psalm* 117. 1-2.

ALLELUIA, Alleluia. O Praise the Lord, all ye heathen; / praise him, all ye nations. For His merciful kindness is ever more and more towards us: / and the truth of the Lord endureth for ever. Praise the Lord. *Alleluia.*

Note that the Alleluias *of the Gradual shall be omitted during Advent and Lent, and other times of Penitence or Solemn Prayer.*

THE GOSPEL. *Saint Matthew* 28. 16-20.

THEN the eleven disciples went away into Galilee, into the mountain where Jesus had appointed them. And when they saw Him they worshipped Him: but some doubted. And Jesus came and spoke to them, saying, All authority is given unto me in heaven and on earth. Go ye therefore, and make disciples of all the nations, baptising them in the Name of the Father, and of the Son, and of the Holy Ghost; teaching them to observe all things whatsoever I have commanded you: and lo, I am with you alway, even unto the end of the world. Amen.

FOR THE UNITY OF
THE CHRISTIAN CHURCH

THE INTROIT. *Psalm* 122. 1-7.

I WAS glad when they said unto me, / We will go into the house of the Lord. Our feet shall stand in thy gates, / O Jerusalem. Jerusalem is built as a city / that is at unity in itself. For thither the tribes go up, even the tribes of the Lord, / to testify unto Israel, to give thanks unto the Name of the Lord. For there is the seat of judgement, / even the seat of the house of David. O pray for the peace of Jerusalem; / they shall prosper that love thee. Peace be within thy walls, / and plenteousness within thy palaces.

GLORY be to the Father, and to the Son, / and to the Holy Ghost;
As it was in the beginning, is now, and ever shall be, / world without end. Amen.

THE COLLECT.

O LORD Jesu Christ, Who didst say unto Thine Apostles, Peace I leave with you, my peace I give unto you: Regard not our sins, but the faith of Thy Church; and grant unto it that peace and unity which is agreeable to Thy will; Who livest and reignest with the Father and the Holy Ghost, one God, world without end. *Amen.*

THE EPISTLE. *Ephesians* 4. 4-16.

THERE is one body, and one Spirit, even as ye are called in one hope of your calling; one Lord, one Faith, one Baptism, one God and Father of all, Who is above all, and through all, and in you all. And unto every one of us is given grace, according to the measure of the gift of Christ; wherefore it is said, He ascended up on high, He led captivity captive, He gave gifts unto men. And when it is said, He ascended, what is it but that He also descended into the lower parts of the earth? He that descended is the same also that ascended up far above all heavens, that He might fill all things. And He gave some, Apostles; and some, Prophets; and some, Evangelists; and some, Pastors and Teachers; for the perfecting of the saints for the work of the Ministry, for the building up of the body of Christ; till we all come, in the unity of the faith and of the knowledge of the Son of God, unto a perfect man, unto the measure of the stature of the fullness of Christ. That we henceforth be no more children, tossed to and fro, and carried about with every wind of doctrine, by the sleight of men, and cunning craftiness, whereby they lie in wait to deceive; but speaking the truth in love, may grow up into him in all things, which is the head, even Christ: from whom the whole body fitly joined together and compacted by that which every joint supplieth, according to the effectual working in the measure of every part, maketh increase of the body unto the edifying of itself in love.

THE GRADUAL. *Psalm* 133. 1-4.

ALLELUIA, Alleluia. Behold, how good and joyful a thing it is, / brethren, to dwell together in unity! It is like the precious ointment upon the head, that ran down unto the beard, / even unto Aaron's beard, and went down to the skirts of his clothing. Like as the dew of Hermon, / which fell upon the hill of Sion. For there the Lord promised His blessing, / and life for evermore. *Alleluia.*

Note that the Alleluias *of the Gradual shall be omitted during Advent and Lent, and other times of Penitence or Solemn Prayer.*

THE GOSPEL. *Saint John* 17. 20-26.

AND Jesus said, Neither pray I for these alone, but for them also that shall believe on me through their word; that they all may be one; as Thou, Father, art in me, and I in Thee, that they also may be one in Us; that the world may believe that Thou hast sent me. And the glory which Thou gavest me, I have given them; that they may be one, even as We are One: I in them, and Thou in me, that they may be made perfect in one; and that the world may know that Thou hast sent me, and hast loved them, even as Thou hast loved me. Father, I will that they also, whom Thou hast given me, be with me where I am; that they may behold my glory, which Thou hast given me; for Thou didst love me before the foundation of the world. O righteous Father, the world hath not known Thee: but I have known Thee, and these have known that Thou hast sent me; and I have declared unto them Thy Name, and will declare it; that the love wherewith Thou hast loved me may be in them, and I in them.

THE EMBER-DAYS

[The Wednesday, Friday, and Saturday: after the Third Sunday in Advent;
after the First Sunday in Lent; within the Whitsun Octave; and after Holy Cross Day.]

THE INTROIT. *Psalm* 122. 1-7.

I WAS glad when they said unto me, / We will go into the house of the Lord. Our feet shall stand in thy gates, / O Jerusalem. Jerusalem is built as a city / that is at unity in itself. For thither the tribes go up, even the tribes of the Lord, / to testify unto Israel, to give thanks unto the Name of the Lord. For there is the seat of judgement, / even the seat of the house of David. O pray for the peace of Jerusalem; / they shall prosper that love thee. Peace be within thy walls, / and plenteousness within thy palaces.

GLORY be to the Father, and to the Son, / and to the Holy Ghost;
As it was in the beginning, is now, and ever shall be, / world without end. Amen.

THE COLLECT.

ALMIGHTY God our heavenly Father, the Giver of all good things, Who of Thy Divine Providence hast appointed divers Orders of Ministers in Thy Church: Call, we humbly beseech Thee, many to serve Thee in the same; and to as many as Thou shalt call give Thy grace; and so pour out Thy Holy Spirit upon them that, replenished with the truth of Thy doctrine and endued with innocency of life, they may faithfully serve before Thee, to the glory of Thy great Name and the benefit of all Thy holy Church; through Jesus Christ our Lord. *Amen.*

THE EPISTLE. *Romans* 12. 1-21.

I BESEECH you therefore, brethren, by the mercies of God, that ye present your bodies a living sacrifice, holy, acceptable unto God, which is your reasonable service. And be not conformed to this world: but be ye transformed by the renewing of your mind, that ye may prove what is that good, and acceptable, and perfect, will of God. For I say, through the grace given unto me, to every man that is among you, not to think of himself more highly than he ought to think, but to think soberly, according as God hath dealt to every man the measure of faith. For as we have many members in one body, and all members have not the same office; so we, being many, are one body in Christ, and every one members one of another. Having then gifts differing according to the grace that is given to us, whether prophecy, let us prophesy according to the proportion of faith; or ministry, let us wait on our ministering; or he that teacheth, on teaching; or he that exhorteth, on exhortation: he that giveth, let him do it with simplicity; he that ruleth, with diligence; he that sheweth mercy, with cheerfulness. Let love be without dissimulation. Abhor that which is evil, cleave to that which is good. Be kindly affectioned one to another with brotherly love, in honour preferring one another: not slothful in business fervent in spirit; serving the Lord; rejoicing in hope; patient in tribulation; continuing instant in prayer; distributing to the necessity of saints; given to hospitality. Bless them which persecute you; bless, and curse not. Rejoice with them that do rejoice, and weep with them that weep. Be of the same mind one toward another. Mind not high things, but condescend to men of low estate. Be not wise in your own conceits. Recompense to no man evil for evil. Provide things honest in the sight of all men. If it be possible, as much as lieth in you, live peaceably with all men. Dearly beloved, avenge not yourselves, but rather give place unto wrath: for it is written, Vengeance is mine; I will repay, saith the Lord. Therefore if thine enemy hunger, feed him; if he thirst, give him drink: for in so doing thou shalt heap coals of fire on his head. Be not overcome of evil, but overcome evil with good.

THE GRADUAL. *Psalm* 59. 1-5.

DELIVER me from mine enemies, O God; / defend me from them that rise up against me. O deliver me from the wicked doers, / and save me from the blood-thirsty men. For lo, they lie waiting for my soul; / the mighty men are gathered against me, without any offence or fault of me, O Lord. They run and prepare themselves without my fault: / arise Thou therefore to help me, and behold. Stand up, O Lord God of hosts, Thou God of Israel, to visit all the heathen; / and be not merciful unto them that offend of malicious wickedness.

THE GOSPEL. *Saint Luke* 10. 1-9.

AFTER these things, the Lord appointed other seventy also, and sent them two by two before His face into every city and place, whither He Himself would come. Therefore said He unto them, The harvest truly is great, but the labourers are few: pray ye therefore the Lord of the harvest, that He would send forth labourers into His harvest. Go your ways: Behold, I send you forth as lambs among wolves. Carry neither purse, nor scrip, nor shoes; and salute no man by the way. And into whatsoever house ye enter, first say, Peace be to this house. And if the son of peace be there, your peace shall rest upon it: if not, it shall turn to you again. And in the same house remain, eating and drinking such things as they give: for the labourer is worthy of his hire. Go not from house to house. And into whatsoever city ye enter, and they receive you, eat such things as are set before you: and heal the sick that are therein, and say unto them, The kingdom of God is come nigh unto you. But into whatsoever city ye enter, and they receive you not, go your ways out into the streets of the same, and say, Even the very dust of your city, which cleaveth on us, we do wipe off against you: notwithstanding be ye sure of this, that the kingdom of God is come nigh unto you.

Here endeth the PROPERS THROUGHOUT THE CHRISTIAN YEAR.

THE grass withereth, the flower fadeth:
but the Word of our God shall stand for ever.
Isaiah 40. 8.

Forms of Prayer with Thanksgiving to Almighty God

For use in all Churches and Chapels within this Dominion, every Year, on the Anniversary of the day of the Accession of the Reigning Sovereign, or on Victoria Day, or on such other day as shall be appointed by Authority.

I.

At the Divine Office

At Divine Service the following Psalms, Lessons, Suffrages, and Collects may be used.

PROPER PSALMS. *Psalms* 20, 101, 121.

PROPER LESSONS.
The First Lesson: *Joshua* 1. 1-10., *or Proverbs* 8. 1-17.
The Second Lesson: *Romans* 13. 1-11., *or Revelation* 21. 22-22. 4.

THE SUFFRAGES NEXT AFTER THE CREED.

Priest.
O LORD, shew Thy mercy upon us.
   Answer. And grant us Thy salvation.
Priest. O Lord, save the Queen.
   Answer. Who putteth her trust in Thee.
Priest. Send her help from Thy holy place;
   Answer. And evermore mightily defend her.
Priest. Be unto her, O Lord, a strong tower;
   Answer. From the face of her enemies.
Priest. Endue Thy Ministers with righteousness.
   Answer. And make Thy chosen people joyful.
Priest. O Lord, save Thy people.
   Answer. And bless Thine inheritance.
Priest. Give peace in our time, O Lord.
   Answer. And ever more mightily defend us.
Priest. O Lord, hear our prayer;
   Answer. And let our cry come unto Thee.

O GOD, Who providest for Thy people by Thy power, and rulest over them in love: Vouchsafe so to bless Thy Servant our Queen, that under her this nation may be wisely governed, and Thy Church may serve Thee in all godly quietness; and grant that she being devoted to Thee with her whole heart, and persevering in good works unto the end, may, by Thy guidance, come to Thine everlasting kingdom; through Jesus Christ Thy Son our Lord, Who liveth and reigneth with Thee and the Holy Ghost, ever one God, world without end. *Amen.*

If the Great Litany be sung or said, these Prayers immediately after the Prayer, We humbly beseech Thee, &c., *shall be used: and if the Great Litany be not said, then these Prayers instead of the Prayers for the Queen and for the Royal Family at Divine Service shall be said instead.*

ALMIGHTY God, Who rulest over all the kingdoms of the world, and dost order them according to Thy good pleasure: We yield Thee unfeigned thanks, for that Thou wast pleased, *as on this day*, to set Thy Servant our Sovereign Lady, Queen *ELIZABETH*, upon the Throne of this Realm. Let Thy wisdom be her guide, and let Thine arm strengthen her; let truth and justice, holiness and righteousness, peace and charity, abound in her days; direct all her counsels and endeavours to Thy glory, and the welfare of her subjects; give us grace to obey her cheerfully for conscience' sake, and let her always possess the hearts and loyalty of her people; let her reign be long and prosperous, and crown her with everlasting life in the world to come; through Jesus Christ our Lord. *Amen.*

O LORD our God, Who upholdest and governest all things by the word of Thy power: Receive our humble prayers for our Sovereign Lady *ELIZABETH*, *as on this day*, set over us by Thy grace and providence to be our Queen; and, together with her, bless, we beseech thee, *Philip* Duke of Edinburgh, *Charles* Prince of Wales, *William* of Duke of Cambridge, Prince *George* of Cambridge, and all the Royal Family; that they, ever trusting in Thy goodness, protected by Thy power, and crowned with Thy gracious and endless favour, may long continue before Thee in peace and safety, joy and honour, and after death may obtain everlasting life and glory, by the Merits and Mediation of Christ Jesus our Saviour, Who with Thee and the Holy Ghost liveth and reigneth ever one God, world without end. *Amen.*

A Prayer for Unity.

O GOD the Father of our Lord Jesus Christ, our only Saviour, the Prince of Peace: Give us grace seriously to lay to heart the great dangers we are in by our unhappy divisions. Take away all hatred and prejudice, and whatsoever else may hinder us from godly union and concord: that, as there is but one Body, and one Spirit, and one hope of our calling, one Lord, one faith, one baptism, one God and Father of us all; so we may henceforth be all of one heart, and of one soul, united in one holy bond of truth and peace, of faith and charity, and with one mind and one mouth glorify Thee; through Jesus Christ our Lord. *Amen.*

ALMIGHTY God, the Fountain of all wisdom, Who knowest our necessities before we ask, and our ignorance in asking: We beseech Thee to have compassion upon our infirmities; and those things, which for our unworthiness we dare not, and for our blindness we cannot ask, vouchsafe to give us for the worthiness of Thy Son Jesus Christ our Lord. *Amen.*

II.

AT THE HOLY EUCHARIST

In the Order of the Administration of the Holy Eucharist, in place of the Introit, Collect, Epistle, Gradual, and Gospel of the day, the following shall be used.

THE INTROIT. *Psalm* 20.

THE Lord hear thee in the day of trouble, / the Name of the God of Jacob defend thee; Send thee help from the sanctuary, / and strengthen thee out of Sion; Remember all thine offerings, / and accept thy burnt-sacrifice; Grant thee thy heart's desire / and fulfil all thy mind. We will rejoice in Thy salvation, and triumph in the Name of the Lord our God; / the Lord perform all thy petitions. Now know I that the Lord helpeth His Anointed, and will hear him from His holy heaven; / even with the wholesome strength of His right hand. Some put their trust in chariots, and some in horses;

/ but we will remember the Name of the Lord our God. They are brought down, and fallen; / but we are risen, and stand upright. Save, Lord, and hear us, O King of heaven, / when we call upon Thee.

GLORY be to the Father, and to the Son, / and to the Holy Ghost;
As it was in the beginning, is now, and ever shall be, / world without end. Amen.

THE COLLECT.

O GOD, Who providest for Thy people by Thy power, and rulest over them in love: Vouchsafe so to bless Thy Servant our Queen, that under her this nation may be wisely governed, and Thy Church may serve Thee in all godly quietness; and grant that she being devoted to Thee with her whole heart, and persevering in good works unto the end, may, by Thy guidance, come to Thine everlasting kingdom; through Jesus Christ Thy Son our Lord, Who liveth and reigneth with Thee and the Holy Ghost, ever one God, world without end. *Amen.*

THE EPISTLE. I *Saint Peter* 2. 11-17.

DEARLY beloved, I beseech you as strangers and pilgrims, abstain from fleshly lusts, which war against the soul; having your conversation honest among the Gentiles, that, whereas they speak against you as evildoers, they may, by your good works which they shall behold, glorify God in the day of visitation. Submit yourselves to every ordinance of man for the Lord's sake; whether it be to the king, as supreme; or unto governors, as unto them that are sent by him, for the punishment of evildoers, and for the praise of them that do well. For so is the will of God, that with well-doing ye may put to silence the ignorance of foolish men: as free, and not using your liberty for a cloak of maliciousness; but as the servants of God. Honour all men. Love the brotherhood. Fear God. Honour the king.

THE GRADUAL. *Psalm* 21. 1-7.

ALLELUIA, Alleluia. The King shall rejoice in Thy strength, O Lord; / exceeding glad shall he be of Thy salvation. Thou hast given him his heart's desire, / and hast not denied him the request of his lips. For Thou shalt prepare his way before him with the blessings of goodness, / and shalt set a crown of pure gold upon his head. He asked life of Thee, and Thou gavest him a long life, / even for ever and ever. His honour is great in Thy salvation; / glory and great worship shalt Thou lay upon him. For Thou shalt give him everlasting felicity, / and make him glad with the joy of Thy countenance. And why? because the King putteth his trust in the Lord, / and in the mercy of the Most High he shall not miscarry. *Alleluia.*
(*Note that the* Alleluias *shall be omitted throughout Advent and Lent.*)

THE GOSPEL. *Saint Matthew* 22. 16-22.

AND they sent out unto Him their disciples, with the Herodians, saying, Master, we know that Thou art true, and teachest the way of God in truth, neither carest Thou for any man: for Thou regardest not the person of men. Tell us therefore, What thinkest Thou? Is it lawful to give tribute unto Caesar, or not? But Jesus perceived their wickedness, and said, Why tempt ye me, ye hypocrites? shew me the tribute-money. And they brought unto Him a penny. And He saith unto them, Whose is this image and superscription? They say unto Him, Caesar's. Then saith He unto them, Render therefore unto Caesar the things which are Caesar's; and unto God the things that are God's. When they had heard these words, they marvelled, and left Him, and went their way.

III.

The following Service may also be used on the same day at any convenient time.

TE DEUM LAUDAMUS

WE praise Thee, O God, / we acknowledge Thee to be the Lord. All the earth doth worship Thee, / the Father everlasting. To Thee all Angels cry aloud, / the heavens and an the powers therein. To Thee Cherubim and Seraphim / continually do cry, Holy, Holy, Holy / Lord God of Hosts; Heaven and earth are full of the Majesty / of Thy glory. The glorious company of the Apostles / praise Thee. The goodly fellowship of the Prophets / praise Thee. The noble army of Martyrs / praise Thee. The holy Church throughout all the world / doth acknowledge Thee; The Father / of an infinite Majesty; Thine honourable, true, / and only Son; Also the Holy Ghost, / the Comforter.

Thou art the King of glory, / O Christ. Thou art the everlasting Son / of the Father. When Thou tookest upon Thee to deliver man, / Thou didst not abhor the Virgin's womb. When Thou hadst overcome the sharpness of death, / Thou didst open the kingdom of heaven to all believers. Thou sittest at the right hand of God, / in the glory of the Father. We believe that Thou shalt come / to be our Judge. We therefore pray Thee, help Thy servants, / whom Thou hast redeemed with Thy precious Blood. Make them to be numbered with Thy Saints / in glory everlasting.

O Lord, save Thy people, / and bless Thine heritage. Govern them, / and lift them up for ever. Day by day / we magnify Thee; And we worship Thy Name, / ever world without end. Vouchsafe, O Lord, / to keep us this day without sin. O Lord, have mercy upon us, / have mercy upon us. O Lord, let Thy mercy lighten upon us, / as our trust is in Thee. O Lord, in Thee have I trusted, / let me never be confounded. Amen.

Then the Priest shall say,
THE Lord be with you.
Answer. And with thy spirit.

Priest. Let us pray.

Lord, have mercy upon us.
Christ, have mercy upon us.
Lord, have mercy upon us.

Then shall the Priest and people together say or sing the Lord's Prayer.
OUR Father, which art in heaven, hallowed be Thy Name. Thy kingdom come. Thy will be done in earth, as it is in heaven. Give us this day our daily bread. And forgive us our trespasses, As we forgive them that trespass against us. And lead us not into temptation, But deliver us from evil. For Thine is the kingdom, the power, and the glory, For ever and ever. Amen.

Then the Priest standing up shall say,
O LORD, save the Queen;
Answer. Who putteth her trust in Thee.
Priest. Send her help from Thy holy place;
Answer. And evermore mightily defend her.
Priest. Let her enemies have no advantage of her,
Answer. Nor the wicked approach to hurt her.

Priest. O Lord, hear our prayer;
Answer. And let our cry come unto Thee.

Priest. Let us pray.

O GOD, Who providest for Thy people by Thy power, and rulest over them in love: Vouchsafe so to bless Thy Servant our Queen, that under her this nation may be wisely governed, and Thy Church may serve Thee in all godly quietness; and grant that she being devoted to Thee with her whole heart, and persevering in good works unto the end, may, by Thy guidance, come to Thine everlasting kingdom; through Jesus Christ Thy Son our Lord, Who liveth and reigneth with Thee and the Holy Ghost, ever one God, world without end. *Amen.*

ALMIGHTY God, Who rulest over all the kingdoms of the world, and dost order them according to Thy good pleasure: We yield Thee unfeigned thanks, for that Thou wast pleased, *as on this day,* to set Thy Servant our Sovereign Lady, Queen *ELIZABETH,* upon the Throne of this Realm. Let Thy wisdom be her guide, and let Thine arm strengthen her; let truth and justice, holiness and righteousness, peace and charity, abound in her days; direct all her counsels and endeavours to Thy glory, and the welfare of her subjects; give us grace to obey her cheerfully for conscience sake, and let her always possess the hearts and loyalty of her people; let her reign be long and prosperous, and crown her with everlasting life in the world to come; through Jesus Christ our Lord. *Amen.*

O LORD our God, Who upholdest and governest all things by the word of thy power: Receive our humble prayers for our Sovereign Lady *ELIZABETH, as on this day,* set over us by Thy grace and providence to be our Queen; and, together with her, bless, we beseech Thee, *Philip* Duke of Edinburgh, *Charles* Prince of Wales, *William* Duke of Cambridge, Prince *George* of Cambridge, and all the Royal Family; that they, ever trusting in Thy goodness, protected by Thy power, and crowned with Thy gracious and endless favour, may long continue before Thee in peace and safety, joy and honour; and after death may obtain everlasting life and glory, by the Merits and Mediation of Christ Jesus our Saviour, Who with Thee and the Holy Ghost liveth and reigneth ever one God, world without end. *Amen.*

O GOD the Father of our Lord Jesus Christ, our only Saviour, the Prince of Peace: Give us grace seriously to lay to heart the great dangers we are in by our unhappy divisions. Take away all hatred and prejudice, and whatsoever else may hinder us from godly union and concord: that, as there is but one Body, and one Spirit, and one hope of our calling, one Lord, one faith, one baptism, one God and Father of us all; so we may henceforth be all of one heart, and of one soul, united in one holy bond of truth and peace, of faith and charity, and with one mind and one mouth glorify Thee; through Jesus Christ our Lord. *Amen.*

Then shall the Priest dismiss them with this Blessing.

THE Blessing of God Almighty, ✠ the Father, the Son, and the Holy Ghost, rest upon you, and remain with you always. *Amen.*

Here end the FORMS OF PRAYER WITH THANKSGIVING TO ALMIGHTY GOD.

A FORM OF SERVICE FOR
DOMINION-DAY
BEING THE ANNIVERSARY OF THE CONFEDERATION OF
THE PROVINCES OF BRITISH NORTH AMERICA
AND THE ESTABLISHMENT OF THE DOMINION OF CANADA
ON THE FIRST DAY OF JULY 1867

The Propers following are appointed to be used at all celebrations of the Holy Eucharist on Dominion-Day, and on the Sunday nearest to Dominion-Day, in all Churches and Chapels throughout Canada, and wheresoever Canadian subjects of Her Majesty The Queen may be gathered together for prayer and worship on those days.

THE INTROIT. *Psalm* 72. 1-8.

GIVE the king Thy judgements, O God, / and Thy righteousness unto the King's Son. Then shall He judge Thy people with righteousness, / and Thy poor with justice. The mountains also shall bring peace, / and the little hills righteousness unto the people. He shall judge the poor of the people, / He shall save the children of the needy, and shall break in pieces the oppressor. They shall fear Thee as long as the sun and moon endure, / throughout all generations. He shall come down like rain upon the mown grass, / as showers that water the earth. In His days shall the righteous flourish; / and abundance of peace so long as the moon endureth. Let His dominion also be from sea to sea, / and from the river unto the world's end.

GLORY be to the Father, and to the Son, / and to the Holy Ghost;
As it was in the beginning, is now, and ever shall be, / world without end. Amen.

THE COLLECTS.

O GOD, Who providest for Thy people by Thy power, and rulest over them in love: Grant unto Thy servant *ELIZABETH* our Queen, and unto all those whom Thou hast set in authority under her, the spirit of wisdom and righteousness, that we may be so godly and wisely governed that Thy Church may serve Thee in all quietness and safety, and all the people of this Dominion, and the Realms and Countries of our Commonwealth, may enjoy the blessings of good government, liberty, prosperity, and peace; through Jesus Christ our Lord and Saviour. *Amen.*

ALMIGHTY God, Who didst lead our forefathers into this land, and didst set their feet in a large room: Give Thy grace, we beseech Thee, to us their children, that we may approve ourselves a people mindful of Thy favour, and glad always to do Thy will. Bless this Dominion with honourable industry, sound learning, and pure manners. Save us from strife, lawlessness, and discord; from pride, hypocrisy, and arrogance; and fashion into one godly Christian people the multitude brought hither out of many kindreds and many tongues. Give to all of us the spirit of loving service and mutual forbearance. In the time of prosperity make us thankful unto Thee, and in the day of trouble suffer not our trust in Thee to fail: so that loving Thee above all earthly things, we may fulfill Thy gracious purpose in this good land; through Jesus Christ our Lord. *Amen.*

THE LESSON. *Joshua* 24. 14-25.

NOW therefore fear the Lord, and serve Him in sincerity and in truth; and put away the gods which your fathers served on the other side of the flood, and in Egypt; and serve ye the Lord. And if it seem evil unto you to serve the Lord, choose you this day whom ye will serve; whether the gods which your fathers served that were on the other side of the flood, or the gods of the Amorites, in whose land ye dwell: BUT AS FOR ME AND MY HOUSE, WE WILL SERVE THE LORD. And the people answered and said, God forbid that we should forsake the Lord, to serve other gods; for the Lord our God, He it is that brought us up and our fathers out of the land of Egypt, from the house of bondage, and which did those great signs in our sight, and preserved us in all the way wherein we went, and among all the people through whom we passed: And the Lord drave out from before us all the people, even the Amorites which dwelt in the land; therefore will we also serve the Lord; for He is our God. And Joshua said unto the people, Ye cannot serve the Lord: for He is a Holy God; He is a jealous God; He will not forgive your transgressions nor your sins. If ye forsake the Lord, and serve strange gods, then He will turn and do you hurt, and consume you; after that He hath done you good. And the people said unto Joshua, Nay; but we will serve the Lord. And Joshua said unto the people, Ye are witnesses against yourselves that ye have chosen you the Lord, to serve Him. And they said, We are witnesses. Now therefore put away, said he, the strange gods that are among you, and incline your heart unto the Lord God of Israel. And the people said unto Joshua, THE LORD OUR GOD WE WILL SERVE, AND HIS VOICE WE WILL OBEY. So Joshua made a covenant with the people that day, and set them a statute and an ordinance in Shechem.

THE GRADUAL. *Psalm* 46.

ALLELUIA, Alleluia. God is our Hope and Strength, / a very present help in trouble. Therefore will we not fear, though the earth be moved, / and though the hills be carried into the midst of the sea; Though the waters thereof rage and swell, / and though the mountains shake at the tempest of the same. The rivers of the flood thereof shall make glad the city of God, / the holy place of the tabernacle of the Most High. God is in the midst of her, therefore shall she not be removed; / God shall help her, and that right early. The heathen make much ado, and the kingdoms are moved; / but God hath shewed His voice, and the earth shall melt away. The Lord of hosts is with us, / the God of Jacob is our Refuge. O come hither, and behold the works of the Lord, / what destruction He hath brought upon the earth. He maketh wars to cease in all the world; / He breaketh the bow, and snappeth the spear in sunder, and burneth the chariots in the fire. Be still then, and know that I am God; / I will be exalted among the heathen, and I will be exalted in the earth. The Lord of hosts is with us / the God of Jacob is our refuge. Alleluia.

THE GOSPEL. *Saint Matthew* 25. 31-46.

WHEN the Son of Man shall come in His glory, and all the holy angels with Him, then shall He sit upon the Throne of His glory: And before Him shall be gathered all nations; and He shall separate them one from another, as a shepherd divideth His sheep from the goats; and He shall set the sheep on His right hand, but the goats on the left. Then shall the King say unto them on His right hand, Come, ye blessed of my Father, inherit the kingdom prepared for you from the foundation of the world: For I was anhungered, and ye gave Me meat: I was thirsty, and ye gave Me drink: I was a stranger, and ye took Me in: Naked, and ye clothed Me: I was sick, and ye visited Me: I was in prison, and ye came unto Me. Then shall the righteous answer Him, saying, Lord, when saw we Thee anhungered, and fed Thee? or thirsty, and gave Thee drink? When saw we Thee a stranger, and took Thee in? or naked, and clothed Thee? or when saw we Thee sick, or in prison, and came unto Thee? And the King shall answer and say unto them, Verily, I say unto you, Inasmuch as ye have done it unto one of the least of these my brothers, ye have done it unto me. Then shall He say unto them on the left hand, Depart from me, ye cursed, into everlasting fire, prepared for the devil and his angels: For I was anhungered, and ye gave me no meat: I was thirsty, and ye gave me no drink: I was a stranger, and ye took me not in: naked, and ye clothed me not: sick, and in prison, and ye visited me not. Then shall they also answer Him, saying, Lord, when saw we Thee anhungered, or athirst, or a stranger, or naked, or sick, or in prison, and did not minister unto Thee? Then shall He answer them, saying, Verily, I say unto you, Inasmuch as ye did it not to one of the least of these, ye did it not unto me. And these shall go away into everlasting punishment: but the righteous into life eternal.

The Epistle and Gospel appointed for Dominion-Day shall be used for the First and Second Lessons respectively at any special Dominion-Day Services which may be held for the general public.

These Propers may also be used at any other times of National Thanksgiving or Witness, and are suitable for State Occasions such as at the Opening of Parliament, or when Her Majesty the Queen is in attendance at Divine Service, or when members of the Royal Family, the Governor-General, a Lieutenant-Governor or other representatives of Her Majesty the Queen are in attendance at the Divine Service or other Acts of the Public Worship of the Church.

THANKSGIVING PRAYERS

The two Prayers following are appointed be said in the place of the hymn Gloria in Excelsis *immediately before the Blessing, and before the General Thanksgiving at Morning and Evening Prayer and any special Dominion Day Services.*

ALMIGHTY and most merciful Lord God, Who in Thy wisdom dost divide to the nations their inheritance: We yield Thee hearty thanks for Thy loving kindness in appointing this good land to be our dwelling-place among the children of men; for the wealth and glory of its plains and mountains, its fruitful fields and teeming waters; for the precious things of heaven, the dew, the sunshine, snow and rain in their season, and the precious things of the earth and the fullness thereof; for a land wherein there is bread without scarceness. For all this, and the opportunities thus vouchsafed to us, we bless and magnify Thy holy Name. And, we pray Thee, grant us grace so to sanctify Thee in our heritage that the world may know that Thou art our God for ever and ever; through Jesus Christ our Lord. *Amen.*

O GOD, Who art the Fountain of all wisdom, we bless and praise Thy holy Name for that Thou didst move our rulers and statesmen to bring together into one great Confederation the scattered communities of our vast Commonwealth on this continent, and to unite them into one Dominion from sea to sea; and we most humbly beseech Thee to grant, O heavenly Father, that the faith and traditions of our early pioneers and forefathers may ever be our inheritance, and that same heritage honoured and faithfully preserved in our time, and thereafter handed down unimpaired and undiminished to our children; and grant that, from generation to generation, until the glorious day when our Lord Jesus shall come again to establish His kingdom, we may always remain a people united, loyal, and true to our ancient Throne, our Sovereign, and our Commonwealth, and, above all other earthly things, to Thee; through the same Thy Son Jesus Christ our Lord. *Amen.*

At the Holy Eucharist, the Blessing shall then be given;
or it being Mattins or Evensong, the General Thanksgiving shall then be said.

Here endeth a FORM OF SERVICE FOR DOMINION-DAY.

AN ORDER OF SERVICE FOR
REMEMBRANCE-DAY

This Order of Service is appointed to be used on Remembrance-Day, and on other days of Remembrance; and may be used immediately before the Dismissal at Divine Service on Remembrance Sunday; and at any Military Funeral in the Church, after the Absolution of the Dead, or at the Graveside.

The Minister shall first say this Sentence of Scripture following.

GREATER love hath no one than this, that a man lay down his life for his friends. *Saint John* 15. 13.

Then shall the Minister say,

BELOVED brethren and friends, we are gathered here together this day, in the sight of God, to remember *all* who gave their lives in the loyal defence of our Sovereign and our Nation; and to beseech Almighty God to bless *their memories*, to grant *them* rest, and to give us all the grace necessary to preserve in our time the sacred principles for which *they* fought, and for which so many died. Let us now remember *those* who served, and honour our fallen.

Then shall the Minister read this Lesson following.

THE LESSON. *Ecclesiastes* 3. 1-8.

TO everything there is a season, and a time to every purpose under the heaven: a time to be born, and a time to die; a time to plant, and a time to pluck up that which is planted; a time to kill, and a time to heal; a time to break down, and a time to build up; a time to weep, and a time to laugh; a time to mourn, and a time to dance; a time to cast away stones, and a time to gather stones together; a time to embrace, and a time to refrain from embracing; a time to get, and a time to lose; a time to keep, and a time to cast away; a time to rend, and a time to sew; a time to keep silence, and a time to speak; a time to love, and a time to hate; a time of war, and a time of peace.

The Minister and Congregation shall say together this Psalm following.

PSALM 46. *Deus noster refugium.*

GOD is our Hope and Strength, / a very present help in trouble. Therefore will we not fear, though the earth be moved, / and though the hills be carried into the midst of the sea; Though the waters thereof rage and swell, / and though the mountains shake at the tempest of the same. The rivers of the flood thereof shall make glad the city of God, / the holy place of the tabernacle of the Most High. God is in the midst of her, therefore shall she not be removed; / God shall help her, and that right early. The heathen make much ado, and the kingdoms are moved; / but God hath shewed His voice, and the earth shall melt away. The Lord of hosts is with us; / the God of Jacob is our Refuge. O come hither, and behold the works of the Lord, / what destruction He hath brought upon the earth. He maketh wars to cease in all the world; / He breaketh the bow, and snappeth the spear in sunder, and burneth the chariots in the fire. Be still then, and know that I am God; / I will be exalted among the heathen, and I will be exalted in the earth. The Lord of hosts is with us; / the God of Jacob is our Refuge.

THE Lord gave, and the Lord hath taken away: /
Blessed be the Name of the Lord.

Then shall the Minister and Congregation stand at attention for the Two Minute's Silence.

The Last Post *may be sounded immediately before the Silence.*

THE TWO MINUTES' SILENCE.

The Two Minutes' Silence ended, Reveille *may be sounded.*

Then shall the Minister say this Prayer following.

O GOD, our heavenly Father, Who didst give Thine only-begotten Son Jesus Christ to die for us, and Who hast taught us in Thy holy Word that greater love no man hath than this, but that he lay down his life for his friends: Regard, we beseech Thee, the prayers and supplications of Thy Church bowed before Thee; forgive us our sins and trespasses; and in Thy mercy behold us who come before Thy Divine Majesty in solemn remembrance of those who gave their lives in the service of our Sovereign, and the defence of our Country and our Commonwealth; and vouchsafe, O Father, to hear our prayers: Grant that their sacrifice will never have been made in vain; grant that they who gave their lives for our liberty and security will never be forgotten by us, nor by the generations yet to come; grant that they who served, and who gave their lives, in the time of War, will be rewarded by Thee in the time of Peace; and grant that, in the Day of Judgement, all may receive of Thee mercy and a just reward who, knowingly or unknowingly, participated in the Sacrifice of Thy Son by giving of their own lives, so that others might thereby live; and this we pray, dear heavenly Father, through Him Who gave His life for us, and rose again, even the same Thy Son Jesus Christ our Lord. *Amen.*

Minister.

THEY will not grow old as we that are left grow old; age will not weary them, nor the years condemn. At the going down of the sun, and in the morning, we will remember them.

People. We will remember them.

Then shall be sung these two verses following of the Royal Anthem of Canada.

GOD save our gracious Queen,
  Long live our noble Queen,
God save the Queen!
  Send her victorious,
Happy and glorious,
  Long to reign over us;
God save the Queen!

Our loved Dominion bless
  With peace and happiness
From shore to shore;
  May our Dominion be
United, loyal, and free:
  True to herself and to Thee
Forever more. Amen.

The Minister.

✠ MAY their souls, and the souls of all the faithful departed, rest in peace.
Answer. And awake to a joyful resurrection.
Amen.

Here endeth an ORDER OF SERVICE FOR REMEMBRANCE-DAY.

A FORM OF THANKSGIVING FOR THE
BLESSINGS OF HARVEST

At Divine Service, the usual order shall be observed except for the following variations.

The Minister shall begin the Office saying these Sentences following.

THE earth is the Lord's, and the fullness thereof. *Psalm* 24. 1.

Rejoice in the Lord, O ye righteous; for it becometh well the just to be thankful. *Psalm* 33. 1.

Praise the Lord, O my soul, and forget not all His benefits. *Psalm* 103. 2.

O give thanks unto the Lord, for He is gracious; because His mercy endureth for ever. *Psalm* 118. 1.

Honour the Lord with thy substance, and with the first-fruits of all thine increase; so shall thy barns be filled with plenty, and thy presses shall burst out with new wine. *Proverbs* 3. 9-10.

One or more of the following Proper Psalms shall be used.

PROPER PSALMS.
Morning Prayer: *Psalms* 65 and 67, or 136.
Evening Prayer: *Psalm* 145, or 147, or 148.

The following Proper Lessons shall be read.

AT A MORNING SERVICE.
First Lesson: *Deuteronomy* 8. 1-20, *or Genesis* 1. 1-31.
Second Lesson: *Saint Luke* 12. 15-34, *or Revelation* 14. 14-19.

*(NOTE: Deuteronomy 8.1-20. may be read at the Holy Eucharist
before the Commandments. Are rehearsed.)*

AT AN EVENING SERVICE.
First Lesson: *Deuteronomy* 16. 9-17, *or Deuteronomy* 28. 1-14.
Second Lesson: II *Corinthians* 9, *or Saint Matthew* 13. 18-30.

THE COLLECTS.
After the Collect of the day, the following Collects shall be said or sung.

O ALMIGHTY God and heavenly Father, we glorify Thee that we are once more permitted to enjoy the fulfilment of Thy gracious promise, that, while the earth remaineth, seed-time and harvest shall not fail. Blessed be Thou, Who hast given us the fruits of the earth in their season. Teach us to remember that it is not by bread alone that man doth live; but grant that we may feed on Him Who is the true Bread which cometh down from heaven even Jesus Christ, our Lord and Saviour; to Whom with Thee, O Father, and Thee, O Holy Ghost, be all honour and glory, for ever and ever. *Amen.*

O MERCIFUL God, at Whose bidding the earth withholdeth her increase, or rendereth her fruits in their season: Give us grace that we may learn, both from Thy mercies and Thy judgements, our entire dependence upon Thee for the supply of our daily bread; and grant that we, remembering that Thy blessings are for our trial as well as for our comfort, may with thankful hearts give unto Thee of

Thine own, ministering gladly to the maintenance of Thy Church, and the relief of the poor and the afflicted, the widow and the orphan, to the glory of Thy holy Name; through Jesus Christ our Lord. *Amen.*

O LORD, we pray Thee, sow the seed of Thy Word in our hearts, and send down upon us the showers of Thy grace, that we may bring forth the fruit of the Spirit; and, at the great day of harvest, may be gathered by the holy angels into the heavenly garner; through Jesus Christ our Lord. *Amen.*

O ALMIGHTY God, Whose dearly beloved Son, after His resurrection, sent His Apostles into all the world; and, on the day of Pentecost, did endue them with special gifts of the Holy Ghost, that they might gather in the spiritual harvest: We beseech Thee to look down from heaven upon the fields, now white unto the harvest, and to send forth labourers to gather fruit unto eternal life. And grant us grace so to help them with our prayers and our offerings, that when the harvest of the earth is ripe, and the time for reaping is come, we, together with them, may rejoice before Thee, according to the joy in harvest; through Jesus Christ our Lord. *Amen.*

At the Holy Eucharist, the following Introit, Collect,
Lesson, Gradual and Gospel shall be used.

THE INTROIT. *Psalm* 34. 1-10.

I WILL alway give thanks unto the Lord / His praise shall ever be in my mouth. My soul shall make her boast in the Lord; / the humble shall hear thereof, and be glad. O praise the Lord with me, / and let us magnify His Name together. I sought the Lord, and He heard me; / yea, He delivered me out of all my fear. They had an eye unto Him, and were lightened, / and their faces were not ashamed. Lo, the poor crieth, and the Lord heareth him; / yea, and saveth him out of all his troubles. The angel of the Lord tarrieth round about them that fear Him, / and delivereth them. O taste, and see, how gracious the Lord is! / blessed is the man that trusteth in Him. O fear the Lord, ye that are His saints; / for they that fear Him lack nothing. The lions do lack, and suffer hunger; / but they who seek the Lord shall want no manner of thing that is good.

GLORY be to the Father, and to the Son, / and to the Holy Ghost;
As it was in the beginning, is now, and ever shall be, / world without end. Amen.

And before the Commandments are read, this Lesson following shall first be read.

THE GREAT LESSON. *Deuteronomy* 8. 1-20.

ALL the commandments which I command thee this day shall ye observe to do, that ye may live, and multiply, and go in and possess the land which the Lord sware unto your fathers. And thou shalt remember all the way which the Lord thy God led thee these forty years in the wilderness, to humble thee, and to prove thee, to know what was in thine heart, whether thou wouldest keep His commandments, or no. And He humbled thee, and suffered thee to hunger, and fed thee with manna, which thou knewest not, neither did thy fathers know; that He might make thee know that man doth not live by bread only, but by every word that proceedeth out of the mouth of the Lord doth man live. Thy raiment waxed not old upon thee, neither did thy foot swell, these forty years. Thou shalt also consider in thine heart, that, as a man chasteneth his son, so the Lord thy God chasteneth thee. Therefore thou shalt keep the commandments of the Lord thy God, to walk in His ways, and to fear Him. For the Lord thy God bringeth thee into a good land, a land of brooks of water, of fountains and depths that spring out of valleys and hills; a land of wheat, and barley, and vines, and fig trees, and pomegranates; a land of oil olive, and honey; a land wherein thou shalt eat bread without scarceness, thou shalt not lack any thing in it; a land whose stones are iron, and out of whose hills thou mayest dig brass. When thou hast eaten and art full, then thou shalt bless the Lord thy God for the good land which He hath given thee. Beware that thou forget not the Lord thy God, in not keeping His commandments, and His judgments, and His statutes, which I command thee this day: lest when thou hast eaten and art full, and hast built goodly houses, and dwelt therein; and when thy herds and thy flocks multiply, and thy silver and thy gold is multiplied, and all that thou hast is multiplied; then thine heart be lifted up, and thou forget the Lord thy God, which brought thee forth out of the land of Egypt, from the house of bondage; Who led thee through that great and terrible wilderness, wherein were fiery serpents, and scorpions, and drought, where there was no water; Who brought thee forth water out of the rock of flint; Who fed thee in the wilderness with manna, which thy fathers knew not, that He might humble thee, and that He might prove thee, to do thee good at thy latter end; and thou say in thine heart, My power and the might of mine hand hath gotten me this wealth. But thou shalt remember the Lord thy God: for it is He that giveth thee power to get wealth, that He may establish His covenant which He sware unto thy fathers, as it is this day. And it shall be, if thou do at all forget the Lord thy God, and walk after other gods, and serve them, and worship them, I testify against you this day that ye shall surely perish. As the nations which the Lord destroyeth before your face, so shall ye perish; because ye would not be obedient unto the voice of the Lord your God.

And after the Commandments are read, the Collect for the Queen's Majesty
and this Collect following shall be said or sung.

THE COLLECT.

O ALMIGHTY and everlasting Lord God, Who crownest the year with Thy goodness, and hast given unto us the fruits of the earth in their season: Give us grateful hearts, that we may unfeignedly thank Thee for all Thy loving-kindness, and worthily magnify Thy holy Name; through Jesus Christ our Lord. *Amen.*

THE LESSON. *Isaiah 55. 1-12.*

HO, every one that thirsteth, come ye to the waters, and he that hath no money; come ye, buy, and eat; yea, come, buy wine and milk without money and without price. Wherefore do ye spend money for that which is not bread? and your labour for that which satisfieth not? hearken diligently unto me, and eat that which is good, and let your soul delight itself in fatness. Incline your ear, and come unto me: hear, and your soul shall live; and I will make an everlasting covenant with you, even the sure mercies of David. For as the rain cometh down, and the snow from heaven, and returneth not thither, but watereth the earth, and maketh it bring forth and bud, that it may give seed to the sower, and bread to the eater: so shall my word be that goeth forth out of my mouth: It shall not return unto me void, but it shall accomplish that which I please, and it shall prosper in the thing whereto I sent it. For ye shall go out with joy, and be led forth with peace: the mountains and the hills shall break forth before you into singing, and all the trees of the field shall clap their hands.

THE GRADUAL. *Psalm 92. 1-4.*

ALLELUIA, Alleluia. It is a good thing to give thanks unto the Lord, / and to sing praises unto Thy Name, O Thou Most High; To tell of Thy loving-kindness early in the morning, / and of Thy truth in the night-season; Upon an instrument of ten strings, and upon the lute, / upon a loud instrument, and upon the harp. For Thou, Lord, hast made me glad through Thy works, / and I will rejoice in giving praise for the operations of Thy hands. Alleluia.

THE GOSPEL. *Saint John* 6. 27-35.

JESUS said, Labour not for the meat which perisheth, but for that meat which endureth unto everlasting life, which the Son of Man shall give unto you: for Him hath God the Father sealed. Then said they unto Him, What shall we do, that we might work the works of God? Jesus answered and said unto them, This is the work of God, that ye believe on Him Whom He hath sent. They said therefore unto Him, What sign shewest Thou then, that we may see, and believe Thee? what dost Thou work? Our fathers did eat manna in the desert; as it is written, He gave them bread from heaven to eat. Then Jesus said unto them, Verily, verily I say unto you, Moses gave you not that bread from heaven; but my Father giveth you the true Bread from heaven. For the Bread of God is He which cometh down from heaven, and giveth life unto the world. Then said they unto Him, Lord, evermore give us this Bread. And Jesus said unto them, I am the Bread of life: he that cometh to me shall never hunger; and he that believeth on me shall never thirst.

PRAYERS AND THANKSGIVINGS

At the Holy Eucharist immediately before the Blessing, and at Divine Service
before the General Thanksgiving, the following Prayers shall be said.

O MOST merciful Father, Who of Thy gracious goodness hast heard the devout prayers of Thy Church, and hast granted us to gather in their season the kindly fruits of the earth, and the harvest of the seas: We give Thee humble and hearty thanks for this Thy bounty; beseeching Thee to continue Thy loving-kindness towards us, that our land may yield her increase; through Jesus Christ our Lord. *Amen.*

ALMIGHTY Father, Who hast watered our fields with the dew of heaven, and poured out upon us the former and the latter rain, according to our need; and hast reserved unto us the appointed weeks of the harvest: We bless and praise Thee that, in love to us Thy children, Thou hast at this season bestowed upon us such an abundant supply for all our necessities. Grant that we may never be destitute of those better gifts which nourish and enrich the soul. Pour down upon us, we beseech Thee, Thy heavenly grace, and endue us with the gifts of Thy Holy Spirit, that we may bring forth abundant fruits to Thy glory; through Jesus Christ our Lord. *Amen.*

This Prayer following may be used when the harvest hath been defective.

ALMIGHTY God and heavenly Father, Who hast in wisdom seen fit to withhold from us at this time Thine accustomed bounty: We most humbly praise Thee for still bestowing upon us far more than we deserve. Make us truly thankful for our many blessings; increase in us more and more a lively faith and love, and a meek and humble submission to Thy blessed will; through Jesus Christ our Lord. *Amen.*

Here endeth a FORM OF THANKSGIVING FOR THE BLESSINGS OF HARVEST.

HOLY BAPTISM
AND CONFIRMATION

The Ministration of
Baptism of Infants

The Parish Priest shall often admonish the people that they bring their children to the Church for Baptism so soon as may be possible after birth; and that, except for urgent cause and necessity, they seek not to have their children baptised in their houses; and also that, so there be no delay in baptising, in the absence of a Priest, it is lawful for a Deacon to baptise.

When there is a Child to be baptised, the parents shall give due notice thereof to the Priest. It is fitting for the Sacrament of Baptism to be administered upon Sundays and other Holy-days at Divine Service, so that the Congregation may witness the receiving of the newly-baptised into the number of Christ's holy Church, and also be reminded of the benefits which they themselves received and the profession which they made at their Baptism. And when Holy Baptism is administered during Divine Service, it shall be either immediately after the Second Lesson at Morning or Evening Prayer, or after the Epistle at the Eucharist. However, this Baptismal Office may also properly be used as a separate Service when, at the discretion of the Priest, it is not possible or convenient to minister Baptism publicly at Divine Service.

There shall be for every male child to be baptised two Godfathers and one Godmother; and for every female child to be baptised one Godfather and two Godmothers. Nevertheless, when three Sponsors cannot be had, one Godfather and one Godmother shall suffice. Parents, if grave necessity so require, may be the Sponsors for their own children. Every Sponsor must be a baptised person and able to make the promises required.

The Priest shall meet the Godparents, with the Child to be baptised, at the Font, which is then to be filled with pure Water in the presence of the people.

A Psalm or hymn may be sung as the Priest proceedeth to the Font.

The Greeting

And standing at the Font, the Priest shall first greet the Godparents,
and all the Congregation there assembled, in the Name of the Lord, saying,
GRACE be unto you, and peace from God our Father, and the Lord Jesus Christ.
Answer. And with thy spirit.

The Declaration of Intention

And then, addressing himself to one of the Godparents, the Priest shall say,
WHAT is your desire?

And the Godparent, answering on behalf of the other Godparents, shall say,
WE desire to confess faith in Jesus Christ on behalf of *this Child*, that *he* might be baptised with Water; and be made thereby *a* very *member* of Christ, *a child* of God, and *an inheritor* of the kingdom of heaven.

The Priest shall then ask concerning each Child to be baptised,
SEEING that we are taught, and do profess, that there is but one Baptism only for the remission of sins; I therefore demand of you, *hath this Child* been already baptised, or no?

And the Godparent shall answer, saying,
No.

However, if the Answer be Yes, the Priest shall surcease from baptising
any Child that hath already been baptised.

315

HOLY BAPTISM

The Preparation of the Child

Then shall the Priest address himself to the Godparents and Congregation present, saying thus,

DEARLY beloved, forasmuch as all men are conceived and born in sin; and that our Saviour Christ saith, None can enter into the kingdom of God, except he be regenerate and born anew of Water and of the Holy Ghost; let us therefore beseech Almighty God our heavenly Father, through His Son Jesus Christ, to prepare *this Child* to receive this holy Sacrament; and that of His bounteous mercy He will grant unto *him* that thing which, by nature, *he* cannot have: that *he* may be baptised with Water and the Holy Ghost, and so be received into Christ's holy Church, and be made *a living member* of the same.

Then shall the Priest anoint each Child *to be baptised,*
anointing him *with the Oil of the Catechumens, and saying,*

WE anoint ✠ this Child, marking *him* with the Sign of Faith, In the Name of the Father, and of the Son, and of the Holy Ghost, and do hereby claim *him* for Jesus Christ the only-begotten Son of God, praying that as *he* is now here outwardly anointed with this Oil of purification and righteousness, so God the Holy Ghost will prepare *him* inwardly with His grace to receive this holy Sacrament of Baptism, and grant unto *him* throughout *his* life wisdom, and strength, and protection from all evil, and everlasting salvation in the life of the world to come; through the same Jesus Christ our Lord. *Amen.*

Then shall the Priest say,
O LORD, hear our prayer.
Answer. And let our cry come unto Thee.

Priest. Let us pray.

Then shall the Priest say these two Prayers following.

ALMIGHTY and everlasting God, Who of Thy great mercy didst save Noah and his family in the ark from perishing by water; and also didst safely lead the children of Israel Thy people through the Red Sea, figuring thereby Thy holy Baptism; and by the Baptism of Thy well-beloved Son Jesus Christ, in the river Jordan, didst sanctify the element of Water to the mystical washing away of sin: We beseech Thee, for Thine infinite mercies, that Thou wilt mercifully look upon *this Child* brought to receive Thy holy Baptism; wash *him* and sanctify *him* with the Holy Ghost, that *he*, being delivered from Thy wrath, may be received into the ark of Christ's Church; and being steadfast in faith, joyful through hope, and rooted in charity, may so pass the waves of this troublesome world, that finally *he* may come to the land of everlasting life, there to reign with Thee world without end. *Amen.*

ALMIGHTY and immortal God, the Aid of all that need, the Helper of all that flee to Thee for succour, the Life of them that believe, and the Resurrection of the dead: We call upon Thee for *this Child*, that *he*, coming to Thy holy Baptism, may receive remission of *his* sins by spiritual regeneration. Receive *him*, O Lord, as Thou hast promised by Thy well-beloved Son, saying, Ask, and ye shall have; Seek, and ye shall find; Knock, and it shall be opened unto you: So give now unto us that ask; let us that seek find; open the gate unto us that knock; that *this Child* may enjoy the everlasting benediction of Thy heavenly washing, and may come to the eternal kingdom which Thou hast promised by Christ our Saviour to all them that believe, and are baptised into His holy Name; through the same Thy blessed Son Jesus Christ our Lord. *Amen.*

The Holy Gospel

Then shall all stand for the reading of the holy Gospel.

And the Minister shall say,
THE Lord be with you.
Answer. And with thy spirit.

Then shall the Minister announce the Gospel, saying,
Hear the words of the Gospel of our Lord Jesus Christ,
written by Saint Mark in the tenth chapter, beginning at the thirteenth verse.

And then shall be said or sung,
GLORY be to Thee, O Lord.

THE GOSPEL. *Saint Mark* 10. 13-16.
THEY brought young children to Christ, that He should touch them; and His disciples rebuked those that brought them. But when Jesus saw it, He was much displeased, and said unto them, Suffer the little children to come unto me, and forbid them not; for of such is the kingdom of God. Verily, I say unto you, Whosoever shall not receive the kingdom of God as a little child, he shall not enter therein. And He took them up in His arms, put His hands upon them, and blessed them.

And then all shall say or sing,
PRAISE be to Thee, O Christ.

Then shall the Minister say,
AND through the Words of the Gospel may our sins be blotted out.

After which the Priest shall say this Exhortation following.
BELOVED in Christ, ye hear in this Gospel the express words of our Saviour Christ, that He commanded the little children to be brought unto Him; how He blamed those that would have kept them from Him; and how He exhorteth all men to follow their innocency. Ye perceive how by His outward gesture and deed He declared His good will toward them; for He embraced them in His arms, He laid His hands upon them, and blessed them. Doubt ye not therefore, but earnestly believe, that He will likewise favourably receive *this present Child*; that He will embrace *him* with the arms of His mercy; that He will give unto *him* the blessing of eternal life, and make *him a partaker* of His everlasting kingdom. Wherefore, we being thus persuaded of the good will of our heavenly Father towards *this Child*, declared by His Son Jesus Christ; and nothing doubting but that He favourably alloweth this charitable work of ours in bringing *this Child* to His holy Baptism; let us faithfully and devoutly give thanks unto Him, and say,

And the Priest and people shall say together,
ALMIGHTY and Everlasting God, heavenly Father, we give Thee humble thanks for that Thou hast vouchsafed to call us to the knowledge of Thy grace, and faith in Thee: Increase this knowledge, and confirm this faith in us evermore. Give Thy Holy Spirit to *this Child* that *he* may be born again, and be made *a member* of Christ, *a child* of God, and *an heir* of everlasting salvation; through our Lord Jesus Christ, Who liveth and reigneth with Thee and the Holy Spirit, now and forever. Amen.

HOLY BAPTISM

The Baptismal Promises

Then shall the Priest speak unto the Godparents on this wise.

DEARLY beloved, ye have brought *this Child* here to be baptised; ye have prayed that our Lord Jesus Christ would vouchsafe to receive *him*, to release *him* from *his* sins, to sanctify *him* with the Holy Ghost, to give *him* the kingdom of heaven, and everlasting life. Ye have heard also that our Lord Jesus Christ hath promised in His Gospel to grant all these things that ye have prayed for: which promises He, for His part, will most surely keep and perform. Wherefore, after this promise made by Christ, *this Child* must also faithfully, for *his* part, promise and vow by you that are *his* Sureties, (until *he* come of age to take it upon *himself*, and publicly profess *his* faith, and be confirmed, following the teaching of the holy Apostles,) that *he* will renounce the devil and all his works, and constantly believe God's holy Word, and obediently keep His commandments. I demand of each of you therefore,

DOST thou, in the name of *this Child*, renounce the devil and all his works, the vain pomp and glory of the world, with all the covetous desires of the same, and the carnal desires of the flesh, so that thou wilt not follow, nor be led by them?

Answer. I renounce them all.

The Priest.

DOST thou believe in God the Father Almighty, Maker of heaven and earth?

And in Jesus Christ His only-begotten Son our Lord? And that He was conceived by the Holy Ghost; born of the Virgin Mary; that He suffered under Pontius Pilate, was crucified, dead, and buried; that He went down into hell, and also did rise again the third day; that He ascended into heaven, and there sitteth at the right hand of God the Father Almighty; and that from thence He shall come again at the end of the world, to judge the quick and the dead?

And dost thou believe in the Holy Ghost; the holy Catholic Church; the Communion of Saints; the Remission of sins; the Resurrection of the flesh; and everlasting Life after death?

Answer. All this I steadfastly believe.

The Priest.

DOST thou desire on behalf of *this Child* to be baptised into this Faith?

Answer. That is my desire.

The Priest.

WILT thou then, on behalf of *this Child*, promise obediently to keep God's holy will and commandments, and to walk in the same all the days of thy life?

Answer. I will endeavour so to do, God being my Helper.

Then shall the Priest extend his right hand over the Child, and say,

O LORD God of hosts, before the might of Whose presence the armies of evil are put to flight, deliver *this Child* from the power of sin, and from every craft and assault of the devil. *Amen.*

GRANT, O merciful Lord, that the old Adam in *this Child* may be so buried in Christ, that the new man may be raised up in *him*. *Amen.*

CAST out of *his* heart, O Lord, every evil imagination, and everything which doth exalt itself against the knowledge of Thee; and bring into captivity every thought to the obedience of Christ. *Amen.*

GRANT, O Lord, that all carnal affections may die in *him*, and that all things belonging to the Spirit may live and grow in *him*. *Amen.*

GRANT, O Lord, that *this Child*, now to be baptised, may through Thee have power and strength to have victory, and to triumph, against the devil, the world, and the flesh. *Amen.*

SEND down, O Lord, upon *this Child* Thy Holy Spirit, that He may make His abode in *him*, and grant that *this Child*, by the effectual working of the power of the Holy Ghost, may be born again, and attain unto everlasting life. *Amen.*

GRANT, that *this Child*, being here dedicated unto Thee by our Office and Ministry, may also be endued with heavenly virtues, and everlastingly rewarded, through Thy mercy, O blessed Lord God, Who dost live, and govern all things, world without end. *Amen.*

THE MINISTRATION OF HOLY BAPTISM

Then shall the Priest proceed to bless the Water, saying,
OUR help standeth in the Name of the Lord.
Answer. Who hath made heaven and earth.
Priest. O Lord, hear our prayer;
Answer. And let our cry come unto Thee.

Priest. Let us pray.

ALMIGHTY and everliving God, our heavenly Father, Whose own most dearly beloved Son our Saviour Jesus Christ, for the forgiveness of our sins, did shed out of His most precious side both Water and Blood, and did give commandment to His disciples, that they should go teach all nations, and baptise them IN THE NAME OF THE FATHER, AND OF THE SON, AND OF THE HOLY GHOST: Regard, we beseech Thee, the supplications of Thy Church, and sanctify this Water to the mystical washing away of sin; and grant that *this Child* now to be baptised therein may receive the fullness of Thy grace, and ever remain in the number of Thy faithful and elect children, through Jesus Christ our Lord. *Amen.*

Then shall the Priest take the Child into his hands, and
shall say to the Godfathers and Godmothers,
Name this Child.

And then naming the Child after them (if they shall certify him that the Child may well endure it),
the Priest shall dip him into the Water discreetly and warily; or else, if it be more convenient
for the well-being of the Child, he shall pour the Water upon the Child, saying,
N. I BAPTISE thee In the Name of the Father, and
of the Son, and of the Holy Ghost.

And all shall answer,
AMEN.

HOLY BAPTISM

Then shall the Priest make a Cross upon the Child's forehead, saying,

WE receive this Child into the Congregation of Christ's flock; and do sign *him* with the Sign of the Cross, in token that hereafter *he* shall not be ashamed to confess the faith of Christ crucified, and manfully to fight under His banner, against sin, the world, and the devil; and to continue Christ's faithful soldier and servant unto *his* life's end. *Amen.*

THE THANKSGIVING AFTER HOLY BAPTISM

Then shall the Priest say,

SEEING now, dearly beloved brethren, that *this Child is* regenerate, and grafted into the body of Christ's Church, let us give thanks unto Almighty God for these benefits, and with one accord make our prayers unto Him, that *he* may lead the rest of *his* life according to this beginning.

Then shall be said the Lord's Prayer as followeth, all devoutly kneeling.

OUR Father, which art in heaven, hallowed be Thy Name. Thy kingdom come. Thy will be done, in earth as it is in heaven. Give us this day our daily bread. And forgive us our trespasses, As we forgive them that trespass against us. And lead us not into temptation, But deliver us from evil. For Thine is the kingdom, the power, and the glory, For ever and ever. Amen.

Then shall the Priest say,

WE yield Thee hearty thanks, most merciful Father, that it hath pleased Thee to bring *this* Thy *Child* to Thy holy Baptism, and to regenerate *him* with Water and the Holy Ghost, to receive *him* for Thine own *Child* by adoption, and to incorporate *him* into Thy holy Church as *a* living *member* of the Body of Thy beloved Son. And humbly we beseech Thee to grant, that *he,* being dead unto sin, and living unto righteousness, and being through Baptism buried with Christ in His death, may crucify the old man, and utterly abolish the whole body of sin; and that, as *he is* made *partaker* of the death of Thy Son, *he* may also be *partaker* of His resurrection; so that finally, with all the elect and faithful remnant of Thy holy Church, *he* may be *an inheritor* of Thine everlasting kingdom; through Jesus Christ our Lord. *Amen.*

THE EXHORTATION TO THE GODPARENTS

Then shall the Priest say to the Godparents this Exhortation following.

FORASMUCH as *this Child* hath promised by you, *his* Sureties, to renounce the devil and all his works, to believe in God, and to serve Him: ye must remember, that it is your part and duty to see that *this Child* be taught, so soon as *he* shall be able to learn, what a solemn vow, promise, and profession, *he hath* here made by you, and be instructed in all other things which a Christian ought to know and believe to his soul's health. And that *he* may know these things the better, ye shall use all diligence to see that *he* be virtuously brought up in the faith and fear of God, so that *he* may lead a godly, righteous, and sober life in Christ, and finally be made *partaker* of His heavenly kingdom. Take care that *he* be taught the Creeds, the Commandments, and the Lord's Prayer, and that *he* be further instructed in the Church's Catechism; and then that *he* be brought to the Bishop to be confirmed by him, so that *he* may be strengthened by the Holy Ghost, and may come to the Lord's Table to receive the Holy Communion of the Body and Blood of Christ our Saviour; and so go forth into the world to serve God faithfully in the fellowship of His holy Church.

WILT thou be faithful in the fulfilment of these duties?

   Answer. I will, the Lord being my helper.

Then shall the Priest say,

A<small>LMIGHTY</small> God, our heavenly Father, who hath given *you* this will to do all these things; Grant also unto *you* wisdom, strength, and power duly to perform the same; through Jesus Christ our Lord. *Amen.*

T<small>HE</small> B<small>LESSING OF THE</small> C<small>HILD</small>

Then shall the Priest say,

D<small>EARLY</small> beloved, let us humbly beseech Almighty God to bless *this Child, his parents, his family, and his home.*

Let us pray.

Then shall the Priest say these Prayers following.

A<small>LMIGHTY</small> God, Whose own most dearly beloved Son did share in Nazareth the life of an earthly home: Bless, we beseech Thee, the home of *this Child,* and grant wisdom, love, and understanding to all who shall have the care of *him,* that *he* may grow up in steadfast love of Thee, and reverence of Thy holy Name; through the same Thy Son Jesus Christ our Lord. *Amen.*

G<small>RANT</small>, O Lord, that *this Child* may, by Thy grace and merciful loving-kindness preparing the way before *him* and working in *him,* grow up in health and wholeness of body, mind, and spirit, and ever live to serve Thee faithfully all the days of *his* life; through Jesus Christ our Lord. *Amen.*

Then shall the Priest pronounce this Blessing.

U<small>NTO</small> God's gracious mercy and protection we commit *thee.* May the Lord bless *thee,* and keep *thee.* May the Lord make His face to shine upon *thee,* and be gracious unto *thee.* May the Lord lift up His countenance upon *thee,* and give *thee* peace, both now and evermore. And so may the blessing of God Almighty, ✠ the Father, the Son, and the Holy Ghost, be upon *thee* and remain with *thee* always. *Amen.*

And if Baptism be ministered as a separate Service,
the Priest shall then conclude it with the Grace.

II *Corinthians* xiii. 14.

T<small>HE</small> grace of our Lord Jesus Christ, ✠ and the love of God, and the fellowship of the Holy Ghost, be with us all evermore. *Amen.*

Here endeth the M<small>INISTRATION OF</small> B<small>APTISM OF</small> I<small>NFANTS.</small>

The Ministration of
Private Baptism

When any Child or Person of Riper Years who hath not received Baptism is critically ill, the Minister of the Parish (or, in his absence, any other lawful Minister) should be called upon to administer the Sacrament without delay; and if no lawful Minister may be had, and the Child is in danger of death, ANY PERSON PRESENT should pour Water upon him and, naming him, say:

N. I BAPTISE thee In the Name of the Father,
and of the Son, and of the Holy Ghost. Amen.

Then shall be said the Lord's Prayer.

Such Baptism shall be forthwith reported to the Parish authorities.

When the Minister himself shall officiate, he shall first say the Lord's Prayer and such other appropriate prayers from the Baptismal Office as the circumstances will allow; and then, the Child or Person who is to be baptised being named by someone that is present, the Minister shall pour Water upon him, saying:

N. I BAPTISE thee In the Name of the Father,
and of the Son, and of the Holy Ghost. Amen.

Then shall he say:

WE yield Thee hearty thanks, most merciful Father, that it hath pleased Thee to regenerate this Child with Thy Holy Spirit, to receive *him* for Thine own Child by adoption, and to make *him* a member of Thy holy Church. Grant, O Lord, that being baptised into the death of Christ, *he* may also be made partaker of His resurrection, so that serving thee here in newness of life, *he* may finally, with all Thy holy Church, inherit Thine everlasting kingdom; through Jesus Christ our Lord. *Amen.*

The Service shall conclude with such prayers from the Office of the Ministry to the Sick as the Minister shall consider suitable, and the Grace.

In the case of an adult Person, the Minister shall first ask the questions provided in the part of the Office for the Ministration of Holy Baptism to those who are of Riper Years.

Here endeth the MINISTRATION OF PRIVATE BAPTISM.

THE PUBLIC RECEIVING
OF SUCH AS HAVE BEEN PRIVATELY BAPTISED

Baptism administered privately in an emergency or for some other reason is lawful and sufficient; and anyone who hath thus received it ought not to be christened again; but should be brought to the Church at such time as the Minister shall appoint, to the intent that the Congregation may be certified that he *hath been truly baptised; and also that* he *may be received publicly into the flock of true Christian people.*

If the Priest did himself administer the Baptism, he shall say to the Congregation:

I CERTIFY you, that according to the due and prescribed Order of the Church, *at such a time, and at such a place*, before divers witnesses, I baptised *this Child.*

*But if some other person did administer the Baptism,
the Priest shall examine whether the same was sufficient, saving to the Sponsors:*

BY whom was *this Child* baptised?
Who was present when *he* was baptised?
Was *he* baptised with Water?
With what words was *he* baptised?

*And if the Priest shall find by the answers of the Sponsors that all things
were done as they ought to be, then shall he say:*

I CERTIFY you that in this particular case all is well done. *This Child* was duly and properly baptised according to the due and prescribed Order of the Church.

Then shall the Minister read the Gospel appointed to be used in the Order for the Ministration of Holy Baptism. He shall then require from the Sponsors the accustomed vows and promises, together with the recitation of the Apostles' Creed, omitting the request for Baptism, first saying:

DEARLY beloved in the Lord, you have brought *this Child* here to be publicly received into the Congregation of Christ's flock. I demand therefore: Dost thou, *etc.*

Then shall he take the Child in his arms, or the Person by his right hand, and say:

WE receive this *Child* into the Congregation of Christ's flock, [*Here the Priest shall make a Cross* ✠ *upon the* Child's *forehead*] and do sign *him* with the Sign of the Cross in token that hereafter *he* shall not be ashamed to confess the faith of Christ crucified, and manfully to fight under His banner against sin, the world, and the devil, and to continue Christ's faithful soldier and servant unto *his* life's end. *Amen.*

Then shall follow the rest of the Order for the Ministration of Holy Baptism.

But if such answers are made at the examination that it cannot appear certain that the Child *was truly baptised with* Water, IN THE NAME OF THE FATHER, AND OF THE SON, AND OF THE HOLY GHOST, *(which are the essential parts of Baptism,) then let the Priest baptise* him *according to the appointed Order, save that instead of the usual words of administration he shall say:*

IF thou art not already baptised, *N.*, I now baptise thee
In the Name of the Father, and of the Son, and of the Holy Ghost. Amen.

*Here endeth the PUBLIC RECEIVING OF SUCH
AS HAVE BEEN PRIVATELY BAPTISED.*

THE PUBLIC RECEIVING OF
A CATECHUMEN

The Candidate *for reception as a Catechumen shall stand at the Church-door. And the Priest, after a time of private prayer, shall come down from the Sanctuary of the Lord to meet the* Candidate *at the Door.*

The Bishop shall first address the Candidate
for the Catechumenate, saying,
DEAR friend, what is your desire?

And the Candidate *shall answer,*
I DESIRE to be received into the order of Catechumens, so that I may receive instruction in the Gospel and Faith of Jesus Christ, and be baptised into His holy Church.

The Priest shall then cause the Candidate *to kneel,*
and shall say this Prayer over him *as followeth.*

ALMIGHTY God, Who willeth not that any should perish, but that all should come to the knowledge of the truth, even of His Son Jesus Christ, and believe on Him and be saved: Grant unto this *Person* whom Thou hast called unto Thee, that *he* shall come to know and confess Jesus Christ Thy Son, Who is the Way, the Truth, and the Life; and that *he* may believe Thy Word and receive instruction in the same, and seek for Thy grace in Baptism; and preserve *him*, O Lord, we humbly beseech Thee that *he* will be brought safely by Thee to that day; through the same Thy Son Jesus Christ our Lord. *Amen.*

Then shall all present kneel down, and the Priest shall say,
O HOLY Lord, Father Almighty, eternal God, regard in Thy compassion this Thy *servant*, who *hath* hitherto wandered and strayed in error and uncertainty, in the midst of the darkness of this evil world. Expel from *him*, we beseech Thee, the spirit of evil; make plain unto *him* the way of truth; enlighten Thou *his* eyes, unstop *his* ears, and open *his* heart, that *he* may know Thee, the One and only true God: the Father, the Son begotten of the Father, and the Holy Ghost proceeding from the Father through the Son, One God in three Persons, the Holy Trinity in Unity and the Holy Unity in Trinity; and grant that *he* may be counted worthy to receive the fruit of this confession, both here and in the world to come; through the same Jesus Christ Thy Son our Lord. *Amen.*

Then shall the Priest stand up, and extending his right hand again
over the Candidate *(still remaining kneeling upon* his *knees), and shall say,*
THE LORD Jesus Christ, our incarnate living God, Who with His finger did cast out devils, and came into the world that He might destroy the works of the devil: Deliver you from Satan, and from all his works, and from all his evil power, and from all his pomps, vanities, and lusts; and cause him to depart from you both now and forever. The Lord deliver you from every evil and unclean spirit; from the spirit of deceit and guile, the spirit of idolatry and covetousness, the spirit of falsehood and all uncleanness: that you may be made meet for the Holy Ghost, and that He may take up His abode in you, and dwell in you forever. *Amen.*

*Then shall the Priest anoint the Candidate upon his forehead
with the Oil of the Catechumens, marking him with the Sign of the Cross, and saying,*

WE anoint you, and receive you as a Catechumen, marking you with the Sign of the Cross with this blessed Oil, ✠ In the Name of the Father, and of the Son, and of the Holy Ghost; and do hereby claim you for Jesus Christ, Crucified, Risen, Ascended, and Glorified; and we beseech Almighty God to grant unto you that as you art here outwardly anointed with this Oil of purification and godliness, so God the Holy Ghost will prepare you inwardly with His grace, to be made ready to receive the holy Sacrament of Baptism, and to make a good confession before heaven and the world of your faith in Christ Jesus, unto righteousness and eternal salvation; through the same Jesus Christ our Lord. *Amen.*

*Then extending his hand over the Catechumen,
the Priest shall say,*
Let us pray.

ALMIGHTY and everlasting God, Father of our Lord Jesus Christ, mercifully regard this Thy *servant* whom Thou hast vouchsafed to call to the rudiments of the Faith, and upon whom we have set Thy Sign in token of Thy good will and gracious purpose towards *him*. Deliver *him*, we beseech Thee, from all unholy and vain desires; remove from *him* all darkness of mind and blindness of heart; instruct *him* in Thy holy mysteries; enable *him* to apprehend and embrace Thy truth; and speedily make *him* meet for the great grace of Thy holy Baptism, and receive *him* unto the same; through the good will and grace of Thine Only-begotten Son, Jesus Christ our Lord, with Whom and Thine all-holy, good, and quickening Spirit, be Thou blessed forever and ever. *Amen.*

Then shall the Priest bless the Catechumen, saying,
MAY the blessing of God Almighty, the ✠ Father, the Son, and the Holy Ghost, be with you, and rest upon you. *Amen.*

A FORM OF BLESSING OF
OIL OF THE CATECHUMENS

When Oil for the anointing of Catechumens is to be blessed prior to the Ministration of Holy Baptism (there being none already blessed by the Bishop and available to be used), the Priest shall bless pure olive Oil (or, if there be no olive Oil at hand to be used, then some other suitable Oil derived solely from plants) according to the Form hereafter following.

The Priest shall extend his hands over the Oil to be blessed, and shall say this Prayer.
O LORD our God, the Protector of all them that believe, and put their trust in Thee: Bless and sanctify, we humbly beseech Thee, this creature of Oil; and grant that all they who shall be anointed therewith may receive from Thee the spirit of godliness, and wisdom, and strength, and the might to eschew evil and to withstand the crafts and assaults of the devil; and give unto them, O Father, a deep and abiding faith in Thee, and a saving comprehension of the truth of Thy Gospel; that as they are prepared for Holy Baptism, and for the manifold graces of Christ, they may be endued by Thee with power to keep their promises and fulfill their vows; through Jesus Christ our Lord. *Amen.*

Here endeth the PUBLICK RECEIVING OF A CATECHUMEN.

THE MINISTRATION OF
BAPTISM TO SUCH
AS ARE OF RIPER YEARS
AND ABLE TO ANSWER FOR THEMSELVES

When any such Persons who are Catechumens, that is to say, who are Believers of riper years and therefore able to answer for themselves, are to be baptised, timely notice shall be given to the Bishop, or the Minister whom he shall appoint for that purpose, a week before at the least, by their Sponsors, or some other discreet persons; that so due care may be taken for their Examination, whether they be sufficiently instructed in the Principles of the Christian Religion; and that they prepare themselves with Prayers and Fasting for the receiving of this holy Sacrament.

It is fitting that adult Catechumens should be baptised at the Liturgy on Easter-Eve, or at Divine Service on Easter-Day or Whitsunday, or some Sunday or Holy-day, following the example of the Primitive Church. And if they shall be found fit, then the Sponsors shall be ready to present them at the Font during Divine Service. This Baptismal Office may also at certain times be used as a separate Service when, at the discretion of the Priest, it is not possible or convenient to minister Holy Baptism at Divine Service.

In the absence of a Priest, it is lawful for a Deacon to be the Minister of Holy Baptism.

The Priest and people may stand throughout the Baptismal Service, if there be no convenient place for them to kneel.

A Psalm or hymn may be said or sung as the Priest proceedeth to the Font.

The Priest shall meet the Persons to be baptised, with their Sponsors, at the Font, which is then to be filled with pure Water in the presence of the people.

THE GREETING

And standing at the Font, the Priest shall first greet the Persons to be baptised with their Sponsors,
and all the Congregation there assembled, in the Name of the Lord, saying,
GRACE be unto you, and peace from God our Father, and the Lord Jesus Christ.
Answer. And with thy spirit.

THE DECLARATION OF INTENTION

And then, addressing himself to each Person to be baptised, the Priest shall say,
WHAT is thy desire?

And each one shall answer the Priest, saying,
I DESIRE to confess faith in Jesus Christ, and be baptised with Water; and be made thereby a very member of Christ, the child of God, and an inheritor of the kingdom of heaven.

The Priest shall then ask of each Person to be baptised,
SEEING that we are taught, and do profess, that there is but one Baptism only for the remission of sins, I therefore demand of thee, hast thou been already baptised, or no?

And that Person shall answer, saying,
No.

However, if the Answer be Yes, the Priest shall surcease from baptising that Person.

326

HOLY BAPTISM

THE PREPARATION OF THE CANDIDATE

Then shall the Priest address himself to the Sponsors *and Congregation present, saying thus,*

DEARLY beloved, forasmuch as all men are conceived and born in sin; and that our Saviour Christ saith, None can enter into the kingdom of God, except he be regenerate and born anew of Water and of the Holy Ghost; let us therefore beseech Almighty God our heavenly Father, through His Son Jesus Christ, to prepare *these Persons* to receive this holy Sacrament; and that of His bounteous mercy He will grant unto *them* that thing which, by nature, *they* cannot have: that *they* may be baptised with Water and the Holy Ghost, and so be received into Christ's holy Church, and be made *living members* of the same.

Then shall the Priest anoint each Person *to be baptised,*
anointing him *with the Oil of the Catechumens, and saying,*

WE anoint this Person, marking *him* with the Sign of Faith, ✠ In the Name of the Father, and of the Son, and of the Holy Ghost, and do hereby claim *him* for Jesus Christ, praying that as *he* is here outwardly anointed with this Oil of purification and godliness, so God the Holy Ghost will prepare *him* inwardly with His grace to receive this holy Sacrament of Baptism, and grant unto *him* all *his* life wisdom, strength, protection from all evil, and everlasting salvation; through the same Jesus Christ our Lord. *Amen.*

Then shall the Priest say,
O LORD, hear our prayer.
Answer. And let our cry come unto Thee.

Priest. Let us pray.

Then shall the Priest say these two Prayers following.

ALMIGHTY and everlasting God, Who of Thy great mercy didst save Noah and his family in the ark from perishing by water; and also didst safely lead the children of Israel Thy people through the Red Sea, figuring thereby Thy holy Baptism; and by the Baptism of Thy well-beloved Son Jesus Christ, in the river Jordan, didst sanctify the element of Water to the mystical washing away of sin: We beseech Thee, for Thine infinite mercies, that Thou wilt mercifully look upon *these* Thy *servants*, wash *them* and sanctify *them* with the Holy Ghost, that *they,* being delivered from Thy wrath, may be received into the ark of Christ's Church; and being steadfast in faith, joyful through hope, and rooted in charity, may so pass the waves of this troublesome world, that finally *they* may come to the land of everlasting life, there to reign with Thee world without end; through Jesus Christ our Lord. *Amen.*

ALMIGHTY and immortal God, the Aid of all that need, the Helper of all that flee to Thee for succour, the Life of them that believe, and the Resurrection of the dead: We call upon Thee for *these Persons,* that *they,* coming to Thy holy Baptism, may receive remission of *their* sins by spiritual regeneration. Receive *them,* O Lord, as Thou hast promised by Thy well-beloved Son, saying, Ask, and ye shall have; Seek, and ye shall find; Knock, and it shall be opened unto you: So give now unto us that ask; let us that seek find; open the gate unto us that knock; that *these Persons* may enjoy the everlasting benediction of Thy heavenly washing, and may come to the eternal kingdom which Thou hast promised by Christ our Saviour to all them that believe, and are baptised into His holy Name; through the same Thy blessed Son Jesus Christ our Lord. *Amen.*

The Holy Gospel

Then shall all stand for the reading of the holy Gospel.

And the Minister shall say,
THE Lord be with you.
Answer. And with thy spirit.

Then shall the Minister announce the Gospel, saying,
✠ Hear the words of the Gospel of our Lord Jesus Christ,
written by Saint John in the third chapter, beginning at the first verse.

And then shall be said or sung,
GLORY be to Thee, O Lord.

THERE was a man of the Pharisees, named Nicodemus, a ruler of the Jews: the same came to Jesus by night, and said unto Him, Rabbi, we know that Thou art come from God; for no man can do these signs that Thou doest, except God be with Him. Jesus answered and said unto him, Verily, verily I say unto thee, Except a man be born again, he cannot see the kingdom of God. Nicodemus saith unto Him, How can a man be born when he is old? can he enter the second time into his mother's womb, and be born? Jesus answered, Verily, verily I say unto thee, Except a man be born of water and of the Spirit, he cannot enter into the kingdom of God. That which is born of the flesh is flesh; and that which is born of the Spirit is spirit. Marvel not that I said unto thee, Ye must be born again. The wind bloweth where it listeth, and thou hearest the sound thereof, but canst not tell whence it cometh, and wither it goeth; so is every one that is born of the Spirit.

And then all shall say or sing,
PRAISE be to Thee, O Christ.

And the Minister shall say,
AND through the Words of the Gospel may our sins be blotted out.

After which he shall say this Exhortation following.
BELOVED in the Lord, ye hear in the Gospel the express words of our Saviour Christ, that except a man be born again of water and of the Spirit, he cannot enter into the kingdom of God. Hearing these words spoken by the Lord Jesus Himself, ye may perceive thereby the great necessity of this Sacrament. Likewise, after our Lord's resurrection from the dead, and immediately before His ascension into heaven (as we read in the last chapter of Saint Mark's Gospel), He gave command to His disciples, saying unto them, Go ye into all the world, and preach the Gospel to every creature. He that believeth and is baptised shall be saved; but he that believeth not shall be damned. These words doth testify unto us the necessity of faith and of baptism as the appointed means whereby we may be saved from damnation, and be made inheritors of the kingdom of God.

For this cause also Saint Peter the Apostle, upon his first preaching of the Gospel, when many were pricked at the heart, and said to him, and to the rest of the Apostles, Men and brethren, what shall we do? Peter replied, and said unto them, Repent, and be baptised every one of you for the remission of sins, and ye shall receive the gift of the Holy Ghost. For the promise is to you, and your children, and to all that are afar off, even as many as the Lord our God shall call. And with many other words did Saint Peter exhort them, saying, Save yourselves from this untoward generation. For (as the same blessed Apostle testifieth in another place) even Baptism doth also now save us, (not the putting away of the filth of the flesh, but the answer of a good conscience towards God,) by the resurrection of Jesus Christ.

Doubt ye not therefore, but earnestly believe, that God will favourably receive *these Persons* here present, truly repenting, and coming unto Him by faith; that He will grant *them* the remission of *their* sins, and bestow upon *them* the Holy Ghost; that He will give *them* the blessing of eternal life, and make *them partakers* of His everlasting kingdom. Wherefore, we being thus persuaded of the good will of our heavenly Father towards *these Persons*, declared by His Son Jesus Christ; let us faithfully and devoutly give thanks unto Him, and say,

Then shall the Priest and people say together,

ALMIGHTY and Everlasting God, heavenly Father, we give Thee humble thanks for that Thou hast vouchsafed to call us to the knowledge of Thy grace, and faith in Thee: Increase this knowledge, and confirm this faith in us evermore. Give Thy Holy Spirit to *these Persons* that *they* may be born again, and be made living *members* of Christ, and *heirs* of everlasting salvation; through our Lord Jesus Christ, Who liveth and reigneth with Thee and the Holy Spirit, now and forever. Amen.

THE BAPTISMAL PROMISES

Then the Priest shall speak to the Persons *to be baptised on this wise.*

WELL-BELOVED, who *are* come hither desiring to receive holy Baptism, *ye have* heard how the Congregation hath prayed, that our Lord Jesus Christ would vouchsafe to receive *you* and bless *you*, to release *you* of *your* sins, to give *you* the kingdom of heaven, and everlasting life. *Ye have* heard also, that our Lord Jesus Christ hath promised in His holy Word to grant all those things that we have prayed for; which promises He, for His part, will most surely keep and perform. Wherefore, after this promise made by our Lord Jesus Christ Himself, *ye* must also faithfully, for *your* part, promise and vow in the presence of these *your* Witnesses, and this whole Congregation, that *you will* renounce the devil and all his works, and constantly believe God's holy Word, and obediently keep His commandments. And now, that this present Congregation here assembled may understand *your minds* and *wills* as *you come* to receive the grace of Christ's holy Baptism, *ye shall each one of you* answer plainly and sincerely to these things which we, in the Name of God, and of His Church, shall demand of *you* touching the profession of *your* Christian faith.

Then shall the Priest demand of each of the Persons *to be*
Baptised, either individually or severally, these Questions following:

DOST thou renounce the devil and all his works, the vain pomp and glory of the world, with all the covetous desires of the same, and the carnal desires of the flesh, so that thou wilt not follow, nor be led by them?

Answer. I renounce them all.

The Priest.

DOST thou believe in God the Father Almighty, Maker of heaven and earth?

And in Jesus Christ His only-begotten Son our Lord? And that He was conceived by the Holy Ghost; born of the Virgin Mary; that He suffered under Pontius Pilate, was crucified, dead, and buried; that He went down into hell, and also did rise again the third day; that He ascended into heaven, and there sitteth at the right hand of God the Father Almighty; and that from thence He shall come again at the end of the world, to judge the quick and the dead?

And dost thou believe in the Holy Ghost; the holy Catholic Church; the Communion of Saints; the Remission of sins; the Resurrection of the body; and everlasting Life after death?

Answer. All this I steadfastly believe.

The Priest.

Wᴵʟᴛ thou be baptised into this Faith?
   Answer. That is my desire.

The Priest.

Wᴵʟᴛ thou then obediently keep God's holy will and commandments, and walk in the same all the days of thy life?
   Answer. I will endeavour so to do, God being my Helper.

Then shall the Priest extend his right hand over them, *and shall say,*

O Lᴏʀᴅ God of hosts, before the might of Whose presence the armies of evil are put to flight, deliver *these Persons* from the power of sin, and from every craft and assault of the devil. *Amen.*

Gʀᴀɴᴛ, O merciful Lord, that the old Adam in *these Persons* may be so buried in Christ, that the new man may be raised up in *them. Amen.*

Cᴀsᴛ out of *their hearts*, O Lord, every evil imagination, and everything which doth exalt itself against the knowledge of Thee; and bring into captivity every thought to the obedience of Christ. *Amen.*

Gʀᴀɴᴛ, O Lord, that all carnal affections may die in *them*, and that all things belonging to the Spirit may live and grow in *them. Amen.*

Gʀᴀɴᴛ, O Lord, that *these Persons*, now to be baptised, may through Thee have power and strength to have victory, and to triumph, against the devil, the world, and the flesh. *Amen.*

Sᴇɴᴅ down, O Lord, upon *these Persons* Thy Holy Spirit, that He may make His abode in *them*, and grant that *these Persons*, by the effectual working of the power of the Holy Ghost, may be born again, and attain unto everlasting life. *Amen.*

Gʀᴀɴᴛ, that *these Persons*, being here dedicated unto Thee by our Office and Ministry, may also be endued with heavenly virtues, and everlastingly rewarded, through Thy mercy, O blessed Lord God, Who dost live, and govern all things, world without end. *Amen.*

Tʜᴇ Mɪɴɪsᴛʀᴀᴛɪᴏɴ ᴏғ Hᴏʟʏ Bᴀᴘᴛɪsᴍ

Then shall the Priest proceed to bless the Water, saying,

Oᴜʀ help standeth in the Name of the Lord;
   Answer. Who hath made heaven and earth.
  Priest. O Lord, hear our prayer;
   Answer. And let our cry come unto Thee.

Priest. Let us pray.

Aʟᴍɪɢʜᴛʏ and everliving God, our heavenly Father, Whose most dearly beloved Son Jesus Christ, for the forgiveness of our sins, did shed out of His most precious side both Water and Blood; and gave commandment to His disciples, saying, All power is given unto me in heaven and in earth, Go ye therefore, and teach all nations, baptising them ɪɴ ᴛʜᴇ Nᴀᴍᴇ ᴏғ ᴛʜᴇ Fᴀᴛʜᴇʀ, ᴀɴᴅ ᴏғ ᴛʜᴇ Sᴏɴ,

330

AND OF THE HOLY GHOST: Regard, we beseech Thee, the prayers and supplications of Thy Church, and sanctify this Water to the mystical washing away of sin; and grant that the Persons now to be baptised therein may receive the fullness of Thy grace, and ever remain in the number of Thy faithful and elect children, through the same Thy Son Jesus Christ our Lord. *Amen.*

Then shall the Priest take each Person to be baptised by the right hand,
and placing him conveniently by the Font, according to his discretion, shall say to his Sponsors,
Name this Person.

And then naming the Person after them, the Priest shall dip him into the Water;
or else, if it be more convenient, he shall pour Water upon his head, saying,
N. I BAPTISE thee In the Name of the Father,
and of the Son, and of the Holy Ghost.

And all the people shall answer,
AMEN.

Then shall the Priest make a Cross upon the forehead
of the newly-baptised Christian, saying,
WE receive this Person into the Congregation of Christ's flock; and do sign *him* with the Sign of the Cross, in token that hereafter *he* shall not be ashamed to confess the faith of Christ crucified, and manfully to fight under His banner, against sin, the world, and the devil; and to continue Christ's faithful soldier and servant unto *his* life's end. *Amen.*

THE THANKSGIVING AFTER HOLY BAPTISM

Then shall the Priest say,
SEEING now, dearly beloved brethren, that *these Persons are* regenerate, and grafted into the body of Christ's Church, let us give thanks unto Almighty God for these benefits, and with one accord make our prayers unto Him, that *they* may lead the rest of *their* life according to this beginning.

Then shall the Priest and people together say the Lord's Prayer, as followeth.
OUR Father, which art in heaven, hallowed be Thy Name. Thy kingdom come. Thy will be done, in earth as it is in heaven. Give us this day our daily bread. And forgive us our trespasses, As we forgive them that trespass against us. And lead us not into temptation, But deliver us from evil. For Thine is the kingdom, the power, and the glory, For ever and ever. Amen.

Then shall the Priest say,
WE yield Thee hearty thanks, most merciful Father, that it hath pleased Thee to bring *these* Thy *servants* to Thy holy Baptism, and to regenerate *them* with Water and the Holy Ghost, to receive *them* for Thine own *Children* by adoption, and to incorporate *them* into Thy holy Church as *living members* of the Body of Thy beloved Son. And humbly we beseech Thee, O heavenly Father, to grant that *they*, being dead unto sin, and living unto righteousness, and being through Baptism buried with Christ in His death, may crucify the old man in *them*, and utterly abolish the whole body of sin; and that, as *they are* made *partakers* of the Death of Thy Son Jesus Christ, *they* may also be *partakers* of His Resurrection; so that finally, with all the elect and faithful remnant of Thy holy Church, *they* may *all* be *inheritors* of Thine everlasting kingdom; through the same Thy Son Jesus Christ our Lord. *Amen.*

The Exhortations and Blessing

Then shall the Priest use this Exhortation following, speaking first to the Sponsors.

FORASMUCH as *these Persons have* promised in *your* presence to renounce the devil and all his works, to believe in God, and to serve Him; *ye* must remember, that it is *your* part and duty to put *them* in mind of what a solemn vow, promise, and profession *they have* now made before this Congregation, and especially before *you their* chosen *Witnesses.* And *ye are* also to call upon *them* to use all diligence to be rightly instructed in God's holy Word, and the true doctrine of His Church; that so *they* may grow in grace, and in the knowledge of our Lord Jesus Christ, and live godly, righteously, and soberly in this present world.

And then, speaking to the newly baptised Persons*, he shall say,*

AND seeing, *Brethren,* that *you* have now by Baptism put on Christ, it is *your* part and duty also, being made *the Children* of God and of the light, by faith in Jesus Christ, to walk in that holy light answerably to *your* Christian calling, and as becometh *the children* of light; remembering always that our Baptism doth represent unto us our profession, which is, to follow the example of our Saviour Christ, and to be made like unto Him; that as He died, and rose again for us, so should all we, who are baptised, die from sin, and rise again unto righteousness; and, taking up our cross and following Him, continually mortify all our evil and corrupt affections, and daily proceed in all virtue and godliness of living. And so, to further this end, *you shall* seek Confirmation without delay, that *you may* be strengthened and sealed by the Holy Ghost, and come to receive the Holy Communion of the Body and Blood of Christ, offering to God continually the sacrifice of worship and service in the fellowship of His one holy Catholic Church of which *you are* now *living members.*

Then shall the Priest pronounce this Blessing over them*, saying,*

UNTO God's gracious mercy and protection we commit *you.* May the Lord bless *you,* and keep *you.* May the Lord make His face to shine upon *you,* and be gracious unto *you.* May the Lord lift up His countenance upon *you,* and give *you* peace, both now and evermore. And so may the blessing of God Almighty, ✠ the Father, the Son, and the Holy Ghost, be upon *you* and remain with *you* always. *Amen.*

And if Holy Baptism be ministered as a separate Service,
the Priest shall then conclude it with the Grace.

II *Corinthians* xiii. 14.

✠ THE grace of our Lord Jesus Christ, and the love of God, and the fellowship of the Holy Ghost, be with us all evermore. *Amen.*

It is expedient that every new baptised Person should be confirmed by the Bishop so soon after his *Baptism as conveniently may be; that so* he *may be admitted without delay to the Holy Communion.*

Here endeth the MINISTRATION OF
BAPTISM TO SUCH AS ARE OF RIPER YEARS.

A CATECHISM,

AN INSTRUCTION TO BE LEARNED OF EVERY PERSON
BEFORE HE BE BROUGHT TO BE CONFIRMED BY THE BISHOP

THE BAPTISMAL COVENANT.

The Catechist shall say,
WHAT is your Name?

And the Candidate for Confirmation shall here answer,
giving his Christian Name to the Catechist.

Question. Who gave you this Name?

Answer. My Godparents in my Baptism; wherein I was made a member of Christ, the child of God, and an inheritor of the kingdom of heaven.

Question. What did your Godparents then for you?

Answer. They did promise and vow three things in my name. First, that I should renounce the devil and all his works, the pomps and vanity of this wicked world, and all the sinful lusts of the flesh, so that I should not follow nor be led by them. Secondly, that I should believe all the Articles of the Christian Faith. And thirdly, that I should keep God's holy will and commandments, and walk in the same all the days of my life.

Question. Dost thou not think that thou art bound to believe, and to do, as they have promised for thee?

Answer. Yes, verily; and by God's help so I will. And I heartily thank God our heavenly Father, that He hath called me to this state of salvation, through Jesus Christ my Saviour. And I pray unto God to give me His grace, that I may ever continue in the same unto my life's end.

THE CHRISTIAN FAITH.

Catechist.
Rehearse the Articles of thy Belief.

Answer.

I BELIEVE in God the Father Almighty, Maker of heaven and earth: And in Jesus Christ His only Son our Lord, Who was conceived by the Holy Ghost, Born of the Virgin Mary, Suffered under Pontius Pilate, Was crucified, dead, and buried, He descended into hell; The third day He rose again from the dead, He ascended into heaven, And sitteth at the right hand of God the Father Almighty; From thence He shall come to judge the quick and the dead. I believe in the Holy Ghost; The holy Catholic Church; The Communion of Saints; The Forgiveness of sins; The Resurrection of the body; And the Life everlasting. Amen.

Question. What dost thou chiefly learn in these Articles of thy Belief?

Answer. First, I learn to believe in God the Father, Who hath made me, and all the world. Secondly, in God the Son, Who hath redeemed me, and all mankind. And thirdly, in God the Holy Ghost, Who sanctifieth me, and all the elect people of God.

THE COMMANDMENTS.

Question. You said that your Godfathers and Godmothers did promise for you, that you should keep God's Commandments. Tell me, how many Commandments there be?

Answer. There are ten Commandments, given by God to Moses on Mount Sinai, as recorded in the Second and Fifth Books of Moses; and there are two Commandments, given unto us by our Lord Jesus Christ, as recorded in the holy Gospels according to Saint Matthew and Saint Mark, which is the whole Summary of the Law.

Catechist.
Rehearse the Commandments of the Law given to Moses on Mount Sinai.

Answer.

I AM THE LORD THY GOD, Who brought thee out of the land of Egypt, out of the house of bondage:

I.   Thou shalt have none other gods but me.

II.   Thou shalt not make to thyself any graven image, nor the likeness of anything that is in the heaven above, or in the earth beneath, or in the water under the earth. Thou shalt not bow down to them, nor worship them: for I the Lord thy God am a jealous God, and visit the sins of the fathers upon the children unto the third and fourth generation of them that hate me, and shew mercy unto thousands in them that love me, and keep my commandments.

III.   Thou shalt not take the Name of the Lord thy God in vain: for He will not hold him guiltless that taketh His Name in vain.

IV.   Remember that thou keep holy the Sabbath-day. Six days shalt thou labour, and do all that thou hast to do; but the seventh day is the Sabbath of the Lord thy God. In it thou shalt do no manner of work, thou, and thy son, and thy daughter, thy man-servant, and thy maid-servant, thy cattle, and the stranger that is within thy gates. For in six days the Lord made heaven and earth, the sea, and all that in them is, and rested the seventh day; wherefore the Lord blessed the seventh day, and hallowed it.

V.   Honour thy father and thy mother, that thy days may be long in the land which the Lord thy God giveth thee.

VI.   Thou shalt do no murder.

VII.   Thou shalt not commit adultery.

VIII.   Thou shalt not steal.

IX.   Thou shalt not bear false witness against thy neighbour.

X.   Thou shalt not covet thy neighbour's house, thou shalt not covet thy neighbour's wife, nor his servant, nor his maid, nor his ox, nor his ass, nor anything that is his.

Catechist.
Rehearse our Blessed Lord's Summary of the Law.

A CATECHISM

Answer.

HEAR, O Israel, THE LORD OUR GOD IS ONE LORD; and thou shalt love the Lord thy God with all thy heart, and with all thy soul, and with all thy mind, and with all thy strength. This is the first and great Commandment. And the second is like unto it: Thou shalt love thy neighbour as thyself. On these two Commandments hang all the Law and the Prophets.

And I beseech the Lord to have mercy upon me;
and to write all these His laws in my heart.

Question. What dost thou chiefly learn by these Commandments?
Answer. I learn two things: my duty towards God, and my duty towards my neighbour.

Question. What is thy duty towards God?
Answer. My duty towards God is, to believe in Him, to fear Him, and to love Him with all my heart, with all my soul, and with all my mind, and with all my strength; to worship Him, to give Him thanks, to put my whole trust in Him, to call upon Him, to honour His holy Name and His Word, and to serve Him truly all the days of my life.

Question. What is thy duty towards thy Neighbour?
Answer. My duty towards my Neighbour is, to love him as myself, and to do unto all men as I would that they should do unto me: To love, honour, and succour my father and my mother: To honour and obey the Queen: To submit myself to all those who have charge over me, my governors and teachers, my spiritual pastors and masters: To order myself lowly and reverently to all my betters: To hurt nobody by word nor deed: To be true and just in all my dealing: To bear no malice nor hatred in my heart: To keep my hands from picking and stealing, and my tongue from evil speaking, lying, and slandering: To keep my body in temperance, soberness, and chastity: Not to covet nor desire other men's goods; but to learn and labour truly to get mine own living, and to do my duty both unto God and my Neighbour in that state of life, unto which it shall please Almighty God to call me.

Question. What is thy duty in regard to those with whom thou keepest company?
Answer. My duty in regard to those with whom I keep company is not to be deceived, but to remember always that evil communications will corrupt good manners. Therefore I must ever take good care, relying on God through prayer, to give me wisdom and right discernment to choose my companions well; for the bad example and companionship of those who would not be obedient to the words and will of Jesus Christ can lead me astray, and take me from the narrow pathway of righteousness which leadeth unto life, and down the broad pathway which leadeth to destruction. For some may come to me in sheep's clothing, but inwardly they are ravening wolves; and as it is with a tree, so it will be that by their fruits I shall know them.

Catechist.

OUR Saviour, on the night in which He was betrayed, said unto His disciples, If ye love me, keep my Commandments. What other new Commandment did our Lord give to His Church?
Answer. Our Lord Jesus Christ said, A new commandment I give unto you, That ye love one another; as I have loved you, that ye also love one another. By this shall all men know that ye are my disciples, if ye have love one to another.

A CATECHISM

THE LORD'S PRAYER.

Catechist.

MY good Child, know this, that thou art not able to do any of these things of thyself, nor art thou able to walk in these Commandments of God, and to serve Him, without His special grace; which thou must learn at all times to call for by diligent prayer. Let me hear, therefore, if thou canst say the Prayer which our Lord Jesus Christ Himself commanded and taught His disciples to pray.

Answer.

OUR Father, which art in heaven, hallowed be Thy Name. Thy kingdom come. Thy will be done, in earth as it is in heaven. Give us this day our daily bread. And forgive us our trespasses, As we forgive them that trespass against us. And lead us not into temptation, But deliver us from evil. Amen.

Question. What desirest thou of God in this prayer?

Answer. I desire my Lord God our heavenly Father, Who is the Giver of all goodness, to send His grace unto me, and to all people; that we may worship Him, serve Him, and obey Him, as we ought to do. And I pray unto God, that He will send us all things that be needful both for our souls and bodies; and that He will be merciful unto us, and forgive us our sins; and that it will please Him to save and defend us in all dangers ghostly and bodily; and that He will keep us from all sin and wickedness, and from our ghostly enemy, and from everlasting death. And this I trust He will do of His great mercy and goodness, through our Lord Jesus Christ. And therefore I say, Amen. So be it.

THE TWO SACRAMENTS OF THE GOSPEL.

The Properties of the Sacraments.

Question. How many Sacraments hath Christ our Lord ordained in His Gospel, as being generally necessary to salvation?

Answer. Christ our Lord hath ordained two Sacraments only as being generally necessary to salvation; that is to say, Baptism and the Supper of the Lord.

Question. What meanest thou by this word Sacrament?

Answer. By this word, I mean an outward and visible sign of an inward or spiritual grace, given unto us and ordained by our Lord Jesus Christ Himself, as a means whereby we verily and indeed receive the same, and a pledge to assure us of the reality thereof.

Question. How many parts are there in a Sacrament?

Answer. There are two parts in a Sacrament: the outward and visible sign; and the inward and spiritual grace, which is the true substance of the Sacrament.

The Sacrament of Baptism.

Question. What is the outward and visible sign of Baptism?

Answer. The outward and visible sign of Baptism is Water, in which the person who is to be baptised is dipped, or else upon whom the Water is poured, together with the form of words, *I baptise thee in the Name of the Father, and of the Son, and of the Holy Ghost.*

A CATECHISM

Question. What is the inward and spiritual grace of Baptism?

Answer. The inward and spiritual grace of Baptism is a death unto sin, and a new birth unto righteousness, through the mystical washing away of sins by the Blood of our Lord Jesus Christ, signified unto us by the Water of Baptism: for being by nature born in sin, and so the children of wrath, we cannot inherit the kingdom of God; yet by the grace imparted unto us in Baptism, we are verily and indeed washed and cleansed by the Blood of Christ, and are made very members of His Body, and the children of grace.

Question. What is required of persons to be baptised?

Answer. Repentance, whereby they who are baptised forsake sin; and Faith, whereby they steadfastly believe the promises of God made unto them in that Sacrament.

Question. Why then are Infants and young Children baptised, when by reason of their tender age they cannot perform them?

Answer. Because Baptism is the outward and visible sign, not only of our regeneration and new life in Christ, but also of our admission thereby into the new Covenant made for us by Him, and sealed with His own Blood; into which holy Covenant the children of Christian parents are admitted, in like manner as the sons of Israel were admitted into the old Covenant, as the seed of Abraham, by their fathers under the Law of Moses; and so they promise, by their Godfathers and Godmothers, who are their Sureties; which promise, when they are come to age, they themselves are bound to perform.

The Sacrament of the Lord's Supper.

Question. Why was the Sacrament of the Lord's Supper ordained?

Answer. The Supper of the Lord was ordained for the continual remembrance of the Sacrifice of the Death of our Saviour Christ, to be shewn forth by His Church until He shall come again; and to partake of the benefits which we receive thereby.

Question. By what other names is the Lord's Supper known?

Answer. The Lord's Supper is also known as the Holy Communion; and the Liturgy wherein that blessed Sacrament is consecrated and ministered to the faithful is called the Holy Eucharist, and also called the Mass.

Question. What is the outward part or visible sign of the Lord's Supper?

Answer. The outward part or visible sign of the Lord's Supper is Bread and Wine, which the Lord Himself hath instituted and commanded to be received.

Question. What is the true and real substance of the Sacrament of the Lord's Supper, that is to say, the inward part or thing signified?

Answer. The true and real substance of the Sacrament of the Lord's Supper is the most precious Body and Blood of our Lord and Saviour Jesus Christ, which are really and truly present under the outward forms or signs of the consecrated Bread and Wine; and which are verily and indeed taken and received by Christ's faithful in the Lord's Supper.

Question. What are the benefits whereof we are partakers in the Lord's Supper?

Answer. The strengthening and refreshing of our bodies and souls, and their preservation unto everlasting life, by the Body and Blood, together with the Soul and Divinity, of our Lord Jesus Christ, which we receive in Holy Communion; and which is the chief means whereby, we are assured, that He doth dwell in us, and we in Him.

Question. What is required of every person that shall partake of the Lord's Supper?

Answer. It is required of every person that shall partake of the Lord's Supper, that he be in a state of grace; that is to say, every communicant must first examine himself, whether he have repented himself truly of his former sins, steadfastly purposing to lead a new life; and if he have committed any deadly sins, to confess them with true contrition; and having received the grace of absolution, to make satisfaction for them; he also must have a lively faith in God's mercy through His only Son Jesus Christ, with a thankful remembrance of His death upon the Cross for our salvation; and be in charity with all men.

The Catechist may conclude the Catechism saying,

THE God of all grace, Who hath called us into His eternal glory by Christ Jesus, make you perfect, stablish, strengthen, settle you. To Him be glory and dominion for ever and ever. *Amen.*

The Parish Priest, and those responsible with him for the education of the children and youth of the Parish, shall diligently, upon Sundays and the greater Holy-days, or at such other times as the Parish Priest himself shall think convenient, instruct and examine the Children of his Parish sent unto him in some part of this short Catechism, as well in the Further Instruction in the Christian Religion which is hereunto appended.

And all Fathers and Mothers, Masters and Dames, Governors and Guardians, shall cause their own Children, Servants, Apprentices, and Wards, to be instructed in this Catechism, until such time as they shall have learned all that is here appointed for them to learn.

So soon as baptised Children are come to a competent age, and can say, in their Mother Tongue, the Creed, the Lord's Prayer, the Ten Commandments, and our Lord's Summary of the Law; and can also answer to the other Questions of this Catechism and those set forth in the Further Instruction in the Christian Religion hereunto appended; they shall then be brought to the Bishop to be confirmed by him. And every one that is confirmed shall have to himself a Sponsor, be it a Godfather or a Godmother, to stand as a Witness of his Confirmation at the hands of the Bishop.

And whensoever the Bishop shall give notice for Candidates to be brought to him for their Confirmation, the Priest shall either bring, or else he shall send in writing, with his hand subscribed thereunto, the names of all such persons within his Parish, as he shall think fit to be presented to the Bishop to be confirmed by him.

FURTHER INSTRUCTION IN THE CHRISTIAN RELIGION

THE CHURCH.

Question. What is the Church?

Answer. The Church is the whole company of all faithful Christian people, called from out of the world by Almighty God; whose members, by Faith and Baptism, through the inner working of the Holy Ghost, are become the Family of God, the Body of Christ, the Temple of the Holy Ghost, the Pillar and Ground of the Truth, and the Communion of Saints.

Question. How is the Church described?

Answer. The Church is described as One, Holy, Catholic, and Apostolic.

Question. Why is the Church described as One?

Answer. Because it hath but one Lord, one Faith, one Baptism, and one God and Father; and there is not, nor can there ever be, any other church than that one Congregation and Body of Christ, made up of all who, by the grace of God, have received the one Baptism into the true Faith of the one Blessed Lord and only Saviour of all mankind.

Question. Why is the Church described as Holy?

Answer. Because in Baptism all sin is washed away; and the Holy Ghost is then given to them that truly believe, sanctifying thereby the whole People of God, and endowing them with His manifold gifts of grace.

Question. Why is the Church described as Catholic?

Answer. Because the Church is universal, and doth exist for all times, and in all places, for all Christian people; and in this holy Catholic Church the one Faith and the whole Truth is held and taught as it was revealed by God to mankind in His Blessed Son Jesus Christ, Who is the same yesterday, to-day, and forever, and Whose Word never faileth.

Question. Why is the Church described as Apostolic?

Answer. Because the Church hath received its sacred mission from Christ Himself through His holy Apostles, and doth continue at all times in their Doctrine and in their Fellowship, built upon their Witness, and governed by their Successors.

Question. What is the work of the Church in the world?

Answer. The work of the Church in the world is to offer up to Almighty God, for itself and on behalf of all mankind, the worship which is His due; to make known to all mankind the Gospel of Christ; to bring into its fellowship all those elect persons who are called by God from out of this world, to instruct them in the Way of salvation, and to prepare them for the Life of the world to come.

THE APOSTOLIC MINISTRY.

Question. How did our Blessed Lord provide for the life and work of His Church?

Answer. Our Blessed Lord gave the Holy Ghost first to His Apostles in the Upper Room, on the evening of Easter-Day; and then He sent down the Holy Ghost upon the Apostles, and other disciples, at Pentecost; thereby endowing His Church with the Presence and gifts of the Comforter.

Question. What Power and Authority did Christ give to His Apostles in the Church?

Answer. Christ gave to His Apostles the fullness of Power and Authority to preach His Word, to minister His Sacraments, to oversee and govern the universal Church, and to feed, care, and provide for all His people until His coming again.

Question. How hath this Ministry been continued in the Church, the Apostles themselves having long since been taken away?

Answer. Through the Bishops of the Church, whom the Apostles themselves had appointed to oversee and govern the particular Churches, and upon whom they laid their hands; and by the Bishops who have succeeded them from generation to generation, also through the laying on of hands, within that one holy Catholic and Apostolic Church.

A CATECHISM

THE FIVE OTHER SACRAMENTS OF THE CHURCH.

Question. Thou hast spoken of the two Sacraments of the Gospel, that were instituted by our Lord Jesus Christ Himself in the Gospels, as being generally necessary for salvation to be received of all Christians: are there any other Sacraments in Christ's Church?

Answer. Yes; there are five other sacred ordinances, or mysteries, commonly called Sacraments, which, like Baptism and the Supper of the Lord, are outward and visible signs of inward and spiritual grace truly imparted to those who rightly and worthily receive them; howbeit, not every Christian is bound to receive them all, as they are not generally necessary for salvation to be received of all Christians; but rather are Sacraments of the Christian life, to be received by each Christian believer according to his own calling in Christ Jesus.

Question. What are these five other Sacraments of the Church?
Answer. Penance, Confirmation, Matrimony, Unction, and Orders.

Question. What is the Sacrament of Penance?
Answer. It is the means whereby God doth pardon all them that confess, and truly repent them of their sins, restoring them to their baptismal innocence and reconciling them to Himself and His Church, through the grace of Absolution, and the performance of such penances as shall be imposed upon them to make satisfaction for the guilt incurred by sin.

Question. What is the Sacrament of Confirmation?
Answer. It is the means whereby God doth confirm and strengthen the faith of baptised Christians, by the inward anointing and sealing of their souls by the Holy Ghost, imparted to them through the laying on of hands, after the example of the holy Apostles.

Question. What is the Sacrament of Matrimony?
Answer. It is the means whereby God doth unite and bind together a man and a woman as one flesh, by a solemn covenant betwixt them made, signified by the pledging of vows, the giving and receiving of rings, and the joining of hands; within which union alone hath God ordained the begetting and nurturing of children.

Question. What is the Sacrament of Unction?
Answer. It is the means whereby God doth heal the sick, through prayer made over them, and by anointing them with Oil in the Name of the Lord, that He may save them, and raise them up; and, if they have committed any sins, they shall be forgiven them.

Question. What is the Sacrament of Orders?
Answer. It is the means whereby God doth set apart men for the threefold sacred Ministry of His Church, through the Laying on of Hands with Prayer, thereby consecrating some Bishops, ordaining some Priests, and making some Deacons; each Minister in the particular Order of his calling, according to the gracious will and purpose of Almighty God.

THE MINISTRY OF THE CHURCH.

Question. What is the work of a Bishop?
Answer. The work of a Bishop is to be the chief Pastor of the flock of Christ committed to his care, exercising the fullness of the sacred Ministry amongst them as an high Priest of the New

Testament, by preaching the Gospel of salvation, and guarding, teaching, and handing on the true Faith; overseeing and presiding in the assembly of the faithful, with fullness of Power and Authority to minister all the Sacraments and other Rites and Ceremonies of the Church, but chiefly those which appertain especially and properly only to his office: the confirming of the baptised faithful; the instituting of Lay-Ministers, and setting apart of Deaconesses; the making, ordaining, and consecrating of Bishops, Priests, and Deacons; and sending them forth as Labourers into the Lord's harvest; all the time following the example of the blessed Apostles from whom he succeedeth in the Ministry of oversight.

Question. What is the work of a Priest?

Answer. The work of a Priest is to minister to the people lawfully committed to his care by the Bishop, and to lead them in the public and private worship of Almighty God; to preach His holy Word; to baptise; to celebrate the Lord's Supper as the Lord Himself hath commanded, and to minister the Holy Communion of His Body and Blood to the faithful; to absolve the penitent; to solemnise Matrimony; to lay hands upon, and to anoint the sick; to set apart the good things of the earth to the service of God, and to consecrate them to a holy use; and to pronounce the blessing and benediction of the Lord upon His people.

Question. What is the work of a Deacon?

Answer. To assist the Bishop or Priest in the Liturgy of the Church, chiefly by reading the Gospel and other Scriptures, and in distributing the Holy Communion to the faithful; and in teaching and preaching; in looking after the sick, the poor, and the needy; and in other ministrations to the People of God.

Question. What is thine own work as a Lay-Member of the Church?

Answer. To take my part in the worship, labour, and councils of the Church, according to the gifts of grace that God hath given me; and to pray, work, and give of my means for the spread of His Gospel and the extension of His kingdom.

THE HOLY SCRIPTURES.

Question. How doth God make known His will in the Church?

Answer. Holy men of old were moved by the Holy Ghost to declare the will of God as it was revealed unto them; and the Word of Almighty God, delivered by them, and contained in the Scriptures of the Old Testament of the Law and the Prophets, were committed to the people of Israel and Judah. These, together with the Gospels of the Evangelists and the Epistles and Revelation of the Apostles in the Scriptures of the New Testament of Jesus Christ, have been preserved in the Christian Church, and handed down to us: and Christ Himself hath set in His Church Ministries for the guidance of His people, in accordance with His written Word. And to all men God beareth witness by the Catholic Church, which is the Pillar and Ground of the Truth, proclaiming His salvation, and blessing the works of His hands.

Question. Why oughtest thou to read the Holy Scriptures?

Answer. Because they tell us of how God hath made Himself known through His creation, and how He hath made Himself known to mankind by His Spirit; and how we may come to know Him, and find our salvation through faith in His Son Jesus Christ.

Question. What doth the Church teach us about the Holy Scriptures?

A CATECHISM

Answer. That the Holy Scriptures are the inspired Word of God, as it was revealed first to Israel and Judah at sundry times and in divers manners, and then in these latter days to His Church; and that nothing may be taught in the Church of God, as necessary to the eternal salvation of mankind, but what may be concluded or proved therefrom.

Question. Where is the Word of God to be found in all its fullness?
Answer. In the Person of our Blessed Lord Jesus Christ, Who is Himself the Word of God Incarnate, the Way, the Truth, the Life, and the only Saviour and Redeemer of mankind; in Whom dwelleth the fullness of the Godhead bodily; Whose words are life and health to them that believe, and put their trust in Him.

THE CHRISTIAN'S VOCATION.

Question. What is the vocation of a Christian?
Answer. The vocation of a Christian is to believe in and to follow Jesus Christ, and to bear witness to Him in this world; to fight manfully under His banner against sin, the world, and the devil, ever continuing His faithful soldier and servant until his life's end; and finally, by God's grace, to lay hold on eternal Life.

Question. What instructions are there for a faithful Christian to follow in the pursuit of his vocation?
Answer. The Church in every place and in every age hath set forth for her children certain Precepts, agreeable to Scripture, as instructions to be followed by all baptised Christians; which, together with the ten Commandments of the Law of Moses, and our Blessed Lord's Summary of the Law, is the duty of every Christian to obey, if he be minded to be a faithful servant of Jesus Christ, and a truly conscientious member of His holy Church.

Question. Tell me how many of these Precepts there are set forth to be observed in this portion of Christ's Church, and what they be?
Answer. There are seven Precepts set forth for us to be observed, which are as followeth:

THE PRECEPTS OF THE CHURCH.

I. Every baptised Christian is bound to keep the First Day of the Week as the Lord's Day, and the Christian's Sabbath-Day; and on that day to worship God in His House, to rest and abstain from all servile and unnecessary labour; and, when and where it may be had, to be present at the Liturgy; and so likewise on every Holy-day appointed to be observed.

II. Every baptised Christian is bound to abstain from meats offered to idols, and from the eating of things strangled, and from blood; and to keep the Days of Fasting and Abstinence appointed by the Church to be observed.

III. Every baptised Christian is bound to confess any mortal sins which he may have at any time committed, and to seek Absolution for them; and to perform such penances as may be duly imposed on him by lawful Authority.

IV. Every baptised Christian is bound to receive worthily the blessed Sacrament of the Holy Communion of Christ's Body and Blood three times every year at the least, of which Easter is appointed to be one.

V. Every baptised Christian is bound to tithe, and to honour the Lord with the first-fruits of all his increase, and to give alms generously, as God shall prosper him; to assist in the support of the Ministry, the work of the Church, and the relief of the poor and destitute.

VI. Every baptised Christian is bound to abstain from fornication, and every other kind of impurity and deadly sin; and to keep the Church's laws concerning Marriage.

VII. Every baptised Christian man is bound to pray or prophesy with his head uncovered, and so likewise is every baptised Christian woman bound to pray or prophesy with her head covered; according to the Apostle's teaching, and the custom of the Churches of God from the Apostles' time.

Catechist.

MY dear Child, in all of these things which we have herein undertaken to teach thee, and which thou hast endeavoured to learn, what are their final purpose and end?

Answer. That I, and all baptised Christian people, may be made perfect in holiness, and be prepared within the Body of the one holy Catholic Church of God for the glorious appearing of our Lord and Saviour Jesus Christ; when He shall be revealed from heaven in like manner as He went up, and the dead in Christ shall be raised, and we which are alive and remain to His coming shall be caught up together with them in the clouds to meet the Lord in the air; and so shall we ever be with the Lord. And in this blessed hope I say, Amen. Even so, come, Lord Jesus.

Saint Jude 24, 25.

NOW unto Him that is able to keep us from falling, and to present us faultless before the presence of His glory with exceeding joy; to the only wise God our Saviour be glory and majesty, dominion and power, both now and ever. *Amen.*

Here endeth a SHORT CATECHISM
and FURTHER INSTRUCTION IN THE CHRISTIAN RELIGION.

THE ORDER OF CONFIRMATION
OR ANOINTING AND LAYING ON OF HANDS
UPON THOSE THAT ARE BAPTISED
AND COME TO YEARS OF DISCRETION

The Sacrament of Confirmation shall be administered only to those Persons who are baptised and are come to years of discretion, that they might receive the grace and seal of the Holy Ghost through Anointing and the Laying on of Hands, and so be permitted to partake of the Lord's Table; for no Person shall be admitted to the Holy Communion until such time as he be confirmed, or be ready and desirous of Confirmation.

Confirmation may be administered alone as a separate Service, or else Confirmation may be administered within the celebration of the Holy Eucharist, or within the Services of Morning or Evening Prayer; and the arrangements for the Service, including the place of the Sermon, and the place and choice of any hymns, shall be subject at all times to the direction of the Bishop.

When the day appointed by the Bishop is come, all them *that* are *then to be confirmed, being placed and standing* in order *before the Bishop, the Rector or Minister in charge of the Parish or Congregation, or some other Minister appointed by the Bishop, shall present* them *unto the Bishop, saying,*

THE PRESENTATION OF THE CONFIRMANDS

RIGHT Reverend Father in God, I present unto you *these Persons* here present to receive the Sacrament of Confirmation.

Bishop. Take heed that the *Persons* whom ye present unto us *have* been duly instructed, and *are* prepared and meet to receive this holy Ordinance.

Minister. They have been duly instructed, and I believe *them* so to be.

Then the Bishop shall read this Preface following.

BRETHREN, *these are they* to whom we purpose, God willing, to administer this day the holy Sacrament of Confirmation; that is to say, anointing *them* with Oil as the outward sign of the seal of the Holy Ghost upon *them* who *are* baptised, and *are* come to years of discretion, together with the laying on of hands upon *them* after the example of the holy Apostles.

The Church hath thought good to order that none shall be confirmed, but such as can say the Apostles' Creed, the Lord's Prayer, the Ten Commandments, and our Blessed Lord's Summary of the Law, and are further instructed in the short Catechism.

We are assured that *these Persons* present, being by Baptism *members* of Christ's holy Church, *have* been duly instructed, and *are* prepared and meet as aforesaid; and we are now here assembled to bless and confirm *them*, by anointing *them* with Oil, and by laying hands upon *them*, with prayer, in the Name of the Lord.

This order is very convenient to be observed.

First. Because it is evident from sundry places in Holy Scripture that the Apostles themselves prayed for, and laid their hands upon, those who were baptised; and the same is agreeable with the usage of the Church from the Apostles' time. This holy rite is reckoned in the Epistle to the Hebrews to be one of the first principles of Christ.

Secondly. In order that baptised persons, having come to the years of discretion, may acknowledge openly the vows made at their Baptism, and so dedicate their lives to the will and service of Almighty God.

CONFIRMATION

Thirdly. In order that by prayer, with the outward anointing, and the laying on of hands, those who are baptised may be sealed and strengthened inwardly by the Holy Ghost, manfully to fight under the banner of Christ crucified, against sin, the world, and the devil, and to continue Christ's faithful soldiers and servants until their life's end.

THE LESSONS

Then either the Bishop himself, or else some other Minister appointed by him, shall read the following three Lessons from the Holy Scriptures.

Hear the Word of God written in the eighth chapter of the Acts of the Apostles, from the fourth to the eighth verse, and from the fourteenth to the seventeenth verse.

THEREFORE they that were scattered abroad went everywhere preaching the Word. And Philip went down to the city of Samaria, and proclaimed unto them the Christ. And the multitudes gave heed with one accord unto the things that were spoken by Philip, when they heard, and saw the signs which he did. For many of those which had unclean spirits, they came out, crying with a loud voice: and many that were palsied, and that were lame, were healed. And there was much joy in that city. But when they believed Philip preaching good tidings concerning the kingdom of God and the Name of Jesus Christ, they were baptised, both men and women. Now when the Apostles which were at Jerusalem heard that Samaria had received the Word of God, they sent unto them Peter and John: who, when they were come down, prayed for them, that they might receive the Holy Ghost: for as yet He was fallen upon none of them: only they had been baptised into the Name of the Lord Jesus. Then laid they their hands on them, and they received the Holy Ghost.

Hear also this written in the nineteenth chapter of the Acts of the Apostles, from the first to the seventh verse.

AND it came to pass, that, while Apollos was at Corinth, Paul having passed through the upper country came to Ephesus, and found certain disciples: and he said unto them, Did ye receive the Holy Ghost when ye believed? And they said unto him, Nay, we did not so much as hear whether the Holy Ghost was given. And he said, Into what then were ye baptised? And they said, Into John's baptism. And Paul said, John baptised with the baptism of repentance, saying unto the people, that they should believe on Him which should come after him, that is, on Jesus. And when they heard this, they were baptised into the Name of the Lord Jesus. And when Paul had laid his hands upon them, the Holy Ghost came on them; and they spake with tongues, and prophesied. And they were in all about twelve men.

And hear also this written in the fifth chapter of the Epistle to the Hebrews, beginning at the twelfth verse, and in the sixth chapter beginning at the first verse.

FOR when by reason of the time ye ought to be teachers, ye have need again that someone teach you the rudiments of the first principles of the oracles of God; and are become such as have need of milk, and not of solid food. Wherefore let us cease to speak of the first principles of Christ, and press on unto perfection; not laying again a foundation of repentance from dead works, and of faith toward God, of the teaching of baptisms, and of laying on of hands, and of the resurrection of the dead, and of eternal judgement. And this we will do, if God permit.

CONFIRMATION

THE RENEWAL OF BAPTISMAL VOWS
AND ADMINISTRATION OF CONFIRMATION

The Lessons ended, the Bishop, sitting in his Chair, shall say to them *that desire to be confirmed,*

DEARLY beloved in the Lord, *ye* who *have* come here this day to be confirmed, (following the example of all faithful Christians, in every place and in every age): Will *ye* here, in the presence of God, and before the face of this Congregation, renew the solemn promises and vows that were made at *your Baptisms*; ratifying and confessing the same in *your* own *persons*, and acknowledging *yourselves* bound to believe, and to do, all those things, which *your* Godfathers and Godmothers then undertook for *you*, or which *you yourselves* did then undertake to believe and perform when *you were* baptised?

And each Person *shall answer, saying,*
I will, the Lord being my Helper.

Then shall the Bishop say,

WE demand *of each one of you* therefore: Dost thou renounce the devil and all his works, the vain pomp and glory of the world, with all the covetous desires of the same, and the carnal desires of the flesh, so that thou wilt not follow, nor be led by them?

Answer. I renounce them all.

The Bishop.

DOST thou believe in God the Father Almighty, Maker of heaven and earth?

And dost thou believe in Jesus Christ His only-begotten Son our Lord? And that He was conceived by the Holy Ghost; and was born of the Virgin Mary; that He suffered under Pontius Pilate, and was crucified, dead, and buried; that He went down into hell, and also did rise again the third day; that He ascended into heaven, and there sitteth at the right hand of God the Father Almighty; and that from thence He shall come again at the end of the world, to judge the quick and the dead?

And dost thou believe in the Holy Ghost, the holy Catholic Church, the Communion of Saints, the Forgiveness of sins, the Resurrection of the body, and everlasting life after death?

Answer. All this I steadfastly believe.

The Bishop.

WILT thou endeavour to keep God's holy will and commandments, and to walk in the same all the days of thy life?

Answer. I will endeavour so to do, God being my Helper.

Then the Bishop, standing up, shall say,

MAY Almighty God our heavenly Father, Who hath given unto *you* the grace to believe, and the will to do, all these things, send down the Holy Ghost upon *you*, to confirm *you* in the faith and fear of Christ and keep and strengthen *you* in the same, preserve *you* from all sin, and make *you* steadfast all the days of *your* life; through Jesus Christ our Lord. *Amen.*

And then shall all *the* Confirmands *be placed* in order *before the Bishop.*

Then shall the Bishop say,
OUR help standeth in the Name of the Lord;
Answer. Who hath made heaven and earth.

CONFIRMATION

Bishop. Blessed be the Name of the Lord;
Answer. Henceforth, world without end.
Bishop. O Lord, hear our prayer;
Answer. And let our cry come unto Thee.

Bishop. Let us pray.

*Then shall the Bishop extend his hands over all them that are
to be confirmed, saying this Prayer following.*

ALMIGHTY and everliving God, our heavenly Father, Who hast vouchsafed to regenerate *these* Thy *servants* by Water and the Holy Ghost, and hast given unto *them* forgiveness of all *their* sins: Pour down upon *them*, O Lord, Thy heavenly blessing, we most humbly beseech Thee; confirm *them*, seal *them*, and strengthen *them*, with the Holy Ghost the Comforter; and daily increase in *them* Thy manifold gifts of grace: the spirit of wisdom and understanding; the spirit of counsel and might; the spirit of knowledge and true godliness; and fill *them*, O Lord, with the spirit of Thy holy fear; now and forever; through Jesus Christ our Lord. *Amen.*

*And then, having received from his Sponsor the name of the Person to be confirmed,
the Bishop shall pronounce that name, and then anoint the forehead of that person, saying,*

N. WE do mark thee, and sign thee, with the mark of the sign of the Cross, and anoint thee with this hallowed and consecrated Oil, ✠ In the Name of the Father, and of the Son, and of the Holy Ghost. Amen. And as thou art anointed outwardly with this holy Chrism, so may God the Holy Ghost bless thee, and confirm thee, and seal thee inwardly with His grace; and preserve thee both in body and soul unto everlasting life; through Jesus Christ our Lord. *Amen.*

And then shall the Bishop lay his hand upon the head of the Confirmand, saying,

DEFEND, O Lord, this Thy *servant* with Thy heavenly grace, that *he* may continue Thine forever; and daily increase in Thy Holy Spirit, more and more, until *he* come unto Thine everlasting kingdom. Amen.

*And then shall the Bishop gently, with his right hand,
strike the newly-confirmed Person on the cheek, saying,*
PEACE be with thee.

And the newly-confirmed Person shall answer,
And with thy spirit.

THE THANKSGIVING AFTER CONFIRMATION

*And then, when all have been confirmed,
the Bishop shall turn to the people and say,*
THE Lord be with you.
Answer. And with thy spirit.
Bishop. Let us pray.

Then shall the Bishop and the Congregation together say the Lord's Prayer, as followeth.

OUR Father, which art in heaven, hallowed be Thy Name. Thy kingdom come. Thy will be done, in earth as it is in heaven. Give us this day our daily bread. And forgive us our trespasses, As we forgive them that trespass against us. And lead us not into temptation, But deliver us from evil. For Thine is the kingdom, the power, and the glory, For ever and ever. Amen.

CONFIRMATION

ALMIGHTY and everliving God, Who makest us both to will and to do those things as be good and acceptable unto Thy Divine Majesty: We make our humble supplications unto Thee for *these* Thy *servants*, whom we have this day anointed, and upon whom, after the example of Thy holy Apostles, we have laid our hands, to certify *them*, by these signs, of Thy favour and gracious goodness towards *them*. Let Thy fatherly hand, we beseech Thee, ever be over *them*; let Thy Holy Spirit ever be with *them*; and so lead *them* in the knowledge and obedience of Thy Word, that in the end *they* may obtain everlasting life; through our Lord Jesus Christ, Who with Thee and the Holy Ghost liveth and reigneth, ever one God, world without end. *Amen.*

O ALMIGHTY Lord, and everlasting God, vouchsafe, we beseech Thee, to direct, sanctify, and govern both our hearts and bodies, in the ways of Thy laws, and in the works of Thy commandments; that, through Thy most mighty protection both here and ever, we may be preserved in body and soul; through Jesus Christ our Lord. *Amen.*

Then shall the Bishop stand up and bless them*, saying,*

GO *ye* forth into the world in the faith and peace of Jesus Christ; be of good courage; hold fast to that which is good; render unto no man evil for evil; love the Lord *your* God with all *your* heart, and with all *your* soul, and with all *your* mind, and with all *your* strength, and *your* neighbour as *yourself*; and serve the Lord *your* God steadfastly and faithfully all the days of *your* life: And may the blessing of God Almighty, ✠ the Father, the Son, and the Holy Ghost, be upon *you*, and remain with *you*, both now and for evermore. *Amen.*

It is an ancient custom that each Confirmand should take upon himself another Christian name, in order to signify his new standing within the Body of Christ, which name is conferred by the Bishop upon the Confirmand at the time of his anointing; and it is also convenient that every candidate for Confirmation have not only his Godparents present at his Confirmation, but also that he shall have at least one Sponsor chosen by him to name him and to present him unto the Bishop when he is confirmed.

Here endeth the ORDER FOR CONFIRMATION.

A FORM OF
RECEIVING A CONFIRMED PERSON
INTO FULL COMMUNION

This Form shall only be used for those who have already been baptised with Water in the Name of the Father, and of the Son, and of the Holy Ghost, and who have been properly confirmed, or are desirous and willing of Confirmation, and have petitioned to be admitted a Communicant in this portion of the One Holy Catholic and Apostolic Church.

It is the right of the Bishop to receive fellow Christians into full Communion with him; nevertheless, in the absence or inability of the Bishop to act, any Priest or Deacon may be authorised to act in his name.

The Bishop speaking to the Petitioner shall say,
MY *brother* in Christ Jesus, what is thy desire?

And the Petitioner shall answer the Bishops, saying,
REVEREND Father in God, it is my desire that I be received by you into full Communion and Fellowship within this portion of the one holy Catholic and Apostolic Church, and to submit myself to the authority and jurisdiction thereof.

The Bishop.
DEARLY beloved *brother*, it is fitting, that before we receive thee into full Communion and Fellowship within this portion of Christ's Church, we should first receive full assurance that thou dost understand what is required of thee in this undertaking. Thou shalt, therefore, answer plainly to these questions:

The Bishop.
DOST thou declare that thou hast been baptised with Water, In the Name of the Father, and of the Son, and of the Holy Ghost; and also that thou dost believe in thy heart and confess with thy mouth the Christian Faith, as the same is set forth in the holy Scriptures of the Old and New Testaments, and the three Creeds of the undivided Catholic Church?
Answer. I do so declare.

The Bishop.
HAST thou received Confirmation at the hands of a true and lawful Bishop of the Catholic Church?
Answer. I have.

The Bishop.
ART thou persuaded that this Congregation of Christian believers is a true part and integral portion of the one holy Catholic and Apostolic Church of God?
Answer. I am so persuaded.

The Bishop.
DOST thou desire to be received into full Communion and Fellowship within this portion of the one Church?
Answer. I do.

CONFIRMATION

The Bishop.

WILT thou endeavour ever to be a loyal communicant, endeavouring always to remain in good standing amongst thy brethren, chiefly by the constant practice of godly charity, and also by accepting and upholding the Faith, Order, and Discipline of this portion of the one Body of Jesus Christ?

Answer. I will endeavour so to do, God being my Helper.

Then shall the Bishop, standing up, say,

ALMIGHTY God, Who hath given thee a will to declare, promise, and do all these things, Grant also unto thee strength and power to fulfill the same, that He may accomplish His work which He hath begun in thee; through Jesus Christ our Lord. *Amen.*

*Then shall the Bishop take the right hand of
the Petitioner in his, and shall say,*

MY *brother,* We receive thee into full Communion and Fellowship in this portion of the one holy Catholic and Apostolic Church, In the Name of the Father, and of the Son, and of the Holy Ghost. Amen.

*Then shall the Bishop gently strike
the new Communicant upon the cheek, saying,*

PEACE be with thee.

And the Communicant shall respond saying,

And with thy spirit.

Then shall the Bishop say this Prayer following.

ALMIGHTY God and heavenly Father, we thank thee for our Fellowship in Christ, and for the bond of peace and unity which is ours within the Communion of His Body the Church: And we beseech Thee, O Lord, to bless this Thy *servant* now admitted into our portion of that One Church, and grant unto *him* that *he* will be faithful to *his* calling, and loyal to *his* brethren, seeking always to fulfill his promises which *he* hath made here in Thy sight this day; through the same Thy Son Jesus Christ our Lord. *Amen.*

Then shall the Bishop bless the new Communicant after this wise.

THE blessing of God Almighty, ✠ the Father, the Son, and the Holy Ghost, rest upon thee, and remain with thee, now and all the days of thy life. *Amen.*

*Here endeth a FORM OF RECEIVING OF A CONFIRMED PERSON
INTO FULL COMMUNION.*

OTHER SACRAMENTS, RITES AND CEREMONIES OF THE CHURCH

HOLY MATRIMONY

A TABLE OF
KINDRED AND AFFINITY
WHEREIN WHOSOEVER ARE RELATED ARE FORBIDDEN BY THE LAWS OF GOD TO MARRY TOGETHER.

A Man may not marry his:
Mother
Daughter
Adopted Daughter
Grandmother
Granddaughter
Sister
Wife's Mother
Wife's Daughter
Father's Wife
Son's Wife
Grandfather's Wife
Wife's Grandmother
Wife's Granddaughter
Grandson's Wife
Father's Sister
Mother's Sister
Brother's Daughter
Sister's Daughter

A Woman may not marry her:
Father
Son
Adopted Son
Grandfather
Grandson
Brother
Husband's Father
Husband's Son
Mother's Husband
Daughter's Husband
Grandmother's Husband
Husband's Grandfather
Husband's Grandson
Granddaughter's Husband
Father's Brother
Mother's Brother
Brother's Son
Sister's Son

In this Table the term 'brother' includes a brother of the half-blood, and the term 'sister' includes a sister of the half-blood.

THE DAYS AND SEASONS
WHEN MARRIAGES ARE FORBIDDEN TO BE SOLEMNISED

I.   Any SUNDAY of the Year; and (except the Ordinary permit):
II. From ADVENT SUNDAY until Eight Days after the EPIPHANY;
III. From SEPTUAGESIMA SUNDAY until Eight Days after EASTER.

A FORM OF
BETROTHAL, OR ENGAGEMENT
OF THOSE INTENDING TO MARRY

This Form ensuing may be used in the Church, or it may be used in the house of the Parents or Friends of the Man or Woman who intend to be married, or in some other suitable place approved by the Parish Priest.

The Man and the Woman shall stand before the Minister, the Man on the right hand, and the Woman on the left; and the Minister shall say,

FORASMUCH as we trust that Almighty God our heavenly Father hath put into your hearts the desire and will to be espoused one to another, seeking for to come together as husband and wife in the Sacrament of Matrimony; you shall now therefore, in the presence of God, and before the face of this company, make your promises either to other to be married if it be the Lord's will according to His laws, and the proper desire of your hearts, so to do; and pray unto Him to give you both the grace and strength to fulfill that solemn engagement of espousal which you here undertake this day.

Then shall the Minister read this Lesson following.
Let us hear the Word of God written in the second chapter of
the First Book of Moses called Genesis, beginning at the eighteenth verse.

THE LESSON. *Genesis* 2. 18-25.

THE Lord God said, It is not good that the man should be alone; I will make him an help meet for him. And out of the ground the Lord God formed every beast of the field, and every fowl of the air; and brought them unto Adam to see what he would call them: and whatsoever Adam called every living creature, that was the name thereof. And Adam gave names to all cattle, and to the fowl of the air, and to every beast of the field. But for Adam there was not found an help meet for him. And the Lord God caused a deep sleep to fall upon Adam, and he slept; and He took one of his ribs, and closed up the flesh instead thereof; and the rib, which the Lord God had taken from man, made He a woman, and brought her unto the man. And Adam said, This is now bone of my bones, and flesh of my flesh: she shall be called Woman, because she was taken out of Man. Therefore shall a man leave his father and his mother, and shall cleave unto his wife: and they shall be one flesh.

The Lesson ended, the Minister shall cause the Man to place a ring on the fourth finger of the Woman's left hand; and being taught by the Minister, the Man shall say,

I, *N.*, in the presence of God, and of this company, do promise thee, *N.*, that, if it be the will of God, according to His Laws, I will take thee unto myself; and so will I wed thee, and make thee my wife, according to His holy ordinance. Amen.

The Minister shall then cause the Woman to place a plain ring on the fourth finger of the Man's right hand; and being taught by the Minister, the Woman shall say,

I, *N.*, in the presence of God, and of this company, do promise thee, *N.*, that, if it be the will of God, according to His Laws, I will accept thee as my husband; and so will I wed thee, and give myself unto thee to be thy wife, according to His holy ordinance. Amen.

Then shall the Man and the Woman join their hands fast together, while the following Canticle is said or sung.

BETROTHAL

Revelation 22. 2 & 3.

AND I, John, saw the holy city, new Jerusalem, coming down from God out of heaven, / prepared as a bride adorned for her husband. And I heard a great voice out of heaven saying, / Behold, the tabernacle of God is with men, And He will dwell with them, and they shall be His people, / and God Himself shall be with them, and be their God.

GLORY be to the Father, and to the Son, / and to the Holy Ghost;
As it was in the beginning, is now, and ever shall be, / world without end. Amen.

Then shall the Minister say,
Let us pray.

Lord, have mercy upon us.
Christ, have mercy upon us.
Lord, have mercy upon us.

OUR Father, which art in heaven, hallowed be Thy Name. Thy kingdom come. Thy will be done, in earth as it is in heaven. Give us this day our daily bread. And forgive us our trespasses, As we forgive them that trespass against us. And lead us not into temptation, But deliver us from evil. For Thine is the kingdom, the power, and the glory, For ever and ever. Amen.

Then shall the Minister say,
O LORD, hear our prayer.
Answer. And let our cry come unto Thee.

The Minister.

O ALMIGHTY God, Who hast put it into the hearts of these Thy servants, to desire to come together as husband and wife, and live together in the holy estate of Matrimony: Vouchsafe unto them, we most humbly beseech Thee, Thy continual protection; and grant that they may fulfill the vows of their espousals, and so, with full purpose of heart and will, come to together in holiness, purity, and mutual love, within the sacred bond of Christian Marriage; and give unto them both grace to enter into that Sacrament reverently, discreetly, advisedly, and soberly, in Thy faith and fear. Bless them both, O Lord, we beseech Thee; and if it be Thy good will that they be joined together as husband and wife, grant that it will not be in word alone, neither only in an outward form, but in truth that they will become one even as Christ and His Church are one, and forever will be one; through the same Jesus Christ our Lord, Who doth love the Church and gave Himself for it, and Who with Thee and the Holy Ghost art ever one God, world without end. *Amen.*

II Corinthians xiii. 14.

✠ THE grace of our Lord Jesus Christ, and the love of God, and the fellowship of the Holy Ghost, be with us all evermore. *Amen.*

And here gifts and other tokens of espousal may
be given and received according to the custom of the place.

Here endeth a FORM OF BETROTHAL, OR ENGAGEMENT.

The Form of
Solemnisation of Matrimony

The Incumbent Minister of the Parish or Congregation shall be responsible for the conduct of the Service, and for the preparation of the Bride and Groom before their Marriage.

It is expedient that timely notice, preferably of no less than three months, shall first be given to the Pastor by those who are intending to marry.

Before solemnising any Marriage, the Minister shall make full inquiry and duly satisfy himself that there be no Impediment of Consanguinity, Affinity, or Status; reference being made to the Constitution and Canons of the Church, and the Table of Kindred and Affinity; and that neither party to the intended Marriage hath been divorced from one who is still living at the time, except a decree of nullity have first been given by the Bishop where nullity hath been proved, or that permission to contract Marriage hath been allowed according to the Word of God and the Canon Law founded thereon.

Where it is the legal responsibility of the Minister so to do, he shall assure himself that all the prerequisite Notices, Consents, and Forms, as required by the Civil Laws of the Province or Territory in which such Marriage is to be solemnised have been given, obtained, and completed.

The Minister shall also assure himself that the Banns of the Persons to be married have been published thrice as required; or in lieu of such publication, that a Licence hath been obtained from the proper Provincial or Territorial authority.

There shall be at every Marriage two Witnesses present who shall sign the Registers and any other required Documents, both of whom must be baptised Christians of lawful age.

Banns of Marriage shall be published, if possible, in the Church on three several Sundays during Divine Service, after the accustomed manner, and in conformity with the ancient usages of the Church.

Where either or both of the parties are accustomed to worship in a Church or Churches other than their own Parish Church, the Banns may be called in the Church or Churches in which they worship.

At the time of Marriage, when asked by the Priest of those present, if any man do allege and declare any Impediment, why they may not be coupled together in Matrimony, by God's Law, or the laws of this Realm; and will be bound, and sufficient Sureties with him, to the parties; or else put in a Caution (to the full value of such Charges as the Persons to be married do thereby sustain) to prove his Allegation: then the Solemnisation of Matrimony must be deferred, until such time as the truth be tried.

Matrimony may not be solemnised for any cause on the Lord's Day, nor upon any day during Holy Week. Matrimony may also not be solemnised on any week-days during Advent or Lent, nor on the Rogation Days, except there be just and urgent cause to the contrary and the Ordinary himself have first given his written approval thereunto.

The Banns

When the Banns are to be published, the Minister shall say,

I PUBLISH the Banns of Marriage between *N.* of . . . and *N.* of . . . If any of you know cause or any just impediment why these two Persons should not be joined together in Matrimony, ye are to declare it. This is the first [*second,* or *third*] time of asking.

MATRIMONY

THE EXHORTATION

At the day and time appointed for solemnisation of the Marriage, the Persons to be married shall come into the body of the Church, with their friends and neighbours, during which time a Psalm or hymn may be sung; and there standing together, the Man on the right hand and the Woman on the left, the Priest shall say,

DEARLY beloved, we are gathered together here in the sight of God and in the face of this Congregation, to join together this Man and this Woman in holy Matrimony.

Matrimony is an honourable estate, instituted of God in the time of man's innocency, signifying unto us the mystical union that is betwixt Christ and His Church; which holy estate Christ adorned and beautified with His presence, and the first miracle that He wrought, in Cana of Galilee; and is commended by Saint Paul to be honourable among all men. Matrimony is therefore not by any to be enterprised, nor taken in hand, unadvisedly, lightly, or wantonly; but reverently, discreetly, advisedly, soberly, and in the fear of God, duly considering the causes for which this holy Sacrament was ordained.

First, Matrimony was ordained for the hallowing of that intimate union betwixt a man and a woman, which is intended by God for the begetting of children; so that their offspring might be conceived in innocency, and brought up in the fear and nurture of the Lord, to the praise of His holy Name.

Second, Matrimony was ordained for a remedy against sin and impurity, and to avoid fornication; so that such persons as have not in themselves the gift of continency might marry, and thereby keep themselves undefiled members of Christ's Body.

Third, Matrimony was ordained for the mutual society, help, and comfort, that one spouse ought to have of the other, both in prosperity and adversity.

It is into this holy estate that these two Persons come now to be joined. Therefore, if any man can shew any just cause, why they may not lawfully be joined together, let him now speak, or else hereafter for ever hold his peace.

THE CHARGE TO THE BRIDAL PAIR

And then, speaking unto the Persons that are to be married, the Priest shall say,

I REQUIRE and charge you both, as ye will answer at the dreadful day of judgement, when the secrets of all hearts shall be disclosed, that if either of you know any impediment, why ye may not lawfully be joined together in Matrimony, ye do now confess it. For be ye well assured, that so many as are coupled together otherwise than God's Word doth allow are not joined together by God; neither is their Matrimony lawful.

THE DECLARATIONS OF INTENTION

There being no impediment alleged, the Priest shall say unto the Man,

N. WILT thou have this Woman to thy wedded wife, to live together after God's ordinance in the holy estate of Matrimony? Wilt thou love her, comfort her, protect, honour, and keep her, in sickness and in health: and, forsaking all other, keep thee only unto her, so long as you both shall live?

The Man shall answer,
I will.

Then shall the Priest say unto the Woman,

N. WILT thou have this Man to thy wedded husband, to live together after God's ordinance in the holy estate of Matrimony? Wilt thou reverence him, and help him, love, honour, and keep him, in sickness and in health: and forsaking all other, keep thee only unto him, so long as you both shall live?

The Woman shall answer,

I will.

Then shall the Priest say to the father of the Woman,
or to her friend that giveth her away,

WHO giveth this Woman to be married to this Man?

And he shall answer,

I do.

THE MATRIMONIAL COVENANT

Then shall the Priest receive the Woman at her father's or friend's hands, and shall cause the Man with his right hand to take the Woman by her right hand. And the Man, being taught by the Priest, shall plight his troth, saying,

I *N.* take thee *N.* to my wedded wife, to have and to hold from this day forward, for better for worse, for richer for poorer, in sickness and in health, to love and to cherish, till death us do part, according to God's holy ordinance: and thereto I plight thee my troth.

Then shall they loose their hands. And the Woman, with her right hand taking the Man by his right hand, and taught by the Priest, shall likewise give her troth, saying,

I *N.* take thee *N.* to my wedded husband, to have and to hold from this day forward, for better for worse, for richer for poorer, in sickness and in health, to love and to cherish, till death us do part, according to God's holy ordinance: and thereto I give thee my troth.

Then shall they again loose their hands;
and they shall exchange Rings in the following manner.

The Priest, receiving the Rings, shall first bless them, saying,

SANCTIFY, O Lord, these Rings, that they may be unto these Thy servants sacred tokens of their vows, and outward signs of the solemn covenant here betwixt them made; and grant that they who wear these Rings may be true and constant in the performance of their vows, and remain faithful one to another, so long as they both shall live; through Jesus Christ our Lord. *Amen.*

Then shall the Priest deliver the Bride's Ring unto the Man, to put it upon the fourth finger of the Woman's left hand. And the Man, being taught by the Priest, shall give the Bride's Ring unto the Woman, saying,

WITH this Ring I thee wed, with my body I thee worship, and all my worldly goods with thee I share: In the Name of the Father, and of the Son, and of the Holy Ghost. Amen.

Then shall the Priest deliver the Bridegroom's Ring unto the Woman, to put it upon the fourth finger of the Man's left hand. And the Woman, being taught by the Priest, shall give the Bridegroom's Ring unto the Man, saying,

WITH this Ring I thee wed, with heart and body I thee honour, and all my worldly goods with thee I share: In the Name of the Father, and of the Son, and of the Holy Ghost. Amen.

Then shall the Priest say,

Let us pray.

MATRIMONY

Then shall the Priest say over them this Prayer following.

O ETERNAL Lord God, Creator and Preserver of all mankind, Giver of all spiritual grace, the Author of everlasting life: Send down Thy blessing upon these Thy servants, this Man and this Woman, whom we bless in Thy Name; that as Isaac and Rebecca lived faithfully together, so also these persons may surely perform and keep the vow and covenant betwixt them made, whereof these Rings given and received are tokens and pledges; and may ever remain in perfect love and peace together, and live according to Thy laws, until death part them; through Jesus Christ our Lord. *Amen.*

Then shall the Priest join their right hands together, and say,

THOSE whom God hath joined together let no man put asunder.

Then shall the Priest speak to the people, saying,

FORASMUCH as *N.* and *N.* have consented together in holy Wedlock, and have witnessed the same before God and this company, and thereto have given and pledged their troth either to other, and have declared the same by giving and receiving of Rings, and by joining of Hands; by the authority committed unto me by Almighty God, I now pronounce that they be Man and Wife together, In the Name of the Father, and of the Son, and of the Holy Ghost. *Amen.*

And the Priest shall add this Blessing.

✠ GOD the Father, God the Son, God the Holy Ghost, bless, preserve, and keep you: the Lord mercifully with His favour look upon you; and so fill you with all spiritual benediction and grace, that ye may so live together in this life, that in the world to come ye may have life everlasting. *Amen.*

Then shall the Register be signed according to the Laws of the Province or Territory, either here or at the end of the Service.

And here a Lesson from the holy Scriptures may be read by the Minister before the newly-married couple proceed to the Altar.

THE PROCESSION TO THE ALTAR

Then the Priest and Clerks, going before the Man and Woman and leading them up to the Lord's Table, shall say or sing one or both of these Psalms following.

PSALM 127. *Nisi Dominus.*

EXCEPT the Lord build the house, / their labour is but lost that build it. Except the Lord keep the city, / the watchman waketh but in vain. It is but lost labour that ye haste to rise up early, and so late take rest, and eat the bread of carefulness; / for so He giveth His beloved sleep. Lo, children and the fruit of the womb / are an heritage and gift that cometh of the Lord. Like as the arrows in the hand of the giant, / even so are the young children. Happy is the man that hath his quiver full of them: / they shall not be ashamed when they speak with their enemies in the gate.

GLORY be to the Father, and to the Son, / and to the Holy Ghost;
As it was in the beginning, is now, and ever shall be, / world without end. Amen.

PSALM 128. *Beati Omnes.*

BLESSED are they that fear the Lord, / and walk in His way. For thou shalt eat the labours of thy hands; / O well it is with thee, and happy shalt thou be. Thy wife shall be as the fruitful vine / upon the walls of thine house; Thy children like the olive-branches / round about thy table. Lo, thus shall the man be blessed, / that feareth the Lord. The Lord from out of Sion shall so bless thee, / that thou shalt see Jerusalem in prosperity all thy life-long; Yea, that thou shalt see thy children's children, / and peace upon Israel.

GLORY be to the Father, and to the Son, / and to the Holy Ghost;
As it was in the beginning, is now, and ever shall be, / world without end. Amen.

Or else this Psalm following may be used in the place of the two foregoing Psalms when the Woman is past child-bearing.

PSALM 67. *Deus misereatur.*

GOD be merciful unto us, and bless us, / and shew us the light of His countenance, and be merciful unto us; That Thy way maybe known upon earth, / Thy saving health among all nations. Let the people praise Thee, O God; / yea, let all the people praise Thee. O let the nations rejoice and be glad; / for Thou shalt judge the folk righteously, and govern the nations upon earth. Let the people praise Thee, O God; / yea, let all the people praise Thee. The earth hath brought forth her increase; / and God, even our own God, shall give us His blessing. God shall bless us; / and all the ends of the world shall fear Him.

GLORY be to the Father, and to the Son, / and to the Holy Ghost;
As it was in the beginning, is now, and ever shall be, / world without end. Amen.

THE PRAYERS BEFORE THE ALTAR

The Psalm ended, the Man and the Woman shall kneel down before the Lord's Table; and the Priest standing at the Altar, and turning his face towards them, shall say,

THE Lord be with you.
Answer. And with thy spirit.

Priest. Let us pray.

Lord, have mercy upon us.
Christ, have mercy upon us.
Lord, have mercy upon us.

Then shall all together say the Lord's Prayer, as followeth.

OUR Father, which art in heaven, hallowed be Thy Name. Thy kingdom come. Thy will be done, in earth as it is in heaven. Give us this day our daily bread. And forgive us our trespasses, As we forgive them that trespass against us. And lead us not into temptation, But deliver us from evil. For Thine is the kingdom, the power, and the glory, For ever and ever. Amen.

Priest. O Lord, save Thy servant, and Thy handmaid;
Answer. Who put their trust in Thee.
Priest. O Lord, send them help from Thy holy place;
Answer. And evermore defend them.
Priest. Be unto them a Tower of strength;
Answer. From the face of their enemy.
Priest. O Lord, hear our prayer.
Answer. And let our cry come unto Thee.

MATRIMONY

The Priest.

O GOD of Abraham, God of Isaac, God of Jacob, bless Thee these Thy servants whom Thou hast joined together in the bond of holy Matrimony, and sow the seed of eternal life in their hearts; that whatsoever in Thy holy Word they may profitably learn, they may indeed fulfill the same. Look, O Lord, mercifully upon them from heaven, and bless them. And as Thou didst send Thy blessing upon Abraham and Sarah, to their great comfort, so vouchsafe to send Thy blessing upon these Thy servants; that they, obeying Thy will, and alway being in safety under Thy protection, may abide together in Thy love unto their lives' end; through Jesus Christ our Lord. *Amen.*

(The Prayer following shall be omitted where the Woman is past child-bearing.

O MERCIFUL Lord and heavenly Father, by Whose gracious gift mankind is increased: Bestow, we beseech Thee, according to Thy gracious will, upon these Thy servants the gift and heritage of children; and grant also that they may live so long together in godly love and honesty, that they may see their children Christianly and virtuously brought up, to the praise and honour of Thy Name; through Jesus Christ our Lord. *Amen.)*

O HEAVENLY Father, we most humbly beseech Thee to bless the home of these Thy servants with Thine abiding presence; that they who dwell therein, being preserved from all evil, may live in holy peace and joy together; through Jesus Christ our Lord. *Amen.*

O GOD, Who hast consecrated the Sacrament of Matrimony to such an excellent mystery, that in it is signified and represented the spiritual marriage and unity betwixt Christ and His Church: Look mercifully upon these Thy servants, that they may love, honour, and cherish each other, and live together in faithfulness and patience, in wisdom and true godliness. O Lord, bless them both, and grant them to inherit Thine everlasting kingdom; through the Merits of Thy Son Jesus Christ our Lord. *Amen.*

ALMIGHTY God, Who at the beginning did create our first parents, Adam and Eve, and did sanctify and join them together in Marriage: Pour upon you the riches of His grace, sanctify ✠ and bless you, that you may please Him both in body and soul, and live together in holy love unto your lives' end. *Amen.*

It is convenient that the new-married Persons should receive the Holy Communion at the time of their Marriage, or at the first opportunity after their Marriage.

AT THE HOLY EUCHARIST

THE COLLECT.

O GOD, the Father of our Lord Jesus Christ, Who didst join together in marriage our first parents: We beseech Thee to sanctify and bless these Thy servants whom Thou hast joined together in holy wedlock; and grant that those whom Thou by Matrimony dost make one, may steadfastly keep the covenant betwixt them made, and so fulfill their vows; and remain in perfect love and peace together; through Jesus Christ our Lord. *Amen.*

THE EPISTLE. *Ephesians 5. 22-33.*

WIVES, submit yourselves unto your own husbands, as unto the Lord. For the husband is the head of the wife, even as Christ is the head of the Church: and He is the Saviour of the Body. Therefore as the Church is subject unto Christ, so let the wives be to their own husbands in everything.

Husbands, love your wives, even as Christ also loved the Church, and gave Himself for it, that He might sanctify and cleanse it with the washing of water, by the Word; that He might present it to Himself a glorious Church, not having spot, or wrinkle, or any such thing; but that it should be holy, and without blemish. So ought men to love their wives as their own bodies. He that loveth his wife loveth himself; for no man ever yet hated his own flesh, but nourisheth and cherisheth it, even as the Lord the Church: for we are members of His Body, of His flesh, and of His bones. For this cause shall a man leave his father and mother, and shall be joined unto his wife; and they two shall be one flesh. This is a great mystery; but I speak concerning Christ and the Church. Nevertheless, let every one of you in particular so love his wife, even as himself; and the wife see that she reverence her husband.

THE GRADUAL.

ALLELUIA, Alleluia. The God of Abraham, the God of Isaac, the God of Jacob be with them: / and may He fulfill His blessing upon them: That they may see their children's children unto the third and fourth generation, / and thereafter may receive eternal life through faith in Jesus Christ. Alleluia.

THE GOSPEL. *Saint Matthew* 19. 4-9.

JESUS answered and said unto them, Have ye not read, that He which made them at the beginning made them male and female, and said, For this cause shall a man leave father and mother, and shall cleave to his wife: and they twain shall be one flesh? Wherefore they are no more twain, but one flesh. What therefore God hath joined together, let not man put asunder. They say unto Him, Why did Moses then command to give a writing of divorcement, and to put her away? He saith unto them, Moses because of the hardness of your hearts suffered you to put away your wives: but from the beginning it was not so. And I say unto you, Whosoever shall put away his wife, except it be for fornication, and shall marry another, committeth adultery: and whoso marrieth her which is put away doth commit adultery.

A HOMILY.
The Homily following may be read at the discretion of the Priest.

ALL ye that are married, or that intend to take the holy estate of Matrimony upon you, hear what the Holy Scripture doth say as touching the duty of husbands towards their wives, and wives towards their husbands.

Saint Paul the Apostle, in his Epistle to the Ephesians, the fifth chapter, doth give his commandment to all married men: Husbands, love your wives, even as Christ also loved the Church, and gave Himself for it, that He might sanctify and cleanse it with the washing of water, by the Word; that He might present it to Himself a glorious Church, not having spot, or wrinkle, or any such thing; but that it should be holy, and without blemish. So ought men to love their wives as their own bodies. He that loveth his wife loveth himself; for no man ever yet hated his own flesh, but nourisheth and cherisheth it, even as the Lord the Church: for we are members of His Body, of His flesh, and of His bones. For this cause shall a man leave his father and mother, and shall be joined unto his wife; and they two shall be one flesh. This is a great mystery; but I speak concerning Christ and the Church. Nevertheless, let every one of you in particular so love his wife, even as himself.

Likewise the same Saint Paul, writing to the Colossians, speaketh thus to all men that are married: Husbands, love your wives, and be not bitter against them. Hear also what Saint Peter, the Apostle of Christ, who was himself a married man, saith unto them that are married: Ye husbands, dwell with your wives according to knowledge; giving honour unto the wife, as unto the weaker vessel, and as heirs together of the grace of life, that your prayers be not hindered.

Hitherto ye have heard the duty of the husband toward the wife. Now likewise, ye wives, hear and learn your duties toward your husbands, even as it is plainly set forth in Holy Scripture.

Saint Paul, in the aforenamed Epistle to the Ephesians, teacheth you thus: Wives, submit yourselves unto your own husbands, as unto the Lord. For the husband is the head of the wife, even as Christ is the head of the Church: and He is the Saviour of the Body. Therefore as the Church is subject unto Christ, so let the wives be to their own husbands in everything. And again he saith, Let the wife see that she reverence her husband.

And in his Epistle to the Colossians, Saint Paul giveth you this short lesson: Wives, submit yourselves unto your own husbands, as it is fit in the Lord. Saint Peter also doth instruct you very well, thus saying: Ye wives, be in subjection to your own husbands; that, if any obey not the Word, they also may without the Word be won by the conversation of the wives; while they behold your chaste conversation coupled with fear. Whose adorning, let it not be that outward adorning of plaiting the hair, and of wearing of gold, or putting on of apparel; but let it be the hidden man of the heart, in that which is not corruptible; even the ornament of a meek and quiet spirit, which is in the sight of God of great price. For after this manner in the old time the holy women also, who trusted in God, adorned themselves, being in subjection unto their own husbands; even as Sarah obeyed Abraham, calling him lord; whose daughters ye are as long as ye do well, and are not afraid with any amazement.

Here endeth the FORM OF SOLEMNISATION OF MATRIMONY.

The Thanksgiving of Women
after Child-birth
commonly called
The Churching of Women

The Woman, at the usual time after her delivery, shall come into the Church decently apparelled with a veil upon her head, and there shall kneel down before the Altar at the Communion rail.

Then shall the Priest say unto her,

Forasmuch as it hath pleased Almighty God of his goodness to give thee safe deliverance, and hath preserved thee in the great danger of child-birth; *and hath bestowed upon thee the gift of a child,* thou shalt therefore give hearty thanks to God, and say with me,

Then shall the Priest and the Woman together recite this Psalm following,

Psalm 116. *Dilexi quoniam.*

I am well-pleased, / that the Lord hath heard the voice of my prayer; That He hath inclined His ear unto me, / therefore will I call upon Him as long as I live. The snares of death compassed me round about, / and the pains of hell gat hold upon me. I found trouble and heaviness, and I called upon the Name of the Lord; / O Lord, I beseech Thee, deliver my soul. Gracious is the Lord, and righteous; / yea, our God is merciful. The Lord preserveth the simple: / I was in misery, and He helped me. Turn again then unto thy rest, O my soul; / for the Lord hath rewarded thee. And why? Thou hast delivered my soul from death, / mine eyes from tears, and my feet from falling. I will walk before the Lord / in the land of the living. I believed, and therefore will I speak; but I was sore troubled: / I said in my haste, All men are liars. What reward shall I give unto the Lord / for all the benefits that He hath done unto me? I will receive the cup of salvation, / and call upon the Name of the Lord. I will pay my vows now in the presence of all His people; / in the courts of the Lord's house, even in the midst of thee, O Jerusalem. Praise the Lord.

Glory be to the Father, and to the Son, / and to the Holy Ghost;

As it was in the beginning, is now, and ever shall be, / world without end. Amen.

Then the Priest shall say,
Let us pray.

Lord, have mercy upon us.
Christ, have mercy upon us.
Lord, have mercy upon us.

Our Father, which art in heaven, hallowed be Thy Name, Thy kingdom come, Thy will be done, in earth as it is in heaven. Give us this day our daily bread; And forgive us our trespasses, As we forgive them that trespass against us; And lead us not into temptation, But deliver us from evil. For Thine is the kingdom, the power, and the glory, For ever and ever. Amen.

Priest. O Lord, save this woman Thy handmaid;
Answer. Who putteth her trust in Thee.
Priest. Be Thou to her a strong tower;
Answer. From the face of her enemy.

CHURCHING OF WOMEN

Priest. O Lord, hear our prayer.
Answer. And let our cry come unto Thee.

Then the Priest shall say,

O ALMIGHTY God, we give Thee humble thanks for that Thou hast vouchsafed to deliver this woman Thy handmaid from the great peril of Child-birth: Grant, we beseech Thee, most merciful Father, that she, through Thy help, may both faithfully live, and walk according to Thy will, in this life present; and also may be partaker of Thine everlasting glory in the life to come; through Jesus Christ our Lord. *Amen.*

Then shall the Priest say this Prayer, or that which followeth.

O GOD, our heavenly Father, we thank Thee and praise Thy glorious Name, for that Thou hast been pleased to bless this Thy handmaid, and to bestow upon her the gift of a child: Grant, we beseech thee, most merciful Father, that she may diligently lead this child in the way of righteousness, to her own great blessing and the glory of Thy Name; through Jesus Christ our Lord. *Amen.*

This Prayer shall be said when the Child hath not survived,

O GOD whose ways are hidden and Thy works most wonderful, Who makest nothing in vain, and lovest all that Thou hast made: Comfort Thou Thy handmaid, whose heart is sore smitten and oppressed; and grant that she may so love and serve Thee in this life, that she may obtain the fullness of Thy promises in the world to come; through our Lord Jesus Christ. *Amen.*

Then shall the Priest bless her, saying,

NOW unto God's gracious mercy and protection we commit thee. ✠ The Lord bless thee, and keep thee. The Lord make His face to shine upon thee, and be gracious unto thee. The Lord lift up His countenance upon thee, and give thee peace, both now and evermore. *Amen.*

The Woman, that cometh to give God her Thanks after Child-birth, must also at that time offer the accustomed offerings; and, if there be a celebration of the Lord's Supper, it is convenient that she and her husband receive the Holy Communion together at that time.

Here endeth the CHURCHING OF WOMEN.

The Form of
Confession and
Absolution of a Penitent

The Penitent shall kneel down in the place where Confessions are appointed to be heard.

The Blessing of the Penitent

The Penitent shall first ask a blessing from the Priest, saying,
✠ BLESS me, Father, for I have sinned.

Then shall the Priest say,

MAY Almighty God bless thee, and have mercy upon thee. May the Lord be in thy heart, and on thy lips, that thou mayest truly and humbly confess thy sins unto Him, In the Name of the Father, and of the Son, and of the Holy Ghost. *Amen.*

And here the Penitent shall tell the Priest how long it hath been
since he made his last Confession, saying,
IT is (*number of days, months, or years*) since I made my last Confession.

The Confession

Then shall the Penitent make his Confession according to the form following.

I CONFESS to GOD ALMIGHTY, the FATHER, the SON, and the HOLY GHOST; and to you, *Reverend* Father: that I have sinned exceedingly, in thought, word, and deed, by omission, and by desire; through my fault, through my own fault, through my own most grievous fault. Especially I accuse myself that *since my last confession* I have committed the following sins: (*Here the Penitent shall confess fully all such particular sins committed by him as may be known unto him*). For these, and for all my sins which I cannot now remember, and for all those sins unknown to me but known unto God, I am heartily sorry; and I humbly beseech Him to grant me pardon and forgiveness, and the grace to amend my life; and from you, Reverend Father, I ask counsel, penance, and absolution. Amen.

Then shall the Priest give such counsel and advice to the Penitent as he shall think necessary; and shall impose upon him such a penance as he shall deem fitting, which the Penitent must first accept before the Priest shall proceed to pronounce Absolution. If the Penitent refuse the counsel and advice of the Priest, or if he shall refuse to perform the Penance imposed upon him, the Priest in that case shall not absolve that Person; but shall advise him that if he do not accept the counsel of the Church and perform the just penance imposed upon him, he shall remain separated from the Congregation of Christ's faithful until such time as he shall submit to the lawful authority of the Church.

An Act of Contrition

The Priest shall then ask the Penitent to say this Act of Contrition following.

O MY God, I am heartily sorry for ever having offended Thee. I detest all my sins, not only because of Thy just punishments, the loss of heaven, and the pains of hell; but because they offend Thee, O my God, Who art all good, and deserving of all my love. I therefore resolve, with the help of Thy grace, to sin no more, and to avoid the near occasions of sin; through Jesus Christ our Lord. Amen.

Then shall the Priest proceed to absolve the Penitent
according to the Form following.

PENANCE

THE ADMINISTRATION OF ABSOLUTION

Then before the Priest shall pronounce the Absolution, he shall say,

O MOST merciful God, Who, according to the multitude of Thy mercies, dost so put away the sins of those who truly repent, that Thou rememberest them no more: Look upon this Thy *servant,* who most earnestly desireth pardon and forgiveness. And forasmuch as *he* putteth *his* full trust only in Thy mercy, impute not unto *him his* former sins, but strengthen *him* with Thy blessed Spirit; and whenever Thou art pleased to take *him* hence, take *him* into Thine everlasting favour; through the Merits of Thy most dearly beloved Son our Lord and Saviour Jesus Christ. *Amen.*

Then shall the Priest absolve him *after this sort,*

OUR Lord Jesus Christ, Who hath left power to His Church to absolve all sinners who truly repent and believe in Him: Of His great mercy forgive thee thine offences. And by His authority committed to me, I absolve thee from all thy sins, In the Name of the ✠ Father, and of the Son, and of the Holy Ghost. *Amen.*

Or this,

OUR Lord Jesus Christ, Who hath left power to His Church to absolve all sinners who truly repent and believe in Him: Of His great mercy forgive thee thine offences. And by His authority committed to me, I absolve thee from all thy sins; and from every censure, bond of excommunication, and interdict, insofar as I am able so to do, and thou hast need thereof; In the Name of the ✠ Father, and of the Son, and of the Holy Ghost. Amen.

THE DISMISSAL

Then shall the Priest dismiss him *with this Blessing.*

MAY the blessed Passion of our Lord Jesus Christ, and His infinite Merits, supply all that is wanting in thy confession; and be also unto thee for the remission of sins, the increase of grace, and the reward of everlasting life: And the blessing of God Almighty, ✠ the Father, the Son, and the Holy Ghost, rest upon thee, and remain with thee, now and for evermore. *Amen.*

Then shall the Priest say,

GO thy way in peace, for the Lord hath put away thy sins.
Penitent. Thanks be to God.

Then shall the Priest say,

AND do thou remember the words of our Saviour Jesus Christ, Go, and sin no more. And therefore so do thou; and pray for me, a sinner. *Amen.*

*Here endeth the FORM OF CONFESSION AND
ABSOLUTION OF A PENITENT.*

A Shorter Form of
the Administration of
The Holy Eucharist

This shorter Form for the Administration of the Holy Eucharist here following is intended for use in private Homes, in Hospitals and Infirmaries, at Sea, in Space, and on the Battlefield, and at such times and under such circumstances as may be required at the discretion of the Priest. This Form may not, however, be used under normal circumstances in the Church as the principal Mass on the Lord's Day or any Holy-day. The foregoing notwithstanding, this shorter Form may be used in the Church at Confirmations, Weddings, and Funerals if necessity or convenience so require. And when using this shorter Form of the Holy Eucharist, all the rubrics pertaining to the celebration of the Holy Eucharist as prescribed in the full Form thereof shall at all times apply.

The Liturgy of the Word of God

The Priest, standing before and facing the Lord's Table, shall say in an audible voice the Lord's Prayer, after which he shall say the Collect thereafter following, the people all devoutly and humbly kneeling.

OUR Father, which art in heaven, hallowed be Thy Name. Thy kingdom come. Thy will be done, in earth as it is in heaven. Give us this day our daily bread. And forgive us our trespasses, As we forgive them that trespass against us. And lead us not into temptation, But deliver us from evil. Amen.

ALMIGHTY God, unto Whom all hearts be open, all desires known, and from Whom no secrets are hid: Cleanse the thoughts of our hearts by the inspiration of Thy Holy Spirit, that we may perfectly love Thee, and worthily magnify Thy holy Name; through Christ our Lord. *Amen.*

The Greeting.
The Priest shall greet the Congregation in the Name of the Lord, saying,
GRACE be unto you, and peace, from God our Father, and the Lord Jesus Christ.
Answer. And with thy spirit.

The Summary of the Law.
Then shall the Priest say,
OUR Lord Jesus Christ said: Hear, O Israel, THE LORD OUR GOD IS ONE LORD; and thou shalt love the LORD thy God with all thy heart, and with all thy soul, and with all thy mind, and with all thy strength. This is the first and great Commandment. And the second is like unto it, Thou shalt love thy neighbour as thyself. On these two Commandments hang all the Law and the Prophets.
People. Lord, have mercy upon us, and write both these Thy laws in our hearts, we beseech Thee.

The Collects.
Then shall the Priest say,
THE Lord be with you.
Answer. And with thy spirit.

Priest. Let us pray.

Then shall the Priest say this Collect for the Queen's Majesty following.

SHORTER EUCHARIST

THE COLLECT FOR THE QUEEN.

ALMIGHTY God, Whose kingdom is everlasting, and power infinite: Have mercy upon Thy people in this Dominion, and all the Realms and Countries of our Commonwealth; and so rule the heart of Thy chosen servant *ELIZABETH*, our Queen and Governor, that she (knowing Whose minister she is) may above all things seek Thy honour and glory : and grant that we, and all her subjects (duly considering Whose authority she hath) may faithfully serve, honour, and humbly obey her, in Thee, and for Thee, according to Thy blessed Word and ordinance; through Jesus Christ our Lord, Who with Thee and the Holy Ghost liveth and reigneth, ever one God, world without end. *Amen.*

THE COLLECT OF THE DAY.
Then shall be said or sung the Collect or Collects appointed to be used that day.

THE EPISTLE.
Then the Priest, or some other Minister, shall read the Epistle or Lesson appointed for that day, first saying, The Epistle [or *The Lesson appointed for the Epistle*] is written in the....chapter of....beginning at the....verse. *And the Epistle or Lesson ended, the Minister shall say,* Here endeth the Epistle [or *Lesson*]: This is the Word of the Lord.

And all shall answer saying,
THANKS be to God.

THE GRADUAL.
Then shall the Gradual be said.

THE GOSPEL.
*Then shall the Priest read the Gospel
appointed for that day.*

And shall the Priest say,
THE Lord be with you.
Answer. And with thy spirit.

Then shall the Priest say,
✠ THE holy Gospel is written in the....chapter of the Gospel
according to Saint....beginning at the....verse.

Then shall be said,
GLORY be to Thee, O Lord.

Then shall the Gospel be read.

The Gospel ended, all shall say,
PRAISE be to Thee, O Christ.

Then the Priest shall say,
AND through the Words of the Gospel,
may our sins be blotted out.

*And here the Apostles' Creed or Nicene Creed may be said,
at the discretion of the Priest.*

369

The Liturgy of the Supper of the Lord

The Preparation of the Faithful

Then shall the Priest or one of the Ministers invite the faithful to the Lord's Table, saying,

YE that do truly and earnestly repent you of your sins, and are in love and charity with your neighbours, and intend to lead a new life, following the commandments of God, and walking from henceforth in His holy ways: Draw near with faith, and take this holy Sacrament to your comfort; and make your humble confession to Almighty God, meekly kneeling upon your knees.

Then shall this general Confession be made by all that are minded to receive the Holy Communion, both the Priest and people together, all humbly kneeling upon their knees, and saying,

ALMIGHTY God, Father of our Lord Jesus Christ, Maker of all things, Judge of all men: We acknowledge and confess our manifold sins and wickedness, Which we from time to time most grievously have committed, By thought, word, and deed, Against Thy Divine Majesty, Provoking most justly Thy wrath and indignation against us. We do earnestly repent, And are heartily sorry for these our misdoings; The remembrance of them is grievous unto us; The burden of them is intolerable. Have mercy upon us; have mercy upon us, most merciful Father; For Thy Son our Lord Jesus Christ's sake, Forgive us all that is past; And grant that we may ever hereafter Serve and please Thee In newness of life, To the honour and glory of Thy Name; Through Jesus Christ our Lord. Amen.

Then shall the Priest stand up and pronounce this Absolution following.

ALMIGHTY God, our heavenly Father, Who of His great mercy hath promised forgiveness of sins to all them that with hearty repentance and true faith turn unto Him: Have mercy upon you; ✠ pardon and deliver you from all your sins; confirm and strengthen you in all goodness; and bring you to everlasting life; through Jesus Christ our Lord. *Amen.*

Then shall the Priest say,

Hear what comfortable words our Saviour Christ saith
unto all that truly turn to Him.

COME unto me all that travail and are heavy laden, and I will refresh you. *Saint Matthew xi.*

So God loved the world, that He gave His only-begotten Son, to the end that all that believe in Him should not perish, but have everlasting life. *Saint John iii.*

Hear also what Saint Paul saith.

This is a true saying, and worthy of all men to be received, That Christ Jesus came into the world to save sinners. I *Timothy i.*

Hear also what Saint John saith.

If any man sin, we have an Advocate with the Father, Jesus Christ the righteous; and He is the propitiation for our sins. I *Saint John ii.*

SHORTER EUCHARIST

THE PREPARATION OF THE LORD'S TABLE

The Priest shall first kiss the Altar, and then shall he say,
THE peace of the Lord be always with you.
Answer. And with thy spirit.

*Then shall the Priest prepare and set in order upon the Lord's Table
all the Bread and Wine which is to be consecrated.*

The Priest shall first take the Bread into his hands, and shall say,
BLESSED art Thou, O Lord our God, Maker and King of heaven and earth; for from Thy bounty we have received this Bread, which we offer unto Thee: Fruit of the earth and the work of men's hands, from which shall be made for us the Bread of eternal life.
Answer. Blessed be God forever.

*Then shall the Priest take the Chalice and, pouring
a little Water into the Wine, shall say,*
O GOD, Who didst wonderfully create, and even yet more wonderfully renew, the dignity of our nature: Grant that, by the mystery of this Water and Wine, we may come to share in the divinity of Christ, Who humbled Himself to partake of our humanity. *Amen.*

Then shall the Priest take the Chalice into his hands, and shall say,
BLESSED art Thou, O Lord our God, Maker and King of heaven and earth; for from Thy bounty we have received this Wine, which we offer unto Thee: Fruit of the vine and the work of men's hands, from which shall be made for us the Cup of everlasting salvation.
Answer. Blessed be God forever.

Then shall the Priest say this Prayer following.
IN a spirit of humility, and with a contrite heart, may we be accepted of Thee, O Lord; and may our sacrifice be so made in Thy sight this day as to be pleasing unto Thee, O Lord our God. *Amen.*

Then shall the Priest wash his hands, saying,
I WILL wash my hands in innocency, O Lord, and so will I go to Thine altar; that I may shew the voice of thanksgiving, and tell of all Thy wondrous works. Lord, I have loved the habitation of Thy house, and the place where Thine honour dwelleth.

Then shall the Priest say,
PRAY, brethren, that this shewing forth of the death of our Lord Jesus Christ, which is my sacrifice and yours, may be acceptable to God the Father Almighty.

And the people shall answer, saying,
MAY the Lord receive the sacrifice at thy hands, to the praise and glory of His Name, and for our good also, and that of all His holy Church. Amen.

*Then shall the Priest turn himself towards the Altar,
and he and the people shall keep silence and pray secretly for a space.*

371

SHORTER EUCHARIST

The Consecration of the Eucharist

Then shall the Priest turn himself again to face the people,
and shall say,

THE Lord be with you.

Answer. And with thy spirit.

Priest. Lift up your hearts.

Answer. We lift them up unto the Lord.

Priest. Let us give thanks unto our Lord God.

Answer. It is meet and right so to do.

Then shall the Priest turn himself again to face the Lord's Table, and say,

IT is very meet, right, and our bounden duty, that we should at all times, and in all places, give thanks unto Thee, Holy Lord, Almighty Father, Everlasting God, Maker and Preserver of all things.

Here shall follow the Proper Preface, if any be specially appointed, after which shall be said,

THEREFORE with Angels and Archangels, and with all the company of heaven, we laud and magnify Thy glorious Name; evermore praising Thee, and saying,

And the Priest and people together shall say,

HOLY, Holy, Holy, Lord God of hosts, Heaven and earth are full of Thy glory: Glory be to Thee, O Lord most high. ✠ Blessed is He that cometh in the Name of the Lord: Hosanna in the highest.

And when the Priest, standing before the Altar, hath so ordered the Bread and Wine, that he may with the more readiness and decency break the Bread, and take the Cup into his hands; he shall say the Prayer of Consecration and the Oblation of the Eucharist, as followeth.

ALL blessing, glory, and thanksgiving be unto Thee, Almighty God, our heavenly Father, Who of Thy tender mercy didst give Thine only Son Jesus Christ to take our nature upon Him, and to suffer Death upon the Cross for our redemption; Who made there, by His one Oblation of Himself once offered, a full, perfect, and sufficient Sacrifice, Oblation, and Satisfaction, for the sins of the whole world; and did institute, and in His holy Gospel command us to continue, a perpetual memory of that His precious Death and Sacrifice, until His coming again. Hear us, O merciful Father, we most humbly beseech Thee; and vouchsafe to send down Thy Holy Spirit upon us, and upon these Thy creatures of Bread and Wine which we set apart according to Thy Son our Saviour Jesus Christ's holy institution, in remembrance of His Death and Passion, that they may become for us His most blessed Body and Blood, and be received by us as He hath commanded: Who, in the same night that He was betrayed, *(Here the Priest is to take the Paten into his hands.)* took Bread; and, when He had given thanks, *(And here the Priest is to make the sign of the Cross over all the Bread to be consecrated.)* He blessed it, *(And here the Priest is to break the Bread.)* and brake it; and gave it to His disciples, saying, *(And here the Priest is to lay his hands upon all the Bread.)* Take, eat;

This is my Body which is given for you:
Do this in remembrance of me.

Likewise, after Supper, *(Here the Priest is to take the Chalice into his hands.)* He took the Cup; and, when He had given thanks, *(And here the Priest is to make the sign of the Cross over every vessel (be it Chalice or Flagon) in which there is any Wine to be consecrated.)* He blessed it, and gave it to them, saying, *(And here the Priest is to lay his hands upon every vessel in which there is any Wine to be consecrated.)* Drink ye all of this;

**For this is my Blood of the New Testament,
which is shed for you and for many for the remission of sins:
Do this, as oft as ye shall drink it, in remembrance of me.**

Then shall the Priest continue, saying,

WHEREFORE, O Father, Lord of heaven and earth, according to the institution of Thy dearly beloved Son our Saviour Jesus Christ, we Thy humble servants, with all Thy holy Church, do celebrate, and make here before the sight of Thy Divine Majesty, with these Thy holy gifts of the Bread of eternal life, and the Cup of everlasting salvation, which we now offer unto Thee, that memory of His blessed Passion and precious Death which in His Gospel He hath commanded us to make; and having also in remembrance His mighty Resurrection and glorious Ascension, and looking for His Coming again in glory, we render unto Thee most high praise and hearty thanks for all the benefits procured unto us by the same. And we most humbly beseech Thee, O Lord, to look with favour upon this our offering unto Thee of the one and all-sufficient Sacrifice of Thy beloved Son, and vouchsafe unto us remission of all our sins; and grant that all we, who shall be partakers of this holy Communion, may worthily receive the same, and be fulfilled with Thy grace and heavenly benediction and preserved both in body and soul unto everlasting life; through the same Thy Son Jesus Christ our Lord, by Whom, and with Whom, in the unity of the Holy Ghost, all honour and glory be unto Thee, O Father Almighty, world without end.

And the Priest and people together shall say,
AMEN.

Then shall the Priest say,
Let us pray.
As our Saviour Christ hath commanded and taught us, we are bold to say:

And the Priest and people together shall then say the Lord's Prayer, as followeth.
OUR Father, which art in heaven, hallowed be Thy Name. Thy kingdom come. Thy will be done, in earth as it is in heaven. Give us this day our daily bread. And forgive us our trespasses, As we forgive them that trespass against us. And lead us not into temptation, But deliver us from evil. For Thine is the kingdom, the power, and the glory, For ever and ever. Amen.

Then shall silence be kept for a space.

Then shall the Priest reverently break the consecrated Bread.

And as the Priest breaketh the consecrated Bread, he shall say this Prayer following.
O LORD Jesu Christ, Who didst say to Thine Apostles, Peace I leave with you, my peace I give unto you: Regard not our sins, but the faith of Thy Church; and grant unto it that peace and unity which is agreeable to Thy will; Who livest and reignest with the Father and the Holy Ghost, ever one God, world without end. *Amen.*

THE PREPARATION FOR HOLY COMMUNION

Then shall the Priest say,
CHRIST our Passover is sacrificed for us, therefore let us keep the feast: Not with the old leaven, neither with the leaven of malice and wickedness; but with the unleavened bread of sincerity and truth.

Then shall the Priest, together with all them that shall receive the Holy Communion,
humbly say this Prayer of humble access to the Lord's Table, as followeth.

WE do not presume to come to this Thy Table, O merciful Lord, Trusting in our own righteousness, But in Thy manifold and great mercies. We are not worthy So much as to gather up the crumbs under Thy Table. But Thou art the same Lord, Whose property is always to have mercy: Grant us therefore, gracious Lord, So to eat the Flesh of Thy dear Son Jesus Christ, And to drink His Blood, That our sinful bodies may be made clean by His Body, And our souls washed through His most precious Blood, And that we may evermore dwell in Him, And He in us. Amen.

Then shall be said,
O LAMB of God, that takest away the sins of the world,
have mercy upon us.
O Lamb of God, that takest away the sins of the world,
have mercy upon us.
O Lamb of God, that takest away the sins of the world,
grant us Thy peace.

THE MINISTRATION OF HOLY COMMUNION

And when the Priest himself hath received the Holy Communion, before he shall proceed to deliver the same to anyone, he shall first take the consecrated Bread and Wine into his hands, and turning himself unto the people, and shewing them the Holy Sacrament, he shall invite them to partake of the Lord's Supper, saying,

BEHOLD, the Lamb of God; behold Him that taketh away the sin of the world: Blessed are they which are called unto the marriage supper of the Lamb.

And all they that shall receive the Holy Communion shall say,

LORD, I am not worthy that Thou shouldest come under my roof; but speak the word only, and my soul shall be healed.

Then shall the faithful come forward to receive the Holy Communion.
And when the Priest delivereth the consecrated Bread to any one, he shall say,

✠ THE Body of our Lord Jesus Christ, which was given for thee, preserve thy body and soul unto everlasting life: Take and eat this in remembrance that Christ died for thee, and feed on Him in thy heart by faith with thanksgiving.

And every one that receiveth the consecrated Bread shall answer, saying,
AMEN.

And the Minister that delivereth the Cup to any one shall say,

✠ THE Blood of our Lord Jesus Christ, which was shed for thee, preserve thy body and soul unto everlasting life: Drink this in remembrance that Christ's Blood was shed for thee, and be thankful.

And every one that receiveth the Cup shall answer, saying,
AMEN.

And here it is also ordered that in the ministering of Holy Communion, the Priest shall place the consecrated Bread either directly into the mouth of each Communicant, or else into his right hand; and the Minister shall not at any time release his hold of the Chalice, but the faithful shall only touch the Chalice with their hands, and guide the same to their mouths. When all have communicated, the Priest shall then return to the Lord's Table, and reverently place upon it whatever remaineth of the Blessed Sacrament of the Body and Blood of Christ covering the same with a fair linen cloth.

SHORTER EUCHARIST

THE THANKSGIVING AFTER HOLY COMMUNION

Then shall the Priest turn to the people, and say,
THE Lord be with you.
Answer. And with thy spirit.

Priest. Let us pray.

Then shall the Priest turn again to face the Altar, and say,
ALMIGHTY and everliving God, we most heartily thank Thee, for that Thou dost vouchsafe to feed us, who have duly received these Holy Mysteries, with the spiritual food of the most precious Body and Blood of Thy Son our Saviour Jesus Christ; and dost assure us thereby of Thy favour and goodness towards us; and that we are very members incorporate in the mystical Body of Thy Son, which is the blessed company of all faithful people; and are also heirs through hope of Thy everlasting kingdom, by the Merits of His most precious Death and Passion. And we most humbly beseech Thee, O heavenly Father, so to assist us with Thy grace, that we may continue in that holy fellowship, and do all such good works as Thou hast prepared for us to walk in; through Jesus Christ our Lord, to Whom, with Thee and the Holy Ghost, be all honour and glory, world without end. *Amen.*

Then the Priest may say this Post-Communion Collect following.
HASTEN, O God, the time when Thou shalt send from Thy right hand Him Whom Thou wilt send; at Whose appearing the Saints departed shall be raised, and we which are alive and remain shall be caught up to meet Him, and so shall we ever be with our Lord. Keep us, we beseech Thee, O Father, unto that day; and grant that at His coming, we may, as One Body, be presented with exceeding joy before the Presence of His glory, holy and unspotted, prepared as a Bride adorned for her Husband; through the same Thy Son Jesus Christ our Lord. *Amen.*

And here Gloria in Excelsis *shall be said or sung,*
or else the proper Dismissal Anthem appointed for use.

THE BLESSING.
Then the Priest shall let them depart with this Blessing.
THE peace of God, which passeth all understanding, keep your hearts and minds in the knowledge and love of God, and of His Son Jesus Christ our Lord: And the blessing of God Almighty, ✠ the Father, the Son, and the Holy Ghost, be amongst you and remain with you always. *Amen.*

Then shall the Priest say,
THE Lord be with you.
Answer. And with thy spirit.
Priest. Let us depart in peace.
Answer. In the Name of the Lord.
Amen.

Here endeth the SHORTER FORM OF
THE ADMINISTRATION OF THE HOLY EUCHARIST.

THE ORDER OF MINISTRATION OF
HOLY COMMUNION

When the Communion is to be ministered to the people outside the Administration of the Holy Eucharist, this Order ensuing shall be used. In the absence of a Bishop or a Priest, a Deacon, or a Subdeacon or Lector authorised by the Ordinary for that purpose, may minister Communion from the Reserved Sacrament. And at all such times when the Minister is not a Bishop or Priest, the Absolution and the Blessing shall remain unsaid.

When a Bishop or a Priest is the Minister of the Sacrament, he shall be vested respectively in Rochet or Surplice with the stole; and likewise a Deacon shall be vested in Surplice with the Stole worn Deacon-wise. And when the Minister is not in holy Orders, he shall wear the Surplice only.

The Minister shall go to the Tabernacle or Aumbry wherein the Blessed Sacrament of the Body and Blood of our Lord Jesus Christ is reserved, and shall reverently remove the same therefrom and carry it to the Altar.

THE PREPARATION FOR HOLY COMMUNION

*And placing the Blessed Sacrament upon the Lord's Table, the Minister shall turn himself
to the people, and shall invite them to receive the Holy Communion, saying,*

YE that do truly and earnestly repent you of your sins, and are in love and charity with your neighbours, and intend to lead a new life, following the commandments of God, and walking from henceforth in His holy ways: Draw near with faith, and take this holy Sacrament to your comfort; and make your humble confession to Almighty God, meekly kneeling upon your knees.

*Then shall this general Confession be made by all that are minded to receive the Holy Communion,
both the Minister and people together, all humbly kneeling upon their knees, and saying,*

ALMIGHTY God, Father of our Lord Jesus Christ, Maker of all things, Judge of all men: We acknowledge and confess our manifold sins and wickedness, Which we from time to time most grievously have committed, By thought, word, and deed, Against Thy Divine Majesty, Provoking most justly Thy wrath and indignation against us. We do earnestly repent, And are heartily sorry for these our misdoings; The remembrance of them is grievous unto us; The burden of them is intolerable. Have mercy upon us; have mercy upon us, most merciful Father; For Thy Son our Lord Jesus Christ's sake, Forgive us all that is past; And grant that we may ever hereafter Serve and please Thee In newness of life, To the honour and glory of Thy Name; Through Jesus Christ our Lord. Amen.

*Then shall the Priest (or the Bishop, if he be present,) stand up,
and turning himself to the people, pronounce this Absolution following.*

ALMIGHTY God, our heavenly Father, Who of His great mercy hath promised forgiveness of sins to all them that with hearty repentance and true faith turn unto Him: Have mercy upon you; ✠ pardon and deliver you from all your sins; confirm and strengthen you in all goodness; and bring you to everlasting life; through Jesus Christ our Lord. *Amen.*

Or, if there be no Priest present, the Minister shall say,

MAY the Almighty and most merciful Lord God grant unto us pardon, ✠ absolution, and remission of all our sins; time for amendment of life, and the grace and comfort of His Holy Spirit; deliver us from all evil; preserve and strengthen us in all goodness; bring us all finally to everlasting life; through Jesus Christ our Lord. *Amen.*

HOLY COMMUNION

Hear what comfortable words our Saviour Christ saith
unto all that truly turn to Him.

COME unto me all that travail and are heavy laden, and I will refresh you. *Saint Matthew xi.*

So God loved the world, that He gave His only-begotten Son, to the end that all that believe in Him should not perish, but have everlasting life. *Saint John iii.*

Hear also what Saint Paul saith.
This is a true saying, and worthy of all men to be received, That Christ Jesus came into the world to save sinners. I *Timothy i.*

Hear also what Saint John saith.
If any man sin, we have an Advocate with the Father, Jesus Christ the righteous; and He is the propitiation for our sins. I *Saint John ii.*

Then shall the Minister say or sing,
Let us pray.

As our Saviour Christ hath commanded and taught us, we are bold to say:

And the Minister and people together shall then say or sing the Lord's Prayer, as followeth.
OUR Father, which art in heaven, hallowed be Thy Name. Thy kingdom come. Thy will be done, in earth as it is in heaven. Give us this day our daily bread. And forgive us our trespasses, As we forgive them that trespass against us. And lead us not into temptation, But deliver us from evil. For Thine is the kingdom, the power, and the glory, For ever and ever. Amen.

And the holy Sacrament being made ready for distribution,
the Minister shall then say or sing,
CHRIST our Passover is sacrificed for us, therefore let us keep the feast: Not with the old leaven, neither with the leaven of malice and wickedness; but with the unleavened bread of sincerity and truth.

Then shall the Minister, together with all them that shall receive the Holy Communion,
humbly say this Prayer of humble access to the Lord's Table, as followeth.
WE do not presume to come to this Thy Table, O merciful Lord, Trusting in our own righteousness, But in Thy manifold and great mercies. We are not worthy So much as to gather up the crumbs under Thy Table. But Thou art the same Lord, Whose property is always to have mercy: Grant us therefore, gracious Lord, So to eat the Flesh of Thy dear Son Jesus Christ, And to drink His Blood, That our sinful bodies may be made clean by His Body, And our souls washed through His most precious Blood, And that we may evermore dwell in Him, And He in us. Amen.

Then shall be said or sung,
O LAMB of God, that takest away the sins of the world,
have mercy upon us.
O Lamb of God, that takest away the sins of the world,
have mercy upon us.
O Lamb of God, that takest away the sins of the world,
grant us Thy peace.

Then shall the Minister first receive the Holy Communion in both kinds himself; and then he shall proceed to deliver the same to the Faithful, all meekly and devoutly kneeling upon their knees; but if anyone cannot receive the Holy Communion kneeling, either due to age or infirmity, he may stand to receive the Blessed Sacrament.

THE MINISTRATION OF HOLY COMMUNION

And when the Minister himself hath received the Holy Communion, before he shall proceed to deliver the same to anyone, he shall first take the consecrated Bread and Wine into his hands, and turning himself unto the people, and shewing them the Holy Sacrament, he shall invite them to partake of the Lord's Supper, saying,

BEHOLD, the Lamb of God; behold Him that taketh away the sin of the world: Blessed are they which are called unto the marriage supper of the Lamb.

And all they that shall receive the Holy Communion shall say,

Lord, I am not worthy that Thou shouldest come under my roof; but speak the word only, and my soul shall be healed.

Then shall the faithful come forward to receive the Holy Communion.

And when the Minister delivereth the consecrated Bread to any one, he shall say,

✠ THE Body of our Lord Jesus Christ, which was given for thee, preserve thy body and soul unto everlasting life: Take and eat this in remembrance that Christ died for thee, and feed on Him in thy heart by faith with thanksgiving.

And every one that receiveth the consecrated Bread shall answer, saying,
AMEN.

And the Minister that delivereth the Cup to any one shall say,

✠ THE Blood of our Lord Jesus Christ, which was shed for thee, preserve thy body and soul unto everlasting life: Drink this in remembrance that Christ's Blood was shed for thee, and be thankful.

And every one that receiveth the Cup shall answer, saying,
AMEN.

And it is hereby ordered that, except for reasons of sickness or infirmity, or some other just cause, the Communion of the Body and Blood of our Lord and Saviour Jesus Christ shall be received by all the Communicants humbly and reverently kneeling at the Communion rail, or in some other convenient place appointed by the Ordinary.

When all have communicated, the Minister shall return to the Lord's Table, and reverently place upon it whatever remaineth of the Blessed Sacrament of the Body and Blood of Christ covering the same with a fair linen cloth. And if any of the consecrated Bread or Wine remain, the same he shall reverently place inside the Tabernacle or Aumbry appointed for that use, and the door thereof shall be securely locked, and covered with a white cloth to indicate the Real Presence of our Lord Jesus Christ in the Blessed Sacrament of the Altar therein reserved.

THE THANKSGIVING AFTER HOLY COMMUNION

The Ministration of Holy Communion ended, the Minister
shall turn himself to face the people, and shall say,
Let us pray.

And turning himself again to face the Lord's Table, the Minister shall say this Prayer following.

ALMIGHTY and everliving God, we most heartily thank Thee, for that Thou dost vouchsafe to feed us, who have duly received these Holy Mysteries, with the spiritual food of the most precious Body and Blood of Thy Son our Saviour Jesus Christ; and dost assure us thereby of Thy favour and goodness towards us; and that we are very members incorporate in the mystical Body of Thy Son, which is the blessed company of all faithful people; and are also heirs through hope of Thy everlasting kingdom, by the Merits of His most precious Death and Passion. And we most humbly beseech Thee, O heavenly Father, so to assist us with Thy grace, that we may continue in that holy fellowship, and do all such good works as Thou hast prepared for us to walk in; through Jesus Christ our Lord, to Whom, with Thee and the Holy Ghost, be all honour and glory, world without end. *Amen.*

And here may follow any Post-Communion Collect appointed to be used.

And here Gloria in Excelsis *or the Dismissal Anthem may be said or sung.*

THE BLESSING.
Then if the Minister be a Priest, he shall let them depart with this Blessing.
THE peace of God, which passeth all understanding, keep your hearts and minds in the knowledge and love of God, and of His Son Jesus Christ our Lord: And the blessing of God Almighty, ✠ the Father, the Son, and the Holy Ghost, be amongst you and remain with you always. *Amen.*

THE DISMISSAL.
Then shall the Minister say,
LET us depart in peace.
Answer. In the Name of the Lord.
Amen.

A COLLECT AFTER COMMUNION.
This Collect following may be used for a Post-Communion Collect when no other Collect is appointed to be said, or after the Collect after Communion, at the discretion of the Minister.
O GRACIOUS Lord God and heavenly Father, Whose only-begotten Son Jesus Christ is truly present in the Blessed Sacrament of the Eucharist: Grant unto us, that when we look upon the outward forms of the consecrated Bread and Wine we may perceive inwardly our Saviour born of the Virgin Mary, who truly suffered, was pierced by the lance, crucified on the Cross, and buried in the sepulchre; and with faith in the truth of His Resurrection, to receive in the holy Supper of His Body and Blood a foretaste of the heavenly Banquet, and be sustained thereby through life, and given grace to persevere in the hour of our death; through the same Thy Son Jesus Christ our Lord. *Amen.*

*Here endeth the ORDER OF THE
MINISTRATION OF HOLY COMMUNION.*

THE ORDER FOR
MINISTRY TO THE SICK
THE VISITATION OF THE SICK

When any Person is sick, notice thereof shall be given to the Parish Priest; and either he,
or some other Priest sent by him, coming into the sick Person's house, shall say,
PEACE be to this house, and to all that dwell in it.

And when he cometh into the sick Person's presence, he shall say,
REMEMBER not, Lord, our iniquities, nor the iniquities of our forefathers: Spare us, good Lord, spare Thy people, whom Thou hast redeemed with Thy most precious Blood, and be not angry with us forever.

And all shall answer,
Spare us, good Lord.

Then shall the Priest say,
Let us pray.

Lord, have mercy upon us.
Christ, have mercy upon us.
Lord, have mercy upon us.

Then shall the Priest and those present say together,
OUR Father, which art in heaven, hallowed be thy Name. Thy kingdom come. Thy will be done, on earth as it is in heaven. Give us this day our daily bread. And forgive us our trespasses, As we forgive them that trespass against us. And lead us not into temptation, But deliver us from evil. Amen.

Priest. O Lord, save this Thy *servant N.*;
  Answer. Who putteth *his* trust in Thee.
Priest. Send *him* help from Thy holy place;
  Answer. And evermore mightily defend *him.*
Priest. Let the enemy have no advantage of *him*;
  Answer. Nor the wicked approach to hurt *him.*
Priest. Be unto *him* a strong tower;
  Answer. From the face of the enemy.
Priest. O Lord, hear our prayer;
  Answer. And let our cry come unto Thee.

Priest.

O LORD, look down from heaven, we beseech Thee, and behold, visit, and relieve this Thy *servant*; look upon *him* with the eyes of Thy mercy; give *him* comfort and sure confidence in Thee; defend and protect *him* from every danger, craft, and snare of the enemy; and keep *him* in perpetual peace and safety; through Jesus Christ our Lord. *Amen.*

HEAR us, we pray Thee, Almighty and most merciful God and Saviour; and vouchsafe to extend Thine accustomed goodness to this Thy *servant* who is grieved *at this time* with sickness. Sanctify, we beseech Thee, this Thy fatherly correction to *him*; that the sense of *his* weakness may add strength to *his* faith, and seriousness to *his* repentance: And grant that, if it shall be Thy good pleasure to restore *him* to *his* former health, *he* may lead the remainder of *his* life in Thy fear, and to Thy glory; or else, give *him* grace so to take Thy visitation, that, after this painful life ended, *he* may dwell with Thee in life everlasting; through Jesus Christ our Lord. *Amen.*

Then shall the Minister exhort the sick Person after this form,
or some other similar words.

DEARLY beloved, know this, that Almighty God is the Lord of life and death, and of all things to them pertaining, as youth, strength, and health, age, weakness, and sickness. Wherefore, whatsoever your sickness is, know you certainly, that it is God's visitation. And for what cause soever this sickness is sent unto you; whether it be to try your patience for the example of others, and that your faith may be found in the day of the Lord laudable, glorious, and honourable, to the increase of glory and endless felicity; or else it be sent unto you to correct and amend in you whatsoever doth offend the eyes of your heavenly Father; know you certainly, that if you truly repent you of your sins, and bear your sickness patiently, trusting in God's mercy, for His dear Son Jesus Christ's sake, and render unto Him humble thanks for His fatherly visitation, submitting yourself wholly unto His will, it shall turn to your profit, and help you forward in the right way that leadeth unto everlasting life.

If the Person visited be very sick, then the Priest may end his exhortation in this place;
or else he may proceed with these words following, or some such similar words.

TAKE therefore in good part the chastisement of the Lord: For (as Saint Paul saith in the twelfth Chapter to the Hebrews) whom the Lord loveth He chasteneth, and scourgeth every son whom He receiveth. If ye endure chastening, God dealeth with you as with sons; for what son is he whom the father chasteneth not? But if ye be without chastisement, whereof all are partakers, then are ye bastards, and not sons. Furthermore, we have had fathers of our flesh, which corrected us, and we gave them reverence: shall we not much rather be in subjection unto the Father of spirits, and live? For they verily for a few days chastened us after their own pleasure; but He for our profit, that we might be partakers of His holiness.

These words, good brother, are written in Holy Scripture for our comfort and instruction; that we should patiently, and with thanksgiving, bear our heavenly Father's correction, whensoever by any manner of adversity it shall please His gracious goodness to visit us. And there should be no greater comfort to Christian persons, than to be made like unto Christ, by suffering patiently adversities, troubles, and sicknesses. For He Himself went not up to joy, but first He suffered pain; He entered not into His glory before He was crucified. So truly our way to eternal joy is to suffer here with Christ; and our door to enter into eternal life is gladly to die with Christ; that we may rise again from death, and dwell with him in everlasting life.

Now therefore, taking your sickness, which is thus profitable for you, patiently, I exhort you, in the Name of God, to remember the profession which you made unto God in your Baptism. And forasmuch as after this life there is an account to be given unto the righteous Judge, by Whom all must be judged, without respect of persons, I require you to examine yourself and your estate, both toward God and man; so that, accusing and condemning yourself for your own faults, you may find mercy at our heavenly Father's hand for Christ's sake, and not be accused and condemned in that fearful judgement. Therefore I shall rehearse to you the Articles of our Faith, that you may know whether you do believe as a Christian man should, or no.

THE MINISTRY TO THE SICK

Here the Priest shall rehearse the Articles of the Faith, saying thus to the sick Person,

DOST thou believe in God the Father Almighty, Maker of heaven and earth? And in Jesus Christ His only-begotten Son our Lord? And that He was conceived by the Holy Ghost, born of the Virgin Mary; that He suffered under Pontius Pilate, was crucified, dead, and buried; that He went down into hell, and also did rise again the third day; that He ascended into heaven, and there sitteth at the right hand of God the Father Almighty; and from thence shall come again at the end of the world, to judge the quick and the dead? And dost thou believe in the Holy Ghost; the holy Catholic Church; the Communion of Saints; the Remission of sins; the Resurrection of the body; and everlasting Life after death?

And the sick Person shall answer,

All this I steadfastly believe.

Then shall the Priest examine whether he repent him truly of his sins, and be in charity with all the world; exhorting him to forgive, from the bottom of his heart, all persons that have offended him; and if he hath offended any other, to ask them forgiveness; and where he hath done injury or wrong to any man, that he make amends to the uttermost of his power. And if he have not before disposed of his goods, let him then be admonished to make his Will, and to declare his debts, what he oweth, and what is owing unto him; for the better discharging of his conscience, and the quietness of his Executors. But men should often be put in remembrance to take order for the settling of their temporal estates, whilst they are in health. And when so doing, the Priest should not omit earnestly to move such sick persons as are of ability to be liberal to the poor.

A FORM OF CONFESSION AND ABSOLUTION

The sick Person may then make a general confession of his sins by saying the Confession following, after which the Priest shall say the Absolution. In times of need, the Priest may say the Confession in the name of the sick Person, who shall say at the end, Amen.

O HEAVENLY Father, I confess unto Thee that I have sinned grievously in thought, word, and deed, against Thy Divine Majesty, and have done that which is evil in Thy sight. And I humbly pray Thee to forgive me all my sins; and to give me grace to repent me truly of all my sins, always to resist temptation, and to do Thy holy will; for Jesus Christ's sake. *Amen.*

Then shall the Priest pronounce this Absolution, saying,

ALMIGHTY God, our heavenly Father, have mercy upon thee, and forgive thee all thy sins, deliver thee from all evil, preserve and strengthen thee in all goodness, and bring thee at the last to everlasting life; through Jesus Christ our Lord. *Amen.*

Or, if the sick Person feel his Conscience troubled with any grave or weighty matter,
he shall be moved to make a special confession of his sins according to the Form following.

The sick Person having first asked for a blessing, the Priest shall bless him, saying,

MAY Almighty God bless thee, and have mercy upon thee. May the Lord be in thy heart, and on thy lips, that thou mayest truly and humbly confess thy sins unto Him, ✠ In the Name of the Father, and of the Son, and of the Holy Ghost. *Amen.*

Then the sick Person shall say,

I CONFESS to Almighty God, that I have sinned against Him in thought, word, and deed, through my own fault. And especially I accuse myself . . . and I pray to God to forgive me all my sins for the sake of Jesus Christ our Saviour. Amen

O MOST merciful God, Who, according to the multitude of Thy mercies, dost so put away the sins of those who truly repent, that Thou rememberest them no more: Look in mercy upon this Thy *servant*, who most earnestly desireth pardon and forgiveness. Renew in *him*, most loving Father, whatsoever hath been decayed by the fraud and malice of the devil, or by *his* own carnal will and frailness; preserve and continue this sick member in the unity of the Catholic Church; consider *his* contrition, accept *his* tears, assuage *his* pain, as shall seem to Thee best and most expedient for *him*. And forasmuch as *he* putteth *his* full trust only in Thy mercy, impute not unto *him his* former sins, but strengthen *him* with Thy blessed Spirit; and, when Thou art pleased to take *him* hence, take *him* into Thine everlasting favour; through the Merits of Thy most dearly beloved Son Jesus Christ our Lord. *Amen.*

After which the Priest shall proceed to absolve the sick Person
(if he humbly and heartily desire it) after this sort.

OUR Lord Jesus Christ, Who hath left power to His Church to absolve all sinners who truly repent and believe in Him, of His great mercy forgive thee thine offences. And by His authority committed to me, I absolve thee from all thy sins; ✠ In the Name of the Father, and of the Son, and of the Holy Ghost. Amen.

Then shall the Priest bless the sick Person, saying

MAY the blessed Passion of our Lord Jesus Christ, and His infinite Merits, supply all that is wanting in thy confession; and be also unto thee for the remission of sins, the increase of grace, and the reward of everlasting life: And the blessing of God Almighty, ✠ the Father, the Son, and the Holy Ghost, rest upon thee, and remain with thee, now and for evermore. *Amen.*

Then shall the Priest say this Psalm following,

PSALM 71. *In te, Domine, speravi.*

IN Thee, O Lord, have I put my trust: let me never be put to confusion / but rid me, and deliver me in Thy righteousness; incline Thine ear unto me, and save me. Be Thou my strong-hold, whereunto I may alway resort, / Thou hast promised to help me; for Thou art my House of defence, and my Castle. Deliver me, O my God, out of the hand of the ungodly, / out of the hand of the unrighteous and cruel man. For Thou, O Lord God, art the thing that I long for; / Thou art my Hope, even from my youth. Through Thee have I been holden up ever since I was born; / Thou art He that took me out of my mother's womb; my praise shall alway be of Thee. I am become as it were a monster unto many; / but my sure trust is in Thee. O let my mouth be filled with Thy praise, / that I may sing of Thy glory and honour all the day long. Cast me not away in the time of age; / forsake me not when my strength faileth me. For mine enemies speak against me, and they that lay wait for my soul take their counsel together, saying, / God hath forsaken him, persecute him, and take him; for there is none to deliver him. Go not far from me, O God; / my God, haste Thee to help me. Let them be confounded and perish that are against my soul; / let them be covered with shame and dishonour that seek to do me evil. As for me, I will patiently abide always, / and will praise Thee more and more. My mouth shall daily speak of Thy righteousness and salvation, / for I know no end thereof. I will go forth in the strength of the Lord God, / and will make mention of Thy righteousness only. Thou, O God, hast taught me from my youth up until now; / therefore will I tell of Thy wondrous works. Forsake me not, O God, in mine old age, when I am grey-headed; / until I have shewed Thy strength unto this generation, and

Thy power to all them that are yet for to come. Thy righteousness, O God, is very high, and great things are they that Thou hast done; / O God, who is like unto Thee?

GLORY be to the Father, and to the Son, / and to the Holy Ghost;

As it was in the beginning, is now, and ever shall be, / world without end. Amen.

And the Priest shall add this, saying,

O SAVIOUR of the world, Who by Thy Cross and precious Blood hast redeemed us;

Answer. Save us, and help us, we humbly beseech Thee, O Lord.

Then shall the Priest say to the sick Person,

THE Almighty Lord, Who is a most strong Tower to all them that put their trust in Him, to Whom all things in heaven, in earth, and under the earth, do bow and obey, be now and evermore thy defence; and make thee know and feel, that there is none other Name under heaven given to man, in Whom, and through Whom, thou mayest receive health and salvation, but only the Name of our Lord Jesus Christ. *Amen.*

*Then may follow any of these Prayers hereafter following,
at the discretion of the Minister.*

PRAYERS FOR THE SICK

A Prayer for a sick Child.

ALMIGHTY God, and merciful Father, to Whom alone belong the issues of life and death: Look down from heaven, we humbly beseech Thee, with the eyes of mercy upon *this child* now lying upon the bed of sickness: Visit *him,* O Lord, with Thy salvation; deliver *him* in Thy good appointed time from *his* bodily pain, and save *his* soul for Thy mercies' sake: and grant that, if it shall be Thy pleasure to prolong *his* days here on earth, *he* may live to Thee, and be an instrument of Thy glory, by serving Thee faithfully, and doing good in *his* generation; or else receive *him* into those heavenly habitations, where the souls of them that sleep in the Lord Jesus enjoy perpetual rest and felicity. Grant this, O Lord, for Thy tender mercies' sake, in the blessed Name of the same Thy Son our Lord Jesus Christ, Who liveth and reigneth with Thee and the Holy Ghost, ever one God, world without end. *Amen.*

A Prayer for a sick person, when there appeareth small hope of recovery.

FATHER of all mercies, and God of all comfort, our only Help in time of need: We fly unto Thee for succour on behalf of this Thy *servant,* here lying under Thy hand in great weakness of body. Look graciously upon *him,* O Lord; and the more the outward man decayeth, strengthen *him,* we beseech Thee, so much the more continually with Thy grace and Holy Spirit in the inner man. Give *him* unfeigned repentance for all the errors of *his* life past, and steadfast faith in Thy Son Jesus Christ; that *his* sins may be done away by Thy mercy, and *his* pardon sealed in heaven, before *he* go from hence, and be no more seen. We know, O Lord, that there is no work impossible with Thee; and that, if Thou wilt, Thou canst even yet raise *him* up, and grant *him* a longer continuance amongst us: Yet, forasmuch as in all appearance the time of *his* dissolution draweth near, so fit and prepare *him,* we beseech Thee, against the hour of death, that after *his* departure hence in peace, and in Thy favour, *his* soul may be received into Thine everlasting kingdom, through the Merits and Mediation of Jesus Christ, Thine only Son, our Lord and Saviour. *Amen.*

THE MINISTRY TO THE SICK

A Commendatory Prayer for a sick person at the point of departure.

ALMIGHTY God, with Whom do live the spirits of just men made perfect, after they are delivered from their earthly prisons, and just punishments for sin: We humbly commend the soul of this Thy *servant*, our dear *brother*, into Thy hands, as into the hands of a faithful Creator, and most merciful Saviour; humbly beseeching Thee, that it may be precious in Thy sight. Wash *him*, we pray Thee, in the Blood of that Immaculate Lamb that was slain to take away the sins of the world; that whatsoever defilements *he* may have contracted in the midst of this miserable and wicked world, through the lusts of the flesh, or the wiles of Satan, being purged and done away, *he* may be presented pure and without spot before Thee. And teach us who survive, in this and other like daily spectacles of mortality, to see how frail and uncertain our own condition is; and so to number our days, that we may seriously apply our hearts to that holy and heavenly wisdom, whilst we live here, which may in the end bring us to life everlasting, through the Merits of Jesus Christ Thine only Son our Lord. *Amen.*

A Prayer for persons troubled in mind or in conscience.

BLESSED Lord, the Father of all mercies, and the God of all comforts: We beseech Thee, took down in pity and compassion upon this Thine afflicted *servant*. Thou writest bitter things against *him*, and makest *him* to possess *his* former iniquities; Thy wrath lieth hard upon *him*, and *his* soul is full of trouble: But, O merciful God, Who hast written Thy holy Word for our learning, that we, through patience and comfort of Thy Holy Scriptures, might have hope; give *him* a right understanding of *himself*, and of Thy threats and promises; that *he* may neither cast away *his* confidence in Thee, nor place it anywhere but in Thee. Give *him* strength against all *his* temptations, and heal all *his* distempers. Break not the bruised reed, nor quench the smoking flax. Shut not up Thy tender mercies in displeasure; but make *him* to hear of joy and gladness, that the bones which Thou hast broken may rejoice. Deliver *him* from fear of the enemy; and lift up the light of Thy countenance upon *him*, and give *him* peace, through the Merits and Mediation of Jesus Christ our Lord. *Amen.*

And before the Priest depart from the house
of the sick Person, he shall say,

NOW unto God's gracious mercy and protection we commit thee. The Lord bless thee, and keep thee. The Lord make His face to shine upon thee, and be gracious unto thee. The Lord lift up His countenance upon thee, and give thee peace, both now and evermore. And the blessing of God Almighty, ✠ the Father, the Son, and the Holy Ghost, be upon you, and remain with you always. *Amen.*

THE COMMUNION OF THE SICK

Forasmuch as all mortal men be subject to many sudden perils, diseases, and sicknesses, and ever uncertain what time they shall depart out of this life; therefore, to the intent they may always be in a readiness to die, whensoever it shall please Almighty God to call them, the Priests shall diligently from time to time (but especially in the time of pestilence, or other infectious sickness) exhort their Parishioners to the often receiving of the Holy Communion of the Body and Blood of our Saviour Christ, when it shall be publicly ministered in the Church; that so doing, they may, in case of sudden visitation, have the less cause to be disquieted for lack of the same. But if the sick Person be not able to come to the Church, and yet is desirous to receive the Communion in his house; then he must give timely notice to the Priest, signifying also how many there are to communicate with him, and having a convenient place in the sick Person's house, with all things necessary so prepared, that the Priest may reverently minister, he shall there celebrate the Holy Eucharist, beginning with the Collect for Purity, and with the Collect, Epistle, and Gospel, hereafter following.

THE MINISTRY TO THE SICK

THE COLLECT.

O LORD and heavenly Father, Who dost relieve those who suffer in soul and body: Stretch forth Thy hand, we beseech Thee, to heal this Thy *servant N.*, and to ease *his* pain; look upon *him* with the eyes of Thy mercy; give *him* comfort and sure confidence in Thee; defend *him* in all danger; and keep *him* in peace; and grant that by Thy mercy, *he* may be restored to health of body and mind, and shew forth *his* thankfulness in love to Thee and service to *his* fellow men; through Jesus Christ our Lord. *Amen.*

THE EPISTLE. II *Corinthians* 1. 3-4.

BLESSED be God, even the Father of our Lord Jesus Christ, the Father of mercies, and the God of all comfort; Who comforteth us in all our tribulation, that we may be able to comfort them which are in any trouble, by the comfort wherewith we ourselves are comforted of God. For as the sufferings of Christ abound unto us, even so our comfort also aboundeth through Christ.

THE GOSPEL. *Saint John* 10. 14-15 & 27-28.

JESUS said, I am the good Shepherd; and I know mine own, and mine own know me, even as the Father knoweth me, and I know the Father; and I lay down my life for the sheep. My sheep hear my voice, and I know them, and they follow me: and I give unto them eternal life; and they shall never perish, and no one shall pluck them out of my hand.

After which the Priest shall proceed according to the Form prescribed in
he celebration of the Holy Eucharist, beginning at these words, Ye that do truly, &c.

If the sick Person be very weak, and necessity so require, it shall suffice to use for this Office, the Confession, the Absolution, the Prayer of Consecration, the Prayer of Humble Access to the Lord's Table, the Form of Delivery of the Sacrament, the Lord's Prayer, and the Blessing. But in case of extreme necessity the Priest may begin with the Prayer of Consecration, and immediately after the delivery of the holy Sacrament to the sick Person, and ending with the Blessing. But and if necessity so require, the Holy Communion may be brought by the Priest to the sick Person from the Sacrament reserved in the Church; in which case the Order shall remain the same save that the Prayer of Consecration shall not be said.

The Form of delivery of the Blessed Sacrament
to those who are in danger of death shall be as followeth.

RECEIVE the sacred Viaticum of the *Body* of our Lord Jesus Christ. May the Lord Jesus Christ, Whom thou hast received, preserve thee, protect thee on thy way, and bring thee to everlasting life. *Amen.*

At the time of the distribution of the Communion, the Priest shall first receive the Sacrament himself and afterward minister unto them that are to communicate with the sick; and last of all to the sick Person. But if any person, either by reason of extremity of sickness, or for want of warning in due time to the Priest, or by reason of extremity of illness, or any other just impediment, do not receive the Sacrament of Christ's Body and Blood, the Priest shall instruct him, that if he do truly repent him of his sins, and steadfastly believe that Jesus Christ both suffered death upon the Cross for him, and shed His Blood for his redemption, earnestly remembering the benefits he hath thereby, and giving Him hearty thanks therefor, and earnestly desiring to receive Christ in Holy Communion, he doth eat and drink the Body and Blood of our Saviour Christ profitably to his Soul's health, although he do not receive the Blessed Sacrament with his mouth. When the sick Person is visited, and receiveth the Holy Communion all at one time, then the Priest, for more expedition, shall cut off the form of the Visitation at Psalm 71; and leaving that Psalm unsaid, he shall go straight to the celebration of the Holy Eucharist. In the time of the plague, sweat, or such other like contagious times of sickness or diseases, when none of the Parish or his neighbours can be gotten to communicate with the sick man, for fear of the infection, the Priest only may communicate with him.

The Form for the Laying on of Hands,
and Anointing of the Sick
which is called
Holy Unction

If after having confessed his sins and having received Absolution, and having duly received the Holy Communion, the sick Person desireth the Laying on of hands and Anointing with blessed Oil, the Priest shall prepare him to receive that holy Sacrament, reading to him these passages of Scripture following. And when the Sacrament of Unction, it is desireable that there be more than one Priest present to join with the Minister in the administration thereof. And in cases of necessity, or for just cause, it shall suffice to anoint the sick Person upon his forehead only.

The Laying on of Hands upon the Sick

The Priest shall say,
BRETHREN, let us hear the words of Holy Scripture.

Saint Matthew 9. 27-31.

AND when Jesus departed thence, two blind men followed Him, crying, and saying, Thou Son of David, have mercy on us. And when He was come into the house, the blind men came to Him; and Jesus saith unto them, Believe ye that I am able to do this? They said unto Him, Yea, Lord. Then touched He their eyes, saying, According to your faith be it unto you. And their eyes were opened.

Saint Luke 4. 40.

NOW when the sun was setting, all they that had any sick with divers diseases brought them unto Him; and He laid His hands on every one of them, and healed them.

Saint Mark 16. 14-18.

AFTERWARD He appeared unto the eleven as they sat at meat, and upbraided them with their unbelief and hardness of heart, because they believed not them which had seen Him after He was risen. And He said unto them, Go ye into all the world, and preach the Gospel to every creature. He that believeth and is baptised shall be saved; but he that believeth not shall be damned. And these signs shall follow them that believe: In my Name they shall cast out devils; they shall speak with new tongues; they shall take up serpents; and if they drink any deadly thing, it shall not hurt them; they shall lay hands on the sick, and they shall recover.

Then shall the Priest say,
THE Lord be with you.
Answer. And with thy spirit.

Priest. Let us pray.

Then shall the Priest say,
O ALMIGHTY God, Whose blessed Son did lay His hands upon the sick and heal them; and did charge His holy Apostles to follow His example, and to do the same: Grant, we beseech Thee, to this Thy *servant* upon whom we now lay our hands in His Name, refreshment of soul and spirit, and, according to Thy gracious will, restoration to health of body and mind; through the same Thy Son Jesus Christ our Lord. *Amen.*

THE MINISTRY TO THE SICK

Then shall the Priest lay his hands upon the head of the sick Person, saying,

N. I LAY my hands upon thee In the Name of our only Lord and Saviour Jesus Christ, and beseech Him humbly that, through His Merits and precious Death, He will grant unto thee forgiveness of all thy sins, relief from all thy pains, and full recovery of health in mind and body; to the glory of His holy Name. *Amen.*

Then shall one of the Priests read these following two passages from the Scriptures.

THE ANOINTING OF THE SICK

The Priest shall say,

BRETHREN, let us once again hear the words of Holy Scripture.

Saint Mark 6. 7, 12, 13.

AND He called unto Him the twelve, and began to send them forth by two and two; and gave them power over unclean spirits. And they went out, and preached that men should repent. And they cast out many devils, and anointed with oil many that were sick, and healed them.

Saint James 5. 14-16.

IS any sick among you? let him call for the priests of the Church; and let them pray over him, anointing him with oil in the Name of the Lord: and the prayer of faith shall save the sick, and the Lord shall raise him up; and if he have committed sins, they shall be forgiven him. Confess your faults one to another, and pray one for another, that ye may be healed. The effectual fervent prayer of a righteous man availeth much.

If the Oil be not already blessed by the Bishop,
the following Prayer of Consecration shall be said over the Oil by the Priest.

O ALMIGHTY Lord and everlasting God, Who hast taught us in Thy holy Word to pray over them that are sick, and to anoint them with Oil in the Name of our Lord and Saviour Jesus Christ, that they may recover their bodily strength and health: Sanctify, we beseech Thee, this Thy creature of Oil; and grant that all that shall be anointed therewith may receive healing and strengthening of body and mind, soul and spirit; through the same Thy Son Jesus Christ our Lord. *Amen.*

Then shall the Priest say,
OUR help standeth in the Name of the Lord;
Answer. Who hath made heaven and earth.
Priest. O Lord, hear our prayer;
Answer. And let our cry come unto Thee.

Then shall the Priest say,

O ALMIGHTY God, Who art the Giver of life and health, and the Aid of them that seek Thee: We call upon Thee for Thy help and goodness mercifully to be shewn upon this Thy *servant*, that being healed of all *his* infirmities of body, mind, and spirit, *he* may give thanks to Thee in Thy holy Church; through Jesus Christ our Lord. *Amen.*

Then, with the blessed Oil on his thumb, the Priest shall anoint the sick Person upon his forehead (and also upon his eyes, ears, nose, and mouth, his hands, breast, and feet, at his discretion, making the sign of the Cross thereupon each time,) while saying,

N. I ANOINT thee with this hallowed Oil, and therewith I do sign thee ✠ with the sign of the Cross upon thy forehead, *and upon thy five bodily senses, and upon thy breast, and upon thy hands, and*

388

upon thy feet, In the Name of the Father, and of the Son, and of the Holy Ghost. Amen. As with this holy Oil thou art anointed outwardly, so may God our heavenly Father grant that thou mayest be anointed inwardly with the Holy Ghost, and healed of all sickness and every disease, and of every weakness and infirmity, of body, mind, and spirit. May Almighty God, of His great mercy, restore unto thee health and strength to serve Him, and send unto thee release from all thy pains and sufferings. May God forgive thee all thy sins, and every trespass; may He preserve thee, and keep thee in all goodness, and finally bring thee to everlasting life; through Jesus Christ our Lord and only Saviour. *Amen.*

Then shall the Priest say these two Prayers following.

O GOD of all grace and power: Behold, visit, and relieve this Thy *servant* upon whom we have laid our hands and anointed with holy Oil, as taught by Thy holy Apostle Saint James; look upon *him* with the eyes of Thy mercy; give *him* comfort and sure confidence in Thee; preserve *him* in body and soul; defend *him* in all danger; and keep *him* in perpetual peace and safety; through Jesus Christ our Lord. *Amen.*

O LORD God and heavenly Father, Who dost relieve those who suffer in soul and body: Stretch forth Thy hand, we beseech Thee, to heal this Thy *servant N.* upon whom we have this day laid our hands, and anointed with holy Oil according to the will of our Lord Jesus Christ and the commandment of His holy Apostle, and to ease *his* pain; that by Thy mercy, *he* may be restored to full health and strength of body and mind, soul and spirit; and then shew forth *his* thankfulness in love for Thee, and for *his* neighbour; through the same Thy Son Jesus Christ our Lord. *Amen.*

Or else this Prayer only, if it be Extreme Unction that is given.

O LORD our heavenly Father, in Whom we live and move and have our being: Grant to this Thy *servant* grace to desire only Thy most holy will; and vouchsafe, we pray Thee, that whether living or dying, *he* may be Thine, and find *his* perfect peace in Thee; for His sake Who loved us and gave Himself for us, Jesus Christ our Lord. *Amen.*

Then shall the Priest bless the sick Person, saying,

NOW unto God's gracious mercy and protection we commit thee. The Lord bless thee, and keep thee. The Lord make His face to shine upon thee, and be gracious unto thee. The Lord lift up His countenance upon thee, and give thee peace, both now and evermore. And the blessing of God Almighty, ✠ the Father, the Son, and the Holy Ghost, be upon you, and remain with you always. *Amen.*

Then the Priest shall discretely dispose of the unused consecrated Oil.

Here endeth the MINISTRY TO THE SICK.

AND HERE IT IS TO BE NOTED, that whensoever at such times, and under such circumstances, as the foregoing Order, or any Order for the Administration of any Sacrament, be not at hand, nor be available to be had, the Priest shall nevertheless administer that Sacrament to the very best of his ability, having always in mind the Intention to do what the Catholic Church hath ever intended to be done, always employing the proper Matter, and using as much of the proper Form as he is able to remember.

A Supplication for
THE DYING OR THE DEAD

This Service following may be used with the dying Person in his last hours, or else after his Death; and at the time of Visitation in the Church or Chapel; and may also be used in the house of the deceased Person, before the Corpse or the Ashes be taken to the Church for the Services of Christian Burial.

The Minister may say these or some other words of Holy Scripture.

THOU wilt keep him in perfect peace whose mind is stayed on Thee. *Isaiah 26. 3.*

COMFORT the soul of Thy servant; for unto Thee, O Lord, do I lift up my soul. *Psalm 86. 4.*

THE Lord is my light and my salvation; whom then shall I fear? The Lord is the Strength of my life; of whom then shall I be afraid? *Psalm 27. 1.*

YEA, though I walk through the valley of the shadow of death, I will fear no evil; for Thou art with me; Thy rod and Thy staff they comfort me. *Psalm 23. 4.*

INTO thy hands I commend my spirit; for Thou hast redeemed me, O Lord, Thou God of truth. *Psalm 31. 6.*

Then shall be said,
✠ IN the Name of the Father,
and of the Son, and of the Holy Ghost. *Amen.*

Minister. Let us pray.

O GOD the Father, Maker of heaven and earth,
Graciously hear us, O Lord.

O God the Son, Redeemer of the world,
Graciously hear us, O Lord.

O God the Holy Ghost, Comforter of the faithful,
Graciously hear us, O Lord.

O Holy Trinity, three Persons and one God,
Graciously hear us, O Lord.

BEHOLD, O Lord, the soul of Thy *servant N.,* and in Thy merciful loving-kindness and of the Thy great pity,
Save him, *and deliver* him, *most good and gracious Lord.*

From all pain of sorrow, and darkness of dismay,
Good Lord, deliver him.

From the power of the devil, and from the consuming fire,
Good Lord, deliver him.

From everlasting condemnation, and from eternal death,
Good Lord, deliver him.

By Thy holy Incarnation and Nativity,
Good Lord, deliver him.

By Thy saving Cross and Passion,
Good Lord, deliver him.

By Thy precious Death and Burial,
Good Lord, deliver him.

By Thy glorious Resurrection and Ascension,
Good Lord, deliver him.

By Thy Coming Again in glory, and the Resurrection of the Dead,
Good Lord, deliver him.

WE sinners do beseech Thee to hear us, O blessed Lord God: and that it may please Thee to pardon and purge away *his* sins,
We beseech Thee, good Lord.

To receive *him* this day into Paradise, and to grant unto *him* refreshment, rest, and peace,
We beseech Thee, good Lord.

To give *him* joy and gladness in Thy courts, with all Thy Saints in light,
We beseech Thee, good Lord.

To accomplish *his* perfecting, and to make *him* fit to receive Thy kingdom,
We beseech Thee, good Lord.

And finally, to raise *him* up clothed in immortality and incorruption, and to bring *him* into Thy Presence, with joy and everlasting glory,
We beseech Thee, good Lord.

O LAMB of God, that takest away the sins of the world,
Have mercy upon him.

O Lamb of God, that takest away the sins of the world,
Have mercy upon him.

O Lamb of God, that takest away the sins of the world,
Grant him *rest and peace.*

Then shall the Minister and all present say together the Lord's Prayer.

OUR Father, which art in heaven, hallowed be Thy Name. Thy kingdom come. Thy will be done, in earth as it is in heaven. Give us this day our daily bread. And forgive us our trespasses, As we forgive them that trespass against us. And lead us not into temptation, But deliver us from evil. Amen.

FOR THE DYING OR THE DEAD

Then shall the Minister say this Prayer following.

O ALMIGHTY God, with Whom do live the spirits of just men made perfect: We humbly commend the soul of this Thy *servant*, our dear *brother*, into Thy hands, as into the hands of a faithful Creator, and most merciful Saviour. Wash *him*, we pray Thee, in the Blood of that immaculate Lamb that was slain to take away the sins of the world; that whatsoever defilements *he* may have contracted in the midst of this miserable and wicked world, through the lusts of the flesh or the wiles of Satan, being purged and done away, *he* may be presented pure and without spot before Thee. Receive *him*, we beseech Thee, O Lord, into the arms of Thy mercy; vouchsafe unto *him* a safe passage, and guide *him* through the valley of the shadow of death; bring *him* into the habitations of light and peace, in the company of Thy most holy Mother, Blessed Mary ever Virgin, and all the faithful departed who are gone before us marked with the sign of Christ: and with them, vouchsafe unto *him* refreshment and quiet rest; and in the day of the resurrection of the just, grant that *he* may be found worthy to be made a partaker of the inheritance of the Saints in light; through the Merits of Jesus Christ Thine only Son our Lord. *Amen.*

This Commendation following may then be said.

DEPART in peace, O thou Christian soul, from out of this world of misery and pain; depart, beyond the reach of temptation, beyond the power of the devil, and beyond the influences of wickedness and sin: In the Name of God the Father, Who created thee; in the Name of God the Son, Who redeemed thee; in the Name of God the Holy Ghost, Who sanctifieth thee. May the Angels, which minister to the heirs of salvation, attend around thee; may the Blessed Virgin Mary the Mother of our Lord, the glorious company of the Apostles, and the goodly fellowship of the Prophets, receive thee; may the noble army of Martyrs, the triumphant band of Confessors, and the multitude of all the Saints which have gone before, welcome thee unto thy rest; wherein thou shalt rejoice in hope of that blessed resurrection wherein, with all the Elect of God, thou shalt receive again thine own body, made like unto Christ's glorious body, and shalt have thy perfect consummation and bliss in the kingdom of His eternal joy, in the Presence of our God. *Amen.*

Minister. ✠ MAY the soul of our dear *brother*, and the souls of all
the Faithful departed, through the mercy of God, rest in peace;
Answer. And awake to a joyful resurrection. *Amen.*

*Here endeth a SUPPLICATION FOR THE DYING
OR THE DEAD.*

THE BURIAL OF THE DEAD

THE SERVICES OF CHRISTIAN BURIAL

The Order for the Burial of the Dead consists of these Services of Christian Burial: the Office of Christian Burial, the Requiem Eucharist, and the Committal at the Grave.

The Pastor of the Parish or Congregation shall be responsible for the conduct of all the Services of Christian Burial, and may be assisted therein by the Curate or other authorised Ministers.

The Office of Christian Burial is intended to be used on the Eve of Burial in the Church or Chapel with the remains of the deceased Person present. And whensoever the Requiem Eucharist shall not be celebrated on the Day of Burial itself, the Burial Office shall be used instead on that day. When the Burial Office is used on the Day of Burial, the Supplication for the Dying or the Dead may be used in place of the Burial Office on the Eve of Burial, together with other suitable Devotions at the discretion of the Minister.

And when a Requiem Eucharist be not celebrated on the Day of Burial itself, it may be celebrated on some other suitable day thereafter following.

Except there be special cause to the contrary, and permission otherwise is duly given by the Ordinary, the Burial Office and the Requiem Eucharist shall be celebrated in the Parish Church.

And here it is to be noted, that the Services of Christian Burial are not to be used for any that die unbaptised, or excommunicate, or by their own wilful act while in a sound state of mind.

THE ORDER OF

THE OFFICE OF CHRISTIAN BURIAL

The Priest and Clerks, meeting the Corpse or Ashes of the departed Person at the Church-door, and going before the same into the Church, shall say or sing the following Sentences.

I AM the Resurrection and the Life, saith the Lord: he that believeth in me, though he were dead, yet shall he live: and whosoever liveth and believeth in me shall never die. *St John* 11. 25-26.

LET not your heart be troubled: ye believe in God, believe also in me. In my Father's house are many mansions: if it were not so, I would have told you. I go to prepare a place for you. *St John* 14. 1-2.

THE eternal God is thy refuge, and underneath are the everlasting arms. *Deuteronomy* 33. 27.

WHETHER we live, we live unto the Lord; or whether we die, we die unto the Lord: whether we live therefore or die, we are the Lord's. For to this end Christ died, and lived again, that He might be Lord of both the dead and the living. *Romans* 14. 8-9.

WE brought nothing into this world, and it is certain we can carry nothing out. The Lord gave, and the Lord hath taken away: blessed be the Name of the Lord. *I Timothy* 6. 7. & *Job* 1. 21.

And the Corpse or Ashes being placed upon the Bier before the Chancel, the Priest may then silently sprinkle the same with holy Water.

THE BURIAL OF THE DEAD

Then shall the Priest say,
THE peace of God be with you.
Answer. And with thy spirit.

Priest. Let us pray.

ALMIGHTY God, we yield Thee hearty thanks for the life of Thy *servant N.,* whom Thou hast commanded to depart from out of this life, delivering *him* thereby from the miseries of this wicked world, from the burden of temptation, and from the weakness of the flesh. And trusting only in Thy mercy, we commend the soul of this our dear *brother* into Thy gracious keeping, praying Thee to grant unto *him* refreshment, rest, and peace, until the day of *his* resurrection from the dead at the coming again of our Saviour Jesus Christ. And in that day, we beseech Thee, O Father, raise up this our dear *brother,* and clothe *him* with immortality and incorruption; and grant that *he,* with all Thine elect and faithful children, may be set altogether at Christ's right hand, and receive that blessing which Thy well-beloved Son shall then pronounce to all that love and fear Thee, saying, Come, ye blessed children of my Father, and possess the kingdom prepared for you from the foundation of the world. Grant this, O merciful Father, we most humbly beseech Thee, through the same Thy Son Jesus Christ our Lord. *Amen.*

THE PSALMS.

Then shall be said or sung one or more of these Psalms following.

PSALM 23. *Dominus regit me.*

THE Lord is my shepherd, / therefore can I lack nothing. He shall feed me in a green pasture, / and lead me forth beside the waters of comfort. He shall restore my soul, / and bring me forth in the paths of righteousness, for His Name's sake. Yea, Though I walk through the valley of the shadow of death, I will fear no evil; / for Thou art with me; Thy rod and Thy staff comfort me. Thou shalt prepare a table before me in the presence of them that trouble me; / Thou hast anointed my head with oil, and my cup runneth over. Surely Thy loving-kindness and mercy shall follow me all the days of my life, / and I will dwell in the house of the Lord for ever.

THE Lord gave, and the Lord hath taken away: /
Blessed be the Name of the Lord.

PSALM 121. *Levavi oculos.*

I WILL lift up mine eyes unto the hills, / O whence cometh my help? My help cometh even from the Lord, / Who hath made heaven and earth. He will not suffer thy foot to be moved; / and He that keepeth thee will not sleep. Behold, He that keepeth Israel / shall neither slumber nor sleep. The Lord Himself is thy Keeper; the Lord is thy Defence upon thy right hand; so that the sun shall not burn thee by day, / neither the moon by night. The Lord shall preserve thee from all evil; / yea, it is even He that shall keep thy soul. The Lord shall preserve thy going out and thy coming in, / from this time forth for evermore.

THE Lord gave, and the Lord hath taken away: /
Blessed be the Name of the Lord.

THE BURIAL OF THE DEAD

PSALM 130. *De profundis.*

OUT of the deep have I called unto Thee, O Lord; / Lord, hear my voice. O let Thine ears consider well / the voice of my complaint. If Thou, Lord, wilt be extreme to mark what is done amiss, / O Lord, who may abide it? But there is forgiveness with Thee, / therefore shalt Thou be feared. I look for the Lord; my soul doth wait for Him; / in His word is my trust. My soul looketh for the Lord more than watchmen for the morning: / yea, more than watchmen for the morning. O Israel, trust in the Lord, for with the Lord there is mercy, / and with Him is plenteous redemption. And He shall redeem Israel / from all his sins.

THE Lord gave, and the Lord hath taken away: /
Blessed be the Name of the Lord.

THE LESSONS.

*Then shall follow the two Lessons: the First Lesson taken from the Old Testament,
and the Second Lesson taken from the New Testament.*

*A hymn or one of the foregoing Psalms may be sung or said
for the Gradual between the Lessons.*

The Minister shall then read the First Lesson, as followeth.

FIRST LESSON. *Wisdom* 3. 1.

THE souls of the righteous are in the hand of God, and there shall no torment touch them. In the sight of the unwise they seemed to die; and their departure is taken for misery, and their going from us to be utter destruction; but they are in peace. For though they be punished in the sight of men, yet is their hope full of immortality. And having been a little chastened, they shall be greatly rewarded; for God proved them and found them worthy for Himself. As gold in the furnace hath He tried them, and received them as a burnt offering. And in the time of their visitation they shall shine, and run to and fro like sparks among the stubble; they shall judge the nations and have dominion over the people, and their Lord shall reign for ever and ever.

Here may follow a Psalm or hymn.

The Minister shall then read the Second Lesson, as followeth.

SECOND LESSON. *Romans* 8. 35.

WHAT shall we say then to these things? If God be for us, who can be against us? He that spared not His own Son, but delivered Him up for us all, how shall He not with Him also freely give us all things? Who shall lay anything to the charge of God's elect? It is God that justifieth; who is he that condemneth? It is Christ that died, yea rather, that is risen again, Who is even at the right hand of God, Who also maketh intercession for us. Who shall separate us from the love of Christ? Shall tribulation, or distress, or persecution, or famine, or nakedness, or peril, or sword? Nay, in all these things we are more than conquerors through Him that loved us. For I am persuaded, that neither death, nor life, nor angels, nor principalities, nor powers, nor things present, nor things to come, nor height, nor depth, nor any other creature, shall be able to separate us from the love of God, which is in Christ Jesus our Lord.

THE BURIAL OF THE DEAD

Then shall be said or sung,

I HEARD a voice from heaven, saying unto me, Write, From henceforth blessed are the dead which die in the Lord: Even so, saith the Spirit, for they rest from their labours; and their works do follow them. *Revelation* 14. 13.

Then shall the Priest say,

BRETHREN, let us now confess the Articles
of our undoubted Christian Faith.

Then shall the people stand; and the Priest and people together shall say,

I BELIEVE in God the Father Almighty, Maker of heaven and earth: And in (*Here everyone shall reverently bow his head.*) **Jesus Christ** His only Son our Lord, Who was conceived by the Holy Ghost, born of the Virgin Mary, suffered under Pontius Pilate, was crucified, dead, and buried; He descended into hell; the third day He rose again from the dead; He ascended into heaven, and sitteth on the right hand of God the Father Almighty; from thence He shall come to judge the quick and the dead. I believe in the Holy Ghost; The holy Catholic Church; The Communion of Saints; The Forgiveness of sins; ✠ The Resurrection of the body, and the Life everlasting. Amen.

THE PRAYERS.

Then shall the Priest say,

BRETHREN, in the comfort of this holy Faith,
let us all together pray to the Lord.

Then shall all devoutly kneel.

Then shall be said or sung,
Lord, have mercy upon us.
Christ, have mercy upon us.
Lord, have mercy upon us.

Then shall the Priest and people say together,

OUR Father, which art in heaven, hallowed be Thy Name. Thy kingdom come. Thy will be done, in earth as it is in heaven. Give us this day our daily bread. And forgive us our trespasses, As we forgive them that trespass against us. And lead us not into temptation, But deliver us from evil. Amen.

Then shall the Priest say these Prayers following.

ALMIGHTY God, with Whom do live the spirits of them that depart hence in the Lord, and with Whom the souls of the faithful, (after they are delivered from the burden of the flesh and just punishment for sin,) are in joy and felicity: We give Thee hearty thanks for that it hath pleased Thee to deliver this our *brother* in Christ Jesus from out of the miseries of this sinful world; and committing the soul of our dear *brother* into Thy gracious keeping, we beseech Thee, O Father, that it may please Thee shortly to accomplish the number of Thine elect, and to hasten Thy kingdom, that we with *him,* and with all those that are departed in the true faith of Thy holy Name, may have our perfect consummation and bliss, both in body and soul, in Thine eternal and everlasting glory; through Jesus Christ our Lord. *Amen.*

O FATHER of all, we pray Thee for those whom we love but see no longer, especially Thy *servant N.,* whom Thou hast taken from this life unto Thyself: Grant unto them Thy peace; and in Thy loving wisdom and almighty power, forgive and purge away their sins; work in them the good purpose of Thy perfect will, and make them fit to receive Thy kingdom and the perfect joys of heaven; through Jesus Christ our Lord. *Amen.*

GIVE rest, O Christ, to Thy *servant* with all Thy Saints, where sorrow and pain are no more, neither sighing; but light, and joy, and peace: where Thou, O Christ, with the Holy Ghost, art most high in the glory of God the Father. *Amen.*

O GOD, Whose days are without end, and Whose mercies cannot be numbered: Make us, we beseech Thee, deeply sensible of the shortness and uncertainty of human life; and let Thy Holy Spirit lead us in holiness and righteousness all our days; that, when we shall have served Thee in our generation, we may be gathered unto our fathers, having the testimony of a good conscience; in the fellowship of the holy Catholic Church; in the confidence of a certain faith; in the comfort of a reasonable, religious, and holy hope; in favour with Thee our God, and in perfect charity with all men. Grant this, O Father, we most humbly beseech Thee, through Jesus Christ our Lord. *Amen.*

O ALMIGHTY God, Father of all mercies and giver of all comfort: Deal graciously, we beseech Thee, with those who mourn; and grant that they may cast upon Thee every care, and evermore know the consolations of Thy boundless and unfailing love; through Jesus Christ our Lord. *Amen.*

GRANT, we beseech Thee, O Lord, that the soul of our dear *brother*, and the souls of all the Faithful departed, through Thy gracious mercy, ✠ may rest in peace, and then awake to a joyful resurrection; through Jesus Christ our Saviour. *Amen.*

THE COMMENDATION OF THE DEPARTED.

*Then shall the Priest proceed to and stand before the Bier, and may here sprinkle the Corpse or Ashes with holy Water. And the Priest standing there shall say this Commendation, the people present answering **Amen** after every Suffrage.*

GO forth, O thou Christian soul, upon thy journey from out of this world:
In the Name of God the Father, Who created thee. *Amen.*
In the Name of God the Son, Who redeemed thee. *Amen.*
In the Name of God the Holy Ghost, Who sanctifieth thee. *Amen.*
May thy rest be this day in peace,
and thy dwelling-place the Paradise of God.
Amen.

Here may follow a Sermon or an Eulogy.

*And if there be no Requiem Eucharist celebrated that day,
the Absolution of the Dead shall follow here.*

Then shall the Priest let them depart with this Blessing following.

✠ THE Lord bless you, and keep you. The Lord make His face to shine upon you, and be gracious unto you. The Lord lift up His countenance upon you, and give you peace, both now and evermore. *Amen.*

Additional Lessons.

The following Lessons may be used in the place of those provided.

For a First Lesson: *Ecclesiastes* 12. 1-7.

REMEMBER now thy Creator in the days of thy youth, while the evil days come not, nor the years draw nigh, when thou shalt say, I have no pleasure in them; while the sun, or the light, or the moon, or the stars, be not darkened, nor the clouds return after the rain: in the day when the keepers of the house shall tremble, and the strong men shall bow themselves, and the grinders cease because they are few, and those that look out of the windows be darkened, and the doors shall be shut in the streets, when the sound of the grinding is low, and he shall rise up at the voice of the bird, and all the daughters of music shall be brought low; also when they shall be afraid of that which is high, and fears shall be in the way, and the almond tree shall flourish, and the grasshopper shall be a burden, and desire shall fail: because man goeth to his long home, and the mourners go about the streets: or ever the silver cord be loosed, or the golden bowl be broken, or the pitcher be broken at the fountain, or the wheel broken at the cistern. then shall the dust return to the earth as it was: and the spirit shall return unto God who gave it.

For a Second Lesson: *Saint John* 5. 24-29.

THEN said Jesus, Verily, verily, I say unto you, He that heareth my word, and believeth on Him that sent me, hath everlasting life, and shall not come into condemnation; but is passed from death unto life. Verily, verily, I say unto you, The hour is coming, and now is, when the dead shall hear the voice of the Son of God: and they that hear shall live. For as the Father hath life in Himself; so hath He given to the Son to have life in Himself; and hath given Him authority to execute judgement also, because He is the Son of Man. Marvel not at this: for the hour is coming, in the which all that are in the graves shall hear His voice, and shall come forth; they that have done good, unto the resurrection of life; and they that have done evil, unto the resurrection of damnation.

The Requiem Eucharist

The Introit. *Psalm* 65. 1-4.

PRAISE is due to Thee, O God, in Sion; / and unto Thee shall the vow be performed in Jerusalem. Thou that hearest the prayer, / unto Thee shall all flesh come. My misdeeds prevail against me: / O be Thou merciful unto our sins. Blessed is the man whom Thou choosest and receivest, / that he may dwell in Thy courts. We shall be satisfied with the pleasures of Thy house, / even of Thy holy temple.

THE Lord gave, and the Lord hath taken away: /
Blessed be the Name of the Lord.

The Commandments shall be omitted.

Kyrie Eleison.

LORD, have mercy upon *him*. / Kyrie, eleison *auton*.
Christ, have mercy upon *him*. / Christe, eleison *auton*.
Lord, have mercy upon *him*. / Kyrie, eleison *auton*.

THE BURIAL OF THE DEAD

THE COLLECT.

O LORD Jesu Christ, our blessed and only Saviour, Who art the Resurrection and the Life: Mercifully hear our prayers; and receive unto Thyself the soul of Thy *servant N.*, our dear *brother* departed, which we commend unto Thy gracious keeping this day; have mercy upon *him*, pardon and deliver *him* from all *his* sins, and grant that *he* may be found worthy finally to attain unto the joy of Thy resurrection, and to live with Thee forever; Who with the Father, and the Holy Ghost, art ever one God, world without end. *Amen.*

FOR THE EPISTLE. *Revelation* 20. 10 - 21. 7.

AND I saw a great white throne, and Him that sat on it, from Whose face the heaven and earth fled away; and there was found no place for them. And I saw the dead, small and great, stand before God; and the books were opened: and another book was opened, which is the book of life: and the dead were judged out of those things that were written in the books, according to their works. And the sea gave up the dead which were in it; and death and hell delivered up the dead which were in them: and they were judged every man according to their works. And death and hell were cast into the lake of fire. This is the second death. And whosoever was not found written in the book of life was cast into the lake of fire. And I saw a new heaven and a new earth: for the first heaven and the first earth were passed away; and there was no more sea. And I John saw the holy city, new Jerusalem, coming down from God out of heaven, prepared as a bride adorned for her husband. And I heard a great voice out of heaven, saying, Behold, the tabernacle of God is with men, and He will dwell with them, and they shall be His people, and God Himself shall be with them, and be their God. And God shall wipe away all tears from their eyes; and there shall be no more death, neither sorrow, nor crying, neither shall there be any more pain: for the former things are passed away. And He that sat upon the throne said, Behold, I make all things new. And He said unto me, Write: for these words are true and faithful. And He said unto me, It is done. I am Alpha and Omega, the beginning and the end. I will give unto him that is athirst of the water of life freely. He that overcometh shall inherit all things; and I will be his God, and he shall be My son.

Or else this that followeth,

THE EPISTLE. I *Thessalonians* 4. 13-18.

BUT I would not have you be ignorant, brethren, concerning them which are asleep, that ye sorrow not, even as others which have no hope. For if we believe that Jesus died and rose again, even so them also which sleep in Jesus will God bring with Him. For this we say unto you by the word of the Lord, that we which are alive and remain unto the coming of the Lord shall not prevent them which are asleep. For the Lord Himself shall descend from heaven with a shout, with the voice of the archangel, and with the trump of God: and the dead in Christ shall rise first: then we which are alive and remain shall be caught up together with them in the clouds, to meet the Lord in the air: and so shall we ever be with the Lord. Wherefore comfort one another with these words.

THE GRADUAL. *Psalm* 112. 4-7.

UNTO the godly there ariseth up light in the darkness: / he is merciful, loving, and righteous. A good man is merciful, and lendeth: / and will guide his words with discretion. For he shall never be moved: / and the righteous shall be had in everlasting remembrance. He will not be afraid of evil tidings: / for his heart standeth fast, and believeth in the Lord.

THE BURIAL OF THE DEAD

THE GOSPEL. *Saint John* 11. 21-27.

THEN said Martha unto Jesus, Lord, if Thou hadst been here, my brother had not died. But I know, that even now, whatsoever Thou wilt ask of God, God will give it Thee. Jesus saith unto her, Thy brother shall rise again. Martha saith unto Him, I know that he shall rise again in the resurrection at the last day. Jesus said unto her, I am the Resurrection and the Life: he that believeth in me, though he were dead, yet shall he live; and whosoever liveth and believeth in me shall never die. Believest thou this? She saith unto Him, Yea, Lord: I believe that Thou art the Christ, the Son of God, which should come into the world.

Or else this that followeth,

THE GOSPEL. *Saint John* 6. 35-40.

AND Jesus said unto them, I am the Bread of life: he that cometh to me shall never hunger; and he that believeth on me shall never thirst; but I said unto you, That ye also have seen me, and believe not. All that the Father giveth me shall come to me; and him that cometh to me I will in no wise cast out. For I came down from heaven not to do mine own will, but the will of Him that sent me. And this is the Father's will which hath sent me, that of all which He hath given me I should lose nothing, but should raise it up at the last day. And this is the will of Him that sent me, that everyone which seeth the Son, and believeth on Him, may have everlasting life: and I will raise him up at the last day.

The Nicene Creed shall be omitted.

THE PROPER PREFACE.

THROUGH Jesus Christ our Lord, in Whom hath shone forth unto us the blessed hope of a joyful resurrection; that they who now mourn the certain condition of their mortality may be consoled by the sure promise of new and everlasting life in the world to come; for unto us, Thy faithful people, life is only changed, and not taken away; and at the dissolution of this earthly tabernacle, a perfect dwelling-place shall be made for us, not made by mortal hands, but made for us by Thee, eternal in the heavens. Therefore with Angels, &c.

And at the Oblation of the Holy Eucharist, the Priest shall say,

AND we entirely desire Thy fatherly goodness mercifully to accept this our sacrifice of praise and thanksgiving: most humbly beseeching Thee to grant that, by the Merits and Death of Thy Son Jesus Christ, which we plead here before Thee, and through faith in His Blood, we and all Thy whole Church, and especially Thy *servant N.*, whom Thou hast commanded to depart from out of this present sinful world, may obtain remission of our sins, and all other benefits of His Passion.

AGNUS DEI.

O LAMB of God, that takest away the sins of the world,
grant *him* rest.
O Lamb of God, that takest away the sins of the world,
grant *him* rest.
O Lamb of God, that takest away the sins of the world,
grant *him* rest and peace.

THE COLLECT AFTER COMMUNION.

The Thanksgiving after Holy Communion ended, the Priest shall say this Collect following.

GRANT, O Lord, that as we are baptised into the death of Thy blessed Son our Saviour Jesus Christ, so by the continual mortifying of our corrupt affections we may be buried with Him; and that, through the grave, and gate of death, we may pass to our joyful resurrection; for His Merits, Who died, and was buried, and rose again for us, Thy Son Jesus Christ our Lord. *Amen.*

THE DISMISSAL ANTHEM.

I HEARD a voice from heaven, saying unto me, / Write, From henceforth blessed are the dead which die in the Lord: Even so, saith the Spirit, for they rest from their labours; / and their works do follow them. O death, where is thy sting? O grave, where is thy victory? / Thanks be to God, which giveth us the victory, through our Lord Jesus Christ.

THE Lord gave, and the Lord hath taken away: /
Blessed be the Name of the Lord.

Then shall the Priest shall proceed directly to the Absolution of the Dead.

THE ABSOLUTION OF THE DEAD

The Priest, standing before the Bier or Catafalque, shall say,

ENTER not into judgement with Thy servant, O Lord, for in Thy sight shall no man living be justified, except Thou grant unto him remission of all his sins. Therefore, we beseech Thee, pronounce not Thy judgement upon that soul, whose cause the faithful prayer of Christian people commendeth unto Thee; but grant, that by the succour of Thy grace, that soul which hath believed on Thee may be found worthy to escape the avenging judgement, who upon earth was sealed with the sign of the Holy Trinity.

The Priest.
Let us pray.

Then shall the Priest say this Absolution over the Body or Ashes, as followeth.

ABSOLVE, O heavenly Father, we humbly beseech Thee, from every bond of sin, the soul of Thy *servant N.,* which we now commend unto Thy gracious keeping: And forasmuch as *he* believed and put *his* trust in Thee, forgive and purge away all *his* sins, washing *him* in the most precious Blood of Thy Son our Saviour Jesus Christ; and like the good thief who died with Him on Calvary, grant also unto Thy *servant* that *he* may be with Thy beloved Son, this day, in Paradise; and vouchsafe unto *him* that there, with all Thy Saints, *he* may enjoy refreshment, rest, and peace, in the blessed hope of *his* resurrection from death to eternal life; through the same Thy Son Jesus Christ our Lord. *Amen.*

Then shall the Priest say,

O SAVIOUR of the world, Who by Thy Cross and precious Blood hast redeemed us;
 Answer. Save us, and help us, we humbly beseech Thee, O Lord.
Priest. Graciously look upon our afflictions, O Lord;
 Answer. Pitifully behold the sorrows of our hearts.
Priest. Grant, O Lord, that our *brother* departed may rest in peace;
 Answer. And awake to a joyful resurrection.

Then shall the Priest say this Prayer of Commendation.

INTO Thy hands, O most merciful Saviour, we commend the soul of Thy *servant N.*, now departed from *his* body. Acknowledge, we beseech Thee, O Lord, a sheep of Thine own fold, a lamb of Thine own flock, a sinner of Thy redeeming; and receive *him* into the arms of Thy mercy. Grant, O Christ, that Thy holy Angels may lead *him* this day into Paradise; and that Thy most holy Mother, Blessed Mary ever Virgin, with the holy Apostles and all the holy Martyrs, may receive *him* at *his* coming; and grant that Thy *servant*, with Lazarus once poor, may have rest from *his* labours, and rise again, at Thy coming, to inherit the kingdom promised to all who in this life have believed and put their trust in Thee. *Amen.*

Then shall the Corpse or Ashes be borne out of the Church,
and thence to the place of burial.

THE COMMITTAL AT THE GRAVE

When they are come to the grave, the Priest shall say,

BLESSED be the God and Father of our Lord Jesus Christ, which according to His abundant mercy hath begotten us again unto a lively hope by the resurrection of Jesus Christ from the dead, to an inheritance incorruptible, and undefiled, and that fadeth not away, reserved in heaven for you.
I *Saint Peter* 1. 3 & 4.

Then shall the Priest say,
O LORD, hear our prayer;
Answer. And let our cry come unto Thee.

Priest. Let us pray.

Then shall the Priest say this Prayer following.

O LORD Jesus Christ, Who by Thy precious burial didst sanctify an earthly sepulchre: Vouchsafe, we beseech Thee, to bless, sanctify, and hallow *this grave*, that it may be a resting-place, peaceful and secure, for the *body* of Thy *servant*, our *brother*, which we are about to commit hereunto, until the great and glorious day when Thou shalt come again to judge the quick and the dead, and the world by fire; Who art the Resurrection and the Life, and Who livest and reignest with the Father and the Holy Ghost, ever one God, world without end. *Amen.*

Then, as the earthly remains of the departed Person are made ready to be laid in the earth,
the Priest shall say or sing, or the Priest together with the people shall say or sing,

MAN that is born of a woman hath but a short time to live, and is full of misery. He cometh up, and is cut down, like a flower; he fleeth as it were a shadow, and never continueth in one stay. In the midst of life we are in death: of whom may we seek for succour, but of Thee, O Lord, Who for our sins art justly displeased? Yet, O Lord God most holy, O Lord most mighty, O holy and most merciful Saviour, deliver us not into the bitter pains of eternal death. Thou knowest, Lord, the secrets of our hearts; shut not Thy merciful ears to our prayer; but spare us, Lord most holy, O God most mighty, O holy and merciful Saviour, Thou most worthy Judge eternal; and suffer us not, at our last hour, for any pains of death, to fall from thee.

THE BURIAL OF THE DEAD

Then, while the earth shall be cast upon the Corpse or Ashes, the Priest shall say,

FORASMUCH as it hath pleased Almighty God, of His great mercy, to take unto Himself the soul of our dear *brother* here departed, we therefore commit *his body* to *the ground*: earth to earth, ashes to ashes, dust to dust; in sure and certain hope of the Resurrection to eternal life, through our Lord Jesus Christ; Who shall change our vile body, that it may be fashioned like unto His glorious body, according to the mighty working whereby He is able to subdue all things unto Himself.

Then shall the Priest say,
Let us pray.

Lord, have mercy upon us.
Christ, have mercy upon us.
Lord, have mercy upon us.

Then shall the Priest and people say together,

OUR Father, which art in heaven, hallowed be Thy Name. Thy kingdom come. Thy will be done, in earth as it is in heaven. Give us this day our daily bread. And forgive us our trespasses, As we forgive them that trespass against us. And lead us not into temptation, But deliver us from evil. Amen.

Then shall the Priest say these Prayers following.

O LORD Jesus Christ, Son of the living God, Who hast opened unto us the gate of everlasting life, and art the Peace and Light of those who rest in Thee: Receive unto Thyself the soul of our dear *brother*, whose *body* we have hereunto committed; and grant that in the company of Thy most holy Mother, the Blessed Virgin Mary, and all Thy Saints, *he* may find rest and peace, and joyfully await with them in the blessed hope of their resurrection to eternal life; Who with the Father and the Holy Ghost livest and reignest, ever one God, world without end. *Amen.*

ALMIGHTY and most merciful Father, we bless Thy holy Name for the life of Thy *servant N.*, and for the lives all Thy servants departed this life in Thy faith and fear, and we beseech Thee to grant unto them Thy peace; and to give unto us Thy grace, that we may follow their good examples; and vouchsafe unto all Thy whole Church, that we may be found worthy to attain unto everlasting life, and also be made partakers of Thy heavenly kingdom. Grant this, O Father, for Jesus Christ's sake, our only Mediator and Advocate. *Amen.*

The Priest may also say the following Prayer.

O HEAVENLY Father, Whose blessed Son Jesus Christ did weep at the grave of Lazarus, His friend: Look with compassion, we beseech Thee, upon those who are now in sorrow and affliction; comfort them, O Lord, with Thy gracious consolations; make them to know that all things work together for good to them that love Thee; and grant unto them evermore sure trust and confidence in Thy love and care for them; through the same Thy Son Jesus Christ our Lord. *Amen.*

II *Corinthians* xiii. 14.

✠ THE grace of our Lord Jesus Christ, and the love of God, and the fellowship of the Holy Ghost, be with us all evermore. *Amen.*

THE BURIAL OF A CHILD

The Priest and Clerks, meeting the Body or Ashes, and going before either,
into the Church or else towards the grave, shall say or sing,

I AM the Resurrection and the Life, saith the Lord: he that believeth in me, though he were dead, yet shall he live: and whosoever liveth and believeth in me shall never die. *Saint John* 11. 25, 26.

HE shall feed His flock like a shepherd: He shall gather the lambs with His arm, and carry them in His bosom. *Isaiah* 40. 11.

BLESSED are they that mourn: for they shall be comforted. *Saint Matthew* 5. 4.

Then shall be said or sung this Psalm following.

PSALM 23. *Dominus regit me.*

THE Lord is my Shepherd; / therefore can I lack nothing. He shall feed me in a green pasture, / and lead me forth beside the waters of comfort. He shall restore my soul, / and bring me forth in the paths of righteousness, for His Name's sake. Yea, though I walk through the valley of the shadow of death, I will fear no evil; / for Thou art with me; Thy rod and Thy staff comfort me. Thou shalt prepare a table before me in the presence of them that trouble me; / thou hast anointed my head with oil, and my cup shall be full. Surely Thy loving-kindness and mercy shall follow me all the days of my life; / and I will dwell in the house of the Lord for ever.

GLORY be to the Father, and to the Son, / and to the Holy Ghost:
As it was in the beginning, is now, and ever shall be, / world without end. Amen.

Then shall follow the Lesson taken out of
the eighteenth chapter of the Gospel according to Saint Matthew.

AT the same time came the disciples unto Jesus, saying, Who is the greatest in the kingdom of heaven? And Jesus called a little child unto Him, and set him in the midst of them, and said, Verily I say unto you, Except ye be converted, and become as little children, ye shall not enter into the kingdom of heaven. Whosoever therefore shall humble himself as this little child, the same is greatest in the kingdom of heaven. And whoso shall receive one such little child in my name, receiveth me. Take heed that ye despise not one of these little ones; for I say unto you, that in heaven their angels do always behold the face of my Father which is in heaven.

Here may be sung a hymn or an anthem.

Then shall the Priest say,
THE Lord be with you.
People. And with thy spirit.
Priest. Let us pray.

And the Priest shall say,
LORD, have mercy upon us.
Answer. Christ, have mercy upon us.
Priest. Lord, have mercy upon us.

Then shall the Minister and people say together,

OUR Father, which art in heaven, hallowed be Thy Name. Thy kingdom come. Thy will be done, in earth as it is in heaven. Give us this day our daily bread. And forgive us our trespasses, As we forgive them that trespass against us. And lead us not into temptation, But deliver us from evil. For Thine is the kingdom, the power, and the glory, For ever and ever. Amen.

> *Minister.* Blessed are the pure in heart;
>   *People.* For they shall see God.
> *Minister.* Blessed be the Name of the Lord;
>   *People.* Henceforth, world without end.
> *Minister.* Lord, hear our prayer;
>   *People.* And let our cry come unto Thee.

O HEAVENLY Father, Whose face the angels of the little ones do always behold in heaven: Grant us to know, and steadfastly to believe, that this Child hath been taken into the safe keeping of Thine eternal love, and will be raised up at the last day; through Jesus Christ our Lord. *Amen.*

O LORD Jesu Christ, Who didst take little children into Thine arms and bless them: Open Thou our eyes, we beseech Thee, that we may perceive that Thou hast now taken this Child into the arms of Thy love, and hast bestowed upon *him* the blessings of Thy gracious favour; who livest and reignest with the Father and the Holy Ghost, ever one God, world without end. *Amen.*

O GOD, Whose ways are hidden and works most wonderful, Who makest nothing in vain, and lovest all that Thou hast made: Comfort Thou, O Father, these Thy servants, whose hearts are sore smitten and oppressed; and grant that they may so love and serve Thee in this life, that together with this Thy Child, they may obtain the fullness of Thy promises in the Life of the world to come; through Lord Jesus Christ our Lord. *Amen.*

THE COMMITTAL AT THE GRAVE

And when they are come to the grave, the Minister shall say,

LIKE as a father pitieth his own children, even so is the Lord merciful unto them that fear Him. *Psalm* 103. 13.

AS one whom his mother comforteth, so will I comfort you. *Isaiah* 66. 13.

Then, while the earth shall be cast upon the body or ashes by some standing by, the Priest shall say,

FORASMUCH as it hath pleased Almighty God of His great mercy to receive unto Himself the soul of this Child, our dear *brother* here departed: we therefore commit *his body* to *the ground*, earth to earth, ashes to ashes, dust to dust; in sure and certain hope of the Resurrection to eternal life, through our Lord Jesus Christ; Who shall change our vile body, that it may be fashioned like unto His glorious body, according to the mighty working whereby He is able to subdue all things unto Himself.

Then shall be said or sung this following.

OUR Lord Jesus Christ said, Suffer little children to come unto me, and forbid them not; for of such is the kingdom of God. *Saint Luke* 18. 16.

Then shall the Minister say,

O HEAVENLY Father, give us grace to entrust the soul of this Child to Thine unfailing care and love, and bring us all to Thy heavenly kingdom; through Jesus Christ our Lord. *Amen.*

ALMIGHTY God, Father of all mercies and Giver of all comfort: Deal graciously, we pray Thee, with all those who mourn, that casting every care on Thee, they may ever know the consolations of Thy love; through Jesus Christ our Lord. *Amen.*

II *Corinthians* xiii. 14.

✠ THE grace of our Lord Jesus Christ, and the love of God, and the fellowship of the Holy Ghost, be with us all evermore. *Amen.*

Here end the SERVICES OF CHRISTIAN BURIAL.

THE ORDINAL

THE FORM AND MANNER OF
MAKING, ORDAINING, AND CONSECRATING OF
BISHOPS, PRIESTS, AND DEACONS
ACCORDING TO THE ORDER OF
THE CHRISTIAN EPISCOPAL
CHURCH OF CANADA

THE PREFACE.

IT is evident unto all men, diligently reading holy Scripture and ancient Authors, that from the Apostles' time, there have been these Orders of Ministers in Christ's Church: Bishops, Priests, and Deacons. Which Offices, being of Divine institution and Apostolic foundation, were evermore had in such reverend estimation, that no man might ever presume to execute any of them, except he were first called, tried, examined and known to have such qualities as are requisite for the same; and also by public Prayer with Imposition of hands, were approved, ordained or consecrated, and admitted thereunto by lawful authority. And therefore to the intent that these three Orders may be continued, and reverently used, and esteemed in this Church: No man shall be accounted or taken to be a lawful and valid Bishop, Priest, or Deacon in this Church, or suffered to execute any of the said Ministries, except he first be called, tried, examined, and admitted thereunto, according to the Form hereafter following, or hath received formerly lawful and valid Episcopal Consecration or Ordination acknowledged as such by this Church.

And none shall be made Deacon except he be twenty three years of age, unless he have a Faculty. And every man which is to be ordered Priest shall be full four and twenty years old. And every man which is to be consecrated Bishop shall be fully thirty years of age.

And the Bishop knowing either by himself, or by sufficient testimony, any person to be a natural born man of virtuous conversation, and without crime, and after examination and trial finding him learned in the Latin tongue, and sufficiently instructed in holy Scripture and the Religion of the Catholic Church, may at the times appointed in the Canon, or else, on urgent occasion, upon some other Sunday or Holy-day, in the face of the Church, make and admit him a Deacon in such manner and form as hereafter followeth.

THE FORM AND MANNER OF
MAKING OF DEACONS

When the day appointed by the Bishop is come; after Morning Prayer is ended, there shall be a Sermon, or Exhortation, declaring the Duty, and Office of such as come to be admitted Deacons; how necessary that Order is in the Church of Christ; and also how the people ought to esteem them in their Office.

THE PRESENTATION

First the Archdeacon or his Deputy shall present unto the Bishop (sitting in his Chair, near to the holy Table) such as are to be made Deacons (each one of them being decently vested in his Albe), saying these words.

REVEREND Father in God; I present unto you these persons present, to be admitted to the Order of Deacons.

The Bishop.

TAKE heed that the persons whom ye present unto us, be apt and meet, for their learning, and godly conversation, to exercise their Ministry duly, to the honour of God, and the edifying of His Church

The Archdeacon shall answer,

I HAVE enquired of them, and also examined them; and think them so to be.

Then the Bishop shall say unto the people,

BRETHREN, if there be any of you who knoweth any Impediment or notable Crime in any of these persons presented to be made Deacons, for the which he ought not to be admitted to that Order of Ministry: Let him come forth in the Name of God, and shew what the Crime or Impediment is.

And if any great Crime or Impediment be objected, the Bishop shall surcease from ordering that person, until such time as the party accused shall be found clear of that Crime.

Then the Bishop (commending such as shall be found meet to be made Deacons, to the prayers of the congregation) shall, with the Clergy and people present, sing or say the Litany as followeth.

THE LITANY

O GOD the Father of heaven: have mercy upon us.
  O God the Father of heaven: have mercy upon us.

O God the Son, Redeemer of the world: have mercy upon us.
  O God the Son, Redeemer of the world: have mercy upon us.

O God the Holy Ghost, proceeding from the Father, and the Son: have mercy upon us.
  O God the Holy Ghost, proceeding from the Father, and the Son: have mercy upon us.

O holy, blessed, and glorious Trinity, three Persons, and one God: have mercy upon us.
  O holy, blessed, and glorious Trinity, three Persons, and one God: have mercy upon us.

REMEMBER not Lord, our offences, nor the offences of our forefathers, neither take thou vengeance of our sins: spare us good Lord, spare Thy people, whom Thou hast redeemed with Thy most precious Blood, and be not angry with us for ever.
  Spare us, good Lord.

Fʀᴏᴍ all evil and mischief; from sin; from the crafts and assaults of the devil; from Thy wrath, and from everlasting condemnation,
Good Lord, deliver us.

From all blindness of heart; from pride, vain glory, and hypocrisy; from envy, hatred, and malice, and all uncharitableness,
Good Lord, deliver us.

From fornication and adultery, and all other deadly sin; and from all the deceits of the world, the flesh, and the devil,
Good Lord, deliver us.

From lightning and tempest; from earthquake, fire, and flood; from plague, pestilence, and famine; from battle, and murder; and from sudden death,
Good Lord, deliver us.

From all sedition, conspiracy, and rebellion; from all false doctrine, heresy, and schism; from hardness of heart, and contempt of Thy Word and Commandment,
Good Lord, deliver us.

Bʏ the mystery of Thy holy Incarnation; by Thy holy Nativity, and Circumcision; by Thy Baptism, Fasting, and Temptation,
Good Lord, deliver us.

By Thine Agony, and bloody sweat; by Thy saving Cross and Passion; by Thy precious Death, and Burial,
Good Lord, deliver us.

By Thy glorious Resurrection and Ascension; by Thy sending of the Holy Ghost; by Thine everlasting Priesthood; and by Thy coming again in glory,
Good Lord, deliver us.

In all time of our tribulation; in all time of our wealth; in the hour of death, and in the day of Judgement,
Good Lord, deliver us.

Wᴇ sinners do beseech Thee to hear us, O Lord God, and that it may please Thee to rule and govern Thy holy Church universal in the right way,
We beseech Thee, good Lord.

To Thee to keep and strengthen in the true worshipping of Thee, in righteousness and holiness of life, Thy servant *ELIZABETH* our most gracious Queen and Governor,
We beseech Thee, good Lord.

To rule and govern her heart in Thy faith, fear, and love, that in all her thoughts, words, and works, she may ever seek Thy honour and glory, and the welfare of her people,
We beseech Thee, good Lord.

To be her defender and keeper, giving her the victory over all her enemies,

We beseech Thee, good Lord.

To bless all the Bishops of Thy Church; and to endue them with Thy Holy Spirit, and fill them with Thy heavenly grace; that they may govern and feed the flock committed to their care according to Thy will,
We beseech Thee, good Lord.

To illuminate all Bishops, Priests, and Deacons, with true knowledge and understanding of Thy Word, and that both by their preaching and living they may set it forth and shew it accordingly,
We beseech Thee, good Lord.

To bless these Thy servants at this time to be admitted to the Order of Deacons; and to pour down Thy Holy Spirit upon them, and so fill them with Thy heavenly grace; that they may duly execute their Office and Ministry to the edifying of Thy Church and the glory of Thy holy Name,
We beseech Thee, good Lord.

To bless all who minister in Thy Name; that each, according to his calling, may duly execute his office to Thy honour and glory, and the edifying of Thy people,
We beseech Thee, good Lord.

To send forth labourers into Thy harvest; to prosper their work by Thy Holy Spirit; to make Thy saving health known unto all nations; and to hasten Thy kingdom,
We beseech Thee, O Lord.

To give to all Thy people an heart to love and dread Thee, and to seek Thy will; and to follow Thy Word and Commandments,
We beseech Thee, good Lord.

To give to all Thy people increase of grace, to hear meekly Thy Word, and to receive it with pure affection, and to bring forth the fruits of the Spirit,
We beseech Thee, good Lord.

To bring into the way of truth all such as have erred and are deceived,
We beseech Thee, good Lord.

To strengthen such as do stand; and to comfort and help the weak hearted; to raise up them that fall; and finally to beat down Satan under our feet,
We beseech Thee, good Lord.

To have mercy upon all men,
We beseech Thee, good Lord.

To forgive our enemies, persecutors and slanderers, and to turn their hearts,
We beseech Thee, good Lord.

To give us true repentance; to forgive us all our sins, negligences, and ignorances; and to endue us with the grace of Thy Holy Spirit, to amend our lives according to Thy holy Word,
We beseech Thee, good Lord,

Son of God: we beseech Thee to hear us.
Son of God: we beseech Thee to hear us.

O Lamb of God : that takest away the sins of the world,
Have mercy upon us.

O Lamb of God: that takest away the sins of the world,
Grant us Thy peace.

O Christ hear us.
O Christ hear us.

*And the Bishop, standing before the Lord's Table,
shall turn himself unto the people, and say,*
THE Lord be with you.
Answer. And with thy spirit.
Bishop. Let us pray.

And the Bishop, turning himself to face the Lord's Table, shall say in an audible voice the Lord's Prayer, and then the Collect following, the people still devoutly and humbly kneeling as before.
OUR Father which art in heaven, hallowed be Thy Name. Thy kingdom come. Thy will be done in earth, as it is in heaven. Give us this day our daily bread. And forgive us our trespasses, as we forgive them that trespass against us. And lead us not into temptation; but deliver us from evil. Amen.

ALMIGHTY God, unto Whom all hearts be open, all desires known, and from Whom no secrets are hid: Cleanse the thoughts of our hearts by the inspiration of Thy Holy Spirit, that we may perfectly love Thee, and worthily magnify Thy holy Name; through Christ our Lord. *Amen.*

THE EUCHARIST

Then shall be sung, or said, the Order for the Administration of the Holy Eucharist, with the Introit, Collect, Epistle, Gradual, and Gospel, as followeth.

THE INTROIT. *Psalm* 135. 1-7.
O PRAISE the Lord, laud ye the Name of the Lord; / praise it, O ye servants of the Lord; Ye that stand in the house of the Lord, / in the courts of the house of our God. O praise the Lord, for the Lord is gracious: / O sing praises unto His Name, for it is lovely. For why? the Lord hath chosen Jacob unto Himself, / and Israel for His own possession. For I know that the Lord is great, / and that our Lord is above all gods. Whatsoever the Lord pleased, that did He in heaven and in earth, / and in the sea, and in all deep places. He bringeth forth the clouds from the ends of the world, / and sendeth forth lightnings with the rain, bringing the winds out of His treasures.
GLORY be to the Father, and to the Son, / and to the Holy Ghost:
As it was in the beginning, is now, and ever shall be, / world without end. Amen.

THE COLLECT.
ALMIGHTY God our heavenly Father, Who through Thy holy Apostles didst institute the Order of Deacons in Thy Church, and didst inspire them to choose into that sacred Order the first Martyr Saint Stephen, with others: Mercifully behold these Thy servants now called to that same Office

and Ministration; and so replenish them with the truth of Thy doctrine, and adorn them with innocency of life, that, both by word and good example, they may faithfully serve Thee in this office, to the glory of Thy Name, and the edification of Thy Church; through the Merits of our Saviour Jesus Christ, Who liveth and reigneth with Thee and the Holy Ghost, now and forever. *Amen.*

Then shall follow the Collect appointed for the Day.

THE LESSON APPOINTED FOR THE EPISTLE. *Acts* 6. 2.

THEN the Twelve called the multitude of the disciples unto them, and said, It is not reason that we should leave the Word of God, and serve tables. Wherefore, brethren, look ye out among you seven men of honest report, full of the Holy Ghost and wisdom, whom we may appoint over this business. But we will give ourselves continually to prayer, and to the ministry of the Word. And the saying pleased the whole multitude. And they chose Stephen, a man full of faith, and of the Holy Ghost, and Philip, and Prochorus, and Nicanor, and Timon, and Parmenas, and Nicholas a proselyte of Antioch; whom they set before the Apostles; and, when they had prayed, they laid their hands on them. And the Word of God increased, and the number of the disciples multiplied in Jerusalem greatly, and a great company of the priests were obedient to the faith.

Or else this,

THE EPISTLE. I *Timothy* 3. 8-13.

LIKEWISE must the Deacons be grave, not double tongued, not given to much wine, not greedy of filthy lucre; holding the mystery of the faith in a pure conscience. And let these also first be proved; then let them use the Office of a Deacon, being found blameless. Even so must their wives be grave, not slanderers, sober, faithful in all things. Let the Deacons be the husbands of one wife, ruling their children and their own houses well. For they that have used the Office of a Deacon well purchase to themselves a good degree, and great boldness in the faith which is in Christ Jesus.

And before the Gospel, the Bishop, sitting in his Chair, shall cause the Ordinands to be brought forward to stand before him, at which time a hymn may be sung.

Then shall the required Oath of Allegiance and the Profession and the Promise of Due Obedience be administered unto every one of them that is to be ordered that day, each one placing his left hand upon the holy Bible, raising his right, and repeating the prescribed Forms as hereafter followeth.

THE OATH OF ALLEGIANCE.

I, *N.*, do testify, and declare in my conscience, that the Queen is the only Supreme Governor of this Dominion, and of all other Her Majesty's Realms and Territories, and hath supreme jurisdiction within her Realms and Territories in all matters and causes pertaining to the government thereof: And that I do hereby solemnly and sincerely promise and swear that I will be faithful, and bear true allegiance to Her Majesty *ELIZABETH* the Second, by the grace of God of the United Kingdom of Great Britain and Northern Ireland, Canada, and all other her Realms and Territories, Queen, Defender of the Faith, Head of the Commonwealth, and to all her rightful heirs and successors according to law. So help me God, and the contents of this Book. Amen.

THE ORDINAL

THE PROFESSION AND THE PROMISE OF DUE OBEDIENCE.

IN the Name of God. Amen. I, *N.*, do hereby and hereon solemnly profess, and promise to hold and maintain, the Doctrine, Sacraments, and Discipline of Christ, as the Lord hath commanded in His holy Word, and as the undivided Church ever received, professed, and set forth the same; and I do here also promise due obedience to the Bishop of this Diocese, and to his Successors. So help me God, through Jesus Christ. Amen.

THE EXAMINATION

Then shall the Bishop examine every one of them that are to be ordered, in the presence of the people, after this manner following.

BRETHREN, before we proceed to admit you to the Order of Deacons, we will examine you in certain articles, to the end that this Congregation present may have a trial, and bear witness, how you be minded to minister in the Church of God.

DO you trust that you are inwardly moved by the Holy Ghost to take upon you this Office and Ministration, to serve God, for the promoting of His glory, and the edifying of His people?

Answer. I trust so.

The Bishop.

DO you think, that you are truly called, according to the will of our Lord Jesus Christ, and the due order of this portion of His Church, to the Ministry of the Church?

Answer. I think so.

The Bishop.

DO you believe the holy Scriptures of the Old and New Testament to be truly the Word of God, and to contain in themselves all things necessary to salvation?

Answer. I do so believe.

The Bishop.

WILL you diligently read the same unto the people assembled in the Church, where you shall be appointed to serve.

Answer. I will.

The Bishop.

IT appertaineth to the Office of a Deacon, in the Church where he shall be appointed to serve, to assist the Priest in Divine Service, and especially when he ministereth the holy Communion, and to help him in the distribution thereof, and to read holy Scriptures and Homilies in the Church; and to instruct the youth in the Catechism; and in the absence of the Priest, to baptise infants (and those of riper years, if necessity so require), to marry, to bury the Dead, to say the Divine Service, and to preach, if he be admitted thereto by the Bishop. And furthermore, it is also his Office, where provision is so made, to search for the sick, poor, and impotent people of the parish, to intimate their estates, names, and places where they dwell, unto the Priest, that by his exhortation they may be relieved with the alms of the parishioners, or others. Will you do this gladly and willingly?

Answer. I will so do, by the help of God.

THE ORDINAL

The Bishop.

WILL you apply all your diligence, to frame, and fashion your own lives, and the lives of your families according to the doctrine of Christ, and to make both yourselves, and them (as much as in you lieth,) wholesome examples of the flock of Christ.

Answer. I will so do, the Lord being my helper.

The Bishop.

WILL you reverently obey your Ordinary, and other chief Ministers of the Church, and them to whom the charge and Government over you is committed; following with a glad mind and will their godly Admonitions.

Answer. I will endeavour myself so to do, the Lord being my helper.

Then shall the Bishop, standing up, say,

ALMIGHTY God, Whose providence hath brought you to this hour: Keep you steadfast by His grace in these your promises; through Jesus Christ our Lord. *Amen.*

THE ORDINATION

Then shall the Bishop say,
OUR help standeth in the Name of the Lord;
   Answer. Who hath made heaven and earth.
Bishop. Blessed be the Name of the Lord;
   Answer. Henceforth, world without end.
Bishop. Lord, hear our Prayer.
   Answer. And let our cry come unto Thee.

And the Bishop still standing, and extending his hands over them who are to be made Deacons, shall then say over them this Prayer following; and they who are to be ordained all humbly kneeling upon their knees.

ALMIGHTY God, Who art the Author and Giver of all good things, and Who hast been pleased to call these Thy servants to the Office and Work of Deacon in Thy holy Church: Send down Thy Holy Spirit upon them, we most humbly beseech Thee; and grant that they may be strengthened by Thy seven-fold gifts of grace, and enabled faithfully to fulfill the Work of this Office unto which it hath pleased Thee to call them; and, that they may duly execute this their Ministry, give unto them all the grace needful for the same. Make them to be modest, humble, and constant in all their ministrations; and to have a good and ready will to observe all spiritual discipline; that they, having always the testimony of a good conscience, may continue ever stable and strong in Thy Son our Saviour Jesus Christ, and be always diligent in their service to Thy Church; through the same Jesus Christ our Lord, to Whom with Thee and the Holy Ghost, be all honour and glory, for ever and ever. *Amen.*

Then the Bishop laying his hands severally upon the head of every one of them,
humbly kneeling before him, shall say,

TAKE thou authority to execute the Office of a Deacon in the Church of God, now committed unto thee by the Imposition of our hands, In the Name of the Father, and of the Son, and of the Holy Ghost. Amen.

Then shall the Bishop deliver to every one of them the New Testament, saying,

TAKE thou authority to read the holy Gospel in the Congregation, and to preach the same if thou be thereto licenced by the Bishop himself.

THE ORDINAL

Then shall each new Deacon be vested according to his Office; and the Bishop may also exchange the Kiss of Peace with each of them in order at that time.

Then shall be said or sung the Gradual as followeth.

THE GRADUAL. *Psalm* 135. 19-21.

ALLELUIA, Alleluia. Praise the Lord, ye house of Israel / praise the Lord, ye house of Aaron. Praise the Lord, ye house of Levi; / ye that fear the Lord, praise the Lord. Praised be the Lord out of Sion / Who dwelleth at Jerusalem. Alleluia.
(And here let it be noted that the Alleluias shall be omitted during Advent and Lent.)

Then one of the newly-made Deacons, appointed by the Bishop, shall read the Gospel.

THE GOSPEL. *Saint Luke* 12. 35-40.

AT that time, Jesus said unto His disciples, Let your loins be girded about, and your lights burning; and ye yourselves like unto men that wait for their Lord, when He will return from the wedding; that when He cometh and knocketh, they may open unto Him immediately. Blessed are those servants, whom the Lord when He cometh shall find watching. Verily I say unto you, that He shall gird Himself, and make them to sit down to meat, and will come forth and serve them. And if He shall come in the second watch, or come in the third watch, and find them so, blessed are those servants. And this know, that if the goodman of the house had known what hour the thief would come, he would have watched, and not have suffered his house to be broken through. Be ye therefore ready also: for the Son of man cometh at an hour when ye think not.

Then shall the Bishop continue in the celebration of the Holy Eucharist; and all they that are made Deacons that day shall receive the Holy Communion with the Bishop.

THE FINAL PRAYERS AND BENEDICTION

The Communion ended, immediately before the Benediction, these two Prayers following shall be said.

ALMIGHTY God, Who hast vouchsafed to accept these Thy servants unto the Order of Deacon in Thy Church: Grant unto them that they may so execute their Ministry that they may ever honour and glorify Thee, and edify Thy people whom Thou hast appointed them to serve; and that they, duly fulfilling their Office, may be found worthy to be called unto the higher Ministries in thy Church, according to Thy will; through the same Thy Son, our Saviour Jesus Christ. *Amen.*

PREVENT us, O Lord, in all our doings with Thy most gracious favour, and further us with Thy continual help; that in all our works, begun, continued, and ended in Thee, we may glorify Thy holy Name, and finally, by Thy mercy, obtain everlasting life; through Jesus Christ our Lord. *Amen.*

Then shall the Bishop let them depart with this Blessing.

THE peace of God, which passeth all understanding, keep your hearts and minds in the knowledge and love of God, and of His Son Jesus Christ our Lord: And the blessing of God Almighty, ✠ the Father, the Son, and the Holy Ghost, be amongst you and remain with you always. *Amen.*

And here it must be declared unto the Deacon, that, if he is to advance in the Ministry he must continue in the office of a Deacon for the space of a whole year, (except for reasonable causes it shall otherwise seem good unto the Bishop,) to the intent he may be perfect and well expert in the things appertaining to the Ecclesiastical Administration.

In the executing whereof if he be found faithful and diligent, he may be admitted by his Diocesan to the Order of Priesthood on the Sundays immediately following the Ember Weeks, or on other such days as shall be appointed by the Bishop, in the face of the Church, in such Manner and Form as hereafter followeth. And if there be just and lawful reason therefor, the Diocesan may request some other Bishop to ordain a candidate for him. And here let it be noted that if there be only one made Deacon that day, the Bishop shall take care to change all words in the preceding Order denoting the plural to those indicating the singular wheresoever that be necessary.

Here endeth the FORM AND MANNER OF MAKING OF DEACONS.

THE FORM AND MANNER OF
ORDERING OF PRIESTS

When the day appointed by the Bishop is come; after Morning Prayer is ended, there shall be a Sermon, or Exhortation, declaring the Duty, and Office of such as come to be admitted Priests; how necessary that Order is in the Church of Christ; and also how the people ought to esteem them in their Office.

THE PRESENTATION

First the Archdeacon or his Deputy shall present unto the Bishop (sitting in his Chair, near to the holy Table) such as are to be ordained Priests (each one of them being decently vested in his Albe), saying these words.

REVEREND Father in God; I present unto you these persons present, to be admitted to the Order of Priests.

The Bishop.

TAKE heed that the persons whom ye present unto us, be apt and meet, for their learning, and godly conversation, to exercise their Ministry duly, to the honour of God, and the edifying of His Church

The Archdeacon shall answer,

I HAVE enquired of them, and also examined them; and think them so to be.

Then the Bishop shall say unto the people,

GOOD people, these are they, whom we purpose, God willing, to receive this day unto the holy Office of Priesthood. For after due examination, we find not to the contrary, but that they be lawfully called to their Function and Ministry and that they be persons meet for the same. But yet if there be any of you, who knoweth any Impediment, or notable Crime in any of them, for the which he ought not to be received into this Order of Ministry: Let him come forth in the Name of God, and shew what the Crime or Impediment is.

And if any great Crime, or Impediment be objected, the Bishop shall surcease from ordering that person, until such time as the party accused shall be found clear of that Crime.

THE LITANY

Then the Bishop (commending such as shall be found meet to be ordered Priests, to the prayers of the congregation) shall, with the Clergy and people present, sing or say the Litany as it is before appointed in the Form of Making of Deacons; save only that in the place of the proper suffrage for Making of Deacons, this suffrage for the Ordering of Priests shall be sung or said instead:

To bless these Thy servants at this time to be admitted to the Order of Priests; and to send down Thy Holy Spirit upon them, and so fill them with Thy heavenly grace; that they may duly execute their Office and Ministry to the edifying of Thy Church and the glory of Thy holy Name,

Answer. We beseech Thee, good Lord.

THE EUCHARIST

Then shall be sung, or said, the Order for the Administration of the Holy Eucharist, with the Introit, Collect, Epistle, Gradual, and Gospel, as followeth.

THE ORDINAL

THE INTROIT. *Psalm* 110.

THE Lord said unto my Lord, / Sit Thou on my right hand, until I make Thine enemies Thy footstool. The Lord shall send the rod of Thy power out of Sion / be Thou ruler, even in the midst among Thine enemies. In the day of Thy power shall the people offer Thee free-will offerings with an holy worship; / the dew of Thy birth is of the womb of the morning. The Lord sware, and will not repent / Thou art a Priest for ever after the order of Melchizedek. The Lord upon Thy right hand / shall wound even kings in the day of His wrath. He shall judge among the heathen; he shall fill the places with the dead bodies / and smite in sunder the heads over divers countries. He shall drink of the brook in the way / therefore shall He lift up His head.

GLORY be to the Father, and to the Son, / and to the Holy Ghost:

As it was in the beginning, is now, and ever shall be, / world without end. Amen.

THE COLLECT.

ALMIGHTY God, Giver of all good things, Who by Thy Holy Spirit hast appointed divers Orders of Ministers in Thy Church: Mercifully behold these Thy servants now called to the Order of Priesthood in Thy holy Church; and vouchsafe, O Lord, to pour down Thy Holy Spirit upon them, giving unto them both power and authority to preach Thy Word, and to minister Thy Sacraments; and replenish them so with the truth of Thy doctrine, and adorn them with innocency of life, that both by word and good example, they may faithfully serve Thee in this Office and Ministry, to the honour and glory of Thy Name, and the edification of Thy Church; through the same Thy Son Jesus Christ our Lord. *Amen.*

Then shall follow the Collect for the Day.

THE EPISTLE. *Ephesians* 4. 7-13.

UNTO every one of us is given grace, according to the measure of the gift of Christ; wherefore He saith, When He ascended up on high, He led captivity captive, and gave gifts unto men. Now that He ascended, what is it but that He also descended first into the lower parts of the earth? He that descended is the same also that ascended far above all heavens, that He might fill all things. And He gave some, Apostles; and some, Prophets; and some, Evangelists; and some, Pastors and Teachers; for the perfecting of the saints for the work of the ministry, for the edifying of the body of Christ; till we all come, in the unity of the faith and of the knowledge of the Son of God, unto a perfect man, unto the measure of the stature of the fullness of Christ.

Or this.

Hebrews 7. 1-28.

FOR this Melchizedek, King of Salem, Priest of the most high God, who met Abraham returning from the slaughter of the kings, and blessed him; to whom also Abraham gave a tenth part of all; first being by interpretation King of Righteousness, and after that also King of Salem, which is, King of Peace; without father, without mother, without descent, having neither beginning of days, nor end of life; but made like unto the Son of God; abideth a priest continually. Now consider how great this man was, unto whom even the patriarch Abraham gave the tenth of the spoils. And verily they that are of the sons of Levi, who receive the office of the priesthood, have a commandment to take tithes of the people according to the law, that is, of their brethren, though they come out of the loins of Abraham: but he whose descent is not counted from them received tithes of Abraham, and blessed him that had the promises. And without all contradiction the less is blessed of the better. And here men that die receive tithes; but there he receiveth them, of whom it is witnessed that he liveth. And as I may so say, Levi also, who receiveth tithes, paid tithes in Abraham. For he was yet in the loins of his father, when Melchizedek met him. If therefore perfection were by the Levitical priesthood, (for under it the people received the law,) what further need was there that another priest should rise after the order of Melchizedek, and not be called after the order of Aaron? For the priesthood being changed, there is made of necessity a change also of the law. For he of whom these things are spoken pertaineth to another tribe, of which no man gave attendance at the altar. For it is evident that our Lord sprang out of Judah; of which tribe Moses spake nothing concerning priesthood. And it is yet far more evident: for that after the similitude of Melchizedek there ariseth another Priest, Who is made, not after the law of a carnal commandment, but after the power of an endless life. For he testifieth, Thou art a Priest for ever after the order of Melchizedek. For there is verily a disannulling of the commandment going before for the weakness and unprofitableness thereof. For the law made nothing perfect, but the bringing in of a better hope did; by the which we draw nigh unto God. And inasmuch as not without an oath he was made priest: (for those priests were made without an oath; but this with an oath by Him that said unto him, The Lord sware and will not repent, Thou art a Priest for ever after the order of Melchizedek:) by so much was Jesus made a surety of a better Testament. And they truly were many priests, because they were not suffered to continue by reason of death: but this Man, because he continueth ever, hath an unchangeable Priesthood. Wherefore He is able also to save them to the uttermost that come unto God by Him, seeing He ever liveth to make intercession for them. For such an high Priest became us, Who is holy, harmless, undefiled, separate from sinners, and made higher than the heavens; Who needeth not daily, as those high priests, to offer up sacrifice, first for his own sins, and then for the people's: for this He did once, when He offered up Himself. For the law maketh men high priests which have infirmity; but the Word of the oath, which was since the law, maketh the Son, Who is consecrated for evermore.

THE GRADUAL. *Psalm* 132. 7-9.

ALLELUIA, Alleluia. We will go into His dwelling-place, / and fall low upon our knees before His foot-stool. Arise, O Lord, into Thy resting-place, / Thou and the ark of Thy strength. Let Thy priests be clothed with righteousness; / and let Thy saints sing with joyfulness. Alleluia.
(And here it is to be noted, that the Alleluias shall be omitted during Advent and Lent.)

THE GOSPEL. *Saint John* 10. 1-16.

VERILY, verily I say unto you, He that entereth not by the door into the sheep-fold, but climbeth up some other way, the same is a thief and a robber. But he that entereth in by the door is the shepherd of the sheep: to him the porter openeth; and the sheep hear his voice, and he calleth his own sheep by name, and leadeth them out. And, when he putteth forth his own sheep, he goeth before them, and the sheep follow him; for they know his voice. And a stranger will they not follow; but will flee from him; for they know not the voice of strangers. This parable spake Jesus unto them: but they understood not what things they were which He spake unto them. Then said Jesus unto them again, Verily, verily I say unto you, I am the Door of the sheep. All that ever came before me are thieves and robbers; but the sheep did not hear them. I am the Door; by me if any man enter in, he shall be saved, and shall go in and out, and shall find pasture. The thief cometh not but for to steal, and kill, and to destroy: I am come that they might have life, and that they might have it more abundantly. I am the good Shepherd: the good Shepherd giveth His life for the sheep. But he that is an hireling, and not the Shepherd, whose own the sheep are not, seeth the wolf coming, and leaveth the sheep, and fleeth; and the wolf catcheth them, and scattereth the sheep. The hireling fleeth, because he is an hireling, and careth not for the sheep. I am the good Shepherd, and know my sheep, and am known of mine. As the Father knoweth me, even so know I the Father: and I lay down my Life for the sheep. And other sheep I have, which are not of this fold; them also I must bring, and they shall hear my voice; and there shall be one flock, and one Shepherd.

The Gospel ended, the Bishop, sitting in his Chair, shall cause the Ordinands to be brought forward to stand before him, at which time a hymn may be sung.

Then shall the required Oath of Allegiance and the Profession and the Promise of Due Obedience be administered unto every one of them that is to be ordered that day, each one placing his left hand upon the holy Bible, raising his right, and repeating the prescribed Forms as hereafter followeth.

THE OATH OF ALLEGIANCE.

I, *N.*, do testify, and declare in my conscience, that the Queen is the only Supreme Governor of this Dominion, and of all other Her Majesty's Realms and Territories, and hath supreme jurisdiction within her Realms and Territories in all matters and causes pertaining to the government thereof: And that I do hereby solemnly and sincerely promise and swear that I will be faithful, and bear true allegiance to Her Majesty *ELIZABETH* the Second, by the grace of God of the United Kingdom of Great Britain and Northern Ireland, Canada, and all other her Realms and Territories, Queen, Defender of the Faith, Head of the Commonwealth, and to all her rightful heirs and successors according to law. So help me God, and the contents of this Book. Amen.

THE PROFESSION AND THE PROMISE OF DUE OBEDIENCE.

In the Name of God. Amen. I, *N.*, do hereby and hereon solemnly profess, and promise to hold and maintain, the Doctrine, Sacraments, and Discipline of Christ, as the Lord hath commanded in His holy Word, and as the undivided Church ever received, professed, and set forth the same; and I do here also promise due obedience to the Bishop of this Diocese, and to his Successors. So help me God, through Jesus Christ. Amen.

THE EXHORTATION AND EXAMINATION

And the Bishop, sitting in his Chair before the Lord's Table, shall then say unto the Ordinands brought to stand before him this Exhortation, as hereafter followeth.

YOU have heard, brethren, as well in your private examination, as in the Exhortation which was made to you, and in the Lessons taken out of the holy Gospel and the writings of the Apostles, of what dignity and of how great importance this sacred Office of Priesthood is, whereunto ye are called.

And now again, we exhort you, in the Name of our Lord Jesus Christ, that you have in remembrance, into how high a Dignity, and to how weighty an Office and Charge ye are called: that is to say, to be the Messengers, Watchmen, and Stewards of the Lord; to teach and to premonish; to feed and provide for the Lord's family, preaching His holy Word and ministering His holy Sacraments unto them; and to seek for Christ's sheep that are dispersed abroad, and for His children who are in the midst of this sinful world, that they may be saved through Christ forever.

Have always therefore printed in your remembrance, how great a treasure is committed to your charge. For they are the sheep of Christ, which He bought with His Death, and for whom He shed His precious Blood. The Church and Congregation whom you must serve is His Spouse and His Body. And if it shall happen the same Church, or any member thereof, to take any hurt or hindrance by reason of your negligence, ye know the greatness of the fault, and also the horrible punishment that will ensue.

Wherefore, consider with yourselves the end of your Ministry towards the children of God, towards the Spouse and Body of Christ; and see that you never cease your labour, your care, and your diligence, until you have done all that lieth in you, according to your bounden duty, to bring all such as are or shall be committed to your charge, unto that agreement in the faith and knowledge of God, and to that ripeness and perfectness of age in Christ, that there be no place left among you, either for error in religion, or for viciousness of life.

Forasmuch then, dear brethren, as this Office is both of so great excellency and of so great difficulty (the execution whereof is the ministration in this world of the heavenly grace of the eternal Priesthood of our Lord Jesus Christ), ye see with how great care and study ye ought to apply yourselves, as well that ye may shew yourselves dutiful and thankful unto that Lord, Who hath placed you in so high a Dignity; as also to beware that neither you yourselves offend, nor be the occasion that others offend. Howbeit, ye cannot have a mind and will thereto of yourselves; for that will and ability is given of God alone.

Therefore ye ought, and have need, to pray for His Holy Spirit. And seeing that you cannot not by any other means compass the doing of so weighty a work, pertaining to the salvation of man, but with doctrine and exhortation taken out of the holy Scriptures, and with a life agreeable to the same; consider how studious ye ought to be in reading and learning the Scriptures, and in framing the manners of both yourselves, and of them that specially pertain unto you, according to the rule of the same Scriptures: and for this self-same cause, how ye ought to forsake and set aside (as much as you may) all worldly cares and studies.

We have good hope, brethren, that you have well weighed and pondered these things with yourselves long before this time; and that you have clearly determined, by God's grace, to give yourselves wholly to this Office, whereunto it hath pleased God to call you: so that, as much as lieth in you, you will apply yourselves wholly to this one thing, and draw all your cares and studies this way; and that you will continually pray to God the Father, by the Mediation of our only Saviour Jesus Christ, for the heavenly assistance of the Holy Ghost; that, by daily reading and weighing of the Scriptures, ye may wax riper and stronger in your Ministry; and that ye may so endeavour yourselves from time to time to sanctify the lives of you and yours, and to fashion them after the rule and doctrine of Christ, that ye may be wholesome and godly examples and patterns for the people to follow.

And now, that this present Congregation of Christ here assembled may also understand your minds and wills in these things, and that this your promise may the more move you to do your duty, you shall answer plainly to these things, which we, in the Name of God, and of His holy Church, shall demand of each one of you touching the same.

Do you think in your heart that you be truly called, according to the will of our Lord Jesus Christ, and the due order of this portion of His holy Church, to the Order and Ministry of Priesthood?

Answer. I think it.

The Bishop.

Are you persuaded that the holy Scriptures of the Old and New Testaments are truly the Word of God, and contain in themselves sufficiently all Doctrine required of necessity for eternal salvation through faith in Jesus Christ? And are you determined out of the said Scriptures to instruct the people committed to your charge, and to teach no doctrine but that true Doctrine which holy Church doth teach, as the same is concluded and proved by the Scripture?

Answer. I am so persuaded, and have so determined by God's grace.

The Bishop.

It appertaineth to the Office of a Priest in the Church of God to preach and teach God's Word, and to preside at Divine Service; to stand before the Table of the Lord, and to shew forth the Sacrifice of His Death in His Supper, and to minister the Sacrament of His Body and Blood to His people; to baptise believers, and their children; to counsel and absolve the penitent; to lay hands upon the sick, and to anoint them with Oil in the Name of the Lord; to solemnise Matrimony; to exhort the sinner, admonish the froward, and rebuke the wicked; to comfort the Dying, and to bury the Dead; and to bless and consecrate the things of this earth for holy use. Will you do all these things gladly and willingly?

Answer. I will so do, God being my Helper.

The Bishop.

Will you then give your faithful diligence always so to minister the Doctrine, Sacraments, and Discipline of Christ, as the Lord hath commanded, and as this portion of His Church hath received and set forth the same, according to the Commandments of Almighty God; so that you may rightly teach the people committed to your cure, and charge them with all diligence to keep and observe the same?

Answer. I will so do, by the help of the Lord.

The Bishop.

Will you be ready, with all faithful diligence, to banish and drive away all erroneous and strange doctrines contrary to God's Word; and to use both public and private monitions, and exhortations, as well to the sick as to the whole, within your cure of souls, as need shall require, and occasion shall be given?

Answer. I will, the Lord being my Helper.

The Bishop.

Will you be diligent in prayers, and in reading of the holy Scriptures, and in such godly studies as shall help to the knowledge of the same, laying aside (as much as shall in you lie by reason of necessity) the study of the world and the flesh?

Answer. I will endeavour myself so to do, the Lord being my Helper.

The Bishop.

Will you be diligent to frame and fashion your own selves, and your families, according to the Doctrine of Christ; and to make both yourselves and them, as much as in you lieth, wholesome examples and patterns to the flock of Christ?

Answer. I will apply myself thereto, the Lord being my Helper.

The Bishop.

Will you maintain and set forward, as much as lieth in you, quietness, peace, and love amongst all Christian people, and especially among them that are or shall be committed to your charge?

Answer. I will so do, the Lord being my Helper.

THE ORDINAL

The Bishop.

WILL you reverently obey your Ordinary, and other chief Ministers, unto whom is or shall be committed the Charge and Government over you, following with a glad mind and will their godly admonitions, and submitting yourselves to their godly judgements?

Answer. I will so do, the Lord being my Helper.

Then shall the Bishop, standing up, say,

MAY Almighty God, Who hath given you this will to do all these things, grant also unto you strength and power to perform the same; that He may accomplish His work which He hath begun in you; through Jesus Christ our Lord. *Amen.*

THE PRAYER FOR THE ORDINANDS

Then shall the Bishop say to the Congregation,

DEARLY beloved, let us pray for these persons now to be Ordained and admitted Priests of our Lord Jesus Christ; that each one may steadfastly keep those solemn promises which he hath here made this day, and faithfully hold the holy Office of Priesthood and duly execute the Ministry, whereunto we trust it hath pleased Almighty God to call them.

After this, the Congregation shall secretly in their prayers make their humble supplications to Almighty God for all these things: for the which prayers silence shall be kept for a space.

Then shall the Bishop say,
O Lord, hear our prayer.
Answer. And let our cry come unto Thee.

Bishop. Let us pray.

Then shall the Bishop say this Prayer following.

ALMIGHTY Father, we most humbly beseech Thee to pour down Thy Holy Spirit upon these Thy servants: Fill them with Thy heavenly grace, and bestow upon them the dignity of the Priesthood of our Lord and Saviour Jesus Christ; make them to be diligent and effectual Ministers of the Gospel and New Testament of Thy Son, and Priests forever after the Order of Melchizedek; and grant unto each one of them, O Lord, that he may so worthily hold this sacred Office, and faithfully execute his holy Ministry, that he may always glorify Thee, and edify Thy Church, by the example of his life and conversation; and finally receive of Thee the crown of glory that fadeth not away; through the same Thy Son Jesus Christ our Lord. *Amen.*

THE INVOCATION OF THE HOLY GHOST

Then shall all those who are to be ordained Priests shall kneel down, and the hymn following, Veni, Creator Spiritus, *shall be sung over them, the Bishop himself beginning, as followeth.*

COME, Holy Ghost, our souls inspire,
    And lighten with celestial fire:
Thou the anointing Spirit art,
    Who dost Thy seven-fold gifts impart.

Thy blessed unction from above
    Is comfort, life, and fire of love.

Enable with perpetual light
  The dullness of our blinded sight.

Anoint and cheer our soilèd face
  With the abundance of Thy grace.
Keep far our foes, give peace at home:
  Where Thou art Guide, no ill can come.

Teach us to know the Father, Son,
  And Thee, of Both, to be but One;
That, through the ages all along,
  This may be our endless song:
Praise to Thine eternal merit,
Father, Son, and Holy Spirit. Amen.

THE ORDINATION

Then shall the Bishop, and all those Priests who shall join with him in the Laying on of hands, stand up. And the Bishop shall stand in the midst of the Priests (who shall stand evenly on either side of him and around the person to be ordained). And the Bishop shall begin as followeth.

The Bishop shall say,
THE Lord be with you.
  Answer. And with thy spirit.
Bishop. Lift up your hearts.
  Answer. We lift them up unto the Lord.
Bishop. Let us give thanks unto our Lord God.
  Answer. It is meet and right so to do.

Then shall the Bishop extend his hands over them that are to be ordained, and shall say,

IT is very meet, right, and our bounden duty, that we should at all times, and in all places, give thanks unto Thee, Holy Lord, Almighty Father, Everlasting God, Maker and Preserver of all things; Who of Thine infinite love and goodness towards us hast given unto us Thine only and most dearly beloved Son Jesus Christ to be our Redeemer and great High Priest, and the Author of everlasting life; Who, after He had made perfect our redemption by His Death, and was ascended into heaven, sent abroad into the world His Apostles, Prophets, Evangelists, Doctors and Pastors, by whose labour and ministry He gathered together a great flock in all parts of the world, to set forth the eternal praise of Thy holy Name. For these so great benefits of Thine eternal goodness, O Lord, and for that Thou hast called these Thy servants to that same Office of Priesthood which Thou hast appointed for the salvation of mankind, we render unto Thee most high praise and hearty thanks, we bless Thee, and we worship Thee.

  Hear us, O merciful Father, we most humbly beseech Thee, and vouchsafe to send down Thy Holy Spirit upon these persons, and so make them Priests of the New Testament of Thy Son Jesus Christ; and, that they may be effectual Ministers of Thy holy Word and Sacraments, give unto them all the grace needful for the due execution of that Ministry whereunto we trust they have been called and now purpose to admit them by the Laying on of our hands, and the hands of the Presbytery.

And grant, Almighty God, unto all which, either here or elsewhere, call upon Thy holy Name, that we may continue to shew ourselves thankful unto Thee for these and all other Thy many benefits; and that we may daily increase and go forwards in the knowledge and faith of Thee and of Thy Son, by the Holy Ghost; so that as well by these Ministers of Thy grace, as by them over whom they shall be appointed Thy Ministers, Thy holy Name may be forever glorified, and Thy blessed kingdom enlarged and extended; through the same Thy Son Jesus Christ our Lord, Who liveth and reigneth with Thee in the unity of the same Holy Ghost, ever one God, world without end. Amen.

When this Prayer is done, the Bishop with the Priests present shall lay their hands severally upon the head of each one that receiveth the Order of Priesthood; the receivers thereof humbly kneeling upon their knees, and the Bishop alone saying,

RECEIVE the Holy Ghost for the Office and Work of a Priest in the Church of God, now committed unto thee by the Imposition of our hands. Whose sins thou dost forgive, they are forgiven; and whose sins thou dost retain, they are retained. And be thou a faithful dispenser of the Word of God, and of His holy Sacraments, In the Name of the Father, and of the Son, and of the Holy Ghost. Amen.

Then shall the Bishop anoint the hands of the new Priest with Chrism, saying,

WE anoint thee with this Chrism, as an outward sign that thou art hereby set apart for the Office and Work of a Priest of the New Testament of our Lord Jesus Christ in the Church of God, In the Name of the Father, and of the Son, and of the Holy Ghost. Amen. And as thou art anointed outwardly with this holy Chrism, so may God the Holy Ghost anoint thee inwardly with His grace, and grant unto thee the power and authority to execute the Office and Work of the Priesthood, according to His holy will; and do thou ever remember by this sacred unction that thou wert this day made a Priest forever after the Order of Melchizedek, that is of our Saviour Christ.

Then shall the Bishop deliver to each one the Chalice and the Paten, saying,

TAKE thou authority to administer the Supper of the Lord, wherein thou shalt shew forth the Death of our Lord Jesus Christ, as He hath commanded; and to offer the same to Almighty God, for the benefit of the quick and the dead.

Then shall the Bishop deliver to him the Bible, saying,

TAKE thou authority to preach the Word of God, and to minister the holy Sacraments in the Congregation, where thou shalt be lawfully appointed thereunto.

Then shall each new Priest be vested according to his Office; and the Bishop may also exchange the Kiss of Peace with each of them in order at that time.

When this is done, the Nicene Creed shall be sung or said; and the Bishop shall after that continue in the administration of the Eucharist, beginning with the Offertory. And all they that have received the Order of Priesthood shall receive the Holy Communion that day with the Bishop, all remaining still in the Chancel until after such time as all have received the Sacrament of Christ's Body and Blood.

THE FINAL PRAYERS AND BENEDICTION

The Communion ended, immediately before the Benediction,
these two Prayers following shall be said.

MOST merciful Father, we beseech Thee to send down Thy heavenly blessing upon these Thy servants whom Thou hast called to the Ministry of Thy Church, and whom we have this day admitted to the Priesthood of our Lord Jesus Christ; and so endue them with the grace of Thy Holy Spirit, that they, preaching Thy Word, may not only be earnest to reprove, beseech, and rebuke with all patience and doctrine; but also may be unto such as believe wholesome examples, in word, in conversation, in love, in faith, in chastity, and in purity; that each one, faithfully fulfilling his course, at the latter day may receive the crown of righteousness, laid up by the Lord the righteous Judge; through the same Thy Son Jesus Christ our Lord, Who liveth and reigneth with Thee and the same Holy Ghost, ever one God, world without end. *Amen.*

PREVENT us, O Lord, in all our doings with Thy most gracious favour, and further us with Thy continual help; that in all our works, begun, continued, and ended in Thee, we may glorify Thy holy Name, and finally by Thy mercy obtain everlasting life; through Jesus Christ our Lord. *Amen.*

THE peace of God, which passeth all understanding, keep your hearts and minds in the knowledge and love of God, and of His Son Jesus Christ our Lord: And the blessing of God Almighty, ✠ the Father, the Son, and the Holy Ghost, be amongst you and remain with you always. *Amen.*

And if there be only one person ordered Priest that day, the Bishop shall take care to change all words in the preceding Order denoting the plural to those indicating the singular wheresoever that may be necessary.

Here endeth the FORM AND MANNER OF ORDERING OF PRIESTS.

The Form of Ordaining and
Consecrating of an
Archbishop or Bishop
Which is always to be performed upon some Sunday or Holy-day.

The Ordaining and Consecrating of an Archbishop or Bishop shall be performed by the Primate, or by the Metropolitan of the Province, who shall be and act as the principal Consecrator unless, for some urgent, just and lawful cause, another Bishop shall be appointed by him or by the Bishops of the National Synod to act in his stead; in which case, the Consecrating Bishop shall act as the representative of the Archbishop.

According to the ancient Canons and the Constitution and Canons of this Church, no less than three Bishops shall be required to lay hands upon any man in order that he be regularly and properly Ordained and Consecrated a Bishop in the Church of God.

When all things are duly prepared in the Church and set in order, after Morning Prayer is ended, the Archbishop or Consecrating Bishop shall begin the Eucharist; in which this Psalm following shall be the Introit.

The Eucharist

The Introit. Psalm 132. 8-18.

ARISE, O Lord, into Thy resting-place; / Thou, and the ark of Thy strength. Let Thy priests be clothed with righteousness, / and let Thy Saints sing with joyfulness. For Thy servant David's sake, / turn not away the presence of Thine Anointed. The Lord hath made a faithful oath unto David, / and He shall not shrink from it: Of the fruit of thy body / shall I set upon thy throne. If thy children will keep my covenant, and my testimonies that I shall teach them, / thy children shall sit upon thy throne for evermore. For the Lord hath chosen Sion; / He hath longed for her to be an habitation for Himself: This shall be my rest forever: / here will I dwell, for I have a delight therein I will bless her victuals with increase, / and will satisfy her poor with bread. I will clothe her priests with salvation, / and her saints shall rejoice and sing. There shall I make the horn of David to flourish: / I have ordained a lantern for mine anointed. As for his enemies, I shall clothe them with shame; / but upon himself shall his crown flourish.

GLORY be to the Father, and to the Son, / and to the Holy Ghost;
As it was in the beginning, is now, and ever shall be, / world without end. Amen.

And this following shall be the Collect.

The Collect.

ALMIGHTY God, Who by Thy blessed Son Jesus Christ didst give to Thy holy Apostles many excellent gifts, and didst charge them to feed Thy flock: Give grace, we beseech Thee, to their successors the Bishops, the Pastors of Thy Church, that they may diligently preach Thy Word, and duly administer the godly discipline thereof; and grant to all Thy people that they may obediently follow the same; that all may receive the crown of everlasting glory; through the same Thy Son Jesus Christ our Lord, Who with Thee and the Holy Ghost, liveth and reigneth ever one God, world without end. *Amen.*

Then shall follow the Collect for the Day.

And another Bishop shall read one of the Lessons following for the Epistle.

THE ORDINAL

THE EPISTLE. I *Timothy* 3. 1-7.

THIS is a true saying, If a man desire the office of a bishop, he desireth a good work. A bishop then must be blameless, the husband of one wife, vigilant, sober, of good behaviour, given to hospitality, apt to teach; not given to wine, no striker, not greedy of filthy lucre; but patient, not a brawler, not covetous; one that ruleth well his own house, having his children in subjection with all gravity; (for if a man know not how to rule his own house, how shall he take care of the Church of God?). Not a novice, lest being lifted up with pride he fall into the condemnation of the devil. Moreover, he must have a good report of them that are without; lest he fall into reproach and the snare of the devil.

Or this.

Titus 1. 1-9.

PAUL, a servant of God, and an apostle of Jesus Christ, according to the faith of God's elect, and the acknowledging of the truth which is after godliness; in hope of eternal life, which God, that cannot lie, promised before the world began; but hath in due times manifested His word through preaching, which is committed unto me according to the commandment of God our Saviour; to Titus, mine own son after the common faith: Grace, mercy, and peace, from God the Father and the Lord Jesus Christ our Saviour. For this cause left I thee in Crete, that thou shouldest set in order the things that are wanting, and ordain presbyters in every city, as I had appointed thee: if any be blameless, the husband of one wife, having faithful children not accused of riot or unruly. For a bishop must be blameless, as the steward of God; not self-willed, not soon angry, not given to wine, no striker, not given to filthy lucre; but a lover of hospitality, a lover of good men, sober, just, holy, temperate; holding fast the faithful word as he hath been taught, that he may be able by sound doctrine both to exhort and to convince the gainsayers.

Then shall this following be said or sung for the Gradual.

THE GRADUAL. *Psalm* 133.

ALLELUIA, Alleluia. Behold, how good and joyful a thing it is, / brethren, to dwell together in unity! It is like the precious oil upon the head, that ran down unto the beard, / even unto Aaron's beard, and went down to the collar of his clothing; like as the dew of Hermon, / which falleth upon the hills of Sion. For there the Lord promised His blessing, / even life for evermore. Alleluia.
(And here let it be noted that the Alleluias shall be omitted during Advent and Lent.)

Then another Bishop shall read one of the following for the Gospel.

THE GOSPEL. *Saint John* 20. 19-23.

THEN the same day at evening, being the first day of the week, when the doors were shut where the disciples were assembled for fear of the Jews, came Jesus and stood in the midst, and saith unto them, Peace be unto you. And when He had so said, He shewed unto them his hands and his side. Then were the disciples glad, when they saw the Lord. Then said Jesus to them again, Peace be unto you: as my Father hath sent me, even so send I you. And when He had said this, He breathed on them, and saith unto them, Receive ye the Holy Ghost: whosesoever sins ye remit, they are remitted unto them; and whosesoever sins ye retain, they are retained.

Or this.

430

THE ORDINAL

Saint John 21. 15-17.

JESUS saith to Simon Peter, Simon, son of John, lovest thou me more than these? He saith unto Him, Yea, Lord; Thou knowest that I love Thee. He saith unto him, Feed my Lambs. He saith to him again the second time, Simon, son of John, lovest thou me? He saith unto Him, Yea, Lord; Thou knowest that I love Thee. He saith unto him, Feed my sheep. He saith unto him the third time, Simon, son of John, lovest thou me? Peter was grieved because He said unto him the third time, Lovest thou me? And he said unto Him, Lord, Thou knowest all things; Thou knowest that I love Thee. Jesus saith unto him, Feed my sheep.

THE PRESENTATION OF THE BISHOP-ELECT

After the Gospel, and the Nicene Creed, and the Sermon are ended, the elected Bishop (vested with his Rochet) shall be presented by two Bishops unto the Archbishop (or the Bishop appointed to be the principal Consecrator), the Archbishop sitting in his Chair, near unto the Holy Table, and the Bishops that present him saying,

MOST Reverend Father in God, we present unto you this godly and well-learned man to be ordained and consecrated Bishop in the Church of God.

Then shall the Archbishop demand the Certificates required before the Consecration of an Archbishop or Bishop, or the Mandate of the Queen, and cause them to be read.

Then shall the Archbishop cause the Bishop-elect to place his left hand upon the Holy Bible, and to raise his right hand, and shall administer to him the Oath of Allegiance and Profession and Oath of Due Obedience to his Metropolitan, as followeth.

THE OATH OF ALLEGIANCE.

I, N., do testify, and declare in my conscience, that the Queen is the only Supreme Governor of this Dominion, and of all other Her Majesty's Realms and Territories, and hath supreme jurisdiction within her Realms and Territories in all matters and causes pertaining to the government thereof: And that I do hereby solemnly and sincerely promise and swear that I will be faithful, and bear true allegiance to Her Majesty ELIZABETH the Second, by the grace of God of the United Kingdom of Great Britain and Northern Ireland, Canada, and all other her Realms and Territories, Queen, Defender of the Faith, Head of the Commonwealth, and to all her rightful heirs and successors according to law. So help me God, and the contents of this Book. Amen.

THE PROFESSION, AND PROMISE OF DUE OBEDIENCE.

IN the Name of God. Amen. I, N., do hereby and hereon solemnly profess, and promise to hold and maintain, the Doctrine, Sacraments, and Discipline of Christ, as the Lord hath commanded in His holy Word, and as the undivided Church ever received, professed, and set forth the same; and I do also promise and profess due obedience to the Metropolitical Archbishop of this Province, and to his lawful successors. So help me God, through Jesus Christ. Amen.

(And here let it be noted that when Consecrating an Archbishop, the foregoing Promise of due Obedience shall not be administered to the Archbishop-elect.)

THE LITANY

Then the Archbishop shall move the Congregation present to pray, saying thus to them,

BRETHREN, it is written in the Gospel of Saint Luke, that our Saviour Christ continued the whole night in prayer, before He did choose and send forth His twelve Apostles. It is written also in the Acts of the Apostles, that the disciples who were at Antioch did fast and pray, before they laid hands on Paul and Barnabas, and sent them forth. Let us therefore, following the example of our Saviour

Christ and His Apostles, first fall to prayer, before we ordain and consecrate, and admit and send forth this person presented unto us, to the Office and Ministration whereunto we trust the Holy Ghost hath called him.

Then the Archbishop shall, with the other Bishops and the Clergy and people present, sing or say the Litany as before in the form of Making of Deacons; save only that after the proper suffrage for the Making of Deacons, this suffrage for the Consecrating of a Bishop shall be sung or said instead:

To bless this our Brother elected; and to pour down Thy Holy Spirit upon him, and so endue him with every necessary grace; that he may duly execute his Office and Ministry whereunto it hath pleased Thee to call him; to the honour, praise, and glory of Thy Name, and the right governing and ordering of Thy Church,

Answer. We beseech Thee, good Lord.

The Litany ended, the Archbishop shall then say this Prayer following.

ALMIGHTY God, Giver of all good things, Who by Thy Holy Spirit hast appointed divers Orders of Ministers in Thy Church: We humbly beseech Thee mercifully to behold this Thy chosen servant now to be admitted to the Order of Bishops, and to bestow upon him all the fullness of the Priesthood of Thy Son our Lord Jesus Christ; and so replenish him with the truth of Thy doctrine, and adorn him with innocency of life, that, both by word and deed, he may faithfully serve Thee in this Office, to the honour and glory of Thy holy Name, and the edifying and well-governing of Thy Church; through the Merits of the same Thy blessed Son Jesus Christ our Lord, Who liveth and reigneth with Thee and the Holy Ghost, ever one God, world without end. Amen.

Then shall the Bishop-elect be brought again to stand before the Archbishop,
at which time a hymn or Psalm may be sung.

THE EXAMINATION

Then the Archbishop, sitting in his Chair, shall say unto him all this that hereafter followeth.

BROTHER, forasmuch as the holy Scriptures and the Canons of the early Church command us that we should not be hasty in the Laying on of hands, and admitting thereby any person to Government in the Church of Christ, which He hath purchased with no less price than the effusion of His own Blood: Before we admit you to the Order of Bishops, we will first examine you in certain articles, to the end that this Congregation here present may have a trial, and bear witness, how you be minded to behave yourself in the Church of God.

ARE you persuaded that you be truly called to this Ministration, according to the will of our Lord Jesus Christ, and the due order of this portion of His holy Church?

Answer. I am so persuaded.

The Archbishop.

ARE you persuaded that the holy Scriptures of the Old and New Testaments are truly the Word of God, and contain sufficiently in themselves all Doctrine required of necessity for eternal salvation through faith in Jesus Christ? And are you determined out of the same Holy Scriptures to instruct the people committed to your charge; and to teach or maintain nothing as required of necessity to eternal salvation, but that which you shall be persuaded may be concluded and proved by the same?

Answer. I am so persuaded, and determined, by God's grace.

The Archbishop.

WILL you then faithfully exercise yourself in the same holy Scriptures, and call upon God by prayer, for the true understanding of the same; so as you may be able by them to teach and exhort with wholesome Doctrine, and to withstand and convince the gainsayers?

Answer. I will so do, by the help of God.

The Archbishop.

Do you profess with your mouth, and believe in your heart, the orthodox Christian Faith as the same is revealed by Almighty God in the aforesaid holy Scriptures, and set forth in the three Creeds and the dogmatic Definitions of the undisputed General Councils of the One undivided Church; and are you ready, with all faithful diligence, to uphold, and to transmit unimpaired, that same true Doctrine, and to banish and drive away all false, erroneous, and strange doctrines that are contrary thereto; and both privately and openly to call upon and encourage others to do the same?

Answer. I do so profess and believe, and am ready so to do, the Lord being my Helper.

The Archbishop.

WILL you deny all ungodliness and worldly lusts, and live soberly, righteously, and godly, in this present world; that you may shew yourself in all things an example of good works unto others, that the adversary may be ashamed, having nothing to say against you?

Answer. I will so do, the Lord being my Helper.

The Archbishop.

WILL you maintain and set forward, as much as shall lie in you, quietness, love, and peace among all men; and such as be unquiet, disobedient, and criminous, within your Diocese, to correct and punish, according to such authority as you have by God's Word, and as to you shall be committed by the Constitution and Canons of this portion of Christ's Church?

Answer. I will so do, by the help of God.

The Archbishop.

IT appertaineth to the Office of a Bishop in the Church of God to judge, to govern, to interpret, and to teach; to proclaim the Gospel of our Saviour Jesus Christ, and to preach His Word; to be instant in season, and out of season; to reprove, to rebuke, and to exhort with all long-suffering and doctrine; to reconcile sinners to God, and to minister the Keys of the kingdom of heaven; to preside over the portion of Christ's Church committed to his care, and to minister the high Priesthood of Jesus Christ in the congregation of His saints; and as chief Pastor of the flock of Christ to confirm, and to ordain, and to consecrate, and to do and perform all other such things as shall pertain to the Work and Ministry of a Bishop in the Church of God. Will you endeavour to be faithful and diligent in the due execution of the same?

Answer. I will endeavour so to be, the Lord being my Helper.

The Archbishop.

WILL you be diligent in Laying your hands upon others, and thereby to confirm baptised persons, make Deacons, ordain Priests, and consecrate Bishops; and likewise to set apart Deaconesses, and admit persons to the several Orders of Lay Ministry in the Church; and in sending forth such Ministers into the Lord's harvest?

Answer. I will so be, by the help of God.

THE ORDINAL

The Archbishop.

WILL you shew yourself gentle, and be merciful for Christ's sake, to poor and needy people, and to all strangers destitute of help; and will you shew yourself patient, kindly, and just to your Clergy and the people of your Diocese; and to be unto them all, as much as shall in you lie, truly both a protector and pastor of souls, and a reverend father in God?

Answer. I will so shew myself, by God's help.

Then the Archbishop, standing up, shall say,

ALMIGHTY God, our heavenly Father, Who hath given you a good will to do all these things, grant also unto you the strength and the power to perform the same; that He accomplishing in you the good work which He hath begun, you may be found perfect and irreprehensible at the latter day; through Jesus Christ our Lord. *Amen.*

THE PRAYER FOR THE BISHOP-ELECT

Then shall the Archbishop say to the Congregation,

DEARLY beloved, let us pray for this our brother now to be Ordained and Consecrated to the Office of Bishop in the Church of God; that, as an high Priest of the New Testament of our Lord Jesus Christ, and chief Pastor and Shepherd of His flock, he may steadfastly keep the solemn promises which he hath made here this day.

After this, the Congregation shall secretly in their prayers make their humble supplications to Almighty God for all these things: for the which prayers silence shall be kept for a space.

Then shall the Archbishop say,
O Lord, hear our prayer.
Answer. And let our cry come unto Thee.

Archbishop. Let us pray.

Then shall the Archbishop say this Prayer following.

ALMIGHTY God, we most humbly beseech Thee to pour forth Thy Holy Spirit upon this Thy chosen servant, and to bestow upon him the highest dignity of Ministry now present in Thy Church (the Apostles having been taken away); and to give unto him that power and authority of Government and Oversight which Thy Son Jesus Christ did bestow upon His Apostles, whom Thy servant hath been elected to succeed in the Office of a Bishop; and so furnish him with every honour, and so sanctify him with the dew of Thy heavenly unction, that he may always serve Thee faithfully in this Office, to the honour and glory of Thy holy Name, and the edifying of Thy Church; through the same Jesus Christ our Lord. *Amen.*

Then shall the Bishop-elect put on the rest of the Episcopal habit; whereafter he shall be placed conveniently before the Archbishop who, assisted by the other Bishops present, shall Ordain and Consecrate him Bishop in the Manner and according to the Form hereafter following.

THE INVOCATION OF THE HOLY GHOST

Then shall the Bishop-elect kneel down, and the hymn following, Veni, Creator Spiritus *shall be said or sung over him, the Archbishop himself beginning, as followeth.*

COME, Holy Ghost, our souls inspire,
And lighten with celestial fire.

Thou the anointing Spirit art,
   Who dost Thy seven-fold gifts impart.

Thy blessed unction from above
   Is comfort, life, and fire of love.
Enable with perpetual light
   The dullness of our blinded sight.

Anoint and cheer our soilèd face
   With the abundance of Thy grace.
Keep far our foes, give peace at home:
   Where Thou art Guide, no ill can come.

Teach us to know the Father, Son,
   And Thee, of Both, to be but One;
That, through the ages all along,
   This may be our endless song:
Praise to Thine eternal merit,
   Father, Son, and Holy Spirit. Amen.

THE ACT OF CONSECRATION.

Then shall the Archbishop stand up, and say,
THE Lord be with you.
   Answer. And with thy spirit.
   Archbishop. Lift up your hearts.
   Answer. We lift them up unto the Lord.
   Archbishop. Let us give thanks unto our Lord God.
   Answer. It is meet and right so to do.

Then shall the Archbishop and Bishops extend their hands over the Bishop-elect,
and the Archbishop shall continue in the Prayer of Consecration of Bishops, saying as followeth,

IT is very meet, right, and our bounden duty, that we should at all times, and in all places, give thanks unto Thee, Holy Lord, Almighty Father, Everlasting God, Maker and Preserver of all things; Who of Thine infinite goodness hast given unto us Thine only and dearly beloved Son Jesus Christ to be our Redeemer and great High Priest, and the Author of everlasting life; Who, after that He had made perfect our redemption by His death, and after His resurrection was ascended into heaven, poured down His gifts abundantly upon men, making some Apostles, some Prophets, some Evangelists, some Pastors and Doctors, within the Priesthood appointed by Him for the salvation of mankind, and for the edifying and making perfect of His body the Church, into which Order of Ministry this Thy servant hath been admitted.

   Hear us, O merciful Father, we most humbly beseech Thee; and vouchsafe to send down Thy Holy Spirit upon this person, and grant unto him all the fullness and perfection of the Priesthood of Thy Son Jesus Christ; and clothe him in innocency, and all the ornaments of holiness and righteousness; sanctify him with Thy heavenly unction, and make him a Bishop in Thy Church; and that he may rightly and duly execute this Office, give unto him all the grace needful for the fulfilment of the same.

And we beseech Thee, O Lord, to endue this Thy servant with that power and authority to oversee and govern wherewith Thou didst endue Thy holy Apostles; that he, following their godly examples, and ever walking in their way, may diligently oversee and govern Thy flock, and evermore be ready to spread abroad Thy holy Gospel, the glad tidings of reconciliation with Thee; and to use the Authority given him, not to destruction, but to salvation; not to hurt, but to help; so that as a wise and faithful servant, giving to Thy family their portion in due season, he may at last be received into everlasting joy; through Jesus Christ our Lord, Who with Thee and the Holy Ghost liveth and reigneth, ever one God, world without end. *Amen.*

Then the Archbishop and Bishops present shall lay their hands upon the head of the elected Bishop kneeling before them upon his knees, the Archbishop saying,

RECEIVE the Holy Ghost, for the Office and Work of a Bishop in the Church of God, now committed unto thee by the Imposition of our hands, In the Name of the Father, and of the Son, and of the Holy Ghost. Amen. And remember that thou stir up the grace of God which is given thee by this Imposition of our hands: for God hath not given us the spirit of fear, but of power, and love, and a sound mind.

Then shall the Archbishop anoint him with Chrism upon his head, saying,

WE anoint thee with this Chrism, as an outward sign that thou art hereby set apart, and consecrated to the Office and Work of an high Priest of the New Testament of Jesus Christ in the Church of God, In the Name of the Father, and of the Son, and of the Holy Ghost. Amen. And as thou art here anointed outwardly with this holy Chrism, so may God the Holy Ghost anoint thee inwardly with His grace; and grant unto thee the power and authority to be a true Bishop and Shepherd of souls, and to oversee that portion of His flock over which it shall please Him to set thee.

Then the Archbishop shall deliver him the Bible, saying,

GIVE heed unto reading, exhortation, and doctrine. Think upon the things contained in this Book. Be diligent in them, that the increase coming thereby may be manifest unto all men. Take heed unto thyself, and to doctrine, and be diligent in doing them; for by so doing thou shalt save both thyself and them that hear thee.

Then shall the Archbishop deliver him the Crosier into his hands, saying,

BE to the flock of Christ a shepherd, and not a wolf; feed them, and devour them not. Hold up the weak, heal the sick, bind up the broken, bring again the outcasts, seek the lost. Be so merciful, that you be not too remiss; so minister discipline, that you forget not mercy: that when the Chief Shepherd shall appear, you may receive the never-fading crown of glory; through Jesus Christ our Lord. Amen.

Then shall the Archbishop and the Bishops present exchange the Kiss of Peace with the newly-consecrated Bishop.

When this is done, the Nicene Creed shall be sung or said; and the Archbishop shall after that continue in the administration of the Eucharist, beginning with the Offertory. And the new consecrated Bishop shall receive the Holy Communion that day with the Archbishop and Bishops, all remaining still in the Chancel until after such time as all have received the Sacrament of Christ's Body and Blood.

The Prayer of Thanksgiving after Communion ended, before Gloria in Excelsis *is sung, the Archbishop shall then invest the newly-consecrated Bishop with the several insignia of the Episcopal Office, as followeth.*

THE ORDINAL

THE INVESTITURES

The Archbishop shall first invest the new Bishop with the Pectoral Cross, saying,

RECEIVE this Cross, the sign of our Redemption; and may it ever rest upon your heart, and speak to you of gain through loss, of triumph through suffering, and of life through death; and may the love of our Lord Jesus Christ, the crucified Redeemer, ever constrain you, and keep you in His care. Amen.

The Archbishop shall then place the Episcopal Ring upon
the fourth finger of his right hand, saying,

RECEIVE this Ring; and may it be unto you a token of the Divine espousals of Christ the Bridegroom and that holy Church which is His Bride, over which you have been chosen to be a Shepherd and Bishop of souls, and which you are charged to love, as Christ doth love her, and for which He gave His life. Amen.

Then shall the Archbishop place the Bishop's Mitre upon his head, saying,

RECEIVE this Crown, which we now set upon your head, as an outward sign of the Helmet of salvation, and the Crown of glory that fadeth not away; and may God grant unto you that, crowned with the horns of both Testaments, you may appear terrible to the gainsayers of truth; and, by the steadfast defence of that holy and saving Faith which was once delivered to the saints, may you be a Champion of God's Word, a Teacher of sound doctrine, and a Protector of the Christian faithful. Amen.

THE FINAL PRAYERS AND BENEDICTION

The Communion ended, immediately before the Benediction,
these two Prayers following shall be said.

MOST merciful Father, we humbly beseech Thee to send down Thy heavenly blessing upon this Thy servant whom we have this day ordained and consecrated Bishop in Thy Church; and so endue him with Thy Holy Spirit, that he, preaching Thy Word, and ministering the Discipline thereof, may not only be earnest to reprove, beseech, and rebuke with all patience and doctrine; but may also be unto such as do believe a wholesome example, in word, in conversation, in love, in faith, in chastity, and in purity; and that, faithfully fulfilling his course, at the latter day he may receive the crown of righteousness laid up by the Lord the righteous Judge, Thy Son Jesus Christ, in Whose blessed Name we make our supplications unto Thee. *Amen.*

PREVENT us, O Lord, in all our doings with Thy most gracious favour, and further us with Thy continual help; that in all our works, begun, continued, and ended in Thee, we may glorify Thy holy Name, and finally by Thy mercy obtain everlasting life; through Jesus Christ our Lord. *Amen.*

THE peace of God, which passeth all understanding, keep your hearts and minds in the knowledge and love of God, and of His Son Jesus Christ our Lord: And the blessing of God Almighty, ✠ the Father, the Son, and the Holy Ghost, be amongst you and remain with you always. *Amen.*

Here endeth the FORM OF ORDAINING AND CONSECRATING OF
AN ARCHBISHOP OR BISHOP.

Standards of Doctrine and Discipline for The Christian Episcopal Church of Canada

THE HOLY BIBLE

THE CHRISTIAN EPISCOPAL CHURCH OF CANADA, following the CHURCH OF ENGLAND, holds the following Books to constitute the Holy Scriptures of the Old and New Testaments:

THE CANONICAL BOOKS OF THE OLD TESTAMENT: The First Book of Moses, called Genesis; The Second Book of Moses, called Exodus; The Third Book of Moses, called Leviticus; The Fourth Book of Moses, called Numbers; The Fifth Book of Moses, called Deuteronomy; The Book of Joshua; The Book of Judges; The Book of Ruth; The First Book of Samuel, otherwise called, The First Book of the Kings; The Second Book of Samuel, otherwise called, The Second Book of the Kings; The First Book of the Kings, commonly called, The Third Book of the Kings; The Second Book of the Kings, commonly called, The Fourth Book of the Kings; The First Book of the Chronicles; The Second Book of the Chronicles; The First Book of Esdras, otherwise called, Ezra; The Second Book of Esdras, otherwise called, Nehemiah; The Book of Esther; The Book of Job; The Book of Psalms; The Proverbs; Ecclesiastes, or, The Preacher; Cantica, or, The Song of Solomon; The Book of the Prophet Isaiah; The Book of the Prophet Jeremiah; The Lamentations of Jeremiah; The Book of the Prophet Ezekiel; The Book of Daniel; Hosea; Joel; Amos; Obadiah; Jonah; Micah; Nahum; Habakkuk; Zephaniah; Haggai; Zechariah; Malachi.

THE APOCRYPHAL BOOKS OF THE OLD TESTAMENT: The Third Book of Esdras; The Fourth Book of Esdras; The Book of Tobias; The Book of Judith; The Rest of the Book of Esther; The Book of Wisdom; Jesus the Son of Sirach; Baruch the Prophet; The Epistle of Jeremy; The Song of the Three Children; The Story of Susanna; Bel and the Dragon; The First Book of Maccabees; The Second Book of Maccabees. These several Books (as *Saint Jerome* saith) the Church doth read for example of life and instruction of manners; but yet doth it not apply them to establish any doctrine.

THE CANONICAL BOOKS OF THE NEW TESTAMENT: The Gospel According to Saint Matthew; The Gospel According to Saint Mark; The Gospel according to Saint Luke; The Gospel According to Saint John; The Acts of the Apostles; The Epistle of Paul the Apostle to the Romans; The First Epistle of Paul the Apostle to the Corinthians; The Second Epistle of Paul the Apostle to the Corinthians; The Epistle of Paul the Apostle to the Galatians; The Epistle of Paul the Apostle to the Ephesians; The Epistle of Paul the Apostle to the Philippians; The Epistle of Paul the Apostle to the Colossians; The First Epistle of Paul the Apostle to the Thessalonians; The Second Epistle of Paul the Apostle to the Thessalonians; The First Epistle of Paul the Apostle to Timothy; The Second Epistle of Paul the Apostle to Timothy; The Epistle of Paul to Titus; The Epistle of Paul to Philemon; The Epistle of Paul the Apostle to the Hebrews; The General Epistle of James; The First Epistle General of Peter; The Second Epistle General of Peter; The First Epistle General of John; The Second Epistle of John; The Third Epistle of John; The General Epistle of Jude; The Revelation of Saint John the Divine.

THE APOSTLES' CREED

I BELIEVE in God the Father Almighty, Maker of heaven and earth: And in JESUS CHRIST His only Son our Lord, Who was conceived by the Holy Ghost, Born of the Virgin Mary, Suffered under Pontius Pilate, Was crucified, dead, and buried, He descended into hell; The third day He rose again from the dead, He ascended into heaven, And sitteth at the right hand of God the Father Almighty; From thence He shall come to judge the quick and the dead. I believe in the Holy Ghost; The holy Catholic Church; The Communion of Saints; The Forgiveness of sins; The Resurrection of the body; And the Life everlasting. Amen.

THE NICENE CREED

I BELIEVE in one God the Father Almighty, Maker of heaven and earth, And of all things visible and invisible. And in one Lord JESUS CHRIST, the only-begotten Son of God, Begotten of His Father before all worlds: God, of God; Light, of Light; Very God, of very God; Begotten, not made; Being of one substance with the Father; Through Whom all things were made: Who for us men and for our salvation came down from heaven, And was incarnate by the Holy Ghost of the Virgin Mary, AND WAS MADE MAN, And was crucified also for us under Pontius Pilate. He suffered and was buried, And the third day He rose again according to the Scriptures, And ascended into heaven, And sitteth on the right hand of the Father. And He shall come again with glory to judge both the quick and the dead: Whose kingdom shall have no end. And I believe in the Holy Ghost, The Lord and Giver of Life, Who proceedeth from the Father and the Son, Who with the Father and the Son together is worshipped and glorified, Who spake by the Prophets. And I believe One Holy Catholic and Apostolic Church. I acknowledge one Baptism for the remission of sins. And I look for the Resurrection of the dead, And the Life of the world to come. Amen.

THE CREED OF SAINT ATHANASIUS

QUICUMQUE VULT.

WHOSEVER would be saved needeth before all things to hold fast the Catholic Faith. Which Faith except a man keep whole and undefiled, without doubt he will perish eternally. Now the Catholic Faith is this, that we worship One God in Trinity, and the Trinity in Unity; neither confusing the Persons, nor dividing the Substance. For there is one Person of the Father, another of the Son, another of the Holy Ghost; but the Godhead of the Father, and of the Son, and of the Holy Ghost is all One, the Glory equal, the Majesty co-eternal. Such as the Father is, such is the Son, and such is the Holy Ghost. The Father uncreated, the Son uncreated, the Holy Ghost uncreated; The Father infinite, the Son infinite, the Holy Ghost infinite; The Father eternal, the Son eternal, the Holy Ghost eternal. And yet there are not three eternals, but One Eternal; As also there are not three uncreated, nor three infinites, but One Infinite, and One Uncreated. So likewise the Father is almighty, the Son almighty, the Holy Ghost almighty; And yet there are not three almighties, but One Almighty. So the Father is God, the Son God, the Holy Ghost God; and yet there are not three Gods, but One God. So the Father is Lord, the Son Lord, the Holy Ghost Lord; And yet there are not three Lords, but One Lord. For like as we are compelled by the Christian verity to confess each Person by Himself to be both God and Lord; So are we forbidden by the Catholic Religion to speak of three Gods or three Lords. The Father is made of none, nor created, nor begotten. The Son is of the Father alone; not made, nor created, but begotten. The Holy Ghost is of the Father and the Son; not made, nor created, nor begotten, but proceeding. There is therefore one Father, not three Fathers; one Son, not three Sons; one Holy Ghost, not three Holy Ghosts. And in this Trinity there is no before or after, no greater or less; But all three Persons are co-eternal together and co-equal. So that in all ways, as is aforesaid, both the Trinity is to be worshipped in Unity, and the Unity in Trinity. He therefore that would be saved, let him thus think of the Trinity. Furthermore, it is necessary to eternal salvation, that he also believe faithfully the Incarnation of our Lord JESUS CHRIST. Now the right faith is that we believe and confess that our Lord JESUS CHRIST, the Son of God, is both God and Man. He is God, of the substance of the Father, begotten before the worlds; and He is Man, of the substance of His Mother, born in the world; Perfect God, perfect Man, of reasoning soul and human flesh subsisting; Equal to the Father as touching His Godhead; less than the Father as touching His Manhood. Who although He be God and Man, yet He is not two, but is one Christ; One however, not by conversion of Godhead into flesh, but by taking Manhood into God; One altogether; not by confusion of substance, but by unity of Person. For as reasoning soul and flesh is one man, so God and Man is one Christ; Who suffered for our salvation, descended into hell, rose again from the dead; Ascended into heaven, sat down at the right hand of the Father; from whence He shall come to judge the quick and the dead. At Whose coming all men must rise again with their bodies, and shall give account for their own deeds. And they that have done good will go into life eternal, and they that have done evil into eternal fire. This is the Catholic Faith, which except a man do faithfully and steadfastly believe, he cannot be saved.

GLORY be to the Father, and to the Son, and to the Holy Ghost;
As it was in the beginning, is now, and ever shall be, world without end. Amen.

THE VINCENTIAN CANON
ANNO DOMINI 434

I HAVE continually given the greatest pains and diligence to inquiring, from the greatest possible number of men outstanding in holiness and in doctrine, how I can secure a kind of fixed and, as it were, general and guiding principle for distinguishing the true Catholic Faith from the degraded falsehoods of heresy. And the answer that I receive is always to this effect; that if I wish, or indeed if anyone wishes, to detect the deceits of heretics that arise and to avoid their snares and to keep healthy and sound in a healthy faith, we ought, with the Lord's help, to fortify our Faith in a twofold manner, firstly, that is, by the authority of God's Law, then by the Tradition of the Catholic Church.

Here, it may be, someone will ask, Since the Canon of Scripture is complete, and is in itself abundantly sufficient, what need is there to join to it the interpretation of the Church? The answer is that because of the very depth of Scripture all men do not place one identical interpretation upon it. The statements of the same writer are explained by different men in different ways, so much so that it seems almost possible to extract from it as many opinions as there are men. *Novatian* expounds in one way, *Sabellius* in another, *Donatus* in another, *Arius, Eunomius* and *Macedonius* in another, *Photinus, Apollinaris* and *Priscillian* in another, *Jovinian, Pelagius* and *Caelestius* in another, and latterly *Nestorius* in another. Therefore, because of the intricacies of error, which is so multiform, there is great need for the laying down of a rule for the exposition of Prophets and Apostles in accordance with the standard of the interpretation of the Church Catholic.

Now in the Catholic Church itself we take the greatest care to hold that which has been believed everywhere, always and by all. That is truly and properly Catholic, as is shewn by the very force and meaning of the word, which comprehends everything almost universally. We shall hold to this rule if we follow universality, antiquity, and consent. We shall follow universality if we acknowledge that one Faith to be true which the whole Church throughout the world confesses; antiquity if we in no wise depart from those interpretations which it is clear that our ancestors and fathers proclaimed; consent, if in antiquity itself we keep following the definitions and opinions of all, or certainly nearly all, Bishops and Doctors alike.

What then will the Catholic Christian do, if a small part of the Church has cut itself off from the communion of the universal Faith? The answer is sure. He will prefer the healthiness of the whole body to the morbid and corrupt limb. But what if some novel contagion try to infect the whole Church, and not merely a tiny part of it? Then he will take care to cleave to antiquity, which cannot now be led astray by any deceit of novelty. What if in antiquity itself two or three men, or it may be a city, or even a whole province be detected in error? Then he will take the greatest care to prefer the decrees of the ancient General Councils, if there are such, to the irresponsible ignorance of a few men. But what if some error arises regarding which nothing of this sort is to be found? Then he must do his best to compare the opinions of the Fathers and inquire their meaning, provided always that, though they belonged to diverse times and places, they yet continued in the faith and communion of the one Catholic Church; and let them be teachers approved and outstanding. And whatever he shall find to have been held, approved and taught, not by one or two only but by all equally and with one consent, openly, frequently, and persistently, let him take this as to be held by him without the slightest hesitation. (Saint *Vincent* of Lerins.)

INSTRUCTIONS CONCERNING THE DISCIPLINE AND LITURGY OF THE ENGLISH CHURCH

From *THE ECCLESIASTICAL HISTORY OF THE ENGLISH NATION.*

SAINT *AUGUSTINE*, BEING MADE BISHOP, SENDETH TO ACQUAINT POPE *GREGORY* WITH WHAT HAD BEEN DONE, AND RECEIVETH HIS ANSWER TO THE DOUBTS HE HAD PROPOSED TO HIM. [ANNO DOMINI 597.]

IN the meantime, *Augustine*, the man of God, repaired to Arles, and, pursuant to the orders received from the holy Father *Gregory*, was ordained Archbishop of the English Nation, by *Ætherius*, Archbishop of that City. Then returning into Britain, he sent *Laurentius* the Priest, and Peter the Monk, to Rome, to acquaint Pope Gregory, that the Nation of the English had received the Faith of Christ, and that he was himself made their Bishop. At the same time, he desired his solution of some doubts that occurred to him. He soon received proper answers to his questions which we have also thought fit to insert in this, our history.

The First Question of *Augustine*, Bishop of the Church of Canterbury: Concerning Bishops, how they are to behave themselves towards their Clergy? or into how many portions the things given by the Faithful to the altar are to be divided? and how the Bishop is to act in the Church?

Gregory, Pope of the City of Rome, answereth: Holy Scripture, in which no doubt you are well versed, testifieth, and particularly the Epistles of the Blessed *Paul* to *Timothy*, wherein he endeavoureth to instruct him how he should behave himself in the house of God; but it is the custom of the Apostolic See to prescribe rules to Bishops newly ordained, that all emoluments which accrue, are to be divided into four portions: one for the Bishop and his family, because of hospitality and entertainments; another for the Clergy; a third for the Poor; and the fourth for the Repair of churches. But in regard that you, my Brother, being brought up under monastic rules, are not to live apart from your Clergy in the English Church, which, by God's assistance, hath been lately brought to the Faith; you are to follow that course of life which our forefathers did in the time of the Primitive Church, when none of them said anything that he possessed was his own, but all things were in common among them.

But if there are any Clerks not received into Holy Orders who cannot live continent, they are to take wives, and receive their stipends abroad; because we know it is written, that out of the same portions abovementioned a distribution was made to each of them according to every one's wants; care is also to be taken of their stipends, and provision to be made, and they are to be kept under ecclesiastical rules, that they may live orderly and attend to singing of Psalms, and, by the help of God, preserve their hearts, and tongues, and bodies from all that is unlawful. But as for those that live in common, why need we say anything of making portions, or keeping hospitality and exhibiting mercy? inasmuch as all that can be spared is to be spent in pious and religious works, according to the commands of Him who is the Lord and Master of all, "Give alms of such things as you have, and behold all things are clean unto you."

Augustine's Second Question: Whereas the Faith is one and the same, why are there different customs in different Churches? and why is one custom of Masses observed in the holy Roman Church, and another in the Gallican Church?

Pope *Gregory* answereth: You know, my Brother, the custom of the Roman Church in which you remember you were bred up. But it pleaseth me, that if you have found anything, either in the Roman, or the Gallican, or any other Church, which may be more acceptable to Almighty God, you carefully make choice of the same, and sedulously teach the Church of the English, which as yet is new in the Faith, whatsoever you can gather from the several Churches. For things are not to be loved for the sake of places, but places for the sake of good things. Choose, therefore, from every Church those things that are pious, religious, and upright, and when you have, as it were, made them up into one body, let the minds of the English be accustomed thereto.

Taken from *Chapter* XXVII of
the First Book of *THE ECCLESIASTICAL HISTORY OF THE ENGLISH NATION*
by the Venerable *Saint Bede of Jarrow*, Anno Domini 731.

SOLEMN DECLARATION 1893

IN the name of the Father, and of the Son, and of the Holy Ghost. Amen.

WE, the Bishops, together with the Delegates from the Clergy and Laity of the Church of England in the Dominion of Canada, now assembled in the first General Synod, hereby make the following Solemn Declaration:

WE declare this Church to be, and desire that it shall continue, in full communion with the Church of England throughout the world, as an integral portion of the One Body of Christ composed of Churches which, united under the One Divine Head and in the fellowship of the One Holy Catholic and Apostolic Church, hold the One Faith revealed in Holy Writ, and defined in the Creeds as maintained by the undivided primitive Church in the undisputed Œcumenical Councils; receive the same Canonical Scriptures of the Old and New Testaments, as containing all things necessary to salvation; teach the same Word of God; partake of the same Divinely ordained Sacraments, through the ministry of the same Apostolic Orders; and worship One God and Father through the same Lord Jesus Christ, by the same Holy and Divine Spirit Who is given to them that believe to guide them into all truth.

And we are determined by the help of God to hold and maintain the Doctrine, Sacraments, and Discipline of Christ as the Lord hath commanded in his Holy Word, and as the Church of England hath received and set forth the same in 'The Book of Common Prayer and Administration of the Sacraments and other Rites and Ceremonies of the Church, according to the use of the Church of England; together with the Psalter or Psalms of David, pointed as they are to be sung or said in Churches; and the Form and Manner of Making, Ordaining, and Consecrating of Bishops, Priests, and Deacons'; and in the Thirty-nine Articles of Religion; and to transmit the same unimpaired to our posterity.

THE SOLEMN DECLARATION 1893 was made by the Bishops and the Delegates from the Clergy and Laity of the Church of England in the Dominion of Canada, assembled together in their First General Synod held at the City of Toronto in the Province of Ontario of the Dominion of Canada, on the Fourteenth day of September in the Year of Our Lord 1893.

THE FUNDAMENTAL PRINCIPLES OF THE ANGLICAN RELIGIOUS SETTLEMENT

The following set of Principles was drawn up and subscribed to by the Primate and Bishops of the Christian Episcopal Church of Canada and the Christian Episcopal Church in the United States of America meeting together at the City of Fort Worth, Texas, on the Nineteenth day of April in the Year of Our Lord 2007.

WE, the Bishops of the Christian Episcopal Churches of North America, gathered together at the City of Fort Worth, in the State of Texas of the United States of America, do hereby make the following Statement in regard to those Fundamental Principles which we hold to constitute and embody the Anglican Religious Settlement established by Law in the reign of Queen *ELIZABETH* , and which have ever governed and guided the Churches of the Anglican Communion, and to which the Christian Episcopal Churches of North America remain fully committed:

WHILE seeking full reconciliation with all historic Branches of the one holy Catholic and Apostolic Church of Jesus Christ, and working for a true restoration of the visible Unity of all orthodox Christians, it is our desire to preserve and maintain our Anglican identity; that is to say, to uphold and remain faithful to the Fundamental Principles of the Anglican Religious Settlement. We deem these Fundamental Principles to be seven in number, and that they may be summarised thus:

I. That the Sacred Scriptures of the Old and New Testaments, being the authentic written record of God's revelation of Himself to the people of Israel, and the complete revelation of Himself to mankind in the Person of Jesus Christ as witnessed to by the Evangelists and Apostles, constitute the Supreme Authority in all matters of Faith and Morals; and that the holy Catholic and Apostolic

Church of Jesus Christ, in every aspect of her mission, must at all times be obedient and faithful to that written revelation which is the Word of God.

II. That each National or Particular Church has the inherent right to oversee its own affairs in all matters of ecclesiastical Government and Order, in relation to its own people, in accordance with the written Word of God and the Tradition of the Catholic Church; and that, while maintaining Unity and Communion with the whole Catholic Church, the Synods, Convocations, Consistories, Councils, and Tribunals of every National or Particular Church have the Authority to exercise their Jurisdiction freely within their own bounds.

III. That the Queen, being the anointed Representative of Almighty God, has supreme and sovereign Authority in all matters of temporal Jurisdiction, whether ecclesiastical or civil, within her Dominions; and that no foreign power has any right to interfere in the affairs of any realm subject to the Queen's Majesty. In regard to the United States of America, this same principle applies, save that the concept of rule by a Christian sovereign was replaced by the concept of rule by the will of the Citizenry guided by the light of natural revelation; and that the constitutional separation of the secular from the religious in all matters of civil government precludes the establishment of a national Church.

IV. That each National or Particular Church has the right to order its Liturgy and Canons in accordance with the written Word of God and the Tradition of the Catholic Church, as may seem best for its own people.

V. That the Clergy, of every Order of the Sacred Ministry, unless voluntarily submitting to the obligations of the religious life, are free to marry as each man shall be moved by God in his heart so to do, within the bounds set forth by Sacred Scripture.

VI. That the Word of God should be read, and the public Liturgy of the Church should be celebrated, in the Common Language of the people; and that the Standard of English for Anglican Christians is the Authorised Version of the Holy Bible of 1611 and the Book of Common Prayer of 1662.

VII. That Our Lord Jesus Christ instituted the Holy Communion in two Kinds; and that, while never denying at any time the Church's doctrine of the concomitance of the Lord's Presence under either Species thereof, the Cup of the Lord is always to be offered to those who wish to receive the Precious Blood at any celebration of the Supper of the Lord.

GIVEN this Nineteenth Day of April 2007, at Fort Worth, Texas.

INSTRUMENT OF COMMUNION

The following Instrument of Communion is the basis upon which the Christian Episcopal Churches are able to enter into full communion and fellowship with other Anglican Churches and particular Ecclesial Jurisdictions of the Anglican tradition.

WE, the undersigned, desiring to walk together in the Way of the Gospel of Jesus Christ, believing and upholding the Christian Faith and Catholic Religion, and particularly as the same was received and set forth by the Church of England as established by Law at the Restoration of King *CHARLES* the Second, and seeking to be in full communion one with another, do hereby agree:

DOCTRINAL STANDARDS

1. That the canonical Holy Scriptures of the Old and New Testaments are Divinely inspired and are the supreme, final, and binding Authority in all matters of Faith and Morals;

2. That the Three Creeds of the One undivided Church, that is to say, *The Apostles' Creed, The Nicene Creed,* and *The Creed of Saint Athanasius,* shall suffice as the authoritative symbols of the Catholic Religion;

3. That the Dogmatic Definitions of the undisputed Ecumenical Councils of the One holy and undivided Catholic and Apostolic Church shall suffice as the authoritative and true expressions of the orthodox Christian Faith;

4. That there are two Sacraments of the Gospel only, that is to say, Holy Baptism and the Lord's Supper (which is also called the Holy Eucharist and the Holy Communion), both of which were instituted by our Lord Jesus Christ, and are generally necessary to be received by all Christians for their eternal salvation;

5. That the true Catholic Doctrines of the Eucharistic Sacrifice and the Real Presence of Christ in the Holy Eucharist are essential for a correct and proper understanding of the meaning, purpose, and function of the Lord's Supper within the Body of Christ's Church;

6. That the other Five sacred Mysteries which are commonly called Sacraments, that is to say, Confirmation, Penance, Matrimony, Orders, and Unction, are also of Divine institution and Apostolic foundation, and are to be esteemed and used as such within the Church of God as real means of grace to be received according to each believer's profession and calling in Christ;

7. That the Three-fold Sacred Ministry consisting of the Orders of Bishop, Priest, and Deacon, and the Apostolic Succession, are likewise of Divine institution and Apostolic foundation, and are absolutely essential for the valid transmission of Sacramental grace, and the perfecting of the Saints thereby;

8. That the Holy Scriptures and the unbroken Tradition of the Church of God require that the conferral of the Three Orders of the Sacred Ministry is to be restricted absolutely only to baptised male Christians;

9. That the sanctity and dignity of Human Life, of Marriage, and of the Family, were established from the beginning by Divine decree and ordinance, and that by their very nature they are sacred, and must be protected, preserved, and upheld as such within both the Church of God and Civil Society;

10. That the Church of God, and every baptised Christian believer within her, ought always to look forward with joyful expectation to the blessed hope of the Lord's Second Coming and the establishing of His kingdom;

11. That the Authorised Version of the Holy Bible in its standard text of 1769, first set forth for use in 1611 during the reign of King James the First of England, is to be accepted and upheld as the one authorised and common translation of the Holy Scriptures appointed to be read at Divine Service and in the Administration of the Sacraments;

12. That the Book of Common Prayer of the Church of England, set forth for use in 1662 during the reign of King Charles the Second of England, is to be accepted and upheld as the common foundation of the Public Liturgy in our Churches.

A Note Concerning

THE NICENE CREED

THE *Nicene Creed* as it is received in the Christian Episcopal Church of Canada agrees with the form which is used in the Church of England and the other Churches of the West. The Churches of the East use the *Nicene Creed* in that form in which it was left by the Council of Constantinople. It does not follow that these two great divisions in the Christian Church are irrevocably opposed on the doctrine involved in that one clause of the *Nicene Creed* which the Western Churches affirm, and which the Eastern Churches abstain from affirming: and it is the position of the Christian Episcopal Church of Canada that, until a competent authority, recognised by the whole Christian Church, shall pronounce thereon, it seems reasonable that either form of the *Nicene Creed* should not be universally imposed upon any particular individual Christian or community of Christians.

THE ORNAMENTS RUBRIC
From *THE BOOK OF COMMON PRAYER OF THE CHURCH OF ENGLAND.*

The Order for

MORNING AND EVENING PRAYER
DAILY TO BE SAID AND USED THROUGHOUT THE YEAR

THE Morning and Evening Prayer shall be used in the accustomed Place of the Church, Chapel, or Chancel; except it shall be otherwise determined by the Ordinary of the Place. And the Chancels shall remain as they have done in times past.

And here is to be noted, that such Ornaments of the Church, and of the Ministers thereof at all times of their Ministration, shall be retained, and be in use, as were in this Church of England by the Authority of Parliament, in the Second Year of the Reign of King *EDWARD* the Sixth.

Forms of Blessing
and Services of Devotion
for Use on
Several Occasions

A Blessing of Water
on the Lord's Day and Holy-Days

*Water and Salt being made ready, the Priest shall proceed to exorcise those elements,
and then to bless them according to the Form hereafter following.*

The Priest shall say,

✠ In the Name of the Father, and of the Son, and of the Holy Ghost. *Amen.*

Then shall the Priest say,

Our help standeth in the Name of the Lord.
Answer. Who hath made heaven and earth.
Priest. O Lord, hear our prayer;
Answer. And let our cry come unto Thee.

The Preparation of the Salt

O gracious heavenly Father, Who art the living God, the true God, the one Holy and Almighty God, by Whom all things were made, we humbly beseech Thee to behold this Thy creature of Salt, and drive from it every evil power and work, and consecrate it to Thy service and the use of Thy holy Church, that it may become a means of salvation, and a wholesome medicine for body and soul, for all believers; and as the dead waters were healed by the Prophet Elisha, and made sweet and pure so that the power of life might be restored therein; grant likewise, O Father, that into whatsoever waters this element of Salt may be, or in any place wheresoever it may be sprinkled, all evil may be put to flight, and every apparition of wickedness, every disposition of villainy, every turn of devilish deceit, and every unclean spirit may be driven out, and adjured by Him will come again in His glorious Majesty to judge the quick and the dead, and the world by fire, even our Lord Jesus Christ. *Amen.*

Priest. Let us pray.

Almighty and everlasting God, we most humbly beseech Thee, of Thine infinite goodness and loving-kindness to bless and sanctify this element of Salt, which Thou didst create and give over to the use of mankind, so that it may become a source of health and healing for all who make use of it; and grant, O Father, that it may rid whatsoever it may touch of all uncleanness, and be a protection for the same from every assault of evil and from all the powers of darkness; through Thy Son Jesus Christ our Lord, Who liveth and reigneth with Thee and the Holy Ghost, ever one God, world without end. *Amen.*

The Preparation of the Water

O Holy, blessed, and glorious Trinity, three Persons and One God, we humbly beseech Thee to hear our prayers and supplications: Behold, O Lord, this Thy creature of Water, and drive from it every evil power, that it may be made useful to Thy service, to put to flight all the power and wickedness of the enemy, and be enabled to root out and to supplant that enemy with all his apostate angels; through our Lord Jesus Christ, Who with Thee O Father, and Thee O Holy Ghost, art ever one God, world without end. *Amen.*

Priest. Let us pray.

BLESSING OF WATER

O GOD our Father, Who for the salvation of mankind hast built Thy greatest mysteries upon this substance of Water: Graciously hear our prayers, we humbly beseech Thee; and in Thy mercy vouchsafe to pour down the power of Thy blessing into this element, making it ready to be used for many kinds of purifications. May this, Thy creature, being renewed and blessed by Thee, become an agent of Thy grace in the service of Thy holy Mysteries, to drive away all evil spirits and to dispel all sickness of every kind, so that everything in the homes and other buildings of the faithful which is sprinkled with this Water may be rid of all uncleanness, and freed from every harm. Let no breath of infection, nor any disease-bearing air, remain in these places. May the wiles of the lurking enemy prove of no avail. Let whatever evil thing that might menace the safety and peace of Christ's faithful be put to flight by the sprinkling of this Water, so that the healthfulness, obtained by calling upon Thy holy Name, may be made secure and sure against all attack; through Thy Son Jesus Christ our Lord, Who liveth and reigneth with Thee and the Holy Ghost, ever one God, world without end. *Amen.*

Then shall the Priest put a little salt into the water, saying,
MAY this Salt and Water be now mingled into one,
even as the Father and the Son are One. *Amen.*

Priest. Let us pray.

O GOD, glorious Creator, invincible Victor, and unconquerable King, Who holdest in check the forces set to dominate and determined to destroy us, Who dost overcome the cruelty of the raging enemy, Who in Thy power dost beat down the wicked foe: We humbly beseech Thee, O Lord, to look with favour upon this Water mingled with Salt which Thou hast created; send down Thy Holy Spirit upon it, shine on it with the light of Thy kindness, and sanctify it with the dew of Thy love; so that, through the invocation of Thy most holy Name, wheresoever this holy Water may be sprinkled, it may turn aside every attack of the unclean spirit and dispel the terror of the poisonous serpent. And wheresoever we may be, O Father, send Thou the Holy Ghost to be present with us, who now implore Thy mercy; through Thy Son our Lord Jesus Christ, Who liveth and reigneth with Thee and the same Holy Ghost, ever one God, world without end. *Amen.*

Then shall the Priest bless the Water, saying,
IN the glorious Name of Jesus Christ, the only-begotten Son of God, our Lord and Saviour, our Redeemer, and our King: we bless, hallow, and sanctify this lustral Water, to the mystical washing away of sin, and the destruction and dissolution of the works, pomps, and vanities of the devil, and all his apostate angels; and for the blessing, hallowing, and sanctification of Christ's faithful people, their homes, the works of their hands, and all the good things of this earth; In the Name of the Father, and of the Son, and of the Holy Ghost. *Amen.*

Then shall the Priest say,
✠ THE grace of our Lord Jesus Christ, and the love of God,
and the fellowship of the Holy Ghost, be with us all evermore. *Amen.*

Here endeth a BLESSING OF WATER.

A Blessing of the Faithful
before the Lord's Supper on the Lord's Day
commonly called
Asperges

*This Service may be used on the Lord's Day and Holy-days
before the principal celebration of the Lord's Supper.*

*The Priest shall first asperse the Altar with holy Water, then himself and the other Ministers,
and then all the people present, whilst one of these Anthems following is sung or said.*

*From Trinity Sunday until Maundy Thursday, during the aspersing,
this Anthem following shall be sung or said.*

HAVE mercy upon me, O God, after Thy great goodness; / according to the multitude of Thy mercies do away mine offences. Wash me thoroughly from my wickedness, / and cleanse me from my sin. Thou shalt purge me with hyssop, and I shall be clean; / Thou shalt wash me, and I shall be whiter than snow. Make me a clean heart, O God, / and renew a right spirit within me.
GLORY be to the Father, and to the Son, / and to the Holy Ghost;
As it was in the beginning, is now, and ever shall be, / world without end. Amen.

*And from Easter-Day until Trinity Sunday, during the aspersing,
this Anthem following shall be sung or said.*

THEN will I sprinkle clean water upon you, and ye shall be clean: / from all your filthiness, and from all your idols, will I cleanse you. A new heart also will I give you, / and a new spirit will I put within you: And I will take away the stony heart out of your flesh, / and I will give you an heart of flesh. And I will put my spirit within you, and cause you to walk in my statutes, / and ye shall keep my judgments, and do them.
GLORY be to the Father, and to the Son, / and to the Holy Ghost;
As it was in the beginning, is now, and ever shall be, / world without end. Amen.

Then shall the Priest say,
O LORD, save us Thy servants;
Answer. Who put our trust in Thee.
Priest. Send us help from Thy holy place;
Answer. And evermore mightily defend us.
Priest. O Lord, hear our prayer;
Answer. And let our cry come unto Thee.

Priest. Let us pray.

GRACIOUSLY hear us, we beseech Thee, Holy Lord, Almighty Father, Everlasting God, and vouchsafe to send Thy holy Angels from heaven to bless this place, and to protect and defend all those who are come into Thy House this day to worship Thee; through Jesus Christ our Lord. *Amen.*

Here endeth ASPERGES.

BLESSING AN ADVENT WREATH

The Advent Wreath shall be set up in the Church nigh unto the Chancel steps. On the wreath there shall be placed four Candles: two Candles of violet, one each for the First and Second Sundays in Advent in Advent; one Candle of rose for the Third Sunday in Advent; and one Candle of purple for the Fourth Sunday in Advent. A fifth Candle of white may also be set up in the midst of the other four to signify the Nativity of our Lord on Christmas-day.

*And going to where the Advent Wreath is placed, the Priest shall then
proceed to bless the same after this Form following.*

The Priest shall first say,
✠ IN the Name of the Father, and of the Son,
and of the Holy Ghost. *Amen.*

The Priest.
THE Lord be with you.
Answer. And with thy spirit.

Priest. Blessed is He that cometh in the Name of the Lord.
Answer. Hosanna in the highest.

Priest.
Let us pray.

O GOD, our Father, by Whose Word all things are made holy: Look down from heaven, we beseech Thee, and behold this Advent Wreath, and send down Thy blessing upon it; and grant that we who look upon it during this season of solemn expectation of the coming of Thy Son both at Christmas, and at His second coming again in glory at the end of the world to judge both the quick and the dead, may be reminded always to be ready to receive Him at His coming, for we know not the time nor the hour thereof; and so give us grace to be found worthy to enter into Thy kingdom, prepared for all who love Thee; through the same Thy Son Jesus Christ our Lord. *Amen.*

And here the Priest shall sprinkle the Advent Wreath with holy Water.

WE bless, hallow, and sanctify this Advent Wreath in the Name of Jesus Christ, the only-begotten Son of God, our Lord and only Saviour, and the Redeemer of all mankind. *Amen.*

O LORD Jesus Christ, Who wast pleased to be born of the blessed Virgin Mary, and to live in this world amongst men as a Man: Send forth, we beseech Thee, O blessed Lord God, the Spirit of truth into our hearts; and grant that we, holding fast and maintaining the true Faith, may be lights of the world in our generation, and stand fast in witness to Thee and the light of Thy Gospel in this dark night of unbelief and sin; Whom with the Father and the Holy Ghost we worship and glorify, One God forever and ever. *Amen.*

Here endeth BLESSING AN ADVENT WREATH.

ADVENT WREATH DEVOTIONS

THE FIRST SUNDAY IN ADVENT

One Violet Candle is lighted.

Minister.
UNTO Thee do I lift up my soul;
Answer. My God, in Thee have I trusted, let me never be confounded.
Minister. Neither let mine enemies triumph over me;
Answer. For all they that look after Thee shall not be ashamed.

Minister.
Let us pray.

O GOD, Who didst send Thine only Son Jesus Christ into the world, and being born of the blessed Virgin Mary, to take our nature upon Him both body and soul: Grant that we who await His coming may be protected from all adversities and dangers spiritual and temporal unto the Day of His appearing; through the same Thy Son Jesus Christ our Lord. *Amen.*

THE SECOND SUNDAY IN ADVENT

Two Violet Candles are lighted.

Minister.
O PEOPLE of Sion, behold the Lord is nigh at hand to redeem the nations;
Answer. And in the gladness of your heart, the Lord shall cause
His glorious voice to be heard.
Minister. Hear, O Thou Shepherd of Israel:
Answer. Thou that leadest Joseph like a sheep.

Minister.
Let us pray.

O GOD, Who hast revealed Thyself unto all mankind in the Person of Thy Son Jesus Christ our Lord, the Word made Flesh: Grant that Thy holy Church may so preach Thy Word to the nations, that all men shall be turned unto Thee, and be saved, and the hearts of Thy faithful people be readied to receive Christ at His coming; through the same Thy Son Jesus Christ our Lord. *Amen.*

THE THIRD SUNDAY IN ADVENT

The two Violet Candles and the Rose Candle are lighted.

Minister.
REJOICE in the Lord always;
Answer. And again, I say, rejoice!
Minister. Let your moderation be known unto all men;
Answer. For the Lord is at hand.

ADVENT WREATH DEVOTIONS

Minister.
Let us pray.

O GOD, Who biddest us not to trust in the things of this world, but to put our whole trust and confidence in Thee: Give us joyful hearts; and let us be careful for nothing, but making our requests unto Thee, look only unto Thee for our sustenance and help, as we await with expectant hope for the coming of Thy Son our Saviour Jesus Christ, in Whose most holy Name we pray. *Amen.*

THE FOURTH SUNDAY IN ADVENT

*The last Violet Candle is lighted, together with
the other two Violet Candles and the Rose Candle.*

Minister.
DROP down, ye heavens, from above;
Answer. And let the skies pour down justice.
Minister. Let the earth open:
Answer. And bring forth a Saviour.

Minister.
Let us pray.

O GOD, Who didst exalt the blessed Virgin Mary far above all women, and didst bring forth from her womb the Saviour of the world: Grant that we, who honour her as the most holy Mother of our Lord and God Jesus Christ, may, at His second coming in power and great glory, be found worthy to be received into His everlasting kingdom; through the same Thy Son Jesus Christ our Lord. *Amen.*

CHRISTMAS-EVE

All Four Candles and the White Candle are lighted.

Minister.
BEHOLD, a Virgin shall conceive and bear a Son,
Answer. And shall call His Name Emmanuel.

Minister.
Let us pray.

O GOD, Who hast sent Thy blessed Son Jesus Christ into the world to save us from our sins: We pray Thee to hear our prayers; and vouchsafe to deliver us, we beseech Thee, O Lord, from every evil past, present, and to come; and grant that by the intercession of our most blessed Lady the Virgin Mary, and all the Saints, we may enjoy peace in our days; and that, by the help of Thine availing mercy, we may be preserved from all sin, and kept safe from all distress, as we await with joyful hope the coming of Thy Son our Saviour Jesus Christ. *Amen.*

Here endeth ADVENT WREATH DEVOTIONS.

THE PROCLAMATION OF THE NATIVITY OF OUR LORD JESUS CHRIST
WHICH MAY BE SAID OR SUNG AT
MIDNIGHT ON CHRISTMAS EVE
OR BEFORE DIVINE SERVICE ON
CHRISTMAS-DAY

This Proclamation of the Nativity of our Lord Jesus Christ may be said or sung before the Holy Eucharist at Midnight on Christmas Eve or before any Service on Christmas-Day.

It is customary that this Proclamation shall be sung or said at the Holy Eucharist immediately before Gloria in Excelsis is sung, or at the Divine Office immediately before the Psalms.

HEAR, O ye people! Hear, all ye people throughout the world! Hear the good tidings of the Nativity of CHRIST the Lord! Upon this day, the five-and-twentieth day of December, in the five thousand one hundred and ninety-ninth year from the creation of mankind, after the time when Almighty GOD in the beginning created the heavens and the earth; in the two thousand nine hundred and fifty-seventh year after the Flood; in the two thousand and fifteenth year from the birth of ABRAHAM; in the one thousand five hundred and tenth year from MOSES and the going forth of the people of Israel from Egypt; in the one thousand and thirty-second year from DAVID being anointed King; in the sixty-fifth week according to the prophecy of DANIEL; in the one hundred and ninety-fourth Olympiad; in the seven hundred and fifty-second year from the foundation of the City of Rome; in the forty second year of the reign of the Emperor OCTAVIAN AUGUSTUS, the whole world then being at peace; in the Sixth Age of the world, JESUS CHRIST the eternal GOD and the only-begotten SON of the FATHER, desiring to sanctify the world by His most merciful coming, being conceived by the HOLY GHOST in the womb of the Virgin MARY, and nine months having passed since His conception, was born at Bethlehem of Judæa of her whom all generations shall call blessed, He being made flesh and dwelling amongst men as a MAN. This is the Nativity of our Lord JESUS CHRIST according to the flesh.

And all shall say or sing,
Thanks be to God.
AMEN.

Here endeth the PROCLAMATION OF THE NATIVITY OF OUR LORD.

BLESSING THE CRÈCHE
AT CHRISTMAS

The Mass ended, the Priest shall proceed to the Crèche,
and shall bless it according to the Form following.

The Priest.
THE Lord be with you.
 Answer. And with thy spirit.
Priest. Let us bless the Lord.
 Answer. Thanks be to God.

Priest. Let us pray.

ALL blessing, glory, and thanksgiving be unto Thee, Almighty God our heavenly Father, for that Thou didst give Thine only-begotten Son our Saviour Jesus Christ to take our nature upon Himself, and as at this time to be born for us, in great humility, of the Blessed Virgin Mary, His most holy Mother: Accept, we beseech Thee, O Father, and bless ✠ to our use, this Crèche that it may set outwardly before our eyes the glorious Nativity our Lord and Saviour Jesus Christ; and grant that inwardly in our souls we may bring with the Shepherds and the Kings our own gifts, and pay unto Him our true devotion; through the same Thy Son Jesus Christ our Lord, to Whom with Thee and the Holy Ghost, be all honour and glory, world without end. *Amen.*

And here the Priest shall sprinkle the Crèche with holy Water.

Then shall the Priest say,

WE bless, hallow, and sanctify this Crèche, In the Name of the Father, and of the Son, and of the Holy Ghost; praying Almighty God that we, who behold here the likeness of the Nativity of His Son, by the power of the Holy Ghost, may have the fire of His love enkindled in our hearts, and be made like unto Him, Who for our sakes was made very Man. *Amen.*

The Priest.
GLORY to God in the highest,
Answer. And in earth peace, good will towards men.
Priest. ✠ May the souls of the faithful departed,
through the mercy of God, rest in peace;
Answer. And awake to a joyful resurrection.
Amen.

Here endeth BLESSING OF THE CRÈCHE AT CHRISTMASTIDE.

THE DEVOTION
ANGELUS DOMINI
AS IT IS APPOINTED FOR USE AT
CHRISTMAS AND EPIPHANY
AND AT OTHER TIMES

The Minister shall say,
THE Angel of the Lord brought tidings unto Mary;
Answer. And she conceived by the Holy Ghost.

O LORD Jesus Christ, Son of God, and Son of Mary:
Have mercy upon us, and give us Thy blessing.
Amen.

Minister. Behold the handmaid of the Lord.
Answer. Be it unto me according to Thy Word.

O LORD Jesus Christ, Son of God, and Son of Mary:
Have mercy upon us, and give us Thy blessing.
Amen.

Minister. And the Word was made flesh;
Answer. And dwelt among us.

O LORD Jesus Christ, Son of God, and Son of Mary:
Have mercy upon us, and give us Thy blessing.
Amen.

Minister. And Mary brought forth her first born Son;
Answer. And wrapped Him in swaddling clothes, and laid Him in a manger.

Minister.
Let us pray.

WE beseech Thee, O Lord, pour Thy grace into our hearts; that, as we have known the Incarnation of Thy Son Jesus Christ by the message of an Angel, so by His Cross and Passion we may be brought unto the glory of His ✠ Resurrection; through the same Jesus Christ our Lord. *Amen.*

Here endeth ANGELUS DOMINI.

Devotions at the Crèche
in Epiphanytide

*The Priest and Ministers shall stand before the Crèche,
and together with the people shall say these devotions following.*

The Priest.
THE Lord be with you.
Answer. And with thy spirit.

Priest. We have seen His star in the east:
Answer. And are come to worship Him.

Priest.
Let us pray.

ALMIGHTY God, Who didst lead the Wise Men by the bright and shining star to the house at Nazareth, wherein dwelt Thine only-begotten Son Jesus Christ, with the Blessed Virgin Mary His Mother; and who, when they found Him there, did worship Him as King and God, offering unto Him their costly gifts of gold, frankincense, and myrrh: Grant that we, also beholding His Divine Majesty, may likewise offer unto Him our own gifts, the poor treasure of ourselves, our souls and bodies; and grant that by the grace and power of Thy Holy Spirit working in us, our offerings may transformed, and be found acceptable in His sight, through Whom we pray unto Thee, and Who with Thee and the Holy Ghost liveth and reigneth, ever one God, world without end. *Amen.*

ALMIGHTY and everlasting God, Who desirest not the death of a sinner, but rather that he may turn away from his wickedness and live: We humbly beseech Thee to deliver all the nations of the earth from sin and disbelief, and bring them unto a true and living faith in Thy blessed Son Jesus Christ; that all mankind may be saved, and true godliness and peace reign upon the earth; through the same Thy Son Jesus Christ our Lord. *Amen.*

Then shall the Priest say,
GLORY be to the Father, and to the Son, and to the Holy Ghost;
Answer. As it was in the beginning, is now, and ever shall be,
world without end. Amen.

Priest. ✠ MAY the souls of the faithful departed,
through the mercy of God, rest in peace;
Answer. And awake to a joyful resurrection.
Amen.

*Here endeth a FORM OF DEVOTIONS AT THE CRÈCHE
AT EPIPHANYTIDE.*

Blessing Flowers
on Mothering Sunday

The Flowers that are to be blessed shall be placed on the Gospel side of the Altar.

And immediately before the Priest shall begin the Service proper, and standing at the Altar, the Priest shall proceed to bless the Flowers there according to this Form following.

The Priest.
The Lord be with you.
Answer. And with thy spirit.
Priest. Let us bless the Lord.
Answer. Thanks be to God.

Priest. Let us pray.

O GOD, from Whom cometh every good and perfect gift, we give Thee humble thanks for all of Thy blessings so freely bestowed upon us; for the fruitful trees and herbs of the field, for their leaves and flowers; and for all the beauty and plenteousness of Thy creation, we praise and magnify Thy holy Name: Bless, we beseech Thee, O Lord, these flowers, which we now set apart in Thy Name, as tokens of Thine unfailing promise that, for as long as the earth shall last, summer and winter, cold and heat, seedtime and harvest, shall never fail; and grant unto us, dear Father, that as these flowers herald the coming of spring in fulfillment of Thy promises, so we may always put our whole trust in Thee, and look forward with a sure faith, and with a blessed hope, to the Resurrection of the dead, and everlasting life in the world to come, for all them that truly believe; through Jesus Christ our Lord. *Amen.*

Here the Priest shall sprinkle the flowers with holy Water.

O LORD God, our heavenly Father, vouchsafe, we beseech Thee, to bless and sanctify these flowers which we have received from Thy bounty; and grant that all who carry them, or have them about their person, or keep them in their homes, may receive of Thee a blessing, and be protected by Thy grace from all evil, and be preserved from all things hurtful and all things ill; through Jesus Christ our Lord and Saviour. *Amen.*

Then shall the Priest say this Collect following.

O BLESSED Lord Jesus Christ, Who through the wonderful mystery of Thy holy Incarnation didst consecrate motherhood to Thy glory: Bless, we beseech Thee, our own mothers, and all women who believe, and put their hope and trust in Thee; make them to be pure and gentle, patient and kind, loving and compassionate, faithful and obedient unto Thee, as was Thine own most Holy Mother the Blessed Virgin Mary; so that, bearing in their hearts the presence of Thy love, their lives may be patterned after the example of her through whom Thou hast wrought the salvation of mankind; Who livest and reignest with the Father and the Holy Ghost, ever one God, world without end. *Amen.*

Here endeth BLESSING FLOWERS ON MOTHERING SUNDAY.

BLESSING BREAD AND EGGS ON EASTER-DAY

The Priest shall first say,

BUT now is Christ risen from the dead, and become the first-fruits of them that slept. For since by man came death, by man also came the resurrection of the dead. For as in Adam all die, even so in Christ shall all be made alive. I *Corinthians* 15. 20-21.

Then shall the Priest shall say,
THE Lord be with you.
Answer. And with thy spirit.

Then shall the Priest say,
MAN shall not live by bread alone;
Answer. But by every word that proceedeth out of the mouth of God.

Priest. Let us pray.

Then shall the Priest bless the Bread, saying,

O HOLY Lord, Almighty Father, Everlasting God, Maker and Preserver of all things, Who hast provided Bread from the earth and the work of men's hands: Vouchsafe, we beseech Thee, to bless this Bread with Thy heavenly benediction; and grant that it may be unto all who partake thereof profitable to the health of their bodies and souls, and a defence against all diseases and every snare of the enemy; through Jesus Christ our Lord, Who is the true and living Bread which came down from heaven and giveth life unto the world, and Who with Thee and the Holy Ghost we worship and glorify, ever one God world without end. *Amen.*

Then shall the Priest say,
I AM the Resurrection and the Life, saith the Lord:
he that believeth in Me, though he were dead, yet shall he live;
Answer. And whosoever liveth and believeth in Me shall never die.

Priest. Let us pray.

Then shall the Priest bless the Eggs, saying,

WE beseech Thee, O Lord, to send down Thy blessing upon these Eggs, each imprinted in itself with the sign of the Blessed Trinity, and the threefold wholeness of our humanity; and grant that all those of Thy faithful people who partake thereof, may find them healthful food in honour of the Resurrection of Thy Son our Saviour Jesus Christ; through the same Jesus Christ our Lord, Who with Thee and the Holy Ghost liveth and reigneth, ever one God, world without end. *Amen.*

Then shall the Priest say,
✠ MAY the souls of the faithful departed, through the mercy of God, rest in peace;
Answer. And awake to a joyful resurrection. *Amen.*

Here endeth BLESSING BREAD AND EGGS ON EASTER-DAY.

BLESSING A HOUSE
DURING
EPIPHANYTIDE AND EASTERTIDE
AND AT OTHER TIMES OF THE YEAR

When the Priest entereth the house, he shall say,
PEACE be to this house, and all who dwell in it.

VISIT this dwelling, we beseech Thee, O Lord, and drive far from it all the snares of the enemy; let Thy holy Angels dwell herein to preserve us in peace; and may Thy blessing and protection be upon us evermore; through Christ our Lord. *Amen.*

Then shall the Priest say,
OUR help standeth in the Name of the Lord;
    Answer. Who hath made heaven and earth.
Priest. O Lord, hear our prayer;
    Answer. And let our cry come unto Thee.
Priest. The Lord be with you.
    Answer. And with thy spirit.

Priest. Let us pray.

WE humbly beseech Thee, O God our Father, for this house and for all who shall dwell herein, both their persons and all their possessions; that it may please Thee to bless them, and to keep them always under Thy constant protection and loving care: Grant, O Lord, unto all them that dwell herein an abundance of the dew of heaven, and of the fatness of the earth, for the sustenance of their life; and so direct the desires of their hearts, that they may obtain Thy mercy. May it please Thee to bless this house with Thy sacred Presence, even as Thou wast pleased to bless the houses of Abraham, Isaac, and Jacob; and within the walls of this house may holy Angels of light continually dwell, to guard it, and all those who dwell in it, from all danger, anxiety, and distress; through Jesus Christ our Lord and Saviour. *Amen.*

GRACIOUSLY hear us, Holy Lord, Almighty Father, Everlasting God, and vouchsafe, in Thy mercy, to send Thy holy Angels from heaven to guard, cherish, protect, visit and defend all who dwell in this house; through Christ our Lord. *Amen.*

BLESS, O Lord God Almighty, this house, that there may be therein health, purity, victory, strength, humility, goodness, meekness, and peace, the joyful fulfilment of the spirit of the Law, and grateful thanksgiving unto Thee, O God the Father, God the Son, and God the Holy Ghost; and may Thy blessing remain upon this house, and upon all those who dwell in it, both now and for evermore. *Amen.*

Then let the house and its inhabitants be sprinkled with holy Water.

Here endeth BLESSING A HOUSE.

AN ORDER OF SERVICE
FOR MARKING THE FOURTEEN
STATIONS OF THE CROSS

The Minister and people shall gather in the Church or Chapel, or some other consecrated place, where the Fourteen Stations of the Way of the Cross are set up or marked out for the devotions of the Faithful.

THE PRAYERS AT THE ALTAR

And the Minister shall stand at the Chancel steps before the Altar.

And the Minister shall say,
✠ IN the Name of the Father, and of the Son, and of the Holy Ghost. *Amen.*

Then shall the Minister and the people all devoutly kneel.

And the Minister shall say,
Lord, have mercy upon us.
Christ, have mercy upon us.
Lord, have mercy upon us.

Minister. Let us pray.

Then shall the Minister and people say together the Lord's Prayer.
OUR Father, which art in heaven, hallowed be Thy Name. Thy kingdom come. Thy will be done, in earth as it is in heaven. Give us this day our daily bread. And forgive us our trespasses, As we forgive them that trespass against us. And lead us not into temptation, But deliver us from evil. Amen.

Then shall the Minister say,
GOD forbid that I should glory,
Answer. Save in the Cross of our Lord Jesus Christ.

Minister. Let us pray.

Then shall the Minister and people together say this Prayer following.
O JESUS, our Saviour and most blessed Redeemer, behold us Thy servants here kneeling at Thy feet, and mercifully hear our prayers and supplications. We implore Thy mercy for ourselves, and for the souls of all those who have departed this life in Thy faith and fear. Grant unto us, and to them, O Lord, we beseech Thee, the infinite merits of Thy Passion, which we are now about to remember and consider as we walk with Thee along the Way of Sorrows, journeying with Thy most blessed Mother, and Thy holy disciples, on the path that led Thee to Calvary, and to death upon the Cross for our salvation. And grant, O blessed Saviour, that as we walk with Thee, our hearts may be so touched with true contrition and sorrow for our sins, and with such a desire to turn in repentance unto Thee, we may be ready to embrace with faith and joy all the crosses, and to persevere in all the sufferings, of this life as may come to us, so that they may be turned from transient trials and passing distress into real means of grace and spiritual comfort, as we make our pilgrimage through this earthly life along the path that shall lead us to our heavenly home. Amen.

STATIONS OF THE CROSS

*This Hymn following, or some other suitable hymn taken from
the Book of Common Praise or other approved Book, may be sung here.*

TAKE up thy cross, the Saviour said,
　If thou wouldst my disciple be;
Deny thyself, the world forsake,
　And humbly follow after me.

Take up thy cross; let not its weight
　Fill thy weak spirit with alarm;
His strength shall bear thy spirit up,
　And brace thy heart and nerve thine arm.

Take up thy cross, nor heed the shame,
　Nor let thy foolish pride rebel;
Thy Lord for thee the Cross endured,
　To save thy soul from death and hell.

Take up thy cross, then, in His strength,
　And calmly every danger brave;
'Twill guide thee to a better home,
　And lead to victory o'er the grave.

Take up thy cross and follow Christ,
　Nor think till death to lay it down;
For only those who bear the Cross
　May hope to wear the glorious crown.

To Thee, great Lord, the ONE in THREE,
　All praise forevermore ascend:
And grant us in our lives to see
　That heavenly life that knows no end.
　　　　　　　　　　　　　　Amen.

Then shall the Minister say,
✠ LET us proceed in peace.
Answer. In the Name of the Lord. *Amen.*

And the Minister and people shall then make their way to the First Station, and thereafter likewise from Station to Station throughout the Church or Chapel, or consecrated place set apart for that purpose, pausing at each Station there to make the appropriate Devotion, until they arrive again at the Chancel steps or the Altar set up at the place whence the procession began.

And as the Minister and people walk from the Chancel steps, or from the place whence the procession is to begin, and thence from Station to Station, they shall sing together a verse of the hymn Stabat Mater Dolorosa *as they proceed.*

AT the Cross, her station keeping,
Stood the mournful Mother weeping,
Where He hung, her dying LORD.

465

I.

THE FIRST STATION:
OUR LORD IS CONDEMNED TO DEATH

*And standing before the Station, the Minister and people
shall bend the knee, and the Minister shall say,*
WE adore Thee, O Christ, and we bless Thee;
Answer. Because by Thy holy Cross, Thou hast redeemed the world.

And then all shall rise, and the Minister shall say,
AND straightway in the morning, the chief Priests held a consultation with the elders and scribes and the whole council, and bound Jesus, and carried Him away, and delivered Him to Pilate. And they all condemned Him to be guilty of death. When Pilate heard that saying, he brought Jesus forth, and sat down in the judgement seat in a place that is called the Pavement, but in the Hebrew, Gabbatha. Then delivered he Him unto them to be crucified. And they took Jesus, and led Him away.

And here all shall pause, and consider briefly the event depicted at the Station.

Then shall the Minister say,
GOD spared not His own Son;
Answer. But delivered Him up for us all.

Minister.
Let us pray.

GRANT, we beseech Thee, Almighty God, that we, who for our evil deeds do worthily deserve to be punished, by the comfort of Thy grace may mercifully be relieved; through our Lord and Saviour Jesus Christ. *Amen.*

And here may follow some other short Prayer or Devotion.

Minister.
GLORY be to the Father, and to the Son, and to the Holy Ghost;
Answer. As it was in the beginning, is now, and ever shall be,
world without end. Amen.

*For her soul of joy bereavèd,
Bowed with anguish, deeply grievèd,
Felt the sharp and piercing sword.*

II.

THE SECOND STATION:
OUR LORD TAKETH UP HIS CROSS

And standing before the Station, the Minister and people
shall bend the knee, and the Minister shall say,
WE adore Thee, O Christ, and we bless Thee;
Answer. Because by Thy holy Cross, Thou hast redeemed the world.

And then all shall rise, and the Minister shall say,
AND He, carrying His Cross, went forth into a place called the place of a skull, which is called in the Hebrew Golgotha. Though He were a Son, yet learned He obedience by the things which He suffered. He is brought as a lamb to the slaughter; and as a sheep before her shearers is dumb, so He openeth not His mouth. Worthy is the Lamb that was slain to receive power, and riches, and wisdom, and strength, and honour, and glory, and blessing.

And here all shall pause, and consider briefly the event depicted at the Station.

Then shall the Minister say,
THE Lord hath laid on Him the iniquity of us all,
Answer. For the transgression of His people was He stricken.

Minister.
Let us pray.

ALMIGHTY God, Whose most dear Son went not up to joy, but first He suffered pain; and entered not into glory before He was crucified: Mercifully grant that we, walking in the way of the Cross, may find it none other than the way of life and peace; through the same Thy Son Jesus Christ our Lord. *Amen.*

And here may follow some other short Prayer or Devotion.

Minister.
GLORY be to the Father, and to the Son, and to the Holy Ghost;
Answer. As it was in the beginning, is now, and ever shall be,
world without end. Amen.

Who on CHRIST's dear Mother gazing,
Pierced by anguish so amazing,
Born of woman would not weep?

III.

THE THIRD STATION:
OUR LORD FALLETH THE FIRST TIME

And standing before the Station, the Minister and people
shall bend the knee, and the Minister shall say,
WE adore Thee, O Christ, and we bless Thee;
Answer. Because by Thy holy Cross, Thou hast redeemed the world.

And then all shall rise, and the Minister shall say,
CHRIST Jesus, being in the form of God, thought it not robbery to be equal with God: but made Himself of no reputation, and took upon Himself the form of a servant, and was made in the likeness of men: and being found in fashion as a man, He humbled Himself, and became obedient unto death, even the death of the Cross. Wherefore God also hath highly exalted Him, and given Him a Name which is above every name: that at the Name of Jesus, every knee should bow, of things in heaven, and things in earth, and things under the earth; and that every tongue should confess that Jesus Christ is Lord, to the glory of God the Father. O come, let us worship and fall down, and kneel before the Lord our Maker, for He is the Lord our God; and we are the people of His pasture, and the sheep of His hand.

And here all shall pause, and consider briefly the event depicted at the Station.

Then shall the Minister say,
SURELY He hath borne our griefs,
Answer. And carried our sorrows.

Minister.
Let us pray.

O GOD, Who knowest us to be set in the midst of so many and great dangers, that by reason of the frailty of our nature we cannot always stand upright: Grant unto us such strength and protection, as may support us in all dangers, and carry us through all temptations; through Jesus Christ our Lord. *Amen.*

And here may follow some other short Prayer or Devotion.

Minister.
GLORY be to the Father, and to the Son, and to the Holy Ghost;
Answer. As it was in the beginning, is now, and ever shall be,
world without end. Amen.

Who, on CHRIST's dear Mother thinking,
Such a cup of sorrow drinking,
Would not share her sorrow's deep?

IV.

THE FOURTH STATION:
OUR LORD IS MET BY HIS BLESSED MOTHER

And standing before the Station, the Minister and people
shall bend the knee, and the Minister shall say,
WE adore Thee, O Christ, and we bless Thee;
Answer. Because by Thy holy Cross, Thou hast redeemed the world.

And then all shall rise, and the Minister shall say,
WHAT shall I testify unto thee? What shall I liken to thee, O daughter of Jerusalem? What shall I compare to thee, that I may comfort thee, O virgin daughter of Sion? For thy ruin is deep as the sea: who can heal thee? Blessed are they that mourn: for they shall be comforted. The Lord shall be thine everlasting light, and the days of thy mourning shall be ended. Hail Mary, full of grace! The Lord is with thee! Blessed art thou amongst women, and blessed is the Fruit of thy womb, Jesus!

And here all shall pause, and consider briefly the event depicted at the Station.

Then shall the Minister say,
BEHOLD, a sword shall pierce through thine own soul also,
Answer. That the thoughts of many hearts may be revealed.

Minister.
Let us pray.

WE beseech Thee, O Lord, pour Thy grace into our hearts; that, as we have known the Incarnation of Thy Son Jesus Christ by the message of an Angel, so by His Cross and Passion we may be brought unto the glory of His Resurrection; through the same Jesus Christ our Lord. *Amen.*

And here may follow some other short Prayer or Devotion.

Minister.
GLORY be to the Father, and to the Son, and to the Holy Ghost;
Answer. As it was in the beginning, is now, and ever shall be,
world without end. Amen.

For His people's sins chastisèd,
She beheld her SON despisèd,
Scourged, and crowned with thorns entwined.

V.

THE FIFTH STATION:
OUR LORD IS HELPED BY SIMON OF CYRENE

And standing before the Station, the Minister and people
shall bend the knee, and the Minister shall say,
WE adore Thee, O Christ, and we bless Thee;
Answer. Because by Thy holy Cross, Thou hast redeemed the world.

And then all shall rise, and the Minister shall say,
AND as they came out, they found a man of Cyrene, Simon by name, coming out of the country, and on him they laid the Cross, that he might bear it after Jesus. If any man will come after me, let him deny himself, and take up his cross and follow me. Take my yoke upon you, and learn of me; for my yoke is easy, and my burden light.

And here all shall pause, and consider briefly the event depicted at the Station.

Then shall the Minister say,
WHOSOEVER doth not bear his cross, and follow me,
Answer. Cannot be my disciple.

Minister.
Let us pray.

O GOD, Whose blessed Son did overcome death for our salvation: Mercifully grant that we who have His glorious Passion in remembrance, may take up our cross daily and follow Him; through the same Thy Son Jesus Christ our Lord. *Amen.*

And here may follow some other short Prayer or Devotion.

Minister.
GLORY be to the Father, and to the Son, and to the Holy Ghost;
Answer. As it was in the beginning, is now, and ever shall be,
world without end. Amen.

Saw Him then from judgement taken,
And in death by all forsaken,
Till His spirit He resigned.

VI.

THE SIXTH STATION:
OUR LORD'S FACE IS WIPED BY SAINT VERONICA

*And standing before the Station, the Minister and people
shall bend the knee, and the Minister shall say,*
WE adore Thee, O Christ, and we bless Thee;
Answer. Because by Thy holy Cross, Thou hast redeemed the world.

And then all shall rise, and the Minister shall say,
HE hath no form nor comeliness; and when we see Him, there is no beauty that we should desire Him. He was despised and rejected of men; a man of sorrows, and acquainted with grief: and we hid as it were our faces from Him; He was despised, and we esteemed Him not. His visage was so marred, more than any man, and His form more than the sons of men. He was wounded for our transgressions, He was bruised for our iniquities: the chastisement of our peace was upon Him; and with His stripes are we healed.

And here all shall pause, and consider briefly the event depicted at the Station.

Then shall the Minister say,
TURN us again, O Lord God of hosts;
Answer. Shew us the light of Thy countenance, and we shall be whole.

Minister.
Let us pray.

O GOD, Who before the Passion of Thine only-begotten Son didst reveal His glory upon the holy mount: Grant unto us Thy servants, that in faith beholding the light of His countenance, we may be strengthened to bear the Cross, and be changed into His likeness from glory to glory; through the same Jesus Christ our Lord. *Amen.*

And here may follow some other short Prayer or Devotion.

Minister.
GLORY be to the Father, and to the Son, and to the Holy Ghost;
Answer. As it was in the beginning, is now, and ever shall be,
world without end. Amen.

*JESU, may her deep devotion
Stir in me the same emotion,
Fount of love, REDEEMER kind.*

VII.

THE SEVENTH STATION:
OUR LORD FALLETH THE SECOND TIME

And standing before the Station, the Minister and people
shall bend the knee, and the Minister shall say,
WE adore Thee, O Christ, and we bless Thee;
Answer. Because by Thy holy Cross, Thou hast redeemed the world.

And then all shall rise, and the Minister shall say,
SURELY He hath borne our grief, and carried our sorrows. All we like sheep have gone astray; we have turned every one to his own way; and the Lord hath laid on Him the iniquity of us all. He was oppressed, and He was afflicted, yet He opened not His mouth: for the transgression of His people was He stricken.

And here all shall pause, and consider briefly the event depicted at the Station.

Then shall the Minister say,
BUT as for me, I am a worm and no man;
Answer. A very scorn of men, and the outcast of the people.

Minister.
Let us pray.

ALMIGHTY and everlasting God, Who, of Thy tender love towards mankind, hast sent Thy Son our Saviour Jesus Christ, to take upon Him our flesh, and to suffer death upon the Cross, that all mankind should follow the example of His great humility: Mercifully grant, that we may both follow the example of His patience, and also be made partakers of His resurrection; through the same Jesus Christ our Lord. *Amen.*

And here may follow some other short Prayer or Devotion.

Minister.
GLORY be to the Father, and to the Son, and to the Holy Ghost;
Answer. As it was in the beginning, is now, and ever shall be,
world without end. Amen.

That my heart fresh ardour gaining,
And a purer love attaining,
May with Thee acceptance find.

VIII.

THE EIGHTH STATION:
OUR LORD IS MET BY THE WOMEN OF JERUSALEM

And standing before the Station, the Minister and people
shall bend the knee, and the Minister shall say,
WE adore Thee, O Christ, and we bless Thee;
Answer. Because by Thy holy Cross, Thou hast redeemed the world.

And then all shall rise, and the Minister shall say,
AND there followed Him a great company of people, and of women which also bewailed and lamented Him. But Jesus turning unto them said, Daughters of Jerusalem, weep not for me, but weep for yourselves, and for your children. For, behold, the days are coming, in the which they shall say, Blessed are the barren, and the wombs that never bare, and the breasts which never nursed. For I have set my face against this city for evil, and not for good, saith the Lord.

And here all shall pause, and consider briefly the event depicted at the Station.

Then shall the Minister say,
THEY that sow in tears,
Answer. Shall reap in joy.

Minister.
Let us pray.

ALMIGHTY and everlasting God, Who hatest nothing that Thou hast made, and dost forgive the sins of all them that are penitent: Create and make in us new and contrite hearts, that we, worthily lamenting our sins, and acknowledging our wretchedness, may obtain of Thee, the God of all mercy, perfect remission and forgiveness; through Jesus Christ our Lord. *Amen.*

And here may follow some other short Prayer or Devotion.

Minister.
GLORY be to the Father, and to the Son, and to the Holy Ghost;
Answer. As it was in the beginning, is now, and ever shall be,
world without end. Amen.

True repentance, JESU, win me;
SAVIOUR print Thy wounds within me:
Brand them on my stubborn heart.

IX.

THE NINTH STATION:
OUR LORD FALLETH THE THIRD TIME

*And standing before the Station, the Minister and people
shall bend the knee, and the Minister shall say,*
WE adore Thee, O Christ, and we bless Thee;
Answer. Because by Thy holy Cross, Thou hast redeemed the world.

And then all shall rise, and the Minister shall say,
O MY people, what have I done unto thee, or wherein have I wearied thee? Testify against me.
Because I brought thee forth from the land of Egypt, thou hast prepared a Cross for thy Saviour.
Because I led thee through the wilderness forty years, and fed thee with manna, and brought thee
into a land exceeding good, thou hast prepared a Cross for thy Saviour. What more could I have
done unto thee that I have not done?

And here all shall pause, and consider briefly the event depicted at the Station.

Then shall the Minister say,
HE is brought as a lamb to the slaughter;
Answer. And as a sheep before her shearers is dumb,
so He openeth not His mouth.

Minister.
Let us pray.

KEEP, we beseech Thee, O Lord, Thy Church with Thy perpetual mercy; and, because the frailty of
man without Thee cannot but fall, keep us ever by Thy help from all things hurtful, and lead us to all
things profitable to our salvation; through Christ our Lord. *Amen.*

And here may follow some other short Prayer or Devotion.

Minister.
GLORY be to the Father, and to the Son, and to the Holy Ghost;
Answer. As it was in the beginning, is now, and ever shall be,
world without end. Amen.

*As Thou bought'st, through tribulation,
In Thy Passion, my salvation,
Let me bear therein my part.*

X.

The Tenth Station:
Our Lord is Stripped of His Garments

And standing before the Station, the Minister and people
shall bend the knee, and the Minister shall say,
We adore Thee, O Christ, and we bless Thee;
Answer. Because by Thy holy Cross, Thou hast redeemed the world.

And then all shall rise, and the Minister shall say,
And when they were come unto a place called Golgotha, that is to say, a Place of a Skull, they gave Him vinegar to drink, mingled with gall: and when He had tasted thereof, He would not drink. And they parted His garments, casting lots: that it might be fulfilled which was spoken by the Prophet, They parted my garments among them, and upon my vesture did they cast lots.

And here all shall pause, and consider briefly the event depicted at the Station.

Then shall the Minister say,
They gave me gall to eat;
Answer. And when I was thirsty, they gave me vinegar to drink.

Minister.
Let us pray.

O blessed Lord God, Whose only Son our Saviour gave His back to the smiters and hid not His face from shame: Grant us grace to take joyfully the sufferings of this present time, in full assurance of the glory that shall be revealed; through the same Thy Son Jesus Christ our Lord. *Amen.*

And here may follow some other short Prayer or Devotion.

Minister.
Glory be to the Father, and to the Son, and to the Holy Ghost;
Answer. As it was in the beginning, is now, and ever shall be,
world without end. Amen.

Let me mourn, O Lord, beside Thee
For the sins which crucified Thee,
While remaineth life in me.

XI.

THE ELEVENTH STATION:
OUR LORD IS NAILED TO THE CROSS

And standing before the Station, the Minister and people
shall bend the knee, and the Minister shall say,
WE adore Thee, O Christ, and we bless Thee;
Answer. Because by Thy holy Cross, Thou hast redeemed the world.

And then all shall rise, and the Minister shall say,
AND when they were come to the place which is called Calvary, there they crucified Him. And with Him they crucified two thieves; the one on His right hand, and the other on His left. And the Scripture was fulfilled, which saith, And He was numbered with the transgressors. O my people, what have I done unto thee? I did raise thee on high with great power: and thou hast hanged me upon the gibbet of the Cross.

And here all shall pause, and consider briefly the event depicted at the Station.

Then shall the Minister say,
AND I, if I be lifted up,
Answer. Will draw all men unto me.

Minister.
Let us pray.

O GOD, Who by the Passion of Thy dear Son hast made the instrument of shameful death to be unto us none other but the means of life and peace: Grant us so to glory in the Cross of our blessed Saviour, that we may gladly suffer shame and loss; for the sake of the same Thy Son Jesus Christ our Lord. *Amen.*

And here may follow some other short Prayer or Devotion.

Minister.
GLORY be to the Father, and to the Son, and to the Holy Ghost;
Answer. As it was in the beginning, is now, and ever shall be,
world without end. Amen.

Take beneath the Cross my station,
And in all Thy tribulation,
I unite myself to Thee.

476

XII.

The Twelfth Station:
Our Lord dieth on the Cross

*And standing before the Station, the Minister and people
shall bend the knee, and the Minister shall say,*
WE adore Thee, O Christ, and we bless Thee;
Answer. Because by Thy holy Cross, Thou hast redeemed the world.

And then all shall rise, and the Minister shall say,
WHEN Jesus therefore saw His mother, and the disciple standing by, whom He loved, He saith unto His Mother, Woman, behold thy son. Then saith He to the disciple, Behold thy mother! When Jesus therefore had received the vinegar, He said, It is finished. And when He had cried with a loud voice, He said, Father, into Thy hands I commend my spirit; and He bowed His head, and gave up the ghost.

And here all shall pause, and consider briefly the event depicted at the Station.

Then shall the Minister say,
CHRIST for our sake became obedient unto death,
Answer. Even the death of the Cross.

Minister.
Let us pray.

O GOD, Who for our redemption didst give Thine only-begotten Son to the death of the Cross, and by His glorious Resurrection hast delivered us from the power of our enemy: Grant us so to die daily from sin, that we may evermore live with Him in the joy of His Resurrection; through the same Thy Son Christ our Lord. *Amen.*

And here may follow some other short Prayer or Devotion.

Minister.
GLORY be to the Father, and to the Son, and to the Holy Ghost;
Answer. As it was in the beginning, is now, and ever shall be,
world without end. Amen.

Let Thy stripes and scourging smite me;
At Thy holy Cross requite me,
Let Thy Blood refresh me there.

XIII.

The Thirteenth Station:
Our Lord is placed in the Arms of His Mother

*And standing before the Station, the Minister and people
shall bend the knee, and the Minister shall say,*
WE adore Thee, O Christ, and we bless Thee;
Answer. Because by Thy holy Cross, Thou hast redeemed the world.

And then all shall rise, and the Minister shall say,
ALL ye that pass by, behold, and see if there be any sorrow like unto my sorrow. Mine eyes do fail with tears, my soul is troubled; my heart is poured out in grief because of the down-fall of my people. Call me not Naomi (Pleasant), call me Mara (Bitter); for the Almighty hath dealt very bitterly with me.

And here all shall pause, and consider briefly the event depicted at the Station.

Then shall the Minister say,
HER tears are on her cheeks;
Answer. She hath none to comfort her.

Minister.
Let us pray.

GRANT, we beseech Thee, merciful Lord, to Thy faithful people pardon and peace; that they may be cleansed from all their sins, and serve Thee with a quiet mind; through Jesus Christ our Lord. *Amen.*

And here may follow some other short Prayer or Devotion.

Minister.
GLORY be to the Father, and to the Son, and to the Holy Ghost;
Answer. As it was in the beginning, is now, and ever shall be,
world without end. Amen.

*JESU, may Thy Cross defend me,
And Thy saving Death befriend me,
Cherished by Thy deathless grace.*

XIV.

THE FOURTEENTH STATION:
OUR LORD IS LAID IN THE SEPULCHRE

And standing before the Station, the Minister and people
shall bend the knee, and the Minister shall say,
WE adore Thee, O Christ, and we bless Thee;
Answer. Because by Thy holy Cross, Thou hast redeemed the world.

And then all shall rise, and the Minister shall say,
WHEN the even was come, there came a rich man of Arimathaea, named Joseph, who also himself was Jesus' disciple; he went to Pilate, and begged the body of Jesus. Then Pilate commanded the body to be delivered. And when Joseph had taken the body, he wrapped it in a clean linen cloth, and laid it in his own new tomb, which he had hewn out in the rock: and he rolled a great stone to the door of the sepulchre, and departed.

And here all shall pause, and consider briefly the event depicted at the Station.

Then shall the Minister say,
THOU shalt not leave my soul in hell;
Answer. Neither shalt Thou suffer Thy holy One to see corruption.

Minister.
Let us pray.

GRANT, O Lord, that as we are baptised into the death of Thy blessed Son our Saviour Jesus Christ, so, by the continual mortifying of our corrupt affections, we may be buried with Him; and that through the grave, and gate of death, we may pass to our joyful resurrection; for His merits, Who died, and was buried, and rose again for us, the same Thy Son Jesus Christ our Lord. *Amen.*

And here may follow some other short Prayer or Devotion.

Minister.
GLORY be to the Father, and to the Son, and to the Holy Ghost;
Answer. As it was in the beginning, is now, and ever shall be,
world without end. Amen.

When the flames of hell would end me
At the Judgement Day, defend me,
Gentle JESU, by Thy love.
Amen.

STATIONS OF THE CROSS

The Prayers before the Altar

Having returned to the Chancel steps, the Minister shall say,
O SAVIOUR of the world, Who by Thy Cross and precious Blood hast redeemed us:
Answer. Save us, and help us, we humbly beseech Thee, O Lord.

Minister.
Let us pray.

Then shall the Minister and the people say this Prayer together.
O BLESSED Saviour, we have walked with Thee the Way of the Cross, in the hope that, by so doing, we shall have shared in some way the mysteries of Thy Passion. Grant, we beseech Thee, O Lord, that the perfect salvation, which Thou hast wrought for us by Thy Death and Resurrection, will so work in our hearts, our souls, and bodies, as to bring forth the good fruit of the Spirit, and so make real in us the effects of Thy redemption. Prepare for us, dearest Lord, we beseech Thee, a place in Thy kingdom with Thee, and make us ready to be received by Thee when our time in this world is ended. All this, we pray Thee to grant, O Blessed Jesus our Lord and our Redeemer, Who with the Father and the Holy Ghost art forever One God, world without end. Amen.

Then shall the Minister say,
NOW unto Him that loved us, and washed us from our sins in His own Blood, and hath made us kings and priests unto God and His Father; to Him be glory and dominion forever and ever. *Amen.*

Minister.
LET us bless the Lord;
Answer. Thanks be to God.
Minister. ✠ May the souls of the faithful departed,
through the mercy of God, rest in peace:
Answer. And awake to a joyful resurrection.
Minister. Let us depart in peace.
Answer. In the Name of the Lord. *Amen.*

Here endeth an ORDER OF SERVICE OF THE WAY OF THE CROSS.

DEVOTIONS BEFORE
THE BLESSED SACRAMENT

*The Blessed Sacrament shall be taken from the Tabernacle or Aumbry,
and then reverently placed upon the Altar of the Lord.*

*Then these two hymns following shall be sung or said
by the Minister and people together, all devoutly kneeling.*

O SAVING Victim, opening wide
    The gate of heaven to man below,
Our foes press on from every side,
    Thine aid supply, Thy strength bestow.

All praise and thanks to Thee ascend
    For evermore, blest One in Three;
O grant us life that shall not end
    In our true native land with Thee.
                                    Amen.

*Here shall the Minister and faithful pause in silent prayer
and adoration before the Blessed Sacrament.*

THEREFORE we, before Him bending,
    This great Sacrament revere;
Types and shadows have their ending,
    For the newer rite is here;
Faith, our outward sense befriending,
    Makes the inward vision clear.

Glory let us give, and blessing,
    To the Father and the Son,
Honour, might, and praise addressing,
    While eternal ages run;
Ever too His Love confessing,
    Who from Both with Both is One.
                                    Amen.

Then shall the Minister say or sing,
THOU gavest them Bread from heaven.
Answer. Containing in itself all sweetness.

Minister. Let us pray.

O GOD, Who in this wonderful Sacrament hast left unto us a memorial of Thy Passion: Grant us, we beseech Thee, so to venerate the sacred mysteries of Thy Body and Blood, that we may evermore perceive within ourselves the fruit of Thy redemption; Who livest and reignest with the Father and the Holy Ghost, ever one God, world without end. *Amen.*

DEVOTIONS

THE DIVINE PRAISES.

*Then shall the Minister rehearse the Divine Praises as followeth,
all the people repeating after him every one.*

BLESSED be God.
 Blessed be His holy Name.
 Blessed be Jesus Christ, true God and true Man.
 Blessed be His Incarnation and Nativity.
 Blessed be His Death and Passion.
 Blessed be His Resurrection and Ascension.
 Blessed be His Coming Again in glory.
 Blessed be the Name of JESUS.
 Blessed be His most sacred Heart.
 Blessed be His most precious Blood.
 Blessed be Jesus in the most holy Sacrament of the Altar.
 Blessed be the Holy Ghost, the Comforter.
 Blessed be the great Mother of God, Mary most holy.
 Blessed be her Conception and Nativity.
 Blessed be her Annunciation and Assumption.
 Blessed be the name of Mary, Virgin and Mother.
 Blessed be Saint Joseph, her most chaste Spouse.
 Blessed be God in His Angels and in His Saints.
 Blessed be God.

Then shall the Minister say,
BLESSED, praised, and adored be Jesus Christ on His throne of Glory in heaven,
in the most holy Sacrament of the Altar, and in the hearts of His faithful people.
Amen.

Then shall the Minister and people together sing or say,
LET us adore forever our Saviour in this holy Sacrament.

PSALM 117. *Laudate Dominum.*
O PRAISE the Lord all ye heathen; praise Him all ye nations. For His merciful kindness is ever more and more towards us; and the truth of the Lord endureth forever. Praise the Lord.
 GLORY be to the Father, and to the Son, and to the Holy Ghost;
As it was in the beginning, is now, and ever shall be, world without end. Amen.

LET us adore forever our Saviour in this holy Sacrament.

Then shall the Blessed Sacrament be reverently returned to the Tabernacle or Aumbry.

Then shall the Minister say,
✠ THE grace of our Lord Jesus Christ, and the love of God,
and the fellowship of the Holy Ghost, be with us all evermore.
Amen.

Here endeth the ORDER OF DEVOTIONS BEFORE THE BLESSED SACRAMENT.

FORMS OF PRAYER
TO BE USED IN
FAMILIES

FAMILY PRAYER

MORNING PRAYERS.

After the reading of a portion of Holy Scripture, let the Head of
the Household, or some other member of the family, say,

O GOD, Thou art my God, early will I seek Thee. In the morning I will direct my prayer unto Thee, and will look up.

Let us pray.

And all shall say together the Lord's Prayer as followeth.

OUR Father, which art in heaven, hallowed be Thy Name. Thy kingdom come. Thy will be done, in earth as it is in heaven. Give us this day our daily bread. And forgive us our trespasses, As we forgive them that trespass against us. And lead us not into temptation, But deliver us from evil. Amen.

Thanksgiving for the gift of another Day.

WE give Thee hearty thanks, O heavenly Father, for the rest of the past night, and for the gift of a new day. Grant that we may so pass the hours of this day in the perfect freedom of Thy service, that at eventide we may again give thanks unto Thee; through Jesus Christ our Lord. *Amen.*

Here may follow the Apostles' Creed and the Collect of the Day,
and then any of the Prayers provided hereafter.

Prayer and Intercession.

O LORD God, Who hast bidden light to shine out of darkness, and Who hast again wakened us to praise Thee for Thy goodness, and to ask for Thy grace: Accept now, we beseech Thee, O Father, the offering of our worship and thanksgiving; and grant unto us all such requests as may be acceptable to Thy holy will. Make us to live as children of the light, and heirs of Thine everlasting kingdom. Remember, O Lord, according to the multitude of Thy mercies, Thy whole Church, all who join with us in prayer, and all our brethren, wherever they may be, and all who stand in need of Thee. Pour down upon us all the riches of Thy grace, so that, redeemed in soul and body through faith in Thy Son, and steadfast in His holy Gospel, we may ever praise Thy wonderful and holy Name; through the same Jesus Christ our Lord. *Amen.*

And before the Grace there may be said by all,

O GOD Almighty, Maker of heaven and earth, and of all things visible and invisible, One Almighty God in Three Persons, FATHER, SON, and HOLY GHOST: We offer unto Thee this day ourselves, our souls and bodies, to be a reasonable, holy, and living sacrifice unto Thee; to Whom be all praise and glory. Amen.

II *Corinthians* xiii. 14.

✠ THE grace of our Lord Jesus Christ, and the love of God, and the fellowship of the Holy Ghost, be with us all evermore. *Amen.*

FAMILY PRAYER

EVENING PRAYERS.

*After the reading of a portion of Holy Scripture, let the Head of
the Household, or some other member of the family, say,*

O LORD, let our prayer be set forth in Thy sight as the incense, and the lifting up of our hands as an evening sacrifice.

Let us humbly confess our sins to Almighty God.

O FATHER Almighty, Lord God of heaven and earth, and Judge of all mankind, we confess that we have sinned against Thee in thought, word, and deed. Have mercy upon us, O Lord, have mercy upon us after Thy great goodness; according to the multitude of Thy mercies do away our offences; wash us thoroughly from our wickedness, and cleanse us from our sins; forgive us all that is past, and give us grace to amend our lives according to Thy holy Word; through Jesus Christ Thy Son our Lord. *Amen.*

For Pardon through the Cross.

ALMIGHTY Father, Who of Thy great love to men didst give Thy dearly beloved Son to die for us: Grant that, through His Cross, our sins may be put away, and remembered no more against us; and that, cleansed by His precious Blood, and mindful always of His sufferings, we may take up our cross daily, and follow Him in newness of life, until we come finally to His everlasting kingdom; through the same Thy Son Jesus Christ our Lord. *Amen.*

*Here may follow the Apostles' Creed and Collect of the Day,
and then the Lord's Prayer, and any of the Prayers provided hereafter.*

OUR Father, which art in heaven, hallowed be Thy Name. Thy kingdom come. Thy will be done, in earth as it is in heaven. Give us this day our daily bread. And forgive us our trespasses, As we forgive them that trespass against us. And lead us not into temptation, But deliver us from evil. Amen.

For Freedom from Worry.

O LORD, Who hast pity for all our weakness: Put away from us all worry and every anxious fear, that, having ended the labours of this day as in Thy sight, and committing our tasks, ourselves, and all we love, into Thy keeping, we may, now that night cometh, receive from Thee Thy priceless gift of sleep; through Jesus Christ our Lord. *Amen.*

And before the Commendation, then may be said by all,

WE will lay us down in peace and take our rest; for it is Thou, Lord, only, that makest us to dwell in safety. Thou, O Lord, art in the midst of us, and we are called by Thy holy Name. Leave us not, O Lord our God; but preserve us waking, and guard us while sleeping, that awake we may watch with Christ, and asleep we may rest in peace. Amen.

The Commendation.

THE Lord Almighty grant us a quiet night, and at the last a perfect end: And the blessing of God Almighty, ✠ the Father, the Son, and the Holy Ghost, be with us this night, and for evermore. *Amen.*

FAMILY PRAYERS.

For the Remembrance of God's Presence.

O HEAVENLY Father, in Whom we live, and move, and have our being: We humbly pray Thee so to guide and govern us by Thy Holy Spirit, that in all the cares and occupations of our daily life we may never forget Thee, but remember that we are ever living and walking in Thy sight; through Jesus Christ our Lord. *Amen.*

For the Family.

O MERCIFUL Saviour, who didst love Martha, and Mary, and Lazarus, hallowing their home with Thy sacred presence: Bless, we beseech Thee, our home, that Thy love may rest upon us, and that Thy presence may be with us. May we all grow in grace, and in the knowledge of Thee, our Lord and Saviour. Teach us to love Thee and one another, as Thou hast given commandment. Help us to bear one another's burdens, and so fulfil Thy Law, O blessed Jesu, Who with the Father and the Holy Ghost livest and reignest, one God, for evermore. *Amen.*

For Relatives and Friends.

O LOVING Father, we commend to Thy gracious keeping all those who are near and dear to us. Have mercy upon any who are sick, and comfort and relieve those who are in pain, anxiety, or sorrow. Awaken all who are careless about eternal things. Bless those who are young and in health, that they may give the days of their strength unto Thee. Comfort the aged and infirm, that Thy peace may rest upon them. Hallow the ties of kindred, that we may help, and not hinder, one another in all such good works as Thou hast prepared for us to walk in; through Jesus Christ our Lord. *Amen.*

For Children.

O LORD Jesus Christ, Who didst take little children up into Thine arms, and blessed them: Bless, we beseech Thee, the children *of this family, and of this Parish;* grant that they may grow up in Thy faith, fear, and love; protect them, and provide for them, O Lord, day by day, with Thy grace, and with all things necessary that they may grow up into the fullness of Thine own stature. Grant this, O blessed Saviour, for Thine own Name's sake. *Amen.*

For a Birthday.

O LORD, our heavenly Father, mercifully hear our prayers; and grant a long and happy life to Thy *servant N.,* whose birthday we remember this day. May *he* grow in Thy grace as *his* years increase; and ever live so as to please Thee, in the faith of Thy Son Jesus Christ, and in the power of Thy Holy Spirit; through the same Jesus Christ our Lord. *Amen.*

For Absent Ones.

O GOD, Who art present in every place: We pray Thee to protect with Thy loving care our dear ones who are away from us. Let Thy fatherly hand direct them; prosper them in the way they should go; grant them their daily bread, and grace and strength for all their daily needs; and inspire in them an unwavering faith in Thee, that they may live always to Thy honour and glory; through Jesus Christ our Lord. *Amen.*

For One Leaving Home.

O GOD, the Refuge and Strength of all who put their trust in Thee: Unto Thy gracious keeping we commit Thy *servant N.,* now going forth from us. Give *him* courage, prudence, and self-control;

raise up for *him* good friends; preserve *him* from loneliness; keep *him*, we beseech Thee, under the protection of Thy good Providence; and make *him* to have a perpetual fear and love of Thy holy Name; through Jesus Christ our Lord. *Amen.*

For Daily Work.

O LORD our heavenly Father, by Whose good providence the duties of men are variously ordered: Grant to us all the spirit to labour heartily to do our work in our several stations, in serving but one Master, and looking for one Reward. Teach us to put to good account whatever talents Thou hast lent to us; and enable us to redeem our time by patience and zeal; through Jesus Christ our Lord. *Amen.*

For Good Stewardship in the Use of this World's Goods.

ALMIGHTY God, Whose loving hand hath given us all that we possess: Grant us grace that we may honour Thee with our substance, and with the first-fruits of all our increase; and, remembering the account which we must one day give, make us to be faithful stewards of Thy creation, and of the bounty which we have received from Thee; through Jesus Christ our Lord. *Amen.*

A RESPONSORY BEFORE MEALS.

Let the head person at the Table say,
THE eyes of all wait upon Thee, O Lord;
And Thou givest them their meat in due season.
Thou openest Thine hand;
And fillest all things living with plenteousness.

And all shall say together,
GLORY be to the Father, and to the Son, and to the Holy Ghost;
As it was in the beginning, is now, and ever shall be, world without end. Amen.

GRACE BEFORE MEALS.

AND when Paul had thus spoken, he took bread, and gave thanks to God in presence of them all: and when he had broken it, he began to eat. *Acts* 27. 35.

O GOD, our heavenly Father, we thank Thee for this food, which we are about to receive from Thy bounty. ✠ Bless, O Lord, this food to our use, and us to Thy service; give us grateful hearts; and make us always mindful of the needs of others; through Jesus Christ our Lord. *Amen.*

GRACE AFTER MEALS.

WHEN thou hast eaten and art full, then thou shalt bless the Lord thy God for the good land which He hath given thee. *Deuteronomy* 8. 10.

FOR all this food which we have received from Thee, O Lord, and for this good land which Thou hast given us to be our home; and for all Thy many and great mercies so freely bestowed upon us, ✠ we thank Thee, we praise Thee, and we bless Thee, O God our heavenly Father; through Christ our Lord. *Amen.*

FAMILY PRAYER

GENERAL PRAYERS.

For a Saint's Day.

O GOD, Who didst bestow upon Thy Saints such marvellous virtue, that they were able to stand fast, and have the victory against the world, the flesh, and the devil: Grant that we, who this day remember Thy blessed *servant* Saint *N.*, may ever rejoice in *his* fellowship; and that, following *his* holy example, and assisted by *his* prayers, we may be enabled, by Thy grace, to fight the good fight of faith, and so lay hold upon eternal life; through our Lord Jesus Christ, Who with Thee and the Holy Ghost liveth and reigneth, one God, for ever and ever. *Amen.*

For the Parish.

MOST merciful Father, we humbly beseech Thee to send down Thy heavenly blessing upon Thy holy Church *in this Parish*, that all its members may dwell together peaceably in unity and brotherly love. Keep far from us all self-will and discord. Endue Thy Ministers with righteousness, and enable them faithfully to dispense Thy holy Word and Sacraments, to bring again the outcasts, and to seek the lost. Grant to us that we may so receive their ministrations, and use Thine appointed means of grace, that in all our words and deeds we may seek Thy glory and the advancement of Thy kingdom; through Jesus Christ our Lord. *Amen.*

A Thanksgiving.

O MOST merciful Father, we humbly and heartily thank Thee for all Thy gifts so freely bestowed upon us: For life, and health, and safety; for power to work, and for leisure to rest; for all that is beautiful in Thy creation, and in the lives of men, we praise and magnify Thy holy Name. But, above all, we thank Thee for our spiritual mercies in Christ Jesus our Lord; for the means of grace, and for the hope of glory. And we pray Thee to fill our hearts with all joy and peace in believing; through Jesus Christ our Lord. *Amen.*

Ephesians 3. 20 & 21.

NOW unto Him that is able to do exceeding abundantly above all that we ask or think, according to the power that worketh in us, unto Him be glory in the Church and in Christ Jesus, throughout all ages, world without end. *Amen.*

A PRIVATE PRAYER.

ΚΎΡΙΕ Ἰησοῦ Χριστέ, Υἱὲ τοῦ Θεοῦ, ἐλέησόν με τὸν ἁμαρτωλόν.

O LORD Jesus Christ, Son of God, have mercy on me a sinner.

THE END.

CPSIA information can be obtained
at www.ICGtesting.com
Printed in the USA
LVHW020717170520
655785LV00009B/399